DELICT

AUSTRALIA
LBC Information Services
Sydney

CANADA and USA
Carswell
Toronto

NEW ZEALAND
Brooker's
Auckland

SINGAPORE and MALAYSIA
Sweet & Maxwell Asia
Singapore and Kuala Lumpur

GREENS CONCISE SCOTS LAW

DELICT

FOURTH EDITION

By

William J. Stewart, LL.B., LL.M., Solicitor
Lecturer, University of Stirling

THOMSON
™
W. GREEN

First published 1989
Reprinted 1990, 1992
Second edition 1993
Third edition 1998

This edition published in 2004 by W. Green & Son Limited
21 Alva Street
Edinburgh EH2 4PS

Typeset by ISL
Gloucester

Printed in Great Britain by
Creative Print & Design (Wales), Ebbw Vale

No natural forests were destroyed to make this product;
only farmed timber was used and replanted.

A CIP catalogue record of this book is available from the
British Library.

ISBN 0414 01556 8

For Mum and Dad

PREFACE

Moving into a fourth edition seemed like a good time for an overhaul rather than a revision. My *Casebook on Delict*, which was first published after the first edition of this book, had been in 24 chapters which had the benefit of breaking the subject up for the student and allowing it to be taught from more easily. I have, accordingly, broken the subject up into more parts linking related areas by enclosing them within sections.

It soon became clear that the first edition of this book was being used by the profession as a kind of noter-up. However, since those days, the profession has available the *Reparation Bulletin* and my own continuously updated looseleaf *Reparation: Liability for Delict* as well as the *Stair Memorial Encyclopaedia* which itself is updated from time to time. After graduation, practical matters for the trainee are now dealt with expertly in Conway, *Personal Injury Practice in the Sheriff Court* (2nd ed., W. Green, 2003), and very little need now be said on that topic. So this edition is now expressly for students only and that has allowed me to unburden the text of some detail in places to allow space for the expansion of the subject as a whole. There is, even now, a substantial aid to last minute revision (or initial orientation) in Mr Cameron's *Basic Delict*, necessitating that this text should be longer and fuller than the first edition which sought to serve all these needs.

More space is released in this edition for delict by the removal of the chapter on restitution. Restitution has a home in delict studies being a non-contractual, non-familial, obediential obligation, but in truth it was there as part of my own efforts in an enrichment revolution. Now that unjust enrichment is liberated from stowaway status in quasi-contract it is probably right that it should not have to squat in delict. This difficult decision was made very easy indeed on the publication of Hector MacQueen's extensive treatment in *Fundamentals of Scots Law* (W. Green, 2003) — intended to be suitable for a broad church of teachers, it meets that aim and is an elegant exposition of a difficult subject which it is hard to imagine could be bettered for that audience. Added to that, the student has access to the authoritative "Unjustified Enrichment" chapter of *Gloag & Henderson*. These two sources mean that this book can focus on its main "delict" mission. Further, the future course of restitution for unjust enrichment will be shaped by the reading of, and debate around, Professor Evans-Jones, *Unjustified Enrichment*, Volume 1, SULI, 2003. In any event, the publication of Professor Birks' *Unjust Enrichment* (OUP, 2003) makes any contribution from me a dangerous, rather than helpful, exercise for undergraduate students.

Thus space has been found for misfeasance in public office (only a little) and for reparation for human rights (quite a lot). I have, at least it may be said, dealt with the major criticism since the first edition by putting all of damages together. Other than that, I have simply expanded the treatment here and there benefiting from my 10 years or so of researches on which is now *Reparation: Liability for Delict*. The existence of *Reparation: Liability for Delict* should make the task of the student and busy teacher in updating between editions very much easier.

Beyond the dreams of the past, students and teachers now have available *historical* treatments of many of the delicts discussed in this book. Teachers no doubt inform their teaching from these essays and good students can consolidate and develop their understanding. I do not mean that in any way to detract from Professor Walker's multi-volume *History*, from which I continue to benefit, simply that that work is probably either beyond the average student or requires too much effort in the crowded curriculum. Illuminating and relatively accessible essays are all found in Reid and Zimmermann, *A History of Private Law in Scotland*, Volume 2, Obligations (Oxford, 2000). Cited as HPLS:

D. Visser & N. Whitty, "The Structure of the Law of Delict in Historical Perspective" 422.
K. Norrie, "The Intentional Delicts" 477.
H. MacQueen and W. Sellar, "Negligence" 517.
R. Zimmermann and P. Simpson, "Strict Liability" 548.
P. Simpson, "Vicarious Liability" 584.
R. Zimmermann and P. Simpson, "Liability among Neighbours" 612.
J. Blackie, "Defamation" 633.

Never before have more resources from more sources, legal and historical, been available to students and teachers, *in Scotland*. The simple things are as difficult and the difficult things more diffuse. On the bright side, more often than not, the Law Commissions make things better, one or other of the Parliaments might make things better rather than worse on a good day and the House of Lords, when it does not choose to act as a 3-2, 4-3, graduate seminar, can muck out the stable, for example, by making barristers liable in negligence and sinking, to the relief even of West of Scotland heretics, the *Polemis*.

For the sake of brevity and cost, previous prefaces are not reprinted. Can I thank again everyone who helped through all these editions — the Strathclyders and others for the first, Jim Logie for the second and third and much more, and Dr Douglas Brodie for this edition. The disclaimer in this case in respect of Dr Brodie must be much more extensive than the "usual disclaimer" — Dr Brodie has had nothing to do with it and does not even know it is being published! However, his recent help with *Reparation: Liability for Delict* has informed this text too. I am very grateful to the colleagues who responded to my unsolicited circular anent the third edition — you know who you are. Thanks to Alison for research assistance. Thanks, this time, and for the last time, to Gerry MacMillan for looking after my professional obligations when I was away from the office doing this when still a partner at MacMillans, Solicitors! Special thanks to Carol Dean who supported me at MacMillans all these years.

Finally, thanks to my new colleagues at the University of Stirling for providing an academic home for this and other texts — and, not least, me.

The law is as at April 30, 2004 but I have tried to include such new material as has come my way.

W.J. Stewart
Hunter's Quay, Summer 2004.

CONTENTS

Page

Preface vii
Table of Cases xiii
Table of Statutes xxxix
Tables of Statutory Instruments xlv

Section I: Introduction
Chapter 1 Introduction 1

Section II: Specific Wrongs
Chapter 2 Wrongs to the Person 23
Chapter 3 Wrongs to Property 33
Chapter 4 Roman Quasi-Delicts 47
Chapter 5 Economic Wrongs 52
Chapter 6 Abuse of Process 70
Chapter 7 Misfeasance in Office 72
Chapter 8 Defamation and Related Actions 74

Section III: Negligence
Chapter 9 Basic Negligence 105
Chapter 10 Economic Loss 130
Chapter 11 Nervous Shock 145
Chapter 12 Public Authorities 153
Chapter 13 Third Party Intervention 162
Chapter 14 Indirect Damage and Injury 166

Section IV: External Wrongs
Chapter 15 Statutory Duty 169
Chapter 16 Reparation for Failed or Inadequate Transposition of
             EU law 177
Chapter 17 Human Rights 182

Section V: Special Applications
Chapter 18 Occupiers Liability 196
Chapter 19 Product Liability 207

Chapter 20 Liability for Animals 217
Chapter 21 Employers' Liability 225
Chapter 22 Professional Liability 247

Section VI: General Matters
Chapter 23 The Litigants 257
Chapter 24 Vicarious Liability 296
Chapter 25 Defences, Transfer and Extinction 308
Chapter 26 Damages and Other Remedies 323

Bibliography 345
Index 357

TABLE OF CASES

A v B PLC [2002] EWCA Civ 337; [2003] Q.B. 195 8–37
A v National Blood Authority; *sub nom.* Hepatitis C Litigation (No. 1), Re [2001] 3 All E.R. 289; [2001] Lloyd's Rep. Med. 187 .... 19–4, 19–5, 19–8
A v United Kingdom [1998] T.L.R. 578 17–3
A v UK [2002] T.L.R. 576 8–19
AB v CD (1904) 7 F. 22 8–9
ADT v UK [2000] T.L.R. 604 17–10
ADT Ltd v BDO Binder Hamlyn [1996] B.C.C. 808 23–19
AG Barr and Co Ltd v MacGheoghegan reported with 1931 S.C. (HL) 1 3–14
A Family v BBC, *Scotsman*, November 6, 1992 26–23
AKZO Chemie BV v Commission of the European Communities (C62/86) [1991] T.L.R. 432 5–10
Aberdeen Bon-Accord Loyal Orange Lodge 701 v Aberdeen City Council, 2002 S.L.T. (Sh. Ct) 52; 2001 G.W.D. 30–1213 17–13
Abouzaid v Mothercare (UK) Ltd [2001] T.L.R. 136 .... 19–4, 19–5, 19–8
Adam v Ward [1917] A.C. 309 8–26
Adams v Guardian Newspapers Ltd, 2003 S.C. 425; 2003 S.L.T. 1058 ...... 8–27, 8–29
Adams v War Office [1955] 1 W.L.R. 1116; [1955] 3 All E.R. 245 23–4
Adamson v Martin, 1916 S.C. 319 25–7
Admiralty Commissioners v North of Scotland and Orkney and Shetland Steam Navigation Co. *See* "Boy Andrew", The v "St Rognvald", The
Advocate (H.M.) v McKean, 1996 J.C. 32; 1996 S.L.T. 1383 8–8
Advocate (H.M.) v R, 2001 G.W.D. 1275 17–21
Advocate (H.M.) v R, [2002] UKPC D3; [2004] 1 A.C. 462; reversing 2002 S.L.T. 834; affirming 2001 S.L.T. 1366; 2001 S.C.C.R. 915 .... 17–1, 17–8
Advocate (Lord) v Glengarnock Iron and Steel Company Ltd, 1909 1 S.L.T. 15 3–2
Advocate (Lord) v NB Ry (1894) 2 S.L.T. 71 .... 3–6, 25–2
Advocate (Lord) v Strathclyde RC, [1990] 2 A.C. 580; [1989] 3 W.L.R. 1346; 1990 S.L.T. 158 23–3
Advocate (Lord) v The Scotsman Publications Ltd, 1988 S.L.T. 490; [1989] 1 F.S.R. 310 5–4
Agnew v Laughlan, 1948 S.C. 656; 1948 S.L.T. 512 23–37
Aiken v Board Of Management Aberdeen College, 2000 G.W.D. 74 21–22
Airedale NHS Trust v Bland [1993] A.C. 789; [1993] 2 W.L.R. 316 23–36
Airnes v Chief Constable, Strathclyde Police, 1998 S.L.T. (Sh. Ct) 15; 1998 Rep. L.R. 19 2–5
Aitken v Finlay (1837) 15 S. 683 6–2
Akenzua v Secretary of State for the Home Department [2002] EWCA Civ 1470; [2003] 1 W.L.R. 741 7–2
Akram v Commission for Racial Equality, 1994 G.W.D. 22–1372 5–13
Al Fagih v HH Saudi Research and Marketing [2001] EWCA Civ 1634; [2002] E.M.L.R. 13 8–27
Al Nakib Investments v Longcroft [1990] 1 W.L.R. 1390; [1990] 3 All E.R. 321 .... 10–4, 10–6
Albert (Prince) v Strange, 2 De G. & Sm. 652 1–19
Alcock v Chief Constable, South Yorkshire; *sub nom.* Jones v Wright [1992] 1 A.C. 310; [1991] 3 W.L.R. 1057; [1991] 4 All E.R. 907 .... 11–1, 11–2, 11–3
Alcock v Wraith [1991] T.L.R. 600 24–7
Allan v Barclay (1864) 2 M. 873 .... 9–25, 9–26, 10–8

Allan v Greater Glasgow Health Board, unreported, November 25, 1993 23–27
Allan's Trs v Allan, 1949 S.L.T. (Notes) 3 23–23
Allardice v Robertson (1830) 2 W. & S. 102 23–7
Allbutt v GMC (1899) 23 Q.B.D. 400 8–28
Allen v Bloomsbury Health Authority [1993] 1 All E.R. 651; [1992] P.I.Q.R.
    Q50 23–27
Allen v Flood [1898] A.C. 1 5–10
Anderson v Advocate (H.M.), 1996 J.C. 29; 1996 S.L.T. 155 22–8
Anderson v Chief Constable, unreported, January 20, 1987 2–5
Anderson v Forth Valley Health Board, 1998 S.L.T. 588; 1998 S.C.L.R. 97 23–27
Anderson v Marshall (1835) 13 S. 1130 2–6
Anderson v Ormiston and Lorain (1750) Mor. 13949 6–2
Anderson v Wilson's Trs, 1965 S.L.T. (Sh. Ct) 35 20–4
Anns v Merton LBC [1978] A.C. 728; [1977] 2 W.L.R. 1024 .... 9–7, 9–8, 10–5, 10–6,
                                                11–2, 12–1, 12–2, 12–3, 12–6
Anwar v Chief Constable, unreported, September 20, 1995 2–5
Arenson v Arenson. *See* Arenson v Casson Beckman
Arenson v Casson Beckman; *sub nom.* Arenson v Arenson [1977] A.C. 405;
    [1975] 3 W.L.R. 815 22–1
Argyll (Duchess of) v Duke of Argyll [1967] Ch. 302; [1965] 2 W.L.R. 790 5–3
Armagas Ltd v Mundogas Ltd S.A.; The Ocean Frost [1986] A.C. 717; [1986]
    2 W.L.R. 1063, (HL) 24–5
Armstrong v Glasgow DC. *See* Armstrong v Moore
Armstrong v Moore; *sub nom.* Armstrong v Glasgow DC, 1996 S.L.T. 690;
    1996 Rep. L.R. 64, (OH) 15–3
Ashcroft's CB v Stewart, 1988 S.L.T. 163, (OH) 25–8
Ashingdane v UK (1985) E.H.R.R. 528 17–5
Ashton v Turner [1981] Q.B. 137; [1980] 3 W.L.R. 736 25–7
Associated Provincial Pictures Houses v Wednesbury Corporation [1948] 1
    K.B. 223 12–8
Atkinson v Aberdeen City Council, 2002 G.W.D. 737 18–5
Atkinson v Newcastle Waterworks Co (1877) 2 Ex. D. 441 15–1
Attia v British Gas [1988] Q.B. 304; [1987] 3 W.L.R. 1101; [1987] 3 All E.R.
    455 11–4
Att.-Gen. v Nissan; *sub nom.* Nissan v Attorney General [1970] A.C. 179;
    [1969] 2 W.L.R. 926; [1969] 1 All E.R. 629 24–2
Att.-Gen. v Guardian Newspapers (No. 2); Observer Ltd, Att.-Gen. v Times
    Newspapers Ltd [1990] 1 A.C. 109; [1988] 3 W.L.R. 776 .... 5–3, 23–6
Axis West Developments Ltd v Chartwell Land Investment Ltd, 1999 S.L.T.
    1416; 1999 G.W.D. 32–1551 3–1

B v Forsey, 1987 S.L.T. 681; 1987 S.C.L.R. 504 2–11
B v Harris, 1989 S.C. 278; 1990 S.L.T. 208 2–4
B v Islington HA [1991] 1 Q.B. 638; [1991] 2 W.L.R. 501 23–24
BT v James Thomson and Sons Ltd, 1997 S.C. 59; 1997 S.L.T. 767 1–11
Baignet v McCulloch, 1997 G.W.D. 16–737 8–23
Baillie v Edinburgh Mags (1906) 14 S.L.T. 344 2–5
Bain v Kings and Co Ltd, 1973 S.L.T. (Notes) 8, (OH) 11–1
Baird v Hamilton (1826) 4 S. 790 24–1
Barker v Murdoch, 1979 S.L.T. 145 26–17
Bank of Scotland v 3i plc, 1992 G.W.D. 6–321 10–4
Bank of Scotland v Fuller Peiser, 2002 S.L.T. 574; 2002 S.C.L.R. 255, (OH) 10–7
Banner's Tutor v Kennedy's Trs, 1978 S.L.T. (Notes) 83, (OH) 25–9
Barratt International Resorts Ltd v Barratt Owners Group, 2003 G.W.D. 19,
    (OH) 5–13, 5–14, 8–1, 8–34
Barnett v Chelsea and Kensington Hospital Management Committee [1969] 1
    Q.B. 428; [1968] 2 W.L.R. 422, QBD 9–20

Barrett v Enfield LBC [2001] 2 A.C. 550; [1999] 3 W.L.R. 79, (HL) 12–5, 17–7
Barrie v Glasgow City Council, 2000 Rep. L.R. 46 21–15
Bartonshill Coal Co v Reid (1858) 3 Macq. 266 24–1
Baume and Co Ltd v Moore [1958] Ch. 907; [1958] 2 W.L.R. 797, (CA) 5–6
Baxter v Pritchard, 1992 G.W.D. 24–1385 24–7
Beck v United Closures and Plastics plc, 2001 S.L.T. 1299; 2002 S.C.L.R. 154,
   (OH) 21–13, 21–14, 21–15
Beggs v Motherwell Bridge Fabricators, 1998 S.L.T. 1215; 1997 S.C.L.R.
   1019; 1997 Rep. L.R. 87, (OH) 21–9
Bell v Gunn (1859) 21 D. 1008 6–2
Bell v McCurdie, 1981 S.C. 64; 1981 S.L.T. 159, 2 Div 23–38
Bell v Scottish Special Housing Association, 1987 S.L.T. 320, 2 Div 9–24
Belmont Laundry Co Ltd v Aberdeen Steam Laundry Co Ltd (1898) 1 F. 45 5–13
Bennett v J Lamont and Sons, 2000 S.L.T. 17; 2000 Rep. L.R. 2, (OH) 14–2, 20–5
Bern's Ex. v Montrose Asylum (1893) 20 R. 859 23–37
Berry v Irish Times [1973] I.R. 368 8–8
Birse v ALPS Electric (Scotland) Ltd, 2002 G.W.D. 513 21–23
Black v Carmichael, 1992 S.L.T. 897; 1992 S.C.C.R. 709 3–16
Black v NB Rly, 1908 S.C. 44 26–3
Blackburn v Sinclair, 1984 S.L.T. 368 10–12
Blackwood v Robertson, 1984 S.L.T. (Sh. Ct) 68, (OH) 23–18
Blake v Lothian Health Board, 1992 G.W.D. 32–1908 25–11
Boal v Scottish Catholic Printing Co Ltd, 1908 S.C. 667 8–10
Bogan's CB v Graham, 1992 S.C.L.R. 920; 1992 G.W.D. 32–1898 ... 23–39, 25–11
Bolam v Friern Hospital Management Committee [1957] 1 W.L.R. 582; [1957]
   2 All E.R. 118, QBD 22–3
Bolitho v City and Hackney HA [1998] A.C. 232; [1997] 3 W.L.R. 1151,
   (HL) 22–3
Bolton v Jameson and Mackay, 1987 S.L.T. 291, reversed on other grounds
   1989 S.L.T. 222 22–7
Bolton v Stone; *sub nom.* Stone v Bolton [1951] A.C. 850; [1951] 1 All E.R.
   1078 .... 9–11, 13–3
Bonser v UK Coal Mining Ltd, 2003 T.L.R. 388 21–7
Bonthrone v Secretary of State for Scotland, 1987 S.L.T. 34, (OH) 2–2, 12–6, 12–7
Borland v Lochwinnoch Golf Club, 1986 S.L.T. (Sh. Ct) 13 23–12
Borowski v Att. Gen for Canada (1987) 39 D.L.R. (4th) 731 23–24
Bourhill v Young, [1943] A.C. 92; [1942] 2 All E.R. 396; 1942 S.C. (HL) 78 9–4,
   9–26, 11–1, 11–2, 23–37
Bowers v Strathclyde RC, 1981 S.L.T. 122, 1 Div 26–17
Boyd and Forrest v Glasgow and South-Western Ry, 1912 S.C. (HL) 93 5–2
"Boy Andrew", The v "St Rognvald", The; *sub nom.* Admiralty Commis-
   sioners v North of Scotland and Orkney and Shetland Steam Navigation
   Co [1948] A.C. 140; [1947] 2 All E.R. 350; 1947 S.C. (HL) 70 9–23
Boys v Chaplin; *sub nom.* Chaplin v Boys [1971] A.C. 356; [1969] 3 W.L.R.
   322 1–5
Brasserie du Pecheur S.A. v Germany (C–46/93) [1996] Q.B. 404; [1996] 2
   W.L.R. 506 .... 16–4, 16–5
Bristol Conservatories Ltd v Conservatories Custom Built Ltd [1989] R.P.C.
   455, (CA) 5–7
British Airways plc v Boyce, 2001 S.L.T. 275 25–18
British Homophone v Kunz [1935] All E.R. 627 5–13
British Motor Trade Association v Gray, 1951 S.C. 586; 1951 S.L.T. 247, 1
   Div 5–13
British Telecom v Thomson, 1997 Rep. L.R. 23 14–1
Brodie of Letham v Sir James Cadel of Morton, March 22, 1707 3–12
Brogan v UK (1989) 11 E.H.R.R. 117 17–5
Brooks v Lind, 1997 Rep. L.R. 83; 1997 G.W.D. 13–570, (OH) 8–9, 8–29

Broom v Ritchie and Co (1904) 6 F. 942 23–37
Brougham v Royal Bank of Scotland, 2002 G.W.D. 449 6–2
Brown v Advocate (Lord), 1984 S.L.T. 146, (OH) 23–5
Brown v D.C. Thomson and Co Ltd, 1912 1 S.L.T. 123 8–5
Brown v East and Midlothian NHS Trust, 2000 S.L.T. 342; 2000 Rep. L.R. 10,
    (OH) 21–23
Brown v Fulton (1881) 9 R. 36 23–35
Brown v Lee Constructions Ltd, 1977 S.L.T. (Notes) 61, (OH) 3–2
Brown v Rolls Royce Ltd, [1960] 1 W.L.R. 210; [1960] 1 All E.R. 577; 1960
    S.C. (HL) 22; 1960 S.L.T. 119 9–15
Brown's Trs v Hay (1898) 25 R. 1112 3–15
Bruce v Clapham, 1982 S.L.T. 386, (OH) 23–17
Bruce v Leisk (1892) 19 R. 482 8–23
Bruce v Smith (1898) 1 F. 327 8–35
Buron v Denman (1848) 2 Ex. 167 24–2
Burrows v Rhodes [1899] 1 Q.B. 816 5–2
Burton Moorhead (1881) 8 R 892 20–2
Burton's Trs v Scottish Sports Council, 1983 S.L.T. 418 26–23
Bush v Belling, 1963 S.L.T. (Notes) 69, (OH) 23–34
Butler v Grampian University Hospital NHS Trust, 2002 S.L.T. 985; 2002 Rep.
    L.R. 83; 2002 G.W.D. 18–610, (OH) 21–12
Byrd v Wither, 1991 S.L.T. 206 2–4
Byrned v Dean [1937] 1 K.B. 818 8–8

C v M, 1923 S.C. 1 8–32
CN v Norsk Pacific Steamship Co., [1992] 1 S.C.R. 1021 10–6
Cairns v Butlins, 1989 G.W.D. 40–1879 .... 18–3, 18–4
Cairns v Harry Walker Ltd, 1913 2 S.L.T. 379 3–15
Caldwell v Monro (1872) 10 M. 717 8–5
Caledonia North Sea Ltd. v London Bridge Engineering Ltd, [2002] UKHL 4;
    [2002] 1 All E.R. (Comm) 321; 2002 S.L.T. 278, (HL); affirming 2000
    S.L.T. 1123; [2000] Lloyd's Rep. I.R. 249 25–17
Caledonian Ry v Greenock Corporation, 1917 S.C. (HL) 56 3–11
Calquhoun v Paton (1859) 21 D. 996 26–23
Caltex Oil Ltd v The Dredge Willemstad (1976) 136 C.L.R. 529; (1977) 51
    A.L.J.R. 270 10–9
Cambridge Water Co Ltd v Eastern Counties Leather plc [1994] 2 A.C. 264;
    [1994] 2 W.L.R. 53, (HL) 3–10
Cameron v Greater Glasgow Health Board, 1993 G.W.D. 6–433 22–5
Cameron v Kvaerner Govan, 2000 G.W.D. 1058 21–16
Cameron v Mortimer (1872) 10 M. 817 6–2
Cameron v Young, 1908 S.C. (HL) 7 18–9
Campbell v MGN Newspapers Ltd [2004] UKHL 22 .... 5–4, 8–37, 17–1, 17–10,
    17–12
Campbell v Muir, 1908 S.C. 387 3–12
Campbell v Ord (1873) 1 R. 149 19–2
Campbell v UK (1993) 15 E.H.R.R. 137 17–10
Campbell and Cosans v UK (1982) 13 E.H.R.R. 441 17–3
Cantwell v Criminal Injuries Compensation Board, 2001 S.L.T. 966 26–5
Caparo Industries plc v Dickman [1990] 2 A.C. 605; [1990] 2 W.L.R. 358;
    [1990] 1 All E.R. 568 10–4
Capital and Counties v Hampshire Council; John Munroe v London Fire
    Authority; Church of Jesus Christ of Latter-Day Saints v West Yorkshire
    Fire Authority [1997] Q.B. 1004; [1997] 3 W.L.R. 331; [1997] 2 All E.R.
    865, (CA) 12–7
Cardle v Mulrainey, 1992 S.L.T. 1152; 1992 S.C.C.R. 658 23–39

Carmichael v Bearsden and District Rifle and Pistol Club, 2000 S.L.T. (Sh. Ct) 49; 2000 Rep. L.R. 55 23–13
Carroll v Andrew Barclay and Sons Ltd, 1948 S.C. (HL) 100 15–6
Carroll v BBC, 1997 S.L.T. (Sh. Ct) 23 8–10
Cassidy v Connachie, 1907 S.C. 1112 8–23
Castle v St Augustine's Links (1922) 38 T.L.R. 615 9–11
Catleugh v Caradon Everest Ltd, 1999 G.W.D. 1554, (OH) 21–6
Cattanach v Melchior, 2001 S.L.T. 446 23–28
Cavanagh v Ulster Weaving Co [1960] A.C. 145; [1959] 3 W.L.R. 262, (HL) 9–15
Century Insurance Co v Northern Ireland Transport Board [1942] A.C. 509; [1942] 1 All E.R. 491, (HL) 24–4
Chadwick v BRB [1967] 1 W.L.R. 912; [1967] 2 All E.R. 945, QBD 11–3
Chahal v UK (1997) 23 E.H.R.R. 413; 1 B.H.R.C. 405 17–5
Chanthall Investments Ltd v FG Minter Ltd, 22 January 1976 (reported on another point in 1976 S.C. 73) 9–26
Chaplin v Boys. *See* Boys v Chaplin
Chapman v Barber, 1989 S.L.T. 830, (OH) 8–26
Chappell v UK (1990) 12 E.H.R.R. 1; [1989] 1 F.S.R. 617 17–10
Chicago (City of) v Tribune Co (1923) 139 N.E. 86 23–6
Christie v Robertson(1899) 1 F. 1155 8–14
Clark v Armstrong (1862) 24 D. 1315 .... 20–2, 20–4
Clark v McLean, 1993 S.L.T. 492, (OH) 25–11
Clark v Maersk Co Ltd, 2000 S.L.T. (Sh. Ct) 9; 1999 G.W.D. 32–1556 18–2
Clayards v Dethick (1848) 12 Q.B. 439 25–9
Clayton v Woodman and Son (Builders) Ltd [1962] 2 Q.B. 533; [1962] 1 W.L.R. 585, (CA) 22–2
Cleland v Lawrie (1848) 10 D. 1372 6–2
Clelland v Robb, 1911 S.C. 253 9–1
Clements v Shell UK Ltd, 1991 G.W.D. 35–2153 9–21
Coclas v Bruce Peebles and Co (1908) 16 S.L.T. 7 23–41
Cohen v Shaw, 1992 S.L.T. 1022; 1992 S.C.L.R. 182, (OH) 23–25, 26–21
Cole v Weir Pumps Ltd, 1995 S.L.T. 12; 1994 S.C.L.R. 580, (OH) 18–4
Coleridge v Miller, 1997 S.L.T. 485 .... 10–8, 14–1
Collins v First Quench Retailing Ltd, 2003 S.L.T. 1220; 2003 S.C.L.R. 205, (OH) 21–8
Colquhoun v Hannah, unreported, October 31, 1942 20–4
Colquhoun and Cameron v Mackenzie (1894) 22 R. 23 26–23
Coltman v Bibby Tankers Ltd [1988] A.C. 276; [1987] 3 W.L.R. 1181, (HL) 21–24
Colvilles Ltd v Devine. *See* Devines v Colville
Comber v Greater Glasgow Health Board, 1989 S.L.T. 639; 1989 S.C.L.R. 515, (OH) 25–11
Comex Houlder Diving Ltd v Colne Fishing Co Ltd, 1987 S.C. (HL) 85; 1987 S.L.T. 443, (HL) 25–17
Comex Houlder Diving Ltd v Colne Fishing Co Ltd (No. 2), 1992 S.L.T. 89, (OH) 25–17
Comingersoll SA v Portugal (35382/97, April 6, 2000) 17–22
Commission v Italian Republic [1989] E.C.R. 143 16–2
Commission v UK C–300/95 [1997] All E.R. (EC) 481 .... 19–3, 19–8
Convery v Lanarkshire Tramway Co (1905) 8 F. 117 1–5
Cope v Sharpe [1912] 1 K.B. 496 .... 3–3, 25–4
Coreck Maritime GmbH v Sevrybokholodflot, 1994 S.L.T. 893, (OH) 23–47
Cossey v UK [1991] 2 F.L.R. 492; [1993] 2 F.C.R. 97; (1991) 13 E.H.R.R. 622 17–10
Costello-Roberts v UK [1994] 1 F.C.R. 65; (1995) 19 E.H.R.R. 112 17–3
Coutts v JM Piggins Ltd, 1983 S.L.T. 320, (OH) 15–5

Coutt's Tr. v Coutts; *sub nom.* Sharp v Coutts, 1998 S.C. 798; 1998 S.C.L.R.
   729 23–40
Cowie v Atlantic Drilling, 1995 S.C. 288; 1995 S.L.T. 1151 26–10
Cowie v Strathclyde RC, 1985 S.L.T. 333, 2 Div 26–23
Cox's Trs v Pegg, 1950 S.C. 117; 1950 S.L.T. 127, 1 Div 23–23
Craig v Glasgow Victoria and Leverndale HBH, (OH), December 1, 1972 2–2
Craig v Inveresk Paper Merchants Ltd, 1970 S.L.T (Notes) 50, (OH) 8–35
Crawford v Adams; Crawford v Dunlop (1900) 2 F. 987 24–2
Crawford v Mill (1830) 5 Mur. 215 3–15
Crofter Hand Woven Harris Tweed Co v Veitch, 1942 S.C. (HL); 1 [1942] A.C.
   435; [1942] 1 All E.R. 147; 1943 S.L.T. 2, (HL); affirming 1940 S.L.T.
   210, 2 Div 1–19, 5–11, 5–12, 25–2
Cropper v Chief Constable, Dumfries, and Galloway Constabulary and
   Secretary of State, 1998 S.L.T. 548; 1997 G.W.D. 22–1106 24–8
Cross v Highland and Islands Enterprise, 2001 S.L.T. 1060; 2001 S.C.L.R.
   547 .... 21–9, 21–11
Crotty v McFarlane, January 27, 1891 8–29
Cruikshank v Fife Council, Cupar Sheriff Court, December 17, 2001 18–3
Cullen v North Lanarkshire Council, 1998 S.C. 451; 1998 S.L.T. 847 21–19
Cullin v London Fire and Civil Defence Authority [1999] P.I.Q.R. P314,
   (CA) 11–2
Cumnock and Doon Valley DC v Dance Energy Associates Ltd, 1992 G.W.D.
   25–1441 3–5
Cunningham v Phillips (1868) 6 M. 926 8–34
Cunningham v Reading Football Club Ltd [1991] T.L.R. 153 13–2
Currie v Clamp's Executor, 2002 S.L.T. 196; 2001 S.C.L.R. 504; 2001 G.W.D.
   319, (OH) 25–8
Cuthbert v Linklater, 1935 S.L.T. 94 .... 8–9, 8–12
Cutler v Wandsworth Stadium Ltd (in liquidation) [1949] 1 All E.R. 544 15–2

DC Thomson v Deakin [1952] Ch. 646; [1952] 2 All E.R. 361 5–14
DM Stevenson and Co v Radford and Bright Ltd (1902) 10 S.L.T. 82. 23–41
D and F Estates Ltd v Church Commissioners for England [1989] A.C. 177;
   [1988] 3 W.L.R. 368, (HL) 9–8, 10–3, 10–4, 10–5, 24–7
Daborn v Bath Tramways Motor Co [1946] 2 All E.R. 333, (CA) 9–13
Dalgleish v Glasgow Corp., 1976 S.C. 32; 1976 S.L.T. 157, 2 Div 26–17
D'Amato v Badger [1996] D.L.R. (4th) 129 10–8
Daniell v Aviemore Station Hotel Co., 1951 S.L.T. (Notes) 76 26–20
Dash Ltd v Philip King Tailoring, 1988 S.C. 87; 1989 S.L.T. 39, 2 Div 5–6
Davenport v Corinthian Motor Policies at Lloyds, 1991 S.L.T. 774; 1992
   S.C.L.R. 221, Ex Div 1–1
Davey v Harrow Corp. [1958] 1 Q.B. 60; [1957] 2 W.L.R. 941; [1957] 2 All
   E.R. 305, (CA) 3–4
Davidson v Kerr, 1996 G.W.D. 40–2296 3–5
Davidson v Upper Clyde Shipbuilders Ltd, 1990 S.L.T. 329, (OH) 26–16
Davie v Edinburgh Corporation, 1977 S.L.T. (Notes) 5, (OH) 18–4
Davie v New Merton Board Mills [1959] A.C. 604; [1959] 2 W.L.R. 331,
   (HL) 21–2, 21–24
Davie v Wilson (1854) 16 D. 956 23–35
Davies v Mann (1842) 10 M. & W. 546 9–23
Dawson v Scottish Power, 1999 S.L.T. 672; 1998 G.W.D. 38–1975, (OH) 18–6,
   18–7
Deane v Lothian RC, 1986 S.L.T. 22, 2 Div 26–23
De freitas v O'Brien [1995] P.I.Q.R. P281; [1995] 6 Med. L.R. 108, (CA) 22–3
Dehler v Ottawa Civic Hospital (1979) 101 D.L.R. (3d) 686 23–24
De Mulder v Jadranska Linijska (Jadrolinija), 1989 S.L.T. 269, (OH) 1–5

Delaney v McGregor Construction (Highlands) Ltd, 2003 Rep. L.R. 56; 2003
G.W.D. 10–290, (OH) 21–19
Dennis and Another v MOD, 2003 T.L.R. 270 .... 3–9, 17–10
Department of the Environment v T. Bates Ltd [1991] 1 A.C. 499; [1990] 3
W.L.R. 457, (HL) 9–8, 10–5
Derbyshire CC v Times Newspapers Ltd [1993] T.L.R. 87 23–6
Derry v Ministry of Defence [1998] T.L.R. 364 23–5
Devines v Colville; *sub nom.* Colvilles Ltd v Devine [1969] 1 W.L.R. 475;
[1969] 2 All E.R. 53; 1969 S.L.T. 154 18–4
Devlin v Strathclyde RC, 1993 S.L.T. 699, (OH) 18–6
Dewar v Fraser (1767) Mor. 12803 3–12
Dick v Grizzel (1566) (see Walker, *History*, Vol.II) 1–17
Dickson v Hygenic Institute, 1910 1 S.L.T. 111 9–19
Dickson v Taylor (1816) 1 Mur 141 5–8
Dickson Minto WS v Bonnier Media Ltd, 2002 S.L.T. 776; 2002 G.W.D.
17–551 .... 8–33, 17–12, 26–23
Dillenkofer v Germany [1996] T.L.R. 564 16–5
Dimbleby and Sons Ltd v NUJ [1984] 1 W.L.R. 427; [1984] 1 All E.R. 751,
(HL) 23–22
Dimond v Lovell [2002] 1 A.C. 384; [2000] 2 W.L.R. 1121 26–5
Dingwall v Walter Alexander and Sons, 1981 S.L.T. 313, 2 Div 26–21
Discovery Communications Inc v Discovery FM Ltd, 2000 S.C. 69; 2000
S.L.T. 212 26–23
Dobbie v Henderson, 1970 S.L.T. (Sh. Ct) 27 20–3
Donaghy v NCB, 1957 S.L.T. (Notes) 35, 1 Div 9–24
Donald v Galloway, 1988 G.W.D. 24–1042 25–11
Donald v Rutherford, 1984 S.L.T. 70, Ex Div 25–11
Donald v Strathclyde Passenger Transport Executive, 1986 S.L.T. 625, 1
Div 25–21
Donlon v Colonial Mutual Group (UK Holdings) Ltd, 1998 S.C. 244; 1997
S.C.L.R. 1088, Ex Div 8–28, 10–5
Donoghue v Stevenson, [1932] A.C. 562; 1932 S.C. (HL) 31, (HL) 9–1, 9–4, 9–5,
9–7, 9–7, 10–3, 10–5, 10–8, 14–2, 19–2, 22–2
Douglas v Advocate (Lord), 1996 G.W.D. 1981 21–16
Douglas and Others v Hello! Ltd and Others, 2003 T.L.R. 239 .... 5–4, 8–37, 17–12
Douglas's CB v Douglas, 1974 S.L.T. (Notes) 7, (OH) 26–10
Downie v Chief Constable, Strathclyde Police, 1998 S.L.T. 8; 1997 S.C.L.R.
603 .... 2–5, 6–3
Dorset Yacht v The Home Office [1970] A.C. 1004; [1970] 2 W.L.R. 1140,
(HL) 1–4, 13–1
Drew v Western SMT, 1947 S.L.T. 92; 1946 S.L.T. (Notes) 30 15–9
Dubai Aluminium Co Ltd v Salaam and Others [2002] UKHL 48; [2003] 2
A.C. 366; [2002] 3 W.L.R. 1913 .... 23–16, 24–5
Dudley v Advocate (H.M.), 2003 J.C. 53; 2003 S.L.T. 597; 2003 G.W.D.
138 17–10
Duff v East Dunbartonshire Council, 1999 G.W.D. 22–1072 18–3
Duff v Highlands and Islands Fire Board, 1995 S.L.T. 1362, (OH) 12–7
Duff v National Telephone Co (1889) 16 R. 675 19–2
Duffy v Lanarkshire Health Board, 2001 G.W.D. 10–368 22–4
Dumbreck v Addie and Sons, 1929 S.C. (HL) 51 18–1
Dumfries Fleshers v Rankine, Dec. 10, 1816, F.C. 23–10
Dunbar v Presbytery of Auchterarder (1849) 12 D. 284 23–10
Dunbar of Kilconzie, Petr, 1986 S.C. (HL) 1; 1986 S.L.T. 463, (HL) 23–23
Duncan v Beattie, 2003 S.L.T. 1243; 2003 G.W.D. 28–798 23–16
Duncan v Ross Harper and Murphy, 1993 S.L.T. 105, (OH) 25–8
Dundas v Livingstone (1900) 3 F. 37 8–24
Dunfermline DC v Blyth and Blyth, 1985 S.L.T. 345, (OH) 25–12

Dunlop v McGowans, 1980 S.C. (HL) 73; 1980 S.L.T. 129, (HL); affirming
1979 S.C. 22; 1979 S.L.T. 34 25–12
Dunlop v Woollahra Municipal Council [1982] A.C. 158; [1981] 2 W.L.R.
693 7–2
Dunlop Pneumatic Tyre Co Ltd v Dunlop Motor Co Ltd, 1907 S.C. (HL) 15 5–6
Dunn v Carlin, 2003 S.L.T. 342; 2003 S.C.L.R. 639; 2003 G.W.D. 5–130 18–5
Dunnet v Nelson, 1926 S.C. 764 8–22
Dunnett v Mitchell (1887) 15 R. 131 23–10
Duport Steels Ltd v Sirs [1980] 1 W.L.R. 142; [1980] 1 All E.R. 529 23–22
Dutton v Bognor Regis UDC [1972] 1 Q.B. 373; [1972] 2 W.L.R. 299 ...... 10–5, 11–2,
                                                                                                                    12–3
Dynamco Ltd v Holland, Hannen and Cubitts (Scotland) Ltd, 1971 S.C. 257;
1972 S.L.T. 38 10–8

EETPU v Times Newspapers Ltd [1980] Q.B. 585; [1980] 3 W.L.R. 98,
QBD 23–21
Eagle v Chambers [2003] EWCA Civ 1107; [2004] R.T.R. 9, (CA) 25–9
Easton v Consafe (Burntisland) Ltd Aberdeen Sh. Ct, April 2, 2002 24–6
Ebsworth v Advocate (H.M.), 1992 S.L.T. 1161; 1992 S.C.C.R. 671 23–39
Edgar v Lamont, 1914 S.C. 277 22–2
Edward Wong Finance Co Ltd v Johnson, Stokes and Master [1984] A.C. 296;
[1984] 2 W.L.R. 1 22–3
Edwards v Butlins, 1998 S.L.T. 500; 1997 G.W.D. 21–1052, 2 Div 21–24
Edwards v NCB [1949] 1 K.B. 704; [1949] 1 All E.R. 743, (CA) 15–7
Edwards v UK [2002] T.L.R. 141 17–2
Elliott v J and C Finney, 1989 S.L.T. 605, 2 Div: affirming 1989 S.L.T. 208,
(OH) 25–11
Elliot v Joicey, [1935] A.C. 209; 1935 S.C. (HL) 57 23–23
Emeh v Kensington, Chelsea and Westminster Area HA [1985] Q.B. 1012;
[1985] 2 W.L.R. 233 23–27
English v Wilsons and Clyde Coal Co, 1937 S.C. (HL) 46 21–1
Erven Warnink v Townend [1979] A.C. 731; [1979] 3 W.L.R. 68, (HL) ... 5–6, 5–7
Esso Petroleum Co Ltd v Hall Russell and Co Ltd, [1989] A.C. 643; [1988] 3
W.L.R. 730; 1988 S.L.T. 874 23–42
Evans v Stein (1904) 7 F. 65 1–5
Evans v Triplex Safety Glass Co Ltd [1936] 1 All E.R. 283, KBD 19–2, 19–4
Ewart v Brown (1882) 10 R. 163 2–3
Ewart v Mason (1806) Hume 633 8–13
Ewing v Mar (1851) 14 D. 314 2–1
Exchange Telegraph v Guilianotti, 1959 S.C. 19; 1959 S.L.T. 293, (OH) 1–2
Express Newspapers Ltd v McShane [1980] A.C. 672; [1980] 2 W.L.R. 89,
(HL) 23–22

F (in utero) [1988] Fam. 122; [1988] 2 W.L.R. 1288 23–24
FC Finance Ltd v Brown and Son, 1969 S.L.T. (Sh. Ct) 41 3–13
Fagan v Commissioner of Police of the Metropolis [1969] 1 Q.B. 439; [1968]
3 W.L.R. 1120, DC 9–3
Fairchild v Glenhaven Funeral Services [2002] UKHL 22; [2003] 1 A.C. 32,
(HL) 9–22, 22–6
Fairlie v Carruthers, 1995 S.L.T. (Sh. Ct) 56 .... 20–6, 20–8, 20–10
Fairly v Earl of Eglinton (1744) Mor. 12780 3–12
Falconer v Edinburgh City Transport Longstone Social Club, 2003 Rep. L.R.
39; 2003 G.W.D. 7–181, (OH) 18–5, 18–7
Farrell v Boyd, 1907 15 S.L.T. 327 8–8
Farry v News Group, 1996 G.W.D. 2–109 8–29
Feely v Co-operative Wholesale Society, 1990 G.W.D. 4–221 18–2
Ferris-Bank (Anguilla) Ltd v Layar and Others [1991] T.L.R. 68 .... 8–33, 26–23

Findlay v Angus (1887) 14 R. 312 19–2
Findlay v Blaylock, 1937 S.C. 21 5–13
Findlay v Ruddiman (1763) Mor. 3436 8–7
Finningham v Peters (1861) 23 D. 260 9–6
Flannigan v British Dyewood Company Ltd, 1971 S.C. 110; 1971 S.L.T. 208,
   (OH) 1–5
Finucane v UK [2003] T.L.R. 437 17–2
Fleming v Hislop (1886)13 R. 43 3–4
Flynn v Advocate (H.M.), 2003 J.C. 153; 2003 S.L.T. 954 17–3
Forbes v Dundee DC, 1997 S.L.T. 1330; 1997 S.C.L.R. 682, (OH) 12–7, 18–11
Ford v Union Insulation Co Ltd, 1989 G.W.D. 16–696 25–11
Forgie v Henderson (1818) 1 Murray 410 26–16
Forsyth v Lothian RC, 1995 G.W.D. 4–204 21–5
Forth Tugs Ltd v Wilmington Trust Co., 1987 S.L.T. 153 23–47
Foskett v McClymont 1998 S.C. 96; 1998 S.L.T. 892; 1998 Rep. L.R. 13,
   (OH) 20–6, 20–8
Fotheringham and Son v British Limousin Cattle Society Ltd, 2002 G.W.D.
   26–867 5–12
Fox v P Caulfield and Co Ltd, 1975 S.L.T. (Notes) 71 23–10
Fox Campbell and Hartley v UK (1991) 13 E.H.R.R. 157 17–5
Francovich v Italian Republic; Danila Bonifaci v Italian Republic C–6190 and
   C–9/90 [1991] E.C.R. I–5357; [1993] 2 C.M.L.R. 66; [1992] I.R.L.R.
   84 .... 16–2, 16–5
Fraser v Greater Glasgow Health Board 1997 S.L.T. 554; 1996 S.C.L.R. 1108;
   1996 Rep. L.R. 58 21–19
Fraser v Lyle, unreported, February 3, 1998, Paisley Sheriff Court 20–4
Fraser v Mirza, 1993 S.C. (HL) 27; 1993 S.L.T. 527, (HL); reversing 1992 S.C.
   150; 1992 S.L.T. 740, 2 Div 8–23
Fraser v Pate, 1923 S.L.T. 457 20–4
Fraser v The Professional Golfers' Association, 2001 G.W.D. 200 10–6
Fraser v State Hospitals Board for Scotland, 2001 S.L.T. 1051; 2001 S.C.L.R.
   357, (OH) 21–6
Friend v Skelton (1855) 17 D. 548 8–8
Frost v Chief Constable [1996] T.L.R. 617 1–9
Frost v Chief Constable [1998] Q.B. 254; [1997] 3 W.L.R. 1194; [1997] 1 All
   E.R. 540 .... 1–9, 11–2
Fry's Metals Ltd v Durastic Ltd, 1991 S.L.T. 689, (OH) 13–3

G (A CHILD), Re. *See* Phelps v Hillingdon LBC
G and A Estates Ltd v Caviapen Trs Ltd (No. 1), 1993 S.L.T. 1037, (OH) 3–11
G B and A M Anderson v White, 2000 S.L.T. 37; 1998 G.W.D. 33–1721,
   (OH) 3–8, 26–23
G Percy Trentham Ltd v Beattie Watkinson and Partners, 1987 S.L.T. 449,
   (OH) 9–19
GKR Karate (UK) Ltd v Yorkshire Post Newspapers Ltd [2000] 1 W.L.R.
   2571; [2000] 2 All E.R. 931, (CA) 8–27
GUS Property Management Ltd v Littlewoods Mail Order Stores Ltd, 1982
   S.C. (HL) 157; 1982 S.L.T. 533, (HL) 23–42
Gall v Slesser, 1907 S.C. 708 8–4
Galt v Philp, 1983 J.C. 51; 1984 S.L.T. 28 26–23
Garden Cottage Foods v Milk Marketing Board [1984] A.C. 130; [1983] 3
   W.L.R. 143, (HL) 5–12, 16–1
Gardiner v Miller, 1967 S.L.T. 29; 1966 S.L.T. (Notes) 80, (OH) 20–4
Garven v White Corries, unreported, June 21, 1989, Fort William Sheriff
   Court 25–8
Gaskin v UK [1990] 1 F.L.R. 167; (1990) 12 E.H.R.R. 36 17–10
Gecas v Scottish Television, 1992 G.W.D. 30–1786 8–17

Gemmell v Bank of Scotland, Glasgow, November 5, 1996 3–16
General Cleaning Contractors v Christmas [1953] A.C. 180; [1953] 2 W.L.R.
    6, (HL) 21–4
George Porteous (Arts) Ltd v Dollar Rae, 1979 S.L.T. (Sh. Ct) 51 25–12
Ghani v Peter T Mccann and Co., 2002 S.L.T. (Sh. Ct) 135; 2002 G.W.D.
    17–578 25–12
Gibson v Anderson (1846) 9 D. 1 26–3
Gibson v Smith (1849) 21 Sc.J. 331 23–11
Gibson v Strathclyde RC, 1993 S.L.T. 1243; 1992 S.C.L.R. 902, RC 18–10
Gibson and Simpson v Pearson, 1992 S.L.T. 894; 1992 S.C.L.R. 771, (OH) 25–18
Gilchrist v Chief Constable, unreported, January 7, 1988, Glasgow Sheriff
    Court 2–5
Gilfillan v Barbour, 2003 S.L.T. 1127; 2004 S.C.L.R. 92; 2003 Rep. L.R. 129;
    2003 G.W.D. 26–747, (OH) 9–13
Gillies v Lynch, 2002 S.L.T. 1420; 2003 S.C.L.R. 467, (OH) 11–1
Gillon v Chief Constable, 1997 S.L.T. 1218; 1996 Rep. L.R. 165, (OH) 9–11
Gillon v Chief Constable, 1997 S.L.T. 1218; 1996 Rep. L.R. 165, (OH) 13–3
Gilmour v East Renfrewshire Council, May 29, 2002 21–13
Girvan v Inverness Farmers Dairy (No. 2), 1998 S.C. (HL) 1; 1998 S.L.T. 21,
    (HL) 26–17
Glasper v Rodger, 1996 S.L.T. 44, 1 Div 25–12
Glass v Leitch (1902) 5 F. 14 23–12
Glassford v Astley (1808) Mor. App No. 7 3–12
Glebe Sugar Refining Company v Lusk (1866) 2 S.L.R. 9; 3 S.L.R. 33 23–10
Globe (Aberdeen) Ltd, The v North of Scotland Water Authority, 2000 S.C.
    392; 2000 S.L.T. 674, Ex Div 3–8
Godfrey v Demon Internet [2001] Q.B. 201; [2000] 3 W.L.R. 1020; [1999] 4
    All E.R. 342, QBD 8–31
Gold v Haringey HA [1988] Q.B. 481; [1987] 3 W.L.R. 649, (CA) 2–2, 22–5
Golder v UK (1979–80) 1 E.H.R.R. 524 17–7
Goldman v Hargrave [1967] 1 A.C. 645; [1966] 3 W.L.R. 513 3–10
Gooda Walker Ltd v Deeny. *See* Henderson v Merrett Syndicates Ltd
Goodes v East Sussex CC [2000] 1 W.L.R. 1356; [2000] 3 All E.R. 603,
    (HL) 12–7, 18–11
Goodwin v UK (1996) 22 E.H.R.R. 123; 1 B.H.R.C. 81 17–12
Gordon v Grant (1765) Mor. 7356 3–12
Gordon v Metaline Company (1886) 14 R. 75 23–10
Gordon v Royal Bank (1826) 5 S. 164 6–2
Gormanley v Evening Citizen Ltd, 1962 S.L.T. (Sh. Ct) 61; (1962) 78 Sh. Ct.
    Rep. 88 23–34
Gorrie v The Marist Brothers, 2002 S.C.L.R. 436; 2001 G.W.D. 39–1484 23–12,
    24–5
Gorris v Scott (1874) L. R. 9 Ex. 125 15–6
Gower v Bromley LBC [1999] T.L.R. 726 24–5
Graham v Hamilton (Duke of) (1868) 6 M. 965 3–2
Graham v Roy (1851) 13 D. 634 8–8
Graham v Hawick Common Riding Committee, 1998 S.L.T. (Sh. Ct) 42; 1997
    S.C.L.R. 917 23–13
Gramophone Co.'s Application, Re [1910] Ch. 423 5–6
Grant v Australian Knitting Mills Ltd [1935] All E.R. 209 19–2
Grant v Lothian RC, 1988 S.L.T. 533, (OH) 18–11
Gray v Dunlop, 1954 S.L.T. (Sh. Ct) 75; (1954) 70 Sh. Ct. Rep. 270 4–3
Greater Nottingham Co-operative Society Ltd v Cementation Piling and
    Foundations Ltd [1989] Q.B. 71; [1988] 3 W.L.R. 396 22–2
Greenfield v Irwin [2001] EWCA Civ 113; [2001] 1 W.L.R. 1279, (CA) 23–28
Gregg v Scott [2002] EWCA Civ 1471; [2003] Lloyd's Rep. Med. 105 26–6
Griffen v George MacLellan Holdings Ltd, 1992 G.W.D. 30–1787 25–11

Grindall v John Mitchell (Grangemouth) Ltd, 1984 S.L.T. 335, (OH) 23–40
Grobbelaar v News Group Newspapers [2002] T.L.R. 423 8–33
Grubb v Mackenzie (1834) 13 S. 717 3–15
Gulf Oil Ltd v Page [1987] Ch. 327; [1987] 3 W.L.R. 166, (CA) 8–33, 26–23
Gunstone v Scottish Women's Athletic Association, 1987 S.L.T. 611, (OH) 23–1
Guy v Strathkelvin DC, 1997 S.C.L.R. 405; 1997 Hous. L.R. 14, (OH) ... 18–4, 18–9

H AND JM BENNETT (POTATOES) v SECRETARY OF STATE FOR SCOTLAND, 1986
    S.L.T. 665, (OH) 5–2
Haggart's Trs v Lord President (1824) 2 Shaw's App. 125 23–7
Haggarty v Glasgow Corp., 1964 S.L.T. (Notes) 54, 2 Div; reversing 1963
    S.L.T. (Notes) 73, (OH) 18–9
Haggerty v EE Caledonia [1997] T.L.R. 69 11–2
Haig v Forth Blending Co, 1954 S.C. 35; 1954 S.L.T. 2, (OH) 5–5, 5–6
Halford v UK [1997] I.R.L.R. 471; (1997) 24 E.H.R.R. 523 17–10
Hall v Watson (1896) 12 Sh. Ct. Rep. 117 2–2
Hall and Co v Simons, [2002] 1 A.C. 615; [2000] 3 W.L.R. 543; [2000] 3 All
    E.R. 673, (HL) 22–8
Hallett v Nicholson, 1979 S.C. 1, (OH) 12–6, 12–7
Hambrook v Stokes Bros [1925] 1 K.B. 141, (CA) 11–1
Hamill v Advocate (Lord), 1994 G.W.D. 33–1960 8–23
Hamilton v Allied Domecq, 2001 S.C. 829; 2001 G.W.D. 13–517, (OH) 22–9
Hamilton v Fife Health Board, 1993 S.C. 309; 1993 S.L.T. 624; 1993 S.C.L.R.
    408, Ex Div; reversing 1992 S.L.T. 1026; 1992 S.C.L.R. 288, (OH) 23–24,
                                                                          23–26
Hamilton v Wilson, 1994 S.L.T. 431; 1993 S.C.C.R. 9 2–9
Hand v North of Scotland Water Authority, 2002 S.L.T. 798; 2002 S.C.L.R.
    493, (OH) 10–8, 23–1
Handy v Bowman, Dundee Sheriff Court, September 22, 1986 2–8
Handyside v UK (1976) 1 E.H.R.R. 737 .... 17–12, 26–23
Hardaker v Newcastle HA [2001] Lloyd's Rep Med 512, QBD 26–6
Hardey v Russel and Aitken, 2003 G.W.D. 2–50 5–4
Harper v Harper, 1929 S.L.T. 187 23–34
Harris v Abbey National, 1996 G.W.D. 33–1993 3–16
Harris v Wyre Forest D.C. [1988] Q.B. 835; [1988] 2 W.L.R. 1173 10–4
Harrison v Michelin Tyre Co [1985] 1 All E.R. 918; [1985] I.C.R. 696,
    QBD 24–4
Harrison v West of Scotland Kart Club, 2001 S.C. 367; 2001 S.L.T. 1171 23–14
Harrods (Buenos Aires) Ltd, Re [1992] Ch. 72; [1991] 3 W.L.R. 397, (CA) 1–5
Haseldine v CA Daw and Son Ltd [1941] 3 All E.R. 156 19–2
Hatherley v Smith, 1989 S.L.T. 316, (OH) 26–20
Hatton v UK , 2003 T.L.R. 401; (2002) 34 E.H.R.R. 1 17–10
Hay's Trs v Young (1877) 4 R. 398 26–23
Hayforth v Forrester-Paton, 1927 S.C. 74 8–4
Hazard v Glasgow Pavilion, 1994 G.W.D. 13–850 18–5
Heath's Garage Ltd v Hodges [1916] 2 K.B. 370 20–4
Heaton's Transport (St Helens) Ltd v TGWU [1972] I.C.R. 308 24–8
Hedley Byrne and Co Ltd v Heller and Partners Ltd [1964] A.C. 465; [1963]
    3 W.L.R. 101, (HL) 8–28, 10–2, 10–3, 10–4, 10–6, 10–7, 10–8, 10–9, 10–11,
                                     12–3, 12–8, 22–2, 22–7, 22–9
Henderson v Chief Constable, Fife Police, 1988 S.L.T. 361; 1988 S.C.L.R. 77,
    (OH) 1–18, 2–10
Henderson v John Stuart (Farms) Ltd, 1963 S.C. 245; 1963 S.L.T. 22, (OH) 20–3
Henderson v Merrett Syndicates Ltd; *sub nom.* McLarnon Deeney v Gooda
    Walker Ltd; Gooda Walker Ltd v Deeny [1995] 2 A.C. 145; [1994] 3
    W.L.R. 761 , (HL) 1–2, 10–2, 10–9, 22–2
Henderson v Rollo (1871) 10 M. 104 6–2

Hendrie v Scottish Ministers, 2002 Rep. L.R. 46; 2002 G.W.D. 2–84, (OH) 13–3
Henning v Hewetson (1852) 14 D. 487 6–2
Hepatitis C Litigation (No. 1), Re. *See* A v National Blood Authority
Hercules Managements Ltd v Ernst and Young [1997] 2 S.C.R. 165 10–6
Heyman v Sutherland Shire Council (1985) 59 A.L.J.R. 564; (1985) 60 A.L.R.
    1 10–6
Highland Dancing Board v Alloa Printing Co., 1971 S.L.T. (Sh. Ct) 50 23–11
Highland Engineering Ltd v Anderson, 1979 S.L.T. 122, (OH) 23–41
Hill v Black, 1914 S.C. 913 23–41
Hill v Chief Constable [1989] A.C. 53; [1988] 2 W.L.R. 1049, (HL); affirming
    [1988] Q.B. 60; [1987] 2 W.L.R. 1126; [1987] 1 All E.R. 1173 .... 12–6, 17–7
Hill v Lovett, 1992 S.L.T. 994 .... 18–5, 20–3
Hillcrest Homecare Services v Tartan Home Care Ltd, 1996 G.W.D. 4–215 5–2
Hislop v Durham (1842) 4 D. 1168 21–1
Hogg v Carrigan's Executrix, 2001 S.C. 542; 2001 S.L.T. 444; 2001 Rep. L.R.
    60, (OH) 26–10
Holland v Lampen-Wolfe [2000] T.L.R. 575 .... 23–47, 23–48
Holmes v Bank of Scotland, 2002 S.L.T. 544; 2002 S.C.L.R. 481; 2002 G.W.D.
    8–269 .... 10–11, 22–7
Home Office v Dorset Yacht Co [1970] A.C. 1004; [1970] 2 W.L.R. 1140,
    (HL) 9–6, 12–6
Honeywill and Stein Ltd v Larkin Bros Ltd [1934] 1 K.B. 191 24–7
Horton v Taplin Contracts Ltd [2002] T.L.R. 492 21–14
Hosie v Arbroath Football Club Ltd, 1978 S.L.T. 122, (OH) 18–5
Hotson v East Berkshire HA [1987] A.C. 750; [1987] 3 W.L.R. 232, (HL) 26–6
Houldsworth v Glasgow Bank (City of) (1880) 7 R. (HL) 53 23–10
Hucks v Cole [1993] 4 Med. L.R. 393, (CA) 22–3
Hudson v Ridge Manufacturing [1957] 2 Q.B. 348; [1957] 2 W.L.R. 948 21–3
Hughes v Advocate (Lord) [1963] A.C. 837; [1963] 2 W.L.R. 779; 1963 S.C.
    (HL) 31, (HL) 9–5, 9–26, 13–1
Hughes' Tutrix v Glasgow DC, 1982 S.L.T. (Sh. Ct) 70 .... 18–4, 18–7, 25–8
Hulton v Jones [1910] A.C. 20, (HL) 8–5
Hunt v Severs [1994] 2 A.C. 350; [1994] 2 W.L.R. 602, (HL) 23–34
Hunter v Canary Wharf Ltd and London Dockland Development Corp. [1997]
    A.C. 655; [1997] 2 W.L.R. 684, (HL) 3–7
Hunter v Hanley, 1955 S.C. 200; 1955 S.L.T. 213, 1 Div 22–2, 22–3, 22–5
Hunter v Murray, 2002 G.W.D. 13–445, (OH) 21–14
Hunter v NSHB, 1989 G.W.D. 15–645 25–11
Hurley v William Muir (Bond 9) Ltd, 2000 G.W.D. 4–158 21–14
Hutchison v Davidson, 1946 S.L.T. 11 26–2

ICI v SHATWELL [1965] A.C. 656; [1964] 3 W.L.R. 329, (CA) 25–7
Inglis v Shotts Iron Co (1881) 8 R. 1006 3–7
Ingram v Ritchie, 1989 G.W.D. 27–1217 .... 9–22, 22–6
International House of Heraldry v Grant, 1992 S.L.T. 1021, (OH) 5–6
Invercargill City Council v Hamlin [1996] A.C. 624; [1996] 2 W.L.R. 367 12–4
Inverness Harbour Trs v BRB, March 31, 1994 3–11
Ireland v United Kingdom (1979–80) 2 E.H.R.R. 25 17–2
Irving v Hiddleston, 1998 S.C. 759; 1998 S.L.T. 912; 1998 S.C.L.R. 350,
    (OH) 25–19

J. BOLLINGER v COSTA BRAVA WINE CO LTD [1960] Ch. 262; [1959] 3 W.L.R.
    966, Ch. D 15–5
Jackson v Harrison [1978] 138 C.L.R. 438; (1977) 16 S.A.S.R. 182 25–8
Jackson v MacKenzie (1875) 3 R. 130 23–40
James Burrough Distillers Plc. v Speymalt Whisky Distributors Ltd, 1989
    S.L.T. 561; 1989 S.C.L.R. 255, (OH) 1–5

Joel v Morison (1834) 6 C. & P. 501 24–4
Johanneson v Lothian RC, 1996 S.L.T. (Sh. Ct) 74; 1996 Rep. L.R. 81 15–3
John Walker and Sons v Douglas Laing and Co., 1993 S.L.T. 156, (OH) 5–6
John Walker and Sons Ltd v Henry Ost and Co Ltd [1970] 1 W.L.R. 917;
   [1970] 2 All E.R. 106, Ch D 5–7
Johnson v Tennant Bros Ltd, unreported, November 19, 1954, (CA) 25–9
Johnstone v Sweeney, 1985 S.L.T. (Sh. Ct) 2 18–3
Johnstone v Traffic Commissioner, 1990 S.L.T. 409, (OH) 12–6
Jones v Hulton and Co [1910] A.C. 20, (HL); affirming [1909] 2 K.B. 444,
   (CA) 8–7
Jones v Lanarkshire Health Board, 1990 S.L.T. 19; 1989 S.C.L.R. 542,
   (OH) 23–27
Jones v Northampton BC [1992] 156 L.G. Rev. 23 23–13
Jones v Wright. *See* Alcock v Chief Constable, South Yorkshire
Jones v Wright [1991] 2 W.L.R. 814; [1991] 3 All E.R. 88 .... 11–1, 11–3
Joyce v Sengupta [1992] T.L.R. 453 8–1
Junior Books v Veitchi Co, [1983] 1 A.C. 520; [1982] 3 W.L.R. 477; 1982
   S.L.T. 492 .... 9–7, 9–8, 10–4, 10–6, 10–8, 10–9, 12–4
Just v British Columbia (1990) 64 D.L.R. (4th) 689 12–4

Kamloops v Nielsen [1984] S.C.R. 2 (S.C.C.) 10–6
Kane v New Forest DC [2001] EWCA Civ 878; [2002] 1 W.L.R. 312, (CA) 12–4
Kay's Tutor v Ayrshire and Arran Health Board, [1987] 2 All E.R. 417; 1987
   S.C. (HL) 145; 1987 S.L.T. 577, (HL) 9–20, 9–22, 22–5
Keen v Tayside Contracts, 2003 S.L.T. 500; 2003 Rep. L.R. 22; 2003 G.W.D.
   9–261, (OH) 11–2, 11–4
Kelly v First Engineering Ltd, 1999 S.C.L.R. 1025; 1999 Rep. L.R. 106,
   (OH) 21–16
Kelly v Kelly, 1997 S.C. 285; 1997 S.L.T. 896, 2 Div 23–24
Kemp v Secretary of State for Scotland, 2000 S.L.T. 471; 2000 S.C.L.R. 10;
   1999 Rep. L.R. 110, (OH) 18–11
Kemp and Dougall v Darngavil Coal Co Ltd, 1909 S.C. 1314 9–1
Kennedy v Allan (1848) 10 D. 1293 8–8
Kennedy v Glenbelle, 1996 S.C. 95; 1996 S.L.T. 1186, 1 Div 1–17, 3–1, 3–8, 3–11
Kennedy v Police Commissioners of Fort William (1877) 5 R. 302 6–2
Kenyon v Bell, 1953 S.C. 125; 1952 S.L.T. (Notes) 78, (OH) 26–6
Kerr v Earl of Orkney (1857) 20 D. 298 3–11
Kidston v Annan, 1984 S.L.T. 279; 1984 S.C.C.R. 20 3–16
King v Carron Phoenix Ltd, 1999 Rep. L.R. 51; 1999 G.W.D. 9–437, (OH) 21–19
King v Phillips [1953] 1 Q.B. 429; [1953] 2 W.L.R. 526; [1953] 1 All E.R.
   617, (CA) 11–1
King v Strathclyde R.C., January 8, 1991, Glasgow 18–10
Kinnes v Adam (1882) 9 R. 698 6–2
Kirby v NCB, 1958 S.C. 514; 1959 S.L.T. 7, 1 Div 24–3
Kirk v Fife Council, 2002 S.L.T. 21 (Note); 2002 S.C.L.R. 407; 2001 G.W.D.
   36–1398 18–4
Kirkintilloch Equitable Co-operative Society Ltd v Livingstone, 1972 S.C.
   111; 1972 S.L.T. 154, 1 Div 23–16
Knott v Newham Healthcare NHS Trust [2002] All E.R. (D) 216 21–23
Kobler v Republik Osterrich [2003] T.L.R. 540 16–5
Kozikowska v Kozikowski, 1996 S.L.T. 386, (OH) 23–34
Kuddus v Chief Constable of Leicestershire [2001] UKHL 29; [2002] 2 A.C.
   122; [2001] 2 W.L.R. 1789, (HL) 26–3
Kuwait Oil Tanker Co SAK and Another v Al Bader and others [2002] 2 All
   E.R. (Comm) 271 .... 5–11, 5–12
Kyle v P and J Stormonth Darling W.S., 1993 S.C. 57; 1994 S.L.T. 191, Ex
   Div 26–6

L, PETR, 1996 S.C.L.R. 538 23–36
Lagden v O'Connor, 2003 T.L.R. 667 26–2
Laird Line v U.S. Shipping Board, 1924 S.C. (HL) 37 25–9
Lamb v Camden LBC [1981] Q.B. 625; [1981] 2 W.L.R. 1038 9–26
Lamond v Glasgow Corporation, 1968 S.L.T. 291, (OH) 9–11, 25–8
Lamont v North East Fife DC,1987 G.W.D. 37–1314 12–6
Lane v Holloway [1968] 1 Q.B. 379; [1967] 3 W.L.R. 1003, (CA) 2–6
Lanford v Hebron [2001] P.I.Q.R. Q160 26–6
Lang Brothers v Goldwell, 1980 S.C. 237; 1982 S.L.T. 309, 2 Div 5–7
Langden v O'Conner [2003] T.L.R. 667 .... 9–25, 9–26
Lange v Atkinson [2000] 1 N.Z.L.R. 257 8–27
Lange v Atkinson (No. 2), 2000 3 N.Z.L.R. 385, (CA) 8–27
Laskey v UK (1997) 24 E.H.R.R. 39 25–7
Latimer v AEC Ltd [1953] A.C. 643; [1953] 3 W.L.R. 259, (HL) 9–14
Launchbury v Morgans [1973] A.C. 127; [1972] 2 W.L.R. 1217, (HL) 24–2
Law Debenture Trust Corp. v Ural Caspian Oil Corp. [1995] Ch. 152; [1994]
    3 W.L.R. 1221; [1995] 1 All E.R. 157, (CA) 5–14
Law Hospital NHS Trust v Advocate (Lord), 1996 S.C. 301; 1996 S.L.T. 848,
    (IH) 23–36, 26–24
Lawless v Ireland (1961) E.H.R.R. 1 17–5
Leadbetter v NCB, 1952 S.C. 19; 1952 S.L.T. 179, 2 Div 23–25
Leask v Burt (1893) 21 R. 32 2–12
Leeds Permanent Building Society v Fraser and Steele, 1995 S.L.T. (Sh. Ct)
    72 26–13
Lees v North East Fife DC, 1987 S.C. 265; 1987 S.L.T. 769, 2 Div 26–23
Leigh v Gladstone (1949) 26 T.L.R. 139 25–4
Leigh and Sillavan Ltd v Aliakmon Shipping Co. Ltd (The Aliakmon) [1986]
    A.C. 785; [1986] 2 W.L.R. 902, (HL) 9–8, 10–8
Liesbosch Dredger v SS Edison [1933] A.C. 449; [1933] All E.R. Rep. 144,
    (HL) 26–2
Leitch v Leydon, 1931 S.C. (HL) 1 .... 3–14, 26–23
Leitch v Lyal (1903) 11 S.L.T. 394 8–25
Lennox v Rose (1824) 2 S. 650 2–5
Leon v Edinburgh Evening News, 1909 S.C. 1014 8–9
Letford v Glasgow City Council, 2002 Rep. L.R. 107; 2002 G.W.D. 23–750 18–10
Liddle v Morton, 1996 J.C. 194; 1996 S.L.T. 1143 2–8
Lister v Romford Ice and Cold Storage Co Ltd [1957] A.C. 555; [1957] 2
    W.L.R. 158; [1957] 1 All E.R. 125, (HL) 25–16
Lister and Others v Hesley Hall Ltd [2001] T.L.R. 308 24–5
Littrell v Government of USA [1993] T.L.R. 589 23–48
Lloyd v Campbell Riddell, March 25, 2003, Glasgow Sheriff Court 25–12
Lloyd v Grace Smith [1912] A.C. 716 23–16
Loch v British Leyland UK Ltd, 1975 S.L.T. (Notes) 67, (OH) 21–24
Logan v Falkirk NHS, 1999 G.W.D. 30–1431, (OH) 21–6
Logan v SRC, unreported, January 12, 1999 21–23
Longworth v Coppas International (UK) Ltd, 1985 S.C. 42; 1985 S.L.T. 111,
    (OH) 21–5
Lonrho v Shell Petroleum Co Ltd (No. 2) [1982] A.C. 173; [1981] 3 W.L.R.
    33, (HL) 5–11
Lonrho plc v Al-Fayed [1992] 1 A.C. 448; [1991] 3 W.L.R. 188, (HL) 5–10, 5–12,
    5–14
Loutchansky v Times Newspapers (No. 2) [2001] EWCA Civ 1805; [2002]
    Q.B. 783; [2002] 2 W.L.R. 640, (CA) 8–27, 8–31
Lumley v Gye (1853) 2 E. & B. 216 .... 5–8, 5–14

MTM CONSTRUCTION LTD v WILLIAM REID ENGINEERING LTD, 1998 S.L.T.
    211; 1997 S.C.L.R. 778, (OH) 24–7

McAllister v ICI Plc, 1997 S.L.T. 351; 1996 Rep. L.R. 136, (OH) 26–19
McArthur v Matthew Cleland Public House Proprietors, 1981 S.L.T (Sh. Ct)
    76 4–4
MacAusland v Dick (1787) Mor. 9246 4–6
McBeath v Halliday, 2000 Rep. L.R. 38; 2000 G.W.D. 2–75, (OH) ... 21–19, 21–23
McCabe v News Group Newspapers Ltd, 1992 S.L.T. 707, (OH) 8–8
McCann v United Kingdom (1995) 21 E.H.R.R. 97 17–23
McCann v UK (1996) E.H.R.R. 97 17–1
McCluskey v Advocate (Lord), 1994 S.L.T. 452, (OH) 18–3
MacColl v Hoo, 1983 S.L.T. (Sh. Ct) 23 4–4
McCormick v Aberdeen DC (City of), 1993 S.L.T. 1123, (OH) 20–3
McDonald v Dickson, 2003 S.L.T. 467; 2003 S.C.C.R. 311 17–5
McDonald v Glasgow Western Hospitals Board, 1954 S.C. 453 24–3
Macdonald v Scottish Stamping and Engineering Co Ltd, 1972 S.L.T. (Notes)
    73, (OH) 9–14
McDonald v Secretary of State for Scotland, 1994 S.L.T. 692; 1994 S.C.L.R.
    318, 2 Div 23–3
MacDougall v Clydesdale Bank Trs. *See* MacDougall v MacDougall's
    Executors
MacDougall v MacDougall's Executors; *sub nom.* MacDougall v Clydesdale
    Bank Trs, 1994 S.L.T. 1178; 1993 S.C.L.R. 832, (OH) 22–7
McDougall v Spiers, 25 February 2003 21–23
McDougall v Tawse, 2002 S.L.T. (Sh. Ct) 10; 2002 S.C.L.R. 160 18–3
McDyer v Celtic Football and Athletic Company Limited (No. 1), 2000 S.C.
    379; 2000 S.L.T. 736, 1 Div 4–3, 18–2
McDyer v Celtic Football and Athletic Company Limited (No. 2), 2001 S.L.T.
    1387; 2001 S.C.L.R. 879, (OH) 4–3, 4–4, 18–2, 18–4
McElroy v McAllister, 1949 S.C. 110; 1949 S.L.T. 139, (IH) 1–5
McErlean v J and B Scotland Ltd, 1997 S.L.T. 1326; 1997 Rep. L.R. 29,
    (OH) 9–14
McFarlane v EE Caledonia Ltd [1994] 2 All E.R. 1; [1994] 1 Lloyd's Rep. 16,
    (CA) 11–2
McFarlane v Tayside Health Board, [2000] 2 A.C. 59; [1999] 3 W.L.R. 1301;
    2000 S.C. (HL) 1; 2000 S.L.T. 154, (HL); reversing 1998 S.C. 389; 1998
    S.L.T. 307; 1998 S.C.L.R. 126, 2 Div 1–15, 23–27
McGeouch v Strathclyde RC, 1985 S.L.T. 321, 2 Div 18–10
McGhee v NCB, [1973] 1 W.L.R. 1; [1972] 3 All E.R. 1008; 1973 S.C. (HL)
    37, (HL) 9–22
McGhee v Strathclyde Fire Brigade, 2002 S.L.T. 680; 2002 Rep. L.R. 29; 2002
    G.W.D. 3–114, (OH) 21–9, 21–13
McGlone v BRB, 1966 S.C. (HL) l; 1966 S.L.T. 2, (HL) 18–1, 18–6
McGregor v AAH Pharmaceuticals, 1995 G.W.D. 32–1656 21–4
McGregor v JS Duthie and Sons, 1966 S.L.T. 133, 2 Div 24–6
McIntosh v Edinburgh Council (City of), 2003 S.L.T. 827; 2003 G.W.D.
    22–664, (OH) 21–23
Mckay v McLean, 1920 1 S.L.T. 34, (OH) 23–35
McKeen v Chief Constable, 1994 S.L.T. 93, (OH) 2–9
McKendrick v. Sinclair, 1972 S.C. (HL) 25; 1972 S.L.T. 110, (HL); affirming
    1971 S.L.T. 234, 2 Div; reversing 1971 S.L.T. 17; 1970 S.L.T. (Notes) 61,
    (OH) 1–7
MacKenzie v Cluny Hill Hydropathic Co Ltd, 1907 S.C. 200 2–10
MacKenzie v Perth and Kinross Council, 2003 G.W.D. 4–101, (OH) 18–11
McKew v Holland and Hannen and Cubitts (Scotland) Ltd, [1969] 3 All E.R.
    1621; 1970 S.C. (HL) 20, (HL); affirming 1969 S.C. 14; 1969 S.L.T. 101;
    1968 S.L.T. (Notes) 99, 2 Div; affirming 1968 S.L.T. 12, (OH) 9–26, 15–9
Mackie v Dundee City Council, 2001 Rep. L.R. 62; 2001 G.W.D. 11–398 21–14
McKillen v Barclay Curle and Co Ltd, 1967 S.L.T. 41, 1 Div 9–26

McKinlay v British Steel Corp., 1988 S.L.T. 810, 2 Div; affirming 1987 S.L.T. 522, (OH) 9–12

McKinney v Chief Constable, Strathclyde Police, 1998 S.L.T. (Sh. Ct) 80; 1998 Rep. L.R. 81 2–12

McKinney v Chief Constable, Strathclyde Police, 2000 G.W.D. 24–919, 1 Div 2–12

Mackintoch v Weir (1875) 2 R. 877 8–8

Mackintosh v Galbraith and Arthur (1900) 3F. 66 3–15

McKnight v Clydeside Buses Ltd, 1999 S.L.T. 1167; 1999 S.C.L.R. 272, (OH) 12–4, 18–11

McLachlan v Bell (1895) 23 R. 126 23–1

McLaren v Procurator Fiscal for Lothian and Borders, 1991 G.W.D. 24–1407 .... 2–11, 24–8

McLarnon Deeney v Gooda Walker Ltd. *See* Henderson v Merrett Syndicates Ltd

McLatchie v Scottish Society for Autism, 2004 G.W.D. 4–67 9–22

McLaughlin v East and Midlothian NHS Trust, 2001 S.L.T. 387; 2000 S.C.L.R. 1108; 2000 Rep. L.R. 87, (OH) 21–15

McLean v Bernstein and Others (1900) 8 S.L.T. 42, (OH) 8–7

McLean v Remploy Ltd, 1994 S.L.T. 687; 1994 S.C.L.R. 406, (OH) 21–3, 24–4

McLean v University of St. Andrews, 2004 G.W.D. 7–152, (OH) 13–3

McLelland v Greater Glasgow Health Board, 2001 S.L.T. 446; 2001 G.W.D. 10–357, Ex Div 23–29

McLeod v Hellyer Bros Ltd [1987] 1 W.L.R. 728; [1987] I.C.R. 526; [1987] I.R.L.R. 232, (CA) 24–3

Macleod v MacAskill, 1920 S.C. 72 2–14

McLoughlin v O'Brian [1983] 1 A.C. 410; [1982] 2 W.L.R. 982, (HL) 11–1, 11–2, 11–3

McManus v Babcock Energy, 1999 S.C. 569; 2000 S.L.T. 655; 1999 G.W.D. 21–1013, (OH) 26–21

McMeechan v Secretary of State for Employment [1997] I.C.R. 549; [1997] I.R.L.R. 353, (CA) 24–3

McMenemy v Argyll Stores Ltd, 1992 S.L.T. 971; 1992 S.C.L.R. 576, (OH) 26–11

McMillan v Advocate (Lord), 1991 S.L.T. 150, (OH) 18–4

McMullan v Glasgow Council, 1998 G.W.D. 17–874, (OH) 21–15

McMullan v Lochgelly Iron and Coal Co, 1933 S.C. (HL) 64 15–4

McMurdo v Ferguson, 1993 S.L.T. 193, (OH) 8–33, 26–23

McNab v Guild, 1989 S.C.C.R. 138 3–3

McNeill v Roche Products Ltd, 1988 S.C. 77; 1988 S.L.T. 704, (OH) 26–10

Mcphee v Heatherwick, 1977 S.L.T. (Sh. Ct) 46 .... 25–18, 25–19

MacPhee v Macfarlane's Executor, 1933 S.C. 163 2–13

McQueen v Hepburn, 1979 S.L.T. (Sh. Ct) 38 26–12

McQueen v Vale of Leven DC, January 24, 1973 18–3

McRostie v Ironside (1849) 11 D. 74 8–9

McSheehy v MacMillan, 1993 S.L.T. (Sh. Ct) 10; 1992 S.C.L.R. 603 .... 25–18, 25–19

McTighe v East and Midlothian NHS Trust, 1998 S.L.T. 969; 1998 S.C.L.R. 203; 1998 Rep. L.R. 21, (OH) 21–9, 21–15

McWilliams v Advocate (Lord), 1992 S.L.T. 1045; 1992 S.C.L.R. 954, (OH) 23–26

Maguire v Charles McNeil, 1922 S.L.T. 193, 1 Div 3–7

Mains v Uniroyal Englebert Tyres Ltd, 1995 S.C. 518; 1995 S.L.T. 1115, Ex Div 21–9

Mair v Wood, 1948 S.C. 83; 1948 S.L.T. 326, 1 Div 23–13, 23–17

Maloco (Smith) v Littlewoods, [1987] A.C. 241; [1987] 2 W.L.R. 480; 1987 S.L.T. 425, (HL); affirming 1986 S.L.T. 272, 1 Div 9–24, 10–4, 13–1

Manners v Whitehead (1898) 1 F. 171 22–9

Marc Rich and Co AG v Bishop Rock Marine Co Ltd and Others (The
  Nicholas H) [1996] A.C. 211; [1995] 3 W.L.R. 227; [1995] 3 All E.R.
  307, (HL) 12–7, 14–1, 14–2
Marco v Merrens, 1964 S.L.T. (Sh. Ct) 74 2–7
Margarine Union GmbH v Cambay Prince Steamship Co (The Wear Breeze)
  [1969] 1 Q.B. 219; [1967] 3 W.L.R. 1569, QBD 10–8
Margrie Holdings Ltd v Edinburgh DC (City of), 1994 S.L.T. 971; 1993
  S.C.L.R. 570, 1 Div 9–26
Marshall v DB Marshall (Newbridge) Ltd, 1991 G.W.D. 30–1807 21–24
Marshall v Sharp, 1991 S.L.T. 114; 1991 S.C.L.R. 104, 2 Div 24–7
Martin v Bell Ingram, 1986 S.C. 208; 1986 S.L.T. 575, 2 Div 10–4, 10–7, 26–12
Martin v Port of Manchester Insurance, 1934 S.C. 143 23–41
Martins Moreira v Portugal (1988) 13 E.H.R.R. 517 17–24
Mason v Orr (1901) 4 F. 220 2–5
Mather v British Telecommunications, May 30, 2000 21–6
Mathews v MOD [2002] 3 All E.R. 513 23–5
Matthew v Perthshire Cricket Club (1904) 12 S.L.T. 635 23–12
Matthew Gloag and Son Ltd v Welsh Distillers Ltd [1998] 2 C.M.L.R. 203;
  [1999] Eu. L.R. 625; [1998] T.L.R. 113; [1998] FSR 718 5–7
Mattis v Pollock [2003] T.L.R. 418 24–5
Matuszczyk v NCB, 1955 S.C. 418; 1955 S.L.T. 101, (OH) 25–18
Mawe v Piggott (1869) Ir. Rep. 4 Cl. 54 8–8
Maxwell v GSW Railway Co (1866) 4 M. 447 26–23
May v Teague Homes, 1996 G.W.D. 23–1344 8–26
Mazure v Stubbs, 1935 S.L.T. 94 8–12
Meek v Burton's Gold Medal Biscuits Ltd, 1989 S.L.T. 338, (OH) 26–11
Meek v SRC, unreported August 23, 2001 18–2
Melrose v Davidson and Robertson, 1993 S.C. 288; 1993 S.L.T. 611; 1993
  S.C.L.R. 365, 1 Div; affirming 1992 S.L.T. 395, (OH) 10–7
Mercury Communication Ltd v Scott-Garner [1984] Ch. 37; [1983] 3 W.L.R.
  914; [1983] I.C.R. 74 23–22
Merivale v Carson (1887) 20 Q.B.D. 275 8–29
Merkur Island Shipping Co v Laughton [1983] 2 A.C. 570; [1983] 2 W.L.R.
  778, (HL) 23–22
Mersey Docks and Harbour Board v Coggins and Griffith (Liverpool) Ltd
  [1947] A.C. 1; [1946] 2 All E.R. 345, (HL) 24–6
Metall and Rohstoff AG v Donaldson Lufkin and Jenrette Inc. [1990] 1 Q.B.
  391; [1989] 3 W.L.R. 563, (CA) 5–11
Miborrow, Petr, 1996 S.C.L.R. (Notes) 314 2–11
Michaels v Taylor Woodrow Development Ltd [2001] Ch. 493; [2001] 2
  W.L.R. 224, Ch D 5–10
Micosta SA v Shetland Islands Council, [1984] 2 Lloyd's Rep. 525; 1986
  S.L.T. 193, (OH) 1–18, 5–15, 5–16, 7–1
Middlebrook Mushrooms Ltd v Transport and General Workers Union [1993]
  T.L.R. 11 5–14
Middleton v Douglass, 1991 S.L.T. 726, (OH) 1–1
Millar v Fife RC, 1990 S.L.T. 651, (OH) 18–4
Miller v Glasgow DC, 1988 S.C. 440; 1989 S.L.T. 44, 1 Div 1–1
Miller v Glasgow DC (City of), 1989 G.W.D. 29–1347 18–4
Miller v Perth and Kinross Council, 2002 Rep. L.R. 22; 2001 G.W.D.
  40–1530 21–12
Milligan v Ayre Harbour Trs, 1915 S.C. 937 23–21
Milligan v Henderson, 1915 2 S.L.T. 156 20–4
Milne v Duguid, 1999 S.C.L.R. 512 23–13
Milne v Express Newspapers [2002] EWHC 2564; [2003] 1 W.L.R. 927,
  QBD 8–30
Milne v Macintosh, 1952 S.L.T. (Sh. Ct) 84; (1952) 68 Sh. Ct. Rep. 301 20–4

Milne v Thomson (1841) 5 D. 759 2–3
Milne v Tudhope, 1981 J.C. 53; 1981 S.L.T. (Notes) 42 3–16
Mineral Transporter; Candlewood Navigation Corp. Ltd, The v Mitsui Lines
  [1986] A.C. 1; [1985] 3 W.L.R. 381, PC 10–9
Mitchell v Campbeltown Shipyard Ltd, 1998 G.W.D. 12–616, (OH) 21–11
Mitchell v Inverclyde DC, 1998 S.L.T. 1157; 1998 S.C.L.R. 191; 1997 Rep.
  L.R. (Quantum) 29 21–16
Mitchell v McCulloch, 1976 S.C. 1; 1976 S.L.T. 2, (OH) 1–5
Mogul Steamship Co Ltd v McGregor, Gow and Co [1892] A.C. 25; [1891–4]
  All E.R. Rep. 263, (HL) 5–10
Monson v Tussauds [1894] 1 Q.B. 671, (CA) 8–4
Monteith v Cape Insulations, 1997 G.W.D. 28–1431 26–19
Montreal Tramways v Leveille [1933] 4 D.L.R. 337 23–23
Moorcraft v W. Alexander and Sons, 1946 S.C. 466; 1946 S.L.T. (Notes) 2 23–25
Moore v Regents of the University of California, 793 P 2d 479 Cal. S.C.
  (1990) 23–38
Moore v Secretary of State for Scotland, 1985 S.L.T. 38, 2 Div 6–3
More v Boyle, 1967 S.L.T. (Sh. Ct) 38 3–12
Morgan Crucible Co plc v Hill Samuel [1991] Ch. 295; [1991] 2 W.L.R. 655;
  [1991] 1 All E.R. 148, (CA) 10–4
Morris v West Hartlepool Steam Navigation Co Ltd [1956] A.C. 552; [1956]
  1 W.L.R. 177, (HL) 9–10
Morrison v Ritchie (1902) 4 F. 645 8–32
Morrisons Associated Companies Ltd v James Rome and Son Ltd, 1962 S.L.T.
  (Notes) 75, (OH) 22–4
Morrow v Neil, 1975 S.L.T. (Sh. Ct) 65 2–8
Morton v Wm Dixon, 1909 S.C. 807 9–15
Moss v Howdle, 1997 J.C. 123; 1997 S.L.T. 782 .... 3–3, 25–4
Moyes v Lothian Health Board, 1990 S.L.T. 444, (OH) 2–2, 22–3, 22–5
Muckarsie v Dixon (1848) 11 D. 4 26–3
Muir v Glasgow Corporation, [1943] A.C. 448; [1943] 2 All E.R. 44; 1943
  S.C. (HL) 3, (HL) 9–9
Muir's Trs v Braidwood, 1958 S.C. 169; 1958 S.L.T. 149, 2 Div 23–40
Mulcahy v Ministry of Defence [1996] T.L.R. 39 .... 21–13, 23–5
Mull Shellfish Ltd v Golden Sea Produce Ltd, 1992 S.L.T. 703 10–8
Mullan v Anderson, 1996 Rep. L.R. 47 25–18
Mullan v Anderson, 1993 S.L.T. 835; 1993 S.C.L.R. 506, (IH) 2–5
Murphy v Brentwood DC [1991] 1 A.C. 398; [1990] 3 W.L.R. 414 .... 9–8, 10–5,
                                             10–6, 12–2, 12–3, 19–2
Murray v Edinburgh DC, 1981 S.L.T. 253, (OH) 18–2
Murray v Fraser, 1916 S.C. 623 2–14
Murray v Harringay Arena [1951] 2 K.B. 529; [1951] 2 All E.R. 320n 25–8
Murray v Nicholls, 1983 S.L.T. 194, (OH) 18–11
Murray v UK (1994) 19 E.H.R.R. 193 17–5
Mustard v Paterson, 1923 S.C. 142 4–8
Myles J Callaghan Ltd v Glasgow DC, 1987 S.C. 171; 1988 S.L.T. 227,
  (OH) 23–41

NACAP LTD v MOFFAT PLANT LTD, 1987 S.L.T. 221 .... 10–8, 23–1, 23–42
Naftalin v L.M.S. Railway, 1933 S.C. 259; 1933 S.L.T. 193, 2 Div 1–5
Napier v Scottish Ministers, June 26, 2001 17–3
Napier v Scottish Ministers, April 26, 2004 17–25
National Bank of Greece v Pinios Shipping Co (No. 1) (The Maria) [1989] 1
  All E.R. 213 22–2
National Coal Board v Thomson, 1959 S.C. 353; 1960 S.L.T. 89 23–42
National Union of Bank Employees v Murray (No. 2), 1949 S.L.T. (Notes) 25,
  (OH) 8–16

Nea Tyhi, The [1982] 1 Lloyd's Rep. 606; [1982] Com. L.R. 9, QBD 10–8
Nelson v Duraplex Industries Ltd, 1975 S.L.T. (Notes) 31, (OH) 26–10
Nelson Holdings Ltd v British Gas [1997] T.L.R. 122 12–7
Nethermere (St Neots) Ltd v Taverna [1984] I.C.R. 612; [1984] I.R.L.R. 240,
 (CA) 24–3
Nettleship v Weston [1971] 2 Q.B. 691; [1971] 3 W.L.R. 370, (CA) 9–16
New Mining and Exploring Syndicate Ltd v Chalmers and Hunter, 1911 2
 S.L.T. 386, Ex Div 23–16
Newcastle Building Society v Paterson, Robertson and Graham, 2001 S.C.
 734; 2002 S.L.T. 747, (OH) 26–13
Nicol v Advocate General for Scotland, 2003 G.W.D. 11–329, (OH) 18–2
Nicol v Blott, 1986 S.L.T. 677, (OH) 26–23
Nicolls v Glasgow (City of), unreported, December 23, 1996, Glasgow Sheriff
 Court 21–19
Nimmo v Alexander Cowan and Sons Ltd, [1968] A.C. 107; [1967] 3 W.L.R.
 1169; 1967 S.L.T. 277 21–9
Nissan v Att.-Gen. *See* Att.-Gen. v Nissan
Norsk Pacific Steamship Co Ltd v Canadian National Ry (1992) 91 D.L.R.
 (4th) 289 10–9
North of Scotland Bank v Duncan (1857) 19 D. 881 23–10
North Scottish Helicopters Ltd v United Technologies Corp. Inc., 1988 S.L.T.
 77, (OH) 10–8, 23–1
North Scottish Helicopters Ltd v United Technologies Corp. Inc., (No. 2), 1988
 S.L.T. 778, (OH) 23–1

O'Briens v Watts, 1987 S.L.T. 101, (OH) 5–6
O'Brien's CB v British Steel, 1991 S.C. 315; 1991 S.L.T. 477, 1 Div 26–15
Observer Ltd and Guardian Newspapers Ltd v UK (1991) A 216, 14 E.H.R.R.
 153 26–23
O'Keefe v The Lord Provost, Magistrates, and Council of the City of
 Edinburgh, 1910 2 S.L.T. 293 12–7
O'Kelly v Trusthouse Forte plc [1984] Q.B. 90; [1983] 3 W.L.R. 605, (CA) 24–3
Oll Ltd v Secretary of State for the Home Dept [1997] 3 All E.R. 897; (1997)
 147 N.L.J. 1099, QBD 12–7
O'Neil v Coyle, 1995 G.W.D. 21–1185 20–8
Ormiston v Redpath Brown and Co (1866) 4 M. 488 6–2
Oropesa, The [1943] P. 32; 1 All E.R. 211, (CA) 9–23
Orr v K, 2003 S.L.T. (Sh. Ct) 70; 2003 Fam. L.R. 26 2–9
Osborne v British Broadcasting Corporation, 2000 S.C. 29; 2000 S.L.T. 150,
 Ex Div 26–23
Osman v UK [1998] T.L.R. 68 17–7
Osman v UK [1999] 1 F.L.R. 193; (2000) 29 E.H.R.R. 245 12–5
Overseas Tankship (UK) v Miller [1967] 1 A.C. 617; [1966] 3 W.L.R. 498,
 PC 9–10
Overseas Tankship (UK) Ltd v Morts Dock and Engineering Co (known as
 "The Wagon Mound (No. 1)") [1961] A.C. 388; [1961] 2 W.L.R. 126 9–25

P's CB v CICB, 1997 S.L.T. 1180; 1997 S.C.L.R. 69, (OH) 9–21, 23–30
PJ and JH v UK, unreported, September 25, 2001, ECHR 17–10
Pacific Associates Inc. v Baxter [1990] 1 Q.B. 993; [1989] 3 W.L.R. 1150,
 (CA) 22–2
Page v Smith [1996] A.C. 155; [1995] 2 W.L.R. 644, (HL) 9–26, 11–2
Paris v Stepney BC [1951] A.C. 367; [1951] 1 All E.R. 42, (HL) 9–12
Park v Tractor Shovels Ltd, 1980 S.L.T. 94, (OH) 24–6
Parker Knoll v Knoll International [1962] R.P.C. 265, (HL) 5–6
Parry v Cleaver [1970] A.C. 1; [1969] 2 W.L.R. 821 26–16
Paterson v Welch (1893) 20 R. 744 .... 8–2, 8–34

Paton v British Pregnancy Advisory Service [1979] Q.B. 276; [1978] 3 W.L.R. 687, QBD 23–24
Paton v Tube Developments Ltd, May 30, 2001 21–14
Paul v Ogilvie, 2001 S.L.T. 171 26–6
Peat v News Group, unreported, March 8, 1996, Outer House 8–9
Peebles v MacPhail, 1990 S.L.T. 245; 1989 S.C.C.R. 410 2–4
Percy v Glasgow Corp., 1922 S.C. (HL) 144 24–2
Perrett v Collins [1998] T.L.R. 393 14–2
Petch v Customs and Excise Commissioners [1993] I.C.R 789 21–6
Phelps v Hillingdon LBC; *sub nom.* G (A Child), Re [2001] 2 A.C. 619; [2000] 3 W.L.R. 776, (HL) 12–8
Phestos Shipping Co Ltd v Kurmiawan, 1983 S.L.T. 388, 2 Div 3–2, 26–23
Philip v Morton (1816) Hume 865 8–35
Phillips v Britannia Hygienic Laundry Co Ltd., 1923 2 KB 832, (CA) 15–5
Phillips v Grampian Health Board, 1988 S.L.T. 628; 1988 S.C.L.R. 363, (OH) 26–19
Pickford v Imperial Chemical Industries Plc. [1998] 1 W.L.R. 1189; [1998] 3 All E.R. 462, (HL) 21–17
Pitts v Hunt [1991] 1 Q.B. 24; [1990] 3 W.L.R. 542, (CA) 25–7
Plato Films v Speidel [1961] A.C. 1090; [1961] 2 W.L.R. 470, (HL) 8–32
Polemis and Furness, Withy and Co Ltd, Re (known as "Polemis") [1921] 3 K.B. 560; (1921) 8 Ll. L. Rep. 351, (CA) 9–25, 15–5
Poliskie v Lane, 1981 S.L.T. 282, (OH) 18–2
Pollack v Workman (1900) 2 F 354 23–38
Pollock v Stead and Simpson Ltd, 1980 S.L.T. (Notes) 76, (OH) 18–2
Pomphrey v James A. Cuthbertson Ltd, 1951 S.C. 147; 1951 S.L.T. 191, 2 Div 26–12
Porteous v Rutherford, 1980 S.L.T. (Sh. Ct) 129 2–8
Porter v Dickie, 1983 S.L.T. 234, (OH) 26–20
Post Office v Morton, 1992 G.W.D. 26–1492 5–2
Potter v McCulloch, 1987 S.L.T. 308, (OH) 26–11
Prentice v Chalmers, 1985 S.L.T. 168, 2 Div 26–20
Pritchard v Tayside Health Board, 1989 G.W.D. 15–643 25–11
Progress and Properties v Craft (1976) 135 C.L.R. 651 25–8
Prole v Allen [1950] 1 All E.R. 476 23–13
Property Selection and Investment Trust Ltd v United Friendly Insurance Plc, 1998 S.C.L.R. 314 3–1
Prophit v BBC, 1997 S.L.T. 745; 1997 G.W.D. 8–332, (OH) 8–31
Pullar v Window Clean, 1956 S.C. 13; 1956 S.L.T. 17, 1 Div 15–1, 15–4
Purdon's CB v Boyd, 1963 S.C. (HL) 1; 1963 S.L.T. 157, (HL) 23–42
Purdie v Glasgow Council (City of), 2002 Rep. L.R. 26; 2002 G.W.D. 1–53, (OH) 21–19

QUILTY v WINDSOR, 1999 S.L.T. 346; 1998 G.W.D. 29–1501, (OH) 8–8
Quinn v McGinty, 1999 S.L.T. (Sh. Ct) 27; 1998 Rep. L.R. 107 .... 1–11, 23–10

R v BOW STREET METROPOLITAN STIPENDIARY MAGISTRATE, ex parte Pinochet Ugarte (No. 3) [2000] 1 A.C. 147; [1999] 2 W.L.R. 827; [1999] T.L.R. 222 23–47
R v H.M. Treasury, ex p. British Telecommunications plc [1996] Q.B. 615; [1996] 3 W.L.R. 203 16–5
R v Kelly [1999] Q.B. 621; [1999] 2 W.L.R. 384; [1998] 3 All E.R. 741, (CA) 23–38
R v Lichniak [2002] T.L.R. 494 17–3
R v Ministry of Agriculture and Fisheries, ex p. Hedley Lomas (Ireland) Ltd [1996] T.L.R. 353 16–5
R v Secretary of State for Transport, ex p. Factortame Ltd (No. 1) [1990] 2 A.C. 85; [1989] 2 W.L.R. 997 16–3

R v Secretary of State for Transport, ex p. Factortame Ltd (No 2) [1991] 1 A.C.
603; [1990] 3 W.L.R. 818 23–3
R (Bernard) v Enfield LBC [2002] T.L.R. 459 17–25
R (KB) v Mental Health Review Tribunal, 2003 T.L.R. 129 17–25
R (Williamson) v Secretary of State [2002] EWCA Civ 1926; [2003] Q.B.
1300; [2002] 1 All E.R. 385 .... 2–4, 17–11
RHM Bakeries v Strathclyde RC, 1985 S.L.T. 214, (HL) 3–8, 3–10, 3–11, 4–4
Racz v Home Office [1994] 2 A.C. 45; [1994] 2 W.L.R. 23, (HL) 7–2
Radford and Bright Ltd v Stevenson (1904) 6 F. 429 23–41
Rae v Chief Constable, Strathclyde Police, 1998 Rep. L.R. 63; 1998 G.W.D.
8–406, (OH) 2–5
Rae v Hay (1832) 10 S. 303 4–6
Rae v Strathclyde Joint Police Board, 1999 S.C.L.R. 793; 1999 G.W.D.
12–571, (OH) 21–9
Ralston v Greater Glasgow Health Board, 1987 S.L.T. 386, (OH) 21–24
Ralston v Pettigrew (1768) Mor. 12808 3–12
Ramsay v Maclay (1890) 18 R. 130 8–2
Reavis v Clan Line Steamers, 1925 S.C. 725; 1925 S.L.T. 538, 1 Div 10–8
Red Sea Insurance Co v Bouygues [1995] 1 A.C. 190; [1994] 3 W.L.R. 926 1–5
Rees v Darlington Memorial Hospital Trust [2003] T.L.R. 568 .... 10–1, 23–28
Rees v UK [1987] 2 F.L.R. 111; (1987) 9 E.H.R.R. 56 .... 17–10, 17–14
Reid v First Glasgow Ltd, unreported, March 4, 2003, Glasgow Sheriff
Court 15–5
Reid v Mitchell (1885) 12 R. 1129 2–1
Reid v Planet Welding Equipment Ltd, 1980 S.L.T. (Notes) 7, (OH) 26–10
Reid v Scott (1825) 4 S. 5 8–15
Reid's Trs v Dashwood, 1929 S.L.T. 619, 1 Div 23–23
Renfrew Golf Club v Ravenstone Securities, 1984 S.L.T. 170, (OH) 25–12
Reynolds v Times Newspapers Ltd [2001] 2 A.C. 127; [1999] 3 W.L.R. 1010,
(HL) 8–27
Ribitsch v Austria (1995) 21 E.H.R.R. 573 17–2
Richardson v LRC Products Ltd [2000] P.I.Q.R. P164; [2000] Lloyd's Rep.
Med. 280, QBD 19–4, 19–5, 19–8
Riddell v James Longmuir and Sons Ltd, 1971 S.L.T. (Notes) 33, (OH) 23–25
Rieley v Kingslaw Riding School, 1975 S.C. 28; 1975 S.L.T. 61, (IH) 26–8
Ritchie v Purdie (1833) 11 S. 771 3–12
Ritchie and Redman v EFT Industrial Ltd, 1997 S.L.T. 865; 1996 S.C.L.R.
955, (OH) 23–41
Riverstone Meat Co Pty Ltd v Lancashire Shipping Co Ltd [1961] A.C. 807;
[1961] 2 W.L.R. 269, (HL) 24–7
Robb v Salamis, 2003 G.W.D. 33–949 25–9
Robbie v Graham and Sibbald, 1989 S.L.T. 870; 1989 S.C.L.R. 578, (OH) 10–7
Roberts v Ramsbottom [1980] 1 W.L.R. 823; [1980] 1 All E.R. 7, QBD 23–39
Robertson v Fleming (1861) 4 Macq. 167 22–7
Robertson v Forth Road Bridge Joint Board, 1995 S.C. 364; 1996 S.L.T. 263,
1 Div 11–2, 11–3
Robertson v Keith (Seven Judges), 1936 S.L.T. 9 .... 2–5, 2–12
Robertson v Ridley [1989] 1 W.L.R. 872; [1989] 2 All E.R. 474, (CA) 23–13
Robertson v Turnbull, 1982 S.L.T. 96, (HL) 10–12
Robertson v Watt and Co, 2nd Division July 4, 1995 22–7
Roe v Ministry of Health [1954] 2 Q.B. 66; [1954] 2 W.L.R. 915, (CA) 9–6
Rondel v Worsley [1969] 1 A.C. 191; [1967] 3 W.L.R. 1666, (HL) 22–8
Rookes v Barnard [1964] A.C. 1129; [1964] 2 W.L.R. 269, (HL) 5–15, 5–16
Rorrison v West Lothian College, 2000 S.C.L.R. 245; 1999 Rep. L.R. 102,
(OH) 21–6
Rose v Plenty [1976] 1 W.L.R. 141; [1976] 1 All E.R. 97, (CA) 24–4

Rose Street Foundry and Engineering Company Ltd v John Lewis and Sons
    Ltd, 1917 1 S.L.T. 153 5–8
Ross v Advocate (H.M.), 1991 J.C. 210; 1991 S.L.T. 564 23–39
Ross v Bryce, 1972 S.L.T. (Sh. Ct) 76 .... 2–6, 25–5
Ross v Secretary of State, 1990 S.L.T. 13, (OH) 12–6
Ross Harper and Murphy v Banks, 2000 S.C. 500; 2000 S.L.T. 699, (OH) 23–18
Rosses v Sir Bhagrat Sinjie (1891) 19 R. 31 1–5
Rossleigh Ltd v Leader Cars Ltd, 1987 S.L.T. 355, (OH) 5–13
Rothfield v NB Ry, 1920 S.C. 805 5–9
Rowling v Takaro Properties Ltd [1988] A.C. 473; [1988] 2 W.L.R. 418 ..... 9–8, 10–3,
    12–2, 26–25
Royal Bank v Bannerman, 23 July 2002 .... 24–5, 24–6
Royal Bank of Scotland Plc v Bannerman Johnstone Maclay, 2003 S.C. 125;
    2003 S.L.T. 181, (OH) 10–4
Runciman v Borders RC, 1987 S.C. 241; 1988 S.L.T. 135, (OH) 9–25
Russell v Dickson, 1997 S.C. 269; 1998 S.L.T. 96, (OH) 23–7
Russell v Motherwell Bridge Fabricators Ltd, 1992 G.W.D. 14–827 21–4
Rylands v Fletcher (1868) L. R. 3 (HL) 330, (HL) 3–10

SW v UK (1996) E.H.R.R. 363 17–9
Saif Ali v Sydney Mitchell and Co [1980] A.C. 198; [1978] 3 W.L.R. 849;
    [1978] 3 All E.R. 1033, (HL) 22–8
Salter v UB Frozen and Chilled Foods Ltd, 2003 S.L.T. 1011 11–2
Sanderson v Paisley Burgh Commissioners (1899) 7 S.L.T. 255 24–7
Schiffahrt and Kohlen GmbH v Chelsea Maritime Ltd (The Irene's Success)
    [1982] Q.B. 481; [1982] 2 W.L.R. 422, QBD 10–8
Scobie v Steele and Wilson Ltd, 1963 S.L.T. (Notes) 45, (OH) 24–2, 24–8
Scorgie v Lawrie (1883) 10 R. 610 2–3
Scotch Whisky Association v JD Vintners [1998] C.L.Y. 352 5–7
Scotsman Publications Ltd v SOGAT, 1986 S.L.T. 646, (OH) 26–23
Scott Lithgow Ltd v GEC Electrical Projects Ltd, 1989 S.C. 412; 1992 S.L.T.
    244, (OH) 1–2
Scottish Australian Emigration Society v Borland (1855) 18 D. 239 23–10
Scott's Trs v Moss (1889) 17 R. 32 12–1
Scottish Milk Marketing Board v Drybrough and Co Ltd, 1985 S.L.T. 253,
    (OH) 5–6
Scottish Old People's Welfare Council, Petrs, 1987 S.L.T. 179, (OH) 23–45
Scottish Whisky Association v Glen Kella Distillers [1997] T.L.R. 186 5–7
Shanks v BBC, 1991 G.W.D. 27–1641 8–8
Sharp v Coutts. *See* Coutt's Tr. v Coutts
Shaw v Morgan (1888) 15 R. 865 8–26
Shell UK Ltd v McGillivray, 1991 S.L.T. 667, (OH) 3–2, 5–10
Sheriff v Wilson (1855) 17 D. 528 8–36
Shetland Line (1984) Ltd v Secretary of State for Scotland, 1996 S.L.T. 653,
    (OH) 7–1, 26–25
Shields v Dalziel (1894) 24 R. 849 25–8
Shore v Ministry for Works [1950] 2 All E.R. 228, (CA) 23–13
Short v J and W Henderson, 1946 S.C. (HL) 24 24–3
Sidaway v Board of Governors of the Bethlem Royal Hospital [1985] A.C.
    871; [1985] 2 W.L.R. 480; [1985] 1 All E.R. 643, (HL) 2–2, 22–3, 22–5
Silver v UK (1983) 5 E.H.R.R. 347 17–10
Sime v Sutcliffe Catering (Scotland) Ltd, 1990 S.L.T. 687, (OH) 24–6
Simmons v British Steel plc [2004] UKHL 20; (2004) 148 S.J.L.B. 540, (HL);
    affirming 2003 S.L.T. 62; 2002 G.W.D. 34–1133, 2 Div; reversing 2002
    S.L.T. 711; 2001 Rep. L.R. 82; 2001 G.W.D. 8–303, (OH) 9–25, 9–26, 15–9,
    21–12, 21–14
Simpson v ICI, 1983 S.L.T. 601, 2 Div 11–1

Simpson and Co v Thomson (1877) 5 R. (HL) 40 .... 10–2, 10–7, 10–8
Sinclair v Muir, 1933 S.N. 42 20–4
Siraj-Eldin v Campbell Middleton Burness and Dickson, 1988 S.C. 204; 1989
    S.L.T. 122, 1 Div 26–6
Skinner v Aberdeen City Council, 2001 Rep. L.R. 118; 2001 G.W.D. 16–657,
    (OH) 21–23
Skipton Building Society v Lea Hough and Co [2000] P.N.L.R. 545, QBD 25–9
Sloan v Triplett, 1985 S.L.T. 294, (OH) 25–8
Smart v Advocate (H.M.), 1975 J.C. 30; 1975 S.L.T. 65 25–7
Smith v Advocate General for Scotland, 2001 G.W.D. 3–139, (OH) 21–6
Smith v Comrie's Exrs, 1944 S.C. 499; 1945 S.L.T. 108, (OH) 26–20
Smith v Crossley Bros Ltd (1951) 95 Sol. Jo. 655 .... 21–3, 21–14
Smith v Eric S. Bush; Harris v Wyre Forrest DC [1990] 1 A.C. 831; [1989] 2
    W.L.R. 790, (HL) 10–4, 10–7
Smith v Goldthorpe, 2002 G.W.D. 10–303, (OH) 23–16
Smith v Jenkins (1970) 119 C.L.R. 397 25–8
Smith and Grady v United Kingdom (33985/96, 33986/96, July 25, 2000) 17–21
Snare v Fife's (Earl of) Trs (1850) 13 D. 286 3–13
Solicitors of Edinburgh v Robertson (1781) Mor. 13935 23–10
Somerville v Hamilton (1541) Mor. 8905 23–31
Somerville v Rowbotham (1862) 24 D. 1187 23–12
Somerville v Thomson, May 19, 1815, F.C. ; 6 Pat. App. 393 6–2
South Australia Asset Management Corporation v York Montague Ltd [1997]
    A.C. 191; [1996] 3 W.L.R. 87; [1996] 3 All E.R. 365, (HL) 26–1, 26–13
Southern Bowling Club Ltd v Ross (1902) 4 F. 405 3–3
Spartan Steel and Alloys Ltd v Martin and Co (Contractors) Ltd [1973] Q.B.
    27; [1972] 3 W.L.R. 502, (CA) 10–8
Spring v Guardian Assurance plc [1992] T.L.R. 628 .... 8–28, 10–5
Spring v Guardian Assurance Plc [1995] 2 A.C. 296; [1994] 3 W.L.R. 354 26–6
Square Grip Reinforcement Co v MacDonald, 1968 S.L.T. 65, (OH) 23–22
Squires v Perth and Kinross DC, 1986 S.L.T. 30, 2 Div 9–24, 12–1
Star Offshore Services plc v National Union of Seamen, 1988 S.L.T. 836,
    (OH) 23–22
Stark v Post Office [2000] T.L.R. 236 21–15
Stedman v Stedman (1744) Mor. 13909 23–34
Steel-Maitland v British Airways Board, 1981 S.L.T. 110, (OH) 3–3
Steele v Scottish Daily Record , 1970 S.L.T. 53, 2 Div 8–36
Stephen v Thurso Police Commissioners (1876) 3 R. 535 24–7
Stevenson v East Dunbartonshire Council, 2003 S.L.T. 97; 2002 G.W.D.
    39–1312, (OH) 21–7
Stevenson v Glasgow Corp., 1908 S.C. 1034 18–6
Stewart v HA Brechin and Co., 1959 S.C. 306; 1959 S.L.T. (Notes) 45,
    (OH) 26–12
Stewart v Thain, 1981 J.C. 13; 1981 S.L.T. (Notes) 2 2–4
Stillie v Wilson, 1990 S.L.T. 145, 2 Div; reversing 1988 S.C.L.R. 108, (OH) 20–7
Stone v Bolton. *See* Bolton v Stone
Stovin v Wise [1996] A.C. 923; [1996] 3 W.L.R. 388, (HL) 1–9, 12–4, 12–7, 18–11
Stratford v Lindley [1965] A.C. 269; [1964] 3 W.L.R. 541; [1964] 3 All E.R.
    102, (HL) 5–13, 5–14
Strathclyde RC v WA Fairhurst, 1997 S.L.T. 658, (OH) 25–12
Strathford East Kilbride Ltd v HLM Design Ltd, 1999 S.L.T. 121; 1997
    S.C.L.R. 877; 1997 Rep. L.R. 112, (OH) 10–4, 10–9, 12–4, 22–8
Stuart v Stephen (1877) 4 R. 873 26–23
Summers v Frost [1955] A.C. 740; [1955] 2 W.L.R. 825, (HL) 15–7, 21–9
Sunday Times v UK (1992) 14 E.H.R.R. 229 17–12
Sutherland v Hatton [2002] EWCA Civ 76; [2002] 2 All E.R. 1; [2002]
    P.I.Q.R. P21, (CA) 21–6

Sutherland Shire Council v Heyman [1955–95] P.N.L.R. 238; 157 C.L.R.
424 12–4
Swan v Andrew Minto and Sons, 1998 Rep. L.R. 42 20–4
Syme v Scottish Borders Council, 2003 S.L.T. 601; 2002 S.C.L.R. 1066,
(OH) 12–7, 18–10, 18–11
Symington v Campbell (1894) 21 R. 434 23–42

TCS Holdings Ltd v Ashtead Plant Hire, 2003 S.L.T. 177; 2003 G.W.D.
2–42, (OH) 10–8, 23–1
TP v UK [2001] 2 F.L.R. 549; [2001] 2 F.C.R. 289 12–5
Tahir v Gosal, Glasgow Sheriff Court, May 16, 1974 2–8
Tahir v Haringey HA [1998] Lloyd's Rep. Med. 104, (CA) 26–6
Tai Hing Cotton Mill Ltd v Liu Chong Hing Bank [1986] A.C. 80; [1985] 3
W.L.R. 317 22–2
Tan Chye Choo v Chong Kew Moi, [1970] 1 W.L.R. 147; [1970] 1 All E.R.
266 15–5
Taplin v Fife Council, 2003 S.L.T. 653; 2003 Rep. L.R. 9; 2003 G.W.D. 1–27,
(OH) 21–7
Tartan American Machinery Corporation v Swan and Co, August 15, 2003 14–1
Tate and Lyle Industries v Greater London Council [1983] 2 A.C. 509; [1983]
2 W.L.R. 649, (HL) 10–4
Taylor v Glasgow (City of), 1997 S.C. 183; 1997 S.L.T. 537; 1997 Rep. L.R.
17, Ex Div; reversing 1996 S.L.T. 701; 1996 Rep. L.R. 69, (OH) 24–5
Taylor v Glasgow City Council, 2002 S.C. 364; 2002 S.L.T. 689, Ex
Div 21–9, 21–10, 21–18, 21–19, 21–21
Teacher v Calder (1899) 1 F. (HL) 39 1–2
Teacher's Trs. v Calder (1900) 2 F. 372 18–4
Telfer v Glasgow DC, 1974 S.L.T. (Notes) 51, (OH) 18–2, 18–4
Thake v Maurice [1986] Q.B. 644; [1986] 2 W.L.R. 337, (CA) 23–27
Thin and Sinclair v Arrol (1896) 24 R. 198 5–2
Thomas v NUM (South Wales Area) [1986] Ch. 20; [1985] 2 W.L.R. 1081, Ch
D 23–22
Thomson v British Steel Corp, 1977 S.L.T. 26, (OH) 24–4
Thomson v Coutts, 2001 G.W.D. 25–923 25–19
Thomson v Devon (1899) 15 Sh. Ct. Rep. 209 2–2
Thomson v Duggie, (1949–50) 83 Ll. L. Rep. 44; 1949 S.L.T. (Notes) 53,
(OH) 23–37
Three Rivers DC v Bank of England (No. 3) [2003] 2 A.C. 1; [2000] 2 W.L.R.
1220 7–2
Thurso Building Society's JF v Robertson, 2000 S.C. 547; 2001 S.L.T. 797,
(OH) 23–43
Thynne, Wilson and Gunnell v UK (1991) E.H.R.R. 666 17–5
Timex Electronic Corporation v Amalgamated Engineering Union, The Scots-
man, April 14, 1993 23–22
Timex Electronics Corporation v AEEU, 1994 S.L.T. 438, 1 Div 26–23
Titchener v British Railways Board, [1983] 1 W.L.R. 1427; [1983] 3 All E.R.
770; 1984 S.L.T. 192 18–6
Todd v British Railways Board, unreported February 24, 1998 18–2
Tolmie v Dewar, December 3, 2002 2–4
Tolstoy v UK [1996] E.M.L.R. 152; (1995) 20 E.H.R.R. 442 .... 8–32, 17–12
Todd v British Railways Board, 1998 G.W.D. 11–568, (OH) 18–4
Topp v London Country Bus Ltd [1991] T.L.R. 552 13–2
Traill and Sons Ltd v Actieselskabat Dalbeattie Ltd (1904) 6 F. 798 23–42
Trans Trust SPRL v Danubian Trading Co [1952] 1 K.B. 285; [1952] 1 All
E.R. 89, KBD 9–26
Transco Plc v Stockport Metropolitan BC [2003] T.L.R. 632 3–10

Trapp v Mackie, [1979] 1 W.L.R. 377; [1979] 1 All E.R. 489; 1979 S.L.T. 126,
(HL) 8–21
Treadwell's Drifters Inc. v RCL Ltd, 1996 S.L.T. 1048, (OH) 5–5, 5–6
Tuttle v Buck (1909) 119 N.W. 946 5–10
Tyrer v UK (1978) 2 E.H.R.R. 1 17–3

UNISON v WESTMINSTER CITY COUNCIL, 2001 T.L.R. 263 23–22
United States v Carroll Towing Co (1947) 159 F (2d) 169 9–10
United Wholesale Grocers Ltd v Sher, 1993 S.L.T. 284, (OH) 24–3
Urquhart v Biwater Industries Ltd, 1998 S.L.T. 576; 1998 S.C.L.R. 198,
(OH) 21–23
Uxbridge Permanent Building Society v Pickard [1939] 2 K.B. 248, (CA) 24–5

VAN DER MUSSELE v BELGIUM (1984) 6 E.H.R.R. 163 17–4
Van Gend en Loos v Nederlandse Tarief Commissie [1963] E.C.R. 1; [1963]
C.M.L.R. 105 16–2
Veedfeld v Arhus Amtskommune [2001] T.L.R. 358 19–8
Vellino v Chief Constable of Manchester [2001] EWCA Civ 1249; [2002] 1
W.L.R. 218, (CA) 25–8

WL TINNEY AND CO LTD v JOHN C. DOUGALL LTD., 1977 S.L.T. (Notes) 58,
(OH) 15–5
Waddell v BBC, 1973 S.L.T. 246, 2 Div 8–33, 26–23
Walker v Eastern Scottish Omnibuses Ltd, 1990 G.W.D. 3–140 18–4
Walker v Gemmill (1846) 8 D. 838 6–2
Walker v Infabco Diving Services Ltd, 1983 S.L.T. 633, Ex Div 26–10
Walker v Northumberland CC [1995] 1 All E.R. 737; [1995] I.C.R. 702,
QBD 21–6
Wallace v Glasgow DC (City of), 1985 S.L.T. 23, 2 Div 18–4
Wallace v Mooney (1885) 12 R. 710 2–5
Wallace-James v Montgomerie and Co (1899) 2 F. 107 26–23
Walsh v Secretary of State for Scotland, 1990 G.W.D. 7–385 2–11
Ward v Cannock Chase DC [1986] Ch. 546; [1986] 2 W.L.R. 660, Ch D 9–26
Ward v Chief Constable, 1991 S.L.T. 292, 1 Div 2–5, 12–6
Wark v Steel, 1946 S.L.T (Sh. Ct) 17 20–4
Waste Systems International Inc v Eurocare Environmental Services Ltd, 1999
S.L.T. 198; 1998 G.W.D. 6–260, (OH) 5–4
Watson v Thompson, 1991 S.L.T. 683; 1992 S.C.L.R. 78, Ex Div; affirming
1990 S.C. 38; 1990 S.L.T. 374, (OH) 23–40
Watt v Jamieson, 1954 S.C. 56; 1954 S.L.T. 56, (OH) 3–7, 3–8
Waugh v Allan [1964] 2 Lloyd's Rep. 1; 1964 S.C. (HL) 102, (HL) 23–39
Waverley Housing Management Ltd v British Broadcasting Corporation, 1993
G.W.D. 17–1117 23–10
Webster v Advocate (Lord), 1985 S.C. 173; 1985 S.L.T. 361, 2 Div; reversing
1984 S.L.T. 13, (OH) 3–4
Weir v East of Scotland Water Authority, 2001 S.L.T. 1205; 2000 G.W.D.
39–1472, (OH) 15–2, 15–4
Weir v JM Hodge, 1990 S.L.T. 266, (OH) 22–7
Weir v Wyper, 1992 S.L.T. 579; 1992 S.C.L.R. 483, (OH) 25–8
Welch v UK (1995) 20 E.H.R.R. 247 17–10
Wells v Wells [1999] 1 A.C. 345; [1998] 3 W.L.R. 329, (HL) 26–15
West v Secretary of State for Scotland, 1992 S.C. 385; 1992 S.L.T. 636, 1
Div 26–25
Western v Eastern Scottish Omnibuses Ltd, 1989 G.W.D. 140 18–4
Whaley v Watson (Lord) of Invergowrie, 2000 S.C. 340; 2000 S.L.T. 475, 1
Div 23–4
Wheeler v New Merton Board Mills Ltd [1933] 2 K.B. 669, (CA) 15–10

White v Chief Constable [1999] 2 A.C. 455 11–1
White v Inveresk Paper Co Ltd (No. 2), 1987 S.C. 143; 1988 S.L.T. 2, (OH) 26–11
White v Jones [1995] 2 A.C. 207; [1995] 2 W.L.R. 187, (HL) 10–2, 10–11, 14–2,
22–7,
Whitefield v Barton, 1987 S.C.L.R. 259 9–11
Wilkie v King, 1911 S.C. 1310 23–21
Wilkinson v Downton [1897] 2 Q.B. 57 5–2
Williams v Hemphill, [1966] 2 Lloyd's Rep. 101; 1966 S.C. (HL) 31, (HL) 24–4
Wills Trs v Cairngorm Canoeing and Sailing School Ltd, 1976 S.C. (HL) 30;
1976 S.L.T. 162, (HL) 26–23
Wilsher v Essex Area HA [1988] A.C. 174; [1988] 2 W.L.R. 557, (HL) 9–19, 9–22,
22–5
Wilson v McCaffrey, 1989 G.W.D. 1–37 12–6
Wilson v Price, 1989 S.L.T. 484, (OH) 25–8
Wilson v Shepherd, 1913 S.C. 300 3–14
Wilsons v McKnight (1830) 8 S. 398 3–15
Wim v Quillan (1899) 2 F. 322 8–8
Winnik v Dick, 1983 S.C. 48; 1984 S.L.T. 185, 2 Div; affirming 1981 S.L.T.
(Sh. Ct) 101; affirming 1981 S.L.T. (Sh. Ct) 23 .... 1–11, 25–8
Winter v News (Scotland) Ltd, 1991 S.L.T. 828, Ex Div 8–32
Wishart Arch Defenders Loyal Orange Lodge 404 v Angus Council, 2002
S.L.T. (Sh. Ct) 43; 2001 G.W.D. 31–1256 17–13
Wolfson v Forrester, 1910 S.C. 675; 1910 1 S.L.T. 318, 1 Div 24–7
Wood v Fullerton (1710) Mor. 13960 24–1
Wood v Wood, 1935 S.L.T. 431, (OH) 23–35
Woodward v Chief Constable, Fife Constabulary, 1998 S.L.T. 1342; 1998 Rep.
L.R. 74, (OH) 2–12
Wooldridge v Sumner [1963] 2 Q.B. 43; [1962] 3 W.L.R. 616; [1962] 2 All
E.R. 978, (CA) 25–8
Woolwich v Inland Revenue [1993] A.C. 70; [1992] 3 W.L.R. 366 26–25
Wormald v HJ Walker and Co., 2004 G.W.D. 55 20–4
Wragg v DC Thomson and Co Ltd, 1909 2 S.L.T. 315, (OH) 8–7
Wright v Outram (1889) 16 R. 1004 8–21
Wright v Paton Farrell, 2002 S.C.L.R. 1039; [2003] P.N.L.R. 20; 2002 G.W.D.
28–988, (OH) 22–8

X v Bedfordshire CC [1995] 2 A.C. 633; [1995] 3 W.L.R. 152; [1995] 3 All
E.R. 353 .... 12–4, 12–5, 12–7, 15–5, 17–7
X v UK (1980) 19 D.R. 244 17–1

Yarmouth v France (1887) 19 Q.B.D. 647 21–24
Yeoman's Executrix v Ferries, 1967 S.C. 255; 1967 S.L.T. 332, (OH) 26–6
Yorkshire Dale SS Co v MOWT [1942] A.C. 691; (1942) 73 Ll. L. Rep. 1,
(HL) 9–21
Young v Ormiston, 1936 S.L.T. 79 23–10
Young, James and Webster v UK (1982) 4 E.H.R.R. 38 17–13
Youssoupoff v MGM (1934) 50 T.L.R. 581; 99 A.L.R. 864, (CA) 8–4
Yuen Kun Yeu v Att.-Gen. Hong Kong [1988] A.C. 175; [1987] 3 W.L.R.
776 .... 9–8, 10–3, 12–3
Yuille v Daks Simpson Ltd, 1984 S.L.T. 115, (OH) 21–24

Z v UK [2001] 2 F.L.R. 612; [2001] 2 F.C.R. 246; (2002) 34 E.H.R.R. 3 .... 12–5, 17–7

TABLE OF STATUTES

1429	Lawburrows Act (c.20)	2–8	
1581	Lawburrows Act (c.22)	2–8	
1686	Winter Herding Act (c.11)	20–2	
1830	Carriers Act (11 Geo. 4 & 1 Will. 4, c.68)	4–6	
1840	Parliamentary Papers Act (3 & 4 Vict., c.9)	8–19	
1847	Harbours, Docks and Piers Clauses Act (10 & 11 Vict., c.27)	15–5	
1855	Bills of Lading Act (18 & 19 Vict., c.111)	10–8	
1857	Crown Suits (Scotland) Act (20 & 21 Vict, c.44)		
	s.1	23–3	
	s.2	23–3	
	s.3	23–3	
1865	Trespass Scotland Act (28 & 29 Vict., c.56)	2–10, 3–2	
1880	Employers Liability Act (43 & 44 Vict., c.42)	21–1	
1881	Married Women's Property (Scotland) Act (44 & 45 Vict., 21)	23–34	
1890	Partnership Act (53 & 54 Vict., 39)	23–16	
	s.10	23–16	
	s.12	23–16	
1893	Sale of Goods Act (56 & 57 Vict., 71)	3–14	
1897	Workmen's Compensation Act (50 & 51 Vict., 41)	21–1	
1906	Dogs Act (6 Edw. 7, c.32)	20–2	
	Trade Disputes Act (6 Edw. 7, c.47)	5–15, 23–22	
1908	Summary Jurisdiction (Scotland) Act (8 Edw. 7, c.65)	2–13	
1911	Coal Mines Act (1 & 2 Geo. 5, c.50)		
	Pt II	15–4	
	s.49	15–4	
1920	Married Women's Property (Scotland) Act (10 & 11 Geo. 5, c.63)	23–34	
1930	Third Parties (Rights Against Insurers) Act (20 & 21 Geo. 5, c.25)	25–15	
1934	Betting, Gaming and Lotteries Act (24 & 25 Geo. 5, c.58)		
	s.11(2)	15–2	
1937	Factories Act (1 Edw. 8 & 1 Geo. 6, c.67)	15–6	
1938	Trade Marks Act (1 & 2 Geo. 6, c.22)	5–6	
1940	Law Reform (Miscellaneous Provisions) (Scotland) Act (3 & 4 Geo. 6, c.42)		
	s.3	9–24	
	s.3(1)	25–16	
	s.3(2)	25–16	
1945	Law Reform (Contributory Negligence) Act (8 & 9 Geo. 6, c.28)	25–9	
1947	Crown Proceedings Act (10 & 11 Geo. 6, c.44)	1–4, 23–3, 24–8, 26–24	
	s.2(1)	23–3	
	s.2(2)	23–3	
	s.10	23–5	
	s.10(1)	23–5	
	s.21(a)	23–3	
	s.43(a)	23–3	
1948	Law Reform (Personal Injuries) Act (11 & 12 Geo. 6, c.41)	24–1	
1949	Civil Aviation Act (12, 13 & 14 Geo. 6, c.67)		
	s.40(1)	3–3	
	s.40(2)	3–3	

1952	Defamation Act (15 & 16 Geo. 6 & 1 Eliz. 2, c.66)	
	s.5	8–17
	s.7	8–28
	s.10	8–20
	s.12	8–32
	s.14	8–34
	Sch.	8–28
	Visiting Forces Act (15 & 16 Geo. 6 & 1 Eliz. 2, c.67)	23–48
1956	Hotel Proprietors Act (4 & 5 Eliz. 2, c.62)	4–7
	s.1	4–7
	s.2	4–8
	Sch.	4–8
1957	Occupiers Liability Act (2 & 3 Eliz. 2, c.31)	18–1
1960	Occupiers Liability (Scotland) Act (8 & 9 Eliz. 2, c.30)	1–8, 13–2, 15–2, 15–10, 18–1, 18–5, 18–8, 20–3, 25–7
	s.1(1)	18–2
	s.1(2)	18–2
	s.1(3)	18–3
	s.2(1)	18–4
	s.2(2)	18–8
	s.2(3)	18–7
	s.3	18–7, 18–9
	s.3(1)	18–9
	s.4	23–3
1961	Human Tissue Act (9 & 10 Eliz. 2, c.54)	23–38
1962	Law Reform (Husband and Wife) Act (10 & 11 Eliz. 2, c.48)	
	s.2	23–34
	Offices Shops and Railway Premises Act (41)	21–9
1964	Diplomatic Privileges Act (c.81)	23–46, 23–47
1965	Trade Disputes Act (c.48)	5–15, 23–22
1967	Tokyo Convention Act (c.52)	
	s.3	2–11
	Police (Scotland) Act (c.77)	
	s.4(1)	6–3
	s.39	24–8
	Abortion Act (c.87)	23–23
1969	Employers Liability (Defective Equipment) Act (c.37)	21–2, 21–24
	s.1(1)	21–24
	Employer's Liability (Compulsory Insurance) Act (c.57)	23–10, 25–15
1971	Carriage of Goods by Sea Act (c.19)	24–7
	Interest on Damages (Scotland) Act (c.31)	26–15, 26–17
	Law Reform (Miscellaneous Provisions) Act (c.43)	
	s.4	26–20
1972	Road Traffic Act (c.20)	25–15
1973	Prescription and Limitation (Scotland) Act (c.52)	25–10
	s.8A	25–17
	s.11	25–12
	s.17	25–11
	s.17(2)(b)(iii)	25–11
	s.17(3)	25–11
	s.19A	25–11
1974	Health and Safety at Work etc.Act (c.37)	1–8, 15–2
	Rehabilitation of Offenders Act (c.53)	
	s.8	8–17
	s.8(3)	8–17
	s.8(5)	8–17
	s.8(8)	8–17
1975	Guard Dogs Act (c.50)	15–2, 20–2, 20–10
	s.1	20–10
	Sex Discrimination Act (c.65)	23–13
	Policyholders Protection Act (c.75)	
	s.6	25–15
1976	Damages (Scotland) Act (c.13)	1–7, 10–12, 23–26, 23–35, 23–37, 26–18, 26–21
	s.1(1)	23–25, 23–26
	s.1(3)	26–20
	s.1(4)	26–21
	s.2	26–18
	s.2(1)	26–18
	s.9	26–15
	s.9A	26–17
	s.9A(1)	26–17
	Sch. 1	26–22

1976 Dangerous Wild Animals
      Act (c.38) 20–8, 20–10
      s.1(3)(a) 20–8
      s.1(3)(b) 20–8
      s.2 20–10
      Sch. 20–8
1977 Unfair Contract Terms
      Act (c.50) 10–7
      s.16 18–7
1978 State Immunity Act
      (c.33) 23–47
      s.2 23–47
      s.3 23–47
      s.3(3) 23–47
      s.9(1) 23–48
      s.13(6) 23–47
1979 Sale of Goods Act
      (c.54) 10–8
1980 Law Reform (Miscella-
      neous Provisions)
      (Scotland) Act
      (c.55) 25–10
      Criminal Justice (Scot-
      land) Act (c.62)
      Pt IV 1–7
1981 Matrimonial Homes
      (Family Protection)
      (Scotland) Act
      (c.59)
      s.14(1) 26–23
      s.15(1) 26–23
1982 Civic Government (Scot-
      land) Act (c.45) 17–13
      Employment Act (c.46)
      s.15 23–21
      Administration of Justice
      Act (c.53) ... 23–35, 26–19,
                                 26–21
      ss.7–9 23–34
      ss.7–10 10–12
      s.8 23–34
      s.8(2) 23–34
      s.8(4) 23–34
      s.9 26–22
      s.10 .... 26–5, 26–16
      s.12 26–11
1983 Representation of the
      People Act (c.2)
      s.106 8–23
1984 Anatomy Act (c.14) 23–38
      Law Reform (Husband
      and Wife) (Scotland)
      Act (c.15)
      s.2(2) 2–9, 23–34
      s.3 23–34

1984 Mental Health (Scotland)
      Act (c.36)
      s.17 2–11
      s.24 2–11
      Trade Union Act
      (c.49) 23–22
      Roads (Scotland) Act
      (c.54)
      s.1(1) 20–5
      s.34 18–11
      s.151 21–12
      Rent (Scotland) Act
      (c.58) 3–1
1985 Law Reform (Miscella-
      neous Provisions)
      (Scotland) Act
      (c.73) 25–10
      s.10(1) 22–9
1986 Corneal Tissue Act
      (c.18) 23–38
      Education Act (c.40) 2–4
      Insolvency Act (c.45)
      ss.8–27 23–41
      s.11(3)(d) 23–41
      s.130(2) 23–41
      Sch. 2, para.5 23–41
1987 Animals (Scotland) Act
      (c.9) 1–8, 15–2, 15–10,
                   18–5, 19–8, 20–1,
                                 20–6
      s.1(8)(a) 20–7
      s.3 20–7
      s.5 20–7
      s.6 20–7
      Crown Proceedings
      (Armed Forces) Act
      (c.25) 23–5, 24–8
      Housing (Scotland) Act
      (c.26)
      Sch. 10 18–9
      Consumer Protection Act
      (c.43) 19–1, 25–10
      s.1(1) 19–3
      s.1(2) 19–4
      s.2(2) 19–4
      s.2(2)(a) 19–6
      s.2(2)(b) 19–6
      s.2(2)(c) 19–6
      s.2(3) 19–2
      s.2(5) 19–6
      s.2(4) 19–4
      s.2(6) 19–3
      s.3(1) 19–5
      s.3(2) 19–5
      s.5(1) 19–7
      s.5(2) 19–7
      s.6(4) 19–8

1987 Consumer Protection Act
  —*cont.*
  Pt 1 .... 15–2, 19–3
  s.24 19–5
  s.45(1) 19–4
  s.45(5) 19–4
1988 Copyright, Designs and
  Patents Act (c.48)
  Pt 1 8–31
  s.1(3) 8–31
  s.1(4) 8–31
  s.1(5) 8–31
  s.1(6) 8–31
1990 Law Reform (Miscella-
  neous Provisions)
  (Scotland) Act
  (c.40) 10–7
1991 Age of Legal Capacity
  (Scotland) Act
  (c.50) 23–31
  s.1(1)(b) 23–31
  s.1(3)(c) 23–31
  s.2(4A) 23–31
  s.2(4B) 23–31
  s.3(3)(d) 23–31
  s.8 .... 25–11, 25–12
  s.9 23–31
1992 Carriage of Goods by Sea
  Act (c.50) 10–8
  Trade Union and Labour
  Relations (Consoli-
  dation) Act (c.52)
  s.1 23–21
  s.10(1) 23–21
  s.20 24–8
  s.20(2) 23–21
  s.22 23–21
  s.23 23–21
  s.30 23–21
  s.219(1) 23–22
  s.219(1)(a) 23–21
  s.219(1)(b) 23–21
  s.219(2) 23–21, 23–22
  s.219(3) 23–22
  s.226 23–22
  s.295 23–21
  s.296 23–21
1993 Damages (Scotland) Act
  (c.5) 23–37, 26–18
  s.3 26–18
  s.5 26–17
  s.7(1) 26–21
  Trade Union Reform and
  Employment Rights
  Act (c.19) 23–22
  Education Act (c.35) 2–4
  Railways Act (c.43) 18–2

1995 Merchant Shipping Act
  (c.21)
  s.105 2–11
  Children (Scotland) Act
  (c.36) 23–31
  s.13 23–31
  Private International Law
  (Miscellaneous Pro-
  visions) Act
  (c.42) 1–5
  s.9 1–5
  s.11(1) 1–5
  s.11(2)(a) 1–5
  s.11(2)(b) 1–5
  s.11(3) 1–5
  s.12 1–5
  s.13(1) 1–5
  s.13(2)(a) 1–5
  s.13(2)(b) 1–5
  Criminal Procedure (Scotland) Act (c.46)
  s.170 2–13
1996 Defamation Act (c.31) 8–7,
                                  8–20
  s.1 8–31
  s.1(2) 8–31
  s.1(3) 8–31
  s.2 26–10
  s.2(1)–(6) 8–30
  s.3 8–30
  s.4 .... 8–30, 26–16
  s.4(5) 8–30
  s.5 26–16
  s.6 26–16
  s.13 8–19
  s.14(1) 8–21
  s.17(1) 8–20
  Sch. 1, para.11(1)(c) 8–20
1997 Social Security (Recovery
  of Benefits) Act
  (c.27) 26–16
  s.3(4) 26–16
  s.6 26–16
  s.8 26–16
  s.15 26–16
  Sch. 2 26–16
  Protection from Harass-
  ment Act (c.40) 2–15,
                                  26–26
  s.8(1) 2–15
  s.8(3) 2–15
  s.8(4)(a) 2–15
  s.8(4)(b) 2–15
  s.8(4)(c) 2–15
  s.12(1) 2–15
  s.12(3) 2–15

1998	Human Rights Act (c.42)	17–1, 17–13, 23–9
	s.6(1)–(6)	17–1
	s.6(1)	17–3
	s.7(1)(a)	17–1
	s.7(1)(b)	17–1
	s.7(4)	17–1
	s.7(5)	17–1, 17–20
	s.8	17–1
	s.8(1)–(4)	17–20
	s.12	17–12, 26–23
	s.12(2)	26–23
	s.12(3)	8–33
	Scotland Act (c.46)	8–20, 23–3
	s.29	17–1
1998	Scotland Act—*cont.*	
	s.40(4)	23–4
	s.53	17–1
	s.57(2)	17–1, 17–3
1999	Employment Relations Act	23–22
2000	Limited Liability Partnership Act (c.12)	23–19
	s.1	23–19
	s.2	23–19
	s.6	23–19
	Sch. 1	23–19
2001	Protection from Abuse (Scotland) Act (asp 14)	2–15
2003	Mental Health (Care and Treatment) (Scotland) Act (asp 13)	2–11

TABLE OF STATUTORY INSTRUMENTS

1965   Rules of the Court of Session (SI 1965/321)
r.89A 26–10

1984   Dangerous Wild Animals
Act 1976 (Modifications) Order (SI 1984/1111)
art.1 20–8

1992   Management of Health
and Safety at Work
Regulations (SI 1992/2051)
reg.3 21–11
reg.15 21–11

Health and Safety (Display Screen Equipment) Regulations
(SI 1992/2792) 21–17
reg.1 21–17
reg.1(4) 21–17
reg.2 21–17
reg.2(1) 21–23
reg.4 .... 21–17, 21–20
reg.4(1)(a) 21–20, 21–22, 21–23
reg.4(1)(b) 21–20, 21–22, 21–23
reg.4(1)(b)(i) 21–20
reg.4(1)(b)(ii) 21–20, 21–23
reg.4(1)(b)(iii) 21–20, 21–23
reg.4(2) 21–20
reg.5 .... 21–17, 21–20
reg.6 21–17
reg.7 21–17

Provision and Use of
Work Equipment
Regulations (SI 1992/2932) 21–14
reg.2 .... 21–13, 21–14
reg.5 ...... 21–9, 21–14, 21–15
reg.5(1) 21–14
reg.5(2) 21–14
reg.5(3) 21–14
reg.6 21–15
reg.8 21–15
reg.9 21–15
reg.11 21–15
reg.12 21–15

1992   Provision and Use of
Work Equipment
Regulations—*cont.*
reg.12(3) 21–15
reg.13 21–15
reg.14 21–15
reg.15 21–15
reg.16 21–15
reg.21 21–15
reg.22 21–15
reg.23 21–15
reg.24 21–15

Personal Protective
Equipment at Work
Regulations (SI 1992/2966) 21–16
reg.2 21–16
reg.3 21–16
reg.4 21–16
reg.5 21–16
reg.6 21–16
reg.7 21–16
reg.8 21–16
reg.9 21–16
reg.10 21–16
reg.11 21–16

Workplace (Health, Safety and Welfare) Regulations (SI 1992/3004)
reg.2(1) 21–12
reg.5 21–12
reg.5(1) 21–13
reg.6 21–12
reg.7 21–12
reg.8 21–12
reg.9 21–12
reg.9(3) 21–12
reg.10 21–12
reg.11 21–12
reg.11(2) 21–12
reg.12 21–12
reg.12(2) 21–13
reg.12(3) 21–12, 21–13
reg.13 21–13
reg.13(5) 21–13
reg.14 21–13
reg.15 21–13
reg.16 .... 21–4, 21–13
reg.17 21–13

1992 Workplace (Health, Safety and Welfare) Regulations—*cont.*
reg.18 21–13
reg.19 21–13
reg.20 21–13
reg.21 21–13
reg.22 21–13
reg.23 21–13
reg.24 21–13
reg.25 21–13
reg.25(3) 21–13
reg.26 21–13
Act of Sederunt (Rules of the Court of Session) (SI 1994/1443 (S.69))
r. 43–9 26–10
1993 Ordinary Cause Rules (SI 1993/3128)
rr. 36.8–36.10 26–10
1997 Social Security (Recovery of Benefits) Regulations (SI 1997/2205) 26–15
1998 Civil Procedure (Modification of Enactments) Order (SI 1998/2940)
para.4 23–34
Scotland Act 1998 (Commencement) Order (SI 1998/3178) 23–4

1999 Scotland Act 1998 (General Transitory, Transitional and Savings Provisions) Order (SI 1999/901) 23–4
Scotland Act 1998 (Transitory and Transitional Provisions) (Standing Orders and Parliamentary Publications) Order (SI 1999/1095) 8–20
Transfer of Property (Scottish Ministers) Order (SI 1999/1104) 23–4
2000 Human Rights Act 1998 (Commencement No. 2) Order (SI 2000/1851) 17–1
2001 Consumer Protection Act 1987 (Product Liability) (Modification) (Scotland) Order (SI 2001/265) 19–4
Solicitors (Scotland) (Incorporated Practices) Practice Rules (SI 1997/645) 23–20
2002 Damages (Personal Injuries) (Scotland) Order (SI 2002/46) 26–15

Section I: Introduction

Chapter 1

INTRODUCTION

Terminology: what is delict?

A cow falls through the ceiling of your shop, some unidentified **1–1** person pours a pot of urine over your head, you fall through the floor of a building or you are butted by a bull over a wall on to stinging nettles having tried to ward it off by tapping it on the nose. You are wrongfully arrested by a police officer, your luggage is missing when you return to your hotel or MegaCorp take all the customers away from your business by offering them a better deal. You are called a liar or your wedding photos are published in the local paper. Your doctor fails to treat your illness in time and your lawyer fails to sue him on time. Your workmates play a prank on you that goes badly wrong. It is with stories like these that the law of delict deals and indeed has had to deal with in the past. But first, it is only fair to explain what is meant by the strange name of the subject.[1]

For the moment, the reader may conveniently consider delict to be the area of law that makes certain legally disapproved conduct by a defender actionable (usually for damages or by interdict) in the civil courts by a pursuer who often, but not always, will have suffered some loss as a result of the conduct. It is about civil wrongs — although not every civil wrong is delictual. It applies to much of the same area of the law as the English "tort". The same subject matter is often considered in Scotland under the heading "reparation" (especially by practitioners), but that term more accurately describes a response to a breach of a legal obligation: one commits a delict; one must make reparation.[2] In practice, both approaches are needed: an injured person will want reparation; a company may want to know

---

[1] " *'Delinquo', supine delictum* means 'to be lacking' or 'fail'. It was already used in classical Latin to mean 'fail in one's duty, offend' ": Birks, "The Concept of a Civil Wrong" in Philosophical Foundations of Tort Law (Owen ed., Oxford, 1995), p.39, n.28. Sabinus was the creator of the category "Delict": *Visser and Whitty HPLS* p.424 n.7 citing P.G. Stein, Romisches Recht und Europa: Die Geschichte einer Rechtskultur (1996), 38.

[2] Reparation is no longer thought to refer to breach of contract: *Miller v Glasgow D.C.*, 1989 S.L.T. 44; *Middleton v Douglass*, 1991 S.L.T. 726. The practitioner publications are called *Reparation Law Reports*, *Reparation Bulletin* and the looseleaf *Reparation: Liability for Delict* all published by W. Green.

what obligations it must fulfil. The wide view of delict taken in this book (coming close to "civil wrongs") is perhaps wider than most.[3]

Calling the subject "delict" is consistent with a division of obligations according to the events which trigger various responses, *i.e.* contract, delict and unjust enrichment. The word "delict" formerly had the same "bad" connotation as has "delinquent" and classically dealt with matters which were essentially crimes and generally required *mens rea*. The term "quasi-delict" is used by the legal community in at least two ways: to describe cases involving actionable conduct not quite so morally wrong as delicts proper, such as, for example, negligence[4]; and, more particularly, to describe those obligations imposed in Scots law that are derived from certain Roman actions.[5]

Relationship with other subjects

Obligations: contract and unjust enrichment

1–2   The traditional explanation is that the commission of a delict is a breach of an obligation created by the law between the wrongdoer and the victim, as opposed to contract where any liability to perform or to pay damages depends upon the consent of the parties or the will of a party (in the case of the unilateral gratuitous obligation). Unjust enrichment,[6] with which delict is frequently associated, has more in common with delict than contract, the obligation being quite clearly imposed by the law: it differs from delictual duties only in that in unjust enrichment cases the duty to pay or to do something arises without the necessity of any wrong being done by the defender.[7] There is the yet unravelled canonist thread that runs through Scots law and in that system restitution for a wrong was the natural starting point because the commission of the delict was a sin.[8] It is only right

---

[3] Many would restrict the use of "delict" to *exclude* related topics and topics such as nuisance, strict liability and statutory liability: *Visser & Whitty HPLS* 464–470.

[4] See Stewart, "Smith's question-mark", 1990 J. R. 71. Current examples are usually as a result of statute or continental usage: see, *e.g. Davenport v Corinthian Motor Policies at Lloyds*, 1991 S.L.T. 774.

[5] See Ch.4.

[6] Until recently misleadingly dealt with under the heading of quasi-contract, this is the body of law which deals with the restitution of gains unjustly made by a defender at the expense of the pursuer, rather than reinstating the pursuer to the position he was in before a wrong was done to him or her, as in delict. A general principle of restitution is recognised in Scotland but the cases are collected under certain categories such as, for example, recompense or repetition.

[7] J. Blackie, "Enrichment and Wrongs in Scots Law'" [1992] Acta Juridica 23; J. Blackie, "Enrichment Wrongs and Invasion of Rights in Scots Law'" in The Limit of the Law of Obligations (Visser ed., 1997). *Teacher v Calder* (1899) 1 F. (HL) 39; *Exchange Telegraph v Guilianotti*, 1959 S.C. 19.

[8] *Zimmerman*, p.1021.

to say that there is considerable academic discussion concerning the interrelation of the various categories of the law of obligations.[9]

One "overlap" question is whether there may be concurrent liability. The case of doctors and other professionals has made it look as if there is no problem but these cases can be explained by a principle whose status and origin is not entirely clear, *spondet peritiam artis*[10] that a person who professes a skill must answer for the failure to deliver it.[11] Cases of carriage are easier and do suggest that Scots law was within a general civilian tradition of allowing concurrent liability.[12] Now that English law has accepted concurrent liability even in claims for economic loss for negligence,[13] it can be said that Scots law most certainly accepts concurrent liability and will do so even in a contractual matrix.[14]

Scots law recognises, in *Contract*, the *jus quaesitum tertio* whereby two parties can contract in favour of a third not a party to the contract. That may sometimes allow a contractual action to take the place of a difficult theoretical delictual action. The fact that such a strong contract law exists may mean that it may not be necessary to extend delict to such a situation. For example, in *Scott Lithgow Ltd v GEC Electrical Projects Ltd*,[15] it was held that where it was sought to establish the constitution of a *jus quaesitum tertio*, it was not sufficient merely that the *jus* be one in which the *tertius* had an interest. It was instead necessary that the *jus* was intended to be of benefit to the *tertius*. Averments merely that a contract referred to a third party and had been concluded for the advancement of that third party's interests were sufficient to plead a relevant case for a *jus quaesitum tertio*. There was, in general, no reason why a *tertius* should not be entitled to sue for damages, but that had to be a matter of the intention of the contracting parties to be ascertained from the terms of their contract.

---

[9] Atiyah, *Rise and Fall* (Oxford, 1979), Ch.20 and Birks, *Introduction to the Law of Restitution* (Oxford, 1989). See the discussions in MacQueen and Thomson, *Contract Law in Scotland*, (LexisNexis, 2000) and M. Hogg, *Obligations* (Avizandum, 2003).

[10] *Et emperitia culpae enumeratur.*

[11] See Chs 10 and 22.

[12] This has been generally ill-articulated. But it is possible to align Scots law more with a German model, where concurrent liability is allowed. In German law liability itself is constrained to certain interests, a line which has not been taken in Scots law in such a dogmatic fashion This is in direct contrast to a French model where concurrent liability is not generally allowed. An explanation for this French position can be found in J. Gordley, "Contract and Delict: Towards a Unified Law of Obligations", (1997) 1 Edin.L.R. 345.

[13] *Henderson v Merrett* [1995] 2 A.C. 145. See P. Cane, "Contract, Tort and the Lloyd's Debacle" in *Consensus Ad Idem* (Rose ed., 1996).

[14] See Ch.10.

[15] 1992 S.L.T. 244.

Crime

1–3   As stated above, Stair made a clear division between these two areas of law which had hitherto been extremely closely related although obviously links remain.[16] What has most certainly gone is any penal aspect of damages in Scotland for delict.

Public law, constitutional and administrative law

1–4   Reparation for delict is a branch of private law. The "farming out" of government functions to private or partly private bodies taken with the Crown Proceedings Act[17] are two major developments that have meant that the State, in some shape or form, finds itself in arguments about reparation.

The landmark case in negligence, *Dorset Yacht v The Home Office*,[18] brought the State more closely into the scope of liability as some of its functions were now thought justiciable and remain so, albeit there has been a general retreat from finding public bodies liable in private law.[19]

New procedures for judicial review allowing a claim for damages for results of an unreasonable or wrongful decision has the look of delict. When the Inner House then made it clear that judicial review was not exclusively a matter of reviewing public bodies, it even more so resembles a new area of delict — that of wrongful administration.[20]

The delicts that control intentional harms are essentially bastions of the constitution. In Scotland, as in England, our Claim of Right and Bill of Rights are not documents upon which the citizen regularly has recourse to protect any civil rights that he or she may have. The Constitution depends upon the fact that people are free to do what is not prohibited and delict is one of the major prohibitions. As Fraser put it, in the first half of the twentieth century:

> "The British subject has no rights which are guaranteed by the constitution. For the protection of his rights to personal freedom, as of all his other rights, the British subject must look to the ordinary law, particularly parts of it dealing with crimes and delicts, and not to any constitutional guarantees. It is an important feature of these branches of the law that they afford protection whether the citizen's rights are wrongfully invaded by a private person or a public official."[21]

---

[16] *Visser and Whitty, HPLS* 432–434.
[17] See para.23–3 below.
[18] [1970] A.C. 1004. See Ch.12.
[19] See discussion below at Ch.12.
[20] See Ch.7.
[21] W.L.R. Fraser, *Constitutional Law* (Hodge, 1938), p.179. See also pp.194 and 200.

Delict as much as crime regulates what we may or may not do the one to the other. Verbal injury is one of the most obvious examples. If free speech is indeed pivotal to civilisation, then in Scotland it is largely verbal injury that regulates it.[22] Rules that seem unfortunate in the context of compensation or insurance or risk may well have significance in maintaining the balance of freedoms in society.[23]

There have been two major developments. First, there is liability from infringement of human rights. This is discussed in context in a later chapter.[24] Secondly, there has emerged or been revived, liability for misuse of public office discussed in context in a later chapter.[25]

Private international law

This is a separate university course.[26] Practically, the first question **1–5** for the practitioner or other analyst ought to be: to what extent does the problem concern the law of Scotland at all, and can the matter be heard a Scottish court? The case may be one to be decided in a different court or according to a different legal system. Delict is treated specially both for jurisdiction and for choice of law. Notably there is a ground additional to domicile allowing actions to be raised "in matters relating to tort, delict or quasi-delict, in the courts for the place where the harmful event occurred",[27] *lis alibi pendens* applies. There are rules in the convention and at common law[28] to prevent two actions running at the same time on related subject-matter. Where proceedings involving the same cause of action between the same parties are brought in the courts of different Contracting States, any court other than the court first seised must, of its own motion, decline jurisdiction in favour of that court.[29] *Forum non conveniens* remains a part of the law of jurisdiction, although the 1982 Act

---

[22] See Ch.8.

[23] P.Q.R. Boberg, *The Law of Delict* (Jutta, 1989), says "the law of delict . . . is close to the core problem of balancing individual freedom against collective security — a balance that it seeks to achieve by tempering broad principles of liability with limiting interpretations of wrongfulness, fault and causation. It follows that a proposition should never be propounded without due regard to its social implications, and that the merit of a rule depends on its functional effects rather than the purity of its ancestry" pp.26–27.

[24] See Ch.17.

[25] See Ch.7.

[26] A.E. Anton and P.R. Beaumont, *Civil Jurisdiction in Scotland* (2nd ed., 1995); A.E. Anton, *Private International Law* (2nd ed., 1990); E. Crawford, *International Private Law* Green, 1998. There is a full treatment in relation to delict in *Stewart, Reparation: Liability for Delict*, Ch.2.

[27] Art.5(3). Brussels and Lugano conventions. Art.5(3) EC Reg.44/2001.

[28] On the details of the plea in a reparation action at common law see *Flannigan v British Dyewood Company Ltd*, 1971 S.L.T. 208.

[29] EC Reg.44/2001 Art.27.

restricts the applicability of it in international cases between Convention countries.[30] The essence of the plea is that there is a more appropriate court to try the case taking into account the interests of the parties and the ends of justice. The result can be a sist or dismissal. It is generally safer to sist because it is not always known what will happen in the other jurisdiction.[31]

Choice of law is about which rules of law govern the case whatever court it is heard in. There is one notable point. The law relating to choice of law has been overhauled by the Private International Law (Miscellaneous Provisions) Act 1995.[32] The old law only applies to delicts committed before the new Act[33] and to defamation actions.[34] Under the old law, the law of the pursuer's domicile was irrelevant.[35] The defender's domicile was equally irrelevant.[36] The claim had to satisfy both the *lex fori* and the *lex loci delicti*. For a long time the rule known as the double actionability or double delict rule applied under which the claim had to be actionable under both systems.[37] The general rule now is that the applicable law is the law of the country in which the events constituting the tort or delict in question occur.[38] Where elements of these events occur in

---

[30] But not in extra-Convention cases: *Re Harrods (Buenos Aires) Ltd* [1992] Ch. 72.

[31] See generally *De Mulder v Jadranska Linijska (Jadrolinija)*, 1989 S.L.T. 269.

[32] There had been criticism in England and Scotland and the matter was dealt with by the Law Commission and the Scottish Law Commission: See, *e.g.* Carter, "Choice of Law in Tort and Delict" (1991) 107 L.Q.R. 405. Black, "Delict and the Conflict of Laws", 1968 J.R. 40, Law Com., No.193; Scot. Law Com., No.129.

[33] Acts or omissions on or after May 1, 1996 apparently regardless of the date of harm.

[34] Section 13(1). This is defined as any claim under the law of any part of the UK for libel or slander of title, slander of goods or of malicious falsehood and any claim under the law of Scotland for verbal injury (s.13(2)(a)) and to claims of the same nature under the law of any country (s.13(2)(b)).

[35] *Convery v Lanarkshire Tramway Co.* (1905) 8 F. 117.

[36] *Naftalin v L.M.S. Railway*, 1933 S.C. 259.

[37] See, *e.g. Rosses v Sir Bhagrat Sinjie* (1891) 19 R. 31; *Evans v Stein* (1904) 7 F. 65; *Naftalin v L.M.S. Ry*, 1933 S.C. 259; and *McElroy v McAllister*, 1949 S.C. 110. *Mitchell v McCulloch* 1976 S.C. 1; *James Burrough Distillers Plc. v Speymalt Whisky Distributors Ltd*, 1989 S.L.T. 561. Exceptions developed, see *Boys v Chaplin* (1971) A.C. 356 and *Red Sea Insurance Co. v Bouygues* [1995] 1 A.C. 190, PC. See Rodger, "Bouygues and Scottish Choice of Law Rules in Delict", 1995 S.L.P.Q. 58.

[38] Section 11(1). See generally Williams and Mead, "Abolition of the Double Actionability Rule: Questions still to be answered" [1996] J.P.I.L. 112. Rules on characterisation are important as a preliminary question. Section 9 provides that that characterisation for the purposes of private international law is a matter for the courts of the forum. The applicable law is to be used for determining issues arising such as whether an actionable tort or delict has occurred. Choice of law rules are excluded from the applicable law. It is provided for the avoidance of doubt that the new law applies to events occurring in the forum as it applies to events occurring in any other country.

different countries there are three rules: in cases of personal injury[39] or death the applicable law is that of the territory where the individual was when the injuries were sustained[40]; for damage to property it is the place where the property was when it was damaged[41]; and for all other cases the territory where the "most significant element or elements of the events"[42] complained of occurred, or failing that, the law of the territory with which the subject matter has the "most real and substantial connection". The general rule may be displaced. If it appears, in all the circumstances, from a comparison of: (a) the significance of the factors that connect a tort or delict with the country whose law would be the applicable law under the general rule; and (b) the significance of any factors connecting the tort or delict with another country, that it is substantially more appropriate for the applicable law for determining the issues arising in the case, or any of those issues, to be the law of the other country, the general rule is displaced and the applicable law for determining that issue or issues (as the case may be) is the law of that other country. The factors that may be taken into account as connecting a tort or delict with a country for the purposes of this section include, in particular, factors relating to the parties, to any of the events which constitute the tort or delict in question or to any of the circumstances or consequences of those events.[43]

Evidence and procedure

The academic student is not fundamentally concerned with proving cases — that is the practitioners problem.[44]   **1–6**

History

Scots law has been influenced by Roman law over the centuries   **1–7** and further reading should, in the first instance, be directed towards some comprehension of that relationship.[45] There are also parallels. The Roman law began by treating delict and crime as much the same

---

[39] This includes disease or any impairment of physical or mental condition: s.11(3).

[40] s.11(2)(a).

[41] s.11(2)(b).

[42] s.11(2)(c).

[43] Section 12.

[44] See generally Conway, *Personal Injury Practice in the Sheriff Court* (W. Green, 2003); Stewart, *Reparation: Liability for Delict*, Chapter 33.

[45] There is now a near complete *History of Scots Law* to the 19th century by Professor Walker. There is a very extensive series of detailed historical, historiographical and theoretical essays in Volume II of *A History of Private Law in Scotland*: *HPLS*. See also Walker, D.M., "The Development of Reparation" (1952) 64 J.R. 101. R. Black, "An Historical Survey of Delictual Liability in Scotland for Personal Injuries and Death", 1975 C.I.L.J.S.A. 46, 189, 316; 1976 9 C.I. L.J.S.A. 57. Evans-Jones, *The Civilian Tradition in Scots Law* (Stair Society, 1995); Zimmerman, *The Law of Obligations: Roman Foundations of the Civilian Tradition* (Oxford, 1996).

thing. The most significant delicts for the Romans were things like assault or theft. In the absence of a State apparatus, such as a police force, to investigate and deal with such matters, the Roman law attempted to control the self-help to which Romans might resort. Roman law arranged for people to be able to buy off vengeance. For example, the first piece of Roman legislation, the Twelve Tables, promulgated about 450 B.C., provided that the killing of an armed thief resulted in no penalty. The law later tried to intercede so that a thief caught red-handed could not have vengeance visited upon him except as permitted by the court. At first the court permitted restricted reprisals, but eventually a monetary penalty was substituted. The penalty was not, however, an amount intended to compensate, as is now the general rule; instead, sometimes two, three or four times the value of the object stolen had to be paid.

Scots law developed in a similar way. In the modern Scots law, theft and assault remain delicts as much as they are crimes. Beginning about the fourteenth century, when a person had killed another as a result of a criminal act, he might be called upon to pay a reasonable sum to the deceased's kin. This remedy became known as "assythment" and was only formally abolished by the Damages (Scotland) Act 1976.[46] (This is one example of a native non-Roman source.) In principle, Scots law parted from crime when Stair, under reference to Romans, xii, 19,[47] was quite clear that the breach of delictual obligations should be visited by an obligation to make reparation and should not be concerned with revenge. Interestingly though, since the Criminal Justice (Scotland) Act 1980, Part IV, a criminal court can in certain circumstances make an order called a compensation order. Such an order makes an offender pay a sum compensating the victim of the crime, as well as any fine or sentence of imprisonment that may be imposed. Compensation orders cannot be made in motor collision cases. The offender who does not pay the order — which can be paid by instalments — can be imprisoned for a specified period.

There are traces running through Scots law of two Roman law remedies that that certainly influenced the systems in the civilian family: the *actio injuriarum* [48] and the *actio legis Aquiliae*.[49] The first gave an action for insult and the second allowed for damages in

---

[46] See Casebook, Appendix, Ext. 11.

[47] I, ix, 2 (Casebook, Ext. 11. 2.1.3).

[48] When reading earlier reports students will note a different and now disapproved use of the term *actio injuriarum*. See *McKendrick v Sinclair*, 1972 S.L.T. 110 (HL); and also in the Court of Session, 1971 S.L.T. 17; T.B. Smith, "Designation of Delictual Actions: Damn Injuria Damn", 1972 S.L.T. (News) 125; "Damn Injuria Again", 1984 S.L.T. (News) 85.

[49] Until relatively recently the modern significance of these antecedents in Scots law were not clearly understood by many: see Stein (1955); T.B. Smith (1972), (1984) (Casebook, Ext. 14).

respect of loss wrongfully caused (*damnum injuria datum*). *Injuria* in the *actio injuriarum* meant affront or insult but meant contrary to law in the context of the *lex Aquilia*.[50] The *lex Aquilia* was an ancient Roman statute, which provided for liability for certain damage to certain property caused in certain ways.[51] Its practical significance is that it is this statute and its interpretation, which attracted the attention of the great Roman Jurists, featured in the *Digest* and was discovered in post-medieval Europe — the start of the *jus* commune period when European states worked with the raw materials of the ancient law to fashion law for their own time and place. Eventually, *injuria* meaning "contrary to law" was expanded to mean blame-worthiness or *culpa*.[52] *Culpa* is a live concept in Scots law and further discussion appears below.[53]

By the time of Erskine it was possible to state the law quite **1–8** broadly:

> "Every one who has the exercise of reason, and so can distinguish between right and wrong, is naturally obliged to make up the damage befalling his neighbour from a wrong committed by himself. Wherefore every fraudulent contrivance, or unwarrantable act by which another suffers damage, or runs the hazard of it, subjects the delinquent to reparation."[54]

This comes close to the position reached in the French Civil Code — a general principle of reparation not requiring nominate heads.[55] There is much scholarly interest in discovering whether and when any such general principle appeared in Scots law.[56]

Economic and Monetary Union with England, and the shared supreme jurisdiction of the House of Lords in most civil matters meant that more and more the influence was from England and the Empire and Commonwealth, and less and less from the *jus* commune countries. It is worth noting that since the UK has been playing a full part in the European Community for over quarter of a century, European solutions are now required for economic reasons and those solutions may often find inspiration from the legal systems of France,

---

[50] D.9.2.5.1 (Ulpian).

[51] See generally Kolbert (1989).

[52] MacCormack, "Aquilian Culpa" in *Daube Noster* (Watson ed., 1974).

[53] See para.1–17.

[54] Erskine, Inst. III, 1, 13 (Casebook, Ext. 12).

[55] Although it should be noted that there are different strands in the civilian tradition: see Zimmerman. Stair has a rights-focused general principle that is similar to the German Code and Erskine's is closer to the French.

[56] See McKenzie, D.W., and Evans-Jones, R., "The Development of Remedies for Personal Injuries and Death" in *The Civilian Tradition in Scots Law* (Evans-Jones ed., Stair Society, supplementary volume 2 (1995)), arguing for a general action in Stair. See however contra, "A general action, and a generalised liability were ideas, the time of which had not yet come." *Visser and Whitty*, 438.

Germany, Italy or Spain, (to name only four) where the foundations are civilian. The new Scottish Parliament has extensive law-making powers in private law of which delict forms part. Thus interest in *jus commune* solutions is growing both academically and practically. That said, moving on one more step, globalisation, whereby everyone speaks English and buys a MacDonalds™ while watching a Hollywood movie chosen on their computer with a Microsoft™ operating system, puts pressure on legislative and other schemes, often of an Anglo-American nature. The Senior Appeal courts in most States will now consider cases from other jurisdictions and systems where there is a new "big issue" under consideration.

Industrialisation brought about more opportunity for loss to be caused in the form of physical injury whether in the factory, the mill, the mine or by the railway or the motor car.[57] Mass production separated the maker from the product and in many cases resulted in no individual being solely responsible for the finished product. In these situations the wrongfulness which triggered liability in theft or assault or in insult was not quite so apparent. More harm was caused through neglect than intent. The concept of fault (*culpa*) recognised in Scots law was a fertile theoretical compost in which liability for lack of care could grow. This rapid change of social factors, which has expanded with production, could not always be accommodated by the common law, which requires a litigation between real parties to declare the law, and often Parliament has been compelled to intervene to provide remedies for appropriate causes, or to remedy perceived deficiencies in the common law as it develops. It shall be seen that many rules of law are no longer found in the common law but in statute or subordinate legislation — for example, the Health and Safety at Work etc. Act 1974, the Occupiers' Liability (Scotland) Act 1960 and the Animals (Scotland) Act 1987 (see Chapter 20). Some of the legislation may now come either directly or indirectly from Europe rather than the UK or Scottish parliaments.

Function: what does delict do?

Deterrence

1–9   Function changes with time.[58] As indicated above, initially, delict had a quasi-criminal function of penalising wrongdoers. To some extent it still has that function: if you strike me or insult me I will get

---

[57] J. McLaren, "Nuisance Law and the Industrial Revolution — Some Lessons from Social History" [1983] 3 O.J.L.S. 155. Some of the great cases, however, "were not of a type peculiar to urban or industrialising society." *MacQueen and Sellar HPLS* 542.

[58] J. Conaghan and W. Mansell, *The Wrongs of Tort*, (Pluto Press, London, 1993) is a good radical look at traditional expositions of Tort (like the treatment of delict in this book!).

damages from you. This is sometimes described as a hortatory/ deterrent function: as well as punishing, the possibility of delictual liability deters people by creating a fear of punishment, encouraging people to organise their behaviour accordingly.[59] But this criminal/ hortatory/deterrent function only operates to a certain extent: if you are unemployed and in receipt of state benefit then you pay no damages and so you may not be so concerned to plan your conduct within the law. If you carelessly run me down in your company car, your employer's insurers pay the damages and it is your employer who loses his "no claims" bonus. The criminal law now fulfils much of the deterrent function: you drive carelessly — you are fined — you may lose your driving licence.

A recent expression of the traditional view can be seen in the judgment of Henry, L.J. in the Court of Appeal in *Frost v Chief Constable*.[60] Deterrence, he said, was part of the public policy behind tort law. Prevention was better than cure and potential defendants should face up to their safety responsibilities before rather than after an accident.[61] Stapleton has demonstrated that the idea of deterrence is perhaps quite deeply entrenched in the modern law.[62] What she has identified is the theme in modern cases denying liability, even where the harm caused could be described as reasonably foreseeable, a theme founded on the idea of "alternative means of protection". She shows that in cases of denial of liability in the face of what might be expected to be liability, deterrence is an issue. Looked at in this way, doctrines of *volenti non fit injuria* and contributory negligence also show deterrence at work — deterring careless behaviour on the part of the pursuer.[63] In economic loss cases, the pursuer must often show that it was reasonable to rely upon the information carelessly given which has caused the loss.[64] Imposing too much liability can result in "over-deterrence". This is the argument often used in professional negligence cases: doctors will do too many, perhaps unnecessary tests. The idea of deterrence may also be a factor in letting some potential defenders escape in order to make sure that liability is focused towards another party whose conduct it is sought to deter, perhaps the negligent builder rather than the busy local authority.[65]

---

[59] This rather unfashionable view is still, it is submitted, valid: see the recent support from Henry, L.J. in *Frost v Chief Constable* [1996] T.L.R. 617.

[60] [1997] 1 All E.R. 540.

[61] *ibid.,* at 567. See also Lord Hoffmann in *Stovin v Wise* [1996] A.C. 923.

[62] J. Stapleton, "Duty of Care: Peripheral Parties and Alternative Opportunities for Deterrence" [1995] 111 L.Q.R. 301. For an argument at an even higher level of theory see R. Wright, "Right Justice and Tort Law" in *Philosophical Foundations of Tort Law* (Owen ed., 1995).

[63] Stapleton, *op cit.*, p.305.

[64] *ibid.*, p.306.

[65] *ibid.*, p.317; See the cases discussed in Chs 10 and 12.

Compensation

1–10   The next major function (and that which concerns the practitioner) is compensation. Instead of concentrating on penalising the wrong-doer we compensate the victim.[66] If compensation is based on fault then not every injured person is compensated and so it might be said that delict is a poor compensation scheme. If a regime of strict liability is applied, more people are compensated.[67] Thus there are often demands for more strict liability and the last 50 years have seen a considerable expansion in such cases. Because a quite significant amount of compensation is achieved through the delict system, those who wish to extend compensation often urge a strict liability regime. Strict liability is also likely to cover the cost of compensating.[68]

Risk allocation

1–11   Aside from penalising some wrongdoers quite effectively (for example, defamation actions between persons with money), delict redistributes the cost of certain accidents within the community — a function most clearly seen in the rule that an employer is vicariously liable for his or her employees (see Chapter 24).

The practice of insuring against certain risks, although it has had a considerable influence on the law, is nonetheless legally irrelevant.[69] It therefore does not matter that a pursuer may already have recovered compensation from his insurers. That said, the availability and practice of insurance may provide a background to a legal approach. For example, if a contractor wrongly cuts a power cable which deprives millions of people of power and causes millions of pounds of financial loss, it would be expensive to insure against such a contingency, whereas if individuals are aware that a power cut is a risk they themselves must carry, they will take steps to minimise the loss they might suffer, for example by buying a petrol-powered generator. Alternatively, people who would suffer from a power cut

---

[66] This is now virtually a subject of study in its own right. The issues and the context are examined fully in P. Cane, *Atiyah's Accidents Compensation and the Law* (6th ed., Butterworths, 1999).

[67] See generally Walker, D.M., "Strict Liability in Scotland" (1954) 66 J.R. 231. D.R. Harris, et al., *Compensation and Support for illness and Injury* (Oxford, 1984); Report of the Royal Commission on Civil Liability and Compensation for Personal Injury, Cmnd. 7054 (1978) P. Cane, *Atiyah's Accidents Compensation and the Law* (6th ed., Butterworths, 1999). P. Cane, "Does No-Fault Have a Future", 1994 J.P.I.L. 302.

[68] See P. Cane, *Atiyah's Accidents Compensation and the Law* (6th ed., Butterworths, 1999). The consultation paper "Compensation for Road Accidents" from the Lord Chancellor's Department (May, 1991) has never been acted upon.

[69] See, *e.g. Winnik v Dick*, 1981 S.L.T. (Sh. Ct) 23. But insurance can be a factor in other enquiries such as fairness: see Lord Rodger in the Outer House in *B.T. v James Thomson & Sons Ltd*, 1997 S.L.T. 767 at 774D.

could arrange insurance themselves.[70] In considering the overall function of the law, insurance is taken into account by the legislature. The delict system would not compensate many injured people if there were not compulsory insurance for drivers and employers. Even that requirement needs to be "patched-up" to meet the function. In road traffic cases there is a Motor Insurers' Bureau scheme to cover cases where a driver is uninsured or unidentified. In employment cases, there is no equivalent safety net but the courts have allowed those who failed to obey the law and take out the insurance, to be sued for breach of their statutory duty.[71]

An enforcement mechanism

The delict or reparation systems are essentially "used" to achieve **1–12** other functions — the best, most recent examples being to meet the demands of European law for a nations failure to transpose directives and the demands of European Human Rights law to provide the citizen with just satisfaction. These topics are embraced in this book because these rules form part of the Scots law of delict or reparation, however alien the source of their content.

Welfare

Even prior to the expansion of the Welfare State after the Second **1–13** World War, the delict system did not act sufficiently broadly to provide welfare for casualties of industrialisation. So while it has and does provide for the welfare of some of the injured — and through establishing liability provides for many more through compelling insurance payments, it is not a cornerstone of the welfare system. There are freestanding systems. People who are the victims of crime may recover compensation under the Criminal Injuries Compensation Scheme[72] and workers injured at work may receive industrial injury benefit. Indeed the welfare system demands recovery from compensation derived from the delict system through compensation recovery.[73]

Differences between Scots law and English law

The English law of torts itself grew out of English criminal law. **1–14** After that its development was closely linked to the forms of action. Basically, unless a person could fit his or her claim into one of the forms of action, there was no remedy. Accordingly, English law is

---

[70] For an excellent examination of this issue, see Davies, "The End of the Affair: Duty of Care and Liability Insurance" (1989) 9 L.S. 67.

[71] See generally Davies, M., "The End of the Affair: Duty of Care and Liability Insurance", 1989 L.S. 67. See *Quinn v McGinty*, 1999 S.L.T. (Sh. Ct) 27.

[72] See Stewart, *Reparation: Liability for Delict*, Chapter 29.

[73] Ch.26.

most appropriately seen as being a series of separate torts and not as a number of frequently occurring instances of a general principle of delictual or tortious liability. On the other hand, with the passage of time, the expansion of each of the torts resulted in there being fewer gaps between the torts, and indeed the extension of existing torts or the creation of new torts seems to have been based on principles similar to those informing Scots law, such as liability based on fault.[74] A common market, constitution and culture and a common Supreme Court had tendencies to assimilate the two systems. While both Law Commissions are committed to their own respective legal systems, consultation and collaboration suggest that often reform can be at least along the same lines in effect. That said, it is fair to say that there are still differences between the two systems — outwith careless conduct, considerable differences. The English law is still affected by precedents, which say that a man acts at his peril, but they have moved away from that in many details. The English law of defamation makes a technical distinction between libel and slander, which Scots law does not. The English courts can award exemplary or penal damages and the rules on prescription and limitation are different. The rules on remoteness of damage are no longer different. The English law in relation to property interests is quite different both in concept and result.[75] The law of trespass is much more significant in England than in Scotland. However, in the most frequently litigated area, that of negligence, it cannot be said that the law is not now the same in both jurisdictions.[76]

General principles

Justice

1–15   Law is an application of justice. Such big issues are seldom discussed in the cases, yet when new big issues arise, the law can and probably should look towards issues of justice as much as internal juridical policy. Delict is essentially about corrective justice — fixing things between person and person. Outlined by Aristotle, it was developed by Grotius and Pufendorf and later by Kant.[77] Gordley, speaking of the Natural Lawyers in this tradition, including Grotius, a great influence on Stair, says:

> "They used an Aristotelian principle of corrective justice that no one should gain through another's loss to explain liability both

---

[74] See Markesinis, B.S., "The not so Dissimilar Tort and Delict" (1977) L.Q.R. 78.
[75] See Torts (Interference with Goods) Act 1977.
[76] See Chs 4 and 5, but especially Rodger, "Lord MacMillan's Speech in *Donoghue v Stevenson*" (1992) 108 L.Q.R. 236.
[77] Owen, "Why Philosophy Matters to Tort Law" and J. Gordley, "Tort Law in the Aristotelian Tradition" in Owen, *ibid*.

for taking another's property and for causing another harm. They gave a unified explanation of causation and fault: one could not say a person was the cause of another's harm unless he chose to harm him by acting intentionally or negligently. They thought that to avoid negligence, a person must weigh the costs and benefits of a course of action, but they did not think the purpose of the law of negligence was to give him the proper incentives to do so."[78]

Distributive justice is the idea that law concerns itself with a just distribution of losses in the community. So far as Scots law is concerned, this is theoretically alien.[79] The law here corrects the wrong done by compelling the defender to make reparation. In addition, leaving aside any view that civilian *culpa* is the organising concept of the law, the main focus in practice, by virtue of the rules on written pleading, is of bringing fault home to the defender. That said, vicarious liability and liberalisations on proof can be seen as distributive. Strict liability, of which there are innumerable examples, many pertaining to the ordinary incidents of everyday life, do in fact place upon one party the burden of the risk of certain activities and to that extent represent distributive justice — the factory owner is obliged to make reparation to his workforce in many situations and, if he manufactures products, to many of his customers or even users of his products who are not customers. The bulk of strict liability is conscious and statutory innovation and thus can legitimately reflect political economic or moral trends. The common law, it is submitted, cannot pick and choose between the mosaic tiles of corrective justice and distributive justice to create whatever picture suits the case in hand.[80]

In "new" cases of negligence the courts, as will be seen, have to ask themselves if it is fair, just and reasonable to impose liability.

At the highest level of generality there is the precept that one person should not harm another. This was one of Justinian's three precepts of the law.[81] Below that is the principle that one should not cause loss wrongfully. "Wrongfully" refers to fault or conduct in

---

[78] Gordley, *ibid.*, p.131.

[79] Views of Lord Steyn in *Macfarlane v Tayside Health Board*, 2000 S.L.T. 154 are not native and are arguably unnecessary for the decision. They do not in any event represent the view of the majority. See generally J.M. Thomson, "Abandoning the Law of Delict," 2000 S.L.T. (News) 43.

[80] This is respectfully the opposite of what Lord Steyn says in *Macfarlane v Tayside Health Board*, 2000 S.L.T. 154 although his analogy is adopted with gratitude.

[81] Inst I, i, 3; originally Ulpian's dictum: D. 1,1,10,1. It was revived to an extent by the natural lawyers such as Pufendorf, De jure naturale et Gentium Lib III, Cap 1,1. See Zimmerman, *The Law of Obligations*, p.1032, n.224. On the face of it such a rule requires strict liability; see Zimmerman, *op. cit.*, p.1033. The natural lawyers began to mitigate that view by reference to imputation, duty and the foreseeability of wrong; *Zimmerman*, p.1033.

breach of a duty of care, or conduct causing reasonably foreseeable harm of the kind which in fact results. However, there are cases where loss is caused but no action is possible — for example, some of the secondary pure economic loss cases.[82] These may be explained on the basis that "wrongfully" can be dependent upon a duty of care, which can only be said to exist in certain limited circumstances or, more convincingly, that sometimes as a matter of public policy, discernible from precedent, the courts will not allow recovery.

Causation

1–16   Causation, in the sense of attribution of responsibility, is deep within the law no doubt as being entrenched within ideas of justice. It is essential in negligence cases,[83] although the last century has seen an easing of what proof is required of things that are themselves difficult or impossible to prove. In cases where there is an intended wrongful act, causation may still play a part where consequences are attributable to other conduct or circumstances, although these discussions may take place under remoteness. Statutory schemes which seek to transfer responsibility often require to take account of causation lest ideas of fault are "smuggled back in". So it is possible that the simple happening of an event can be a sufficient condition for liability or there may have to be some link which can more neutrally be expressed as "attribution".

Culpa

1–17   *Culpa* is the strongest contender for a general principle. What is not settled in the literature is what *culpa* actually means.[84] Its relevance comes from the *jus* commune approach to the *lex Aquilia* of the old Roman law. *Culpa*, in the sense of blameworthiness, appears in the Digest as a supplement to the *injuria* of *damnum injuria datum*.[85] Ulpian's examples are cases where the act is *ex facie* wrongful as infringing the potential pursuer's rights but which are not within the Aquilian liability because the defender is not blameworthy — the lunatic and the infant being examples.[86] This idea

---

[82] See para.10–6.
[83] See Ch.9.
[84] See J.J. Gow, "Is *culpa* amoral?" (1953) 65 J.R. 17; W.A. Elliot, "What is *culpa*?" (1954) 66 J.R. 6.; G. MacCormack, "Aquilian Culpa" in *Daube Noster* (Watson ed., 1974).; G. MacCormack, "*Culpa* in the Scots Law of Reparation", 1974 J. R. 13; W.W. McBryde, "The Advantages of Fault", 1975 J.R. 32. W.J. Kamba, "Concept of Duty of Care and Aquilian Liability in Roman Dutch Law", 1975 J. R. 252. F. McManus, "*Culpa* and the Law of Nuisance", 1997 J.R. 259. F. McManus, "*Culpa* and the Law of Nuisance", 1995 J.R. (note) 462.
[85] D.9.2.5.1 (Ulpian)
[86] For a broad and deep discussion see P. Birks, "The Concept of a Civil Wrong" in *Philosophical Foundations of Tort Law* (Owen ed., 1995), pp.42–45.

grew out of and could easily assimilate the various defences to an *injuria* based action — self-defence, necessity and consent for example.[87] But what was this blameworthiness denoted by *culpa*? MacCormack puts the point clearly:

> "*Culpa* is to be translated as fault and not negligence. Where a jurist presents the facts of the case and draws the conclusion that there has, or has not, been culpa, he is not asking, do these facts constitute negligence? His approach is to ask, do these facts constitute a fault? From this one may infer that where *culpa* is used as a criterion of liability in a general context without the addition of facts which explain what is meant, it should be taken as fault. The texts frequently state that a person is liable under the *lex Aquilia* for *dolus* and/or *culpa*. Such statements do not contrast loss brought about through intention and loss brought about through negligence. The mention of *dolus* in no way shows that culpa is negligence. As in other contexts it means fault, specifically fault not falling within the ambit of *dolus*. Whether *culpa* is taken as negligence or as fault is important. To say that someone is at fault implies that he has behaved in some way that he should not have behaved but leaves open the nature of the behaviour. To say that someone has been negligent implies that he has acted in a careless fashion and that he ought to have foreseen that what he did would cause damage."[88]

Carelessness was a way in which fault could be established.[89] "Under the *lex Aquilia* even the slightest degree of fault counts".[90] The crucial point is also made, "there is fault when what could have been foreseen by a diligent man was not foreseen."[91] Sometimes *culpa* includes *dolus* and sometimes it is excluded.[92] Zimmerman, summarising the further development of the actio, states that: "by the end of the seventeenth century ... the modern law in action no longer reflected the Aquilian delict of the *corpus juris*."[93] The end of the seventeenth century is a critical time for Scots lawyers being the

---

[87] *Zimmerman*, pp.998–1004.

[88] *Zimmerman*, p.202.

[89] *ibid.*

[90] D.9.2.44.pr.

[91] D.9.2.31.

[92] *Zimmerman*, p.201.

[93] *Zimmerman*, p.1018. He explains that Thomasius put the matter as strongly as saying that the action then current bore as little resemblance to the *lex Aquilia* as a bird to a beast — that an action for damage done was hiding behind an *Aquilian* mask. Note Zimmerman's verdict is that historically Thomasius was wrong but purely dogmatically he had a point, p.1031.

time in which Stair was working on the Institutions.[94] Foreseeability
was an aspect of the necessary imputability.[95] Thus for a system to
have an action for recovery of damage based on the *lex Aquilia*, it
need not be called that.[96] It is not clear to what extent delict cases of
the nineteenth and twentieth centuries were actually decided on the
basis of civilian *culpa*. Professor MacCormack has made some very
good points:

> "Statements which assert that the law of reparation is founded.
> upon a principle of *culpa* derived from the Roman law are of a
> fairly late date";

> "The judges have simply taken the word *culpa* and used it in the
> construction of arguments which consider the incidence of fault
> or negligence"; and finally,

> "the sporadic reliance on texts from the Digest or the Institutes
> which use the term *culpa* does not prove that Scots law
> extracted from the Roman sources and applied a principle of
> *culpa*".[97]

One recent nuisance case has provided an opportunity for a restatement of the civilian approach. *In Kennedy v Glenbelle*,[98] Lord
President Hope said:

---

[94] There is very little of liability for lack of care before Stair. Professor Walker finds
what we would now describe as case allowed on relevancy, where the dispute was
whether the defender was negligent or whether it was heavy weather that caused the
loss of a ship as long ago as 1492, Walker, *History*, II, p.737 (when of course the
world was flat). He also finds a questionable Scots Privy Council case in 1566:
Dick v Grizzel in which a person injured by an accidentally dropped plank was
compensated. *Zimmerman*, summarises that natural law school of which Stair is one
of the least well-known members as moving away from looking at the injured party
to looking at the injuring party and their duty, above, p.1033.

[95] *Zimmerman*, p.1034.

[96] Nor need it any longer comply with any of the rules applicable to that remedy at any
particular time. However, in systems which codify the view of the remedy at the
time of codification is entrenched and whether or not better rules or more efficient
or more just rules can be arrived at may become a matter of legislation rather than
permissible judicial development. One major divergence is that German law on one
view still differentiates fault and unlawfulness whereas the French do not.
Markesinis, *The German Law of Torts*, p.58. There is justification for that approach
because the German Code specifies certain protected interests. If Scots law treated
Stair as "the codification that never was" then the enumerated rights would provide
a foundation for a similar approach in Scots law. This is a preliminary enquiry for
then it must be established that there was intention to harm or a lack of reasonable
care. Yet by interpretation it is argued that the imputability idea should mean that
lack of care itself can constitute the wrongfulness. *Markesinis*, p.60.

[97] MacCormack, "*Culpa* in the Scots Law of Reparation", 1974 J.R. 13 at 14, 18,
27.

[98] 1996 S.L.T. 1186 at 1188.

"*Culpa* which gives rise to a liability in delict may take various forms. In *Stair Memorial Encyclopaedia,* vol 14, "Nuisance" para 2087 it is stated that the usual categories of culpa or fault are malice, intent, recklessness and negligence. To that list there may be added conduct causing a special risk of abnormal damage where it may be said that it is not necessary to prove a specific fault as fault is necessarily implied in the result".

Protection of rights and interests

It has been seen that Stair spoke in terms of certain rights being **1–18** protected.[99] Those which are not recognised are not reparable.[1] Such an approach is not a Roman law doctrine but comes from the civilian tradition. It found at its peak and present significance in its incorporation in the German Code:

"A person who wilfully or negligently injures the life, body health, freedom, property, or other right of another contrary to law is bound to compensate him for any damage arising therefrom."[2]

New issues test these apparently clear and principled divisions. Thus, the Germans have had to consider whether nervous shock relates to health.[3] Economic loss (non-derivative) is generally unrecoverable because of the wording of the code entrenching eighteenth century thinking.[4] The apparently wide "other rights" applies only to absolute rights like patents and not relative rights like contractual rights.[5] It should also be appreciated that if one is following this kind of analysis, right and interest cannot necessarily be equiparated.[6] Although even for civilians duty, right and interests are different paths in the same enquiry.[7]

There are two good examples of an explicit interest based approach. In *Henderson v Chief Constable, Fife Police,*[8] a female worker was asked to remove her bra in the cells for her own safety, the concern being that she might do herself a mischief. Lord Jauncey said:

---

[99] Professor Walker points out that such an approach was hinted at in the Digest and appeared in Grotius and Van Leeuwen. Walker, *History,* IV, p.695.

[1] That can be seen carried through to Bell who speaks in terms of rights being protected.

[2] Markesinis, *The German Law of Torts,* p.10.

[3] *ibid.,* pp.35, 95–109.

[4] *ibid.,* pp.37–43, 148–239; *Zimmerman,* p.1037, nn.255 and 256.

[5] *Markesinis,* pp.51–58.

[6] *ibid.,* p.56.

[7] P.Q.R. Boberg, *The Law of Delict* (Jutta, 1989), pp.31–32.

[8] 1988 S.L.T. 361.

"such removal must amount to an infringement of liberty. I see no reason why the law should not protect the individual from this infringement just as it does from other infringements".

Yet another important dictum appears in *Micosta S.A. v Shetland Islands Council*.[9] The case was unusual in that the wrong alleged was a deliberate misuse of a statutory power by a public body. Lord Ross, approving a statement of general principle by Professor Walker[10]:

"The validity of a claim such as that made by the present pursuers does not depend upon there being any precise Scottish authority. There is no such thing as an exhaustive list of named delicts in the law of Scotland. If the conduct complained of appears to be wrongful, the law of Scotland will afford a remedy even if there has not been any previous instance of a remedy being given in similar circumstances. As Professor Walker puts it at p.9: 'The decision to recognise a particular interest, and consequently to grant a remedy for its infringement, is a question of social policy, and the list recognised has grown over the years. In considering whether or not to recognise particular interests the courts have had regard to such factors as the moral obliquity of the defenders' conduct, the capacity of the parties to bear the loss, and the consistency of recognition with what is conceived to be public policy.' In my opinion, deliberate misuse of statutory powers by a public body would be actionable under the law of Scotland at the instance of a third party who has suffered loss and damage in consequence of the misuse of statutory powers, provided that there was proof of malice or proof that the action had been taken by the public authority in the full knowledge that it did not possess the power which it purported to exercise."[11]

1–19 Another much more significant example might be the *Crofter* case[12] in which conspiracy was developed to protect business interests but also respecting other legitimate interests.[13] However, it is not obvious that case or the others in the area of economic delicts are truly the reflection of a general protection of economic interests rather than discrete delicts which have that effect. The thinking has essentially all been done in England and so it would not be surprising if an interests based approach was not intended. In a penetrating review,

---

[9] 1986 S.L.T. 193.
[10] *Delict*, p.9.
[11] *Micosta* at 198. The English tort considered was misfeasance in public office.
[12] *Crofter Hand Woven Harris Tweed Co. v Veitch*, 1942 S.C. (HL) 1. Discussed in Ch.5.
[13] See Ch.5.

Weir concludes that the Germans require immorality, the French, unreasonableness and the Americans impropriety — all signs of a more general interests based approach. But the English law, does not he tells us, take that path but a more conduct-orientated regime.[14] As will be seen in a later chapter, one interest that might have been expected to be afforded protection has not. That is privacy.[15] It would be expected for social reasons. Its failure to thrive in England can easily be ascribed to the force of precedent.[16] A principled system based on rights and interests could easily have recognised such an interest or right but it has not happened in Scotland, casting doubt perhaps on the extent to which this principle is an effective source of remedies. The "interests" theory has predictive value. It is principled in the sense that new cases in the same branch can be decided on the basis of a general rule. It is practically flexible if and only if new interests can be recognised relatively quickly.[17] The introduction of European Human Rights law could become a foundation for the recognition of new wrongs based on infringement of these rights.[18]

So the civilian heritage must always be kept in view. However, the law of delict — especially if widely defined as in this book — is neither explained nor predicted by any one theory. The student's task is very well described by Lord Cullen's analogy:

> "The subject [delict] might suggest the image of a large mansion to which many additions have been made over the years in response to changing conditions in society. Some but not all of its rooms are interconnected — haunted no doubt by the benign ghost of the reasonable man. Some rooms are plain: others are richly elaborate. Some are thronged and familiar: others rarely visited."[19]

The law of delict for is a large amount of precedent and a quantity of statutory provision on top of some solid principle, a body of norms which are not always consistent. Taking that view there are areas where the law is reasonably clear because of precedent, or institutional authority. In other areas the law is less clear but there are

---

[14] T. Weir, *Economic Torts* (1997), Ch.3.

[15] L. Blom-Cooper, "The Right to be Let Alone" [1989] J.L.S. 402; A.J. Bonnington, "Privacy: Letting the Right Alone", 1992 S.L.T. (News) 289; G.T. Laurie, "Privacy, Paucity and the Press", 1993 S.L.T. (News) 285; D.L. Carey Miller, and H. Lardy, "Calcutt II: Comments from a Scots Perspective", 1993 S.L.T. (News) 199; M.A. Hogg, "Privacy: A Valuable and Protected Interest in Scots Law", 1992 S.L.T. 349.

[16] Albeit, ironically, it was an English case which founded the article that founded the tort in England: *Prince Albert v Strange*, 2 De G. & Sm. 652.

[17] Less than a generation and more than a general election!

[18] See Ch.17.

[19] McManus Russell et al., *Delict: A comprehensive Guide to the Law*, Wiley, *xvii*.

themes — if not precepts or principles — that run through much of the authority that can assist a court, practitioner or student in determining the law. It is all a matter of emphasis: there is no danger in saying that the law of delict is based upon certain principles, so long as one is aware of all of the exceptions and anomalies. The law of delict is largely in the cases (and statutes) — the first task for the student is to know them.

> "Hence we shall insist no further, but come to the obligations by delinquence, which are civilly cognoscible by our custom, according to their known names and titles in our law; which though they do rather signify the acts or actions whereby such obligations are incurred or prosecute, than the obligations themselves, yet will they be sufficient to hold out both."[20]

Following this practical and sensible approach, in the next seven chapters we look at a large number of delicts which have recognised names and associated cases.

---

[20] Stair, I, ix, 5. See this in context, Casebook, Ext. 11.

Section II: Specific Wrongs

Chapter 2

WRONGS TO THE PERSON

Assault

Assault is an overt act intended to insult or harm another done **2–1** without justification or excuse. The *actio injuriarum* root of Scots law infuses the delict of assault as much as any development of the *lex Aquilia*. Accordingly, assault as a delict includes notional assaults, such as threats of harm, if sufficiently immediate.[1] Assault includes conduct that might also be criminal. However, the issue of *mens rea* (guilty mind) in the criminal law does not feature to any significant extent in the civil law. Where four farm labourers were building a straw stack and three of them began frolicking, when one of the frolicking workers hit the labourer who had continued to work, this was held to be an assault. Lord Young treated it as a case of assault:

> "Technically he assaulted him, although he did it playfully and without any bad intention, for if a man playfully attacks another to make him engage in sport, I am of the opinion that that is an assault, and if harm results that is an actionable wrong."[2]

An accident is not actionable as assault.[3]

Motive and consent

Even a good motive does not justify an assault; thus medical **2–2** treatment without a patient's consent is an assault and actionable.[4] However, in an English case,[5] the court refused to impose a rule that

---

[1] See the charge to the jury of Lord President Boyle in *Ewing v Mar* (1851) 14 D. 314.

[2] *Reid v Mitchell* (1885) 12 R. 1129.

[3] *Hall v Watson* (1896) 12 Sh. Ct. Rep. 117; although a negligence action might attack some "accidents".

[4] *Thomson v Devon* (1899) 15 Sh. Ct. Rep. 209.

[5] *Sidaway v Board of Governors of the Bethlem Royal Hospital* [1985] A.C. 871, (HL); and see also *Gold v Haringey Health Authority* [1987] 3 W.L.R. 649. For Scotland see the case *Bonthrone v Secretary of State for Scotland*, 1987 S.L.T. 34; *Craig v Glasgow Victoria and Leverndale HBH*, (OH), December 1, 1972; *Moyes v Lothian Health Board*, 1990 S.L.T. 444.

a patient's consent has to be fully informed, a rule that does apply in some of the United States of America.[6] The rationale of the informed consent doctrine is that if to touch is *prima facie* actionable as assault, then if the patient's consent has been obtained on the basis of misinformation or a withholding of available information, the consent given is vitiated and the treatment given thereafter becomes actionable even if the treatment that follows is carried out without fault or negligence. While this reasoning appears quite sound, it was rejected by a majority in the House of Lords on the basis that the whole matter fell to be dealt with on principles of negligence, asking the question: Would a reasonable doctor have given more information than that upon which the consent was based? There is support for this approach in Scotland.[7]

Causation

2–3 Causation arises as an issue. A person who allegedly kicked a boy was assoilzied, the death being caused by a fall, the boy surviving for over two years.[8] In negligence it is appreciated that causation and remoteness of damage are connected and it is more likely in cases of assault that chains of events would be dealt with on the basis of remoteness. Some authority for that might be found in *Scorgie v Lawrie*,[9] where it was held that although paralysis of a pupil's thumb was caused by a blow with the cane, it was not attributable to the fault of the headmistress. *Ewart v Brown*[10] is even clearer in that the schoolmaster who hit a boy on the head with a pointer was held liable for damages for being at fault in hitting him, but not for his subsequent illness.

Defences

Justification

2–4 There are many justifications for assault both at common law and by statute. Many of the statutory protections are connected with arrest or detention and are noted below. A recent example was the

---

[6] For a perspective from another jurisdiction see A.C. Malcolm, (The Hon David K.), "The High Court and Informed Consent: The Bolam Principle Abandoned" (1994) 1 Tort L. Rev. 81.

[7] The Outer House decision in *Moyes v Lothian Health Board*, 1990 S.L.T. 444 is support for the *Sidaway* case: indeed it is argued that Scots law had already come down against the need in all cases for informed consent. For further reading see K. Norrie, "Informed consent and duty of care", 1985 S.L.T. (News) 289. L. Sutherland, "A Relationship of Mutual Trust", Rep. L.B. 5–4; for England, P.M.D. Grundy, A.P. Gumbs, "Bolam, Sidaway and the Unrecognised Doctrine of Informed Consent: A Fresh Approach' " [1997] J.P.I.L. 211. See 22–5.

[8] *Milne v Thomson* (1841) 5 D. 759.

[9] (1883) 10 R. 610.

[10] (1882) 10 R. 163.

decision of the Inner House that where the prison rules permitted visual examination of the external parts of the body, it was not an assault to part a prisoners buttocks to examine his anus.[11] Scots law allows a defence to a claim of assault (both criminal and civil) in the case of certain instances assaulting of children. The defence applies in criminal cases and probably in the same way to civil cases. However, the defence is limited to reasonable chastisement — it is supposed to be a disciplinary matter. The defence is available to parents of children and to others having a position of authority and responsibility over the child, such as teachers[12] and probably cohabitants.[13] What is or is not considered reasonable is a matter for the court and clearly there is likely to be uncertainty as a result.[14] In the case of teachers, the defence was limited by the Education Act 1986 in the public sector and removed completely for all schools by the Education Act 1993. It is not corporal punishment, however, to strike a child out of the way of immediate danger of harm or to prevent immediate danger to property of a person, as by rugby tackling a child about to throw a brick through the windscreen of someone's car. There are often proposals for reform, with some favouring complete abolition and others fearing many spoiled children. The debate continues into the twenty-first century with human rights arguments from freedom of religious expression. It has been held that the UK ban on corporal punishment in schools did not infringe the religious rights of others who did want the right to punish: there was a distinction between a religious belief or practice and an action motivated by religious belief.[15]

The police

The police do not have a special immunity in relation to assault, **2–5** but where they are using force in the exercise of their duty, it is necessary to aver that the conduct is outwith the scope of the duty.[16] *Mason v Orr*[17] purports to lay down some guidance in such cases. Mason was bundled down his own stairs from his own pavement as an officer tried to clear the pavement of Mason and his workforce who were watching a royal visit. The Lord Ordinary allowed an

---

[11] *Tolmie v Dewar*, December 3, 2002.
[12] *Stewart v Thain*, 1981 S.L.T. (Notes) 2.
[13] *Byrd v Wither*, 1991 S.L.T. 206.
[14] *B. v Harris*, 1990 S.L.T. 208; *Peebles v MacPhail*, 1990 S.L.T. 245.
[15] *R (Williamson and Others) v Secretary of State*, [2002] 1 All E.R. 385. A valuable examination of the religious issues which will no doubt continue to emerge. For a consideration of the issue under other Rights systems see the note, J. Eekelaar, "Corporal Punishment, Parents' Religion and Children's Rights", 2003 L.Q.R. 370.
[16] *Lennox v Rose* (1824) 2 S. 650; *Wallace v Mooney* (1885) 12 R. 710.
[17] (1901) 4 F. 220.

issue, but on reclaiming the case was held to be irrelevant. Lord McLaren in whose opinion the rest of the division concurred said:

> "To make a relevant case of assault on the part of a police officer on duty it appears to me to be necessary to aver either (1) that the order which the officer was seeking to enforce was unlawful, that is, not within the scope of his duty; or (2) that the pursuer was willing to comply with the order, in which case the use of force would be unnecessary; or (3) that the force used was manifestly in excess of the requirements of the case."[18]

The test is the balance of probabilities,[19] the view sometimes expressed that the evidence of the officer has to be of "more than ordinary persuasive weight" only means that the officer is assumed, as any other citizen, to be honest and truthful until the evidence is heard tested and scrutinised. There have been far too many cases in which the police have not been believed in recent years for any general rule of law to be acceptable.[20] Although there is clear authority that it is necessary to aver and prove malice and want of probable cause when suing the police, that applies where the conduct complained of is, on the face of it, within the competence of the officer concerned.[21] However, where it is not there is no need to aver malice and want of probable cause.[22]

Provocation

2–6   Provocation is not a defence, but will serve to mitigate (reduce) the damages.[23]

---

[18] *ibid.,* at 223. See also *Baillie v Edinburgh Magistrates* (1906) 14 S.L.T. 344.

[19] *Anwar v Chief Constable,* Unrep., September 20, 1995; *Ward v Chief Constable,* 1991 S.L.T. 292; *Mullan v Anderson,* 1993 S.L.T. 835; *Anderson v Chief Constable,* unreported, January 20, 1987; *Gilchrist v Chief Constable,* Unrep., Glasgow Sheriff Court, January 7, 1988.

[20] *Downie v Chief Constable, Strathclyde Police,* 1998 S.L.T. 8; *Airnes v Chief Constable, Strathclyde Police,* 1998 S.L.T. (Sh. Ct) 16; *Rae v Chief Constable, Strathclyde Police,* 1998 G.W.D. 8–406.

[21] *Ward v Chief Constable, Strathclyde Police,* 1991 S.L.T. 292.

[22] *Robertson v Keith* (Seven Judges), 1936 S.L.T. 9. It is submitted that this is also established by *Mason v Orr* (1901) 4 F. 220, where the Lord Ordinary had thrown out the argument: "This is an action for damages for assault, and if assault be well averred there is no need for an averment or an issue of malice or want of probable cause." This argument was not taken further although it was suggested that there needed to be "an averment to make him responsible analogous to the averment of malice in a case of wrongful apprehension" at 222.

[23] *Ross v Bryce,* 1972 S.L.T. (Sh. Ct) 76; See *Anderson v Marshall,* (1835) 13 S. 1130; See contra in England, *Lane v Holloway* [1968] 1 Q.B. 379.

Self-defence

Self-defence is a complete defence. Where parties are involved in **2–7**
a brawl, there is no defence where one party clearly becomes an
assailant, as where one man hit another with a bottle at a time when
he had ample opportunity to disengage.[24]

Contravention of lawburrows

A person who has been required to find caution (a sum of money **2–8**
or an insurance bond for a sum of money) not to harm another or his
family (called "lawburrows") may, if he contravenes the non-
molestation order, be sued in an action of contravention of lawburrows for forfeiture of the caution.[25] This procedure, it may be
said, is not often used, but that may simply be because few are aware
of it. It is today still used in disputes between neighbours.

In *Liddle v Morton*,[26] the defender admitted breaking the pursuers'
windows. He threatened violence and shook his fist. He left a gate off
its hinge so that it would fall. It did — but on the postman. A log was
thrown through the pursuers' front window. The sheriff granted
lawburrows. On appeal to the High Court of Justiciary, counsel for
the appellant accepted, as did the Court, that the test for granting
lawburrows was that set out by Sheriff Macphail in *Morrow v Neil*[27]:
"The pursuer must establish that he has reasonable cause to appre-
hend that the defender will harm the person or property of the
pursuer or his family, tenants or servants." The "reasonableness"
aspect of this may require to be reviewed if challenged — such
subtlety was not a feature of fifteenth-century Scottish jurisprudence.[28]

Relatively recently it has been unsuccessfully used in two tene-
ment disputes.[29] In 1986, an unsuccessful attempt was made to have
a chief constable find caution for the alleged behaviour of his
officers: it was held that lawburrows would only be granted in respect
of the personal behaviour of the defender and not on the basis of his
vicarious responsibility.[30] That named delicts can cover more than
one interest is demonstrated in that lawburrows was designed to
protect against intrusion on property as well as injury to the
person.

---

[24] *Marco v Merrens*, 1964 S.L.T. (Sh. Ct) 74.
[25] Lawburrows Acts 1429 and 1581. See generally Walker, *Legal History*, Vol.II,
pp.615–616.
[26] 1996 S.L.T. 1143.
[27] 1975 S.L.T. (Sh. Ct) 65 at 67.
[28] See *Porteous v Rutherford*, 1980 S.L.T. (Sh. Ct) 129; and *Tahir v Gosal*, Glasgow
Sheriff Court, May 16, 1974.
[29] *Morrow v Neil*, 1975 S.L.T. (Sh. Ct) 65; *Porteous v Rutherford*, 1980 S.L.T. (Sh. Ct)
129.
[30] *Handy v Bowman*, Dundee Sheriff Court, September 22, 1986.

There are divergent views as to whether it is an elegant remedy or an absurd form.[31]

Enticement

2–9 A right of action exists where a person, even a relative, entices a member of someone's family away from him or her, without justification. There is now, however, no delictual liability in the most common instance of enticement-where a person has induced someone's spouse to leave, or remain apart from, the other spouse.[32] This delict might provide a remedy in cases where children are "attracted" to a religious cult. Contrary to that view is the case of *McKeen v Chief Constable*,[33] where a man was claiming a sum for the intervention of the police in taking away his child during a custody dispute with his wife. A particular statement of Professor Walker's was relied upon: "A claim may even lie against a parent not entitled to custody who seeks to entice a child out of the custody of the parent lawfully entitled thereto,[34] Lord Morton thought that if such a right existed it was strange that it had not come before the court.[35] He hazarded the opinion that there might be social reasons why recognition of such a right might be inappropriate. It is submitted that the authorities on enticement generally support Professor Walker's view. Contempt of court and criminal sanctions (plagium) might explain why such cases are rare — although even plagium has difficulty with the "new" contact/residence.[36]

Physical detention and arrest

2–10 Generally, the simple act of preventing a person moving around freely is actionable and sounds in damages for the affront caused. In *MacKenzie v Cluny Hill Hydropathic Co. Ltd*,[37] in which the pursuer was prevented from leaving a room for 15 minutes, the apparently attractive *de minimis* argument was rejected until, if at all, after proof. Lord Low said:

> "I have no doubt that a wrong and in my view not a trifling wrong, has been averred. It is averred that the manager detains

---

[31] See generally W.J. Stewart, "Lawburrows: Elegant Remedy or Absurd Form," 1988 S.L.T. 181 and related correspondence; SME "Lawburrows"; Norrie, *HPLS* 497–500 and Jamieson, *Summary Applications* GPL (W. Green, 2000).

[32] Law Reform (Husband and Wife) (Scotland) Act 1984, s.2(2).

[33] 1994 S.L.T. 93.

[34] *Delict*, p.713.

[35] 1994 S.L.T. at 96A.

[36] See, *e.g. Hamilton v Wilson*, 1994 S.L.T. 431. In *Orr v K*, 2003 S.L.T. (Sh. Ct) 70 the Sheriff refused to treat a mother's failure to return a child on time after contact, as plagium.

[37] 1907 S.C. 200.

this lady in his room for fifteen minutes after the assault had been committed, and refused to let her go until she made an apology. If that be true it was an outrage, and a relevant case has been stated."[38]

Perhaps the most practical modern significance of this particular delict relates to store detectives detaining persons suspected of shoplifting. Wrongful detention is enough to constitute the delict. There is no need to establish defamation of character.

Henderson v Chief Constable[39] is a good illustration of how the law applies. Indeed it might be seen as advancing the law: the reasoning is directed at the individual's interest in personal integrity. Some workers barricaded themselves in their employer's laboratory. Action was taken by the police under the Trespass (Scotland) Act 1865. They arrested the workers, who sued for damages on four counts: (1) the arrest and detention were unjustified; (2) if detention was justified there was no need to detain in cells; (3) if detention in cells was necessary then the removal of one worker's brassiere was unjustified; (4) there was no justification for handcuffing one of the individuals. It was held that, in terms of the 1865 Act, the police had been given a discretion to arrest or detain and that they had exercised it reasonably. Moreover, it was also reasonable in the circumstances to keep the admittedly intelligent and articulate employees in cells. However, the claim in respect of the request to remove the brassiere succeeded. Although there had been no previous case where a request to remove clothing had been held to be actionable, Lord Jauncey, then in the Outer House, said that such a request, "must amount to an infringement of liberty . . . I see no reason why the law should not protect the individual from this infringement, just as it does from other infringements." It was conceded that it was wrongful in the circumstances to handcuff one of the workers. The case illustrates how this delict, like many others, is based upon the protection of the legitimate interests of the citizen.

Statutory detention

In many cases it may be permissible to detain a person either at **2–11** common law or under a statute, for example, where someone wants to leave in breach of contract; or a child may be detained so far as reasonable and necessary in his interests. The master of a ship may detain people for the preservation of good order or the safety of persons, property or the vessel itself, and a mentally ill person may

---

[38] *ibid.* at 204.
[39] *Henderson v Chief Constable, Fife Police*, 1988 S.L.T. 361.

be detained if a danger to himself.[40] Commanders of aircraft have statutory powers ever more requiring to be exercised as a result of a recent phenomenon of "air-rage".[41] To keep a person in prison longer than necessary is a form of wrongful detention.[42] The opinion has been expressed that detention based on identification of a person's photograph as resembling a perpetrator, together with another accusation, was not unlawful.[43] The courts will scrutinise statutory powers carefully.[44]

Arrest

2–12   A special form of detention is arrest. Police officers have powers of arrest and if properly exercised no wrong is done. It is important to distinguish between cases of unlawful arrest simpliciter and cases where there was a power or warrant to arrest but one which turned out to be ineffective. In the former case there is no need to aver malice and want of probable cause; in the latter case the pursuer must prove malice and want of probable cause.[45] In *Robertson v Keith*,[46] the Lord President (Normand) said:

> "It is not doubtful that any unwarranted and unlawful proceedings by a public officer resulting in injury to anyone will subject him to liability, and that in such a case proof of malice or want of probable cause is not required of the pursuer."[47]

In *Leask v Burt*,[48] where a man was arrested without warrant and many months after the alleged offence, the case was relevant without averment of malice. In the recent case of *McKinney v Chief Constable*,[49] decided by the Inner House, the police got it wrong when they, with some reason, thought they had a power of arrest in

---

[40] Merchant Shipping Act 1995, s.105 and the Mental Health (Scotland) Act 1984, ss.17 and 24. The new legislation, the Mental Health (Care and Treatment) (Scotland) Act 2003 has received the Royal Assent but is not yet in force. H. Patrick, "New Act Heralds Major Reform of Scottish Mental Health Law", 2003 S.L.T. (News) 255: "It is expected that the new Act will come into effect in early 2005". For a full discussion of issues of principle see *B. v F.*, 1987 S.L.T. 681. 27.

[41] Tokyo Convention Act 1967, s.3.

[42] *Walsh v* Secretary of State for Scotland, 1990 G.W.D. 7–385.

[43] *McLaren v Procurator Fiscal for Lothian and Borders*, 1991 G.W.D. 24–1407.

[44] *Miborrow Petitioner*, 1996 S.C.L.R. (Notes) 314.

[45] This point was made in *McKinney v Chief Constable, Strathclyde Police*, 1998 S.L.T. (Sh. Ct) 80 and rejected by Lord Kingarth in *Woodward v Chief Constable, Fife Constabulary*, 1998 S.L.T. 1342. *McKinney* was upheld on appeal by the First Division: 2000 G.W.D. 24–919.

[46] 1936 S.C. 29.

[47] *ibid.*, at 41.

[48] (1893) 21 R. 32.

[49] 1998 Rep. L.R. 82.

a matrimonial interdict case but did not in fact have that power. It was conceded the arrest was unlawful in this sense. Therefore, the defenders could not insist upon the pursuer showing malice and want of probable cause.

Wrongful imprisonment

To be actionable the imprisonment has to be shown to have been **2–13** legally unjustifiable in the first place. Superior court judges are immune. Magistrates may be liable for a grossly *ultra vires* sentence, without proof of malice or lack of probable cause but not for an honest error in statutory interpretation. In *MacPhee v Macfarlane's Executor,*[50] Lord President Clyde thought it clear that there could be no liability for an honest error in statutory interpretation. In that particular case, if there had been an error in interpretation of the Summary Jurisdiction (Scotland) Act 1908, it would have been one that magistrates all over the country would have been applying since 1908 and so would not be actionable as grossly *ultra vires*. Generally, in terms of section 170 of the Criminal Procedure (Scotland) Act 1995, the wrongfully imprisoned pursuer must aver and prove both malice and lack of probable cause, and the action must be commenced within two months of the act complained of.

Seduction

Seduction is a delict perhaps not litigated nearly as often as it is **2–14** committed. Professor Walker defines it as "obtaining sexual relations with a virgin by fraud, circumvention, guile, misrepresentations or other persuasive practices and deflowering her."[51] The difference between seduction and fornication (or adultery in particular) is that in the latter there is genuine and full consent. In rape, which is itself actionable, consent is never given at all. In seduction, there is consent, but it is vitiated by the trickery or wiles involved. An example is *Murray v Fraser,*[52] where the pursuer was a headmaster's daughter and alleged that sexual intercourse took place on two occasions, once in a bicycle shed and another time in a wood. She became pregnant. The defender was a tenant farmer about 30 years of age. He was a friend of the family. He said he regarded the girl as a child and the girl said he treated her as such. She was ignorant of sexual matters and believed his assurance that she would come to no harm. Lord Dundas pointed out that the popular meaning of seduction is different from its legal meaning. In general speech, full consent is implied. What he considered important was the defender's relationship with the family and the girl's amazing ignorance of

---

[50] 1933 S.C. 163.
[51] Walker, p.698. 31 1916 S.C. 623.
[52] 1916 S.C. 623.

matters sexual. Other examples of wiles are promises to marry not later implemented, courtship with apparent intention to marry and taking advantage of the woman's dependency, as when she is in the man's employment.[53]

This seems like a paternalistic, sexist anachronism, although many things that were once thought much less important by changes in Christian society in the 1960's might be things which are thought important by other religionists in our increasingly multi-cultural society. The issue then becomes whether the modern state should simply be entirely secular.

Harassment and abuse

2–15   Under the Protection from Harassment Act 1997, every individual in Scotland has a right to be free from harassment and, accordingly, a person must not pursue a course of conduct which amounts to harassment of another and — (a) is intended to amount to harassment of that person; or (b) occurs in circumstances where it would appear to a reasonable person that it would amount to harassment of that person.[54] Conduct includes speech.[55] Harassment of a person includes causing the person alarm or distress.[56] A course of conduct must involve conduct on at least two occasions.[57] It is not otherwise defined and the matter is for the courts.

There is a defence as a result of the Secretary of State certifying that the conduct related to national security, the economic well-being of the United Kingdom or the prevention or detection of serious crime.[58] Alternatively, it is a defence to show that the conduct complained of was pursued for the purpose of preventing or detecting crime.[59] The other defences are legal authority[60] and that the conduct was reasonable.[61] The Scottish Parliament moved to meet similar mischief. Scottish courts now have power in terms of the Protection from Abuse (Scotland) Act 2001 to attach a power of arrest to an interdict where there is the threat of abuse defined as including violence, harassment, threatening conduct, and any other conduct giving rise, or likely to give rise, to physical or mental injury, fear, alarm or distress. For these purposes, "conduct" includes speech and presence in a specified place or area.

---

[53] *Macleod v MacAskill*, 1920 S.C. 72.
[54] s.8(1).
[55] s.8(3).
[56] *ibid.*
[57] s.8(3).
[58] s.12 (1). The certificate is conclusive. A certificate which purports to be of such type is presumed to be so unless the contrary is proved: s.12(3).
[59] s.8(4)(b).
[60] s.8(4)(a).
[61] s.8(4)(c).

CHAPTER 3

WRONGS TO PROPERTY

HERITABLE PROPERTY

Ejection and intrusion

Ejection is where someone enters on to lands and removes another **3–1** or stays on when his right to stay there has expired. Intrusion is sneaking on to the subjects when the possessor holds *animo* (by will) rather than *corpore* (in person):

> "they differ in this; that intrusion is the entering in possession, being for the time void, without consent of the parties interested, or order of law... but ejection... is not only the unwarrantable entering in lands, but the casting out violently of the then possessor."[1]

The remedies are: (a) summary ejection[2]; (b) violent profits, being the greatest profit the pursuer could have made if in possession[3]; and (c) actual compensatory damages. Caution for violent profits may be made a condition of proceedings. It was delicts such as these that lawburrows was introduced to prevent. Two modern cases show these wrongs are still live.

In *Axis West Developments Ltd v Chartwell Land Investment Ltd*,[4] the pursuers claimed reparation from the defenders, for wrongful encroachment, because they had constructed a drainage pipe on the pursuers' land without the pursuers' consent. The Lord Ordinary allowed a proof before answer on quantum only. However, after reviewing the land ownership and title issues, the Inner House granted dismissal and an appeal to the House of Lords was refused. In *Property Selection and Investment Trust Ltd v United Friendly Insurance Plc*,[5] the pursuers were heritable proprietors of adjacent subjects. The pursuers' subjects were destroyed by fire and they

---

[1] Stair, 1, ix, 25.
[2] Subject to, *inter alia*, the Rent (Scotland) Act 1984.
[3] This is arguably an instance of restitution for wrongs.
[4] 1999 S.L.T. 1416.
[5] 1998 S.C.L.R. 314.

discovered rock anchors in their own subjects supporting the defenders' buildings. The pursuers were unable to say when the anchors were placed and the defenders had no knowledge of them at all until the building work. The pursuers sued for the losses involved in exploring and removing the rock anchors. Lord Penrose[6] held that in these circumstances, the encroachment itself would not justify damages and that there had to be averments of *culpa*. The action was amended and debated of new before Lord MacFadyen. Because the pursuers failed to satisfy his Lordship that they had relevant averments sufficient to make it clear that the defenders were responsible for the workings, the reparation case had to fail. The anchors had in any event become the legal property of the pursuer![7]

Trespass

3–2   Trespass, in Scotland, is a temporary intrusion without permission or justification, such as entering upon someone else's property.[8] The Trespass (Scotland) Act 1865, as amended, criminalises certain trespasses, being "an Act to provide for the better Prevention of Trespass in Scotland." The Act is important in making conduct "wrongful" but it has not been decided whether it can be founded on in a breach of statutory duty case.

Because land is owned *a caelo usque ad centrum* (from the heavens to the centre of the earth), the law is concerned as much with the pursuer's airspace and the ground under his property as with the surface. The matter was considered in *Brown v Lee Constructions Ltd*[9] in which a homeowner petitioned for interdict against builders to restrain the respondents' crane sweeping over the petitioner's property. The builders argued that there was a difference between a permanent overhang and a transient one. The interdict was granted. The court mentioned that there was some risk of personal injury, but quite properly did not treat that as important, for trespass essentially protects the pursuer's interest in his land. Damages are not recoverable for trespass where no damage is done to the property, especially if the trespassing is innocent. But there are interesting arguments as to whether a loss of a chance of a wayleave that might have been charged is a reparable loss or whether a restitutionary award might be made for the wrong.[10] Interdict is possible if repetition is feared and self-help is allowed so long as reasonable in the circumstances.

---

[6] Influenced by *Kennedy v Glenbelle*, 1986 S.L.T. 1186.

[7] 1999 S.L.T. 975.

[8] For a full up-to-date treatment see Stewart, *Reparation: Liability for Delict*.

[9] 1977 S.L.T. (Notes) 61.

[10] *Graham v Duke of Hamilton* (1868) 6 M. 965; *Lord Advocate v Glengarnock Iron and Steel Company Ltd*, 1909 1 S.L.T. 15.

Shell UK Ltd v McGillivray[11] is a notable case. Trespass was pled as the basis of an action for interdict (an interdict, incidentally, which in preventing continued occupation had the positive result of requiring the respondents to leave on transport becoming available). The action was against workmen of contractors of the petitioners who were "occupying" oil installations where they worked. It was argued for the respondents that as the property was moveable the law of trespass did not apply. Lord Cameron of Lochbroom applied dicta in a case dealing with non-heritable property.[12] He said:

> "In my opinion, the use of the word trespass has no particular significance in these petitions other than indicating that the actings of the respondents are averred to be wrongful acts of occupation of parts of property of which the petitioners have the exclusive right of occupation."

He then proceeded on the basis that such occupation was a delict.[13] It is support, like *Henderson* above, for a more generalised view of wrongful conduct being actionable in general, without a nominate head.

Defences

Lady Matilda Steel-Maitland claimed against three airline com- **3–3** panies in respect of damage to her castle for damage caused by vibration and by droplets of aviation fuel.[14] She met the defence provided by Civil Aviation Act 1949, s.40(1) which provides that there is to be no liability in respect of normal flight (as defined) in nuisance. However, making up for this there is a provision in s.40(2), which provides a right to damages in cases where material loss or damage is caused by an aircraft or by an article or (alarmingly) a person falling from a plane. In these circumstances there is no need to prove negligence or intention nor any other cause of action. There is mention of contributory negligence and sole fault and it may be assumed (but it is not clear) that a small amount of contributory negligence does not bar the defender entirely. The Scottish Court accepted a view that is certainly explicable against the background of English law, quoting from MacNair's *Law of the Air* (4th ed.) p.107, in relation to the two provisions: "they represent a compromise or bargain which can be summed up as establishing no liability for technical legal injury (if any), but absolute liability for actual material injury".[15] Thus the case for interdict was unsuccessful, but

---

[11] 1991 S.L.T. 667.
[12] *Phestos Shipping Co. Ltd v Kurmiawan*, 1983 S.L.T. 388.
[13] 1991 S.L.T. 667 at 669.
[14] *Steel-Maitland v British Airways Board*, 1981 S.L.T. 110.
[15] *ibid.*, Quoted with approval by Lord Jauncey at 112.

the case for damages was allowed to proceed to a proof before answer.[16]

Necessity and justification, as by having a legal warrant, are defences: a fireman can crash through your gate and axe your door — providing, of course, there is a fire![17]

Nuisance

What is a nuisance?

3–4   Nuisance arises where a person uses their land in such a way that it is more than the pursuer should have to tolerate.[18] A nuisance is a continuing harm and not an isolated incident. A trivial matter will not be actionable. The nuisance must not be a matter of nature and must therefore be as a result of the defender's acts or omissions.[19] Functionally, it can be seen as a matter of legal protection of the environment.[20] *Webster v Lord Advocate*[21] is an example. The pursuer moved into her flat in 1977. She sought interdict because of the noise involved in the construction nearby of the grandstand for the Edinburgh Tattoo. The Tattoo had been going on for some time before the complainer moved in. Both sides accepted that the simple fact that the conduct had been going on before the complainer arrived was not a defence.[22] The court had to balance the various circumstances and interests: "I was left in no doubt that the Tattoo is a spectacle appreciated by the public and a valuable publicity and commercial asset to the city."[23] But the court was clear that it was not generally the case that the greater good would allow a nuisance — in this case the noise involved in erecting the grandstand rather than the Tattoo itself — to continue. It rejected the contention that Miss Webster could reduce the effect of the noise by closing her windows

---

[16] For nuisance see below para.3–4 *et seq.*

[17] *Cope v Sharpe* [1912] 1 K.B. 496 (necessity); *Southern Bowling Club Ltd v Ross* (1902) 4 F. 405 (justification). Necessity called "duress of circumstances" has recently been reinvigorated in the criminal law. Taking into account the close relationship of crime and intentional delicts these cases may be helpful in future delictual cases. See *McNab v Guild*, 1989 S.C.C.R. 138 and *Moss v Howdle*, 1997 S.L.T. 782.

[18] For a full judicially approved treatment see N. Whitty, "Nuisance", *Stair Memorial Encyclopaedia*, Vol. 14. However, see *Zimmerman and Simpson HPLS II* 612–632 for a fresh perspective.

[19] *Davey v Harrow Corp.* [1957] 2 All E.R. 305.

[20] J. Steele, "Private law and the environment: nuisance in context", 1995 L.S. 236.

[21] 1984 S.L.T. 13, and on appeal at 1985 S.L.T. 361.

[22] And see *Fleming v Hislop* (1886)13 R. 43: "It is clear that whether the man went to the nuisance or the nuisance came to the man the rights are the same."

[23] 1984 S.L.T. 13, *per* Lord Stott at 14.

or having double-glazing: "one of the nice things about summer is that you are able to open your windows." Interdict was granted.

The essence of the delict is that the defender's conduct is, in the circumstances, more than the pursuer should reasonably have to tolerate, *i.e.* that the conduct is *plus quam tolerabile*.[24] In a recent case, it was held that a "rave" — an all-night dance party with very loud music — held in an isolated location did not exceed what was *plus quam tolerabile,* being a one-off event.[25] A next-door neighbour failed when all that could be shown was noise arising from normal domestic use such as would not seriously disturb nor substantially inconvenience an average reasonable person in the locality.[26]

Coming to the nuisance

The court in *Webster* reiterated the long-established point that it is **3–5** not a good defence to plead that the pursuer came to the nuisance. Thus long practice of a nuisance does not give a potential defender a right to continue it when one acquires a new neighbour. On the other hand, the different point should be noted that if someone has put up with a nuisance for the 20 years of the long negative prescription then, so long as the behaviour has not changed, the potential pursuer has no right to interdict or damages. But it would be open to some other person in the same neighbourhood to complain.

Statutory authority

A possible defence is statutory authority, *i.e.* the "nuisance" is **3–6** really obedience to some Act of Parliament or subordinate legislation. A distinction has to be made between cases where a statute actually permits some conduct to be done even though it is a nuisance, and statutes which require certain matters to be carried out but which need not be carried out in such a way as to cause a nuisance.[27] Statutory authority will not be a defence if the act carried out could have been executed without causing a nuisance.

Neighbourhood and locality

The Scots law is reflected in the maxim *sic utere tuo ut alienum* **3–7** *non laedas* (so use your own property in a way that you do not harm another). As Lord President Cooper said:

---

[24] It transpires the Latin does not signify any deep civilian root: N. Whitty, "The Source of the Plus Quam Tolerabile Concept in Nuisance," 2003 7 Edin L.R. 218.

[25] *Cumnock & Doon Valley District Council v Dance Energy Associates Ltd*, 1992 G.W.D. 25–1441.

[26] *Davidson v Kerr*, 1996 G.W.D. 40–2296.

[27] *Lord Advocate v N.B. Ry* (1894) 2 S.L.T. 71.

> "If any person so uses his property as to occasion serious disturbance or substantial inconvenience to his neighbour or material damage to his neighbour's property, it is in the general case irrelevant as a defence for the defender to plead merely that he was making a normal and familiar use of his own property."[28]

Nuisance is a delict that arises from the interests involved in the ownership or occupation of property.[29] It probably also protects the interests of the individual even temporarily in the neighbourhood of the property in his or her life and health.[30] It seems closely connected to neighbourhood. It is largely a matter of fact and degree depending upon the circumstances of the case whether or not a nuisance has been or is being committed. One guide is the locality principle: "Things which are forbidden in a crowded urban community may be permitted in the country. What is prohibited in enclosed land may be tolerated in the open."[31] In *Maguire v Charles McNeil*,[32] the locality principle was considered by the First Division. The site occupied by the defenders had been used as a forge. They bought more adjacent property and installed heavy drop hammers which were alleged to be causing noise and vibration. The pursuers, churchmen and teachers complained. Lord President Clyde declared the locality to be "one of a familiar kind in a great centre of commerce such as the City of Glasgow."[33] He continued: "The doctrine of locality is a concession made by the law to that social necessity which (particularly in towns) drives people into close neighbourhood, not only with each other, but also with the work by which they earn their living." He explained that a considerable sacrifice is required in a society as "the price of the advantages which close neighbourhood to others, and to remunerative employment brings with it."[34] However, that did not mean that "the small but indispensable section of brain workers in the community must suffer torture without hope of protection, however close to the ears the industrial babel may be brought."[35] It was held that in this case the doctrine would not have applied, but there had not been proof of sufficient inconvenience, although if there had been proof of noise at night that might have been different.

---

[28] *Watt v Jamieson*, 1954 S.C. 56 at 58.

[29] German law approaches the matter from the point of view of land law: *Zimmerman and Simpson, HPLS II*, 615, n.34.

[30] Lord Hope in an English appeal agreed with his brethren that a licensee was not protected by the law of nuisance: *Hunter v Canary Wharf Ltd and London Dockland Development Corp.*, [1997] A.C. 655.

[31] *Inglis v Shotts Iron Co.* (1881) 8 R. 1006 at 1021, *per* Lord Shand.

[32] 1922 S.L.T. 193.

[33] *ibid.*, at 200.

[34] *ibid.*

[35] *ibid.*, at 201.

Interdict will be granted to prevent a nuisance being continued or repeated and damages will be granted in respect of loss caused by it.

The basis of liability

Until recently the view was often expressed that nuisance was an **3–8** example of strict liability, in that it was not open to a defender to show that he had taken all reasonable care to prevent the nuisance, *i.e.* that he was not at fault. The position has now been resolved by the House of Lords' decision in *R.H.M. Bakeries v Strathclyde Regional Council.*[36] A bakery was flooded as the result of the collapse of a sewer. The pursuers sued for damages but did not allege that the flood was the defenders' fault, just that they had committed a nuisance. The House held that this was not sufficient — it was essential to allege some degree of fault. However, in nuisance cases it will often be very simple to infer fault from the happening of the incident and the onus will be upon the defender to show that the nuisance was not his fault.[37] This, it must be said, is not the same as saying that negligence will be inferred!![38]

The law was subject to further review in *Kennedy v Glenbelle.*[39] Building work was done on the pursuers' premises by the first-named defenders on advice from the second-named defenders (who had been engaged by the first defenders). It caused damage to the pursuers' subjects. The Lord President said that negligence is not required for nuisance although *culpa* is. For a damages action, other conduct may infer the necessary responsibility. When taken with conduct *plus quam tolerabile,* that can be nuisance.[40] The *culpa* is nuisance *culpa.*[41] As Lord Hope explained:

> "*Culpa* which gives rise to a liability in delict may take various forms. In Stair Memorial Encyclopaedia, Vol. 14, 'Nuisance', para 2087 it is stated that the usual categories of *culpa* or fault are malice, intent, recklessness and negligence. To that list there may be added conduct causing a special risk of abnormal damage where it may be said that it is not necessary to prove a specific fault as fault is necessarily implied in the result".[42]

---

[36] 1985 S.L.T. 214.

[37] *ibid.* at 219.

[38] For a discussion on the relationship between negligence and nuisance see B.S. Markesinis, "Negligence, nuisance and affirmative duties of action", (1989) 105 L.Q.R. 104; P.F. Davidson, "Nuisance and Negligence", 1986 J.R. 107.

[39] 1996 S.L.T. 1186.

[40] See generally para.1–17.

[41] See generally F. McManus, "*Culpa* and the law of Nuisance", 1995 J.R. (note) 462.

[42] 1996 S.L.T 1186 at 1188.

Accordingly, nuisance is still special. In some nuisance cases at least the onus of proof of specific fault is reversed.[43]

Damages for losses consequent upon damage caused by nuisance are recoverable. In *G B & A M Anderson v White*,[44] it was held that *culpa* had been relevantly pled in that the pursuers averred that a deliberate act on the part of the defenders caused the water level to rise, that the resulting condition was maintained by the parties taking over control of the dam and that the defenders had actual or constructive knowledge of the damage caused because of the complaints made to them. The nature of the loss was that the water table had been raised, causing flooding in low lying fields, which prevented their normal use for grazing of cattle and growing hay and silage. So it is submitted it is reasonable to categorise this as consequential loss upon the physical damage of the flooding. Potentially more expansive is the decision of an extra division in *The Globe (Aberdeen) Ltd v North of Scotland Water Authority*.[45] There was a claim for financial loss not clearly following upon physical damage: the loss of customers put off by prolonged sewage works. The Sheriff, taking the approach in negligence cases to economic loss, dismissed the cause. However, it was held, on appeal, that this could proceed to proof before answer.

A distinction can be made between cases where interdict is sought, on the one hand, and cases where damages are sought, on the other. In the case of interdict the court will generally look at the matter from the point of view of the complainer, concentrating less on the issue of fault and more on the issue of whether the defender is going to continue to do the act complained of.[46]

Human rights and nuisance

3–9   As will be seen below, there is a human right to a family life and enjoyment of property. The conduct that comprises a nuisance can infringe those rights. If the law of nuisance is the mode of obtempering the ECHR obligations, then cognisance needs to be taken of that jurisprudence. In *Dennis and Another v MOD*,[47] it was held that training flights by the RAF were a nuisance and engaged Article 8 and Article 1 of protocol 1 infringing the right to family life. The common law damages of £950,000 (to cover the period until 2012) were sufficient to constitute just satisfaction.

---

[43] Whitty, "Nuisance", para.2107. See also the discussion in *Zimmerman and Simpson HPLS II* 631–632.

[44] 2000 S.L.T. 37.

[45] 2000 S.L.T. 674.

[46] 1985 S.L.T. at 218; *Watt v Jamieson* is accordingly still good authority on the question of interdict.

[47] 2003 T.L.R. 270.

Non-natural use of land and the escape of dangerous things from land

Since the decision of the House of Lords in *R.H.M. Bakeries v* **3–10** *Strathclyde Regional Council,* it is now possible to deal with this formerly awkward category of cases very briefly. As a general rule, liability for nuisance is based on *culpa.* Generally, there is no rule, as applies in some circumstances in England, that a man acts at his peril.[48] However, where, for example, someone brings something inherently dangerous like dynamite on to his or her land and damage results from its escape (*e.g.* by explosion), the action is based on his or her fault in so bringing it on and his or her fault in not preventing it from exploding, or his or her fault in not taking steps to prevent parties who would foreseeably interfere with it from doing so, and such fault will be easily inferred-indeed the defender will have to explain why it is not his or her fault.

Diversion of the natural course of a stream

When the House of Lords was restating the law of nuisance in **3–11** *R.H.M. Bakeries,* it distinguished an earlier House of Lords' case in a Scots appeal: *Caledonian Ry v Greenock Corporation.*[49] Greenock Corporation altered the channel of a burn to make a paddling pool. Rainfall which was exceptional for Greenock, but not for Scotland, caused it to flood and damage occurred to the railway company's property. The corporation were held liable. Lord Fraser acknowledged that the House of Lords, in making that decision, may have applied strict liability rather than liability based upon *culpa*; because the decision was not strictly in point, the House did not require to overrule the case. *In Kennedy v Glenbelle Ltd,*[50] it was accepted this

---

[48] *Rylands v Fletcher* (1868) L. R. 3 H.L. 330 applied that principle to establish a strict liability for the escape of dangerous things where there was a non-natural use of land. Even in England there is a trend to restrict the application of this type of liability to cases where the whole danger is man-made and in other cases to impose liability based on fault: *Goldman v Hargrave* [1967] 1 A. C. 645. The House of Lords in *Cambridge Water Co. Ltd v Eastern Counties Leather plc* [1994] 2 A.C. 264 held that the case should be restricted to isolated escapes from land and not extended to be a rule of strict liability for ultra-hazardous operations on land. It was also said that even under this head there had to be foreseeability of damage of the type which occurred. The exercise of due care is not, however, a defence. See J.G. Fleming, "The Fall of the Crippled Giant" (1995) 3 Tort L. Rev. 56. F. McManus, "Bye-bye Rylands-Again!", 1995 J.R. 194. The House of Lords has again refused to depart from the case: *Transco Plc v Stockport Metropolitan BC* [2003] T.L.R. 632. However, it had to be read according to modern conditions and piping water into a block of flats did not fall within the rule.

[49] 1917 S.C. (HL) 56; cases which the court reconsidered and explained as being truly based upon *culpa* included what could be called a "Scottish Rylands": *Kerr v Earl of Orkney* (1857) 20 D. 298, where the language of strict liability was used, especially at 302.

[50] Discussed above.

may be an anomalous category of case. It seems to have been accepted in principle in *G. & A. Estates Ltd v Caviapen Trustees Ltd (No. 1)*.[51] Accordingly, it remains the case that while liability for non-natural use of land or the escape of dangerous things is now based on *culpa*, liability may remain strict where damage is caused by the alteration of the natural direction of a stream, at least until a case in point comes before the House of Lords.[52]

Use of land in aemulationem vicini

3–12   This is a recognised but difficult area of liability.[53] According to Johnstone there are six important eighteenth century cases.[54] He considers that the reception of *aemulationem vicini* never faltered and became an established doctrine of Scots law. Its roots are in the *jus* commune rather than Roman law itself.[55] In one of the first modern cases, *Ritchie v Purdie*,[56] Lord Gillies said:

> "It is a valuable rule of our law that a man cannot use his property in aemulationem vicini. He may attempt to do so by positive acts, and this is the most common form perhaps in which such an abuse of the right of property is attempted. But he may also attempt it, as in this instance, negatively, by endeavouring to retrain the rights of his neighbour, to this injury of that neighbour, and without any benefit whatever to himself. In this case, as well as in the other, the Court will refuse their sanction to the nimious and emulous enforcement of a right to the hurt of another."[57]

Under this head there is liability for harm caused by a legitimate and non-continuing use of land that is carried out with malice and spitefully to harm a neighbour. It is clearly associated with nuisance,

---

[51] 1993 S.L.T. 1037.

[52] See Gordon D.L. Cameron, "Strict Liability and the Rule in *Caledonian Railway Co v Greenock Corporation*," 2000 (5) S.L.P.Q. 356, considering *inter alia*, the unreported case of *Inverness Harbour Trustees v BRB*, March 31, 1994 and related English authority. He also usefully considers the aspects of the law of property which may apply to cases of this nature.

[53] Johnston, "Owners and Neighbours: from Rome to Scotland" in The Civil Law Tradition in Scotland (Evans-Jones ed., 1995), Stair Society Supplementary Volume 2, p.176.

[54] *Brodie of Letham v Sir James Cadel of Morton*, March 22, 1707; *Fairly v Earl of Eglinton* (1744) Mor. 12780; *Gordon v Grant* (1765) Mor. 7356; *Dewar v Fraser* (1767) Mor. 12803; *Ralston v Pettigrew* (1768) Mor. 12808; *Glassford v Astley* (1808) Mor. App No. 7.

[55] D. Johnston, "Owners and Neighbours: from Rome to Scotland" in The Civil Law Tradition in Scotland (Evans-Jones, ed. Supplementary Vol.2), p.197.

[56] (1833) 11 S. 771.

[57] *ibid.*, at 774–775.

but differs in that one incident is sufficient and that the defender's mental state must be demonstrated.[58]

An example is *Campbell v Muir*.[59] The defender was exercising his entitlement to fish from a boat in a river. He did so in such a way as to prevent anglers on the opposing bank from being able to cast. It was held that to do this spitefully was actionable and amenable to interdict.

MOVEABLE PROPERTY

Spuilzie and wrongful interference with moveables

Spuilzie (pronounced, approximately, "spoolly") both describes: **3–13** (a) the act of interfering with property, namely, spoliation; and (b) a remedy known to the law of Scotland in respect of such actings. It is a delict said by some to be obsolete, but which may yet be found to be useful.[60] It long ago ceased to be important in relation to heritage. It is committed by a person who takes away moveables without the consent of the possessor or without order of law. It is not even necessary for the pursuer to establish ownership of the property, so long as there is a right of possession or custody.[61] The primary obligation is to restore the goods to the pursuer, but there is also a liability to violent profits. These are the profits that could have been made with the goods value originally by the pursuer's own oath.

Although there is an urge to interpret this remedy as combination of restitution and damages for delict, this may be misleading. It is the element of violent profits that is of interest. This is not necessarily a matter of delictual damages. Indeed the exciting thing about such a claim is that it means that the pursuer does not have to show the loss that would be required if the case were based on loss wrongfully caused. The better rationalisation might be that this award is essentially restitutionary and is an example of restitution for wrongs.[62] The recognition of loss of use as a head of claim in ordinary delictual actions makes it unlikely that spuilzie arguments will be heard often. There have been some intersting cases and some debate as to the relevance of spuilzie in cases of hire purchase.[63]

If we look now at the wider notion of wrongful interference, it can be said that spuilzie is a species of this wider delictual concept

---

[58] See Hume, Lectures, III, 208.

[59] 1908 S.C. 387. Another is *More v Boyle*, 1967 S.L.T. (Sh. Ct) 38.

[60] For a fuller up-to-date treatment see Stewart, *Reparation: Liability for Delict.*

[61] Stair, I, ix, 16.

[62] See p.2, n.7.

[63] *F.C. Finance Ltd v Brown & Son* 1969 S.L.T. (Sh. Ct) 41. Rodger, "Spuilzie in the Modern World", 1970 S.L.T. (News) 33.

(which is likely to have both proprietary and restitutionary aspects). There are sufficient markers in the Scots authorities for this wider notion. In *Snare v The Earl of Fife's Trustees*,[64] Snare, a bookseller in Reading, bought a picture that he discovered to be Charles I, by Velasquez. He exhibited it and produced pamphlets showing it to have been in the possession of the Earl of Fife. The result of this information was that the Earl of Fife's trustees petitioned the sheriff that the picture had been stolen or surreptitiously abstracted from their possession and craved (i) restitution or (ii) warrant to the clerk of court to take possession and retain until caution found. Warrant was granted, the painting seized and retained, and eventually returned. Snare claimed for damages for loss of exhibition. The court allowed the case to go to trial on the basis of the wrongful detention — they "obtained and acted upon an illegal warrant". Neither did they require to aver malice and lack of probable cause.

3–14   Even more interesting are the bottle cases. An interdict was granted in *Wilson v Shepherd*,[65] where one trader allowed people to fill another's bottles with paraffin. While there is an element of the law of property about this, the interdict was granted on the basis of a wrong to property and therefore was essentially a delict for which damages could be sought. In a later case, *Leitch v Leydon*,[66] a grocer filled bottles belonging to another with aerated water. It had already been intimated to him that the owners retained ownership. It would have taken a careful glance to check the origin of a bottle. It was held there was no duty to inspect bottles. For Viscount Dunedin there was no *culpa*. Interdict was refused. Although Wilson was cited in argument, the respondents were not called upon and the case was not mentioned in the speeches. There was no mention of the provisions of the Sale of Goods Act 1893 that allowed a non-owner to pass title if a buyer was in possession of the goods, although the notice on the bottle might well deprive the "consumer" of the right to rely upon it. So far as it goes, the case is correct, but the real issue is whether, if it were clear *ex facie* that a bottle was one of a specific type that was always sold under a retention if there was no specific intimation that the owners expressly prohibited refilling, interdict or damages should be granted.

In modern life it seems strange that we can do what we like with a bottle that says "Property of X — do not refill, return or destroy", but cannot do as we please with a video cassette or computer disk. The analysis used by the software "vendors" is that the "buyer" pays for a licence rather than the property.

---

[64] (1850) 13 D. 286.

[65] 1913 S.C. 300.

[66] 1931 S.C. (HL) 1. This case ran along with, and was reported with, *A.G. Barr & Co. Ltd v MacGheoghegan* and was decided in exactly the same way.

The law does require a revision to create a coherent wrongful **3–15** interference with moveable property and to incorporate the miscellaneous wrongs that already apply. It could also be an opportunity to recognise which interests in moveables are reparable when harmed — something which would have a consequence for negligence for economic loss. Just now a summary is as follows:

1. Property destroyed

The *lex Aquilia* principle applies — loss wrongfully caused. In this case (for a long time) deliberate destruction has fallen clearly within the idea of wrongfulness. This does not depend in any way upon the law of negligence. Examples include the destruction of a horse[67] and the destruction of stakenets.[68] Spuilzie is not appropriate in destruction simpliciter for there is no taking.

2. Property of another taken

It is the kind of activity which would have been struck at by spuilzie and in modern times attracts an award of damages albeit damage need not be proved in the sense of loss but rather by proving that the property was taken and evidence given as to its value. The loss of use is an independent head of damages.

3. Property of another used without permission

In addition to the bottle cases discussed above there is *Brown's Trustees v Hay*.[69] Hay was an employee of a firm of solicitors who, while involved with an estate, discovered papers which he thought implicated the estate in false returns to the revenue. He was held liable in damages for the ultroneous use of the property even although there was no actual loss and no taking. A defender who took possession of a car in a sale from a trustee of a garage proprietor which had not been included in the sale was held liable in damages to the owner of the car.[70] That case may come within this category because the taking was permitted. In *Cairns v Harry Walker Ltd*,[71] the owners of a ship were fined for an excise offence. The cause was the conduct of the steward in conjunction with the defenders. They were held to be liable for the wrongful and illegal use of the ship.

---

[67] *Wilsons v McKnight* (1830) 8 S. 398.
[68] *Grubb v Mackenzie* (1834) 13 S. 717.
[69] (1898) 25 R. 1112.
[70] *Mackintosh v Galbraith & Arthur* (1900) 3F. 66.
[71] 1913 2 S.L.T. 379

4. Property detained

In addition to *Snare,* cited above, a person who stopped a coach taking people to a funeral was held liable in damages.[72]

Another approach

3–16 As the issue in these cases is intentional violation of interests in moveables, the general theme that all crimes are delicts might help in this sphere. The Scots indigenous criminal law has developed carefully over the years, while the civil counterpart has been obscured by negligence and duties of care. Thus it is submitted that in cases where the facts fit *Milne v Tudhope*[73] or *Kidston v Annan*[74] or *Black v Carmichael,*[75] civil liability based on wrongfulness ought to succeed without difficulty. Looking at cases in that way means that they can become rather simple, as in *Gemmell v Bank of Scotland,*[76] where the bank repossessed and the pursuers' goods were missing. The learned sheriff thought it did not matter that the case was one of spuilzie or restitution — there would be damages including damages for loss of use.[77]

---

[72] *Crawford v Mill* (1830) 5 Mur. 215.

[73] 1981 S.L.T. (Notes) 42.

[74] 1984 S.C.C.R. 20.

[75] 1992 S.C.C.R. 709.

[76] Glasgow, November 5, 1996.

[77] Compare with *Harris v Abbey National,* 1996 G.W.D. 33–1993 in which the pursuer was also successful.

CHAPTER 4

THE ROMAN QUASI-DELICTS

The Roman quasi-delicts is a special category of obligations that **4–1** certainly arise *ex lege* and are, therefore, appropriately treated in the law of delict.[1] Unfortunately they have little in common in either Roman or Scots law. However, when it is remembered that the term "delict" originally had a morally blameworthy connotation, this may help explain why they were put together, in that in these cases the defender has not been especially bad (as opposed to the actual person who poured, threw, placed or suspended the offending item). With perhaps the difficult exception of the *judex qui litem suam fecerit* (the judge who makes a cause his own), they involve liability being established without proof of fault on the part of the defender and have suggestions of vicarious liability. Their reception into Scots law is not, as shall be seen, without difficulty. The interests protected are sometimes the integrity of the person, but extend also to property. As there are no Scots cases directly in point on the strict liability of the *judex,* that head of liability is not dealt with in this book.[2]

The *actio de effusis vel dejectis* and the *actio de positis vel suspensis*

Roman law imposed a penalty on the occupier of premises (i) from **4–2** which something was poured or thrown out, striking the victim (the *actio de effusis vel dejectis*), and (ii) where something was placed or suspended from a building which fell causing loss, injury or damage (the *actio de positis vel suspensis*).

Poured and thrown

The remedy has been recognised as part of Scots law, but not **4–3** clearly so.[3] In *Gray v Dunlop*,[4] the pursuer's pupil son was walking

---

[1] For a fuller up-to-date treatment see Stewart, *Reparation: Liability for Delict.*

[2] See Walker, pp.285–286.

[3] Bankton, I, iv, 32; Kames, I, i, 1; Hume, Lectures, iii, 186; and see P. Stein, "*The actio de effusis vel dejectis* and the Concept of Quasi-Delict in Scots Law" (1955) 4 I.C.L.Q. 356.W.M. Gordon, "Householders' Liabilities" (1982) 27 J.L.S.S. 253.

[4] 1954 S.L.T. (Sh. Ct) 75.

along a street about 5pm when some, understandably unidentified, person emptied a pot of urine upon him. An action was raised against the occupier of the premises, which were a model lodging house (a sort of hostel for down-and-outs). No fault could be proved against the occupier and so it was important for the pursuer that strict liability should be established. The sheriff refused to accept that there could be liability without fault and refused the claim. Notwithstanding that decision, Professor Walker and Professor Stein incline to the view that the *actio de effusis vel dejectis* is part of the law of Scotland.[5] This case must now be read subject to the dicta in the Opinion of the Court in *McDyer v Celtic Football and Athletic Company Limited*,[6] discussed below. While that case dealt with the *actio de posito et suspenso*, it is clear that the preferred view was that these two quite different heads of liability have come into Scots law in some kind of related way.

Placed and suspended

4–4   The *actio de positis vel suspensis* was considered *in MacColl v Hoo*,[7] Miss MacColl discovered that her motor car had been dented by a slate that had fallen from premises occupied by Mr Hoo. She sued relying on the *actio*. The sheriff at first instance allowed the claim, accepting that it was part of the law of Scotland, and did not require proof of fault. On appeal, the sheriff principal rejected the claim, taking the view that there can be no liability without fault. In *McArthur v Matthew Cleland Public House Proprietors*,[8] another lady was unsuccessful in claiming for damages for injury caused by a slate falling from the roof of the defenders' public house. The sheriff had allowed the case to proceed on the basis of the possibility of *res ipsa loquitur* being established. The sheriff correctly rejected *res ipsa loquitur* because the fall of a slate could be explained other than by the defenders' negligence. However, it may well be that if there had been more facts alleged in the pleadings sufficient to infer fault, the case would have proceeded — averments that the roof was generally in a poor state of repair prior to the accident, or (in the sheriff principal's view) that the building was newly built.[9]

The *actio de posito* came up for consideration before the Inner House in *McDyer v Celtic Football and Athletic Company Limited*.[10] The pursuer was injured in the defenders stadium when attending the European Summer Special Olympic Games. A piece of wood fell on

---

[5] Stein and Walker, n.58 above.
[6] 2000 S.L.T. 736. The subsequent proof is noted at 2001 S.L.T. 1387.
[7] 1983 S.L.T. (Sh. Ct) 23.
[8] 1981 S.L.T. (Sh. Ct) 76.
[9] *ibid.* at 77. In *MacColl* the home was completed in July 1979 and the slate fell in December of that year.
[10] 2000 S.L.T. 736. The subsequent proof is noted at 2001 S.L.T. 1387

him from a temporary construction attached to the roof. One of the grounds pled by the pursuer was that there was strict liability to the pursuer in terms of the *actio de positis vel suspensis* for causing or allowing a piece of timber to be placed or suspended from the said stadium canopy where it could fall upon the pursuer who was in a part of the stadium where the public were likely to pass or congregate. The *actio* was the subject of learned debate and consideration. It seems the Inner House was convinced that the *actio* had been received. In this case, however, it would not be applicable because the incident took place *inside* the stadium.[11] The Occupiers Liability Act would apply and thus averments of strict liability were irrelevant. These special factual situations have come into Scots law as instances of liability providing there is *culpa*. We then reach the difficult question since *R.H.M. Bakeries* albeit with the assistance of *Kennedy*, namely to determine "what is *culpa*?" If there is nuisance-*culpa*, is there roman "quasi-delict *culpa*"? There seems little point in admitting that the law has infused special cases but in no way treats them specially. It is thus possible that the practical result is that the defender in such cases has more explaining to do and that the burden of averment on the pursuer is lifted at least to some extent.[12] It may be that they are treated as simple cases of "negligence or inadvertency" and only of merit in identifying some situations where it might be easier to establish liability — at least to the extent of establishing *prima facie* liability against which the defender must offer averment and — if after the pursuers proof there is a case to answer — proof. As a matter of convenience, on that analysis, a court could ordain a defender to learn at proof.

The praetorian edict *nautae caupones stabularii*

The praetor was a Roman magistrate elected annually. When he **4–5** demitted office, his edicts were handed down to the next praetor and eventually this grew into a body of law equivalent to legislation — most praetors being content to leave the previous edicts alone. This particular edict related to the liability of sailors (*nautae*), innkeepers (*caupones*) and stable keepers (*stabularii*).[13] These particular trades are said to have been singled out because of the propensity of people involved in them to be in league with pirates or highwaymen. The hotel keeper or carrier could arrange to have the guest's baggage or the consigned goods stolen for a share in the booty. The carrier or innkeeper would then be able to plead that it was not his fault. To

---

[11] This conclusion is disputed on analysis of the Roman law: Tammo Wallinga, "*Effusa vel deiecta* in Rome and Glasgow", 2002 Edin. L.R. Vol.6, 123. He goes so far as to say the Praetor would have found strict liability.

[12] This is largely the same problem encountered not only with nuisance but with the discussion of the divertion of the natural course of a stream discussed above.

[13] J. MacKintosh, "The Edict *nautae caupones stabularii*" (1891) 3 J.R. 306.

remedy this, the edict imposed strict liability for the simple happening unless there had been a *damnum fatale*. In its modern form in
Scots law, it applies to carriers of goods (not carriers of passengers),
hotel keepers and stable keepers.

While the law of contract will often be applicable in many such
cases, since we are concerned with liability in delict it is not essential
that a contract exists: for example, in a case where a purported
contract for accommodation is void, if goods are stolen from the
hotel there is still liability under the edict. The liability of both the
carrier and hotel proprietor has been adjusted by statute.

Carriers

4–6   *Nautae,* or carriers by sea, are strictly liable unless they can show
the damage to goods was caused by *damnum fatale* or act of the
Queen's enemies.[14] It is, therefore, to no avail to show that all
reasonable precautions were taken.[15] The particular law is, however,
substantially modified and stated in international conventions and
legislation and is not dealt with in this book.[16] The common carrier
of goods (but not of people) by land is, by analogy, held strictly liable
for the goods carried. It is no defence to show that the goods were
stolen.[17] Only the defences of *damnum fatale* and act of the Queen's
enemies are available. The Carriers Act 1830 affects the edictal
liability. It prevents the carrier excluding liability by advertisement
or notice. It does allow special contracts to be made so long as
reasonable care is taken to bring the terms to the attention of the
consignor. It also excludes the carrier's liability for certain specified
goods,[18] unless their nature and value, if over £10, was declared
when deposited.

Hotel proprietors

4–7   The Hotel Proprietors Act 1956 now regulates the inn keeper's
liability: "An hotel within the meaning of this Act shall, and any
other establishment shall not, be deemed to be an inn." Hotel "means
an establishment held out by the proprietor as offering food, drink
and, if so required, sleeping accommodation, without special contract, to any traveller presenting himself who appears able and
willing to pay a reasonable sum for the services and facilities
provided and who is in a fit state to be received."[19] On such a

---

[14] Mackenzie Stuart, "Liability of Common Carriers" (1926) 3 8 J.R. 205.
[15] *Rae v Hay* (1832) 10 S. 303.
[16] See Gloag and Henderson, *The Law of Scotland* (11th ed, W. Green, 2001) Chs 25,
26 and 27.
[17] *MacAusland v Dick* (1787) Mor. 9246.
[18] For example, jewellery, watches and lace.
[19] s.1.

proprietor there falls strict liability subject to the defences of *damnum fatale* and act of the Queen's enemies. But the Act offers additional protections to the hotel proprietor: sleeping accommodation has to have been booked at the time of the loss; and the loss must have occurred between the midnight before arrival and the midnight after departure. There is no special strict liability in respect of motor vehicles in hotel car parks. The proprietor can limit his liability to £50 for any one article and £100 in aggregate if he has conspicuously displayed a notice in terms of the Schedule to the Act.[20] But the restriction does not apply: where fault or vicarious liability is actually established; where the property was deposited for safe custody; or if the goods were offered for deposit and not accepted.

Stable keepers

Stable keepers have not received the benefit of any special **4–8** legislation and are strictly liable for any damage to the beast subject to the defences of *damnum fatale* and act of the Queen's enemies.[21]

---

[20] s.2.
[21] See *Mustard v Paterson*, 1923 S.C. 142.

CHAPTER 5

ECONOMIC WRONGS

5–1 This Chapter deals with a number of delicts, some of which have been described in England as economic torts.[1] This is by no means a closed nor a clearly identified category. However, what these delicts do have in common is that they all define the limits of legal trading and so are usefully considered together. As will be seen, attempts have been made to harmonise some or all of the wrongs.

Fraud

5–2   Fraud is a machination or contrivance to deceive.[2] There is no substantial body of purely delictual cases.[3] This delict protects the infringement of many different interests. It may, for example, cause someone nervous shock[4] or result in their becoming involved in some dangerous escapade.[5] Often it is encountered in commerce. Fraud involves the making of a false representation of fact without belief in its truth, intending that the person to whom it is made should act in reliance thereon, which causes a consequent loss.[6]

Frequently it is encountered in connection with contracts — the fraud inducing a contract either with the person perpetrating the fraud or with another party. Damages are recoverable whether or not the contract can be rescinded, emphasising the independent nature of

---

[1] For a fuller treatment see Stewart, *Reparation: Liability for Delict*, Ch.8. For England see Clerk and Lindsell, Chs 15, 24, 26 and 27.

[2] Ersk., III, i, 16.

[3] Although there is a longer history in connection with Bankruptcy, Norrie, *HPLS II*, 495. In England it is thought that the similar tort of deceit can be subsumed into the proposed tort of intentional infliction of harm by unlawful means: P. Sales and D. Stilitz, "Intentional Infliction of harm by Unlawful Means," (1999) 115 L.Q.R. 411.

[4] *Wilkinson v Downton* [1897] 2 Q.B. 57.

[5] See *Burrows v Rhodes* [1899] 1 Q.B. 816, which arose from the Jameson raid. Sir Leander Starr Jameson led a raid against the Transvaal to support rebels (mainly British) to advance Cecil Rhodes' colonial ambitions. Jameson was captured and handed over to the British. The reasoning might be a little coloured by the circumstances.

[6] See generally *Boyd & Forrest v* Glasgow & South-Western Ry, 1912 S.C. (HL) 93.

the delict.[7] Fraud can be carried out in an infinite number of ways, and in particular it is possible to commit the delict without words, but to do so by actions or deeds. A good recent example is *Hillcrest Homecare Services v Tartan Home Care Ltd.*[8] The pursuers alleged that the defenders had induced them to purchase a nursing home by arranging matters so that they and their surveyor were fooled into thinking there were more occupants than actually there were!

An illustration of the technical nature of the wrong can be seen in *H & J.M. Bennett (Potatoes) v Secretary of State for Scotland.*[9] The government department provided a certificate saying that certain potatoes were found or believed by the inspector to be free from potato cyst eelworm. The potatoes were sold by the pursuers to buyers not parties to the action, who rejected the goods because they were infected. The tests carried out could not have determined whether the problem existed or not. At first sight, the impression would be that this was an example of negligence. It is at least that (in the sense of carelessness), but the law on reparation for negligence makes the usual fraud losses/economic losses difficult. In this case, by making the statement there had been an intentional act. Taking into account the wide definition of fraud, the official was "guilty" of fraud because he knew the certificate was not stating the true position, albeit another technical person might have read the certificate in a less stringent fashion. There was no need to establish an intention to cheat.

Breach of confidence

This was not, until very recently, a well-defined delict. Matters **5–3** have moved on from the review undertaken by the Scottish Law Commission, which nonetheless remains valuable reading for the student.[10] There is a core of cases in commercial contract matters where, for example, an employee has access to trade secrets. The interest for delict is in cases where this contractual basis may be missing.

The law moved on in the House of Lords' decision in the *Spycatcher* litigation.[11] So far as the case in the House of Lords is concerned, the essential facts were that a former secret service operative, Mr Peter Wright, published a book in Australia that

---

[7] *Thin & Sinclair v Arrol* (1896) 24 R. 198; and see *Post Office v Morton*, 1992 G.W.D. 26–1492.

[8] 1996 G.W.D. 4–215.

[9] 1986 S.L.T. 665.

[10] Scottish Law Commission, No. 90, Cmnd 9385 (1984), p.8.

[11] *Att.-Gen. v Observer Ltd, Att.-Gen. v Times Newspapers Ltd* [1988] 3 W.L.R. 776. For the background to this case and an enjoyable read see Turnbull, *The Spycatcher Trial* (Heinemann, London, 1988). See also Jones, "Breach of Confidence after Spycatcher" [1989] C.L.P. 49.

revealed information that he had obtained while working for the British security service. The Crown sought to restrain publication in the United Kingdom by injunction. In the House of Lords, Lord Keith took the view that the law had long recognised an obligation of confidence arising out of relationships such as doctor and patient, priest and penitent, solicitor and client, and banker and customer. Presumably from the standpoint of English law, Lord Keith said: "The obligation may be imposed by an express or implied term in a contract but it may also exist independently of any contract on the basis of an equitable principle of confidence." In his opinion, an invasion of personal privacy was sufficient to justify the law's interference. In stating this, he referred to the granting of an injunction in England arising out of the Scottish divorce between the Duke and Duchess of Argyll.[12] This case was also cited to justify the proposition: "It is a general rule of law that a third party who comes into possession of confidential information which he knows to be such, may come under a duty not to pass it to anyone else." The obligation may be quite wide:

> "Further as a general rule it is in the public interest that confidences should be respected and the encouragement of such respect may in itself constitute a sufficient ground for recognising and enforcing the obligation of confidence even where the confider can point to no specific detriment to himself."

In the *Wright* case, the *Sunday Times* newspaper sought to justify its publication of the material it knew well was confidential, on the basis that it was to be published in America. The House of Lords did not regard this as acceptable: according to the House, "[t]he fact that a primary confidant [Wright], having communicated the confidential information to a third party [*Sunday Times*] in breach of obligation, is about to reveal it similarly to someone else [*US publishers*], does not entitle that third party to do the same." Accordingly, *Times Newspapers* was held to be in breach of an obligation of confidence in publishing the information and were liable to account for the profits resulting from the breach.

5–4   The next advance was *Lord Advocate v The Scotsman Publications Ltd*.[13] In this case, another secret service agent wrote a book. *The Scotsman*, among others, wanted to print details of the book. By the time the case reached the Inner House, the issue was whether the mere fact of publication was sufficiently contrary to national interests (represented by the Crown), regardless of the nature of the actual material in the book, to be prohibited — *i.e.* the emphasis was not on anything actually said in the book. It was not surprising, therefore,

---

[12] *Duchess of Argyll v Duke of Argyll* [1967] Ch. 302.
[13] 1988 S.L.T. 490.

that interdict was refused, apparently on the basis of the lack of interest of the Crown in restraining non-prejudicial matters. However, the court was of the opinion that confidential information did not cease to be confidential merely because it had been disclosed in breach of obligation. Further, the Inner House considered that there was probably an obligation in Scots law to prevent a third party obtaining and publishing confidential information and knowing it to be so. The obligation may be based on equity, as it is in England. Nothing was said about damages. The House of Lords dismissed the Lord Advocate's appeal.[14] Nevertheless, it was made clear that if the book had contained prejudicial matter and there had been no previous publication, the result would probably have been different.

While the cases discussed involve the State, confidentiality also applies in relation to private individuals,[15] and commercial contracts often include confidentiality clauses that could provide the necessary foundation for a case against a third party.[16] The mode of acquisition raises interesting problems — often found as much in exam papers as real life.[17] An example of a "non-State" application is in *Douglas and Others v Hello! Ltd and Others*,[18] in which it was held that the wedding of two celebrities could be regarded as a commodity and protected as a trade secret. As was pointed out, treating a sacrament in this way was justified by the fact that two parties had *bid* for the rights to photograph it — and the parties getting married has offered to sell the rights — it was no ordinary wedding. Where the press took unauthorised pictures, this could be a breach of commercial confidence — not privacy. Because the press were involved, Article 10 ECHR was engaged, but as the conduct in this case was in breach of the Press Complaints Commission Code, the balance was in favour of the plaintiffs existing right under the law of confidence not being eroded by Article 10. Just as this book went to press, *Campbell v MGN Newspapers Ltd*[19] was decided and it is now clearly recognised that confidence does not require a pre-existing relationship, and that it may operate in the private sphere as protecting misuse of private information."[20]

---

[14] 1989 S.L.T. 705.

[15] Proof before answer was allowed in a case alleging solatium for breach of confidence in obtaining the pursuers medical records in a case involving not him but his mother: *Hardey v Russel & Aitken*, 2003 G.W.D. 2–50.

[16] *Waste Systems International Inc v Eurocare Environmental Services Ltd*, 1999 S.L.T. 198.

[17] G. Wei, "Surreptitious Takings of Confidential Information", 1992 L.S. 302.

[18] 2003 T.L.R. 239.

[19] Unreported, May 6, 2004. [2004] UKHL 22.

[20] para.14. See the fuller discussion below at paras 8–37 and 17–10.

There are many English cases supporting a public interest right to disclose, which could well be followed here.[21]

Passing off

5–5   This well-recognised and often utilised delict can be used to obtain an interdict or damages or both where one party has represented his goods or services as being those of another in a way calculated to deceive the public, divert custom and cause loss of business to the other. Sometimes, as we shall see, this element of calculating to deceive will easily be inferred from the circumstances. It can result in damages or a restitutionary remedy for the wrong of an account of profits.[22]

In *Haig v Forth Blending Co.*[23] the court reviewed the existing authorities and provided a useful set of propositions applicable to these cases:

(1) It is not permissible to sell goods in such a way that the public may be confused into thinking that the goods are those of the complainer.

(2) A trader must show that his goods are recognised by the public or a particular section of it and that any name, mark or get-up is associated in their minds with his goods alone.

(3) The trader must show a likelihood of confusion although he need not actually show that any particular member of the public has been confused — certainly where the remedy sought is interdict.

(4) There is no right of property in any name, mark or get-up: the essence of the delict is the defender's attempt to appropriate the pursuer's goodwill.

(5) "Get-up" includes design, labels and generally the way the thing is packaged for the public — a special design of a useful part of an article may form part of the get-up.

(6) In considering whether the public has been deceived, a member of the public is "a person of reasonable apprehension and proper eyesight."

(7) A bottle may be part of the get-up and it may be associated with a single trader.

(8) If the goods of a trader have, from a peculiar mark or get-up, become known by a particular name, the adoption by

---

[21] Clerk and Lindsell, 27–37.

[22] It has been held that a pursuer must claim either an account of profits or damages: *Treadwell's Drifters Inc. v RCL Ltd*, 1996 S.L.T. 1048 (decided in 1993).

[23] 1954 S.C. 35.

another of any mark or get-up which will cause his goods to attain the same name is actionable.

(9) An innocent manufacturer may have to answer for a dishonest retailer if the manufacturer provides a weapon for the dishonest retailer.

(10) Even if there is no intention to deceive on the part of a retailer, he may be interdicted if the public are being misled.

The Haig case was an action by a whisky company against blenders and retailers. The complainers were trying to prohibit the use of a bottle of triangular shape similar to one they had used for a long time. There was material before the court that indicated that barmen and customers were confused, thinking that the defenders' product was the complainer's "Dimple". Interdict was granted.

A more recent statement of the nature of the delict in the House of **5–6** Lords casts some doubt on the possibility of an innocent trader being held liable and tries to focus less on the appropriation of goodwill and more on the elements of loss and misrepresentation. It constitutes an attempt to find a broader principle behind the rules of passing off. In doing so, it admits of the possibility of an expansion of the rules. Lord Diplock, in *Erven Warnink v Townend*,[24] indicated that the following five elements would have to be present to support an action:

(1) a misrepresentation;[25]

(2) made by a trader in the course of a trade;

(3) to prospective customers of his or ultimate consumers of goods and services supplied by him;

(4) which is calculated to injure the business or goodwill of another trader (in the sense that this is a reasonably foreseeable consequence); and

(5) which causes actual damage to the business or goodwill of the trader by whom the action is brought, or which will probably do so.

Thus it is not even permissible to use one's own name in trade if used fraudulently or to create avoidable confusion.[26] Interdict might be available if it can be shown that one's own name has attached to some particular product.[27] It is usually permissible to use a word or

---

[24] [1979] A.C. 731.

[25] It has been held in Scotland following this authority that a mere misrepresentation is not sufficient: *Treadwell's Drifters Inc. v RCL Ltd*, 1996 S.L.T. 1048 (decided in 1993).

[26] *Baume & Co. Ltd v Moore* [1958] Ch. 907; *O'Briens v Watts*, 1987 S.L.T. 101.

[27] *Parker Knoll v Knoll International* [1962] R.P.C. 265. See Clive, "Goods by Any Other Name", 1963 S.L.T. (News) 106.

name that is part of the English language for a product and so it is essential for the complainer to show that any word has become associated with his product alone. For this reason, a trader is well advised to register any new word he or she has invented under the Trade Marks Act 1938 (as amended). If this is not done there is a danger that a concocted word may lose its distinctiveness, becoming by enthusiastic marketing a generic term for products of that kind. Browsing through the *Concise Oxford Dictionary of Current English* (9th ed.) one can find "Sellotape: transparent cellulose or plastic tape" and "Hoover: a vacuum cleaner", showing this process in action.[28]

Cases tend to turn on different issues and to an extent the principles set out in the *Forth Blending* case are not exhaustive. In deciding whether there is a likelihood of confusion, the market in which the parties operate is usually important.[29] The geography of the market may be an important factor. Thus, in the case of the *Dunlop Pneumatic Tyre Co. Ltd v Dunlop Motor Co. Ltd,*[30] although both companies had similar names, it was held that the citizens of Kilmarnock were unlikely to be confused between the pursuers, the Dunlop tyre company from England, and the defenders, a family business in Kilmarnock. In any event, the sort of work carried out by the two companies was, in the main, different. That the market sector is quite often crucial can be seen from the case of *Scottish Milk Marketing Board v Drybrough & Co. Ltd,*[31] where the pursuers, who had sold butter under the name "Scottish Pride" for some considerable time, tried to prevent the defenders from selling a lager by the

---

[28] Although it is equally interesting to note that among much erudite philological information in the introduction to the dictionary the following also appears: "This dictionary includes some words which have, or are asserted to have, proprietary status as trade marks or otherwise. Their inclusion does not imply that they have acquired for legal purposes a non-proprietary or general significance, nor any other judgement concerning their legal status. In cases where the editorial staff have some evidence that a word has proprietary status this is indicated in the entry for that word by the abbreviation propr., but no judgement concerning the legal status of such words is made or implied thereby." Both "Sellotape" and "Hoover" are so marked. See *Re Gramophone Co.'s Application* [1910] Ch. 423. Further researches reveal the position to be even more interesting. It transpires that "Proprietary terms are of more than usual concern to lexicographers since such terms are often the subjects of protracted correspondence or even threatened litigation": Burchfield, "Controversial Vocabulary in the Oxford English Dictionary" in Unlocking the English Language (Faber, 1989), p.96. His further exposition indicates that passing-off would be unlikely to be successful against a dictionary as the publisher is not trying to sell the product. It is the use of dictionaries by Trade Marks registrars and the like that gives the proprietor of a mark an interest in the publication of the word with a lower case first letter indicating generic use.

[29] J. Phillips, and A. Coleman, "Passing Off and the Common Field of Activity" (1985) 101 L.Q.R. 242.

[30] 1907 S.C. (HL) 15.

[31] 1985 S.L.T. 253.

same name. They were unsuccessful on the basis that confusion was unlikely to result. They were also unsuccessful in a slightly more subtle argument. The dairy company had been sponsoring sporting events to associate, in the public mind, their product with health. They complained that the defenders' actions would damage that advertising. This did not seem to carry much weight at the interim hearing.

Where the market area is narrow, confusion is much more likely, as where the International House of Heraldry were able to restrain the use of "International Art of Heraldry".[32] In *Dash Ltd v Philip King Tailoring*,[33] it was argued that the confusion that was said to exist in the case was only such as to amount to the possibility of confusion, whereas the *Haig* case required a likelihood of confusion. Lord McDonald, giving the opinion of the court, stated that the *Haig* case dealt with the similarity of goods rather than names. The court did, however, consider that in the case before it, if the test were likelihood, it had been met. There seems to be no reason why the principles expounded in *Haig* should not apply to names as much as get-up — the test should be the same whether a trader obtains another's sale by using a name or a get-up. "Likelihood", it is submitted, is still the better verbal formulation.[34]

The delict has widened in that the pursuer is permitted to claim in **5–7** circumstances where the defender, rather than actually pretending to sell someone's goods, pretends that his goods are in some way the same as the pursuer's or by his actions tries to appropriate exclusiveness and style. The Scottish case of *John Walker & Sons Ltd v Henry Ost & Co. Ltd*[35] supports this broader view in that the court accepted that a producer was entitled to protect his product from sales of non-Scotch whisky on the basis that there would be damage to his sales where someone tasted the inferior product and decided not to try the real thing. This case need not be restricted to mere geographic appropriation, but applies to the whole image of a product.[36] So far as whisky itself is concerned, there is a definition of the drink in European Law.[37] It has been held in *Scottish Whisky Association v Glen Kella Distillers*[38] that this regulation was intended not only to

---

[32] *International House of Heraldry v Grant*, (OH), 1992 S.L.T. 1021.

[33] 1989 S.L.T. 39.

[34] And see *John Walker & Sons v Douglas Laing & Co.*, 1993 S.L.T. 156 in which likelihood as opposed to probability was considered sufficient in breach of interdict proceedings. This case, although reported in 1993, was decided in 1976.

[35] [1970] 1 W.L.R. 917; and see *Lang Brothers v Goldwell*, 1982 S.L.T. 309

[36] See H.L. MacQueen, "Wee McGlen and the Action of Passing Off", 1982 S.L.T. (News) 225; H.L. MacQueen, "The Wee McGlen case: Representations of Scottishness — Passing off and Unfair Trading" (1983) 5 E.I.P. R. 18. See Casebook cover for the Wee McGlen bottle and generally, Q. Stewart, "The Law of Passing-Off — A Scottish Perspective" (1983) 5 E.I.P.R. 64.

[37] Regulation 1576/89 [1989] O.J. L160/1.

[38] [1997] T.L.R. 186.

protect the public, but also producers who would have title to sue for injunction for breach of the regulation. An injunction was granted where the defendants sold "white whisky". It was produced by re-distilling ordinary whisky. It had not been re-matured after distillation. It would thus constitute passing off, commencing an insidious process of erosion of the integrity and aura of true whisky. The regulation was founded upon, again in protection of Scotch Whisky in *Matthew Gloag and Son Ltd v Welsh Distillers Ltd.*[39] The defendants sold a Welsh whisky called "Swyn y mor" with a big red dragon on the bottle. It said: "Welsh whisky . . . is a spirit unique in taste and origin — a superb blend of malt and grain whiskies blended and bottled by the Welsh Whisky Co. Brecon, Wales, UK, Product of Wales, UK, Blended in the Principality for the world to enjoy." It was not in dispute that the contents were Scotch whisky. It was held that this was extended passing off on the basis of *Erven Warnick*[40] and *Bristol Conservatories Ltd v Conservatories Custom Built Ltd.*[41] It was accepted that there had been a breach of the European regulation but it was argued that only consumers had a right of action under the regulation. On the basis of *Glen Kella*[42] and an unreported case, *Scotch Whisky Association v J.D. Vintners*,[43] Laddie, J found for the Scottish Whisky Companies.

Attempts can be made to use passing off as a way of protecting intangible "rights".[44]

Harbouring employees

5–8   It is a wrong for an employer to employ a worker when he knows that the worker is already under contract to another. In *Rose Street Foundry and Engineering Company Ltd v John Lewis & Sons Ltd*,[45] the Inner House reviewed the authorities in relation to this wrong. The pursuers sued their former employee Clark and his subsequent employers, the defenders. Interestingly, the defenders complained that Clark had previously worked for them but had been induced by the pursuers to leave. When the matter came before the court, the inducement issue was not live. The Lord Justice-Clerk (Scott-Dickson) reviewed and stated the law which is accurate today albeit there do not appear to be any reported Scottish cases:

---

[39] [1998] T.L.R. 113; [1998] FSR 718.
[40] *Erven Warnick B.V. v Townend* [1979] A.C. 731.
[41] [1989] R.P.C. 455.
[42] *Scotch Whisky Association v Glen Kella Distillers* [1997] T.L.R. 186.
[43] [1998] C.L.Y. 352.
[44] See, *e.g.* P. Russell, "The Commercial Exploitation of Fictitious Names" (1980) 130 N.L.J. 256. C. Waelde, "Wet? Wet? — a little mystery unresolved", 1996 S.L.T. (News) 1.
[45] 1917 1 S.L.T. 153.

"I hold that the facts that A., knowing that B. is under a contract of service with C., takes B. into his service or continues to employ him during part of the period embraced in said contract and while C. desires implement thereof constitute 'harbouring,' and a legal wrong against the original employer".[46]

Wrongful refusal to contract

Usually it is not a delict to refuse to contract. But for a long time **5–9** it has been recognised that persons in certain occupations were compelled to contract, namely the carrier of goods and the innkeeper. An innkeeper, for example, must provide accommodation, food and drink unless: (a) no security for the bill is proffered if requested; (b) the "guest" is accompanied by an animal causing alarm to other guests; (c) the complainer is not actually on a journey; (d) the traveller refuses to pay or is of undesirable character; or (e) there is no available accommodation.[47] The rules relating to carriers are now usually considered as part of the law relating to carriage of goods.[48] It has been suggested that this delict, "should be kept apart from the economic torts as they develop".[49]

CONSPIRACY, INTERFERENCE IN CONTRACT AND INTIMIDATION

These are, strictly speaking, three separate delicts but, as the leading **5–10** modern cases often involve more than one, they may usefully be considered together. They are frequently found in cases of industrial conflict. It has to be said that these delicts are becoming ever more interrelated, so much so that some writers have begun to speak of a general delict of wrongful interference with trade, or causing loss by unlawful means.[50] They have been joined by the English legal profession. The existence of such a tort was pled and conceded in the House of Lords in *Lonrho plc v Al-Fayed*.[51] It was accepted in the House that the tort exists but that its definition is as yet uncertain. It

---

[46] *ibid.*, at 155–156, relying, *inter alia*, on *Lumley v Gye* (1853) 2 E. & B. 216 and *Dickson v Taylor*, (1816) 1 Mur 141.

[47] See *Rothfield v N.B. Ry*, 1920 S.C. 805.

[48] See Gloag and Henderson, *The Law of Scotland* (11th ed., W. Green, 2001) Chs 25, 26 and 27.

[49] H. Carty, "Intentional Violation of Economic Interests: the Limits of Common Law Liability" (1988) 104 L.Q.R. 242 at 284. H. Carty, *An analysis of the Economic Torts* (OUP, 2001).

[50] See generally, J. Adams, "Is There a Tort of Unfair Competition?" 1985 J.B.L. 26; H. Carty, "Intentional Violation of Economic Interests: the Limits of Common Law Liability" (1988) 104 L.Q.R. 242. P. Sales, and D. Stilitz, "Intentional Infliction of harm by Unlawful Means" (1999) 11 L.Q.R. 411. J. Holyoak and F. Mazzocchetti, "The Legal Protection of Economic Interests", (1993) 1 Tort L.R. 185.

[51] [1991] 3 W.L.R. 188.

was briefly considered in a Scottish case which appeared to recognise the wider tort: *Shell UK Ltd v McGillivray*.[52] This idea of a general wrong and special wrongs is not difficult if the relationship is clear. At this stage of development, in England, it is difficult. Weir says:

> "I believe that the tort of inducing a breach of contract has now been absorbed into the general tort of causing harm by unlawful means. To the extent it has recently developed distinctive rules, because such absorption has been ignored, this development should promptly be put into reverse."[53]

Sales and Stilitz argue for the recognition of a general head of liability, which would go wider than mere economic cases and set up a complimentary principle to that of negligence: the intentional infliction of harm by unlawful means.[54] If there is to be any juridical consistency, then at the very least one might agree with Laddie, J. that what is unlawful means for one of these wrongs, should also be unlawful means for the others.[55]

Each of them should be viewed against the background that the law in England, and probably the law of Scotland, generally prefers to leave people free to participate in a competitive free market. Thus, in *Mogul Steamship Co. Ltd v McGregor, Gow & Co.*[56] it was held not to be actionable for the defendants to put the plaintiffs out of business by undercutting their competitors, offering rebates to those exclusively dealing with them and restricting their own agents from dealing with competitors. Shortly afterwards, in *Allen v Flood*,[57] a union official was held not to be liable for telling his employers that if certain workers were not dismissed, the union workers would not work. The workers were employed on a daily basis and were under no obligation to sign on for work the next day.

On the other hand, the law of Scotland recognises a doctrine, from the civil law of *aemulationem vicini*,[58] which would generally suggest that the malicious infliction of harm would be actionable, even if the conduct complained of is, on the face of it, lawful. A similar line has been taken in the United States.[59] The European

---

[52] 1991 S.L.T. 667.

[53] T. Weir, *Economic Torts* (1997), p.28.

[54] P. Sales and D. Stilitz, "Intentional Infliction of harm by Unlawful Means," (1999) 115 L.Q.R. 411.

[55] *Michaels v Taylor Woodrow Development Ltd* [2001] Ch. 493.

[56] [1892] A.C. 25.

[57] [1898] A.C. 1. "Perhaps the most important (case) in the whole of the law of torts": R. Heuston, "Judicial Prosopography" (1986) 102 L.Q.R. 90 at 97.

[58] See para.2.20 and see L.J. Bowen in *Mogul Steamship*, cited above. D.E.L. Johnston, "Owners and Neighbours: From Rome to Scotland" in The Civil Law Tradition in Scotland (Evans-Jones ed., Stair Soc. Sup. 2, 1995).

[59] *Tuttle v Buck* (1909) 119 N.W. 946. But see the comments on the case in Weir, *Economic Torts* (Oxford, 1997), pp.72–74.

Court of Justice has held that not all price competition can be regarded as legitimate and has penalised predatory pricing.[60]

The following interrelated delicts should, therefore, be seen as exceptions to a general approach that permits harm to others as a result of the lawful conduct of business.

Conspiracy

There are two forms of this wrong of combination: (1) conspiracy **5–11** to injure by lawful means, in which the predominant purpose must be to injure the plaintiff and; (2) conspiracy to injure by unlawful means,[61] which does not require a predominant purpose to injure.[62]

The most significant Scottish case is *Crofter Hand Woven Harris Tweed Co. Ltd v Veitch*,[63] a decision of the House of Lords that is now considered to be the leading authority in this area in both Scotland and England. The facts are quite complicated. The Crofter Company marketed cloth woven by the Isle of Lewis crofters using yarn imported from the mainland. Yarn was also spun on the island itself. The island spinners were members of the TGWU. The union tried to get a higher rate of pay for its members who spun yarn on the island. The island employers said they could not afford to pay their members more money; the TGWU ordered its members not to handle the yarn of the mainland producers. The House of Lords held that this conduct was not actionable, but a number of propositions can be taken from it:

(1) Conspiracy of one variety consists in the agreement of two or more to do an unlawful act or to do a lawful act by unlawful means so long as the acts are actually carried out in pursuance of the conspiracy to the damage of the pursuer.

---

[60] *AKZO Chemie B.V. v Commission of the European Communities* (C 62/86), [1991] T.L.R. 432.

[61] The subject of agonising jurisprudence in the anglo-american world (see Clerk and Lindsell Ch.24) but which has not seriously troubled the Scots courts. Issues arise for example as to whether a simple breach of a statutory provision is enough or whether it is necessary to consider each provision in its own context. That may well be because the major protagonists — trades unions, the Government and employers take a UK wide view and take advice based on mainly English decisions to avoid reaching the courts at all.

[62] See generally *Kuwait Oil Tanker Co. SAK and Another v Al Bader and others*, [2002] 2 All E.R. (Comm) 271.

[63] 1942 S.C. (HL) 1. For a review of the case and conspiracy generally see J.M. Thomson, "An Island Legacy — the Delict of Conspiracy" in Comparative and Historical Essays in Scots Law (Carey Miller & Mayers, eds, Butterworths, 1992), p.137.

(2) Conspiracy of the other variety consists in a "conspiracy to injure" with a predominant purpose to injure where injury is actually caused even where there are no unlawful means or unlawful acts. This differs from a "set of acts dictated by business interests" which is not actionable.

(3) There is nothing unlawful in giving a warning or intimation that if the party addressed pursues a certain course of conduct, others may act in a manner he will not like, so long as nothing unlawful is threatened or done.

(4) It is possible for something that would not be actionable if done by one person to be actionable if he conspires to do it with another. This may be anomalous, but it is said to be firmly entrenched in the law.

(5) It is not conspiracy (absent unlawful means) if the predominant motive is not unlawful. It was this last proposition which proved decisive in the Crofter case: the union's predominant motive was to advance the members' interests.

A distinction has been made between cases where the conspiracy is to use unlawful means which, if harm results, will be actionable regardless of motive, and "simple" cases, where, as in *Crofter*, there are no unlawful means and where only the absence of a legitimate predominant motive will make conspiracy to do something not in itself illegal, actionable.[64]

5–12 The law in England continues to grow. In *Kuwait Oil Tanker Co. SAK v Al Bade*,[65] it was held that conspiracy to injure by unlawful means was a tort. The agreement needed to be proved as did the unlawful means. Each unlawful act had to be proved as being carried out pursuant to the conspiracy. The state of the law at this time was stated to be that there are two distinct torts: (1) conspiracy to injure by lawful means, in which the predominant purpose must be to injure the plaintiff and; (2) conspiracy to injure by unlawful means, which did not require a predominant purpose to injure. In this case, it was argued that where the unlawful means were themselves tortious, by the doctrine in English law of merger, the conspiracy action could not stand. That argument was rejected. The facts related to fraudulent schemes to obtain money.

---

[64] A speech by Lord Diplock was interpreted in the Court of Appeal as meaning that a justifiable predominant purpose would excuse even an unlawful means conspiracy (*Lonrho v Shell Petroleum Co. Ltd (No. 2)* [1982] A.C. 173; see also *Metall and Rohstoff A.G. v Donaldson Lufkin and Jenrette Inc.* [1990] Q.B. 391). This error was set right by the House of Lords, the leading speech being by Lord Bridge who had sat with Lord Diplock on the Appellate Committee in the *Lonrho v Shell* case: *Lonhro Ltd v Al-Fayed* [1991] 3 W.L.R. 188.

[65] [2000] 2 All E.R. (Comm) 271.

Another development that may make simple cases less common is Lord Diplock's view that breach of the competition provisions of the EEC Treaties amounts to a breach of duty, which is actionable. If so it would be actionable for an individual or group of individuals to unduly restrict competition within the common market or to abuse a dominant position within the common market.[66] The Competition Act in the United Kingdom is modelled on the European Union Treaty provisions and may in time make such conspiracy cases even less common.[67] In an important decision, *Fotheringham & Son v The British Limousin Cattle Society Ltd*[68] a proof before answer was allowed against an attack on the competency as well as the relevancy of the case, it is submitted correctly, in a case alleging wrongful competition in the sense of being against the Competition Act. There are many ways of looking at this. It could be a statute that requires reparation for its enforcement, it could be the act creates a business interest that deserves protection by reparation or it could be considered to inconsistent to allow a case or reparation based on the European progenitor of our act and not upon an Act of our own saying largely the same thing. A reclaiming motion was refused.[69]

Inducing breach of contract

It is an actionable wrong knowingly to induce a person to break his **5–13** lawful, valid and subsisting contract with another. This was apparent from some dicta in *Crofter*, but was applied in the case of *British Motor Trade Association v Gray*[70]:

> "After the second world war there was a shortage of motor vehicles. The BMTA was formed, consisting of manufacturers and their distributors. They developed a scheme whereby every purchaser of a new car signed an agreement undertaking not to resell the car within a specified period. It was alleged that the respondent had purchased such vehicles within the specified period knowing full well that a covenant had been executed, *i.e.* he had induced the original purchaser of the car to break his covenant with BMTA."

The court allowed the case to proceed: "if damage results, it is an actionable wrong for a third party knowingly and unjustifiably to induce a breach of a lawful contract." Lord President Cooper said that although such conduct had never been stated as a delict in the

---

[66] *Garden Cottage Foods v Milk Marketing Board* [1984] A.C. 130.
[67] See K.G. Middleton, "Reform of UK Competition Law", 1998 S.L.T. (News) 47.
[68] 2002 G.W.D. 26–867.
[69] Unreported, April 8, 2004.
[70] 1951 S.C. 586.

law of Scotland, that was just a coincidence. Cases where people were held liable for enticing employees away from their employers[71] were just examples of this broader principle. In any event, it was assumed that there was such a delict in *Crofter.*

It is clearly established that the defender must be aware that there is a valid contract.[72] That said, the courts will judge the defender by the standard of knowledge he ought to have had: thus a defender cannot say that he was unaware that the men working in a factory were under a contract with the factory owner simply because the specific contracts are not known to him.[73] On the other hand, in the Outer House it has been held that there had to be knowledge on the part of the defender of the existence of the contract and that recklessness or turning a blind eye was not sufficient unless it was tantamount to intention.[74] There must be loss before there can be liability, but this will easily be inferred. It is, as in cases of conspiracy, a defence to have a legitimate interest in inducing the breach and this is illustrated by the case of *Findlay v Blaylock,*[75] where a woman failed in an action against the father of the man to whom she had been engaged. At the time the case was decided, engagement was a legal contract, breach of which would sound in damages. The father was held entitled as the curator of his minor son to look after his interest by persuading the son to break off the engagement with the pursuer, whom he considered to be unsuitable. In *Akram v Commission for Racial Equality,*[76] a proof before answer was allowed where it was alleged that the pursuer had been told to resign or be dismissed as a result of a proposal agreed between the defenders, the pursuer's employer and the regional and district councils. Distinguishing *Findlay v Blaylock,*[77] it was considered that the defenders had to aver and prove justification.

In *Barratt International Resorts Ltd v Barratt Owners Group,*[78] the defenders remained contractually tied to the pursuers by management contracts. The defenders were unhappy at the pursuers performance and complained in many different ways. The pursuers *inter alia* sought interdict against the defenders interfering with the committees established under the management contracts. They failed against a background of some human rights discussion and his Lordships robust view of language.

---

[71] See, for example, *Belmont Laundry Co. Ltd v Aberdeen Steam Laundry Co. Ltd* (1898) 1 F. 45.
[72] *British Homophone v Kunz* [1935] All E.R. 627.
[73] See *Stratford v Lindley* [1964] 3 All E.R. 102.
[74] *Rossleigh Ltd v Leader Cars Ltd,* 1987 S.L.T. 355 at 360, *per* Lord Mayfield.
[75] 1937 S.C. 21.
[76] 1994 G.W.D. 22–1372.
[77] 1937 S.C. 21.
[78] 2003 G.W.D. 19.

In the English case of *D.C. Thomson v Deakin*,[79] three ways of **5–14** committing the delict were set out: (1) direct persuasion, which covers cases such as the defender enticing the pursuer's contracting partner[80]; (2) direct intervention by striking at the other contracting partner (for example, if the defender imprisoned the pursuer's contracting partner) — it is not clear whether the interference need be unlawful to be actionable because the interference in this case is direct[81]; (3) indirect intervention, in the sense that it is not the other contracting partner who is interfered with directly, will be actionable where loss is caused if, but only if, the means used are unlawful. This could be where the defender destroys the pursuer's contracting partner's machinery. "Unlawful means" for the purposes of this delict may be conduct in breach of the criminal law, a statutory provision, or indeed a breach of some other contract. This area of liability may be extending to unlawful interference in contract, whether or not there is a breach. These cases have been adopted and approved since *Lonrho v Fayed*.[82] This "interference with contract" is robustly critiqued by Weir: "The law should address the wrong of a defender having another person wrong the pursuer rather than asking if the pursuer's right to contractual services has been interfered with."[83] He quotes Lord Bingham dealing with the same distinction pithily: "In concentrating on the right ... the judge did take his eye off the wrong."[84] Weir considers *Torquay* as wrongly decided, submitting there was liability for causing harm through unlawful means — the procuring of breach by the drivers.[85]

The freedom to trade can conflict with other freedoms. In *Middlebrook Mushrooms Ltd v Transport and General Workers Union*[86] it was held that handing out leaflets urging potential customers not to buy the plaintiffs' mushrooms was not tortious. It was not direct interference because the leaflets were addressed to the customers not to the supermarket managers. It would require unlawful means to make the conduct actionable. These issues of course were similar to those discussed in *Barratt International Resorts Ltd v Barratt Owners Group*,[87] which latter had the added factor of human rights issues.

---

[79] [1952] 2 All E.R. 361.
[80] Often described in England by reference to the first major case on the subject: *Lumley v Gye* (1853) 2 E. & B. 216.
[81] See *Stratford v Lindley* [1964] 3 All E.R. 102.
[82] [1991] 3 W.L.R. 188.
[83] T. Weir, *Economic Torts*, p.29.
[84] *ibid.*, at p.30, citing *Law Debenture Trust Corp. v Ural Caspian Oil Corp.* [1995] 1 All E.R. 157.
[85] *ibid.*, at p.37.
[86] [1993] T.L.R. 11. Weir agrees with this decision: Economic Torts, p.42.
[87] 2003 G.W.D. 19.

Intimidation

5–15   In *Rookes v Barnard*,[88] the plaintiff was a skilled draftsman working in a closed shop for BOAC. He left his union and eventually his workmates intimated that if he was not removed in three days they would withdraw their own labour. In view of this and the possibility that other workers would come out in sympathy, BOAC suspended and then dismissed Mr Rookes. As between BOAC and Rookes, the dismissal was lawful. The jury found that a conspiracy existed, that the defendants were a party to it and that it had caused his dismissal. Because there was a "no strike" agreement the threat to withdraw their labour was a threat by the employees to breach their contracts with BOAC. It was held in the House of Lords that the threat to breach their contracts amounted to intimidation and that Rookes could sue his workmates for the loss of his job. Intimidation included not just threats to commit a tort, but also threats to breach a contract. It is worth noting that the union was protected from liability for strikes that broke contracts in pursuance of a trade dispute (under the Trade Disputes Act 1906), but were not given immunity to intimidate. The effect of *Rookes* was altered by the Trade Disputes Act 1965, which gave immunity for one form of intimidation — the threatening to procure a breach of contract.

Rookes is highly persuasive authority for a delict of intimidation. Stair himself considered it a delict following the Roman law:

> "Extortion signifies the act of force, or other means of fear, whereby a person is compelled to do that which of their proper inclination they would not have done. It doth also imply the obligation of the injurer to the injured, to repair his loss and damage by such acts."[89]

It has to be said, though, that he may not have had in mind the threat to commit a breach of contract.[90]

The "tort of intimidation" was expressly relied on in *Micosta S.A. v Shetland Islands Council*.[91] It was alleged that a public body, the harbour authority, wrongfully threatened terminal operators and the charterers with statutory powers should they refuse to cancel a charterparty. The threat worked — the charterers cancelled and caused loss to the pursuers. (They did not, or more probably could not, complain of the breach by the charterers in view of the terms of the charter-party). It does appear that Lord Ross accepted Professor Walker's view that intimidation was actionable. However, the threat

---

[88] [1964] A.C. 1129.
[89] Stair, I, ix, 8.
[90] See J.T. Cameron, "Intimidation and the Right to Strike", 1964 S.L.T. (News) 81.
[91] 1986 S.L.T. 193.

had to delictual in itself and in this case there had been good faith and use of the statutory powers would have been perfectly lawful.[92]

Rookes is an example of what is called three-party intimidation: **5–16** A threatens B in order to hurt C. There is no clear authority in Scotland, other than the statement by Stair above, and some dicta in *Micosta* (above) for the existence of two-party intimidation, *i.e.* where A threatens B causing him loss. While it seems reasonable where the intimidation is criminal or delictual, to permit a delictual remedy where the threat is to break a contract would have potentially profound effects upon the law of contract. Weir[93] argues that such behaviour does constitute actionable intimidation (standing that often there will be a remedy for the breach of the contract itself), whereas Wedderburn[94] considers that this upsets the object of the law. Two-party intimidation now seems to be established in England.[95]

Finally, if the intimidation is to make someone *enter* a contract, it may be the case that the Scottish courts would uphold the concept of economic duress as vitiating the contract and permitting of restitution.[96]

---

[92] *ibid.* at 199–200.
[93] [1964] C.L.J. 225.
[94] (1964) 27 M.L.R. 257.
[95] Clerk and Lindsell, 24–85.
[96] See A. Thomson, "Economic Duress," 1985 S.L.T. (News) 85, E. McKendrick, "Economic Duress — A Reply," 1985 S.L.T. (News) 277, R. Bigwood, "Economic Duress by (Threatened) Breach of Contract," (2001) 117 L.Q.R. 376.

CHAPTER 6

ABUSE OF PROCESS

6–1 Abuse of process is a rarely encountered wrong for obvious reasons — solicitors, advocates, sheriff officers, messengers at arms and prosecutors are educated, trained and ethical. Most cases that arise are of wrongful diligence where it is said someone has tried to enforce a decree against the wrong person or against the "right" person for the wrong debt.

Civil litigation

6–2 In civil litigation, the only penalty for failure in an action is generally an award of expenses as taxed.[1] Generally, a party having title and interest to oppose can oppose any proceedings he wishes subject only to an award of expenses being made against him.[2] In civil cases, two early cases suggest that clear evidence of malice and want of probable cause is required.[3] Using process moderately and in good faith results in no liability and there must be an averment of malice and want of probable cause.[4] The basic rule applies:

> "Where a person acts in the exercise of a legal right and in the ordinary use of legal forms of procedure, and where it is said that he has abused that right, the law holds that malice or an intention to injure must be proved, and also that it must be shewn that he had no probable cause for what he did."[5]

In relation to the use of diligence (enforcement), the creditor is always liable even although he has employed independent contractors.[6] No one is liable for enforcing an *ex facie* regular decree.[7]

---

[1] *Kennedy v Police Commissioners of Fort William* (1877) 5 R. 302 *per* Lord Gifford at 307: "The costs of suit are the damages for bringing a groundless claim."

[2] *Gordon v Royal Bank* (1826) 5 S. 164; (1846) *Walker v Gemmill* 8 D. 838.

[3] *Somerville v Thomson*, May 19, 1815, F.C.; 6 Pat. App. 393; *Cleland v Lawrie* (1848) 10 D. 1372.

[4] *per* Lord President Inglis in *Kinnes v Adam* (1882) 9 R. 698 at 702. This claim was founded on a sequestration which had been recalled on purely technical grounds.

[5] *Henning v Hewetson* (1852) 14 D. 487, *per* Lord Justice-Clerk Hope at 488.

[6] *Anderson v Ormiston and Lorain* (1750) Mor. 13949.

[7] *Aitken v Finlay* (1837) 15 S. 683.

An incompetent warrant does not protect the creditor.[8] It is wrongful to do diligence when it has been agreed to delay such.[9] If the creditor has exaggerated the sum, he and neither the agent nor the messenger is liable.[10]

It is accepted that there is a distinction to be made between diligence done as of right, in which malice and want of probable cause must be shown and other cases, such as interdict where the creditor requires to make a representation to the court to obtain the order.

Crime

In criminal matters it has long been settled that a public prosecutor **6–3** can only be liable on proof of malice and want of probable cause. It is a prerequisite that the pursuer has been acquitted of the charge or the charge has been abandoned against him.[11] It is not possible by seeking reparation to review a decision of the High Court of Justiciary.[12]

---

[8] *Bell v Gunn* (1859) 21 D. 1008; *Ormiston v Redpath Brown & Co.* (1866) 4 M. 488. A case of wrongful diligence was dismissed as recently as 2002 where the diligence was done on the basis of a valid decree from a competent court: *Brougham v Royal Bank of Scotland*, 2002 G.W.D. 449.

[9] *Cameron v Mortimer* (1872) 10 M. 817.

[10] *Henderson v Rollo* (1871) 10 M. 104.

[11] The pursuer in *Downie v Chief Constable, Strathclyde Police*, 1998 S.L.T. 8 had been acquitted of charges of charges of breach of the peace and a contravention of s.41(1) of the Police (Scotland) Act 1967. It was admitted this was a malicious prosecution and damages awarded at £1500 under this head.

[12] *Moore v Secretary of State for Scotland*, 1985 S.L.T. 38.

CHAPTER 7

MISFEASANCE IN OFFICE

7–1 Public officers may be a category of person who can be held liable for abuse of power — notwithstanding the law of negligence.[1] The difficulty in establishing negligence liability against public authorities[2] makes this approach of interest to pursuers.

Scotland now has a very well developed system of judicial review. Within that system damages or reparation may be claimed. It remains of course that judicial review is only a procedure and it is still possible to ask what is the substantive right. Often it may well be abuse of power or misfeasance in public office and these are the wrongs for which reparation may be ordered.[3]

There was an early discussion, based on Professor Walker's work, in a case argued before Lord Ross:

"The expression 'a tort which is called misfeasance in public office' sounds strange to Scottish ears. However, the question which arises is whether some equivalent would be recognised by the law of Scotland . . . The validity of a claim such as that made by the present pursuers does not depend upon there being any precise Scottish authority. There is no such thing as an exhaustive list of named delicts in the law of Scotland. If the conduct complained of appears to be wrongful, the law of Scotland will afford a remedy even if there has not been any previous instance of a remedy being given in similar circumstances. As Professor Walker puts it at p.9: 'The decision to recognise a particular interest, and consequently to grant a remedy for its infringement, is a question of social policy, and the list recognised has grown over the years. In considering whether or not to recognise particular interests the courts have had regard to such factors as the moral obliquity of the defenders' conduct, the capacity of the parties to bear the loss,

---

[1] C.T. Reid, "Damages for Deliberate Abuse of Power" 1988 S.L.T. (News) 121. The future of these heads of liability will be charted in Stewart, *Reparation: Liability for Delict.*

[2] See Ch.12.

[3] See the discussions in *Micosta S.A. v Shetland Islands Council*, 1986 S.L.T. 193 and *Shetland Line (1984) Ltd v Secretary of State for Scotland*, 1996 S.L.T. 653.

and the consistency of recognition with what is conceived to be public policy.' In my opinion, deliberate misuse of statutory powers by a public body would be actionable under the law of Scotland at the instance of a third party who has suffered loss and damage in consequence of the misuse of statutory powers, provided that there was proof of malice or proof that the action had been taken by the public authority in the full knowledge that it did not possess the power which it purported to exercise. I have reached this conclusion on a consideration of the English authorities referred to above and having regard to the general principles applicable under the law of Scotland to abuse of legal process which are referred to by Professor Walker in Ch.24 of his work on Delict."[4]

Recent developments have been in the Commonwealth and in England. A public officer may be liable for loss injury and damage resulting from action known to be unlawful and likely to cause harm.[5] The claim can succeed on recklessness — conduct in the face of a serious risk of loss due to an act or omission that was known to be unlawful but which was deliberately disregarded — it not essential to prove spite, ill-will or specific intent to injure.[6] It may be raised against a public authority or a public officer. In England, the class of public officers is wide and can in some circumstances include police officers. Again in England, there is the suggestion that a "police" case could circumvent the probable cause requirement there.[7] It might also assist in circumventing some judicial protection of social work departments and the like.[8] Bad faith is of the essence.

7–2

---

[4] *Micosta S.A. v Shetland Islands Council*, 1986 S.L.T. 193 at198.

[5] *Dunlop v Woollahra Municipal Council* [1982] A.C. 158; *Racz v Home Office* [1994] A.C. 158.

[6] *Three Rivers DC v Bank of England (No.3)* [2003] 2 A.C. 1, *Akenzua v Secretary of State for the Home Department*, [2003] 1 W.L.R. 741.

[7] Clerk and Lindsell, 17–138.

[8] Clerk and Lindsell, 17–141.

CHAPTER 8

DEFAMATION AND RELATED ACTIONS

Introduction

8–1   Actions for "verbal injuries" and "slander" have been permitted in the Scottish courts for a very long time. Indeed, there is a record of a case of slander coming before the Court of Session as early as 1542.[1] That, however, was exceptional, for at that time the Church courts had jurisdiction in such matters. Stair considered fame, reputation and honour to be among the interests that the law protects and described them, somewhat enigmatically, as being "in some way reparable".[2] The last centuries have seen a considerable English influence. Unfortunately, our law of verbal injuries is not clear. One reason is that this is not simply an application of the *lex Aquilia*, but there was an influence from the Roman *actio injuriarum* for insult, affront or (as it is sometimes known) *contumelia*. The history of the subject — that it was dealt with by Church courts — makes it likely that it has become something of a mixture of doctrines. A recent critical history will help anyone trying to discover why the law appears so very "organic".[3] Because legal aid is not available[4] for such actions, it is usually only seen in disputes between public figures and celebrities from the entertainment industry against newspapers and broadcasting organisations — there are accordingly few opportunities for the law to be tested and restated. The Human Rights Act will have some effect over the coming years and its influence has already been felt. It may be that the need to make this area of the law human rights compliant could bring about a useful complete overhaul.

By far the most serious problem is the identification of different wrongs within the overall rubric. Professors Walker and T.B. Smith alerted the community to these problems. Professor Norrie attempted a more fundamental partial deconstruction.[5] Professor Blackie has

---

[1] Stair Society, Vol. 20, "Delict", p.268.

[2] I, ix, 4.

[3] *Blackie, HPLS II*, 633.

[4] In one English case an action was raised on the basis of malicious falsehood which did attract legal aid: *Joyce v Sengupta* [1992] T.L.R. 453.

[5] K. Norrie, "Hurts to Character, Honour and Reputation: a Reappraisal", 1985 J.R. 163.

succeeded in explaining why so many terms have such fluid meanings. Hardly any terms have been stable throughout history making older cases very difficult to place. For the purpose of this basic exposition, the structure is essentially based on that said to be settled in Scots law set out by Lord Wheatley in *Barratt International Resorts Ltd v Barratt Owners Group*.[6] Students, however, should not fail to be wary of the warnings in the aforementioned writings when confronted with any case outside the core of meaning:

> "The term 'verbal injury' is therefore distinct from defamation, which is the remedy available to someone whose personal reputation has been injured by the expression of written or verbal falsehoods. It is also distinct from convicium which is concerned with the hurt to an individual's feelings and public reputation, by being brought into public hatred, contempt and ridicule. Further, there are various types of slanders, recognised principally in the English authorities, but which are of no concern in the present case. Different considerations clearly apply to these various kinds of action."[7]

That gives us defamation, *convicium*, Scottish verbal injury and **8–2** English slanders (malicious falsehoods). The aspirant wrong of infringement of privacy is considered here being often a wronging by words or pictures, but also because the human right to privacy is engaged in many discussions of verbal injury. Lord Wheatley explained "verbal injury":

> "The ingredients of such an action are that false statements, either written or verbal, must be maliciously communicated to third parties, which are calculated or likely to produce, and which in fact do produce, actual damage to the pursuers' business interests."[8]

That is a workable framework, but there is real difficulty in outside of "core" defamation and "core" "false-malicious-business harming". Some cases involving public hatred do fall within *convicium*, but some could and have been said to fall within the verbal injury category. (Verbal injury can be used as the name for this whole branch of the subject as much as a division of it — here it is used as a branch of the subject.) It is a workable arrangement because most activity is around defamation and the others are less often encountered. It also sets up a situation where if *convicium* does not exist —

[6] 2003 G.W.D. 19.
[7] Transcript para.25.
[8] Transcript para.26.

the cases can go into "verbal injury" as can the "English" slander
—malicious falsehood cases. That would be extremely "neat".
Where Lord Wheatley's verbal injury excludes non business cases,
then that requires the expansion of *convicium* to include the non-
business hatred cases, whereas if such cases were allowed in "verbal
injury", there would be little left in *convicium*. Professor Blackie
convincingly demonstrates that *Paterson v Welch* is a business case
and that being critical to the *Barratt* divisions, in this book, *Paterson*
goes into "verbal injury" even though it is arguably in a *convicium*
line.

DEFAMATION

8–3   To support an action of defamation there needs to have been
communication of a defamtory imputation of and concerning the
pursuer. It is a powerful restraint on free speech because if the
statement falls within the scope of defamatory remarks then there is
a *prima facie* case that the defender must escape. So the delict creates
an atmosphere of restraint and a need for caution. That said, free
speech is then protected by the considerable range of defences — the
most prominent in the balancing exercise being *veritas*, that the
statement was in fact substantially true. Privilege and qualified
privilege allow for the free exchange of information in certain
circumstances.

Communication

8–4   The statement must have been communicated to someone. In
Scotland, it is sufficient that the statement has been communicated to
the pursuer alone, as in the case of *Ramsay v Maclay*.[9] A former debt
collector sued because his former associates wrote asking why he
had not accounted for some money he had collected. The letter said
there would be serious consequences and that the matter would be
reported. The court agreed the case could proceed even though the
letter had been seen only by the pursuer. *Gall v Slessar*[10] was a
straightforward case of a letter being written by one man to another
that was held actionable. The damages, £30 in those times, were
intended not to be a large sum but not a nominal sum either.[11] The
methods or means of communication are various. For example, a
wax effigy has been held sufficient means of communication,[12] as has

---

[9] (1890) 18 R. 130.
[10] 1907 S.C. 708.
[11] *ibid., per* Lord Low at 715.
[12] *Monson v Tussauds* [1894] 1 Q.B. 671.

a cinema film.[13] Most cases turn on spoken or written communication. In England, this distinction is technically important, spoken defamation being slander and written defamations being libels. Anyone who transmits a defamation is liable for it.[14] For convenience, in this book the term "statement" is used to cover all communications.

Of and concerning the pursuer

It is essential that the defamatory statement is of and concerning **8–5** the pursuer. This is in opposition to humanity in general and a group of individuals in particular. *Browne v D.C. Thomson & Co Ltd*[15] was an action for slander by the Roman Catholic Bishop of Cloyne, Ireland and other individuals against publishers of the *Dundee Courier* in relation to an article that stated that "the Roman Catholic religious authorities" in Queenstown, County Cork, had instructed that all Protestant shop assistants were to be dismissed and further that any Roman Catholic shopkeeper who refused to comply had been ruined. *Hulton v Jones*[16] was followed, the Lord President (Dunedin) deciding that it was for the jury to decide whether the pursuers were the persons understood to be referred to as "the Roman Catholic religious authorities". That is that it had to be shown that these pursuers were themselves damnified by these words not merely as members of a group itself damnified — a fine distinction. In *Caldwell v Monro*,[17] the defender had not identified any particular person with the alleged defamatory remark; he said a letter was a forgery. It took some tortuous averments to make that allegation appear by a process of deduction to be that to the audience in question only the pursuer could be the target.

Falsity

The statement complained of must be a false statement. The law in **8–6** this area is intimately connected with procedural issues. If the statement is defamatory, it is assumed to be untrue and the defender must prove that it is true, if necessary by putting a counter-issue to a jury. In effect, if the defender does not positively prove the truth of the statement, his defence will fail even if the pursuer fails to prove it was false. For that reason the matter is better examined from the

---

[13] *Youssoupoff v MGM* (1934) T.L.R. 581.
[14] *Hayforth v Forrester-Paton*, 1927 S.C. 74.
[15] 1912 1 S.L.T. 123.
[16] [1910] A.C. 20; see above.
[17] (1872) 10 M. 717.

defender's point of view and so is dealt with under the defence of *veritas* (truth),[18] known in England as "justification".

Intention

8–7 Students, faced with the largest part of their course being given over to negligence, may be concerned as to where lack of care comes in. In principle, it does not. From the point of view of a person defamed, it is irrelevant whether or not the maker intended to make the statement because the damage is done. From the point of view of the maker, there is a considerable difference: there are very strict controls over liability for negligently caused harm and especially so over negligently caused economic loss. The difficult case is defamation where malice is presumed. The law in Scotland is that defamation can be committed accidentally, that is without meaning to injure the pursuer. There is old authority in support of that.[19] The recent authority is equally clear and was directly influenced by the leading English case. In *Wragg v D.C. Thomson & Co. Ltd*,[20] the Lord President said that in view of the then recent decision of the House of Lords in the English case of *Jones v Hulton & Co.*,[21] the Court was not prepared to withhold an issue. In the Scottish case, *Wragg*, the facts were that the defender newspaper proprietors published a report stating "George Reeves shoots wife twice then ends his own life". That the report did not refer to the pursuer is vouched for the fact that he raised the action for slander against the paper. Mr Wragg was a music hall artiste and comedian, known professionally as George Reeves. The article was "lifted" from an American paper and the defence was that it was clear it did not apply and that there was no intention to refer to the pursuer. The Lord Ordinary allowed the issue to proceed without need for proof of intention.[22] However, as will be seen below, there is a defence of sorts for unintentional defamation as a result of the Defamation Act 1996.[23]

---

[18] See para.8–17.
[19] *Findlay v Ruddiman* (1763) Mor. 3436.
[20] 1909 2 S.L.T. 315 and 409. See also *McLean v Bernstein and Others* (1900) 8 S.L.T. 42 concerning an action of slander against the first defender who caused an advertisement to be published in the *Daily Record*. The proprietors were also called as additional defenders and they argued at debate that the action was irrelevant as laid against them. They argued that they could only be liable if the advertisement was plainly libellous or such as to put a publisher on his guard. The pursuer was not mentioned by name in it. It was held that the action was relevant against them although the Lord Ordinary (Stormonth Darling) made it clear that when the matter went to the jury the case would be considered differently in relation to each defender.
[21] [1909] 2 K.B. 444, aff. (HL) December 6,1909.
[22] *Wragg v D.C. Thomson & Co.*, at 316–317.
[23] See para.8–31.

The statement must be defamatory

The distinction between fact and law here is important.[24] Whether **8–8** words are reasonably capable of being defamatory is a question of law; it is then a matter of fact (perhaps for a jury to determine) whether in all the circumstances the statement is actually defamatory. That said, there is no strict legal definition of what is or is not defamatory. A phrase used in the English law conveys the idea inherent in many of the cases: the statement can be defamatory if it tends to lower the plaintiff in the estimation of right-thinking members of society generally. That said, there are other cases — the "shunning" cases where it can be defamatory to describe a person wrongly as within a class that most people — uncharitably, uncaringly and ignobly perhaps — would shun, *e.g.* the leper or the unconvicted paedophile. The example of the informer is a good example. On the face of it, right-thinking people might think an informer a good person, one who helps with the administration of justice. On the other hand, it is an unpleasant way of earning a living involving deception. It has been held that to call a person an informer is defamatory. In *Kennedy v Allan*,[25] the Inner House held an allegation relevant that the defender circulated a letter from the stamp office penalising him for having granted an unstamped receipt to the pursuer and his colleagues on the Stock Exchange. Members of the Stock Exchange dealt in unstamped documents. In *Graham v Roy*,[26] the allegation was that the defender had informed on the pursuer to the exciseman. It was expressly argued that this could not be defamatory, an informer being a legal officer, and it could not be defamatory to say that a person gave information to repress an illegal act like smuggling. Lord Fullerton said: "It may be legitimate to give information, but an informer is by no means a popular character."[27]

The Lord President focused on what is perhaps a more important point — the pursuer alleged that the defender had suggested the informing was done for reward.[28] In *Wim v Quillan*[29] it was held that to call a man an informer was derogatory where the sting was that the pursuer, an Irishman, had given evidence to the Crown. These cases raise the tension between right-thinking and shunning. In an Irish case, an allegation that a man had denounced the Fenian Conspirators was held not to be defamatory.[30]

---

[24] Not least because defamation cases may still be heard by a jury, unless special cause is shown: see *Shanks v BBC*, 1991 G.W.D. 27–1641; *McCabe v News Group Newspapers Ltd*, 1992 S.L.T. 707.

[25] (1848) 10 D. 1293.

[26] (1851) 13 D. 634.

[27] *ibid.,* at 636.

[28] *ibid.*

[29] (1899) 2 F. 322.

[30] *Mawe v Piggott* (1869) Ir. Rep. 4 Cl. 54. See also *Berry v Irish Times* [1973] I.R. 368; *Byrned v Dean* [1937] 1 K.B. 818.

Some commentators consider that the "right-thinking member" of society is quite enlightened. Professor Norrie says the right-thinking person is "a contemporary person who moves with the times and who does not maintain attitudes of 20 or even 10 years ago." However, that could be that such a test would give over defamation to the trendy or politically correct or fashionable notions of the time — fame has usually been thought to be a longer and deeper asset. It is always a matter of balance and time does have its effect. Perhaps the best recent example in support of Norrie's faster-moving view is the question whether it is defamatory to call a person a "homosexual".[31] Another might be to consider whether it was defamatory to call someone AIDS-infected, or indeed nowadays, a leper. About a hundred years ago there was no dispute in *Farrell v Boyd*,[32] that to say of a person to his employer that he suffered from gonorrhoeal rheumatism was defamatory.[33]

Certain instances have appeared more often than others and for convenience can be collected.[34] They must be evaluated in case they have been overtaken by the times.

8–9   Statements imputing *immorality or criminality*[35] can be defamatory, as where it is suggested that someone has committed a crime or behaved less than decorously. Perhaps the most extreme case (in the sense of being favourable to a pursuer) is *Cuthbert v Linklater.*[36] Mrs Cuthbert raised an action against the author Eric Linklater in respect of the publication of his novel, *Magnus Merriman*. One of his characters, Beaty Bracken, removed a Union Jack from a castle and placed it in a public urinal. Mrs Cuthbert was a famous Scottish Nationalist who had come to the public attention when she had removed a Union Jack from Stirling Castle and tossed it to a guard (which is not the same as putting it in a public urinal). Her action was allowed to proceed.

Another quite clear category is where a statement is made about someone's *fitness for their occupation or profession*, as where a solicitor was accused of conducting cases for his own benefit rather than that of his clients,[37] or a football manager said to treat his players like dirt, break promises and to be parsimonius in paying

---

[31] See, *e.g.* the remarks of Lord McLean in *H.M. Advocate v McKean*, 1996 S.L.T. 1383; And in one recent Outer House it was held that to call a person a homosexual was not defamatory: *Quilty v Windsor*, 1999 S.L.T. 346 (Lord Kingarth).

[32] 1907 15 S.L.T. 327.

[33] See also *Friend v Skelton* (1855) 17 D. 548 (habitual drunkenness). *Mackintoch v Weir* (1875) 2 R. 877, sometimes cited, is of no real value on the allegation of insanity.

[34] This "collecting" has a history — see Blackie 687.

[35] *Leon v Edinburgh Evening News*, 1909 S.C. 1014.

[36] 1935 S.L.T. 94. For background to this case, see Casebook, Ext. 82.

[37] *McRostie v Ironside* (1849) 11 D. 74.

wages.[38] Accusing a councillor of sheer lunacy and gross malad-ministration was not defamatory,[39] but alleging malicious misuse of public money was.[40]

Imputations about *solvency* have produced considerable litigation. A solicitor in a county town, who held a number of important positions involving trust in the community, brought an action against a local manufacturer. It was alleged that the manufacturer had said that the solicitor had "been cleaned out and lost his all".[41] The court allowed the case to proceed on the basis that the words could affect the solicitor's reputation and credit. Interestingly, the Lord President opined that, "If the pursuer had been living on his private means the statement in a railway carriage that he was reported to have 'lost his all' might have excited compassion, but it would not have injured him in his public reputation or purse." In that hypothetical case, the remedy open to the pursuer would be to try to make out some other head of verbal injury such as *convicium*.

Innuendo

Sometimes words may not on their face be defamatory. It is **8–10** permissible to allege facts extrinsic to the statement to illuminate the words used and show that as used they are able to convey a defamatory imputation. The innuendo has to be averred and proved. In short, an innuendo makes clear the defamatory point of an apparently non-defamatory statement. In *Boal v Scottish Catholic Printing Co. Ltd*,[42] Samuel Boal, a journalist and lecturer, brought an action against the defenders for alleged defamation in their news-paper. A report of a charitable home being founded and in which the pursuer was involved asked: "what guarantee is there that the money subscribed does not go to the private profit of . . . the scribbling Boal?" Now it is possible to answer that question by saying: "there is none, for none is needed, Boal is an honest man." But it was held that the statement was capable of a defamatory meaning, namely that the pursuer was the kind of person who would swindle a charity in some way. Once allowed, it is for the jury to decide which of the two possible interpretations the words were intended to have. "Stranger to the truth" has been held a clear enough way of saying "liar" such as not to require an innuendo.[43] The technical nature of innuendo is illustrated by the fact that it is essential to innuendo a statement made in a foreign language.

---

[38] *Peat v News Group*, unreported, Outer House, March 8, 1996.
[39] *Brooks v Lind*, 1997 Rep. L.R. 83.
[40] *ibid.*
[41] *AB v CD* (1904) 7 F. 22.
[42] 1908 S.C. 667.
[43] *Carroll v BBC*, 1997 S.L.T. (Sh. Ct) 23, albeit it was held by the sheriff principal not to be defamatory of a solicitor.

Defences to defamation actions

8–11   Many "defences" are simply denials of elements of the delict —
for example, to deny that the words were used or that the words were
issued with the defender's authority; others are more specialised,
applying only to this area of the law.

1. Disclaimer

8–12   In meaning to do no harm a writer might well try to disclaim any
intention of defaming another. This is unlikely to meet with any
success. Lord Shaw commented on the strategy in the blacklist case
Mazure v Stubbs[44]:

> "A conditioned or specialised slander of that kind is not known
> to the law; the results of a calumnious falsehood arise from the
> impression which it — all of it, including reservations, cautions
> and all the rest — makes upon the minds of the readers, an
> impression which may be quite apart from any artificial restric-
> tion which the author of the falsehood sought to impose. It is for
> those results that the author or promulgator of the libel is
> responsible. The law itself is not inconsiderate of all the
> legitimate excuses for error in such publications, but it cannot
> accept the will of the author of a wrong as the measure of the
> consequence of that wrong."[45]

That was a case of a black-list. Another common example is in
artistic works where it is often said that: "Any reference to any
person living or dead is purely coincidental." On the basis of
Cuthbert v Linklater,[46] discussed above,[47] the longer the disclaimer,
the more it looks like a smoking gun.

2. Apology

8–13   Palinode or public withdrawal and admission of falsity was the
essential remedy in the early days of defamation.[48] A horse dealer
who had insulted others when informed of what he had said, having
himself forgotten, immediately offered to apologise in any terms
sought by the others. Sensibly, there was held to be no ground for an
action of defamation.[49] It is likely that where there has been no
publication beyond the recipient, this will still be the case. An early

---

[44] 1935 S.L.T. 94.
[45] *ibid.,* at 165.
[46] *Cuthbert v Linklater*, 1935 S.L.T. 94.
[47] See para.8–18 above.
[48] For an example see Walker, *History, V,* p.240 n.285.
[49] *Ewart v Mason* (1806) Hume 633.

apology that reaches all those who hear or read a statement should mitigate damages.

3. *In rixa*

The essence of this defence is that the words were uttered in the **8–14** heat of an argument as an angry retort or as mere abuse. This is especially so if the words are such as are usually uttered in this context. *Christie v Robertson*[50] is an example. The parties were at an auction sale at a farm. Each thought a particular horse had been knocked down to him. The pursuer saw the defender walking away with the horse and made insinuations to the effect that the defender was trying to steal the horse. The pursuer went to fetch a policeman. The defender then said words to the effect that the pursuer should have been in the hands of the police 20 times during the last five years. The pursuer was awarded £1 damages in the Outer House but lost completely on appeal. However, the court made each party pay his own expenses, perhaps to discourage others from taking similar action.

4. *Vulgar abuse*

Reference to the section above provides sufficient authority for the **8–15** proposition that mere vulgar abuse is not defamatory and the same reasons apply. It is because those hearing the slander disregard it. Various derogatory slang works would be defamatory if treated as a statement of fact, but may now be common parlance, and would not be actionable if used simply as vulgar abuse.[51] In older times, "whore" was not actionable in a quarrel.[52]

5. *Fair retort*

The essence of this defence is that readers or eye-witnesses should **8–16** be aware that the defender has been wounded and is fighting back. In *National Union of Bank Employees v Murray*,[53] Lord Birnam said:

> "I am further of opinion that in stating that the pursuers' misrepresentations were deliberate, the defenders honestly believed, and had good reason to believe, that this was so and that they did not issue the leaflet maliciously but in good faith and by way of fair retort to the pursuers' attack."

---

[50] (1899) 1 F. 1155.
[51] See the US rapper Ice Cube, quoted in R. Abel. "Speech and Respect", 44th Hamlyn Lectures (Sweet & Maxwell)
[52] *Reid v Scott* (1825) 4 S. 5.
[53] 1949 S.L.T. (Notes) 25.

Like the other defences some immediacy is suggested, and time to reflect will make the defence ever more difficult.

6. Veritas

8–17   This is a complete defence. The defender simply proves what he said was true — the onus of proof, on balance of probabilities, in this respect being upon the defender.[54] The position at common law was that the defender had to prove the truth of all material statements, thus justifying everything in the alleged defamatory communication. The position is now regulated by the Defamation Act 1952, s.5 which provides:

> "In an action for defamation in respect of words containing two or more distinct charges against the pursuer, a defence of veritas shall not fail by reason only that the truth of every charge is not proved, if the words not proved to be true do not materially injure the pursuer's reputation having regard to the truth of the remaining charges."[55]

Another major statutory intervention is contained in the Rehabilitation of Offenders Act 1974, s.8. The Act sets out to allow certain offences to be treated as not having taken place after a period of time has past and they have become "spent" and the offender accordingly rehabilitated. The general rule is that the circumstances surrounding the offence cannot be used against a rehabilitated person, but the Act does allow the defence of *veritas* to be pled in defamation actions so long as the original publication was not made with malice.[56]

7. *Absolute privilege*

8–18   As a matter of law, deriving from public policy, certain statements, although affecting someone in their reputation or causing them dreadful loss, are just not actionable.

Parliament

8–19   Statements in either House and reports in *Hansard* are completely protected in the interest of free speech in the chambers. As a

---

[54] For a modern example of a successful plea of *veritas*, see *Gecas v Scottish Television*, 1992 G.W.D. 30–1786.

[55] As verbally altered by the Scottish s.14. See Casebook, App. Ext. 5; and Gecas, above.

[56] Sections 8(3), (5) and (8); the Act, in allowing publication, interestingly reflects a sentiment expressed in the Digest (47, 10, 18): "It is not right or just to condemn anyone for bringing a wrongdoer into disrepute, for it is necessary and proper for the offences of wrongdoers to be known."

corollary, repetition outside the Houses is not so privileged. The protection may be waived by an MP for a particular case, allowing the defenders to plead *veritas*.[57] Reports and proceedings published under the authority of either House are, however, protected.[58] The UK rule of absolute Parliamentary privilege for statements made in the Houses of Parliament was held not to be in contravention of *inter alia* Art.8 of the ECHR.[59]

Scottish Parliament

By virtue of a statutory instrument,[60] temporary provision was **8–20** made for privilege of Parliamentary papers. The Scotland Act itself amended the Defamation Act 1952, section 10 on limitation on privilege at elections to make provision for the Scottish Parliament. The Defamation Act 1996 was amended by inclusion in section 17(1) (interpretation), in the definition of "statutory provision", to include a provision contained in an Act of the Scottish Parliament or in an instrument made under such an Act. A member of the Scottish Executive was treated as a Minister of the Crown in paragraph 11(1)(c) of Schedule 1 on qualified privilege.

Judicial proceedings

Absolute privilege attaches to all statements made in judicial **8–21** proceedings whatever the court or the rank of the person sued. It also extends to proceedings in tribunals if the procedures are similar in essence to a court.[61] As Lord Diplock said:

> "No single touchstone emerges from the cases; but this is not surprising for the rule of law is one which involves the balancing of conflicting public policies, one general: that the law should provide a remedy to the citizen whose good name and reputation is traduced by malicious falsehoods uttered by another; the other particular: that witnesses before tribunals recognised by law should ... 'give their testimony free from any fear of being harassed by an action of an allegation, whether true or false, that they acted from malice'."[62]

---

[57] Defamation Act 1996, s.13. A double-edged "sword of truth".
[58] Parliamentary Papers Act 1840.
[59] *A v UK*, [2002] T.L.R. 576.
[60] SI 1095/1999. The Scotland Act 1998 (Transitory and Transitional Provisions) (Standing Orders and Parliamentary Publications) Order 1999.
[61] *Trapp v Mackie*, 1979 S.L.T. 126.
[62] *ibid.*, at 129.

Fair and accurate reports of judicial proceedings are probably absolutely privileged at common law,[63] and are given statutory absolute privilege if contemporaneous (as defined).[64]

8. Qualified privilege

8–22   In certain circumstances, a defender enjoys what is known as "qualified privilege". The defender will have a defence *unless it can be shown that the statement was motivated by express or actual malice.* Since people are presumed to act honestly, the pursuer must have sufficient evidence to infer malice.

Qualified privilege attaches to circumstances as opposed to any particular person. The list of privileged categories is not closed but changes with time. That said, there has been a dramatic development in the recognition of a new category of qualified privilege that is not based on an occasion — it may be called, responsible journalism privilege or *Reynolds* privilege after the case which declared it and it is discussed below.[65] As a general rule, a statement is protected, *absent malice*, if honestly made by a person in the discharge of a public or private duty of some kind or in his own affairs in a matter where his interest is concerned.[66] Categories that are well established are now discussed, concluding with a discussion of the analytically different *Reynolds* privilege.

Discharge of a duty

8–23   A proper complaint to the appropriate authority will attract qualified privilege. Thus, for example, it was held that there could be qualified privilege when a complaint was made to a chief constable about the conduct of a sergeant.[67] The privilege extends to statements made about candidates in elections.[68] The House of Lords has considered the effect and extent of privilege and in particular in relation to a complaint against the police. Mirza complained that he was arrested by Fraser because he, Mirza, was a Pakistani and a justice of the peace. What Mirza intended to convey by this was that he had been arrested on no reasonable grounds, something that it had been held Mirza knew to be untrue. However, the statement only supported an innuendo of prejudice in respect of which no malice

---

[63] *Wright v Outram* (1889) 16 R. 1004.

[64] Defamation Act 1996, s.14(1). A court includes any tribunal or body exercising the judicial power of the state, all UK courts, the ECJ and the ECHR.

[65] See para.8–27.

[66] *Dunnet v Nelson*, 1926 S.C. 764.

[67] *Cassidy v Connachie*, 1907 S.C. 1112.

[68] *Bruce v Leisk* (1892) 19 R. 482. Note the Representation of the People Act 1983, s.106, which makes it an offence to make a false statement about a candidate's personal character or conduct for the purpose of affecting the candidate's return at an election.

could be shown. The House held that the existence of the knowing falsehood was sufficient to evidence malice albeit not in relation to the actual defamatory statement. The malice was enough to constitute a misuse of the occasion giving rise to the qualified privilege.[69]

Something more than negligence is required for the defence to be lost — the occasion of complaint must not be misused.[70] A complaint needs to be directed towards the proper source to have the privilege. So a complaint about a nursing home might have been protected if made to the Health Board rather than to a BBC documentary.[71]

Protection of the interests of another

If someone asks for information or a character reference about **8–24** another individual, then that is an occasion that attracts qualified privilege to the extent that the reply deals with relevant matter.[72]

Between persons having a common interest

Qualified privilege attaches where a communication is made **8–25** between parties, one who has an interest in making it and the other having an interest to receive it, so long as they are in good faith and the statement is not published more widely than is necessary.[73]

Protection of one's own interests

This heading permits statements replying to attacks on oneself so **8–26** long as pertinent.[74] A recent case provides a very practical example of what this defence is about. *Chapman v Barber*[75] was a case between two company directors. Chapman sent Barber draft minutes of a board meeting. Barber thought the minutes suggested that Barber had been conducting himself improperly and responded by accusing Chapman of acting against company policy and misleading the board with a malicious and inaccurate minute. Chapman pointed out that Barber's version had been seen by non-director staff. The court held that the statements were covered by qualified privilege and the fact of others seeing the document, which had, after all, been marked

---

[69] *Fraser v Mirza*, 1993 S.L.T. 527, reversing 1992 S.L.T. 740.

[70] *Hamill v Lord Advocate*, 1994 G.W.D. 33–1960.

[71] *Baignet v McCulloch*, 1997 G.W.D. 16–737

[72] *Dundas v Livingstone* (1900) 3 F. 37.

[73] *Leitch v Lyal* (1903) 11 S.L.T. 394.

[74] See *Shaw v Morgan* (1888) 15 R. 865; *Adam v Ward* [1917] A.C. 309.

[75] 1989 S.L.T. 830.

private and confidential and sent in the usual way, did not result in the privilege being lost. Rules like this prevent storms in teacups.[76]

9. *Responsible journalism or* Reynolds *privilege*

8–27 In *Reynolds v Times Newspaper Ltd*,[77] the House of Lords reviewed qualified privilege. It decided not to recognise a new category of qualified privilege of political information, but in view of the new legal landscape after Human Rights, protection could be given to the press where taking into account the necessary balances it was correct so to do.[78]

Lord Nicholls identified matters which might be relevant when a court was deciding whether or not to grant this new privilege:

> "Depending on the circumstances, the matters to be taken into account including the following. The comments are illustrative only. 1. The seriousness of the allegation. The more serious the charge, the more the public is misinformed and the individual harmed, if the allegation is not true. 2. The nature of the information, and the extent to which the subject matter is a matter of public concern. 3. The source of the information. Some informants have no direct knowledge of the events. Some have their own axes to grind, or are being paid for their stories. 4. The steps taken to verify the information. 5. The status of the information. The allegation may have already been the subject of an investigation which commands respect. 6. The urgency of the matter. News is often a perishable commodity. 7. Whether comment was sought from the plaintiff. He may have information others do not possess or have not disclosed. An approach to the plaintiff will not always be necessary. 8. Whether the article contained the gist of the plaintiff's side of the story. 9. The tone of the article. A newspaper can raise queries or call for an investigation. It need not adopt allegations as statements of fact. 10. The circumstances of the publication, including the timing."[79]

It was observed by Lord Hope dissenting and others since that this is a departure from traditional thinking, whereby the occasion is privileged or not. That distinction was important in allowing it to be

---

[76] The defence was also held applicable where there was an entry in company accounts "defalcation by director": *May v Teague Homes*, 1996 G.W.D. 23–1344.

[77] [2001] 2 A.C.127

[78] This defence is a new jurisprudential creature: *Loutchansky v Times Newspapers (No.2)* [2002] 2 W.L.R. 640.

[79] At 205. See the difference in the New Zealand position in the Privy Council, *Lange v Atkinson* [2000] 1 N.Z.L.R. 257 and later in the *Court of Appeal Lange v Atkinson (No.2)*, 2000 3 N.Z.L.R. 385.

decided as a matter of law whether there was potential privilege and as a matter of fact whether it had been lost.[80]

Reynolds was fully considered in Scotland in *Adams v Guardian Newspapers Ltd*,[81] although it should be noted that acceptance of much common ground meant the case would not be a fundamental re-examination. The press reported an allegation that one member of parliament had alleged that the pursuer, also a member of parliament, had leaked an allegedly confidential matter. The press took no view on it themselves. On this point, Lord Reed noted that parties were agreed that the starting point was the ten points of Lord Nicholls — applications of the general rule that publication had to be of sufficient value that in the public interest, it should be protected (absent malice). He noted the subsequent jurisprudence, but it was common ground before him that the Nicholls guidance in *Reynolds* should be followed. Then, it was also common ground that in applying *Reynolds*, the approach of the Court of Appeal in *Loutchansky v Times Newspapers Ltd (Nos 2–5)* should be followed, namely: (i) if *Reynolds* privileged that will inevitably preclude a finding of malice; (ii) setting the standard of journalistic responsibility too low would be dangerous and ultimately the press itself would be undermined if many untruths were ultimately published; (iii) setting the standard too high would frighten the press. In *Adams* itself, it was impossible to draw from the *pursuers* averments the conclusion that the standard had been satisfied — indeed there were averments the other way. In any event this was a case where evidence would be needed to gauge the press conduct.

10. Published reports

This is a recognised head of qualified privilege at common law and **8–28** includes reports about parliamentary proceedings, the court or quasi-judicial bodies so long as fair and accurate.[82] The Defamation Act 1952, s.7, however, expressly provides for "qualified privilege of newspapers":

> "The publication in a newspaper [any paper containing public news or observations thereon or consisting wholly or mainly of

---

[80] In *GKR Karate (UK) Ltd v Yorkshire Post Newspapers Ltd* [2000] 2 All E.R. 931 (an allegation that the plaintiffs were selling karate lessons by unqualified instructors for full fees) it was held in the Court of Appeal that if the judge decides that the occasion was not privileged, the issue of malice does not arise. If the judge decides that the occasion was privileged, he must have decided that, in all the circumstances, at the time of the publication, the public was entitled to know the particular information available. A case could be decided in England as a preliminary issue. For another example see *Al Fagih v HH Saudi Research and Marketing* [2001] EWCA Civ 1634.

[81] 2003 S.L.T. 1058.

[82] See, generally, *Allbutt v GMC* (1899) 23 Q.B.D. 400.

advertisements, which is printed for sale and is published in the United Kingdom either periodically or in parts or numbers at intervals not exceeding 36 days] of any such report or other matter as is mentioned in the Schedule to this Act shall be privileged unless the publication is proved to be made with malice."

This necessitates consideration of the Schedule, which divides newspaper statements into two categories. The reason for this is that Part 1 statements are entitled to qualified privilege without explanation or contradiction, whereas Part 2 statements do require explanation or contradiction to obtain qualified privilege. If the statement is a Part 2 matter, then the Act is not a defence if the paper has refused to publish a reasonable explanation or contradiction. Generally, too, the statement must not be unlawful or of no public benefit. Part 1 matters cover, *inter alia*: legislative acts; international organisations; courts martial; courts; and official notices. Matters set out in Part 2 cover, *inter alia*: transactions of public associations for business sports and the like; public meetings, whether the audience is public or restricted; local authorities; and tribunals.

The defence is an aid to free speech, allowing honest mistakes to be made on these important occasions. This policy was strong enough to allow the English Court of Appeal to refuse to apply the law relating to negligent mis-statements to a reference which was "so strikingly bad as to amount to ... 'the kiss of death'" to the plaintiff's career. There had been no malice in the preparation — the defendant was a fool and not a rogue.[83] However, in the House of Lords' the view was taken that as there could be liability for making a mistaken good reference; as in *Hedley Byrne,* there was no reason why a mistaken bad reference should not be actionable too. That decision has now been applied in Scotland by an Extra Division in *Donlon v Colonial Mutual Group (UK Holdings) Ltd.*[84]

11. Fair comment

8–29   This is a defence in its own right although it is closely related to qualified privilege. Unlike qualified privilege, the facts stated have to be truly stated. The protection is against the innuendo or inference that can arise from the stated facts. The protected statement must therefore be a comment and not a statement of fact. Where it is impossible to detect any comment severable from fact, then the defence is doomed.[85] The defence arises from the individual's

---

[83] *Spring v Guardian Assurance plc* [1992] T.L.R. 628.
[84] 1997 S.C.L.R. 1088. K. Norrie, "Defamation, Negligence and Employers' References" (1994) 39 J.L.S.S. 418.
[85] *Adams v Guardian Newspapers Ltd*, 2003 S.L.T. 1058.

interest in commenting upon public matters and so the matter discussed must be to do with the public interest. It is also essential that the comment be honestly and fairly made as opposed to being inspired by malice. A good example is *Merivale v Carson*.[86] The plaintiff and his wife were authors of a play called *The Whip Hand*. A review appeared in the *Stage* magazine:

> "The Whip Hand ... gives us nothing but a hash-up of ingredients which have been used ad nauseam, until one rises in protestation against the loving, confiding, fatuous husband with the naughty wife and her double existence, the good male genius, the limp aristocrat, and the villainous foreigner."

The innuendo alleged was that the review suggested that the play was immoral. The court said that every latitude should be allowed to comment on a matter of public interest (which included the play as it was being performed to the public) even if opinionated or prejudiced, unless the writing was done with an indirect and dishonest intention to injure the plaintiff. In one of the most important Scottish cases, *Crotty v McFarlane*,[87] it was said that criticisms were to be examined to see whether they expressed honest opinions, however unjust, or whether they were couched in language so reckless and exaggerated that no reasonable man could possibly have entertained the opinion or used the language. It was held that the language in the case was acceptable even though it was hostile or even if it was grossly unjust. It has been held more recently that calling a sports administrator a "dictator" might fall within the defence as the phrase no longer had the connotation of murder associated with Hitler or Stalin[88]; "malicious misuse of public money" said of a councillor was fair comment if defamatory.[89]

12. Offer of amends

A person who has published a statement alleged to be defamatory **8–30** may offer to make amends in relation to the statement generally or in relation to a specific defamatory meaning, which the person making the offer accepts that the statement conveys (to be called a qualified offer).[90] The offer must be in writing, expressed to be an offer in terms of the Act, and if it is a qualified offer it must state the defamatory meaning concerned.[91] The offer must be to make a

---

[86] (1887) 20 Q.B.D. 275.
[87] January 27, 1891; Casebook, Ext. 86.
[88] *Farry v News Group*, 1996 G.W.D. 2–109.
[89] *Brooks v Lind*, 1997 Rep. L.R. 83.
[90] Deformation Act 1996, s.2(1) and (2). Section 2 is not in force at time of writing.
[91] *ibid.*, s.2(3).

suitable correction and a sufficient apology, to publish the correction and apology in a reasonable manner practicable in the circumstances, and to pay the victim compensation and costs.[92] An offer cannot be made after serving a defence.[93] An offer can be withdrawn before acceptance and a renewal is treated as a fresh offer.[94] Once accepted, the victim cannot bring or continue proceedings. If the details are not agreed, the court can make the necessary orders and can settle the damages on the common-law basis.[95] Unless it can be shown that the offeror knew or had reason to believe that the statement related to the victim and was both false and defamatory, the offer is a defence if the publisher wants to use it — but if he does, he may not use any other defence.[96] The offer may be relied on in mitigation of damages whether or not relied on as a defence.[97]

It has been held that for the plaintiff to attack the defendants defence of an offer of amends, the claimant has to go so far as to establish bad faith in the publication and to demonstrate actual knowledge.[98]

13. Unintentional defamation

8–31   Innocent disseminators (other than authors, editors and publishers as defined) have a statutory defence.[99] A broadcaster with no effective control over a live programme is entitled to the defence.[1] An internet service provider (as opposed to Internet publisher) is also entitled to the defence. In defamation proceedings, a person has a defence if he or she shows that: (a) he was not the author, editor or publisher of the statement complained of; (b) he took reasonable care in relation to its publication; and (c) he did not know, and had no reason to believe, that what he did caused or contributed to the publication of a defamatory statement.[2] The "author" is the originator of the statement, but does not include a person who did not intend that his statement be published at all; "editor" means a person having editorial or equivalent responsibility for the content of the statement or the decision to publish it; and "publisher" means a commercial publisher whose business is issuing material to the public, or a section of the public, who issues material containing the statement in

---

[92] *ibid.,* s.2(4).
[93] *ibid.,* s.2(5).
[94] *ibid.,* s.2(6).
[95] *ibid.,* s.3.
[96] *ibid.,* s.4.
[97] *ibid.,* s.4(5).
[98] *Milne v Express Newspapers* [2003] 1 W.L.R. 927.
[99] Defamation Act 1996, s.1.
[1] s.1(3). For the kind of facts this might in future cover, see *Prophit v BBC*, 1997 S.L.T. 745.
[2] s.1(1).

the course of that business.[3] A person is not to be considered the author, editor or publisher of a statement if he or she is only involved: (a) in printing, producing, distributing or selling printed material containing the statement; (b) in processing, making copies of, distributing, exhibiting or selling a film or sound recording[4] containing the statement; (c) in processing, making copies of, distributing or selling any electronic medium in or on which the statement is recorded, or in operating or providing any equipment, system or service by means of which the statement is retrieved, copied, distributed or made available in electronic form; (d) as the broadcaster of a live programme containing the statement in circumstances in which he or she has no effective control over the maker of the statement; and (e) as the operator of or provider of access to a communications system by means of which the statement is transmitted, or made available, by a person over whom he or she has no effective control. In a case not within paragraphs (a) to (e) the court can have regard to those provisions by way of analogy in deciding whether a person is to be considered the author, editor or publisher of a statement.[5] Employees or agents of an author, editor or publisher are in the same position as their employer or principal to the extent that they are responsible for the content of the statement or the decision to publish it.[6] In determining for the purposes of this section whether a person took reasonable care, or had reason to believe that what he did caused or contributed to the publication of a defamatory statement, regard shall be had to: (a) the extent of his responsibility for the content of the statement or the decision to publish it; (b) the nature or circumstances of the publication; and (c) the previous conduct or character of the author, editor or publisher.[7]

In *Godfrey v Demon Internet*,[8] it was held that the defenders, an internet service provider, were not commercial publishers of an item on a news server and so were not publishers for the purposes of defamation. However, they were liable because they failed to show that they met the requirements of subss (1)(b) and (1)(c) of the Act. Essentially, it seems that they did not act quickly enough when made aware of the possibly defamatory quality of the news posting. In *Loutchansky v Times Newspapers Ltd and Others (No.2)*,[9] the publishers were not entitled to a defence for their internet archive — once alerted to the defamatory potential they ought to have attached a warning notice to the archive matter. In this way, scholarship and

---

[3] s.1(2).
[4] As defined in Part I of the Copyright, Designs and Patents Act 1988.
[5] s.1(3).
[6] s.1(4).
[7] s.1(5). This section does not apply to any cause of action which arose before the section came into force: s.1(6).
[8] [1999] 4 All E.R. 342.
[9] [2002] 2 W.L.R. 640.

research are not inhibited — history is not rewritten, but reputations are protected.

Damages

8–32 Damages will always be awarded for a defamatory statement. Either there will be damages based on the *lex Aquilia* action for loss of business or damage to reputation, or there will be an award of *solatium* for the hurt feelings following the *actio injuriarum,* or both. The more difficult problem in this area is that certain factors are treated as increasing the award that should be made and others as decreasing or mitigating the damages.

The award may be aggravated where the statement has been repeated after a warning that it was false.[10] It is inappropriate to attempt to make a direct comparison between an award of *solatium* for pain and suffering caused by physical injury and an award of *solatium* for injury to feelings and reputation.[11] While it is proper for a court to take account of levels of award made in Scottish defamation cases, no assistance can be derived from a consideration of English cases in which awards are assessed on very different principles.[12]

Certain factors may mitigate the award of damages. In defamation cases, malice is irrelevant unless qualified privilege is pleaded or unless it has increased the injury, but damages may be reduced if it is shown that there was indeed no malice in making the defamatory statement. That the statement was repeated as a general report or that an offer of apology was made may also mitigate. Provocation may mitigate. Section 12 of the Defamation Act 1952 allows the unsuccessful defender to lead evidence of damages already awarded to the pursuer in mitigation — as where someone defamed by the "Moon" newspaper is also defamed by the "Looking-Glass" newspaper and has received compensation from the "Moon" newspaper. Most dramatically, it is possible to show that the pursuer's character is such that it did not suffer damage from the statement. The court keeps this line within close bounds and the evidence of bad character must be bad character in relation to the matter in issue. In *Plato Films v Speidel,*[13] the plaintiff was at the time of the action the Supreme Commander of Allied Land Forces in Central Europe, but had held a number of important positions in the German army before and during the Second World War. The defendants were Plato Films and Stanley Forman. The action concerned a film called *Operation*

---

[10] *Morrison v Ritchie* (1902) 4 F. 645.
[11] *Winter v News (Scotland) Ltd*, 1991 S.L.T. 828.
[12] *ibid.*
[13] [1961] A.C. 1090.

Teutonic Sword. The defendants admitted that they had said that the plaintiff had been privy to the murder of King Alexander of Yugoslavia and others and that he had betrayed Field Marshal Rommel. They pled justification (or *veritas*). But, alternatively, in mitigation, they claimed that the film accused him of lots of other things, including being a war criminal, and if he was not prepared to deny these allegations he could not have much of a character. The House of Lords allowed the allegation that "the plaintiff had a bad reputation as a man who was party to and/or responsible for acts which were war crimes and/or against humanity and/or atrocities" to remain in the pleadings, *i.e.* the House did not say it was inadmissible. At the same time, it was stated that the suggestion that the plaintiff had to complain of every libel in a given work or be held to have admitted it was said to be wholly improper. However, the court held that, in this case, the allegation involved character in relation to the matter at issue. On the other hand, the good character of the pursuer does not aggravate damages, for every pursuer is presumed to be of good character. Previous malice is irrelevant and, as already indicated, bad character in an area not relevant to the issue before the court is not considered.[14] As Lord Radcliffe put it in Plato Films: "Life not being a morality play or a Victorian Melodrama, men do not enjoy reputations for being bad or good simpliciter."[15]

Under the European Convention of Human Rights, a system must make sure that damages awards are necessary and that there are suitable controls on excess.[16]

If the jury (or a court on appeal!) take a dim view of the character of the pursuer in relation to the actual matter in question, damages of a farthing were famously awarded and that tradition has recently been approved by the House of Lords albeit inflation has raised the legendary farthing to one pound sterling.[17]

Interdict

There has been a reluctance, especially in England to allow **8–33** plaintiffs to restrain publication in advance — it stifles free speech before it is uttered. The general rule there is that interim injunctions should not be issued where the defendant raises a defence, whether of justification, fair comment on a matter of public interest or privilege.[18] English law permits an exception where the publication

---

[14] *C v M*, 1923 S.C. 1.
[15] [1961] A.C. 1090 at 1130.
[16] English law fell foul: *Tolstoy v UK*, unreported, ECHR, July 13, 1995.
[17] *Grobbelaar v News Group Newspapers* [2002] T.L.R. 423.
[18] Clerk and Lindsell, 30–21.

is part of a conspiracy to injure,[19] but this exception is narrowly construed.[20]

So far as Scots law is concerned, *McMurdo v Ferguson*[21] seems to show a much more favourable attitude to a pursuer and a correspondingly more worrying attitude to freedom of speech. Lord Murray appears to have asked only whether or not the statement was *prima facie* defamatory. In the earlier case of *Waddell v BBC*,[22] the Inner House clearly also considered an application competent, but the balance of convenience was in favour of the publisher publishing in the public interest.

Professor Walker is no doubt correct to say that "interdict against repetition of a given statement, already held defamatory, is quite competent."[23]

Human Rights law has already had an impact, not least because of the express terms of section 12(3) of the HRA.[24]

VERBAL INJURY

8–34 In *Paterson v Welch*,[25] the pursuer was a governor of college A. The defender was a governor of college A but also a chairman of the school board of B. The defender made the statements complained of at a meeting of the school B and at another meeting. Here it was alleged that a false report was made of the pursuer's comments at a meeting of the governors of college A. So the complaint is that the pursuer says that the defender said that the pursuer said the pupils from the board schools would contaminate the genteel children attending college A. The defamatory claim (slander) was held not to apply on the facts. Lord President (Robertson) said:

> "But assuming, as I now do, that the words sued on do not found a claim of damages on the head of slander, it by no means follows that they are not actionable. The true case of the pursuer is this — he says to the defender, 'You publicly asserted that I said certain things; your assertion was false; it was made with design to injure me, and I have been injured.' In my opinion that is a good claim in damages. In judging of the relevancy of such a claim, it is of course necessary that the words ascribed to the pursuer should be such as reasonably support the essential

---

[19] *Gulf Oil Ltd v Page* [1987] Ch. 327. Tony Weir has recently described this case as egregious and disgraceful: Weir, *Economic Torts* (Oxford, 1997), pp.19–20.

[20] *Ferris-Bank (Anguilla) Ltd v Layar and Others* [1991] T.L.R. 68, injunction refused.

[21] 1993 S.L.T. 193.

[22] 1973 S.L.T. 246.

[23] Delict, p.453.

[24] *Dickson Minto WS v Bonnier Media Ltd*, 2002 G.W.D. 551.

[25] (1893) 20 R. 744. See also *Cunningham v Phillips* (1868) 6 M. 926.

averments, that the attributing of them to him was done with an intention to injure, and with the result of injuring. But subject to this observation, it seems to me that when speech is ascribed to A by B, A will have an action if: (1) the statement of B is false; (2) the statement was made with design to injure; and (3) injury has resulted. The pursuer's case complies with these conditions. He begins by saying that he never used the words ascribed to him. These words are invidious words, to utter which may well be supposed to bring down on him, who was alleged to have used them, the hatred of his neighbours. The pursuer goes on to say that the defender ascribed these words to him, because the defender calculated their effect, and desired to inflict that injury on him. He ends by saying that the falsehood did its work; that he has become an object of public hatred; that the people have tried to burn him in effigy at his own door; that his personal comfort and public influence have been impaired; and all this through the falsehood of the defender."[26]

The case involves a false statement, an ascription of an unpopular view and public hatred. Professor Blackie adduces convincing reasons for saying that the case actually involved specific business losses and was not simply about *solatium*.[27]

A current statement of this head of liability can be found in *Barratt International Resorts Ltd v Barratt Owners Group*[28]:

"An action for verbal injury arises out of harm said to be done to a person in his business relations by written or verbal falsehoods . . . In respect of an action for verbal injury the delict consists in 'maliciously communicating written or oral falsehoods calculated in the ordinary course to produce, and in fact producing, actual damage' (Walker p.902). The ingredients of such an action are that false statements, either written or verbal, must be maliciously communicated to third parties, which are calculated or likely to produce, and which in fact do produce, actual damage to the pursuers' business interests. It is not necessary for the pursuers to aver and prove that the defenders knew that the statements were false . . . Accordingly, to succeed in the ordinary case of verbal injury the pursuers must prove two things. Firstly, they must prove that the statements made by the defenders are false. Secondly, the pursuers must prove that the communication of these statements was malicious. In the context of this kind of action, malice comprises three elements. Firstly, the malice consists in the

---

[26] *ibid.,* at 749.
[27] Blackie, *HPLS II*, 705.
[28] 2003 G.W.D. 19.

deliberate utterance of a false statement. Again it will be noted that this does not mean that the maker of the statement necessarily knew that it was false. Secondly, the falsehood must be uttered with the intention and design of injuring the pursuer. This may be evidenced by 'spite, or malevolence, or other improper motive, or intent to injure the pursuers' business, or at least a lack of honest belief in the truth of the statement made' (Walker, p.902). Knowledge of the falsity of a statement may go a long way to demonstrate an intention of injuring the pursuers. Finally, the falsehood maliciously uttered must be calculated or likely to cause the pursuers some actual damage. It is accepted that it is not necessary now for the pursuers to show that they have suffered actual or special damage (Defamation Act 1952 section 14); it is sufficient if the pursuers offers to prove a general damage or loss to the business . . . essentially the quality of malice requires some positive element of ill-will or intent to injure as either a principal or a significant element in the expression of any untrue statements. Such malice must therefore be evidenced by something more than the expression of a statement subsequently found to be untrue and uttered with the intention of causing injury or damage. The expression of the statement must certainly be deliberate and made with the intent of injuring the party about whom it is made. That malice is also present may be evidenced in the circumstances by the knowledge that the statement is false, or made with such recklessness that it amounts to the same thing; or by averments of improper motive, malevolence, ill-will, or other evidence of a malicious willingness to injure the reputation of the party at whom the false statements are directed. It may be significant to consider how central the statements are to any dispute ongoing between the parties. It may be easier to infer malice from statements which do not go to the heart of any such dispute but which are rather essentially adventitious in nature. The lack of honest belief in the truth of a statement may in the circumstances go a long way to demonstrate that malice is present. But such considerations — separate from the mere transmission of an untrue statement — must be separately found. In addition the question of whether the statement is malicious or not will require to be considered against the need to recognise that parties must be able to exercise their views with reasonable freedom in any debate which legitimately concerns them, and an action of personal injury should not be used to stifle a debate however vigorous between parties in conflict over their respective rights."[29]

---

[29] Transcript 25.

MALICIOUS FALSEHOOD: "ENGLISH" SLANDER CASES

This species of verbal injury is probably an offshoot from the English **8–35** law of defamation. There is not all that much Scottish authority for it but it seems quite unobjectionable in principle — indeed it could as easily be a form of Scottish verbal injury. The requisites are an actually spiteful communication, which is false, and which causes or is calculated to cause damage. It differs from *convicium* in that the statement must be false, and from defamation in that the statement need not lead to a lowering of the victim's reputation in the estimation of right-thinking subjects. It is known under four heads: slander of title (in the sense of legal ownership); slander of property (in the sense of physical land or buildings); slander of goods (moveables); and slander of business. Of course, none of these are slanders as the term is presently used, which implies defamation. An example is *Bruce v Smith*.[30] In this case, a builder sued in respect of an article in the Glasgow *Evening News*, which said:

> "People . . . in the city have discovered a new distraction in watching the rents which are appearing in the frontage of a new property still unoccupied. A year or so ago the building collapsed due to an insecure foundation, but it has been run up again. Signs of fresh weakness are already evident, and there is much speculation as to the future of the part of small crowds which gather in the evening, and gaze blankly at the building. The master of works may hear that his services are required — when the tenement comes down with a run for the second time."

The building was, therefore, becoming difficult to sell or to let. The claim was held to be relevant and indeed the court did not require the pursuer to prove malice, merely that the statement was false and calumnious.

In *Philip v Morton*,[31] it was said the pursuer did not own goods he was selling. *Craig v Inveresk Paper Merchants Ltd*,[32] is the kind of case which is often encountered in practice. It was alleged that the defenders were saying the pursuers would be going out of business.[33]

---

[30] (1898) 1 F. 327.
[31] (1816) Hume 865.
[32] 1970 S.L.T. (Notes) 50.
[33] The case failed only on vicarious liability. It is described in the report as a "verbal injury" case.

CONVICIUM

8–36 *Convicium* consists in maliciously abusing a person or holding him up to public ridicule or contempt and causing him loss or hurt to his feelings. The roots of this head of liability are in the *Digest*.[34] The Praetor says: "Nothing shall be done to bring a person into hatred, ridicule or contempt." Guthrie Smith describes this as a species of verbal injury:

> "a specially aggravated kind — the loud and public denunciation of an individual by different persons, one or more, acting in concert. To be hooted and insulted in this way on the public street is evidently a worse wrong than any form of private scandal. It, may, moreover, often lead to public disturbance; and hence, while the truth of the libel is a good plea in all other cases, in this case the maxim applies *veritas convicii non excusat*".[35]

There is a line of relevant cases, the foundation case being *Sheriff v Wilson*.[36] A series of articles was published vilifying the pursuer. The Lord Justice-Clerk considered that a man could be driven to a state of almost desperation by such conduct.[37] It was thus actionable. The basis was that it would have been punished under the old law and there was authority in Erskine. Glegg goes to considerable trouble to demonstrate the existence of this type of liability.[38] While this is considered by Professor Walker to be part of the law of Scotland, other commentators are very much more doubtful.[39] The state has been reached whereby it is described as a myth in the *Stair Memorial Encyclopaedia*.[40]

An example of the kind of case that could be described as *convicium* is *Steele v Scottish Daily Record*.[41] Counsel before the Inner House agreed to describe the action as one for verbal injury and so the Division did not analyse the matter. This action was based on an article appearing in the "Judge" section of the *Sunday Mail*. The paper reported that the pursuer, a motor dealer, had insisted upon

---

[34] 47, 10, 15. Or even in the Twelve Tables: Smith, "When the Truth Hurts", 1998 S.L.T. (News) 1.

[35] Guthrie-Smith, *The Law of Damages*, p.241.

[36] (1855) 17 D. 528.

[37] *ibid.,* at 531.

[38] Blackie, *HPLS II* at 702 demonstrates an innocent misinterpretation or misunderstanding by Glegg of the development of the Roman law in the *jus commune*.

[39] Walker, p.736 *et seq*; see contra, Norrie (1995) n.3 above, at pp.35 *et seq.*

[40] *Stair Memorial Encyclopedia*, Vol.15, para.558, "The non-existence of convicium".

[41] 1970 S.L.T. 53.

holding a man to his contractual obligations. Part of the report stated:

> "But fair's fair — did your firm have to make him take a car he didn't want, a car he can't afford to run? A car that he's going to find very hard to sell with the coining of winter? You're in the big time, Mr Steele. Probably you didn't know the tough times young Mr McLeod was going through. Come on . . . let's show us that the big time has a big heart too."

Note that this could not be a defamation case as the facts stated did not allege dishonourable or immoral conduct. In the event, the court held the case of *convicium* was not made out because the pursuer had not shown that the article intended to have the pursuer ridiculed or treated with contempt. An alternative test equivalent to that in defamation — a lowering in public esteem —was rejected.

More difficult is the question whether the maxim *veritas convicium non excusat* (truth does not excuse *convicium*) applies. There were indications in *Steele* that it might not. *Barratt* appears to leave the matter open. Professor Blackie has offered a cogent explanation for how it could be that it was thought by Glegg (mistakenly) that this could be the case.[42] If there is to be a "hooting down" delict, then it is not much use if it only applies to false statements. Nor would recognition of a delict of infringement of privacy help if the matter were already public — like the hunchback, or neither true nor false — where the statements were simply vilificatory. It is true that criminal legislation is gradually appearing to control *inter alia* "hate speech" and, indeed in the modern world, it may be that what is needed is a statutory restatement on this narrow point without the need for a fundamental review of the entire law of defamation and related obligations. It could either be declared to be non-existent or given a modern existence. That would allow "verbal injury" (narrow) to develop more clearly. Nor must it be assumed that the publication of the truth is an absolute right. Criminal law, regulatory provisions and human rights law all restrain the truth that the press may publish and to prevent them publishing abusive hurtful hooting and hounding material hardly restrains the press in its questioning role — merely the manner in which it does it.

PRIVACY

The last quarter century has seen considerable debate about the right **8–37** to privacy. Clearly if such a right exists, it has similarities to some of

---

[42] Blackie, *HPLS II* at 702.

the law already discussed in that it might restrain free speech. It would, however, cover conduct not covered by any of the "expression" delicts — an example being surveillance. *Convicium* was mentioned some time ago as a possible source of protection of privacy.[43] Explanations of why there should be this increased debate will not be found here — the increase in printed and televisual media may have something to do with it, for they tend to seek out information about those in whom they think the public may be interested.

The recent attention turns mainly on the Human Rights Act. However, it is probably still worth considering governmental material and commentary predating this.

In 1990, the first Calcutt report was published.[44] It was established as a result of public concern about intrusions into the private lives of individuals by the press. Three criminal offences were proposed, which encompassed trespassing for a story, using surveillance devices and taking photographs or recordings without consent with a view to publication. Consideration was to be given to the law of Scotland to see if it required to be extended. No statutory right of reply was introduced. A tort of infringing privacy was not recommended for immediate introduction. The press was given a last opportunity to show that self-regulation worked. The offences proposed have not to date been introduced.

A government review was published in 1993.[45] It recommended the special offences be introduced in England but said nothing at all about Scotland. The review is an excellent source for the reader keen to consider the various problems that it is argued the law might address. The main interest for this book is recommendation (3), that consideration be given to introducing a tort of infringement of privacy.

---

[43] "The Right to be Let Alone" (1989) 34 J.L.S.S. 402.

[44] The Report of the Committee on Privacy and Related Matters, Cmnd 1102 (June 1990).

[45] Review of Press Self-Regulation, Cmnd 2135 (January 1993). For a discussion, see Carey Miller and Lardy, "Calcutt 11: Comments from a Scots Perspective", 1993 S.L.T. (News) 199. The Lord Chancellor's Department and the Scottish Office have (post-Calcutt II) published a discussion paper, Infringement of Privacy, July 1993, Central Office. The quotation this time is Milton: "For solitude sometimes is best society, and short retirement urges sweet return." For comment, see G.T. Laurie, "Privacy, Paucity and the Press", 1993 S.L.T. (News) 285. For a full review, see Hogg, "The Very Private Life of the Right to Privacy" (EUP, 1994), Hume Paper Vol.2, No.3. See generally, Kilbrandon, Lord, "The Law of Privacy in Scotland" (1971) 2 Cambrian L.R. 35. M.A. Hogg, "Privacy: A Valuable and Protected Interest in Scots Law", 1992 S.L.T. (News) 349, A.J. Bonnington, "Privacy: Letting the Right Alone", 1992 S.L.T. (News) 289, A.P. McKenzie, "Privacy: A New Right in UK law?" 2002 S.L.T. (News) 98.

In *Douglas and Others v Hello! Ltd and Others*,[46] it was held that the wedding of two celebrities could be regarded as a commodity and protected as a trade secret. Where the press took unauthorised pictures this could be a breach of commercial confidence — not privacy. Because the press were involved, Article 10 of the ECHR was engaged, but as the conduct in this case was in breach of the Press Complaints Commission Code, the balance was in favour of the plaintiffs existing right under the law of confidence not being eroded by Article 10. Then in a further development, in *Campbell v MGN Newspapers Ltd*,[47] the House of Lords supported a famous[48] model in her case against a newspaper for publishing details of her treatment for drug addiction and revealing she had lied about her condition in the past. At trial and to the end of the case, it had been accepted that the *Mirror* was entitled to publish the fact that Miss Campbell was a drug addict and was having therapy. She had publicly denied any involvement with illegal drugs, in particular in a television interview after an admission to a clinic in America in 1997, and the paper was entitled to put the record straight. It was also entitled, even obliged, to balance that disclosure with the fact that she was addressing the problem by having therapy. But, it was argued, the paper was not entitled to disclose that she was attending meetings of Narcotics Anonymous, or that she had been doing so for some time and with some frequency. Nor was it entitled to illustrate the story with covert photography of Miss Campbell in the company of other participants in the meeting.[49]

In the House, Lord Nicholls[50] said:

> "The continuing use of the phrase 'duty of confidence' and the description of the information as 'confidential' is not altogether comfortable. Information about an individual's private life would not, in ordinary usage, be called 'confidential. The more natural description today is that such information is private. The essence of the tort is better encapsulated now as misuse of private information."[51]

The long anticipated influence of the ECHR was influential:

> "The time has come to recognise that the values enshrined in Articles 8 and 10 are now part of the cause of action for breach

---

[46] 2003 T.L.R. 239.

[47] Unreported May 6, 2004. [2004] UKHL 22.

[48] "Even the judges know who Naomi Campbell is" Baroness Hale, 127.

[49] para.129 *per* Baroness Hale.

[50] Although he would have refused the appeal and the House was divided, they were largely united on the law applicable.

[51] para.14.

of confidence. As Lord Woolf CJ has said, the courts have been able to achieve this result by absorbing the rights protected by Articles 8 and 10 into this cause of action: *A v B plc* [2003] Q.B. 195, 202, paragraph 4. Further, it should now be recognised that for this purpose these values are of general application. The values embodied in Articles 8 and 10 are as much applicable in disputes between individuals or between an individual and a non-governmental body such as a newspaper as they are in disputes between individuals and a public authority."[52]

Lord Hope in the majority expressed the practical test: "what a reasonable person of ordinary sensibilities would feel if she was placed in the same position as the claimant and faced with the same publicity."[53]

---

[52] para.17. Referring to G. Phillipson's "Transforming Breach of Confidence? Towards a Common Law Right of Privacy under the Human Rights Act" (2003) 66 M.L.R. 726, 726–728.
[53] para.99.

SECTION III: NEGLIGENCE

CHAPTER 9

BASIC NEGLIGENCE

INTRODUCTION

Many scholars have written on the history and development of **9–1** liability generally, and in this area in particular.[1] While it is impossible to summarise the different views and the detailed history here, there are some propositions that are worth noting. The first is that the current law in Scotland is that which has been decided in the House of Lords in the twentieth and twenty-first centuries, in English as well as Scottish appeals.[2] Today, the main focus is on the existence of a duty of care. There is no liability for a failure to take reasonable care unless there was a duty to take care in the first place. This was not necessarily the Scots view.[3] However, after clearly demonstrating this, Black,[4] in a particularly penetrating historical analysis of the law, accepted that the duty of care concept is part of the law of Scotland.

Secondly, *culpa* is still discussed in Scottish cases, but usually in the negative sense of there being no liability without fault. *Culpa* itself is something of a compromise notion involving a question very like that of a notional duty of care. *Culpa* may have been an application, a more detailed expression, of *injuria,* the wrongfulness, in the sense of "against the law" of the *lex Aquilia* upon which the Scottish law was undoubtedly modelled. Kamba's conclusion for South African law, "[t]hat the English law concept of notional duty

---

[1] See the articles footnoted in this Chapter as well as those about *culpa* in Chapter 1.

[2] See Rodger, "Lord MacMillan's Speech in Donoghue v Stevenson" (1992) 108 L.Q.R. 236 for an earlier "Scottish" draft of the *Donoghue* speech.

[3] See Lord Kinnear in *Kemp & Dougall v Darngavil Coal Co. Ltd*, 1909 S.C. 1314 at 1319 and Lord President Dunedin in *Clelland v Robb*, 1911 S.C. 253 at 256 for the language of duty: Rodger, *op. cit.*, p.249.

[4] Black, *Historical Survey*, p.326. This is accepted too in the most recent historical survey, H. MacQueen and W.D.H. Sellar, "Negligence," *HSPL* 517 although they do not agree with Professor Black's explanation and offer their own. Interestingly an English academic has recently argued that the stage has now been reached such that the duty concept should be abandoned and replaced by a fault principle: B. Hepple, "Negligence: the Search for Coherence" [1998] C.L.P. 69 at 93. Note that he proposes that compensation for personal injury and death would be removed from the tort system.

of care is in substance the equivalent of the Roman-Dutch law requirement of wrongfulness (*injuria*) but the approach in the two systems of law is significantly different", may well be valid for Scots law — save that the approach to key "big issues" is now largely the same in Scotland and England. Although, expanding English horizons will often see cases from Germany, and sometimes France, considered along with the Commonwealth cases, when big issues are involved.

A person is only liable for being careless if they were legally obliged to take care in the first place.

It was one decision, *Donoghue v Stevenson*,[5] which laid the foundation for cases to be taken on the basis of negligence in new situations.[6] There were many negligence cases before and it was some time after the case before a more general approach emerged. That case is clearly established authority in both Scotland and in England, but controversy still exists over what exactly is its *ratio decidendi*. As well as clearly establishing the head of liability for unintentional physical harm, it has provided a workable conceptual framework for handling most cases involving clearly protected interests such as property or the person. It all began in a cafe in Paisley. Mrs Donoghue had gone along to the cafe with a friend who bought her an opaque bottle of ginger beer. The shopkeeper poured some ginger beer over ice cream in a glass from which Mrs Donoghue drank. Then her friend poured out the remainder which was when Mrs Donoghue alleged she saw a decomposed snail in the bottle and as a result (she alleged) she suffered a serious illness. As this was an example of a case proceeding only upon legal debate, the averments are assumed to be true. Mrs Donoghue did not have a contract with the seller nor with the manufacturer of the goods and so her only possible remedy was in delict against the manufacturer on the basis of his fault in not taking care in the production of the product.[7] The House of Lords held that the case was one which could proceed to a proof before answer (which means that it was not unsound in law). One thing that should be mentioned first is that at the time the most important thing the case did was to avoid the so-called heresy that there could be no delictual liability upon a defender if they had supplied goods under a contract — that in effect he was only liable to the customer. Instead the manufacturer of the product was held to owe a duty to take care because of the

---

[5] 1932 S.C. (HL) 31; for the whole story, see Rodger, 1988 C.L.P. 1.

[6] Although it should be appreciated that both jurisdictions allowed recovery for negligence before it.

[7] This case is justly famous and was celebrated by the Canadian Bar Association. The resulting "Paisley Papers" are a valuable collection of essays on negligence but also reveal some interesting background to the case. See also Rodger, "Mrs Donoghue and Alfenus Varrus", 1988 C.L.P. 1 and (1992) 108 L.Q.R. 236.

relationship between himself and the ultimate consumer — a relationship of proximity or "neighbourhood". This principle of liability is sometimes known as the "neighbourhood principle" after the following celebrated passage in Lord Atkin's speech. Although not a definition, this passage is often considered to express the principle upon which delictual liability for negligence proceeds:

> "The rule that you are to love your neighbour becomes in law, you must not injure your neighbour; and the lawyer's question, Who is my neighbour? receives a restricted reply. You must take reasonable care to avoid acts or omissions which you can reasonably foresee would be likely to injure your neighbour. Who, then, in law, is my neighbour? The answer seems to be-persons who are so closely and directly affected by my act that I ought reasonably to have them in contemplation as being so affected when I am directing my mind to the acts or omissions which are called into question."[8]

From the speeches in *Donoghue* and the treatment of it in later **9–2** cases, it is possible to set out something of a formula or algorithm for working out whether there may be an action for negligence (difficulties inherent in this framework are discussed in the next chapter):

(1) There must be a duty of care owed by the defender to the pursuer.
(2) There must be a breach of the duty.
(3) The breach must cause a loss.

Within each of these essential components there are other issues that have to be addressed. In so doing it must be appreciated that there is no such thing as negligence in the air — every case turns on its own facts — and that the categories of negligence are never closed: except in cases where the courts have actually excluded recovery as a matter of policy or precedent, it is always possible to argue that there is a ground of action.

1. DUTY OF CARE

"Neighbourhood" and reasonable foreseeability

From Lord Atkin's dictum, it can be seen that very much depends **9–3** upon whether the defender should reasonably have foreseen that his acts or omissions would cause harm to the pursuer. At this stage it

---

[8] *Donoghue, per* Lord Atkin at 44.

should be made clear that "acts or omissions" is not a phrase devoid of difficulty. Generally, there is no liability for a pure omission — that is a failure to do anything to prevent harm where there is no duty owed as where I see you about to walk off the edge of a cliff.[9] What is or is not reasonably foreseeable depends upon the foreseeability of the "reasonable man". The reasonable man has a place in many areas of the law, but certainly now spends most of his time as a legal device for determining whether or not there is liability for unintentional harm. The reasonable man is not the average man, for quite often he is far more rigorous in the conduct of his affairs than is the average man. Reasonable foreseeability is partly an objective test — we do not ask: did this defender foresee the harm; but neither do we assume a completely objective approach and say the reasonable man does or does not foresee X or Y. Instead we ask whether a reasonable man in the position of the defender would have contemplated the harm — a technique that might conveniently be described as "defender objectivity". We put the reasonable man in the defender's position and ask him what he can see. What is required is the application of reason and not prophecy.

A duty owed to a particular pursuer

9–4   Shortly after *Donoghue* the conceptual framework for negligence cases was developed further. *Bourhill v Young*[10] highlights these points. A motorcyclist who overtook in a way that a reasonable road user would not have done was sued by a woman who suffered nervous shock as a result of seeing the aftermath of the resulting accident. She had gone to see what had happened. It was held that she could not succeed. While the motorcyclist was careless in his actions and owed a duty not to be careless to, for example, other road users, he did not owe a duty of care to, and thus could not be said to be legally negligent towards, this particular pursuer. This was because she was outwith the ambit or the scope of the duty of care. The motorcyclist would not, in the Atkinian sense, have had her in his contemplation. He could have contemplated harm to people he might have struck with his cycle or even, perhaps, people who might have been struck by debris from a collision because they were in the

---

[9] See para.5.40; Logie, "Affirmative Action in the Law of Tort: the Case of the Duty to warn" (1989) 48 C.L.J. 115; Markesinis, "Negligence, Nuisance and Affirmative Duties of Action" (1989) 105 L.Q.R. 104. The other difficulty is characterisation: if I accidentally park my car on your foot and do not move it when you shout "Ouch, my foot!" is that an act or an omission? See *Fagan v Commissioner of Police of the Metropolis* [1969] 1 Q.B. 439.

[10] 1942 S.C. (HL) 78. This case has now had its human dimension explored. See W.W. McBryde, "Bourhill v Young: the Case of the Pregnant Fishwife" in Comparative and Historical Essays in Scots Law (Carey Miller and Meyers, eds, Butterworth, 1992), p.66.

vicinity, but not persons who only later came to the scene. This case was significant for Scots law because a civilian approach would be to achieve the same result by saying the motorcyclist was at fault, sufficient in itself for liability, but that the harm was too remote. The House, however, dealt with the matter on the basis that the deceased motorcyclist had not owed a duty to the pursuer. The remoteness issue is, however, a legitimate one in considering whether or not there is a duty of care at all. This is because the reasonable man would not contemplate an injury too remote from the act or omission. Thus remoteness of injury (as contrasted with the entirely different problem of remoteness of damage[11]) is part of the duty inquiry.[12] Negligence is therefore something different from carelessness, which is often used as a legally neutral word.[13] It is dangerous to use the word "negligence" other than in the sense of legally actionable carelessness. There must be a duty owed to the particular pursuer by the actual defender.

What is to be foreseen?

Just as it is from *Donoghue* that liability is judged on the basis of **9–5** the use of reason, so too from *Donoghue* it can be taken that what is to be foreseen is the injury to the pursuer.[14] "Injury" is not a helpful word in this context because as liability is based on *damnum injuria datum,* injury might be thought to relate *to injuria* whereas actually it is related to *damnum* (loss), often in the shape of personal injury (injury to the person in body or feelings). "Harm" signifies more accurately the object of foreseeability. Foreseeability is just like crystal ball-gazing. Courts who look at these problems after they have happened (*ex post facto*) are in the same position. If one had the gift of foresight, one might see the following sequence of events:

(1) Post office workers uncover a manhole in a public road.
(2) They erect a canvas shelter.
(3) They stop for a tea break.
(4) They remove the ladder from down the hole.
(5) They close the shelter with a tarpaulin.
(6) They place paraffin fuelled red warning lamps around the shelter and leave.
(7) Two young children remove the tarpaulin.
(8) They take up a paraffin lamp.

---

[11] See para.9–25.
[12] And see the discussion at para.9–5.
[13] Lawyers tend to use the word "accident" to cover incidents where there is loss or damage but no fault — the layman does not discriminate. He says, "I have had an accident — it was your fault."
[14] F. Bates, "What must be foreseen?" 1970 S.L.T. (News) 97.

(9) They enter the shelter.

(10) One knocks the lamp over.

(11) The paraffin unexpectedly vaporises and bursts out in a rush of flame.

(12) The boy loses his balance and falls, burning himself.

Looking at these events, it is clear that a line could conceivably be drawn at any event. One could say: you must not open manholes or you pay if someone gets harmed, or going on to number (3) you must not open a manhole and leave it unattended, and so on. In this case, the foresight that reason would permit us (as opposed to crystal ball-gazing) might fade around number (6) or (7) or (8) and certainly reason is strained at about (10), (11) and (12): it could be said that almost everything is foreseeable but not everything reasonably foreseeable. The facts set out above are basically those of *Hughes v Lord Advocate*.[15] The House of Lords decided that while the explosion might have been unforeseeable, the danger of an explosion and the harm it might cause was not different in kind to the harm that actually resulted. There was a reasonably foreseeable danger of harm by fire in some form if an open manhole, lamps and equipment were left about that were obvious allurements to young children. So in assessing what is reasonably foreseeable (or put another way, what is too remote to be reasonably foreseen) we are to look at the harm that actually occurred. In this case then, as the harm that occurred was injury by fire, the foreseeability required need only extend to about number (6) above. It should be appreciated that this is significantly different from saying that one must reasonably foresee what actually happened: that places the point of foresight at number (12) and would deny recovery, unlike *Hughes* where recovery was allowed.

The test is particularly difficult to apply in cases that involve a third party, largely because there is then the possibility of saying that the third party was the cause of the harm rather than the defender. This involves the question of causation, which is discussed below, but is usually approached, at least as a first step, by asking if there is a duty or whether harm of the kind which actually resulted should reasonably have been foreseen. Again, imagine our soothsayer consults the crystal ball and sees the following:

(1) Some borstal boys are working on an island.

(2) They are being supervised by borstal officers.

---

[15] 1963 S.C. (HL) 31. For a background account of the case, see Walker, "Reflections on a Leading Case" (1992) 37 J.L.S.S. 394.

(3) The supervisors go to bed instead of supervising the boys.
(4) Seven of the boys escape.
(5) They go on a yacht and crash into another yacht damaging it.

The owner of the second yacht sues the persons legally responsible **9–6** for the supervision of the boys. The problem in this case is that, as between the pursuer and the defender, the defender himself has not actually done anything to the pursuer. But that does not matter — we ask if there is a duty of care. It is reasonably foreseeable that borstal boys, if not guarded, will escape and that they, being on an island, will damage a yacht. The reasonable man foresees as far as number (4) and that is enough to establish the duty. And so the House of Lords held in a case on (basically) these facts.[16] It can, therefore, be said that before there can be a duty of care, the defender must be held to have been able reasonably to foresee that his acts or omissions would result in harm occurring of the kind that did actually result, it being unimportant that the actual harm resulted partly by the agency of the pursuer himself (*Hughes*) or by a third party (*Dorset Yacht*).

Often it is not necessary to take such a rigorous analytical approach to resolve such problems. If no ordinary reasonable man would be aware of the risk, he cannot be held reasonably to have foreseen it. Thus where patients developed spastic paraplegia caused by phenol entering molecular cracks in ampules containing local anaesthetic, it was held that as this was not a known hazard at the time it could not reasonably be foreseen: "We must not look at the 1947 accident with 1954 spectacles."[17] This pithy dictum of Lord Denning was anticipated in Scotland as long ago as 1861 when Lord Justice Clerk Inglis said:

"It is not sufficient to subject a party to liability for the consequences of an accident when people after the accident see how it might have been prevented, and say that he was bound to have seen that before the accident. There are many precautions adopted on the teaching of accidents such as this, and yet the omission of such precautions may not amount to that want of due precaution or that neglect for which an employer is responsible."[18]

---

[16] *Home Office v Dorset Yacht Co.* [1970] A.C. 1004.
[17] *Roe v Ministry of Health* [1954] 2 Q.B. 66.
[18] *Finningham v Peters* (1861) 23 D. 260 at 264.

This emphasises that although the court has the benefit of hindsight and can see the whole series of facts, reasonable foreseeability may well stop before any harm can be foreseen.

Outline of developments in the concept of the duty of care

9–7   The existence of a duty of care has been recognised in an ever widening set of circumstances but so, too, has it been recognised that in new cases it cannot be assumed in establishing new duties that reasonable foreseeability of harm or proximity alone will suffice. So while the *Donoghue* "neighbour principle" is seen as establishing a general duty to take reasonable care to avoid foreseeable direct physical injury or damage to property, other cases have gone further, but the potential scope of the principle has also been restained in other areas.

In *Hedley Byrne & Co. Ltd v Heller & Partners Ltd*,[19] the court held that there was a duty not to cause foreseeable economic loss even where there was no damage to the pursuer's person or property, if the pursuer received information from a person who knew that if it was wrong and reliance was placed upon it, and reliance was reasonably placed upon it, the pursuer would suffer loss.

The position had eventually come so far that Lord Wilberforce was able to say, in *Anns v Merton London Borough Council*,[20] that:

"Through the trilogy of cases in this House, *Donoghue v Stevenson*, *Hedley Bryne & Co. Ltd v Heller & Partners Ltd* and *Home Office v Dorset Yacht Co. Ltd*, the position has now been reached that in order to establish that a duty of care arises in a particular situation it is not necessary to bring the facts of that situation within those of previous situations in which the duty of care had been held to exist. Rather the question has to be approached in two stages. First one has to ask whether, as between the alleged wrongdoer and the person who suffered the damage, there is a sufficient relationship of proximity or neighbourhood such that, in the reasonable contemplation of the former, carelessness on his part may be likely to cause damage to the latter-in which case a prima facie duty of care arises. Secondly, if the first question is answered affirmatively, it is necessary to consider whether there are any considerations which ought to negative, or to reduce or limit the scope of the duty or the class of person to whom it is owed or the damages to which a breach of it may give rise."

---

[19] [1964] A.C. 465.
[20] [1978] A.C. 728 at 751.

In the Scottish appeal *Junior Books v The Veitchi Co.*[21] a duty was found to exist in a case where the defenders, who had no direct contract with the pursuers, did some work on the pursuers' property that was defective as opposed to dangerous: *i.e.* it was not within the principle of *Donoghue,* there being no harm to person or property. Since the case proceeded on the basis that there was no physical damage to his property, effectively the pursuer recovered a pure economic loss. Such a decision could have had enormous implications for the law relating to contracts generally, and consumer contracts in particular, so the House of Lords was careful to limit the decision to the special facts of the case. These matters are considered in more detail in the next chapter.

In the next chapter it will also be seen that the law has refused to **9–8** extend the duty of care established in *Junior Books. Junior Books* owned the building, the floor of which was defectively laid. In a later case the House of Lords preferred to follow a long line of precedent, stating that someone who did not own goods at the time they were damaged could not sue in delict.[22]

Then in two cases where consideration had been given to the duty of care, the Privy Council advised that reasonable foreseeability of economic loss was not itself a sufficient basis for establishing a duty of care; there has to be a close and direct relationship between the pursuer and the defender, such as was explicitly held to exist in *Junior Books.*[23] The House of Lords, in one English appeal, indicated that in future the two-stage test in *Anns* was not to be regarded in all circumstances as a suitable guide to the existence of a duty of care.[24] In two subsequent English appeals heard consecutively, the House of Lords departed from *Anns.*[25] In cases where a completely new kind of duty is sought to be imposed, the favoured test is now to ask if it is "fair, just and reasonable" so to do. Matters have gone so far from the high point generality of *Anns,* to the state where a case of careless damage to property caused indirectly was refused.[26] The working out of some of these developments is kept for the following chapters in this section.

---

[21] 1982 S.L.T. 492. For the kind of issues involved see J.G. Fleming, "Tort in a Contractual Matrix" (1995) 3 Tort L. Rev. 12.

[22] *Leigh and Sillavan Ltd v Aliakmon Shipping Co. Ltd (The Aliakmon)* [1986] 2 W.L.R. 902.

[23] *Yuen Kun Yeu v Att.-Gen. Hong Kong* [1988] 1 A.C. 175; *Wallace Edward Rowling et al. v Takaro Properties Ltd* [1988] 2 W.L.R. 418.

[24] *D. & F. Estates Ltd v Church Commissioners for England* [1989] A.C. 177. See R. Kidner, "Resiling from the *Anns* principle: the variable nature of proximity in negligence" (1987) 7 L.S. 319.

[25] See para.5.16; *Murphy v Brentwood D.C.* [1991] 1 A.C. 398; *Department of the Environment v Bates* [1991] 1 A.C. 499 the effect for general theory being that the trilogy of cases still stands, as does *Junior Books,* but the reasonable foreseeability *prima facie* test is seriously disapproved as a mode of determining new duties.

[26] See below at Ch.14.

2. Breach of a Duty

Reasonable care: the reasonable man (sic)

9–9   Once a duty is established a breach of that duty must also be present. Again the reasonable man is to the fore. This time he[27] is asked what he would or would not have done had he been in the defender's position, to eliminate the risk, which in the exercise of his reasonable foreseeability, he had identified. The nature of this requirement was examined in the Scottish case, *Muir v Glasgow Corporation*.[28] A church party obtained permission to use the defenders' tearoom. The tea-urn was carried by two men, McDonald and Taylor. For some unexplained reason, the urn was dropped and young Eleanor Muir was severely burned. The action was based on the fault of the manageress in allowing the urn to be carried through the tearoom or for not clearing the children out of the way.

It was accepted that the defenders owed a duty to the pursuer: the question was whether or not there had been a breach of this duty. The House of Lords made it clear that the standard to be used was the conduct of the reasonable man. This was said to be an impersonal test. "It eliminates the personal equation and is independent of the idiosyncrasies of the particular person whose conduct is in question." However, Lord MacMillan went on to add an important qualification:

> " . . . but there is a sense in which the standard of care of the reasonable man involves in its application a subjective element. It is still left to the judge to decide what, in the circumstances of the particular case, the reasonable man would have had in contemplation, and what, accordingly, the party sought to be made liable ought to have foreseen."

There is one comment that should be made about this reappearance of the reasonable man. In this context, the focus is not simply on whether it is possible for some harm of the kind suffered to result; instead "[t]he court must be careful to place itself in the position of the person charged with the duty, and to consider what he or she should have reasonably anticipated as a natural and probable consequence of neglect."[29] In the circumstances of *Muir*, it was held that the manageress had taken reasonable care: her duty was only to

---

[27] The reasonable man is linguistically embedded in the language of the law. The test is of course that of the reasonable person. L. Bender, "A Lawyer's Primer on Feminist Theory and Tort" (1988) 38 J. Legal Educ. 3. I am indebted to Wright, "Standards of Care in Negligence Law" in Philosophical Foundations of Tort Law (Owen, ed., 1996) for this trail.

[28] 1943 S.C. (HL) 3.

[29] *per* Lord Thankerton at 8.

take reasonable care, not to prevent all accidents occurring on the premises.

Reasonable care: risk and economics

The issue of breach of duty is usually considered in a more **9–10** practical way by assessing the various options that the reasonable man considers relevant. Economists can look at this exercise as a calculus of risk — assessing the probability of injury against the difficulty, expense and other factors involved in preventing or avoiding the injury. This, after all, is the sort of thing the reasonable man would do when directing his mind to the acts or omissions that are called into question — particularly so if "he" is a legal person like a large employer or a railway operator. It has to be said that it is seldom that judges actually or, rather, explicitly decide cases in this way. It may be that what follows reasonably represents the mechanism of their intuition or unarticulated thoughts. So, for example, when a seaman on a grain ship was sent below to fetch some timber and fell from a stair, he alleged breach of duty to provide a handrail. His employer stated that no other employers in that business erected such rails. The reasonable man is not, however, the average man and the court said:

> "If a real risk is one which would occur to the mind of a reasonable man and which he would not brush aside as far fetched ... then surely he would not neglect such a risk if action to eliminate it presented no difficulty, involved no disadvantage and required no expense."[30]

Again, in *Morris v West Hartlepool Steam Navigation Co. Ltd*,[31] it was said that in considering whether some precautions should be taken against a foreseeable risk, the duty is "to weigh on the one hand the magnitude of the risk, the likelihood of an accident happening and the possible seriousness of the consequences if an accident does happen, and on the other hand the difficulty and expense and any other disadvantage of taking precautions." A modern formulation of the factors to be considered in taking such a scientific approach[32] is as follows:

---

[30] *Overseas Tankship (UK) v Miller* [1967] 1 A.C. 617, *per* Lord Reid at 642.

[31] [1956] A.C. 552 at 574.

[32] The scientific approach is often called the "Learned Hand formula". It is called this after the US judge whose name was Learned Hand and who set it out in *United States v Carroll Towing Co.* (1947) 159 F (2d) 169 at 173: "If the probability [or harm] be called P; the [gravity of] injury L; and the burden [of adequate precautions] B; liability depends upon whether B is less than L multiplied by P; i.e. whether B<PL."

"First, the degree of probability that damage will be done by the conduct which is challenged; secondly, the magnitude of the harm which is likely to be done if the risk unfortunately materializes; thirdly, the value or utility of the object to be achieved by the conduct in question; and fourthly, the burden in terms of cost, time and trouble, of taking precautions against the risk of damage."[33]

Cases can be found that focus on one or other of these "elements" or more grandly, "variables".

1. The degree of probability

9–11 In *Bolton v Stone,*[34] for example, a woman was struck by a ball hit for six out of a cricket ground. She was walking on a quiet road adjacent to the park. The ball went over a 17-foot fence, which was about 80 yards from the batsman. The victim herself was about 100 yards from the batsman. Such a stroke had been played only some six times in 30 years and no one had been hit. The plaintiff failed.[35] There are many Scottish examples. In *Lamond v Glasgow Corporation,*[36] a pedestrian on a path alongside a golf course was struck by a ball. At proof it was established that about 6,000 shots went out of bounds each year, although no one had previously been struck. It was held that the injury was foreseeable. Although the path was never busy, there were various pedestrians using it between 9am and 5pm. Lord Thomson held there to be a real risk of injury. The cost/benefit analysis was accepted.[37] It was held that either a fence could have been built or the course redesigned.[38] In *Gillon v Chief Constable,*[39] the pursuer was a police officer who was injured when a footballer came off the field and knocked her over to her injury. She had been under orders to face away from the pitch. The case was essentially one of employers' liability, but it was held, after a consideration of

---

[33] Atiyah, *Accidents, Compensation and the Law* (3rd ed., 1980), p.44. Compare with *Hatton* guideline No.8 at para.21–6.

[34] [1951] A.C. 850.

[35] A claim in nuisance also failed. Prior to *Bolton*, but in different circumstances, a claim in nuisance had been successful where golf balls had regularly been hit out of bounds (*Castle v St Augustine's Links* (1922) 38 T.L.R. 615) and recently another similar claim based on negligence was successful in Scotland: *Whitefield v Barton,* 1987 S.C.L.R. 259, in which Bolton was considered and the sheriff principal appeared to be following *Castle*. See also the similar case of *Lamond v Glasgow Corp.*, 1968 S.L.T. 291.

[36] 1968 S.L.T. 291.

[37] *ibid.,* at 293.

[38] See *Whitefield v Barton*, 1987 S.C.L.R. 259 for another consideration in the sheriff court, this time for damage to a car by a golf ball.

[39] 1997 S.L.T. 1218.

Bolton and relevant evidence, that the happening was unforeseeable on the basis that there were no reported happenings. With respect this is a more simple case where it seems obvious that if you make people stand with their backs to an obvious and foreseeable hazard such as players coming off the pitch, which they do in every game, an accident is inevitable. This is reminiscent of the famous case in the *Digest* of the barber who shaves a person next to a place where people are playing ball.[40]

2. The magnitude of the harm

This factor is illustrated by *Paris v Stepney Borough Council*.[41] **9–12**
The plaintiff was blind in one eye as a result of enemy action during the war, but this was not known by his employers until discovered by the firm's medical officer. He was given notice. Before leaving the firm, he hit a bolt with a steel hammer and a piece of metal hit his good eye and he lost his sight in it, leaving him blind. The court accepted that there was a duty to supply goggles to this particular employee, taking into account the employer's knowledge of his disability, the seriousness of the injury and the likelihood of total blindness occurring. There would have been no breach of duty, on the evidence of practice at the time, if the pursuer had had two good eyes.

3. The value of the activity

If there is some extraordinary benefit that can be achieved this will **9–13**
allow an abnormally high risk to be assumed. In *Daborn v Bath Tramways Motor Co.*,[42] the defendants were responsible for the driving of an ambulance with a defective signalling system. There was, however, a sign at the back of the vehicle that said: Caution left hand drive. The court held that in wartime there was a necessity of using all possible vehicles and said it was necessary to balance the risk against the consequences of not assuming that risk and in *Daborn* that calculation was thought to work out in favour of the plaintiff. More recently, in Scotland, it was accepted (*obiter*) that less care may be taken in an emergency and even absent an emergency, a police driver legitimately in a hurry will not be held liable for a mere error of judgement.[43]

---

[40] D.9.2.11. Pr.
[41] [1951] A.C. 367; see also *McKinlay v British Steel Corp.*, 1987 S.L.T. 522; 1988 S.L.T. 810.
[42] [1946] 2 All E.R. 333.
[43] *Gilfillan v Barbour*, 2003 G.W.D. 26-747. The police driver and the other driver were held liable to each other with 50% contribution.

4. Knowledge of, availability of, or expense involved in taking, precautions

9–14   This factor may allow fewer precautions to be taken. For example, a large factory was flooded by an unusually heavy rainstorm. The water mixed with an oily liquid usually gathered in channels. The company spread sawdust on the floor, but they did not have enough to cover the whole area. The plaintiff slipped and a barrel he was rolling went over his leg. The only precaution that would actually have prevented the injury was to close the factory at great expense, when the risk had not been that likely. The court held that there was insufficient evidence that a reasonable employer would have closed the factory.[44]

While it will always be remembered that a serious personal injury is something to be avoided, the cost/benefit analysis sometimes finds favour. In *McErlean v J & B Scotland Ltd*,[45] a woman was injured while trying to clear a production line. The case raises some of the other points considered above, which are broadly within the economic/Learned Hand approach The dismissal of the case below was upheld on appeal. The following point was made in support of acquitting the defenders of negligence:

> "Accordingly the proper approach to this case is, I think, simply to ask whether the employers did, in all the circumstances, fail to take reasonable care. In considering that question, the circumstances to be taken into account include the magnitude of the risk, the seriousness of any injury which may result, and the difficulty and practicability of any measures required to eliminate it. In this case, there was a known risk, but it was a risk of minor injury."[46]

All I would say about this case is that while that dictum may be correct, a jury may take a quite different view of what is or is not a *serious* injury — not just in the familiar way of awarding higher damages, but in making the decision as to what a reasonable man would or would not do. Read the case and ask yourself where you would put the cost benefit balance if (a) you were the employer and (b) the injured person were a friend or a member of your family.

Reasonable man: usual practice

9–15   A related issue is that of usual practice. Once this was very important: if the defender could show that he followed usual practice,

---

[44] *Latimer v AEC Ltd* [1953] A.C. 643.

[45] 1997 S.L.T. 1326

[46] At 1330. Compare this case with *Macdonald v Scottish Stamping and Engineering Co. Ltd*, 1972 S.L.T. (Notes) 73.

this would indicate, as a matter of law, that he had not breached his duty.[47] The courts have, however, rectified that approach and usual practice is now simply a factor, albeit quite a significant one, in assessing whether the duty has been breached. In *Cavanagh v Ulster Weaving Co.*,[48] a labourer sued his employer. He had been wearing rubber boots provided by his employer and had fallen from a crawling ladder, which had no handrail, on to a glass roof while carrying a bucket of cement. The rubber boots had become wet and slippery. Expert evidence (which was unchallenged) was led to the effect that the system was perfectly in accord with good practice. The House of Lords held that on the evidence the jury had been entitled to find for the worker since the evidence as to trade practice alone could not be treated as conclusive in favour of the defendants. The other side of the coin is that simply not to follow a common practice will not constitute negligence if it is otherwise clear that reasonable care has been taken.[49] Overall, the issue is a practical one and the economic approach is only of use as a guide in identifying relevant factors.

Reasonable care: A lower standard for the below average?

It might be asked whether children, the infirm or the uneducated **9–16** need live up to a standard that is actually unattainable for them. The defender objectivity test would suggest that a child should be judged by the standard of the reasonable man in the position of a child, or if the defender is blind, then the reasonable man unable to see. With certain activities, especially if there is compulsory insurance, the temptation is to find the child or the blind man who, driving a lorry, runs down the pursuer. With the blind man it is possible to find liability based on the antecedent negligence in driving at all. So too with an ill person who becomes more ill whilst driving. With the child or the adult incapax it would be best to exculpate but find the person charged with the care of the person liable.[50] Alternatively some of the cases can be seen as exceptions. In the often cited case of *Nettleship v Weston*,[51] the Court of Appeal held a learner driver to owe the skill and care of the ordinary driver to the passenger who sat

---

[47] This approach was often called the "Dunedin formula": "Where the negligence of the employer consists of what I may call a fault of omission, I think it absolutely necessary that the proof of that fault of omission should be one of two kinds, either to skew that the thing which he did not do was a thing which was commonly done by other persons in like circumstances, or to shew that it was a thing which was so obviously wanted that it would be folly in anyone to neglect to provide it." *Morton v Wm Dixon*, 1909 S.C. 807.

[48] [1960] A.C. 145.

[49] *Brown v Rolls Royce Ltd*, 1960 S.C. (HL) 22; 1960 S.L.T. 119.

[50] Or the person in charge of the vehicle on a third party intervention case if careless or jointly if he permitted the use on the basis of he does who causeth do.

[51] [1971] 2 Q.B. 691.

in with her, but by a majority allowed a deduction of 50 per cent contribution because of his awareness of the risks. The correct approach, it is submitted, is that the standard should be lower — the reasonable man who cannot drive, being asked to drive like a good driver. It is possible on the principle *ars spondet artiam* to heighten the duty when a specially skilful task is considered. Driving is such a task as is vouched by the need to pass a test.

Reasonable care: a higher standard for the above average?

9–17   The reasonable man cannot, with any hope of success carry out brain surgery. As the reasonable man test is an objective test, to apply this test to cases of skilled persons would be to allow them to escape liability in all but the most gross cases where the conduct was such that no care could reasonably be exercised — as in the case of a drunken surgeon. So the law applies a higher standard based on that of the ordinary practitioner practising in the profession. This matter is discussed at length in the context in which it normally occurs — that of professional negligence.[52]

Reasonable care: impractical and immoral standards

9–18   Sometimes a standard cannot be set for lack of evidence. It may also be the case that a standard cannot be set on grounds of policy. The court will not set the standard of the reasonable burglar for the reasonable man does not burgle and the court would not want to hear such evidence. Such cases are normally considered under the *ex turpi* defence.

Reasonable care: multi-layered standards

9–19   The days of the guild are nearly gone. Professions share each others' functions. Nurses do what doctors did. Estate agents do what lawyers did. Professions are encouraged to be multi-disciplinary and persons to be multi-skilled. Demarcation in the workplace has gone. The one-stop shop is everywhere. Banks sell insurance. Insurers sell financial services. Against that background, an early contract case based on negligence against a company for dentistry work is helpful. The defenders argued that they were only expert in supplying and fitting false teeth, not in removing the teeth in relation to which they only had to do their poor untrained non-qualified best as their operatives were not qualified dentists.[53] It was held that the practitioner holding himself out to do dentistry had to meet the standard of a dentist. Done well, the one-stop shop can be very beneficial. There is

---

[52] Ch.22.
[53] *Dickson v Hygenic Institute*, 1910 1 S.L.T. 111.

the potential for confusion of responsibilities or a gap in responsibility.[54] Obviously, the practical answer to avoid these difficulties is either contractual provisions or statements defining obligations, but they will continue to arise so long as multi-disciplinary operations continue. Within a profession the same principle applies. The less experienced member of the profession, who holds himself out as a specialist or the trainee who does the qualified person's work, is judged by the higher standard, not his own level of competence.[55]

3. CAUSATION

The alleged breach of duty must in fact have been the real **9–20** predominant or effective cause of the occurrence that resulted in the pursuer's loss, injury or damage. In older cases it will be seen as the question whether the breach is the *causa causans* and not simply a *causa sine qua non* of the accident. That is question-begging labelling. Causation is no more than another aspect of attribution of responsibility. This element of the claim for unintentional harm has been severely criticised and should be looked at as simply another method of controlling potential liability. The law states what can or cannot be a legally effective cause and the inquiry into the fact is whether or not the breach of duty or wrongful act actually did cause the loss. This issue is also intimately connected with the issue of remoteness of damage. The reason there is this other enquiry is that the cases in which it arises are cases where there is another competing cause. On the predominant view of the world, if some effect is being examined it has a cause (whether identified or not). The pursuer must show that the defenders' breach caused the loss. The cases are really a category of successful challenges by defenders to theories of causation, arguments from common sense that fail or diversion of responsibility to some other cause — real or imagined.

If the harm would have occurred without the breach of duty then the breach is not even a *sine qua non* and is legally irrelevant. In *Barnett v Chelsea and Kensington Hospital Management Committee*[56] the plaintiff's husband had a cup of tea. Then he vomited persistently for three hours. A hospital doctor was contacted, who told the man to go home and see his own doctor. The plaintiff's husband died and indeed had been murdered! The action against the doctor for not treating the man failed because it was not shown that if treated immediately he would have lived — because of the nature of the poison introduced into the tea he would have died anyway. The

---

[54] *G. Percy Trentham Ltd v Beattie Watkinson and Partners* 1987 S.L.T. 449.
[55] *Wilsher v Essex Area Health Authority* [1988] A.C. 174.
[56] [1969] 1 Q.B. 428.

failure to treat, although a breach of duty, did not in any sense cause the harm. This is often called the "but for" test. The test applies in most cases, but it has been pointed out[57] that in the case of omissions and in the case of harm arising from multiple causes, the test is not so useful: in the case of a person shot in the head by two gunmen, neither is a cause utilising the "but for" test. The validity of causation in this sense is demonstrated by comparing it to *Dorset Yacht*. The borstal boys caused the damage, like the poisoner in *Barnett*, but the failure to supervise was an anterior cause of the borstal boys' damage; the posterior failure of the hospital was no cause at all. The competing cause that exculpates the defender can be nature itself — or anything, as it is the pursuer who must establish causation on balance of probabilities. In *Kay's Tutor v Ayrshire and Arran Health Board*,[58] the pursuer's son went to hospital suffering from meningitis. By a mistake in the treatment, the child was given a massive overdose of penicillin. As an immediate result the child suffered convulsions and hemiparesis. However, as a result of prompt remedial action the child soon recovered from these effects and recovered from the meningitis but turned out to be deaf. Evidence that the penicillin itself would damage the hearing nerve was rejected. Indeed, there was no known case where deafness had been caused by a penicillin overdose and very many where deafness had been caused by meningitis.

9–21   It has been well said that "[t]he choice of the real or efficient cause from out of the whole complex of the facts must be made by applying common-sense standards. Causation is to be understood as the man in the street, and not as either the scientist or the metaphysician would understand it."[59] The Second Division recently considered the common sense of causation in *Clements v Shell UK Ltd*.[60] The tenant of a salmon netting station alleged that Shell, whilst laying a pipeline, had allowed the channel to be blocked and silted up. The court, however, considered that the silt that blocked the river was produced by a natural mixing of salt water and fresh water. So while the concurrence of the silting and the laying of the pipe happened about the same time, they were coincidental and not linked in any way. Common suspicion that they might be was displaced by expert testimony, which was accepted of a natural cause. In *P.'s Curator Bonis v CICB*[61] a child was born as a result, it was alleged, of incestuous rape. One point that is made below is that the

---

[57] Atiyah, pp.116–121.

[58] 1987 S.L.T. 577.

[59] *Yorkshire Dale S.S. Co. v MOWT* [1942] A.C. 691 at 706. See Mullany, "Common-sense Causation — an Australian View", 1992 O.J.L.S. 431. This article concludes that "modern psychological research indicates that it is unlikely that there is any consistent common-sense notion of what constitutes a cause" p.436.

[60] 1991 G.W.D. 35–2153.

[61] 1997 S.L.T. 1180.

injuries were caused by the incestuous genetic element rather than the act of violence. Lord Osborne said:

> "I do not think it is disputed that the court ought to adopt the common sense approach to causation referred to in a number of decisions . . . The message which emerges from these cases is that causation is not to be examined in any metaphysical or scientific sense, but in the wider and more liberal sense in which the matter would be understood by the man in the street applying commonsense standards . . . the respondents draw a distinction between the birth of the child, which they accept was directly attributable to an act of rape, and the 'injuries'. It appears to me that a jury or the ordinary man would not draw such a distinction. I consider that they would accept that the birth of the child and its disabilities were both directly attributable to the same criminal act, namely the acknowledged act of rape."[62]

Material contribution

The breach, need not be only the whole complete cause — it is **9–22** sufficient that it has materially caused the harm. This was decided in *McGhee v NCB.*[63] A labourer whose normal duties were in a pipe kiln was sent to work in a brick kiln, where the working conditions were hotter and dustier. The workman later contracted dermatitis and sued, *inter alia*, on the basis that his employer failed to provide showering facilities at the work place. By the time the case reached the House of Lords, it was admitted that there had been a breach of a duty of care. The House found that as the breach of duty had materially increased the risk of the harm, this was sufficient to establish causation.

In *Kay's Tutor v Ayrshire and Arran Health Board,*[64] the pursuer's son was taken into hospital with meningitis. By mistake, he was given a massive overdose of penicillin. As an immediate result he suffered convulsions and hemiparesis. He recovered from that and the meningitis and but was now deaf. The evidence was that there were many cases where meningitis caused deafness and none caused by a penicillin overdose. The defenders admitted that the doctor was negligent (*i.e.* had breached his duty) and accepted responsibility for the convulsions and hemiparesis. The answer was in the negative. It could not be a cause at all. In the House of Lords, attempts were

---

[62] *ibid.,* at 1200.
[63] 1973 S.C. (HL) 37.
[64] 1987 S.L.T. 577. In a relatively recent case a lady who suffered a stroke six days after starting a course of contraceptive pills could not establish that they were the cause and absolvitor was granted: *Ingram v Ritchie,* 1989 G.W.D. 27–1217.

made to rely on *McGhee*. This was held not to be possible because:

> "The principle in *McGhee* would only fall for consideration if it was first proved that it was an accepted medical fact that penicillin in some cases caused or aggravated deafness."[65]

So, for a time, *McGhee* was thought to be of very narrow application. However, it was dramatically rehabilitated in a most perplexing case. In *Fairchild v Glenhaven Funeral Services*,[66] the facts were complicated, but the legal issue came down to this. The plaintiff contracted mesothelioma; 90 per cent of such cases are preceeded by asbestos use. It needs only the smallest amount of asbestos to bring about the condition. The plaintiff worked for more than one employer who exposed him to asbestos. However, he could not bring fault home to any one employer. He could not say it was employer A's dust as opposed to that of B or C. Accordingly, *all* the employers were released. The House of Lords, however, held that the claims were not doomed on causation, *inter alia*, by accepting that *McGhee* had moved the law on. While some parts of the various speeches in the House try to limit the case to its very own facts, it is submitted that *Fairchild* cannot be treated as applying only to mesothelioma cases. It is, however, reasonably limited to cases where the claimant has proved all that he possibly can. There must have been an increased risk of injury to the actual plaintiff. The increased risk must actually have been a cause of injury in the actual case.[67] The case has already been discussed in Scotland.[68]

Novus actus interveniens

9–23   This phrase identifies a particular type of causation problem — that which arises when another cause (often but not necessarily an act of a third party) results in harm to the pursuer after the defender has breached his duty. Generally, there is a presumption against a subsequent act being a *novus actus*. This is because if it is treated as

---

[65] *per* Lord Griffiths at 581. In the later case of *Wilsher v Essex Area Health Authority* [1988] 2 W.L.R. 577 the House seemed to go even further in restricting the scope of *McGhee*. In *McLatchie v Scottish Society for Autism*, 2004 G.W.D. 4–67, it was expressly mentioned that doubts expressed in *Wilsher* had been dispelled by *Fairchild*.

[66] [2003] 1 A.C. 32. For a full analysis of the speeches, see R. Milligan, "*Fairchild v Glenhaven Funeral Services*," 2002 46 Rep. B. 1. See also S. Arnell, "Causation reassessed," 2002 S.L.T. 265, A Gore, "Asbestos claims" [2002] J.P.I.L. 105.

[67] See *Wilsher*.

[68] A vibration white finger case succeeded in *McKenna v British Railways Board*, 2003 G.W.D. 743, which included a valuable (obiter) discussion of the applicability of *Fairchild* in Scotland. In *McLatchie v Scottish Society for Autism*, 2004 G.W.D. 67, it was accepted that the case had swept away the doubts that had been cast over *McGhee*.

a *nova causa*, the original wrongdoer is completely discharged. There are no definite rules of law fixing what is or is not a *novus actus*:

> "There are certain propositions that I think are well established and beyond question in connection with this class of case. One is that human action does not per se sever the connected sequence of acts . . . The question is not whether there was new negligence but whether there was a new cause . . . It must always be shown that there is something which I will call ultroneous, something unwarrantable, a new cause coming in disturbing the sequence of events, something that can be described as either unreasonable or extraneous or extrinsic. I doubt very much whether the law can be stated more precisely than that."[69]

The courts take a flexible approach to such questions and the rather rigid, last opportunity rule,[70] which ascribed causality to the actor who had the last opportunity to avoid an accident, is only of use as a guide, if at all, to cases where one of the participants is stationary. The proper approach is that taken in *The "Boy Andrew" v The "St Rognvald"*.[71] A steamship was doing nine knots trying to overtake a drifter doing eight knots. The ships were apart by a lateral distance of 100 feet. The stern of the steamship was nearly level with the stern of the drifter. The drifter, without warning, made a move to starboard, which immediately became a sharp swerve. The master of the steamship gave the order "hard starboard" and rang the engine room to stop. Unfortunately the drifter was struck aft and 15 feet from the stern, killing the whole crew. What was the cause of the loss of the life? Was it the drifter in turning off its course? Was it the steamship for trying to overtake without leaving the other vessel a wide berth? It was held that both ships' actions were causes of the loss. The last opportunity rule was therefore not applied and said to be of a very limited value.

It is open to the court then to find a *novus actus* as a result of the **9–24** actings of a third party and thereby exonerate the defender. At this stage the inquiry resembles and overlaps the remoteness of injury question. In short, the intervention of a third party will not operate as a *novus actus* if it is the very kind of thing that the defender was supposed to take reasonable care to prevent. The position on this point is not absolutely clear, particularly as to the degree of likelihood of the intervention — this, it would seem, is a matter of fact to be left to the tribunal of fact. Two divisions of the Inner House

---

[69] *The Oropesa* [1943] P. 32; 1 All E.R. 214.
[70] *Davies v Mann* (1842) 10 M. & W. 546.
[71] 1947 S.C. (HL) 70.

had taken fixed and divergent views, one holding that the intervention had to be very likely, the other that it was sufficient if it were likely.[72] The House of Lords indicated that the position is more fluid:

> "Unless the judge can be satisfied that the result of the human action is highly probable or very likely he may have to conclude that all that the reasonable man could say was that it was a mere possibility. Unless the needle that measures the probability of a particular result flowing from the conduct of a human agent is near the top of the scale it may be hard to conclude that it has risen sufficiently from the bottom, to create the duty reasonably to foresee it."[73]

This leaves the matter quite at large for the fact-finding tribunal. The broader issues involved in the intervention of third parties are discussed in Chapter 13.

Another aid to flexibility is the Law Reform (Miscellaneous Provisions) (Scotland) Act 1940, s.3, which provides:

> "(1) Where in any action of damages in respect of loss or damage arising from any wrongful acts or negligent acts or omissions two or more persons are ... found jointly and severally liable in damages or expenses, they shall be liable inter se to contribute to such damages or expenses in such proportions as the jury or the court ... may deem just ...
>
> (2) Where any person has paid any damages or expenses ... he shall be entitled to recover from any other person who, if sued, might also have been held liable in respect of the loss or damage on which the action was founded, such contribution, if any, as the court may deem just."

The pursuer's own actings may be such that he has caused his own loss despite some breach of duty by the defender, and so a claim will fail. Lawyers say in cases like this, rather quaintly, that the pursuer is the "author of his own misfortune". This is the result where, for example, a worker does not use or would not have used a safety device that the employer has failed to provide in breach of duty and which the workman alleges would have prevented his injuries.[74] If his conduct falls short of being causative to the exclusion of the

---

[72] *Squires v Perth & Kinross District Council*, 1986 S.L.T. 30; *Maloco v Littlewoods Organisation Ltd*, 1986 S.L.T. 272; and see also *Bell v Scottish Special Housing Association*, 1987 S.L.T. 320 and *Maloco (Smith) v Littlewoods*, 1987 S.L.T. 425, *per* Lord Mackay at 433.

[73] *Maloco (Smith) v Littlewoods*, 1987 S.L.T. 425, *per* Lord Mackay at 433.

[74] *Donaghy v NCB*, 1957 S.L.T. (Notes) 35.

defender's liability, then it may be sufficient lack of care for his safety to amount to the defence of contributory negligence.[75]

REMOTENESS OF DAMAGE

Remoteness of damage (as opposed to remoteness of injury) operates **9–25** throughout the law of damages and is essentially a method of preventing a wrongdoer having to pay for all the results of his wrongdoing. It operates to protect someone in breach of contract as much as someone who has been in breach of a delictual duty. The issue of remoteness of damage in delict can only come into play once it has been established that a legal wrong has taken place, *i.e.* that some loss or injury has occurred.

An *obiter* remark of Lord Kinloch is often cited in this area. It has recently been agreed that, properly interpreted, it is a useful starting point.[76] He said:

> "The grand rule on the subject of damages is, that none can be claimed except such as naturally and directly arise out of the wrong done; and such, therefore, as may reasonably be supposed to have been in the view of the wrongdoer."[77]

Although quite pithy, this statement does not set out one clear test. In the first part it espouses a direct and natural consequences test, but in the second part it introduces the reasonable foresight of the wrongdoer. The House of Lords has now unanimously decided in a Scottish appeal, *Simmons v British Steel plc*,[78] that, properly interpreted, this is a test of reasonable foreseeability.

In this student textbook, there is a real temptation to go over again the great cases that led English law to this conclusion some time ago, but there are new difficulties and new disputes and it seems proper to take the benefit given by the House and to say that these old cases and debates are now relegated to further study for the dedicated student.[79] Any new problems should be soluble by application of the

---

[75] See para.25–9.

[76] *Simmons v British Steel plc*, [2004] UKHL 20, *per* Lord Rodger paras 60 and 66. *Per* Lord Hope at 19.

[77] *Allan v Barclay* (1864) 2 M. 873 at 874; for a more recent application see *Runciman v Borders R.C.*, 1988 S.L.T. 135.

[78] [2004] UKHL 20. Indeed when this book was in manuscript there was a sign that such a development could take place. See *Langden v O'Conner* [2003] T.L.R. 667.

[79] Re *Polemis and Furness, Withy and Co. Ltd* (known as "*Polemis*") [1921] 3 K.B. 560. *Overseas Tankship (UK) Ltd v Morts Dock & Engineering Co.* (known as "*The Wagon Mound (No.1)*") [1961] A.C. 388. M. Davies, "The Road from Morocco: Polemis, Donoghue, No Fault" (1982) 45 M.L.R. 534. R. Kidner, "Remoteness of Damage: the Duty Interest Theory and the Re-interpretation of The Wagon Mound", 1989 L.S. 1. See the literature and cases discussed in *Simmons* itself.

Grand Rule, the following *Simmons* guidelines, and the existing law and developments in England where there has been more experience with this rule.

9–26 The present state of the law is now as set out by Lord Rodger in *Simmons v British Steel plc*[80]:

> "These authorities suggest that, once liability is established, any question of the remoteness of damage is to be approached along the following lines which may, of course, be open to refinement and development. (1) The starting point is that a defender is not liable for a consequence of a kind which is not reasonably foreseeable: *M'Kew v Holland & Hannen & Cubitts (Scotland) Ltd,* 1970 S.C. (HL) 20, 25 *per* Lord Reid; *Bourhill v Young*, 1942 S.C. (HL) 78, 85 *per* Lord Russell of Killowen; *Allan v Barclay* (1864) 2 M 873, 874 *per* Lord Kinloch. (2) While a defender is not liable for damage that was not reasonably foreseeable, it does not follow that he is liable for all damage that was reasonably foreseeable: depending on the circumstances, the defender may not be liable for damage caused by a *novus actus interveniens* or unreasonable conduct on the part of the pursuer, even if it was reasonably foreseeable: *M'Kew v Holland & Hannen & Cubitts (Scotland) Ltd*, 1970 S.C. (HL) 20, 25 *per* Lord Reid; *Lamb v Camden London Borough Council* [1981] Q.B. 625; but see *Ward v Cannock Chase District Council* [1986] Ch 546. (3) Subject to the qualification in (2), if the pursuer's injury is of a kind that was foreseeable, the defender is liable, even if the damage is greater in extent than was foreseeable or it was caused in a way that could not have been foreseen: *Hughes v Lord Advocate*, 1963 S.C. (HL) 31, 38, 40 *per* Lord Reid. (4) The defender must take his victim as he finds him: *Bourhill v Young*, 1942 S.C. (HL) at p.92 *per* Lord Wright; *M'Killen v Barclay Curle & Co Ltd*, 1967 S.L.T. 41, 42, *per* Lord President Clyde. (5) Subject again to the qualification in (2), where personal injury to the pursuer was reasonably foreseeable, the defender is liable for any personal injury, whether physical or psychiatric, which the pursuer suffers as a result of his wrongdoing: *Page v Smith* [1996] 1 A.C. 155, 197F–H, *per* Lord Lloyd of Berwick."[81]

It may also be assumed that Lord Hope's position in the earlier English case of *Langden v O'Conner*,[82] a case of consequential damage to moveable property, will now apply here. In the course of his speech Lord Hope said:

---

[80] [2004] UKHL 20.
[81] *per* Lord Rodger at para.67.
[82] [2003] T.L.R. 667.

"The same approach has been adopted in Scotland. In *Chanthall Investments Ltd v FG Minter Ltd*, 22 January 1976 (reported on another point in 1976 S.C. 73) Lord Keith, sitting in the Outer House of the Court of Session, said: 'I am of opinion that in each case where the matter arises it is a question of fact, in the particular circumstances, whether loss associated with the impecuniosity of the party claiming to have suffered loss was within the contemplation of the parties. Authority for this proposition is to be found in *Trans Trust SPRL v Danubian Trading Co* [1952] 1 K.B. 285.' This statement was approved by the Inner House in *Margrie Holdings Ltd v City of Edinburgh District Council*, 1994 S.L.T. 971, 976-977, where the Lord President (Hope), delivering the opinion of the court said that the proper approach, consistent with the modern authorities, was to ask whether the loss was or was not foreseeable and that this was ultimately a question of fact in each case."[83]

---

[83] [2003] UKHL 64 para.58.

CHAPTER 10

ECONOMIC LOSS

10–1 When delicts and torts were first growing, wealth was in land and in the person's ability to sell his labour. So the law had delicts and torts that protected land and the person. The shift of wealth to contract and to capital is a shift to the less tangible. While a contract may be written on paper, it need not be and its worth can be more than the largest estate. The ostensible castle may be mortgaged to the turret and the shares in the company holding that mortgage worth more than the castle. Other aspects of life begin to seek protection. The other pressure is that negligence as a ground of liability has caught on. Once lack of care is actionable in many situations it is then asked, why should it matter what form the loss takes? Once people are being made to pay for their bungles, it is suggested that they should pay for them all. I break the tip of your little finger by accident and I have to pay; what if I accidentally ruin you by giving you poor advice? In one case the loss is bearable although-strictly speaking and for the ancient Romans — irreparable, whereas the other is reparable simply by paying money. Yet the law baulks. Now we turn to the rules and themes and "principles" to see what the law says. The present writer does not consider that the law has yet "settled", regardless of what the House of Lords has said, and so to state the law as it is or will be in the next big case requires not a dogmatic statement of a view or any particular dicta but, so far as is in keeping with the concise mission of the text, an exposition of the rules and themes and such principles as have emerged.[1]

One juridical point that should not be missed, as we have already seen,[2] is that the law is "canny" about the protection it gives to intentional harm to economic interests — to give more protection where the wrongdoer was merely negligent would cause juridical problems.

The law quite happily awards damages for what could be called "economic loss" in many cases. What is easily compensated is a

---

[1] The House of Lords itself appears to have realised that it should not change its mind too often but it remains the case that 3:2 majorities are common. Of course the case in which it decided not to change its mind too often was decided 4:3! *Rees v Darlington Memorial Hospital Trust* [2003] T.L.R. 568.
[2] Ch.5.

person's loss of wages while he is injured, or the loss of use of an item while it is being repaired. These are economic losses but losses that are well recognised as beyond dispute. The law has no difficulty with such claims because they are closely derived from previously legally recognised interests — a person is injured or property damaged and other losses follow. Such consequential loss is quite easily and reasonably foreseeable and likely to be limited to an amount of money bearing some proportional relationship to the person or thing damaged. After that the law scatters and principle is difficult to organise. It is possible to detect two sets of cases that may or may not reflect some form of complex principle — they do offer predictive value.[3] There are then other cases!

For the purposes of this concise exercise, it is hoped that no **10–2** serious injustice is done to the complexity of the subject if these are treated as follows:

(1) *Hedley Byrne* liability (assumption of liability/special relationship cases).
(2) *Simpson v Thomson* bright line non-liability cases (economic loss derived from non-pursuer).
(3) *Henderson v Merrit* liability (expanded *Hedley Byrne* liability).
(4) *Miscellaneous: White v Jones* liability.

It is possible to treat the failed sterilisation type of cases[4] and the indirect damage cases[5] as types of difficult economic loss case and in any full review that should be considered.

1. *Hedley Byrne* liability (assumption of liability/special relationship cases)

The foundation case, as important as *Donoghue*, is *Hedley Byrne* **10–3** *& Co. Ltd v Heller and Partners*.[6] It established that there could be liability for a negligent misstatement and at the same time clarified a number of other matters. The plaintiffs were a firm of advertising consultants. They booked advertising for clients on the basis that they (*Hedley Byrne*) themselves would be contractually liable to the

---

[3] I am obliged to A.B. Wilkinson, and Forte, A.D.M., "Pure Economic Loss — a Scottish Perspective", 1985 J. R. 1, which, some time ago now, clearly identified for me these two lines of cases. Students should still find the article helpful once they have surveyed the main cases. Two other key analytical articles that will help with the current law are Hogg, "Relational Loss, the Exclusory Rule and the High Court of Australia" (1995) 3 Tort L. Rev. 26; Cane, "Contract Tort and the Lloyd's Debacle" in Consensus in Idem (Oxford, 1996). And for a full Scottish analysis see Hogg, *Obligations*, (Avizandum, 2003).
[4] See para.23–27.
[5] See Ch.14.
[6] [1964] A.C. 465.

advertiser. Accordingly, it was important for them to make inquiry into the creditworthiness of their customers. In this case, they did so by contacting their own bankers, who in turn contacted the defenders, who were the bankers of the client company, Easipower. In reply, the defendants said that Easipower were believed to be "respectably constituted and considered good for its normal business engagements" and that it "would not undertake any commitments they were unable to fulfil." A later inquiry obtained a similar response by letter with a statement that the letter was "without responsibility".

The actual decision in the case was that there should be no recovery of damages because of the effect of the disclaimer in the letter, but that decision implied that the court accepted the following propositions: (1) there can be liability for words as much as for deeds; (2) despite the absence of a contract there can be liability in respect of negligent mis-statements if a special relationship exists; (3) there can be recovery for a pure economic loss even where it does not arise from damage to the pursuer's property.

It is the existence or otherwise of this special relationship that filters cases out. Not every loss through a misstatement will attract liability. Whether or not a special relationship exists will depend on each case. Sometimes this will be very obvious, especially if there is an existing relationship such as in the case of solicitor and client. But *Hedley Byrne* is authority for recognising a non-contractual special relationship where two factors are present: (1) the pursuer reasonably relies on the statement made by the defender; and (2) it was reasonable that the defender should know that the pursuer would rely on the statement. It is this element of *reliance* that allowed the disclaimer to be effective. At the very time the statement was made, there was a disclaimer made that would prevent the reasonable man in the position of the recipient taking advantage of it. The relevance of this formulation of the duty of care to the professions is that quite often they will exhibit or profess a certain skill and in so doing will almost automatically engender reliance.

In the many years that have passed, this case has been interpreted and reinterpreted. Following *Yuen Kun Yeu*,[7] it was, and sometimes still is, interpreted more from the defender's point of view, the question asked being simply, "Has the defender assumed responsibility for the statement complained of?"

10–4 It should be added here, parenthetically, that doubts that *Hedley Byrne* might not extend to Scotland or that it might be restricted to certain particular trades or professions were set aside by the case of *Martin v Bell-Ingram*,[8] which both established *Hedley Byrne* liability

---

[7] [1988] W.L.R. 175; and see also *Rowling v Takaro Properties Ltd* [1988] 2 W.L.R. 418; and *D. & F. Estates Ltd v Church Commissioners for England* [1988] 3 W.L.R. 368.

[8] 1986 S.L.T. 575.

in Scotland and made it clear that surveyors could be liable to persons other than those who instructed them. Surveyors in that case were held liable to a disappointed purchaser who bought on the basis of the survey and found that he had purchased a property worth far less than the surveyor had indicated. The complicating factor had been the fact that the survey had been prepared on the instructions of the building society that was lending money to the purchaser, not the purchaser himself. There was no contract and so only delict could provide a remedy. Liability was established on the basis that a reasonable purchaser would rely on the report given to the lender. In *Martin*, a disclaimer was issued, just as in *Hedley Byrne*,[9] except the disclaimer came in writing after the initial misstatement and after the pursuer had suffered his loss by contracting to buy the house. The disclaimer was held ineffective.

This idea of the foreseeability of the misstator that the statement would be relied upon by the actual pursuer harmed reached the House of Lords in *Caparo Industries plc v Dickman*.[10] Accountants were auditors to a company. There are statutory requirements for such an audit. The plaintiffs alleged that on the basis of the accounts they bought more shares and took over the company. The accounts, they alleged, were negligently prepared and they suffered loss. The House of Lords held that there was no duty of care between the accountants and potential purchasers of shares. The accountants owed a duty to the shareholders as members of the company to prepare the accounts properly to the extent that the shareholders could utilise the accounts to judge the health of their company; they did not owe a duty to potential purchasers of shares. The difficulty of this distinction can be illustrated by the example of the shareholder who sells his shares as a result of wrongly prepared accounts. Lord Bridge distinguished the two types of investment decision in such a way that, although not decided, the case of sale might be decided differently. If specific representations are made to a potential acquirer with the intent to induce reliance, then a case is statable on the basis of this proximity, the potential pursuer being identifiable.[11] Indeed, in a Scottish case, a proof before answer has been allowed against auditors since.[12]

---

[9] *Harris v Wyre Forest D.C.* [1988] 2 W.L.R. 1173 and on appeal [1989] 2 W.L.R. 790.

[10] [1990] 1 All E.R. 568; see the discussion and application of the case in *Al Nakib Investments v Longcroft* [1990] 3 All E.R. 321 and in the Scottish case *Bank of Scotland v 3i plc*, 1992 G.W.D. 6–321.

[11] *Morgan Crucible Co. plc v Hill Samuel* [1991] 1 All E.R. 148.

[12] *The Royal Bank of Scotland Plc v Bannerman Johnstone Maclay*, 2003 S.L.T. 181.

A high point of liability based on *Hedley Byrne* is measured by a Scottish case, *Junior Books v The Veitchi Co.*[13] The pursuers, who owned a factory, entered into a contract with Ogilvie (Builders) Ltd for the laying of a floor in the production area. Ogilvie sub-contracted to the Veitchi Co. as specialist sub-contractors. Junior Books sued for the losses due to bad workmanship, which they said resulted in them obtaining a floor which was defective, although not dangerous, and which would involve expense in being put right. Thus they were suing over the head of their contracting party — Ogilvie — and for a floor which was defective, but which had not caused danger to the health or safety of any person nor risk of damage to any other property belonging to the owner of the floor. This case has been much analysed and discussed. It raised a very large number of points, the most important of which can be set out as follows: (1) Is there liability for carelessly done work which will foreseeably cause economic loss as a result of its defective condition? (2) Is there a difference between houses and goods? (3) Is the fact that the defender has or may have contractual exemptions a relevant factor in formulating his duty to the pursuer who was not a party to the contract? The answers given in the case were: (1) yes, in certain circumstances but not by any means all; (2) yes; (3) possibly, but the point did not require to be decided. These answers decided very little save the point in the case, particularly because of the terms of the leading speech which concentrated on the facts of the case. However, the attitude to the first and primary question made and makes the case of the first significance. In achieving that positive answer, considerable doubt was again cast upon the floodgates argument: that if the case were successful there might be, in Cardozo's phrase, "liability in an indeterminate amount for an indeterminate time to an indeterminate class." Answers (2) and (3) above can be seen in the speeches of the "nearly dissenter" Lord Keith and the "dissent" of Lord Brandon of Oakbrook. Lord Keith agreed with the majority decision, but expressed considerable reservations. First, he considered that the case could not and should not be used to develop a liability for defective products generally; and secondly, he agreed with Lord Brandon that there might be difficulties in formulating the duty of care where there are exemption clauses in the contract under which the work is done initially. Lord Brandon dissented and would have allowed the appeal resulting in the case being dismissed. The majority refused the appeal and allowed the case to proceed to a proof before answer. The decision is clearly right and is so on the expressed basis, that of the proximity of the parties. Lord Roskill came to his conclusion based on eight points of proximity, which included factors such as that the potential

---

[13] 1982 S.L.T. 492.

pursuer was known precisely by the defender and that the pursuer relied upon the defender and that the defender was aware the pursuer was relying upon him. The case was quickly taken up by litigants and almost as quickly denounced by commentators and courts.[14] It was called "a damage to property case", which clearly it was not.[15] It was said to depend very largely on its own facts, said (with respect rather exaggeratedly) to be unique, and unable to lay down any principle in the law of delict.[16] It has been suggested that the House succumbed too easily to a proximity test.[17] However, the case is now even more secure, than it has been in view of the decision in *Henderson* noted below.[18] That said, it is very unlikely that in such a case the defenders would not now put in issue the contract between the pursuer and the absent third party (*e.g.* the Ogilvie figure).

The scope of cases falling within the arguments relating to primary **10–5** economic loss expanded because the House of Lords correctly reclassified certain losses as economic losses rather than damage to property cases. In *D. & F. Estates v Church Commissioners*,[19] plaster was incorrectly applied by sub-contractors (Hitchins) to a wall. The court at first instance held the main contractor (Wates) liable for a series of losses resulting from the defect. Both the Court of Appeal and the House of Lords disagreed. The loss was held to be pure economic loss, which is not itself recoverable under *Donoghue*. That was correct. In another landmark case, *Murphy v Brentwood District Council*,[20] the House of Lords departed from *Anns* on the fundamental question of the duty owed by a local authority and this aspect of the case is dealt with later in this chapter.[21] The importance of the case in this context is that it firmly established a line between economic loss and physical damage. A building that falls down and causes damage is dangerous and covered by *Donoghue v Stevenson.* The collapse of the building is not actionable damage under *Donoghue* because it does not damage other property; it is damage to the thing-in-itself. The error in *Anns*, which itself originated in the

---

[14] See, generally, Logie, "The Final Demise of Junior Books", 1989 J.R. 5 (Casebook, Ext. 42).

[15] *Tate & Lyle Industries v Greater London Council* [1983] 2 A.C. 509.

[16] *D. & F. Estates v Church Commissioners* [1988] 3 W.L.R. 368, *per* Lord Bridge.

[17] *Maloco v Littlewoods Organisation Ltd*, 1987 S.L.T. 425, *per* Lord Goff.

[18] See 5.46. For a recent Scottish consideration after Henderson, see the valuable discussion of recent authorities in *Strathford East Kilbride Ltd v HLM Design Ltd*, 1997 Rep. L.R. 112, decided on the basis of an absence of an assumption of liability.

[19] [1988] 3 W.L.R. 368.

[20] [1990] 3 W.L.R. 414. *Al-Nakib Investments v Longcroft* [1990] 3 All E.R. 321.

[21] The decision was instantly applied to the case of a builder: *Department of the Environment v T. Bates Ltd* [1990] 3 W.L.R. 457. This case was argued before *Murphy* but decided immediately after it.

judgment of Lord Denning in *Dutton v Bognor Regis UDC*,[22] was to say that imminent danger to health or safety meant that money spent in preventing such was recoverable under *Donoghue* as preventing physical injury.

In an independent development, the *Hedley Byrne* doctrine has shown its strength in the overall picture of the law in the House of Lords decision in *Spring v Guardian Assurance plc*,[23] in which by a 4-1 majority it was held that the *Hedley Byrne* principle applied to an employment reference notwithstanding that if the case had been brought in defamation a defence of qualified privilege could have been run successfully. Abbreviating the facts, the plaintiff was unsuccessful in gaining employment because of a bad reference — a kiss of death. As a result of inadequate investigation into the material in the reference, information had been given which was untrue. The economic loss caused was reasonably foreseeable and so *Hedley Byrne* was applicable. This decision was arrived at notwithstanding the long-standing rule in the law of defamation that references were entitled to qualified privilege. *Spring* has been applied in Scotland by the Inner House.[24]

Fair, just and reasonable

10–6   *Anns* had been used by teachers, students, practitioners and judges for some time as a guide at least. An important court full of jurists, removing that guide in *Murphy*, had to offer something else. "Proximity" was an associated concept, still used to require more than reasonable foreseeability by trying to find connections in the case — *Junior Books* being a good example. The answer was based on some efforts that had been canvassed in other cases: in cases of new duties — like those to take care not to cause economic losses — it has to be fair, just and reasonable to impose a duty. This test is now extensively used for any difficult new[25] duty not just economic loss. As noted in the preceding chapter, it was applied in a physical damage case, *Marc Rich*, and the implications of that are dealt with below.[26] However, while in a new type of primary economic loss case it might be appropriate to consider this test, a case falling within *Hedley Byrne* does not require such an exercise. It is probably worth noting here that the *Anns* approach — foreseeability, proximity and

---

[22] [1972] 1 Q.B. 373.
[23] [1995] 2 A.C. 296.
[24] *Donlon v Colonial Mutual Group (UK Holdings)*, 1997 S.C.L.R. 1088.
[25] New in the sense of a new category of liability — not a new factual varient of a well-known duty.
[26] See Ch.14.

policy has continued to find favour elsewhere in the Common-wealth.[27]

There are many examples of the application of the test in this and the next four chapters. Cases which fail are those which do not fit into the existing categories and where it cannot be shown to be fair just and reasonable to impose one. A recent example, is *Fraser v The Professional Golfers' Association*.[28] The pursuer failed his golf-pro exam because he failed to fix a ladies putter. *Inter alia* he alleged a delictual duty to have prevented his economic loss. It was held that it would not have been fair just and reasonable to impose a duty. There was an element of discretion in setting examinations. It is also worth noting that the existence of a contract was a factor in the case.

Excursus: disclaimers

The actual decision in *Hedley Byrne* was that the disclaimer **10–7** prevented actionable reliance. That is perfectly in accord with principle. Until I say "put all your money on black, the odds of winning are 100-1 in your favour",[29] I have no liability at all as your roulette adviser. If I say at the same time, "but I don't accept any liability for saying that", there seems to be a symmetrical justice about denying the person relying on the advice the right to sue for it. It was generally considered that disclaimers would usually work and that is still the starting point. As explained above in discussing the *Martin* case, the disclaimer has to come into the transaction as close to the roulette example as possible to be potentially effective in preventing reliance — if it comes after reliance (*faites vos jeux, s'il vous plaît, messieurs, mesdames*), it is too late.

Parliament decided some time ago that some disclaimers of liability had to be prevented or prohibited under the Unfair Contract Terms Act 1977. As the name suggests, this was about contract rather than delict but contracts can exclude delictual liability. The English provisions clearly covered non-contractual disclaimers, but it did not appear that the Scottish provisions did so too. Lord Weir in *Robbie v Graham & Sibbald*,[30] expressed regret that he had no control over the disclaimers in the case as would have been the case if the English provisions applied. The Act was amended by the Law Reform

---

[27] Especially the Supreme Court of Canada: *Kamloops v Nielsen*, [1984] S.C.R. 2 (S.C.C.). *CN v Norsk Pacific Steamship Co.*, [1992] 1 S.C.R. 1021; *Hercules Managements Ltd v Ernst & Young* [1997] 2 S.C.R. 165. Australia did not favour *Anns*: *Heyman v Sutherland Shire Council* (1985) 59 A.L.J.R. 564, (1985) 60 A.L.R. 1.

[28] 2004 G.W.D. 200.

[29] Note — the odds are (nearly) evens, so the advice is bad.

[30] 1989 S.L.T. 870.

(Miscellaneous Provisions) (Scotland) Act 1990.[31] The Act now applies to matters other than contracts and covers notices and disclaimers. It must be fair and reasonable to rely on the provision. The time at which this is tested is the time when the liability arose or would apart from the notice or disclaimer have arisen.[32]

The House of Lords, in two joined English cases, analysed the issues and rejected the view that disclaimers can completely destroy a duty arising at all and thus prevent the possibility of applying the Unfair Contract Terms Act 1977.[33]

Disclaimers are still effective and a very good example with a full analysis of principle can be found in *Bank of Scotland v Fuller Peiser*.[34] The defender surveyors provided a report for their client. The client needed it for a business loan. When it was late the bank phoned and asked for it to be sent to them (the bank) direct. When the property had to be sold to realise the security, it did not realise what the Bank had hoped based on the report. The report carried a "disclaimer" that "no responsibility whatsoever to any party other than the client." Lord Eassie dismissed the action. The disclaimer was, it is submitted correctly, treated as a "non-constituter" — it prevented liability arising at all. The *domestic* conveyancing contortions of *Smith v Bush* did not arise and that case could be distinguished. Nor did the clause fail the fair and reasonable test of the Unfair Contract Terms Act.

2. *Simpson v Thomson* bright line non-liability cases (economic loss derived from non-pursuer)

10–8   Wilkinson and Forte identified this category of case[35]: "By secondary, or derivative loss is meant loss which arises as a consequence of physical injury to the person or property of another [*i.e.* someone other than the pursuer]." Scots law had for a long time refused to allow damages in delict for an economic loss resulting from a person's contractual losses — that is, losses that are losses because the pursuer has the right to another person's services or

---

[31] See Casebook, Ext. 95 and para.12.2.5.

[32] See *Melrose v Davidson & Robertson*, 1992 S.L.T. 395, on appeal 1993 S.L.T. 611 for a case where it was held that the unamended Act could control terms in a contract to which the party complaining was a party but the party complained against was not (that party being sued and being the beneficiary of the exclusion).

[33] By then applying the Act it was possible for a disclaimer not to apply in relation to advice concerning the purchase of a dwelling as opposed to a commercial transaction: *Smith v Eric S. Bush* and *Harris v Wyre Forrest D.C.* [1989] 2 W.L.R. 790.

[34] 2002 S.L.T. 574.

[35] 1985 J.R. 1 at 8.

another person's property. So it had been held that an employer could not recover for the loss of his employee's services when he had been injured by the defender.[36] The House of Lords refused to allow a claim where a person suffered loss as a result of damage to property but where the pursuer did not own that property.[37]

The decisions in *Donoghue* and *Hedley Byrne* obviously required that rule to be reconsidered for it was clear after *Hedley Byrne* that there was no absolute rule against the recovery of *pecuniary* loss. Such a reconsideration took place in *Dynamco Ltd v Holland, Hannen and Cubitts (Scotland) Ltd*.[38] Occupiers of a factory raised an action against contractors, who were working nearby and had cut the electricity cable leading to the factory. The claim was one for a purely financial loss on the ground that the plant was unable to operate for over 15 hours. The cable belonged to the state provider of electricity. The court preferred to follow a traditional analysis, expressing the view that even if a duty of care did exist, the loss was too remote. While this may be satisfactory, it is submitted that the court did not fully take into account cases like *Donoghue* and *Hedley Byrne*, which bring into the duty question all or most of the limiting factors. The same result obtained in a substantially similar English case, *Spartan Steel & Alloys Ltd v Martin & Co. (Contractors) Ltd*.[39] The same process of cross-argument took place in England bringing about an unsuccessful challenge in which the non-recovery rule was supported.[40] The decision in *Anns*, among other cases, brought two successful challenges, at first instance suggesting that the distinction between economic losses might collapse.[41] By the time the secondary economic loss issue came to the House of Lords, the reaction to *Junior Books* and Lord Wilberforce's dictum in *Anns* (discussed above) had begun to set in.

The bright line non-recovery rule in secondary economic loss was re-emphasised and further entrenched in *Leigh and Sillivan Ltd v*

---

[36] *Allan v Barclay* (1864) 2 M. 873 and *Reavis v Clan Line Steamers*, 1925 S.L.T. 538. The point is still being (unsuccessfully) argued: *D'Amato v Badger* [1996] D.L.R. (4th) 129.

[37] *Simpson & Co. v Thomson* (1877) 5 R. (HL) 40.

[38] 1972 S.L.T. 38.

[39] [1973] Q.B. 27. Ironically, in a recent cable case it is arguable there was far too much reanalysis of basic principles: *Coleridge v Miller*, 1997 S.L.T. 485. Interested students can find a German power cable case, a French power cable case and a gas main case in Van Gerven, *Cases, Materials and Text on National, Supranational and International Tort Law*, (Hart, 2000).

[40] *Margarine Union GmbH v Cambay Prince Steamship Co.* [1969] 1 Q.B. 219 (The Wear Breeze).

[41] *Schiffahrt & Kohlen GmbH v Chelsea Maritime Ltd (The Irene's Success)* [1982] Q.B. 481 (now overruled); The Nea Tyhi [1982] 1 Lloyd's Rep. 606 (obiter) (now disapproved).

Aliakmon Shipping Co. Ltd.[42] The legal background was extremely complicated and depends upon a good knowledge of the law relating to the carriage of goods by sea or at least the law of sale of goods. Suffice it to say that normally the risk (the economic burden) of accidental destruction of property passes from the seller to the buyer when ownership passes.[43] Under the Sale of Goods Act 1979, there is no need to transfer the goods to transfer ownership. Commercial dealers will, therefore, make sure they do not carry the risk or will obtain insurance cover. In *Aliakmon*, due to some alterations being made in a complex contract, the net effect of these was that buyers of a cargo of steel coils did not acquire property nor a possessory title to the goods. The goods were damaged due to the negligence of the ship owners or their servants. The effect of this was that the plaintiffs fell within the aforementioned authorities which stated that there was no right to sue for a loss as a result of damage to property if the plaintiff did not own the property or have a similar proprietary title to it at the time it was damaged. Despite the precedent against the plaintiffs, they argued that the cases like *Hedley Byrne, Anns*, and *Junior Books* had so changed the law that the old cases should be ignored and the plaintiffs should recover from the parties who caused the loss. The unanimous decision of the House of Lords was to refuse the claim. Lord Brandon, who had dissented in *Junior Books*, made the only reasoned speech. Passing over *Junior Books* as not being in point, he held that the policy of the law had been to refuse such claims and this generated certainty in the law which is of value to commerce. He pointed out that cases where this problem arose were unusual.

However, the urge to do justice between the parties where there appears to be no water behind the floodgates continues and the right to recover was allowed in a case heard after *Aliakmon* where the pursuer was the hirer of a helicopter.[44] In yet another case, a proof

---

[42] [1986] 2 W.L.R. 902. The actual law applicable to cases like this one and those cited above, has to be read against the repeal of the Bills of Lading Act 1855 and its replacement by the Carriage of Goods by Sea Act 1992 — a measure introduced to the Lords by Lord Goff of Chieveley based on a report of the Law Commissions.

[43] J. Adams and R. Brownsword, "The *Aliakmon* and the Hague Rules", 1990 J.B.L. 23.

[44] *United Technologies Corp. Inc. v North Scottish Helicopters Ltd*, 1988 S.L.T. 77; and (No.2) at 778. The case was not followed and *Nacap* (below) applied in *TCS Holdings Ltd v Ashtead Plant Hire*, 2003 S.L.T. 177 in which tenants under a registered lease of lands served by a sewer laid on the lands but which connected to the main public sewer underneath the adjoining subjects sued the neighbours for damage where the sewer ran under the defenders property. The pursuers did not have exclusive use or possession. A proof before answer was however allowed in *Hand v North of Scotland Water Authority*, 2002 S.L.T. 798, which includes a valuable review of the authorities — here a tenant of public house lost revenue as the result of the influx of sewage.

before answer was allowed in respect of damage done to mussels. However, it appears that the case is right on the border, for the pursuers had no property in the mussels until they settled on ropes. Their loss, at least to some extent, was to their contractual right to be able to attract mussel larvae.[45] In another case (Inner House), no recovery was allowed where the damage was done to a pipe owned by a third party, upon which the pursuers were working, and for which they were contractually responsible.[46] These decisions turn on the interpretation of an *obiter dictum* of Lord Penzance, which stated that an action could only be raised by someone having ownership of or possession of the property — for example, a lien or hypothec.[47]

In secondary economic loss cases involving one item of damaged **10–9** property where the only reason the case becomes an economic loss case is the separation of property from risk, there is a way of allowing the wrongdoer to compensate the victim without opening any floodgates. The control is the principle of transferred loss enunciated by Goff L.J. (as he then was) in the Court of Appeal decision in *Aliakmon*.[48] It is as follows:

> "There is a recognisable principle underlying the imposition of liability, which can be called the principle of transferred loss. Furthermore, that principle can be formulated. For the purposes of the present case, I would formulate it in the following deliberately narrow terms, while recognising that it may require modification in the light of experience. Where A owes a duty of care in tort not to cause physical damage to B's property, and commits a breach of that duty in circumstances in which the loss of or physical damage to the property will ordinarily fall on B but (as is reasonably foreseeable by A) such loss or damage by reason of a contractual relationship between B and C, falls upon C, then C will be entitled, subject to the terms of any contract restricting A's liability to B, to bring an action in tort against A in respect of such loss or damage to the extent that it falls on him, C."

This argument failed in the House of Lords in *Aliakmon*, which is unfortunate because it seems to be a sensible rule that would not distort the law.

In other jurisdictions the *Hedley Byrne, Junior Books, Anns* approach has swept into these secondary cases. In *Caltex Oil Ltd v*

---

[45] *Mull Shellfish Ltd v Golden Sea Produce Ltd*, 1992 S.L.T. 703.
[46] *Nacap Ltd v Moffat Plant Ltd*, 1987 S.L.T. 221. See Young, "Rights of Relief", 1992 S.L.T. (News) 225 for comment on the use of assignation in such cases.
[47] In *Simpson & Co. v Thomson* (1877) 5 R. (HL) 40.
[48] [1985] Q.B. 350 at 399, quoted by Lord Brandon of Oakbrook in [1986] 2 W.L.R. 902 at 917.

The Dredge Willemstad,[49] the dredger negligently broke a pipeline owned by the Australian Oil Refining Ltd which crossed Botany Bay. Caltex sued for the extra cost of having to transport oil around the bay. They were held entitled to recover. The basis was that there was no floodgates fear in this case because those in charge of the dredger knew whose pipe it was and where it went — it was not like a general electricity cable. There were many other factors, one of the most significant being that the skipper of the dredger was given a chart showing the pipe so that he might avoid it. Put another way, the class of possible plaintiffs was ascertainable and not general. This case was not followed in this country when it could have been in *Aliakmon*, having been disposed of as virtually without a *ratio decidendi* by Lord Fraser in *The Mineral Transporter; Candlewood Navigation Corp. Ltd v Mitsui Lines*.[50]

The Supreme Court of Canada, too, relaxed its approach. In *Norsk Pacific Steamship Co. Ltd v Canadian National Ry*,[51] a tug, *The Jervis Crown*, owned by the defendants, was towing a barge down the Fraser River when, through its admitted carelessness, it collided with and damaged the New Westminster Railway Bridge. The bridge was owned by Public Works Canada and used by four railway companies including the plaintiffs, Canadian National Railway. The railway company sued for costs incurred because of the closure of the bridge. The plaintiffs' case was upheld by the Supreme Court.[52] The basis was the proximity. The trial judge's finding of proximity, based on a checklist not unlike that of Lord Roskill *in Junior Books*, was upheld. While some of the dicta adopt a reasoning wider than that of *Caltex*, the basis is very similar — that of the identifiability of the plaintiff. Again, in this case the defendant actually knew the plaintiff would suffer loss by his carelessness.[53]

3. *Henderson v Merrit liability*

10–10 This liability is founded on *Hedley Byrne* to the extent that it would never have happened without it. The case was between Lloyds names and those whom they said had negligently caused them to lose on their Lloyds investment.[54] Superficially, the scheme operates by

---

[49] (1976/77) 136 C.L.R. 529, known both as the Caltex case and as The Willemstad.

[50] [1986] A.C. 1.

[51] (1992) 91 D.L.R. (4th) 289.

[52] Albeit by a 4-3 decision.

[53] Lord McLean considered that the *Murphy* departure from *Anns* meant that in cases not covered by the ratio of *Murphy*, commonwealth authority including *Norsk* should not be considered: *Strathford East Kilbride v HLM Design*, 1997 S.C.L.R. 877 at 887A.

[54] The background is very complex and there have been exponential developments: see P. Cave, "Contract, Tort and the Lloyd's Debacle" in *Consensus ad Idem* (Rose ed., Sweet & Maxwell, 1996), p.5.

the "name" agreeing to be responsible to an unlimited amount, being worth a certain sum and depositing a fraction of it. Normally this was easy money and becoming a Lloyds name carried a cachet. Bad weather in the United States and large damages claims — ironically probably based on tort — brought about enormous losses. The names case, at its most honourable, was that they did not mind losing but the way their involvement was handled by their agents and sub-agents was negligent — lacking all care for their interests. Liability was established on the basis of *Hedley Byrne*, but on at least one view[55] went a step further by accepting that liability extended to careless or dilatory omissions as well as to careless acts. It imposes liability for the underlying professional conduct rather than any particular manifestation of it in words.

4. Miscellaneous: *White v Jones* liability

A says he wants to leave his money to P (pursuer). His lawyer D **10–11** (defender) goes and leaves it to B. A dies. B gets the money. P finds out. In *White v Jones*,[56] D had to pay P.[57] How does this fit into the main division into two categories of case? It simply does not and attempts to do so make any theoretical framework impossible. This is not an obvious economic loss case because economically there has been no loss — the estate remains in existence. No one is out of pocket — the pursuer has not had a windfall gain. *Hedley Byrne* cannot apply save by extension. It is thus quite clear that it was necessary for the decision that the defendants were solicitors and if there were no imposition of liability the bunglers would get off. It appears to be an application of the principle that a professional person should answer for his lack of care. *White* undoubtedly applies in Scotland.[58]

This category is called miscellaneous so that it is not felt necessary to fit other cases into existing cases that are relatively well understood. This is all the more important in an era of incrementalism — when it is important to know what is a *new* case. In doing that, new duties from all areas may be cross cited.

Excursus: a statutory case

There is a statutory intervention which allows the recovery of an **10–12** economic loss — the Administration of Justice Act 1982, ss.7 to 10,

---

[55] That of Lord Mustill (dissenting) in *White v Jones*.

[56] [1995] 2 A.C. 207.

[57] See generally K. Norrie, "Liability of Solicitors to Third Parties", 1988 S.L.T. (News) 309, 317. J. Blaikie, "Negligent Solicitors and Disappointed Beneficiaries", 1989 S.L.T. (News) 317; "The Dilatory Solicitor and the Disappointed Legatee", 1993 S.L.T. (News) 329; "Professional negligence: the dilatory solicitor and the disappointed legatee", 1996 S.L.P.Q. 245.

[58] *Holmes v Bank of Scotland*, 2002 S.L.T. 544.

which provide that services rendered to an injured person by a relative, unless it is expressly agreed that no sum shall be payable, will be a head of loss allowing recovery of reasonable remuneration and repayment of reasonable expenses. This Act reversed the common law.[59] However, the title to sue approach is respected by refusing the relative who suffers the economic loss title to sue. Instead the loss is recovered in a claim made by the injured person, who is placed under an obligation to account to the person suffering the loss. This, incidentally, is an example of how procedure can remedy some of the concerns on some economic loss cases. One of the worries is that if a non-owner is compensated, the wrongdoer can be met with a double liability if later sued by an owner, an example being *Blackburn v Sinclair.*[60] The 1982 Act offers one model and the Damages (Scotland) Act 1976 another. A Rule of Court, which ordained a person claiming secondary economic loss to aver the identity of the owner at the time of the damage and to show evidence of intimation of proceedings, might meet some of the worries of those who oppose the recovery of economic loss in cases where another person's property is damaged.

---

[59] *Robertson v Turnbull*, 1982 S.L.T. 96.
[60] 1984 S.L.T. 368 (Casebook, Ext. 96).

CHAPTER 11

NERVOUS SHOCK

When lawyers speak of "nervous shock" it is a symbol for cases of **11–1** actionable non-physical personal injury. Nervous shock is always, for a lawyer, a recognised medical condition.[1] It is something different and more serious than simply getting a fright. While it may be that the same accident results in some people suffering a fright and others a nervous shock, only the latter are eligible to be compensated in either the Scottish or English courts. A clear illustration of this is apparent in the case *Simpson v ICI.*[2] There was an explosion at the pursuers' place of work. It was a big one: there were flames, breaking glass and a wall fell down. The defenders admitted responsibility for the accident. The Inner House held that some of the claims could not be sustained. Lord Robertson said: "It is not enough . . . for the pursuers in each case to show simply that they got a fright and suffered an emotional reaction, if no visible disability or provable illness or injury followed."

Simply proving such an eligible injury is not in itself sufficient. The reason is that over the years the courts have been circumspect in allowing claims to proceed, probably on the basis that it might impose a very wide liability on a wrongdoer and his insurers. There are two justifications for this fear. First, quite a number of people may sustain nervous shock as the result of the one accident. Secondly, there is a possibility that claims might be fabricated sufficiently well to overcome the first eligibility hurdle and so increase the number of persons claiming.

---

[1] One of the reasons that the law has had to move on is that psychiatric views have changed — many more mental problems being recognised. A real difficulty arises because doctors are making diagnoses to treat patients and lawyers are using these to establish "injury". One of the most commonly encountered "mental shocks" is post-traumatic stress disorder or PTSD. However others appear. In *Gillies v Lynch*, 2002 S.L.T. 1420 the court allowed issues in a claim for a pathological grief reaction amounting to a psychiatric illness. See generally L.S. O'Brien, "The Validity of the Diagnosis of Post-Traumatic Stress Disorder" [1994] J.P.I.L. 257. G.J. Turnbull, "Post-Traumatic Stress Disorder — a Psychiatrist's Guide" [1997] J.P.I.L. 234. For a full up-to-date treatment including any developments after publication of this book see Stewart: *Reparation: Liability for Delict.*

[2] 1983 S.L.T. 601 at 605.

Delict

The law has a long history of interesting cases but, equally, great effort has gone into establishing a workable framework in recent decades. That framework is complicated enough itself and so it is now — to an extent — counter-productive to learn the law chronologically, although to understand how the present position has been arrived, at study of the older cases and commentary thereon is necessary.[3] A landmark case was the Scottish appeal to the House of Lords, *Bourhill v Young*.[4] A motorcyclist was driving carelessly, collided with a motor car and was killed. The pursuer was a pregnant fishwife who heard the collision and later saw the bloodstained road, but she had not actually seen the accident. She alleged that she suffered shock and later miscarried. The difficulty in this case was that undoubtedly the motorcyclist owed a duty of care to other road users to drive carefully. He had not driven with due care. The court held that the fishwife could not recover. Other cases denied recovery, the themes discussed usually involving the ideas of closeness to the impact, or presence at the aftermath — factors that might indicate that a pursuer was in some way more likely to be in the contemplation of the defender.[5] Effectively, the court was looking at proximity in the sense of foreseeability more than in any much narrower way of asking, for example, whether the pursuer could himself have been harmed by the defender's acts. The next major landmark was *McLoughlin v O'Brian*.[6] The House of Lords opened up the possibility of recovery and, by imposing *control mechanisms*, overcame the "floodgates fear". Subsequent developments have seen *McLoughlin*, itself positioned in the new structure and for ease of understanding that case is discussed later in its new place. Finally, *Alcock et al. v Chief Constable, South Yorkshire*[7] — arising out of a disaster at a football stadium — developed these control mechanisms

---

[3] H. Teff, "Liability for Negligently Inflicted Nervous Shock" (1983) 99 L.Q.R. 100. Lord Hoffmann sums up the problems just now and after his own efforts as follows in *White v Chief Constable* [1999] 2 A.C. 455 at 503: "My Lords, this story of the ebb and flow of tort liability for psychiatric injury has often been told and I have recounted it again at some length only because I think it must be borne in mind when we come to deal with the authorities. In order to give due weight to the earlier decisions, particularly at first instance, it is necessary to have regard to their historical context. They cannot simply be laid out flat and pieced together to form a timeless mosaic of legal rules. Some contained the embryonic forms of later developments; others are based on theories of liability which had respectable support at the time but have since been left stranded by the shifting tides."

[4] 1942 S.C (HL)78. The "story" of this case can be read in McBryde, "Bourhill v Young: The Case of the Pregnant Fishwife," in *Comparative and Historical Essays in Scots Law*, Carey-Miller and Meyers eds. (Butterworths, 1992) p.66.

[5] See *Hambrook v Stokes Bros* [1925] 1 K.B. 141; *King v Phillips* [1953] 1 All E.R. 617; *Bain v Kings & Co. Ltd*, 1973 S.L.T. (Notes) 8.

[6] [1983] A.C. 410. H. Teff, "Liability for Negligently Inflicted Nervous Shock" (1983) 99 L.Q.R. 100.

[7] [1991] 4 All E.R. 907; reported below as *Jones v Wright* [1991] 2 W.L.R. 814; [1991] 3 All E.R. 88.

but also set up a distinction between *primary* and *secondary* cases. The detail follows but, broadly, primary cases are easier because the pursuer is a participant; secondary cases are more difficult because they are subject to the control mechanisms.[8]

Primary victims

In *Page v Smith*,[9] a teacher who had for some years suffered from **11–2** a condition at the time of the case called M.E. was in a collision of moderate severity with the defender. He was not physically injured, but within about three hours his condition returned in a virulent way, preventing him from working. The leading speech is that of Lord Lloyd of Berwick, in whose speech the 3:2 majority concurred. He accepted a factual distinction between primary and secondary victims and that this distinction should have legal consequences.[10] The primary victim is directly involved, but others who suffer through what they see or hear are secondary victims. The previous big cases — *Bourhill*, *McLoughlin* and *Alcock* — were secondary cases. Lord Lloyd followed the judge at first instance and tried to treat the case simply. It is recognised that drivers owe a duty to other road users and that the defender was in breach of that duty in the sense that he drove carelessly. Had he so much as bruised the plaintiff, he would have been liable for some damages and there would have been no question of reopening the question of duty. It thus goes against common sense (which is often mentioned as a touchstone of proximity or duty[11]) that just because (luckily) he was not physically injured he could not succeed. There was one more critical point dividing the House. That is the question of reasonable fortitude or the customary phlegm. The majority seem to have applied what is truly a remoteness test in the thin-skull cases, which establish that the victim must be taken as found and applied that to the liability inquiry. A final point in favour of the dissent is that the majority view bears a worrying resemblance to the *Anns/Dutton* heresy that economic loss can be treated as property damage even although the property did not actually fall down and hurt anyone. That logic was clearly persuasive at the time and for some time. Is the majority in *Page* guilty of the same logical error, namely mental illness = physical injury? No, if it can be accepted that the interest in one's mental health is equivalent to the security of one's arms and legs.

Page was followed by a 2:1 majority in *Frost*[12] in the Court of Appeal to allow the claim of a policeman who suffered shock in the

---

[8] This distinction has nothing at all to do with the distinction between primary and secondary economic loss.

[9] [1996] 1 A.C. 155.

[10] Following Lord Oliver in *Alcock*, pp.410–411.

[11] Although it is not that common and seldom is it sensible.

[12] *Frost v Chief Constable South Yorkshire* [1997] 1 All E.R. 540.

same football stadium disaster as had brought about the *Alcock* litigation. Lord Justice Rose saw the policeman as a primary participant. This was because the police were employees in the course of their employment and because they were rescuers (who had traditionally been treated more favourably). Dissenting, Lord Justice Judge could not see the mopping-up exercise as involving participation. The same kind of argument that succeeded in *Frost* had been unsuccessful before many of these developments in the First Division, in *Robertson v Forth Road Bridge Joint Board*,[13] in which workmen claimed when, while working, one saw a colleague blown off the defendant's bridge and another heard a loud noise and then noticed the deceased was missing. Even had a *Frost* approach been taken (which, it not having been decided it could not), it is unlikely that the Division would have accepted that, on the facts, these employees were "participating" enough. In a *later* case in the Outer House, a different result was reached. The facts were probably stronger for the pursuer. In *Salter v UB Frozen & Chilled Foods Ltd*,[14] the pursuer worked a forklift. When there was a stock take he had to lift workmate stocktakers. Through no fault of his own, one of his workmates got horribly crushed and he saw some of the consequences. There was no risk of physical injury to the pursuer so the pursuer was doomed as a secondary victim. Was he a primary victim? Not if some dicta were followed — especially Lord Griffiths in *Frost*. *Frost* and to and extent *Robertson* may have required the primary victim to have been potentially injured. Reid, T.J. relied on passages from Lord Oliver in *Alcock* to focus on *involvement* in the incident. Guilt or self-blame were not essential elements. Reid, T.J. required distinction between involuntary cause cases and participant cases. Inspired perhaps by Lord Goff's speech in *Frost*, Reid, T.J. considered that participation was of the essence in employment cases to constitute a person a primary victim. Here there was sufficient participation.

Rescuers, who on the basis of *Frost* may be treated as primary victims need not be in physical danger themselves, nor need they perceive themselves, as being in fear of their own safety.[15] In view of that, a case like *Haggerty v E.E. Caledonia*[16] might be more difficult. This was the case of an off-duty worker on a supply ship who witnessed the Piper Alpha disaster. It seems he was some 500m away and a fireball fizzled out some 50m in front of him. The Court of

---

[13] 1996 S.L.T. 263. Lord Cowie nearly dissented: 271. Rose L.J. thought it doubtful in Frost. Henry L.J. would have accepted that view of the case in *Frost*.

[14] 2003 S.L.T. 1011. See also the note D. Kinloch, "*Salter v UB Frozen and Chilled Foods Ltd.*" 2003 S.L.T. (News) 261.

[15] *Cullin v London Fire & Civil Defence Authority* [1999] P.I.Q.R. P314. See generally, D. Brodie, "Nervous Shock and Professional Rescuers" (1997) Rep. B. 13-2.

[16] [1997] T.L.R. 69.

Appeal held that the decision that he was not a primary victim was correct — his fear for his own life was not a rational one.[17] Recently, in a Scottish case, *Keen v Tayside Contracts*,[18] a worker who was sent to set up a road diversion at the scene of a crash failed in his PTSD claim. In a straight application of the above noted system — especially from *Frost* — it was held he was a secondary victim who failed to satisfy all of the established control mechanisms.

Secondary cases

Here the search is for reasonable foreseeability of the harm to get **11-3** the pursuer off the ground and then a search for control mechanisms. These were first elucidated and organised by the House of Lords in an English appeal, *McLoughlin v O'Brian*,[19] when of course it was not known that this was a secondary case! The plaintiff's husband and three children were involved in a road accident. The accident took place at 4pm. The wife heard about the accident from a neighbour about 6pm and was taken to the hospital. She was told that her youngest daughter had been killed and learned the nature and extent of the injuries to the rest of her family. She was able to see her relatives. Subsequently, she suffered severe shock followed by a psychiatric illness.

At first instance, it was held that there was no duty owed as the possibility of the plaintiff suffering nervous shock was not foreseeable. The Court of Appeal held that it was reasonably foreseeable that she would suffer nervous shock but that on the authorities it was settled law that, as a matter of policy, the duty was limited to persons or owners of property at or near the scene of an accident and directly affected by the negligence. The House of Lords reversed the Court of Appeal. Lord Wilberforce considered all of the themes. He dismissed the fear that there might arise "an industry of lawyers and psychiatrists who will formulate a claim for nervous shock" on the basis that courts should be able to deal with unmeritorious claims in this sphere as in any other. This case established that foreseeability of shock is generally sufficient, subject to three possible control mechanisms. First, the class of persons may be a restriction: claims might not be successful if an injury is to some stranger as opposed to a member of a person's family. Secondly, pursuers should generally be close in time and space to the accident. Thus the aftermath doctrine is

---

[17] *Compare McFarlane v EE Caledonia Ltd*, [1994] 2 All E.R. 1. See generally, See J. Blaikie, "Nervous Shock: Traumatised Fellow Workers and Bystanders", 1994 S.L.T. (News) 297.

[18] 2003 S.L.T. 500.

[19] [1983] A.C. 410. H. Teff, "Liability for Negligently Inflicted Nervous Shock" (1983) 99 L.Q.R. 100.

acceptable.[20] Thirdly, the medium by which the shock is caused may be relevant to restrict liability, the main emphasis here being that normally knowledge of the event causing the shock should come directly to the pursuer. *McLoughlin* undoubtedly made the law clearer and swept away any notions of impact theory in favour of reasonable foreseeability. These mechanisms were further elaborated in *Alcock v Chief Constable, South Yorkshire*,[21] the case arising out of a football stadium disaster. It involved some 16 actions raised by people who were not at the actual incident: some were in the stadium, some saw it on television and one actually saw it on television but on a bus just outside the ground.[22] It was held that the category of plaintiff was not limited to husband and wife and parent and child. The closeness of tie has to be proved by the plaintiff although it can be assumed in many cases. Thus it was held that in the case of brothers and sisters-in-law there was no special tie of affection. A parent and a fiancé were within the close ties. Three members of the House would consider the claim of a bystander who was not within the special class of rescuer, which has for some time been within the bounds of proximity largely to encourage rescuers.[23] On the communication, point the House considered that, in general, presence was required and more distant communication was not sufficient. People who saw the incident on the television and not the actual loved ones were not sufficiently proximate, this being even more restrictive than the first instance decision, which allowed live television as a mode of communication, although not recorded highlights nor radio.

Other cases

11–4   Before the recent flourish of activity, further development had in any event taken place as a result of the decision of the Court of Appeal in *Attia v British Gas*.[24] In this case, the plaintiff witnessed her home (with its contents) burning down as a result of the defendants' alleged negligence. The plaintiff suffered nervous shock. The court accepted that a claim could be made in such circumstances and that it was not essential that the shock resulted from witnessing damage to property as opposed to persons, or as a result of fear for one's own safety.

---

[20] But in *Alcock* [1991] 4 All E.R. 907, discussed below, the viewing of a corpse eight hours after was not within the aftermath.
[21] [1991] 4 All E.R. 907; reported below as *Jones v Wright* [1991] 2 W.L.R. 814; [1991] 3 All E.R. 88.
[22] The 16 were test cases for some 150 similar claims; only 10 went on appeal to the House.
[23] *Chadwick v BRB* [1967] 1 W.L.R. 912. A unanimous First Division excluded bystanders and the argument that fellow employees fell within an actionable relationship under the authorities then prevailing; *Robertson v Forth Road Bridge Joint Board*, 1996 S.L.T. 263.
[24] [1987] 3 All E.R. 455.

Workers' "stress" cases are now safely treated as an aspect of the employment duty,[25] although in some cases, like *Keen v Tayside Contracts*,[26] both approaches may be argued.[27]

Reform

Both the English and Scottish Law Commissions have worked on **11–5** this topic.[28] So intractable appears the mission of providing a common law bright line that attempts have been made to resolve the matter by statute. The English Law Commission issued a consultation paper.[29] That has recently been followed by a report which may well be influential in this area.[30] The Commission accepts that foreseeability cannot be the only test in all cases — the floodgates fear is alive and well. The Commission proposes to abolish the need for victims to be close in space and time. The distinction is not strictly between primary and secondary victims, but between immediate victims and others. To mirror the present state of the law, an *Anns*-like policy defence is proposed in a new post-*Murphy* form whereby the court can disapply the duty if it is found to be just and reasonable not to apply a duty. It recommends the abolition of the requirement for shock. The Royal College of Psychiatrists Mental Health Law Group said that the idea of shock-induced illness had no scientific or clinical merit.[31] In place of an open-ended test of a tie of love and affection, the Commission proposes to fix a list of guaranteed claimants[32] with others having to show their entitlement. However, it is worth saying that the present state of the law was arrived at by the House of Lords taking into account the work of the Law Commission and it may be that the present structure is workable.

The Scottish Law Commission has issued a valuable discussion **11–6** paper, taking account of the work of the English Commission.[33] In so far as there is the possibility of using the Damages (Scotland) Act categories of relatives to assist in drawing lines, consideration must

---

[25] See para.21–6.

[26] 2003 S.L.T. 500.

[27] Both unsuccessfully in that case.

[28] Law Commission Consultation Paper on Liability for Psychiatric Illness, 1995 CP No.137; Report on Liability for Psychiatric Illness, Law Com No.249; Scottish Law Commission Discussion paper on Damages for Psychiatric Injury, 2002 S.L.C. DP No.120.

[29] No.137. For comment in Scotland see M. O'Carroll, "Nervous Shock: Proposals for Reform" (1995) 40 J.L.S. 231; for a practitioner-orientated comment see K. Wheat, "Nervous Shock: Proposals for Reform" [1994] J.P.I.L. 207.

[30] Liability for Psychiatric Illness (Law Com. No.249, 1998).

[31] *ibid.*, para.5.29(2).

[32] Spouse, parent, child, sibling, co-habitant of two years or more including homosexual co-habitants.

[33] Scottish Law Comm. Report 2002 No.120.

also be given to the Scottish Law Commission's report on Title to Sue for Non-patrimonial Loss.[34]

One interesting point arising out of the discussion paper which has not arisen in a case is the problem of the defender who had a defence against the primary victim — should some or all of these be available against the secondary victim? The tradition of this claim is that it is an independent right against the wrongdoer. The English Law Commission has come down against allowing the defence to be used, but the Scottish Law Commission has come to the provisional view that the defence should be allowed.

---

[34] Scottish Law Comm. Report 2002 No.187. For any future developments after publication see Stewart, *Reparation: Liability for Delict*.

CHAPTER 12

PUBLIC AUTHORITIES

As has been demonstrated above, there are difficulties enough with **12–1** the concept of the duty of care in the context of private law — that is, the law between persons. However, the matter becomes even more complicated when there is an element of public law involved. Public law, of course, concerns the relationship between the individual and the State.[1] Sometimes — indeed perhaps quite often — public authorities cause loss to individuals through their actings or their failure to act. Sometimes the matter is not difficult, as where the authority is under a statutory duty[2] to act or refrain from acting. However, it can be difficult to deal with a case where the authority has failed to act because often there may be very good political reasons for not acting — such as a lack of resources. So there is a principal issue as to whether the case in question is justiciable by the courts at all.

While *Anns v Merton LBC*[3] became famous for the so-called Wilberforce dictum on the scope of liability generally (which has now been dissapproved in the UK), the actual *ratio* was concerned with the liability of a public authority. The essential facts were that a builder was under a statutory duty to notify the council before the foundations of a house were covered up. The council was alleged to have been negligent in failing to take reasonable care to inspect the foundations to ensure they were of sufficient depth, and in breach of duty imposed under byelaws to ensure that the building was built in accordance with the plans. The court considered that:

> "it must be in the reasonable contemplation not only of the builder but also of the local authority that failure to comply with the byelaws' requirement as to foundations may give rise to a hidden defect which in future may cause damage to the building

---

[1] See generally J. Sopinka, "The Liability of Public Authorities: Drawing the Line" (1993) 1 Tort L. Rev. 123. D. Brodie, "Public Authorities and the Duty of Care", 1996 J.R. 127. J.J. Doyle, "The Liability of Public Authorities (1994) 1 Tort L. Rev. 189. For an up to date treatment of developments after publication see Stewart, *Reparation: Liability for Delict*.

[2] See Ch.15.

[3] [1978] A.C. 728.

affecting the safety and health of owners and occupiers. And as the building is intended to last, the class of owners and occupiers likely to be affected cannot be limited to those who go in immediately after construction."[4]

The reasonable foreseeability which, generally, is so important in the establishment of liability, is apparent here. But that is not, in such cases, the end of the matter. Lord Wilberforce in *Anns* itself identified a difficulty that had not been properly considered in the lower courts: that the powers and duties of the council were definable in terms of public rather than private law. He said:

"The problem which this type of action creates is to define the circumstances in which the law should impose, over and above, or perhaps alongside, these public law powers and duties, a duty in private law towards individuals such that they may sue for damages in a civil court."

12–2 That remains the case. The court noted one common distinction made in public authority cases: namely that between a discretionary area (where the authority has a discretion to do or not to do something) and an operational area (where it is doing something it has decided to do — for example, where a council decides to have five lorries grit roads, but then forgets to send a memo to the appropriate department sending the gritting lorries out). Lord Wilberforce issued a caution:

"Although this distinction between the policy area and the operational area is convenient, and illuminating, it is probably a distinction of degree, many 'operational' powers or duties have in them some element of discretion. It can safely be said that the more 'operational' a power or duty may be, the easier it is to superimpose on it a common law duty of care."

However, that is not the end of the matter. According to the House of Lords in *Anns*, even where a discretionary power or duty is in question, the council must avail itself of the discretionary power whenever and as often as it may be of the opinion that the public interest will be promoted by its exercise. Thus in the example of the gritting lorries, if empowered to spend money on lorries and grit and drivers for them, on the basis of the *Anns* formulation there could be a case made out if the council did nothing at all during an extended period of icy, snowy weather. The framework set out in *Anns* was criticised, distinguished and eventually departed from in a later House of Lords' decision: *Murphy v Brentwood*,[5] which is discussed

---

[4] [1985] A.C. 210.
[5] [1991] 1 A.C. 398.

below. Before that there were notable decisions showing a desire to protect public bodies.

In *Rowling v Takaro Properties Ltd*,[6] a property developer was refused damages for the delay of a Minister in dealing with an application in connection with the financing of a development. In the lower court, it was held that there was a duty but no breach. While Lord Keith said that it was unnecessary to decide if there was a duty because no breach had been established, his *obiter* comments are of interest. In particular, he dealt with the discretion/operational distinction:

> "This distinction does not provide a touchstone of liability, but rather is expressive of the need to exclude altogether those cases in which the decision under attack is of such a kind that a question whether it has been made negligently is unsuitable for judicial resolution, of which notable examples are discretionary decisions on the allocation of scarce resources or the distribution of risks . . . If this is right, classification of the relevant decision as a policy or planning decision in this sense may exclude liability; but a conclusion that it does not fall within that category does not . . . mean that a duty of care will necessarily exist."

Instead, he suggested that courts should just look at all the circum- **12–3** stances.[7] In *Yuen Kun Yeu v Att.-Gen. Hong Kong*,[8] a commissioner registered a company as a deposit-taking company under an ordinance, the company went into liquidation and an action was brought by plaintiffs who had lost money as a result of relying on the company's status. Lord Keith, again, this time giving the advice of the board, refused to allow the claim. First he disposed of the wider ratio of *Anns*: "for the future it should be recognised that the two-stage test in *Anns* is not to be regarded as in all circumstances a suitable guide to the existence of a duty of care." This time, however, Lord Keith was more constructive and gave guidance as to how cases like these and, indeed, any novel cases, should be considered. It was necessary that a close and direct relationship between the parties be established before liability in tort could arise. All circumstances had to be taken into account including reasonable contemplation of harm, although foreseeability of injury by itself is insufficient to create a

---

[6] [1988] 2 W.L.R. 418.
[7] See generally S.H. Bailey, and M.J. Bowman, "The Policy/Operational Dichotomy — a Cuckoo in the Nest", 1986 C.L.J. 430. Feldthusen, "Failure to Confer Discretionary Public benefits: The Case for Complete Negligence Immunity", 1997 Tort L. Rev. 17. S.H. Bailey, and M.J. Bowman, "Public Authority Negligence Revisited," 2000 C.L.J. 59(1), 85.
[8] [1988] 1 A.C. 175.

duty. In the case before the board it was held that there had not been sufficient close and direct relationship between the official and the disappointed investors. *Obiter,* cases like *Hedley Byrne* were explained on the basis of a voluntary assumption of liability.

In *Murphy v Brentwood*,[9] the House of Lords departed from its previous decision in *Anns* on the particular finding of a duty being encumbent upon the council, in the particular case of its implementation of building control.[10] A strong theme in the decision was to restrict recovery for economic loss generally and to preserve the so-called logic that if *Anns* were right, then there would be liability in respect of chattels or goods, which is something the law must not allow. Nonetheless, a major part of the decision was also that the building legislation did not intend to create or found such a liability.

12–4   The preponderent trend since in English cases has been to evince an enthusiasm for protection of public bodies, although it may be now be no surprise to the student to discover that this being a difficult area for social and political reasons, the 3:2 decision is still encountered. A recent reaffirmation in the House of Lords is *Stovin v Wise.*[11] Stovin, on his motorbike, collided with Mrs Wise who was not keeping a good lookout. She settled with him but called the council as third parties due to the state of the crossroads where the accident took place. There had been three previous accidents. The council's surveyor examined the site and agreed it was dangerous and that work should be done. This was approved by the council providing the owners of the land would agree to the work being done. Nothing was achieved, but if the council had not delayed the works could have been done because the owners would have agreed to the work without the need for the council to exercise its statutory powers. By a 3:2 majority the House of Lords denied the claim. For the majority this was a case involving omissions. Lord Hoffmann left open the question whether the *Anns* decision was wrong — that the courts could impose common law duties. It was, however, clear that the policy/operational distinction was inadequate to be a guide to liability.[12] On an examination of the facts of the case, there are certainly grounds for thinking this not to be one crying out for a finding of liability. Despite the decision having been taken that the work ought to be done, there was no time scale for it. It could have been done in one, two or three years. That would put it in a different budgetary cycle. The cost had not been ascertained. The judge at first

[9] [1991] 1 A.C. 398.
[10] It overruled *Dutton v Bognor Regis UBC* [1972] 1 Q.B. 373 and all cases subsequent to *Anns* decided on the basis of it.
[11] [1996] A.C. 923. See also the important *X. v Bedfordshire C.C.* [1995] 3 All E.R. 353.
[12] At 951.

instance did not make a finding that the decision was irrational. There was a computer system that identified black spots. This was not such a black spot.[13] Indeed, even in England, where the local authority by their layout effectively create a dangerous road junction, they will not be able to have a claim struck out.[14]

Looking around the common law world, it is notable that members of the judicial committee of the House of Lords sitting as the Board of the Privy Council on an appeal from New Zealand, on a case very like *Murphy*, declined to follow it on the immunity point: *Invercargill City Council v Hamlin*.[15] It was said that conditions and expectations in New Zealand were different in this area of building control, which can be seen as involving some degree of public protection.[16] *Murphy* itself was based on an anti-liability decision from Australia.[17] Canada which, as has been seen in relation to economic loss, is much more like the House of Lords in its *Junior Books* phase in its approach to liability, has none the less respected the immunity.[18] Commonwealth cases are extremely influential in the House of Lords and Privy Council.[19] One day, Scotland could take its own course.[20]

Child protection

These cases are not in principle different from the roads or any **12–5** other cases, but they have concentrated minds of late. The basic approach has been to protect the local authorities. In the leading case *X v Bedfordshire CC*[21] one set of children claimed that the Council failed to take them into care when it should have. (A pre-care decision — the children not being in care.) This case, as opposed to others, was argued on the basis of the Council's own liability rather than vicarious liability. The decisions in question were justiciable, there was proximity but the House of Lords held it was not fair just and reasonable to recognise a duty of care. In a later "post-care" decision (the children being in care), *Barrett v Enfield, LBC*,[22] the

---

[13] At 956.
[14] *Kane v New Forest DC* [2002] 1 W.L.R. 312. For Scotland see *McKnight v Clydeside Buses Ltd*, 1999 S.L.T. 1167.
[15] [1996] A.C. 624.
[16] See generally U. Cheer, "New Zealand Court of appeal rejects the 'Murphy' approach to tort liability for defective buildings" (1995) Tort L. Rev. 90. S. Todd, "Negligence Liability of Public Authorities: Divergence in the Common Law" (1986) 102 L.Q.R. 370.
[17] *Sutherland Shire Council v Heyman* (1985) 157 C.L.R. 424.
[18] *Just v British Columbia* (1990) 64 D.L.R. (4th) 689.
[19] But did not attract Lord Maclean in *Strathford East Kilbride Ltd v HLM Design Ltd*, 1997 Rep. L.R. 112 at 27–07.
[20] See para.12–6 *et seq*.
[21] [1995] 3 All E.R. 353.
[22] [2001] 2 A.C. 550.

House of Lords held that the Council could be liable. The facts would usually need to be explored. There remains a human rights dimension to such cases where there is a family life question. There may now be an independent HRA action in such cases regardless of the approach to negligence. *Barrett* may reflect the fact that notwithstanding convolusions in the European Court and Commission of Human rights,[23] trial of the facts is likely to be required.

Scotland

12–6   One curious feature is that this whole topic hardly appeared in Scotland at all. It is hard to say why. The propositions expounded in *Anns* were adopted for Scots law by Lord Dunpark in *Hallett v Nicholson*.[24] The case concerned the acts and alleged omissions of a fire authority. The statutory framework was set out and the discretion/operation distinction noted. Lord Dunpark set out three propositions which he took from *Anns* and *Dorset Yacht Co. v Home Office*:

> "(1) Acts or omissions committed by a statutory authority in the proper exercise of its statutory duties or powers do not found a cause of civil action . . .   (2) Acts or omissions which are committed by a statutory authority in the course of an improper exercise of its statutory duties or powers and which infringe the rights of third parties may be actionable at civil law. (3) For such an exercise to be improper, it must be either (a) not authorised by statute or (b) not made bona fide in the interests of the public within the limits of any statutory discretion."[25]

In *Bonthrone v Secretary of State for Scotland*,[26] a fourth proposition was put forward:

> "When the exercise of a statutory power confers a discretion on the authority entitled to exercise it as to the manner in which, or the means by which it is to be exercised, then if the discretion is exercised within the ambit of the power, and in bona fide, albeit the exercise of it can be shown to display an error of judgement, a person who suffers loss as a result of the exercise of the power will not have an action of damages against the authority which exercised it . . . the taking of reasonable care in connection with the exercise of a statutory power . . . does not

---

[23] *Osman v UK*, (2000) E.H.R.R. 245; *Z. v UK* [2001] 2 F.C.R. 246 and *TP and KM v UK* [2001] 2 F.L.R. 549.

[24] 1979 S.C. 1.

[25] 1979 S.C. at 9.

[26] 1987 S.L.T. 34; see also *Lamont v North East Fife D.C.*,1987 G.W.D. 37–1314.

arise until the discretionary stage of its exercise has ceased and the executive stage has begun."[27]

The *Hallett/Bonthrone* formulation — different in style and perhaps in substance than the formulations presently discussed in England — has formed the basic framework in Scottish cases for some time.[28]

In *Duff v Highlands and Islands Fire Board*,[29] the fire brigade left **12–7** after they thought they had put out a fire. It broke out again and burnt down the property and one beside it. Lord Macfadyen rejected arguments of public immunity. While on the evidence the brigade were assoilzied, the fact that the brigade had gone into action meant that ordinary principles of liability applied. It is respectfully submitted that this decision is correct. Interestingly, the anti-liability approach of the House of Lords in recent years has been reinforced in the English Court of Appeal in a series of cases involving the fire brigade refusing liability, mainly on the rationale that liability would cause defensive practices.[30] *Forbes v Dundee Council*,[31] represented the arrival in Scotland of the recent English approach. *Hallet* and *Bonthrone* are seldom even discussed but the principal English cases like *Stovin* are. In *Forbes*, a woman lost her footing when leaving a large shop. She did not trip on a dangerous step but her rhythm of walking was broken by the irregular spacing of the steps, not conforming in this regard (it was alleged) to the building regulations which the defenders were charged by statute to apply. Lord Nimmo-Smith dismissed the action. He accepted that the issue of reasonable foreseeability of harm of the kind that happened was sufficiently stated to entitle the pursuer to a proof before answer. There was no duty following the English cases.[32] Timorously, but fairly, his lordship considered that the trend was away from imposing civil liabilities on local authorities. He did not think that there was enough in *Duff* to support the dicta in favour of liability in that case. It is

---

[27] 1987 S.L.T. at 41.

[28] *Johnstone v Traffic Commissioner*, 1990 S.L.T. 409; *Ross v Secretary of State*, 1990 S.L.T. 13; *Wilson v McCaffrey*, 1989 G.W.D. 1–37. No reference was made to this line in *Ward v Chief Constable*, 1991 S.L.T. 292 but probably for the good reason that this was a case where action was implemented on the ground and the police were protected by the need for the pursuer to prove malice and want of probable cause. It is not, therefore, a Scottish equivalent of *Hill v Chief Constable*, [1987] 1 All E.R. 1173 in which there was no liability for a failure to properly investigate crime.

[29] 1995 S.L.T. 1362.

[30] *Capital and Counties v Hampshire Council*; *John Munroe v London Fire Authority*; *Church of Jesus Christ of Latter-Day Saints v West Yorkshire Fire Authority* [1997] 2 All E.R. 865. See also *Nelson Holdings Ltd v British Gas* [1997] T.L.R. 122; *Oll Ltd v Secretary of State for the Home Dept* [1997] 3 All E.R. 897.

[31] 1997 S.L.T. 1330.

[32] *X. v Bedfordshire* being expressly mentioned.

submitted that the decision in *Forbes* cannot be justified by the cases
mainly relied upon. The injury was a physical injury. As explained in
more detail below,[33] *Marc Rich* is not correctly understood as
overruling *Donoghue*, not even for property damage.[34] Leaving that
essential point aside, *Duff* is correct in its application of the *Murphy*
principle and without a doubt also correct on the *Pullar* line.[35]

The trend of adopting the arguments from the English cases
continued and was effective in *Syme v Scottish Borders Council*,[36]
albeit the case was a dismissal and relied expressly on Scots pleading
requirements. The pursuer slipped on a road, which had not been
gritted according to the defenders own plan. *Stovin* was influential as
was a similar Enlgish case, *Goodes v East Sussex County Council*.[37]
Heretofore, Scots courts had tended to look at these operational cases
more favourably, and it is submitted rightly so.[38] Ironically, it appears
that as a result of *Goodes* in England, the UK Government intends to
review and legislate to clarify the law.[39] So in cases relying on *Syme*,
consideration will need to be given to the fact that *Goodes* was relied
on.

Litigation far from impossible

12–8   So there is a present a trend to protect public bodies from extra
common law liability. But many cases can still succeed. First it must
not be forgotten that *Hedley Byrne* liability is independent and at the
very least public bodies can be vicariously liable for the failures of
their professional or skilled staff,[40] and that now vicarious liability is
very widely applied.[41] Secondly, misfeasance in office has been
rediscovered and is not affected by these decisions.[42] Thirdly, public
authorities are liable directly under the Human Rights legislation.[43]
Fourthly, public authorities are emanations of the State for *Brasserie*
cases.[44] Fifthly, judicial review cases allow the court to award

---

[33] 5.44.

[34] Lord Nimmo-Smith may have been deflected by the argument noted at 1335, which
it is submitted is erroneous.

[35] See Ch.15.

[36] 2003 S.L.T. 601.

[37] [2000] 1 W.L.R. 1356.

[38] *O'Keefe v The Lord Provost*, Magistrates, and Council of the City of Edinburgh,
1910 2 S.L.T. 293.

[39] G. Junor, "Road Authorities on Ice: A postscript or new chapter?" 2003 50 Rep. B.
4.

[40] *Phelps v Hillingdon LBC* [2001] 2 A.C. 619.

[41] See Ch.24.

[42] See Ch.7.

[43] See Ch.17.

[44] See Ch.16.

reparation in cases where there has been an illegal decision in the sense of *Wednesbury* and judicial review cases since. Against that background it is easy to see why some judges confronted with a neglect case will say "and why not for carelessness as well?" especially where personal injury is concerned.

CHAPTER 13

THIRD PARTY INTERVENTION

13–1 Third party intervention is another difficult area where the law has to reconcile the desire to compensate individuals who have suffered harm with other compelling interests.[1] It will occasion no surprise that this is done by using the duty of care to determine who shall and who shall not recover. The cases also raise questions as to the significance of reasonable foreseeability in determining the existence of a duty of care. The root of the problem is that English law has for a long time had a general rule that there is no liability for what is called a pure omission — a failure to prevent a person coming to harm in the absence of a duty to prevent it.[2]

The *Dorset Yacht* case[3] made it clear that a defender could be liable for the acts — even the criminal acts — of a third party.[4] Foreseeability of harm to the yacht owners if the boys went unsupervised was enough to create the necessary duty — there was no pre-existing relationship between the yacht owner and the employers of the probation officers. Add to that the pre-*Dorset Yacht, Hughes* case,[5] where all the law required was that the reasonable foreseeability sufficient to establish a duty is foreseeability of harm of the kind that actually occurred, and there is a framework that can allow a pursuer to recover damages from a person who has in some way culpably allowed other people to cause him harm.

The issue was sharply raised in Scotland by *Squires v Perth and Kinross DC*.[6] A burglar robbed the pursuer's jewellers shop. Contractors employed by the District Council were working on flats above the pursuer's premises. They neglected the security of the building and the flats were left unsecured. They put up scaffolding. It had been removed before the theft, but it had alerted the thief (who

---

[1] For an up-to-date treatment of developments after publication, see Stewart, *Reparation: Liability for Delict.*

[2] See Logie, "Special Relationships, Reasonable Foreseeability and Distinct Probabilities: the Duty to Prevent Damage to the Property of Others", 1988 J.R. 77.

[3] See paras 9–5 to 9–6.

[4] Although the Scots law had recognised a similar liability in *Scott's Trs v Moss* (1889) 17 R. 32.

[5] See paras 9–5 to 9–6.

[6] 1986 S.L.T. 30.

himself gave evidence!) to the possibility of a burglary. The Inner House found the Council liable on the basis that the theft was reasonably foreseeable. That the thief did not carry out the theft in a foreseeable way was unimportant because of the decision in *Hughes v Lord Advocate*.[7] The court, in allowing the claim, had held that the third party intervention had to be "very likely to" occur. However, in the later case of *Maloco v Littlewoods*,[8] the Inner House held that it was sufficient that the intervention be *likely*. The facts of *Maloco* were that some third parties, probably young children, set a fire that burnt down a derelict cinema, which Littlewoods had purchased. The fire spread to damage Mr Maloco's cafe and the church in the charge of Mr Smith, who also sued Littlewoods. When *Maloco* came to the House of Lords, Lord Mackay settled that point by indicating that it is essentially a question of fact and that the intervention should be high on a scale of probability before there can be liability.

In the *Maloco* case, while it was perhaps likely that vandals could gain entry and that they might start a small fire, it was not likely that they would start a conflagration which would engulf an entire building. So far as the court was concerned, the building did not contain readily combustible materials, at least in the sense that they would set fire to this particular building.[9] It would have been very difficult for the court to hold that harm of the kind that did occur was foreseeable: it is a matter of comparing the flammability of the materials with the material of the building — the result would perhaps have been different if the building had been made of wood or if there had been drums of petrol lying about in a concrete building. Nor is it entirely accurate to suggest that Lord Mackay equated reasonably foreseeable in this context with highly probable — instead the pursuers had failed to establish that harm of the kind that had occurred was reasonably foreseeable. The focus of the reasonable foreseeability test is on harm of the kind that results — the acts of third parties should be thought of as mere cogs in the mechanism of liability. There was quite a difference between the speeches of Lord Mackay and Lord Goff in *Maloco*.[10] Lord Goff was concerned that foreseeability should not impose duties on individuals in their ordinary lives — elderly gardeners leaving french doors open, stone-deaf asthmatics leaving windows open or old ladies leaving their windows open for their cats while they (the old ladies)

---

[7] 1963 S.C. (HL) 31

[8] 1986 S.L.T. 272.

[9] See the Lord President, 1986 S.L.T. at 276J: "There was nothing about the building, so far as we know . . . to suggest that it could easily be set alight"; and Lord Mackay, 1987 S.L.T. at 429B: "The type of film used in the cinema was non-inflammable"; see generally Logie, 1988 J. R. 77.

[10] Lord Keith agreed with both!

visit their married daughters. It may be national divisions or it may be that Glasgow fundamentally differs from Ambridge.

Cases since *Maloco*

13–2   It is an interesting question to ask whether there has been a divergence along national lines.

In England, in *Topp v London Country Bus Ltd*,[11] the owners of a minibus stolen by unknown persons were held not to be liable to the husband of a person run down by the bus. The case was argued on the basis of allurement: the ignition key was left in the lock and the vehicle left unattended. The court held that foreseeability was not enough. The fact that the allurement and danger argument was taken shows the influence of Lord Goffs speech — the attempt was to bring the case within his catalogue of situations in which there could be liability. Lord MacKay's test could, however, bring about the same decision because the need for the needle to be high might rule this case out — it is not like untrained borstal boys trying to sail boats. Even if it was foreseeable that the car would be stolen, the next stage — driving such as to injure another — is not perhaps probable: most people, most of the time do not run people down. On the other hand, there are car thieves and there are car thieves — some are excellent and careful drivers who safeguard their booty; others may be young "neds" who may never actually have learned to drive. The harm of the kind which resulted was not the harm reasonably to be foreseen, namely injury after car theft. However, in another English case a decision was reached, albeit against the background of the Occupiers' Liability (Scotland) Act 1960, which fits more into the "foreseeability with high probability" model. In *Cunningham and Others v Reading Football Club Ltd*,[12] the plaintiffs were injured at a football match by bits of terracing thrown at the police. Four months earlier, concrete had been thrown. The club knew it was a local derby and knew that trouble might arise. The club was held liable.

13–3   In *Fry's Metals Ltd v Durastic Ltd*,[13] a company entered into a lease with another company of factory and office premises for the six-month period to March 23, 1984. Two separate alarm systems protected the premises: a conventional bell system mounted on an exterior wall manually set by a key, and a private system installed by a security company at the request of the tenants, connected to the offices of the security company by landline. The tenants notified the security company that cover would not be required after March 30. On April 2, the tenants sought to hand over the keys to the landlords.

[11] [1991] T.L.R. 552.
[12] [1991] T.L.R. 153.
[13] 1991 S.L.T. 689.

The keys were refused because electricity and gas meters were required to be read before the handover was complete. This took place on April 9. On April 7, the premises were broken into and vandalised. Both alarm systems failed to operate. The landlords sued the tenants for loss caused by the failure of the private alarm system. It was argued, on the basis of Lord MacKay's speech, that there is a duty in delict to take care in respect of the occupation of premises to prevent damage by the action of a third party, which arises if, but only if, the injury or damage by third parties arising from the act or omission of the person against whom the duty of care is alleged is highly probable. Lord Dervaird held that test met. In Scotland, in *Gillon v Chief Constable*,[14] a police officer on the track who was told to stand with her back to the playing surface was "run-down" by an enthusiastic footballer. She sued her employer and lost on the basis of *Bolton v Stone* unlikeliness. But it is an example of the fact that, although there was another human being (in this case a footballer) in the chain of events, a case could be made out. In *Hendrie v Scottish Ministers*,[15] half a million pounds was awarded to a prison officer who injured his back intervening in a fight between two inmates. There has been a fight before between them. There has been enough time to separate them. However, the scope of the duty can reach only so far. In *McLean v University of St Andrews*,[16] the pursuer, a student at the defender's institution, claimed she had been raped by three Russian soldiers while an exchange student in Odessa. She had been outside the accommodation provided for her at the time (although allegedly because of a fight there). It was known to be a dangerous area and the University could only be held responsible to provide safe accommodation.

---

[14] 1996 Rep. L.R. 165.
[15] 2002 G.W.D. 2–84.
[16] 2004 G.W.D. 7–152.

CHAPTER 14

INDIRECT DAMAGE AND INJURY

14–1 Indirect damage and injury could be a very large category, but it is restricted to one relatively new category, which it is submitted has been ill-understood.[1] In *Marc Rich & Co. A.G. and Others v Bishop Rock Marine Co. Ltd and Others (The Nicholas H)*,[2] a tanker developed a crack in its hull carrying a cargo incorporating the Hague-Visby rules. It was inspected by a surveyor acting for the vessels classification society. The surveyor recommended permanent repairs in dry-dock there and then, but was persuaded to change his mind, allowed temporary repairs and the vessel to sail. The Nicholas H sank as a result of the temporary welding failing. After sundry claims the cargo owners were still carrying a loss and sued the classification society. For the purposes of the legal argument on duty, the parties accepted that the plaintiffs had title to sue, it was foreseeable that lack of care was likely to expose the cargo to physical damage, that the damage suffered was physical damage and that the damage was as a result of the carelessness of the surveyor. At first instance the plaintiffs were successful. The Court of Appeal allowed an appeal on the basis that the cargo having been sent under the Hague-Visby rules meant that the ship owner (and not the defendants) was under a duty. The House of Lords decided by a 4:1 majority to agree with the Court of Appeal and refused the appeal. The importance of the case is that the new duty ("fair, just and reasonable" test) was used in a case where it appears the loss was damage to property rather than economic loss. This case looks a little like a primary economic loss case and it also has features of the public authority cases. It would have been better if it had been decided on these two lines.

In Scotland, it was taken as allowing theoretical issues from primary economic loss cases to be brought to bear on a property damage case. In *British Telecom v Thomson*,[3] a sub-contractor's work caused property damage (in this respect unlike *Junior Books*), yet the case was argued as if it were an economic loss case. The claim was

---

[1] For developments after publication see Stewart, *Reparation: Liability for Delict*.
[2] [1995] 3 All E.R. 307.
[3] 1997 Rep. L.R. 23.

refused and upheld on appeal by a 2:1 majority. In *Coleridge v Miller*,[4] there was another case of simple property damage which was burdened by a consideration of what it is thought *Murphy* did to the law. Once the defender has damaged the pursuer's property in a reasonably foreseeable way, causing harm of the kind that was envisaged, only remoteness of damage can save the wrongdoer. The effect of *Marc Rich* was felt in the *Tartan American Machinery Corporation v Swan & Co*.[5] Both parties accepted, and his Lordship approved, the application of the fair, just and reasonable test in this case. In view of the existence of *Marc Rich*, that was probably inevitable. However, with respect, the case of a professional supervising the packing of goods seems to fall within well recognised categories and could perhaps be dealt with once the facts have been heard on existing principles — such as that of the supervising architect as urged by the pursuers. The pursuers were selling goods. Others were to pack and send them. When they arrive they were damaged and need remedial work. While the pursuers obtained decree against the agents who arranged for the packing and dispatch, it was worthless. This debate was about the liability of the marine surveyors who had been instructed by the agents to supervise, photograph and supply a written report on the packing and securing of the cargo. That said, in this case the court allowed a proof before answer as to whether they had a duty.

What then does *Marc Rich* do? It is probably best understood as **14–2** applying only, to *indirect* property damage cases. In such a situation it may well be that more consideration is required than a simple *Donoghue* analysis.

The effect of *Marc Rich* was most clearly questioned in a subsequent case that dealt not with indirect property damage as indirect personal injury. In *Perrett v Collins*,[6] the plaintiff claimed damages for injuries sustained when the plane in which he was a passenger crashed. He sued, *inter alios*, the inspector who inspected it for a certificate of airworthiness and the certifying authority. It was accepted that the harm was reasonably foreseeable and there had been carelessness. The defendants understandably founded on *Marc Rich*. They argued the fair, just and reasonableness test applied. Hobhouse, L.J. said that *Marc Rich* was of no assistance as it was an economic loss case and not a personal injury case. This is, with respect, dodging the issue, which has been discussed above. It is submitted that although indeed *Marc Rich* was like an economic loss case, it was a *property* damage case (and property of the pursuer) and as such could and probably should have been dealt with under the neighbour principle. In short, it is submitted that the defenders were

---

[4] 1997 S.L.T. 485.
[5] August 15, 2003.
[6] [1998] T.L.R. 393.

right to submit the *Marc Rich* rule was applicable. Then it is possible to say with Hobhouse, L.J. that a further balkinisation could be carried out by saying that *Perrett* is about indirect physical injury and that the rule for indirect physical injury is different to the rule for indirect property damage. That would be the logical, although unsatisfactory, exposition. The difficulty would then be whether it is right to have different rules. Because the Court of Appeal did not confront the issue directly, the position is presently unclear.[7] It is submitted that while there can be two opposite rules some justification would have to be forthcoming other than that personal injury is sometimes sadder than property damage. Sometimes it is, but not if one compares the broken finger with the wrecked core business asset, bankruptcy and ruin. The two cases can be seen as cases of the liability of professionals exercising special skills, and in that there is a loss in both cases, they are more compelling of relief than *White v Jones*, which, while anomalous on the nature of the loss, is clear on the liability of the skilled individual.

---

[7] *Marc Rich* was influential in the dismissal of a personal injury case by T.G. Coutts, T.J. in *Bennett v J Lamont & Sons*, 2000 S.L.T. 17, decided in 1999 without reference to *Perrett*.

Section IV: External Wrongs

Chapter 15

STATUTORY DUTY

Most of the duties considered so far came from the common law in **15-1** the cases. Duties are also imposed by statutes, but often without saying whether or not there is civil liability. The fundamental position in Scotland was set out some time ago, albeit on the basis of many English authorities:

> "It has long ago been decided that the mere fact that a duty has been created by a statute will not entitle a person injured by the breach of that statutory duty to claim damages from the person upon whom the duty is imposed (*Atkinson v Newcastle Water-works Co.* (1877) 2 Ex. D. 441 *per* Lord Cairns, L.C., at p.448), and the Courts have frequently had to determine whether a particular statutory obligation does or does not confer a right upon a person injured by its breach to damages for that injury. The solution in each case must depend upon what the intention of Parliament was in enacting the obligation in question, and what persons consequently have a right to enforce it or to found upon it as a basis for a claim of damages."[1]

There are two ways of looking at this type of liability: the one, that it is an instance of common law delict, the only difference being that the duty is imposed by Parliament instead of by the common law; the other, that the statute creates the entire obligation and the delict system of the common law merely provides the mechanism for its enforcement. Professor Walker prefers the second view on the persuasive basis that sometimes Parliament imposes duties that do not accord with the common law and sometimes it imposes duties that are not civilly actionable.[2]

There are three types of statutory duties with which this chapter is **15-2** *not* concerned. The first is where Parliament clearly intends for there to be civil liability, examples being the Occupiers' Liability (Scotland) Act 1960, the Animals (Scotland) Act 1987 and Part I of the

---

[1] *Pullar v Window Clean*, 1956 S.L.T. 18, *per* Lord President Clyde at 21. For an up-to-date review of developments after publication, see Stewart, *Reparation: Liability for Delict*.
[2] Walker, Delict, pp. 296–297.

Consumer Protection Act 1987. Secondly, there are statutes that impose duties, but which expressly declare that there is no intention of creating civil liability, for example the Health and Safety at Work etc. Act 1974 and the Guard Dogs Act 1975. The third category is cases where a statute imposes some duty on a public authority, in which case the element of public law has to be taken into account.[3] Instead, we are concerned with the more difficult case where Parliament has said nothing at all about civil liability. This is, therefore, a specialised area of statutory interpretation.[4] A good example is *Cutler v Wandsworth Stadium Ltd (in liquidation)*.[5] This was an action raised by a bookmaker for damages against a licensed dog track for their refusal to allow him space on their premises to carry on bookmaking. The bookmaker founded on the Betting, Gaming and Lotteries Act 1934, section 11(2), which provided that so long as a totalisator (state bookmaking system) was being lawfully operated from a licensed dog track, the occupier could not exclude any person from the track by reason only that he proposes to carry on bookmaking on the track; and had to take such steps as are necessary to secure that . . . there is available for bookmakers space on the track where they can conveniently carry on bookmaking. Every person who contravened or failed to comply with, any of the provisions was made guilty of an offence. Now, while it is clear that Parliament was imposing a duty on the stadium proprietor it is not clear from reading the Act when, if at all, and in what circumstances, a person might be able to sue in the civil courts for a failure to carry out the duty. In the House of Lords, Lord Reid identified certain issues that can help to determine the question. He asked: for whose benefit was this sub-section intended? And, as Law Lords usually do, he provided an answer to his own question: I think that it was primarily intended for the protection of those members of the public who might wish to bet on these tracks. Not for bookmakers. The idea was to provide competition for the state-run totalisator. Another factor for Lord Reid was that, "if the legislature had intended to create such [civil] rights, [one] would expect to find them capable of reasonably precise definition." This the bookmaker was unable to do since, for example, there were many answers to the question "How many bookmakers must be allowed in?"— all that ask, or just enough to leave enough space for the dogs? Lord Reid concluded by pointing out that the statute imposed a criminal penalty that was "appropriate and sufficient for the general obligation imposed." That, then, is the sort of issue with which this head of liability deals. Other issues arise in

---

[3] A treatment.of *everything* to do with statutory duty—including the connection with common law negligence is now available: Stanton et al. *Statutory Torts*, (Sweet & Maxwell, 2003).

[4] D.M. Walker, The Scottish Legal System, (7th revised ed.), 1997 at 395 *et seq.*

[5] [1949] 1 All E. R. 544. This case was influential and approved in *Pullar*, above.

other cases and it is possible to set out a list of requirements the presence of which might lead to success, and the absence of which are likely to bring defeat for the pursuer. As Lord McCluskey recently put it, "It is essential to look at the statute founded upon."[6]

1. There must be a statutory duty in force and applicable to the defender

The statute must tell the defender to do or refrain from doing **15–3** something. It is not enough that it permits or allows the defender to do or refrain from doing something. It must also be applicable to the facts of the case, so where an Act imposed a duty relevant to a "factory" it was held not to cover a trawler. This decision was not as obvious as at first it might seem. Initially, the court's attention was directed to a definition section that included drydocks within the definition of "factory". This test was not met in *Johanneson v Lothian Regional Council*,[7] in which no regulations had yet been made. In *Armstrong* v Moore,[8] it was held that as the particular regulation founded on had been revoked and not re-enacted, there was no relevant averment that the new building complained of had breached any relevant building standards regulation or did not comply with any condition on which the warrant had been granted, and accordingly the authority could not be under any duty to refuse to grant the completion certificate.

2. The duty must be intended to protect the pursuer

This point is illustrated by *Cutler* above, where although there may **15–4** have been some intention by Parliament to help bookmakers generally, it was essentially members of the public who were being protected. In *McMullan v Lochgelly Iron and Coal Co.*[9] the court held that section 49 of the Coal Mines Act 1911 protected a workman on the basis that the section occurred in Part II of the Act, the heading of which was "Provisions as to Safety", and the purpose of section 49 was to ensure the safety of the workmen employed in the mine. In the leading case of *Pullar v Window Clean*,[10] the idea of a class of persons protected of which the pursuer must be a member was explained by Lord President Clyde:

"If the class of persons for whose protection it is alleged that the duty was imposed is indefinite and difficult to define, this would

---

[6] *Weir v East of Scotland Water Authority*, 2001 S.L.T. 1205 at 1210.
[7] 1996 S.L.T. (Sh. Ct) 7.
[8] 1996 S.L.T. 690.
[9] 1933 S.C. (HL) 64.
[10] 1956 S.L.T. 18.

tend to exclude the construction of the section which would give a right to civil damages for breach . . . and would favour the view that the legislature intended the sanction of prosecution for a penalty as appropriate and sufficient for the obligation imposed by the section . . . But where the predominant purpose of the statute is manifestly the protection of a particular class of workmen by imposing on their employers for instance the duty of taking special measures to secure their safety then the inference is readily drawn that the legislature intended to confer on these workmen a right to sue for damages where the duty is not fulfilled . . . Accordingly, before a right to civil damages can arise out of the statutory duty imposed there must be a manifest or clear intention to confer such a right and a definite class of persons upon whom the right is so conferred."[11]

In *Pullar*, the pursuer could not establish a sufficiently clear class of persons. The applicable Dean of Guild legislation although it provided for measures which would provide safety for some window cleaners in some buildings, it was not "designed to constitute a charter for window-cleaners."[12]

In *Weir v East of Scotland Water Authority*,[13] the duty on the defenders to provide a supply of wholesome water was held to be owed to every domestic consumer within the defenders area and thus not a sufficiently defined limited class of the public. Is this not a question of a big defined class — they are defined by having pipes into their houses and perhaps paying water rates?

3. It must be a duty that the statute intends to be enforced by civil action

15–5 Again *Cutler* is an illustration of this point in that the obligation was one regulated by the criminal law. There are no fixed rules in these matters. Sometimes some sections of an Act have been held civilly actionable, whereas others have not. If there is another remedy in the Act or clearly envisaged by the Act, then that will usually exclude an action based on the statute. In the case of *J. Bollinger v Costa Brava Wine Co. Ltd*,[14] there was an attempt by French champagne producers seeking an injunction against a Spanish company using the name "champagne", to found on the Merchandising Marks Act 1887, which provided penalties against persons for false trade descriptions and the like. However, the Act preserved the right of a party to proceed with a passing-off action and accordingly

---

[11] *ibid.*, at 22.
[12] *Pullar, ibid.* at 17.
[13] 2001 S.L.T. 1205.
[14] [1960] Ch. 262.

could not be used in support of a civil action based on breach of the statute. It is also worth noting that the statute was held intended to protect the public from false trade descriptions rather than offering a protection to rival traders. In *Coutts v JM Piggins Ltd*,[15] where there was a claim for *inter alia* damages in respect of an allegation of breach of the duty under Harbours, Docks and Piers Clauses Act 1847, the pursuer's complaint was that the defenders refused to handle consignments of goods from the pursuer which were to be shipped or to operate cranes for the pursuer or persons driving the pursuer's lorries. The pursuer was not able to carry out his business because of this. It was held that Act imposed only a criminal penalty and did not imply civil liability.[16]

Perhaps surprisingly, legislation providing for motor vehicles to be kept in a safe condition has not supported breach of statutory duty cases.[17]

It can be said that where protection of a specific class is clear, and there is no mention of a civil or criminal sanction, that is the very kind of case where a civil action is necessarily upheld to give effect to the duty.[18]

4. The intention must be to guard against the harm that has occurred

This is another particular application of statutory interpretation. It **15–6** may be that the pursuer is the sort of person who is supposed to be protected by the Act and the defender may have a duty incumbent upon him which Parliament intends to give rise to civil liability, but no action will lie if the harm is not within the scope of the protection offered by the Act. *Carroll v Andrew Barclay and Sons Ltd*[19] demonstrates the point. The Factories Act 1937 provided that every part of the transmission machinery should be securely fenced. A workman was injured when a belt forming part of the transmission machinery broke. One of the ends hit his head. The belt had been enclosed but not fenced. It was held that the employers were not in breach of section 13 as that provided only for fencing which would prevent persons from coming into contact with the machinery but not fencing which would protect them from broken parts of the machinery coming out to strike them.[20]

---

[15] 1983 S.L.T. 320.
[16] See also *W. L. Tinney & Co. Ltd v John C. Dougall Ltd*, 1977 S.L.T. (Notes) 58.
[17] *Phillips v Britannia Hygienic Laundry Co. Ltd*, 1923 2 KB 832, *Tan Chye Choo v Chong Kew Moi*, 1970 1 W.L.R. 147, *Reid v First Glasgow Ltd*, Unreported, Glasgow Sh. Ct. 4/3/03
[18] Lord Browne-Wilkinson in *X v Bedfordshire County Council* [1995] 3 All E.R. 353.
[19] 1948 S.C. (HL) 100.
[20] See also *Gorris v Scott* (1874) L. R. 9 Ex. 125.

5. Breach of duty

15–7 The pursuer must still show a breach of the duty imposed. The content of the duty is a matter of interpretation of the legislation. This is a specialised matter of pleading. Sometimes the standard required will be reasonable care as in common-law liability, but other standards exist, mainly because statutes have usually been passed to impose a higher degree of care. Thus, sometimes there is absolute liability[21] or cases where something must be achieved so far as it is reasonably practicable, or an Act may allow a defence of impracticality only, regardless of how unreasonable it would be to take certain steps. Examples of these can be seen in the treatment of the Factories Act. In *Edwards v NCB*,[22] the following formulation of reasonable practicability was offered:

> "Reasonably practicable is a narrower term than physically possible and seems to me to imply that a computation must be made by the owner in which the quantum of risk is placed in one scale and the sacrifice involved in the measures necessary for averting the risk (whether in money, time or trouble) is placed in the other, and that, if it be shown that there is a gross disproportion-the risk being insignificant in relation to the sacrifice — the defendants discharge the onus on them . . . The questions he has to answer are: (a) what measures are necessary and sufficient to prevent any breach . . . (b) are these measures reasonably practicable?"

If the duty is an absolute one then only the happening need be proved. Overall though, the courts have no place in "double-guessing" the statutory provision:

> "All that it is necessary to show is duty to take care to avoid injuring; and if, the particular care to be taken is prescribed by statute, and the duty to the injured person to take the care is likewise imposed by statute, and the breach is proved, all the essentials of negligence are present. I cannot think that the true position is, as appears to be suggested, that in such cases negligence only exists where the tribunal of fact agrees with the legislature that the precaution is one that ought to be taken. The very object of the legislation is to put that particular precaution beyond controversy."[23]

---

[21] See *Summers v Frost* [1955] A.C. 740.

[22] [1949] 1 K.B. 704.

[23] *McMullan v Lochgelly Iron and Coal Co.*, 1933 S.C. (HL) 64 at 67, *per* Lord Atkin.

6. Causation

Normally it is essential to show that the harm was caused by the **15–8** breach of the statutory duty.[24] A statute can make proof of causation unnecessary.

7. Damage

There seems to be no clear direct authority on remoteness of **15–9** damage in statutory liability cases. Probably the same approach would be taken as in the general law. Some suggestions that the same rule does apply can be found in *Drew v Western SMT*.[25] A boy was killed as a result of a breach of a statutory regulation as to the lighting of vehicles. Lord McKay in the Second Division said: "So much explained, then, it is enough to say by preliminary that I cannot find any grounds whatever in fact or in law for giving the benefit of 'remoteness' whether that be treated as remoteness in time, or remoteness in logic, to the maintenance, contrary to a safety statute, of an unlit obstacle in the full and public path likely to be taken by approaching traffic from behind."[26] In the Outer House, in the well-known *McKew v Holland & Hannen & Cubitts (Scotland) Ltd*,[27] Lord Robertson applied traditional remoteness of damage doctrine to what was both a common law and statutory claim. The leading English text book suggests the possibility that an "old" remoteness rule such as that in *Polemis* might apply in these cases, even although that rule was departed from some time ago in England for ordinary negligence cases.[28] In view of the decision in *Simmons v British Steel*,[29] it unlikely that there would be enthusiasm for that, but it is true to say that different considerations might apply.

8. Defences

There remains only one more speciality of liability for breach of **15–10** statutory duty and that is that the defence of *volenti non fit injuria* does not normally apply, on the basis that if Parliament had intended a duty to be so restricted, it would have said so. This is well illustrated by the case of *Wheeler v New Merton Board Mills Ltd*.[30] A boy was employed to clean the blades of a machine. There was a lever that he was to use to stop the machine to let him do this. Either through pressure of work or over eager application to his task, his practice was to try to clean the blades while the machine was still in

---

[24] *Wardlaw v Bonnington Castings*, 1956 S.C. (HL) 26.
[25] 1947 S.L.T. 92.
[26] *ibid.*, at 95.
[27] 1968 S.L.T. 12.
[28] See the discussion in *Stanton* et al para.9.025.
[29] [2004] UKHL 20.
[30] [1933] 2 K.B. 669.

operation. Scrutton L.J. takes up the story: "He went on for three months taking shaving out of the knives while the machine was still working, and by good luck he did so for three months without having his fingers cut off, but at last the evil day came when he lost his hand and fingers." The court held that he was not defeated by the plea of *volenti*. It should be noted that Parliament can include such a defence should it so wish, as it has in the Occupiers' Liability (Scotland) Act 1960 and the Animals (Scotland) Act 1987. That Parliament does this indicates that the inapplicability of the *volenti* defence is not restricted to cases under the Factories Acts.

It is possible for conduct to amount to contributory negligence reducing or completely excluding liability.

CHAPTER 16

REPARATION FOR FAILED OR INADEQUATE TRANSPOSITION OF EUROPEAN UNION LAW

Known for obvious reasons as "Eurotort" or "Eurorep," this head of **16–1** liability has been described as a new and emerging tort. It is included here because it is similar to statutory liability in that (a) there may be no express provision for damages, indeed no UK provision at all, and (b) it is the national system of law, particularly that dealing with compensation in the civil courts, that gives effect to the right of damages on breach. The first manifestation was in relation to the competition policy of the European Community.[1] It was suggested in one case that a breach of these provisions might be actionable in the United Kingdom courts for damages.[2]

Francovich

The next development is in relation to the enforcement of **16–2** Community law generally. The methods provided by the Treaty have not always been adequate. The decision in the landmark case *Van Gend en Loos v Nederlandse Tarief Commissie*[3] declared that certain Treaty Articles could have direct effect[4] in the Member States and later decisions declared that regulations and directives[5] can have this effect too. That is not the end of the matter, for the problem with directives is that, as they are frequently addressed to a Member State with instructions to achieve an objective, there is the possibility, that the Government will not implement or will improperly implement the directive. This failure heretofore had been thought only challengeable at the supranational level of the Commission suing the Member State before the European Court of Justice. Some directives, indeed many directives, allow the Member State some considerable

---

[1] For Community law generally, see "European Community Law and Institutions", The Laws of Scotland. *Stair Memorial Encyclopaedia*, Vol.10.
[2] *Garden Cottage Foods v Milk Marketing Board* [1984] A.C. 130.
[3] [1963] 1 C.M.L.R. 105.
[4] See *Stair Memorial Encyclopaedia*, Vol.10, para.81.
[5] *ibid.*, paras 89–93.

discretion. If it is not exercised then there is a gap in the Community enforcement mechanism.[6] This was plugged in *Francovich*.[7] The case arose out of Directive 80/987, which was intended to provide workers with a minimum level of protection in the event of the insolvency of their employers. The deadline for implementation was October 23, 1983. The Italian Government failed to implement the directive and was sued by the Commission, who obtained a ruling against Italy. Nonetheless, nothing had been done by May 1991. *Francovich* is in fact two cases, raised separately and later joined, whereby workers who were uncompensated sought damages against the State for payment of wages as provided by the directive or alternatively for compensation for the loss as a result of the failure of the State to implement the directive.[8] On a preliminary ruling,[9] it was held that the directive just failed to meet the twin criteria for direct effect as the State had a considerable discretion. The court did allow the compensation claim: The full effectiveness of rules of Community law would be undermined and the protection of the rights which they create weakened if individuals were unable to obtain reparation when their rights were infringed as a result of Member State's violation of Community law.[10] There are three conditions for such a case:

(1) the result prescribed by the directive must involve the attribution of rights to individuals;
(2) the content of those rights must be identifiable from the provisions of the directive;
(3) a causal link must exist between the violation of the Member State's obligation and the damage suffered by the injured person.[11]

It is for the national courts to decide the form of the reparation process. However, the national systems must designate the competent courts and forms of proceedings which may be used to pursue such Eurorep cases.

---

[6] What follows is indebted to G.H. Downie, "New Right to Damages in Community Law" (1992) 37 J.L.S.S. 424; see also C. Boch and R. Lane, "A New Remedy in Scots Law: Damages from the Crown for Breach of Community Law", 1992 S.L.T. 145.

[7] *Commission v Italian Republic* [1989] E.C.R. 143.

[8] C–6190 and C–9/90, *Andrea Francovich v Italian Republic*; *Danila Bonifaci & Others v Italian Republic* [1992] I.R.L.R. 84.

[9] See *Stair Memorial Encyclopaedia*, Vol.10, paras 239–244.

[10] para.34.

[11] para.40.

Factortame

The European Court of Justice took the law a stage further in two **16–3** joined cases.[12] In *R. v Secretary of State for Transport, ex parte Factortame Ltd*,[13] companies owned and operated by Spanish citizens sought judicial review complaining of the illegality of a UK statute and related regulations. A first ECJ reference declared that any national rules precluding remedies enforcing Community law were inapplicable and so injunctions could be brought against the Crown and national courts could declare UK legislation inapplicable. In the second reference, the UK legislation was ruled to have been contrary to EU law. It was changed by the UK Parliament as a result. The plaintiffs then sought the damages they had claimed in the original judicial review — they had, after all, been precluded (they said) from fishing by what had been declared to be illegal legislation. It was held that such a right to damages did arise.

Brasserie

In *Brasserie du Pecheur S.A. v Germany*,[14] French brewers **16–4** complained that the German law on beer duty was contrary to EU law and that they had sustained a loss as a result. They, too, were entitled to recover damages. The ECJ based its rules for establishing liability on its existing rules on non-contractual liability of the Community. Community law confers a right to reparation where three conditions are met:

(1) the rule of law infringed must be intended to confer rights on individuals;
(2) the breach must be sufficiently serious;
(3) there must be a direct causal link between the breach of the obligation resting on the state and the damage sustained by the injured parties.

In deciding whether the matter was sufficiently serious the decisive test is whether the Member State had manifestly and gravely disregarded the limits on its discretion. Certain factors can be taken into account (so can others not listed by the Court) in approaching that question:

(a) the clarity and precision of the rule breached;
(b) the measure of discretion left to the Member State;

---

[12] For a detailed analysis see Upton, "Crown Liability in Damages under Community Law [Parts 1 & 2]", 1996 S.L.T. (News) 175 and 211.
[13] [1990] 2 A.C. 85, (HL); [1991] 1 A.C. 603, ECJ (C–48/93).
[14] C–46/93; [1996] 2 W.L.R. 506.

(c) whether the infringement and any damage caused were intentional or voluntary;

(d) whether any error of law was excusable;

(e) the contribution, if any, a Community institution might have made;

(f) the adoption or retention of national measures.

Where there has been (a) a judgment finding an infringement established; (b) a preliminary ruling; or (c) an established body of ECJ jurisprudence, then the breach is sufficiently serious.

A number of practical points were also laid down in the joint cases. The obligation to make reparation did not depend on a condition based on any concept of fault (intentional or negligent) beyond that of a serious breach of community law. The extent of reparation must be commensurate. The local system may set the criteria but they must not be less favourable than those applying to similar claims based on domestic law and must not be such as in practice make it impossible or excessively difficult to obtain reparation. Damages for loss of profit could not be ruled out as many cases involve commerce. Exemplary damages, where they apply nationally, could not be ruled out either. The date from which damages would be payable was not cut off at the date of a decision — there was no temporal limitation.

Beyond

16–5   An example based on the foregoing jurisprudence is *Dillenkofer v Germany*.[15] The plaintiffs lost money when their holiday companies went bust. They sued the State for failure to have implemented the directive on package travel swiftly enough to have covered their cases. The court referred to the *Brasserie* criteria and the *Francovich* criteria. The court explained that although *Francovich,* another non-transposition case, did not expressly mention the need for serious breach, it was implied within it. Thus failure to transpose within the set time-limit is *per se* a serious breach. In this case, the rights conferred and the persons on whom they were conferred was clear.[16]

Another example, this time showing the wide reach of the liability, is *Kobler v Republik Osterrich*,[17] in which the ECJ held that the *Brasserie* criteria could apply to the decision of a court at last

---

[15] [1996] T.L.R. 564.

[16] The UK joined the case to argue that late transposition should not be a matter of liability *per se* and that it would have to be shown that it was a manifest and grave breach. The directive was implemented by the UK in the the Package Travel, Package Holiday and Package Tours Regulations 1992 (SI 1992/3288).

[17] [2003] T.L.R. 540.

instance as being part of the state apparatus. To be actionable, the *Brasserie* criteria still have to be met and in *Kobler* — an interpretation of a length of service increment — the breach was not sufficiently manifest. This head of liability will increase as the years go by.[18]

---

[18] See also *R.v Ministry of Agriculture and Fisheries, ex p. Hedley Lomas (Ireland) Ltd* [1996] T.L.R. 353; *R. v H.M. Treasury, ex p. British Telecommunications plc* [1996] 3 W.L.R. 203. The increased size of the Community will naturally generate more litigation.

CHAPTER 17

HUMAN RIGHTS

17–1 The introduction explained that this book came close to considering all civil wrongs. It also explained that on one view delict is about protecting rights and interests. That must be so regardless of the original source of the rights and interests. The European human rights are as much rights as any domestic rights. They are legal and are thus juridical or juristic. Breach of them to the extent they apply is wrongful.[1] This section only deals with the effect of the Human Rights Act 1998 on the availability of reparation,[2] although for practical and historical reasons the overall context of the discussion is "just satisfaction."[3] The Act provides additional remedies to those already provided by the law.[4] There is an express mechanism for cases involving a public authority. It is unlawful for a public authority to act in a way which is incompatible with a convention right.[5] A person who is a victim of the unlawful act[6] can bring proceedings against the authority under the Act[7] or rely on the convention rights in any legal proceedings[8]

There are important debates as to whether this law affects the rights of citizens against others citizens as opposed to just the citizen

---

[1] For a fuller treatment and developments after the date of publication, see Stewart, *Reparation: Liability for Delict.*

[2] The Scottish Parliament and Executive was set up in such away that it immediately required to have regard for Human Rights: Scotland Act 1998: ss.29, 53 and 57(2). These provisions remain in force. They may in some circumstances provide a different route to compensation as where a claim for damages is attached to a judicial review of a decision. The Human Rights Act 1998 came into effect on October 2, 2000 (SI 2000/1851). A "delictual" type of action such as discussed herein does not necessarily involve a devolution issue: *HM Advocate v R*, 2001 S.L.T. 1366. See also Fairgrieve, "The Human Rights Act 1998, Damages and Tort law," [2001] P.L. 695.

[3] Human Rights Act, s.8.

[4] Art.11 of ECHR.

[5] Section 6(1). Subject to the detailed provisions of subs.(2)–(6), mainly permitting action in respect of judicial acts but exempting Parliament.

[6] If proceedings are brought by way of judicial review then a person is only to have title and interest to sue if he is a victim: s.7(4). Victim of an unlawful act is specially defined: s.7(7).

[7] Section 7(1)(a). This envisages a special procedure and rules. It envisages a one year prescription with an equitable override: s.7(5).

[8] Section 7(1)(b).

and the State. If it is the case that the Scots law of reparation can operate by virtue of the recognition of an interest by the courts,[9] then these rights and freedoms are the very things — now part of the law in a formal sense — that can be used directly or in combination to recognise new reparable interests.[10] This is often called a horizontal effect. More advanced analysis argues that there can be weak or strong horizontality: the weak, where the courts take into account the convention rights in developing the law; the strong, where the courts are compelled to make the common law compatible.[11] The House of Lords' decision in *Campbell v MGN Newspapers Ltd*,[12] discussed below,[13] supports at least weak horizontality.

Accordingly, these outline treatments should be seen not only as sensitising the student to potential instances of reparation against the State, but also as potentially affecting the scope of the existing law. The cases from many countries over many years provide a vast relevant jurisprudence. I have preferred to select those most relevant to delict and from the UK.[14]

Right to life

Everyone's right to life must be protected by law. No one should **17–2** be deprived of his or her life intentionally, save in the execution of a sentence of a court following his or her conviction of a crime for which this penalty is provided by law.[15] In *Edwards and Another v UK*,[16] the ECHR held that there had been a breach of Article 2 where the prison authorities put a dangerous prisoner with mental problems in a cell with another. Non-pecuniary compensation was set at £20,000, In *Finucane v UK*,[17] the UK's failure to promptly and effectively investigate the death of an individual was held by the ECHR to be a breach of Article 2.

---

[9] See the discussion in Chapter 1 at para.1–18.

[10] See generally, D. Brodie, "Negligence in the Convention," in A Practical Guide to Human Rights Law in Scotland, ed. Reed, (W. Green, 2001).

[11] H. MacQueen and D. Brodie, "Private Rights, Private Law and the Private Domain", in Human Rights and Scots Law: Comparative Perspectives on the Incorporation of the ECHR, Ed. Boyle, Himsworth et al (Hart, 2002). See the many papers and books on the topic referred to therein.

[12] Unreported May 6, 2004. [2004] UKHL 22.

[13] See para.17–12.

[14] Many more examples relevant to reparation are available in *Stewart: Reparation for Delict*, Chapter 17.

[15] Article 2(1). Deprivation of life shall not be regarded as inflicted in contravention of this Article when it results from the use of force which is no more than absolutely necessary: (a) in defence of any person from unlawful violence; (b) in order to effect a lawful arrest or to prevent the escape of a person lawfully detained; (c) in action lawfully taken for the purpose of quelling a riot or insurrection: Art. 2(2). See *McCann v UK* (1996) E.H.R.R. 97; *X v UK* (1980) 19 D.R. 244.

[16] [2002] T.L.R. 141.

[17] [2003] T.L.R. 437.

Prohibition of torture, etc.

17–3   No one should be subjected to torture or to inhuman or degrading treatment or punishment.[18] In *A v United Kingdom*,[19] the applicant had been caned by his step-father sufficient to cause bruising. The step-father was acquitted by a jury on the defence of reasonable chastisement. It was held that the chastisement was excessive by European standards. It was further held that the United Kingdom was liable for not having taken steps to protect persons such as the applicant. The United Kingdom was held liable for damages and costs.

The mandatory life sentence for murder applicable in the UK was not in contravention of the ECHR, according to the House of Lords.[20] For Scotland see, the Convention Rights (Compliance) (Scotland) Act 2001 (asp 7).[21]

In Scotland a case was raised against the Scottish Ministers complaining of the practice of "slopping out" in Barlinnie prison: *Napier v Scottish Ministers*.[22] The principal thrust of the case was for judicial review.[23] The background to the case was set out by the petitioner based on the Report to the UK Government on a visit carried out by the European Committee for the Prevention of Torture and Inhumane or Degrading Treatment or Punishment in May 1994. Barlinnie Prison was the subject of unfavourable conduct and reference was made to the fact that slopping-out was to have ended by 1999. So far as interim measures were concerned, the court granted in the petitioner's favour an order on the Scottish Ministers to secure the transfer of the petitioner to conditions of detention that complied with Article 3 of the Convention, whether within HM Prison Barlinnie or in any other prison, and that within 72 hours. Eventually the case proceeded to proof. It was held in

---

[18] Article 3. See also *Ireland v United Kingdom* (1979–80) 2 E.H.R.R. 25; *Ribitsch v Austria* (1995) 21 E.H.R.R. 573 (assault in police custody).

[19] [1998] T.L.R. 578. See also *Tyrer v UK* (1978) 2 E.H.R.R. 1; *Costello-Roberts v UK* (1993) 19 E.H.R.R. 112; *Campbell and Cosans v UK* (1982) 13 E.H.R.R. 441.

[20] *R. v Lichniak*, [2002] T.L.R. 494.

[21] And the decision of the High Court on Appeal in *Flynn v HM Advocate*, 2003 S.L.T. 954.

[22] June 26, 2001.

[23] The petitioner sought *inter alia*: declarator that the conditions of his detention are contrary to Article 3 of the Convention, being conditions which cause him to be subjected to inhuman or degrading treatment; declarator that the failures of the Governor of the prison and of the Scottish Ministers to secure that his conditions of detention are not contrary to Article 3 are acts or failures to act incompatible with his rights under that Article, and are accordingly unlawful by virtue of section 6(1) of the Human Rights Act 1998 and (as regards the Scottish Ministers) section 57(2) of the Scotland Act 1998; an order on the Scottish Ministers to secure his transfer to conditions of detention compliant with Article 3, whether within the prison or in any other prison; and for such an order *ad interim*; and damages.

Napier v The Scottish Ministers[24] that indeed there had been an infringement of the petitioner's human rights.[25]

Prohibition of slavery and forced labour

No one can be held in slavery or servitude.[26] No one shall be **17–4** required to perform forced or compulsory labour.[27]

Right to liberty and security

Everyone has the right to liberty and security of person. No one **17–5** can be deprived of his liberty save in the following cases and in accordance with a procedure prescribed by law: (a) the lawful detention of a person after conviction by a competent court; (b) the lawful arrest or detention of a person for non-compliance with the lawful order of a court or in order to secure the fulfilment of any obligation prescribed by law; (c) the lawful arrest or detention of a person effected for the purpose of bringing him before the competent legal authority on reasonable suspicion of having committed an offence or when it is reasonably considered necessary to prevent his committing an offence or fleeing after having done so; (d) the detention of a minor by lawful order for the purpose of educational supervision or his lawful detention for the purpose of bringing him before the competent legal authority; (e) the lawful detention of persons for the prevention of the spreading of infectious diseases, of persons of unsound mind, alcoholics or drug addicts or vagrants; (f) the lawful arrest or detention of a person to prevent his effecting an unauthorised entry into the country or of a person against whom action is being taken with a view to deportation or extradition.[28] Everyone who is arrested shall be informed promptly, in a language which he understands, of the reasons for his arrest and of any charge against him.[29] Everyone arrested or detained in accordance with the provisions of paragraph 1(c) of this Article must be brought promptly before a judge or other officer authorised by law to exercise judicial power and is entitled to trial within a reasonable time or to release

---

[24] Unreported, Lord Bonomy, April 26, 2004.
[25] See below on "just satisfaction".
[26] Art.4(1).
[27] Art.4(1). "For the purpose of this Article the term 'forced or compulsory labour' shall not include: (a) any work required to be done in the ordinary course of detention imposed according to the provisions of Article 5 of this Convention or during conditional release from such detention; (b) any service of a military character or, in case of conscientious objectors in countries where they are recognised, service exacted instead of compulsory military service; (c) any service exacted in case of an emergency or calamity threatening the life or well-being of the community; (d) any work or service which forms part of normal civic obligations": Art.4(3). See *Van der Mussele v Belgium* (1984) 6 E.H.R.R. 163.
[28] Art.5(1). For Art.5(1)(f) see *Chahal v UK* (1997) 23 E.H.R.R. 413.
[29] Art.5(2).

pending trial. Release may be conditioned by guarantees to appear for trial.[30] Everyone who is deprived of his liberty by arrest or detention is entitled to take proceedings by which the lawfulness of his detention must be decided speedily by a court and his release ordered if the detention is not lawful.[31] Then there is a clear reparation provision: "Everyone who has been the victim of arrest or detention in contravention of the provisions of this Article shall have an enforceable right to compensation."[32] That is not to say either that this is the only provision which will result in reparation merely that this is a clear instance.

In *McDonald v Dickson*,[33] an accused was granted bail on condition, *inter alia*, that he remained in his house except between 10am and noon. In the context of a devolution minute the High Court held that this did not infringe Article 5. It was a severe restriction on his freedom but not complete. He had *not* been placed in detention.

Right to a fair trial

Generally

17–6   In the determination of his civil rights and obligations or of any criminal charge against him, everyone is entitled to a fair and public hearing within a reasonable time by an independent and impartial tribunal established by law. Judgment must be pronounced publicly, but the press and public may be excluded from all or part of the trial in the interest of morals, public order or national security in a democratic society, where the interests of juveniles or the protection of the private life of the parties so require, or to the extent strictly necessary in the opinion of the court in special circumstances where publicity would prejudice the interests of justice.[34]

Civil cases

17–7   This Article has already caused considerable controversy. In *Osman v United Kingdom*,[35] the applicants complained that the

---

[30] Art.5(3). There are extensive derogations mainly applicable to this Article in respect of the civil insurrection in Northern Ireland which is regulated internally by successive Prevention of Terrorism Acts. See Sch.3 to the Human Rights Act 1998 (c.46). See *Lawless v Ireland* (1961) E.H.R.R. 1; *Fox Campbell and Hartley v UK* (1991) 13 E.H.R.R. 157; *Brogan v UK* (1989) 11 E.H.R.R. 117; *Murray v UK* (1994) 19 E.H.R.R. 193.

[31] Art.5(4). See, *e.g. Ashingdane v UK* (1985) E.H.R.R. 528; *Thynne, Wilson and Gunnell v UK* (1991) E.H.R.R. 666.

[32] Art.5(5).

[33] 2003 S.L.T. 467.

[34] Art.6(1).

[35] [1998] T.L.R. 68. See also *Golder v UK* (1979–80) 1 E.H.R.R. 524 (entitlement of prisoner to consult a lawyer to raise civil proceedings).

police had been negligent in their investigation of a teacher, who eventually shot and killed a pupil's father, shot and injured a pupil, shot and injured the headmaster and shot and killed the headmaster's son. They lost their damages action before the English Court of Appeal on the authority of the exclusionary rule in *Hill v Chief Constable of West Yorkshire*.[36] The European Court of Human Rights held that the *automatic* application of *Hill* was contrary to Article 6(1) of the Convention. The fact that they could have sued the killer or the psychiatrists was not to the point, the applicant had not had the chance to have a determination on the conduct of the police. The applicants were awarded damages for the loss of the chance to have sued the police. As a result, the House of Lords accepted that the practice of striking-out is not Convention friendly in relation to negligence cases where the court has the task of weighing up interests.[37] However, where there is a clear rule of law established that is itself ECHR compliant, striking out or dismissal at debate is not a breach.[38] While Scots law some time ago reached the stage where *personal injury* reparation cases are not supposed to be dismissed on relevancy, the dispensation for relevancy does not apply to specification. Cases other than personal injury cases may require to take account of the attenuated position originally enforced by the ECHR and accepted in the House of Lords in *Barrett*.

Criminal cases

The substantive protection given in Scots Criminal Law and **17–8** Procedure to comply with the Convention is not the subject of this text. The concern here is for cases where there may be a claim for reparation or just satisfaction arising out of an inadequacy of the already very compliant procedures. Everyone charged with a criminal offence is presumed innocent until proved guilty according to law.[39] Everyone charged with a criminal offence has the following minimum rights: (a) to be informed promptly, in a language which he understands and in detail, of the nature and cause of the accusation against him; (b) to have adequate time and facilities for the preparation of his defence; (c) to defend himself in person or through legal assistance of his own choosing or, if he has not sufficient means to pay for legal assistance, to be given it free when the interests of justice so require; (d) to examine or have examined witnesses against him and to obtain the attendance and examination of witnesses on his behalf under the same conditions as witnesses against him; (e) to

---

[36] [1989] A.C. 53.

[37] *Barrett v Enfield L.B.C.* [1999] 3 W.L.R. 79.

[38] It was held in *Z and Others v UK*, (2002) 34 E.H.R.R. 3, the ECHR sequel to *X v Bedfordshire* [1995] 2 A.C. 633 that disposal of the case without proof was not in itself, in this case, a breach of Article 6.

[39] Art.6(2).

have the free assistance of an interpreter if he cannot understand or speak the language used in court.[40]

So far as criminal cases are concerned, it is usually the case that the human rights are respected and protected *in the criminal process*.[41]

No punishment without law

17–9 No one can be held guilty of any criminal offence on account of any act or omission that did not constitute a criminal offence under national or international law at the time when it was committed. Nor shall a heavier penalty be imposed than the one that was applicable at the time the criminal offence was committed.[42]

Right to respect for private and family life

17–10 Everyone has the right to respect for his private and family life, his home and his correspondence.[43] There must be no interference by a public authority with the exercise of this right except such as is in accordance with the law and is necessary in a democratic society in the interests of national security, public safety or the economic well-being of the country, for the prevention of disorder or crime, for the protection of health or morals, or for the protection of the rights and freedoms of others.[44] The ECHR held that an increase in the level of noise by increased flights from Heathrow airport constituted a breach of the applicants right to family life.[45] Later the Grand Chamber held that the Heathrow night-flying scheme did not in fact interfere with the applicants human rights under Article 8. There was a finding under Article 13 because, until the HRA was in force, there had been no way of the applicants taking their arguments under domestic law.[46] In *ADT v UK*,[47] the ECHR ruled that the UK liberalisation of

---

[40] Art.6(3).

[41] *HMA v R.*, 2003 S.L.T. 4 (Privy Council). It may well be the case that where a "criminal" resolution cannot be achieved, just satisfaction may still be sought by way of reparation as suggested by Lord Reed below, 2001 S.L.T. 1366.

[42] Art.7(1). This Article does not prejudice the trial and punishment of any person for any act or omission which, at the time when it was committed, was criminal according to the general principles of law recognised by civilised nations: Art.7(2). See, *e.g. Welch v UK* (1995) 20 E.H.R.R. 247; *SW v UK* (1996) E.H.R.R. 363.

[43] Art.8(1). See, *e.g. Rees v UK* (1997) 9 E.H.R.R. 56; *Cossey v UK* (1991) 13 E.H.R.R. 622.

[44] Art.8(2). See, *e.g. Gaskin v UK* (1990) 12 E.H.R.R. 547; *Chappell v UK* (1990) 12 E.H.R.R. 1; *Silver v UK* (1983) 5 E.H.R.R. 347; *Campbell v UK* (1993) 15 E.H.R.R. 137; *Halford v UK* (1997) 24 E.H.R.R. 523.

[45] *Hatton v UK* (2002) 34 E.H.R.R. 1.

[46] *Hatton v UK*, 2003 T.L.R. 401. See also *Dennis and Another v MOD*, 2003 T.L.R. 270 in which it was held that training flights by the RAF were a nuisance and engaged Article 8 and Article 1 of protocol 1. The common law damages of £950,000 were sufficient to constitute just satisfaction.

[47] [2000] T.L.R. 604.

homosexual activity was inadequate where it still prohibited male group sex. This was a violation of Article 8. The pursuer was awarded reparation of £20,929 in that he had been convicted and conditionally discharged for two years. Legislation providing for the monitoring of inmates telephone calls was not contrary to Article 8 of the ECHR.[48] In *Campbell v MGN Newspapers Ltd*,[49] the House of Lords took account of the ECHR to ensure that the existing law of breach of confidence could equally be treated as abuse of private information, which would safeguard the Convention right as between individuals as much as between the individual and the State.

Freedom of thought, conscience and religion

Everyone has the right to freedom of thought, conscience and **17–11** religion; this right includes freedom to change his religion or belief and freedom, either alone or in community with others and in public or private, to manifest his religion or belief, in worship, teaching, practice and observance.[50] Freedom to manifest one's religion or beliefs is subject only to such limitations as are prescribed by law and are necessary in a democratic society in the interests of public safety, for the protection of public order, health or morals, or for the protection of the rights and freedoms of others.[51] The UK ban on corporal punishment in schools did not infringe the religious rights of others who did want the right to punish corporeally: there was a distinction between a religious belief or practice and an action motivated by religious belief.[52]

Freedom of expression

Everyone has the right to freedom of expression.[53] This right **17–12** includes freedom to hold opinions and to receive and impart information and ideas without interference by public authority and regardless of frontiers. This Article must not prevent States from requiring the licensing of broadcasting, television or cinema enterprises.[54] The exercise of these freedoms, since it carries with it duties

---

[48] *Dudley v HM Advocate*, 2003 G.W.D. 138; 2003 S.L.T. 597. (Distinguishing *PJ and JH v UK*, ECHR, September 25, 2001, unreported).

[49] Unreported, May 6, 2004. [2004] UKHL 22.

[50] Art.9(1).

[51] Art.9(2).

[52] *R (Williamson and Others) v Secretary of State* [2002] 1 All E.R. 385. A valuable examination of the religious issues which will no doubt continue to emerge. For a consideration of the issue under other rights systems see the note, J. Eekelaar, "Corporal Punishment, Parents' Religion and Children's Rights", 2003 L.Q.R. 370.

[53] See, *e.g. Handyside v UK* (1976) 1 E.H.R.R. 737; *Goodwin v UK* (1996) 22 E.H.R.R. 123; *Sunday Times v UK* (1992) 14 E.H.R.R. 229; *Tolstoy v UK* (1995) 20 E.H.R.R. 442.

[54] Art.10(1).

and responsibilities, may be subject to such formalities, conditions, restrictions or penalties as are prescribed by law and are necessary in a democratic society, in the interests of national security, territorial integrity or public safety, for the prevention of disorder or crime, for the protection of health or morals, for the protection of the reputation or rights of others, for preventing the disclosure of information received in confidence, or for maintaining the authority and impartiality of the judiciary.[55] In *Douglas and Others v Hello! Ltd and Others*,[56] it was held that the wedding of two celebrities could be regarded as a commodity and protected as a trade secret. Where the press took unauthorised pictures, this could be a breach of commercial confidence — not privacy. Because the press were involved, Article 10 ECHR was engaged but, as the conduct in this case was in breach of the Press Complaints Commission Code, the balance was in favour of the plaintiffs' existing right under the law of confidence not being eroded by Article 10. The detailed application of the extent to which the press are allowed to "abuse private information" is considered in *Campbell v MGN Newspapers Ltd*.[57] Finally, the ECHR was influential in supporting a refusal of interdict against anticipated publication of allegedly defamatory material.[58]

Freedom of assembly and association

17–13   Everyone has the right to freedom of peaceful assembly and to freedom of association with others, including the right to form and to join trade unions for the protection of his interests.[59] No restrictions shall be placed on the exercise of these rights other than such as are prescribed by law and are necessary in a democratic society in the interests of national security or public safety, for the prevention of disorder or crime, for the protection of health or morals or for the protection of the rights and freedoms of others. This Article does not prevent the imposition of lawful restrictions on the exercise of these rights by members of the armed forces, of the police or of the administration of the State.[60] A Scots example is *Aberdeen Bon-Accord Loyal Orange Lodge 701 v Aberdeen City Council*,[61] in which the pursuers were aggrieved that they were prevented from marching. The defenders were able to plead in defence the Civic

---

[55] Art.10(2). Nothing in this Article may be regarded as preventing the States from imposing restrictions on the political activity of aliens: Art.11.

[56] 2003 T.L.R. 239.

[57] Unreported, May 6, 2004. [2004] UKHL 22.

[58] *Dickson Minto WS v Bonnier Media Ltd*, 2002 G.W.D. 551. Section 12 of the HRA.

[59] Art.11(1). See, *e.g. Young, James and Webster v UK* (1982) 4 E.H.R.R. 38.

[60] Art.11(2). Nothing in this Article may be regarded as preventing the States from imposing restrictions on the political activity of aliens: Art.11.

[61] 2001 G.W.D. 1213.

Government (Scotland) Act 1982, which permits restrictions on parades. It was held that this legislation was indeed compatible with the HRA where correctly applied, because it provides a proportionate and reasonable response to public order risks. In this particular case, however, the Council had not made out its reasons properly and an appeal against a ban was upheld.[62]

Right to marry

Men and women of marriageable age have the right to marry and **17–14** to found a family, according to the national laws governing the exercise of this right.[63]

Prohibition of discrimination

The enjoyment of the rights and freedoms set forth in the **17–15** Convention must be secured without discrimination on any ground such as sex, race, colour, language, religion, political or other opinion, national or social origin, association with a national minority, property, birth or other status.[64]

Protection of property

Every natural or legal person is entitled to the peaceful enjoyment **17–16** of his possessions. No one may be deprived of his possessions except in the public interest and subject to the conditions provided for by law and by the general principles of international law. The preceding provisions do not, however, in any way impair the right of a State to enforce such laws as it deems necessary to control the use of property in accordance with the general interest or to secure the payment of taxes or other contributions or penalties.[65]

Right to education

No person can be denied the right to education. In the exercise of **17–17** any functions which it assumes in relation to education and to teaching, the State shall respect the right of parents to ensure such education and teaching in conformity with their own religious and philosophical convictions.[66]

---

[62] See also *Wishart Arch Defenders Loyal Orange Lodge 404 v Angus Council*, 2001 G.W.D. 31–1256.

[63] Art.12. See, *e.g. Rees v UK* (1987) 9 E.H.R.R. 66.

[64] Art.14. Nothing in this Article may be regarded as preventing the States from imposing restrictions on the political activity of aliens: Art.11.

[65] First Protocol Art.1.

[66] First Protocol Art.2.

Right to free elections

17–18   The High Contracting Parties undertake to hold free elections at reasonable intervals by secret ballot, under conditions which will ensure the free expression of the opinion of the people in the choice of the legislature.[67]

The death penalty

17–19   The death penalty is abolished. No one may be condemned to such penalty or be executed.[68]

REPARATION FOR INFRINGEMENT

The basic structure

17–20   Sections 8(1) to (4) of the HRA provide: (1) In relation to any act (or proposed act) of a public authority which the court finds is (or would be) unlawful, it may grant such relief or remedy, or make such order, within its powers as it considers just and appropriate. (2) But damages may be awarded only by a court which has power to award damages, or to order the payment of compensation, in civil proceedings. (3) No award of damages is to be made unless, taking account of all the circumstances of the case, including (a) any other relief or remedy granted, or order made, in relation to the act in question (by that or any other court), and (b) the consequences of any decision (of that or any other court) in respect of that act, the court is satisfied that the award is necessary to afford just satisfaction to the person in whose favour it is made. (4) In determining (a) whether to award damages, or (b) the amount of an award, the court must take into account the principles applied by the European Court of Human Rights in relation to the award of compensation under Article 41 of the Convention.

The Act does seem to suggest that the HRA remedy is not "subsidiary".[69] This provides that proceedings under the HRA must be brought within 12 months of the date on which the act complained of took place. If no declarator is required of infringement, it may well be actions could be lost. Until there is jurisprudence on the matter, practitioners should consider raising and sisting cases.

---

[67] First Protocol Art.3.

[68] Sixth Protocol Art.1. A State may make provision in its law for the death penalty in respect of acts committed in time of war or of imminent threat of war; such penalty shall be applied only in the instances laid down in the law and in accordance with its provisions. The State shall communicate to the Secretary General of the Council of Europe the relevant provisions of that law: Sixth Protocol Art.2.

[69] s.7(5) of the HRA.

Just satisfaction

The heads of claim

The Strasbourg Court awards damages as just satisfaction under **17–21** three heads pecuniary loss, non-pecuniary loss, and costs and expenses. In practice, the Court does not always separate its awards into these respective heads of damage, and it has often awarded global sums which combine all of the applicant's losses into a single figure. This is reminiscent of the Scots cases where there have been *solatium* "employability" awards, which have a pecuniary element but insufficient to establish a patrimonial award.

The Law Commissions[70] note that the European Jurisprudence is opaque on this issue. That said, this does have a resonance with *solatium* in Scots law, which is our domestic non-pecuniary satisfaction. It is submitted that Scots courts will find it as easy as the ECHR to take a case by case view of the suffering of the victims. The kind of approach that might be expected can be seen in *Smith and Grady v United Kingdom*[71] (concerning homosexuals banned from military service) in which the Strasbourg Court noted that it was not possible to make a precise calculation of the amount necessary to make complete reparation for the applicants' loss of future earnings because of "the inherently uncertain character of the damage flowing from the violations". Again, however, substantial awards (£19,000 to each applicant) were made for non-pecuniary loss. The Commissions' researches show, "Non-pecuniary awards have included compensation for pain, suffering and psychological harm, distress, frustration, inconvenience, humiliation, anxiety and loss of reputation. There appears to be no conceptual limit on the categories of loss which may be taken into account, and the Strasbourg Court is often prepared to assume such loss, without direct proof." Sometimes just satisfaction may require a civil claim for damages as opposed to the protection from criminal prosecution.[72]

Who may claim?

Any victim may claim. Corporate entities may suffer non-pecu- **17–22** niary loss. Account should be taken of the company's reputation, uncertainty in decision-planning, disruption in the management of the company (for which there is no precise method of calculating the consequences) and the anxiety and inconvenience caused to the members of the management team.[73]

---

[70] Law Comm. 266.
[71] (33985/96, 33986/96, July 25, 2000).
[72] *HM Advocate v R*, 2001 G.W.D. 1275.
[73] *Comingersoll SA v Portugal* (35382/97, April 6, 2000).

The character and conduct of the pursuer

17–23   Reminiscent of our domestic CICA scheme, the character and conduct of the applicant may affect the amount of any award. This is most clearly seen in *McCann v United Kingdom*.[74] The applicants had made claims in respect of the killing of three IRA terrorists suspected of planning a bomb attack in Gibraltar. The ECHR found a violation of Article 2. However, the Court rejected the claim for compensation: the victims were intending a terrorist attack. Accordingly, an award of damages was inappropriate. It is more likely that a judgment will itself be held to provide just satisfaction where the applicant is a criminal or a suspected criminal.

Causation

17–24   The approach to causation will bring about interesting arguments. The Commissions explain that the view is strict. It is, however, tempered by a flexible approach to loss of opportunity. In *Martins Moreira v Portugal*,[75] the applicant complained that the proceedings in which he sought damages for personal injury were not completed within a reasonable time. The defendant became insolvent. The ECHR held that it was reasonable to conclude that, as a result of the long delay, the applicant he suffered a loss of opportunities that warranted an award of just satisfaction in respect of pecuniary damage.

The UK experience thus far

17–25   In *R (KB) v Mental Health Review Tribunal*,[76] it was said that the ECHR approach was to be taken first. There is no reason for lower awards but it is right even where there is no comparable tort to look at ordinary awards in general. *R (Bernard and Another) v Enfield LBC*[77] is noteworthy as one of the first domestic human rights damages cases. Sullivan J. in the Queens Bench declined to follow Law Commission guidance, that is by starting from a tort award. The Council had not sufficiently acted to provide accommodation for over 20 months for a disabled person. He considered that damages, in this case against a public authority, should not be minimal or lower than tort damages. There was, in any event, no directly related tort. Instead he looked towards Ombudsman findings of maladministration.

---

[74] (1995) 21 E.H.R.R. 97.
[75] (1988) 13 E.H.R.R. 517.
[76] 2003 T.L.R. 129.
[77] [2002] T.L.R. 459.

One of the first Scottish cases, *Napier v The Scottish Ministers*[78] was a case where there were in fact physical results from the treatment complained of. In view of that and in view of the fact that a financial award was made, that, together with the declaration of the infringement, was sufficient for just satisfaction.

[78] Unreported, Lord Bonomy, April 26, 2004.

CHAPTER 18

OCCUPIERS' LIABILITY

18–1 The liability of an occupier is now mainly a matter of statutory liability, in particular the Occupiers' Liability (Scotland) Act 1960, although the precise residual position of the common law is not yet resolved, notwithstanding the terms of the legislation.[1] The Act was passed to alter the Scots common law, which had been strongly influenced by English principles imposed by the House of Lords.[2] It is submitted that this is now a matter of legal history; but in reading pre-Act decisions, it should be borne in mind that the classification of the injured person, as either licensee, invitee or trespasser, was crucial. Although that is no longer the case, it is still a circumstance that must be considered as affecting what care a reasonable occupier would actually take.[3] The broad purpose of the Act is to provide that occupiers must take reasonable care for persons entering on their premises. It does not create a general liability upon an occupier of the property to take any care for persons who have not entered on the property, such as adjoining proprietors or passers-by. Such individuals are protected by general principles of liability for unintentional harm and nuisance and other related delicts. It is not a duty of insurance although the more dangerous the activity the more care must be taken. There is a cluster of cases discussing whether Employers' Liability regulations also give protection to non-workers entering the workplace.[4]

Who is liable?

18–2   The first question is usually to determine who is the occupier. Here we gain some assistance from the Act.[5] It defines "occupier of premises" as "a person occupying or having control of land or other premises." However, we still require to know what is meant by

---

[1] For a full up-to-date statement including developments after the date of publication see Stewart, *Reparation: Liability for Delict*.

[2] *Dumbreck v Addie & Sons*, 1929 S.C. (HL) 51. The position in England changed, although not so far as to make it identical to the law in Scotland: see the Occupiers' Liability Act 1957.

[3] See *McGlone v BRB*, 1966 S.C. (HL) 1.

[4] See Stewart, *Reparation: Liability for Delict*, para.A19–001.

[5] Occupiers' Liability (Scotland) Act 1960 (the "1960 Act"), s.1(1).

occupying or having control. To resolve this question regard is had to the law as it applied before the Act. This is still effectively determined by the common law which is expressly saved in the statute[6] The test is a matter of possession and control and will be a matter of fact in each case. An example is *Telfer v Glasgow D.C.*[7] The Co-operative Society was in the course of selling property to Glasgow District Council. Both the Council and the Society were sued in respect of an injury sustained on the property. It was held, *inter alia,* that the Society was the occupier. It had the keys and the *de facto* power to exclude others. Ownership is not necessary nor indeed is any form of title however limited, as can be seen in *Poliskie v Lane,*[8] where an independent contractor was held to be liable. Nor does the involvement of an independent contractor mean that the "primary" employer escapes liability.[9] Nor is ownership sufficient, as was made clear in *Pollock v Stead & Simpson Ltd*[10] in which a case against one of the defenders based solely on infeftment was dismissed.[11] In *Murray v Edinburgh District Council,*[12] the pursuer was a home help and was injured when a wooden panel containing a ventilator fell onto her wrist when she was working in a council house tenanted by an individual. The case under section 2(1) failed as it was not averred that the defenders were in occupation and control. In *Todd v British Railways Board,*[13] the pursuer alleged that he slipped on a pavement in Waverley station while employed as a conductor. The issue arose because it was not clear whether British Railways Board or Railtrack were responsible partly due to the allocation of functions set up under the Railways Act 1993. While that Act transferred ownership, Lord Penrose correctly thought that irrelevant. It was held that the case was relevant under the Act on the basis that it was said that the premises were a train station. The pursuer is not always so fortunate in these multiple-defender cases. In *Meek v SRC,*[14] the pursuer fell on to a concrete "beach" when the promenade gave way. The Regional Council, District Council and "Scotrail" were all released at legal debate. It is open to a court to find all or some defenders liable and apportion liability.[15]

The special case of the landlord of premises is discussed below.

---

[6] 1960 Act, s.1(2).

[7] 1974 S.L.T. (Notes) 51. See also *Feely v Co-operative Wholesale Society,* 1990 G.W.D. 4–221. And see also for an independent contractor pursuer himself being in control: *Poliskie v Lane,* 1981 S. L.T. 282.

[8] 1981 S.L.T. 28.

[9] *McDyer v The Celtic Football and Athletic Co Ltd,* 2000 S.L.T. 736.

[10] 1980 S.L.T. (Notes) 76.

[11] See also comments in *Clark v Maersk Co Ltd,* 2000 S.L.T. (Sh. Ct) 9.

[12] 1981 S.L.T. 253.

[13] Unreported, February 24, 1998.

[14] Unreported, August 23, 2001.

[15] *Nicol v Advocate General for Scotland,* 2003 G.W.D. 11–329.

Liable in respect of what subjects or objects?

18–3   The next question is to ask what is meant by premises ("land" being apparently self-explanatory). This is not defined in the Act and is a matter to be determined in each case. The Act also imposes liability for certain areas that (as they have been separately described) are not premises and may be described as notional premises.[16] So the following are covered by the Act: fixed or moveable structures, including any vessel, vehicle or aircraft. This provision in its terms covers most modes of transport and it will be a question of statutory interpretation whether, for example, a hoist or a ski-tow fall within the statutory definitions. An open area of land attracted liability when Mrs Cairns, a grandmother, tripped in a concealed hole at a Butlins camp. The defenders denied the existence of a hole on the basis of regular inspections. The court held there was a hole and because they had regular inspections they must have been negligent and missed it![17] The Act was mentioned in *McCluskey v Lord Advocate*,[18] where the Forestry Commission was held not to be liable to a woman who slipped off a footpath and fell on to a rock. The path was not one of the Forestry Commission's paths. The idea that there exists a right of way over land otherwise in possession and control was rejected in a sheriff court case reviewing the authorities and referring to a still unreported Inner House case.[19] The act applies to a footpath running along a grass embankment, which path was unlit and hazardous, the fall to the side being of the order of eight feet.[20] The act applies to *exits* from premises, presumably where the pursuer has already entered on the premises.[21] Roads and pavements under public control are generally thought to be treated outside the scope of the Act. These are discussed at the end of this section.

Duty and standard

18–4   The duty and the standard of care are laid down by the Act. To succeed the pursuer must bring himself within the terms of the Act[22]:

---

[16] 1960 Act, s.1(3).

[17] *Cairns v Butlins*, 1989 G.W.D. 40–1879.

[18] 1994 S.L.T. 452. There is a full discussion of this general topic and some very interesting comparative material in D. Mckenzie et al., "Civil Liability for Injury and Damage Arising from Access to the Scottish Countryside'" (1997) 2 S.L.P.Q. 214.

[19] *Johnstone v Sweeney*, 1985 S.L.T. (Sh. Ct) 2. The unreported case is *McQueen v Vale of Leven District Council,* January 24, 1973. See the tangential discussion in *McDougall v Tawse*, 2002 S.L.T. (Sh. Ct) 10 and see Cusine and Paisley, Servitudes and Rights of Way.

[20] *Cruikshank v Fife Council*, Cupar Sheriff Court, December 17, 2001.

[21] See *Duff v East Dunbartonshire Council*, 1999 G.W.D. 22–1072; First Division, June 28, 2002.

[22] 1960 Act, s.2(1).

"The care which an occupier of premises is required, by reason of his occupation or control of the premises, to show towards a person entering thereon in respect of dangers which are due to the state of the premises or to anything done or omitted to be done on them and for which the occupier is in law responsible shall, except in so far as he is entitled to and does extend, restrict, modify or exclude by agreement his obligations towards that person, be such care as in all the circumstances of the case is reasonable to see that that person will not suffer injury or damage by reason of any such danger."

While this provision can be summarised to the effect that the occupier must take such care as is reasonable in all the circumstances, it is nevertheless a statutory duty and it is important to try to fit specific cases into the statutory definition of the duty. Despite the positive formulation of the duty, it seems now to be settled that it imposes no evidentiary burden upon the occupier. The pursuer will still have to show the circumstances which give rise to the duty; a pursuer cannot merely aver that he has suffered an accident on premises and put the onus on the defender to prove that he took reasonable care.[23] However, in *McDyer v The Celtic Football and Athletic Co Ltd*[24] the Inner House allowed the doctrine of *res ipsa loquitur* to apply to the extent of allowing that the doctrine meant that the pleadings that narrated control and an accident were sufficient where an item fell on the pursuer from above.[25]

Previously decided cases can illustrate what the rule set out in the statute means. It certainly would cover many a derelict building,[26] poor lighting[27]; leaving things lying about over which people can trip[28]; the failure to find a hole during regular inspections of land,[29] leaving a surface slippery because wet.[30] A failure to mark unexpected steps can incur liability as where a salesman fell and the steps were not marked by either a notice or a warning strip.[31] In the case of a landlord, an example is leaving a toilet bowl damaged.[32] In *Kirk*

---

[23] See *Wallace v City of Glasgow D.C.*, 1985 S.L.T. 23; *Walker v Eastern Scottish Omnibuses Ltd*, 1990 G.W.D. 3–140; *Miller v City of Glasgow D.C.*, 1989 G.W.D. 29–1347. For notes on the law in practice see Kinloch, "Slippery Substances", 1995 Rep. B. 4–7.

[24] 2000 S.L.T. 736.

[25] Applying *Devines v Colvilles*, 1969 S.L.T. 154.

[26] *Telfer v Glasgow D.C.*, 1974 S.L.T. (Notes) 51.

[27] *Millar v Fife Regional Council*, 1990 S.L.T. 651; although it is perfectly possible to descend a stair in the dark and it may only be where the absence of light is unexpected that there may be liability: *Teacher's Trs. v Calder* (1900) 2 F. 372.

[28] *McMillan v Lord Advocate*, 1991 S.L.T. 150.

[29] *Cairns v Butlins*, 1989 G.W.D. 40–1879.

[30] *Todd v British Railways Board*, 1998 G.W.D. 11–568.

[31] *Cole v Weir Pumps Ltd*, 1995 S.L.T. 12; 1994 S.C.L.R. 580.

[32] *Hughes' Tutrix v Glasgow District Council*, 1982 S.L.T. (Sh. Ct) 70.

v Fife Council,[33] the pursuer was injured when he slipped playing
five-a-side football. It was established there had been water on the
floor such that under their policy the defenders ought to have called-
off the game. Whether or not safe common stairs should be lit is a
matter of fact and degree.[34] A man succeeded when he fell down
stairs leaving premises he had visited as a salesman. It was held that
the steps were dangerous because of the lack of a warning, either by
notice or by a coloured warning strip.[35] A woman who fell when the
signpost she was leaning on gave way did not succeed as it was not
established that the defenders should have known of the defect.[36]
Allowing a house to become damp such that it affected a child's
asthma has fallen within the Act.[37]

Actings of others

18–5   Liability extends to a failure to take into account the actings of
other parties. In *Hosie v Arbroath Football Club Ltd*,[38] the club was
held liable when fans forced down a door by their sustained pressure
injuring the pursuer. There were safety devices available and in use
that would have prevented the door being lifted off.[39] The facts of
Hazard v Glasgow Pavilion[40] are unusual. A person fell from a stage
after being hypnotised by a performer and a proof before answer was
allowed. A pursuer was unsuccessful where his car was hit by a gate
from premises, but he could not explain how it got loose, evidence
having been accepted that it had been earlier secured.[41] While cases
involving dog bites or other injuries by animals are now likely to be
dealt with under the Animals (Scotland) Act 1987, in principle, the
Occupiers' Liability (Scotland) Act 1960 applies to an occupier's
conduct in keeping animals on premises and it was so held in the
Outer House in *Hill v Lovett*.[42] In *Dunn v Carlin*,[43] the Inner House
upheld a finding of liability on an occupier in respect of his having
petrol exposed that did ignite and injure the pursuer, who later died.
The pursuer had not proven that one of the employees of the defender
had been smoking while decanting petrol. However, the Inner House

---

[33] 2001 G.W.D. 36–1398.
[34] *Davie v Edinburgh Corporation,* 1977 S.L.T. (Notes) 5.
[35] *Cole, ibid.*
[36] *Western v Eastern Scottish Omnibuses Ltd,* 1989 G.W.D. 140.
[37] *Guy v Strathkelvin D.C.,* 1997 S.C.L.R. 405.
[38] 1978 S.L.T. 122.
[39] *ibid.,* at 124–125. Another case based on the act, that the club should have had more
turnstiles and all of them manned, was on the facts alleged, unsuccessful.
[40] 1994 G.W.D. 13–850.
[41] *Atkinson v Aberdeen City Council,* 2002 G.W.D. 737.
[42] 1992 S.L.T. 994. It was also opined that there may well have been employer's
liability upon one defender for failing to provide a safe place of work, *per* Lord Weir
at 997.
[43] 2003 G.W.D. 5–130.

made very clear that the act relates to the state of the premises, which *with the exposed petrol* was dangerous. The occupier cannot take care of things about which he does not know or ought not to know. In *Falconer v Edinburgh City Transport Longstone Social Club*,[44] the pursuer slipped on residual body oil from a male strip show. Her case failed because there was neither averment nor proof that the occupiers knew or ought to have known that there would be oil on the floor at the interval. In such a situation, a case against the showmen might have been indicated but, of course, they may be difficult to find or convene.

The status of the pursuer

As a result of there being no express categories of victim, it does **18–6** not matter, in principle, whether someone is on the premises by invitation or as a trespasser: the standard of care, in both cases, is still reasonable care. However, as a matter of fact and circumstance, the pursuer's mode of entry is still relevant. These points were considered in *McGlone v British Railways Board*.[45] A boy aged 12 climbed up a transformer belonging to the board. It was surrounded on three sides by a large fence and on the other by the railway. A gap between the fence and a wall was restricted by barbed wire in a fan shape. There were signs saying, "Danger — overhead live wires." The boy was badly burned as a result of an electric shock sustained when he came into contact with one of the wires high up the transformer. The court held that although the barrier was not impenetrable, it indicated to the victim that he would be in danger and that was enough to implement the duty of care. Lord Reid expressed the view that the degree of care to be shown could vary depending on whether the person was trespassing or not. Lord Reid's opinion has not, in any way, resulted in an under-the-table categorisation of victims: instead it usefully serves to make courts and advisers remember that the Act refers every case back to its own circumstances.

McGlone was considered again by the House of Lords in *Titchener v British Railways Board*.[46] A girl was struck by a train as she crossed a busy railway line. She was aware that it was such and usually looked both ways. She alleged the board should have inspected for gaps in the fence and repaired them. It was held that the existence and extent of a duty to fence will depend upon the circumstances of the case, including the age and intelligence of the particular person entering on the premises. Thus the board owed no duty to that particular pursuer in these particular circumstances to

---

[44] 2003 G.W.D. 181, 2003 Rep. L.R. 39.
[45] 1966 S.L.T. 2.
[46] 1984 S.L.T. 192; followed in *Devlin v Strathclyde R.C.*, 1993 S.L.T. 699.

repair the fence. Indeed, Lord Fraser said that if it had been necessary to do so, he would have held that the board owed her no duty to provide a fence at all. This applies generally so that an obvious danger does not require to be fenced or signposted.[47] A final, and more routine example is *Dawson v Scottish Power*,[48] in which the pursuer's 11-year-old son was injured when he went to retrieve his football which landed on the defenders' substation. He tried to climb over and impaled his finger on a spike at the top of the fence. The fence was six-feet high but had reduced effectively to four feet as a result of the build up of rubble. It was as a matter of common sense and the evidence of a health and safety expert reasonably foreseeable that a boy would try to go over a fence for his ball and six feet or two metres was the safe height.

Notices, assumption of risk and consent

18–7   It is possible to exclude the duty by agreement but not by a simple notice or warning. However, such notice or warning will be a circumstance to be accorded whatever weight is appropriate.[49] Further, there is statutory control of agreements where premises are used as business premises. Section 16 of the Unfair Contract Terms Act 1977 provides:

> "Where a term of a contract purports to exclude or restrict liability for breach of duty arising in the course of any business or from the occupation of any premises used for business purposes of the occupier, that term — (a) shall be void in any case where such exclusion or restriction is in respect of death or personal injury; (b) shall in any other case, have no effect if it was not fair and reasonable to incorporate the term in the contract."

There is no obligation to a person entering on the premises in respect of a risk which that person has willingly accepted as his.[50] There was an extensive evaluation of the law in *Hughes' Tutrix v Glasgow District Council*,[51] a landlord's case in which a child injured her hand on a broken toilet bowl:

---

[47] *Stevenson v Glasgow Corp.*, 1908 S.C. 1034.
[48] 1999 S.L.T. 672.
[49] *McGlone*, above.
[50] 1960 Act, s.2(3).
[51] 1982 S.L.T. (Sh. Ct) 70. See also *Dawson v Scottish Power*, 1999 S.L.T. 672 in which the boy had been warned of the danger by his father and understood the risk. However, Lord MacLean commented section 2(3) was not pled. There was a finding of contributory negligence.

"Since the 1960 Act, the old law no longer exists, and this case is not raised in contract. The defence of *volenti* is specifically retained in the 1960 Act, by virtue of s.2(3) . . . The landlord's obligation under s. 3 is the same as is required of an occupier in terms of s.2, and so s.2(3) would apply in this case. Professor Walker says of that section: 'The application of the maxim [*volenti non fit injuria*] to landlord and tenant cases is probably further limited by the effect of the Occupiers' Liability (Scotland) Act, 1960, s.3, which imposes on a landlord towards his tenants and sub-tenants the duties of care owed by an occupier towards his visitors, so that only clear evidence of voluntary acceptance of specific known risks (s.2 (3)) could be sufficient to make the maxim applicable' (Delict, p.352). I accept that in this case there was a specific known risk, but I think that it is open to me to hold that the defenders have not shown that, in all the circumstances, the pursuer 'willingly' accepted the danger, far less that it can be inferred that she agreed to what would be tantamount to a variation of her contract (*c.f.* Rankine on Personal Bar, pp.76–87) to the effect of relieving the defenders of their obligation to repair the bowl."[52]

In *Titchener* (above), it was reiterated that the part of the Act which deals with acceptance of risk merely put into words the principle expressed by the maxim *volenti non fit injuria* . In *Titchener*, it was stated that if there had been a duty of care this "*volenti*" subsection would have applied to exclude liability. In evidence, the pursuer had said that she had known she was "taking a chance". In the case of the male strippers discussed above, had the occupiers been liable for allowing body oil on to the floor upon which the pursuer slipped, the pursuer would not have been held to have assumed that risk.[53]

Higher duties

The 1960 Act does not relieve an occupier of any higher duty of **18–8** care incumbent upon him[54] such as the employer's duty to provide for his employees under employers' liability legislation.

Landlord and tenant

The Act makes special provision for cases involving landlord and **18–9** tenant. This is important, for the tenant is the person in actual occupation and would seem to be the occupier for the purposes of the Act. The landlord under a lease may, however, be the one who has

---

[52] *ibid.*, per Sheriff Gordon at 73.
[53] *Falconer v Edinburgh City Transport Longstone Social Club*, 2003 G.W.D. 181, 2003 Rep. L.R. 39.
[54] 1960 Act, s.2(2).

the responsibility for certain aspects of the state of the premises. While the tenant is entitled to pursue a claim against the landlord for a breach of an obligation under the lease, this is a contractual right which would not be available to his guests or members of his family. Accordingly, the Act makes the landlord liable instead of the tenant, if under the lease the landlord is responsible for the maintenance or repair of the premises.[55] The most important question is, of course, whether the landlord is responsible in the first place: this will be determined by the contract of lease. Apart from any special terms in the lease there are two major implied conditions:

(1) There is an implied warrandice that the subjects let are fit for the purpose for which they are let. In an urban lease the landlord is impliedly obliged to maintain the subjects in a tenantable and habitable condition, having put them in such a state at entry.

(2) There is a statutorily implied condition that subjects are and will be maintained reasonably fit for human habitation.[56]

Accordingly, in most cases where someone is injured in a council house they will have a possible delictual remedy against the landlord even if they do not have a contractual right under the lease. Lord Johnston has recently decided in the Outer House that section 3 of the Act effectively overruled the effect of the existing common-law rule which relied upon privity to deny the tenant's claim.[57]

Roads and footpaths

18–10 Historically, liability in respect of roads developed separately from occupiers' liability, while liability for premises was subject to the older "English" tripartite system. Accordingly it is still thought that a different regime applies to public roads and footpaths. This may be on the basis of history or because authorities do not have sufficient possession and control to fall within the plain words of the Act.

In practice, despite a brave attempt by the then Sheriff Principal at Glasgow to state the law in a an open ended way in *King v Strathclyde R.C.*,[58] the Inner House balkanised pavement cases in the daily cited case of *Gibson v Strathclyde R.C.*[59] The following, sometimes obvious, practical propositions can be extracted from that

---

[55] 1960 Act, s.3(1).

[56] Housing (Scotland) Act 1987, Sch.10, and see *Haggarty v Glasgow Corp.*, 1963 S.L.T. (Notes) 73; 1964 S.L.T. (Notes) 95.

[57] *Guy v Strathkelvin D.C.*, 1997 S.C.L.R. 405 — the common-law rule was in *Cameron v Young*, 1908 S.C. (HL) 7.

[58] Glasgow, January 8, 1991.

[59] 1993 S.L.T. 1243.

case: (1) Liability is for fault; (2) The general rule applies that a pursuer's personal injury case should not be dismissed on relevancy unless it is bound to fail if proved, the onus of establishing that being on the defender[60]; (3) A daily inspection case cannot normally be supported by a bald averment it would be reasonable and practicable to do that[61]; (4) It is possible to establish a daily inspection case without averments of proper practice giving rise to an inference of negligence although the circumstances should be, on one view, special, exceptional and obvious,[62] or perhaps better the subject of averment.[63] The arguments often made by pursuers were made in this case and largely rejected, particularly the point that the pursuer seldom has the knowledge of what is reasonable or practicable, the daily burden of roads administration being beyond their knowledge and in the absence of private or public funding, that of their professional advisers. Older cases, quite naturally, suggesting that defects in roads infer fault were not adopted, although depending on the circumstances. That said, it is possible to establish a case based on prior reports of danger.[64] The Sheriff Principal at Glasgow has recently emphasised, it is submitted correctly, that an averment of *a dangerous state* does not require *Gibson* averments anent inspection (save in the alternative).[65] However, most cases have to rely on the arguing that the defenders have failed to meet the standard they themselves have currently agreed.[66] Proving the case requires information held by the defenders.[67]

As public authorities are involved in roads and pavement cases, it **18–11** should not be forgotten that general principles of liability apply, albeit the "great" cases are not generally cited and discussed.[68] Although the wording of the Roads (Scotland) Act 1984, s.34 (which provides that a roads authority must take such steps as they consider reasonable to prevent snow and ice endangering the safe passage of

---

[60] Lord Justice-Clerk Ross at 1245H-K.

[61] Lord Justice-Clerk Ross at 1246A; Lord Weir at 1248B.

[62] Lord Weir at 1248A.

[63] Lord Justice-Clerk Ross at 1246H.

[64] *McGeouch v SRC*, 1985 S.L.T. 321; *Syme v Scottish Borders Council*, September 24, 2002, Lord Clarke.

[65] *Letford v Glasgow City Council*, 2002 G.W.D. 23–750.

[66] Delivering the Best Value in Highway Maintenance: Code of Practice for Maintenance Management, July 2001 reported and discussed in R. Conway, *Personal Injury Practice in the Sheriff Court*, (2nd ed., W Green, 2003), Chapter 18.

[67] The issues are discussed for England in D. Turner, "Pre-action protocol: tripping up over disclosure", 2003 P.I.L.J. August p.2 and there is a style specification in Conway, "Personal Injury Practice in the Sheriff Court, (2nd ed., W Green, 2003) p.303.

[68] *Stovin v Wise* [1996] A.C. 923, although an English House of Lords' case is still important but is not in point where there is already a duty of care recognised in Scotland by an authority. *Forbes v Dundee*, 1997 S.L.T. 1330 imports these *Stovin* arguments into a Scots discussion but on the facts the basis of the case may have merited such an argument.

pedestrians and vehicles over public roads) seems more helpful requiring the authority to take steps, it has been held to reflect the common law and there is no fault where a reasonable system is in place.[69] The power to mark roads and the like and the existence of foreseeability of injury is not itself sufficient to create a duty to mark roads, although it might be possible to make a case if there is evidence of special risks known to the authority.[70] In *Kemp v Secretary of State for Scotland*,[71] it was held that the roads authority was liable for having a raised kerb at the edge of a footpath that caused the pursuer to fall into the path of traffic. There was evidence from a police office and a consulting engineer that the design was a hazard.[72] It was held in *McKnight v Clydeside Buses Ltd*[73] that the roads authority was under an obligation to mark low bridges where it knew or ought to have known it constituted a danger, such as in this case where there had been many accidents before. Roadworks need to be properly marked and regard may be had to the "traffic signs manual".[74]

---

[69] *Grant v Lothian Regional Council*, 1988 S.L.T. 533, *Syme v Scottish Borders Council*, September 24, 2002. In England there may be no right at all: *Goodes v East Sussex County Council* [2000] 1 W.L.R. 1356. See G. Junor, "Claims against Road Authorities on Ice in England", 2002 Rep. B. 45–4 It appears that as a result of *Goodes* the government intend to review and legislate to clarify the law: G. Junor, "Road Authorities on Ice: A postscript or new chapter?" 2003 Rep. B. 50–4. So in cases relying on *Syme* consideration will need to be given to the fact that *Goodes* was relied on.

[70] *Murray v Nicholls*, 1983 S.L.T. 194.

[71] 1999 Rep. L.R. 110.

[72] There was one-third contributory negligence as the pursuer was drunk.

[73] 1999 S.L.T. 1167.

[74] *MacKenzie v Perth and Kinross Council*, 2003 G.W.D. 4–101.

Chapter 19

PRODUCT LIABILITY

Product liability like many other areas now involves the application **19–1** of both the common law and statute.[1] It is another area which usually involves unintentional harm. The general common-law duty to take reasonable care has been supplemented by a special statutory form of strict liability by the Consumer Protection Act 1987.[2] Not all cases are covered by the Act, so the common law is still relevant.

The common law

Scots law did recognise delictual liability outwith contract in **19–2** respect of injuries caused by products in some circumstances. In one case, the liability was upon the person who left a dangerous machine in a public place.[3] In another case, the owner was liable even although the pursuer's injuries were the result of the acts of another: two children played with the door of a shed on waste ground and it fell on another as a result of its insufficiency.[4] It would not have fallen if the boys had not climbed up the door and lifted a drop bar. On the other hand, where the goods were intrinsically safe, there was no liability.[5] Mention has already been made of the case of *Donoghue v Stevenson* in the context of liability for unintentional harm generally.[6] However, while that case has a wide ratio establishing proximity as a basis of liability, it also has a narrow ratio which is a suitable beginning from which to look at product liability. That narrow ratio is apparent from a dictum of Lord Atkin:

> "A manufacturer of products, which he sells in such a form as to show that he intends them to reach the ultimate consumer in the form in which they left him, with no reasonable possibility of intermediate examination, and with the knowledge that the

---

[1] For developments after publication, see Stewart, *Reparation: Liability for Delict.*
[2] This only applies to damage attributable to defective products arising after March 1, 1988, where the product has been supplied after that date.
[3] *Campbell v Ord* (1873) 1 R. 149.
[4] *Findlay v Angus* (1887) 14 R. 312.
[5] *Duff v National Telephone Co.* (1889) 16 R. 675.
[6] 4.6 above.

absence of reasonable care in the preparation or putting up of
the products will result in an injury to the consumer's life or
property, owes a duty to the consumer to take that reasonable
care."[7]

It has been accepted that the principle could apply to services as
much as goods.[8]

The intermediate examination point requires some clarification. In
Donoghue, the seller of the ginger beer could not be expected to open
the bottles to check for decomposed snails. However, if the bottle had
been translucent, the retailer might have been expected to check for
obvious impurities. In the case of *Grant v Australian Knitting Mills
Ltd*,[9] the issue was whether it was possible to recover in respect of
dermatitis contracted as a result of injurious chemicals being present
in the plaintiff's underwear. The difference between this case and
Donoghue was that the retailer took the underpants from their pack
and placed them on his shelves, whereas the alleged snail in
Donoghue remained in its bottle all the time. The Privy Council
refused to accept the significance of that distinction. There was no
need for the product to remain as it had been put out. On the other
hand, it was stated that the defect in the product has to remain
"hidden and unknown to the consumer". The *Grant* case is also of
interest because it was held that the plaintiff did not have to prove the
mechanism of the harm — it was possible to establish the cause by
an inference from the proven facts. The issue of intermediate
examination and the general question of causation are interrelated.
The issue of intermediate examination can be analysed as whether
the cause of the accident was the fault of the manufacturer or due to
another cause.[10] The case of *Evans v Triplex Safety Glass Co. Ltd*[11]
illustrates this. It is also a convenient example of how the common
law fails to offer what many consider to be adequate protection for
the consumer. Mr Evans bought a car. The manufacturers of the car
fitted a windscreen manufactured by the defenders. When Mr Evans
was driving his car the windscreen disintegrated and injured people
in the car. The accident could have been due to faulty fitting of the
windscreen or could have been due to other causes such as faulty
manufacture of the windscreen. Because *Evans* failed to prove fault
on the part of the manufacturer either of the car or of the windscreen,

---

[7] 1932 S.C. (HL) 31 at 57. Lord Rodger has traced the legal ancestry of the *Donoghue*
snail back to a cigar stub in a Coca-Cola bottle in Tennessee: "Lord Macmillan's
Speech" (1992) 108 L.Q.R. 236 at 244.
[8] *Haseldine v C.A. Daw & Son Ltd* [1941] 3 All E.R., 156.
[9] [1935] All E.R. 209.
[10] For a discussion of the modern relevance of intermediate examination, see *Murphy v
Brentwood D.C.* [1990] 3 W.L.R. 414.
[11] [1936] 1 All E.R. 283.

he lost his case. It was such difficulties that led to calls for liability independent of fault, to which we now turn.

The Consumer Protection Act 1987, Part I

This statute implements an EEC Directive[12] and it is expressly **19–3** stated in the Act that it has to be construed to comply with the Directive.[13] For some time there had been moves to introduce some form of strict liability, but no domestic solution had come to fruition.[14] There are many matters of policy reflected in such a system. In the main, liability is placed on the person most able to prevent an accident in the first place — the producer. Secondly, the cost of an accident is removed from the consumer, who generally would find it expensive to insure, and passed to someone else more likely to be able to obtain insurance cover on reasonable terms. The Act provides a limited form of strict liability for defective products, which does not, however, replace any existing liability in delict.[15] Broadly speaking, there is strict liability on a producer for damages caused by a defective product. Each of the key elements in this liability is defined by the statute. The following treatment is intended to give a broad view of the Act, but does not deal with every aspect of it.

---

[12] Dir. No. 85/374/EEC.
[13] s.1(1). This is no platitude. It had been anticipated that the Commission might challenge the UK's implementation of the directive as being too restrictive to liability in places. Such a case did emerge, *Commission v UK* [1997] All E.R. (EC) 481, and this very provision convinced the Court that the UK had complied, for if this provision were given effect to the UK law would comply with EC law. That is an optimistic view of the approach of UK courts to legislation! See generally Clark, *Product Liability* (Sweet & Maxwell, 1989); J. Blaikie "Product Liability" (1987) 32 J.L.S. 325; A. Clark, "Liability for Defective Products" (1981) 26 J.L.S. 398; A. Clark, "Product Liability: The New Rules", 1987 S.L.T. (News) 257; A. Clark, "Conceptual Basis of the Product Liability" (1985) 48 M.L.R. 325; A. Clark, "US Product Liability" (1982) 27 J.L.S. 514; W.C.H. Ervine, "Product Liability and Part 1 of the Consumer Protection Act 1987" (1988) SCOLAG 21; P.R. Ferguson, "Pharmaceutical Products Liability", 1992 J.R. 226; P.R. Ferguson, "Compensation for Alleged Vaccine Injury" (1994) 39 J.L.S. 80; C. Newdick, "The Future of Negligence in Product Liability" (1987) 103 L.Q.R. 288; C. Newdick, "The Development Risk Defence" 1988 C.L.J. 455; J. Stapleton, "Products Liability Reform — Real or Illusory", 1986 6 O.J.L.S. 392; D. Powles, "Product Liability — A Novel Dimension in Scots Law", in A.J. Gamble (ed.), Obligations in Context (1990, W. Green) at p. 33, R Freeman "Product Liability, defective goods" [2001] J.P.I.L. 26, G. Junor, "Beyond the Common Law — The (potential) reach of product liability" 2001 Rep. B. 41–5. P. Balen, "An introduction to product liability claims" [2002] J.P.I.L. 3.
[14] The Strasbourg Convention: Dir/Jun (76) 5; the Scottish and English Law Commissions: Cmnd 6831 (1977); the Pearson Commission: Cmnd 7054 (1978).
[15] s.2(6).

Product

19–4 "Product" means any goods or electricity and includes any goods comprised in another product whether by virtue of being a component part or raw material or otherwise.[16] Thus both the car and the windscreen in a case like *Evans* would be products. "Goods" is further defined as including "substances, growing crops and things comprised in land by virtue of being attached to it and any ship, aircraft or vehicle."[17] for Scotland the reference to "attached" means becoming heritable by accession to heritable property.[18] There is no liability in respect of any defect in any game or agricultural produce, which is defined as being any produce of the soil or stock farming or fisheries so long as the supply was at a time when it had not undergone an industrial process.[19] A new European Union directive included agricultural produce too.[20]

It has been held to apply to vaccine,[21] to an elasticated strap,[22] and, in principle, to a condom.[23]

Defect

19–5 The Act provides a definition of "defect", which exists "if the safety of the product is not such as persons generally are entitled to expect."[24] Realising that this would not answer every problem or might lead to diverging judicial opinions, the Act provides that while all the circumstances of the case should be taken into account, the following must be considered:

> (a) the manner in which and purposes for which, the product has been marketed, its get-up, the use of any mark in relation to the product and any instructions for, or warnings

---

[16] s.1(2). See also J. Stapleton, "Software, Information and the Concept of Product" (1989) 9 Tel Aviv Stud. in Law 47; R. Colbey, "Personal Injury Claims Arising out of Food Poisoning" [1994] J.P.I.L. 294.

[17] s.45 (1).

[18] s.45(5).

[19] ss.2(4) and 1(2).

[20] "Extension of Product Liability Directive" (1998) 43 J.L.S. 45. Directive 1999/34. "Article 1 Directive 85/374/EEC is hereby amended as follows: 1. Article 2 shall be replaced by the following: "Article 2 For the purpose of this Directive, 'product' means all movables even if incorporated into another movable or into an immovable. 'Product' includes electricity." 2. In Article 15, paragraph 1(a) shall be deleted." Given effect in England and Wales by The Consumer Protection Act 1987 (Product Liability) (Modification) Order 2000 and in Scotland (late) by the Consumer Protection Act 1987 (Product Liability) (Modification) (Scotland) Order 2001.

[21] *A and Others v National Blood Authority* [2001] 3 All E.R. 289.

[22] *Abouzaid v Mothercare (UK) Ltd*, [2001] T.L.R. 136.

[23] *Richardson v LRC Products Ltd.*, [2000] P.I.Q.R. P164.

[24] s.3(1).

with respect to, doing or refraining from doing anything with or in relation to the product;

(b) what might reasonably be expected to be done with or in relation to the product; and

(c) the time when the product was supplied by its producer to another." [25]

This is sometimes referred to for convenience as a consumer expectation test. In *A and Others v National Blood Authority*,[26] the plaintiffs had been infected with Hepititis C as a result of transfusions. The defendants' argument was based simply on the focus of the legislation — the consumer expectation test. They said that consumers would not expect anything other than reasonably available precautions. Burton J. made his decision based on the distinction between standard and non-standard products and then asked whether the non-standard risk was accepted. He held it was not. In *Abouzaid v Mothercare (UK) Ltd*,[27] the plaintiff injured his eye as the result of the recoil of an elasticated strap on the defenders product. In the Court of Appeal, the judge's decision that this was a breach of the consumer expectation test was upheld and it was emphatically pointed out that this was so even though there was no negligence. In *Richardson v LRC Products Ltd*,[28] it was held that a consumer would not expect a condom to be 100 per cent safe from bursting.

Producers and suppliers

In the first place, liability is on the producer. This includes the **19–6** manufacturer, but may also include the person who wins or abstracts raw materials. Someone who processes agricultural products is a producer. Someone who simply packages goods is not a producer.[29] As well as the producer, other persons may be liable in respect of the same product,[30] namely any person who holds himself out as the producer by putting his brand on the goods (sometimes known as an "own brander") and a person who imports goods from outside the European Community in the course of his business to supply them to another (an "importer").[31] Further, in addition to those liable above

---

[25] s.3(2). See Stoppa, "The Concept of Defectiveness in the Consumer Protection Act 1987: a critical analysis", 1992 L.S. 210.

[26] [2001] 3 All E.R. 289. See generally, J.M. Williams, "Product Liability — Hepatitis C litigation" [2001] J.P.I.L. 238.

[27] [2001] T.L.R. 136.

[28] [2000] P.I.Q.R. P164.

[29] s.2(2)(a), although he may be liable under another head.

[30] s.2(2)(b); s.2(2)(c).

[31] It goes without saying that students must be familiar with the ever increasing membership of the European Community.

as producers, there is liability too on the supplier of goods, for example, a retailer, but only if: (a) the victim requests that the supplier reveal one or more of the producers; (b) that request is made within a reasonable time after damage occurs, and at a time when it is not reasonably practicable for the victim to identify all of the producers himself; and (c) the supplier fails to identify the producer or the person who supplied to him.[32] The value of this provision is to encourage the supplier to reveal the person who produced the article. Once the provision is appreciated in the business community, it is likely that steps will be taken to record the source of products and components so that liability can be avoided by a supplier by complying with the request and naming the person who supplied to him. Any persons who are liable are liable jointly and severally.[33] These provisions make it likely that a person in the position of the plaintiff in *Evans*[34] would suceed. He could sue either the car manufacturer or the windscreen manufacturer, both of whom are prima facie liable.

Damages

19-7   The damages recoverable are limited by the Act. Damages are recoverable for personal injuries, death or damage to the pursuer's property. Damage to the product itself or damage to a product caused by one of its defective component parts, is not recoverable.[35] Damages can only be recovered in respect of property, which is:

> "of a description of property ordinarily intended for private use, occupation or consumption; and intended by the person suffering the loss or damage mainly for his own private use, occupation or consumption."

In any event, even if not a business asset, the value of the property damaged must exceed £275. However, it should be noted that this limit does not apply to personal injuries or death.

Defences

19-8   It is crucial to know the defences for they affect the scope of liability significantly. They are:

> (1) *Compliance with any requirement imposed by or under any enactment or with any Community obligation.* This is self explanatory.

---

[32] s.2(3).
[33] s.2(5).
[34] [1936] 1 All E.R. 283.
[35] s.5(1) and (2).

(2) *The defender did not supply.* This covers a situation where someone takes the product away from the defender, as by theft or mistake. The point was litigated in *Veedfeld v Arhus Amtskommune,*[36] an ECJ case on a preliminary ruling from Denmark. The product in question was kidney flushing fluid used in kidney transplants. It was argued, *inter alia,* by the defendants that they were not liable as the product had not been "put into circulation" in terms of the directive. That argument failed.

(3) *The supply is not in the course of a business by someone who is not one of the producer class or, if he is, he is so by virtue of things not done with a view to a profit.* Blaikie has well explained this provision by saying, "the commercial producer who gives his product away for nothing . . . cannot rely on this defence. However the lady who makes confectionery for the cake and candy stall at the church sale of work would not be liable."[37] In the same way, it is perfectly permissible to make a present for a person's birthday, without attracting strict liability. In the case of *Veedfeld v Arhus Amtskommune,*[38] noted above, an ECJ case on a preliminary ruling from Denmark, the product in question was kidney flushing fluid used in kidney transplants, It was argued, *inter alia,* by the defendants that they were not liable as the product had not been manufactured for an "economic purpose" in terms of the directive. That argument failed. This was not a charitable supply as envisaged by Article 7(c).

(4) *The defect did not exist at the relevant time.* Generally, the relevant time is the time of supply. This will allow a defence where it can be shown that someone else has tampered with the product.

(5) *The state of scientific and technical knowledge at the relevant time was not such that a producer of products of the same description as the product in question might be expected to have discovered the defect if it had existed in his products while they were under his control.* This is often known as the "development risks defence".[39] The directive provided that the Commission would review in 1995 whether Member States should be allowed to continue to permit this and other provisions. There are arguments for and against it. Not to have it inhibits

---

[36] [2001] T.L.R. 358.

[37] Blaikie, "Product Liability" (1987) 32 J.L.S.S. 325 at 328.

[38] [2001] T.L.R. 358.

[39] P. Spink, "The Consumer Protection Act the State of the Art Defence" (1997) 42 J.L.S.S. 416.

entrepreneurs and inventors or at least puts their costs up.[40]

There was concern during the passage of the legislation that the United Kingdom's form of the defence narrated above did not properly implement the Directive.[41] Article 7(e) of the Directive provides a defence that "the state of scientific and technical knowledge at the time when he put the product into circulation was not such as to enable the existence of the defect to be discovered."[42] Eventually this divergence led to a challenge by the Commission before the ECJ in *Commission v United Kingdom*.[43] The ECJ treated the Commission's argument as being that the United Kingdom had converted the intended strict liability regime into a negligence liability. The United Kingdom did not challenge the submission that the Directive set out an objective test but argued instead that read together the United Kingdom's version interpreted in the light of section 1(1) of the Act did not infringe the obligation to deliver the directive. The ECJ agreed. In so doing, the court accepted that the directive defence (and thus the United Kingdom's defence) required it to be shown that the producer had complied with the most advanced knowledge available on an objective analysis, but the producer would be able to argue that the knowledge was not accessible. This is nowhere near saying that the court agreed with a negligence standard. Most people familiar with the way in which United Kingdom's courts construe United Kingdom legislation will be surprised that the ECJ thought that the United Kingdom's courts would ignore the generous words of the United Kingdom's defence to impose a liability based on section 1(1). Semantically, the United Kingdom defence seems to allow more room for danger than the EC Directive even as more liberally explained by the court, especially in cases where information was reasonably accessible, but a reasonable producer

---

[40] See Goldberg, "The Development Risk Defence and Medicinal Products" (1991) 36 J.L.S.S. 376. See n.48 above for the challenge by the Commission on the UK formulation.

[41] See, *e.g.* A. Clark, Product Liability (Sweet & Maxwell, 1989), Ch.8; J. Blaikie, "Product Liability" (1987) 32 J.L.S. 325; W.C.H. Ervine, "Product Liability and Part 1 of the Consumer Protection Act 1987" (1988) SCOLAG 21; C. Newdick, "The Future of Negligence in Product Liability" (1987) 103 L.Q.R. 288; J. Stapleton, "Products Liability Reform_Real or Illusory" (1986) 6 O.J.L.S. 392.

[42] Note the comments in W.A. Wilson, "The Product Liability Directive", 1980 S.L.T. 1 which suggests that the final UK version was one which had been rejected even before the directive came into being.

[43] C–300/95; [1997] All E.R. (E.C.) 481.

did not find it. United Kingdom courts in all fairness ought, of course, now to interpret the United Kingdom statute, not according to the semantics of United Kingdom statutory interpretation, but by the hermeneutics of the United Kingdom in Europe. In *A and Others v National Blood Authority*,[44] a defence was taken under direct reference to Article 7(e). The pursuers had contracted hepititis C from the defender's vaccine. This was a case where the risk was known, but it was not possible to identify which particular item among many would be dangerous — in that the defender's knew that some blood would be dangerous but not that any particular blood was dangerous. The defence failed. In *Abouzaid v Mothercare (UK) Ltd*,[45] doubt was expressed as to whether a database showing an absence of previous incidents came within the category of scientific or technical knowledge.

It was said (*obiter*) in *Richardson v LRC Products Ltd*[46] that this defence would not have availed condom manufacturers:

"unless the case had shown that there was a defect of which the leading evidence of available scientific knowledge was ignorant. The test provided by the statute is not what the defendants knew, but what they could have known if they had consulted those who might be expected to know the state of research and all available literature sources. This provisions is . . . not apt to protect a defendant in the case of a defect of a known character, merely because there is no test which is apt to reveal its existence in every case."[47]

(6) *Defect in a product in which the defender's product is comprised.* This is a defence only if the defect is wholly attributable to the design of the subsequent product or to compliance by the defender with instructions given by the final producer. Again this would cover cases like *Evans*. It is a valuable protection for component makers who do not know what their product is to be used for — where bolts are subjected to inordinate stress and strains by the "assembling" manufacturer.

---

[44] [2001] 3 All E.R. 289. See J.M. Williams, "Product Liability — Hepatitis C litigation," [2001] J.P.I.L. 238.
[45] [2001] T.L.R. 136.
[46] [2000] P.I.Q.R. P164.
[47] *per* Ian Kennedy, J. at P172.

(7) *Contributory negligence is recognised.*[48]

It can be seen then that it is impossible to understand fully the scheme of strict liability without comprehending the defences, a position which obtains equally in the other new strict liability scheme under the Animals (Scotland) Act 1987.

Time bar

19–9   There are complicated time-bar provisions providing broadly that there shall be a limitation period of three years from the time the victim was aware, or it was reasonably practicable for him to be aware, of the essential facts to ground an action. There is a long-stop prescriptive period of 10 years.

---

[48] s.6(4), and see [11.21].

CHAPTER 20

LIABILITY FOR ANIMALS

There is an interesting history[1] to the liability for animals and some **20–1**
interesting comparative work.[2] Historically, the law has treated
animals specially. This is unsurprising when most legal systems have
their historical roots in essentially agricultural communities: animals
constitute stock, machinery and wealth in such communities. Some
animals clearly and notoriously can be so harmful to person or
property that taking reasonable care that they do not cause harm is
not perceived as being sufficient for the welfare of the community.
Thus there is a tradition of the imposition of stricter forms of liability
— a tradition that continues to the present day. Animals in law are
things, but things capable of considerable independent action —
perhaps only slaves, and robots raise similar problems for the law.[3]
Scots law was systematically and extensively reformed by the
Animals (Scotland) Act 1987.[4]

Strict liability before the 1987 Act

A person in charge of a wild animal or an animal that could be **20–2**
shown to have vicious propensities was strictly liable for the harm
that it caused. The fact that reasonable care was taken was not a
sufficient defence — effective precautions had to have been taken. So
when a dog with vicious propensities managed to break its chain and
then bit a passer-by, it was not sufficient to show that the chain
looked strong and usually held the dog.[5] Certain animals were
deemed to have the vicious propensities required to attract the strict
liability and were described as *ferae naturae* (such as lions, tigers,
elephants, bears and boars). This was in distinction to animals

---

[1] B.S. Jackson, "Liability for Animals in Scottish Legal Literature", 1 J.R.139.

[2] See D.L. Carey Miller, "A Statutory Substitute for Scienter" (1973) J.R. 61; D.L.
Carey Miller, "The Scottish Institutional Writers on Animal Liability" (1974) J.R.
1; Blackie, "The Provoking Dogs Problem 2" 1993 J.L.S. 148.

[3] The Germans have gone so far as to recast the BGB to provide a separate section
for animals: See J. Blackie, "The Provoking Dogs Problem 2" 1993 J.L.S. 148; See
also P. Handford, "The Dog Act in the New South Wales Court of Appeal" 1995
Tort Law Rev. (Note), p.5.

[4] For a full and up-to-date treatment including developments after publication, see
Stewart, *Reparation: Liability for Delict.*

[5] Burton Moorhead (1881) 8 R 892 .

domitae naturae (such as dogs, cats, and cattle including bulls!),[6] whose damage did not attract strict liability unless they could be shown to have previously exhibited dangerous propensities. These categories were categories of law and it was not competent to show that a particular animal *ferae naturae* was, as a matter of fact, domesticated.

Defences were available to a defender who could show (1) that the beast was provoked by the complainer, (2) that the beast was actually still under control, (3) that the animal was improperly loosed by a third party, or (4) *damnum fatale*.

The Dogs Act 1906 rendered the owner of a dog liable in damages for injury done to cattle including horses, sheep, oats and swine without proof of negligence or vicious propensities.[7] The Guard Dogs Act 1975 was expressly stated not to create any civil liability but is now to an extent incorporated in the 1987 Act.

Common law: negligence

20–3   Whether or not we are concerned with the new statutory liability, the general principles of negligence are still relevant. This was certainly the case where there was strict liability at common law. In *Henderson v John Stuart (Farms) Ltd*[8] a farmworker, who was an experienced stockman, was fatally injured by a Friesian dairy bull. He had been cleaning out its box, which was not fitted with baffles or escape gaps. It was not averred that the bull (which is, of course, *domitae naturae*) had dangerous propensities. It was held that there was no need to aver dangerous propensities to state a relevant case. The action was founded on the employer's breach of duty to his employee by failing to follow normal practice in relation to looking after bulls.

Where fault is required, it is not so easily inferred from the happening of an incident as where a bull escaped unexplained.[9] It was held, however, in *Hill v Lovett*[10] that at common law and under the Occupiers' Liability (Scotland) Act 1960 there was liability for the lack of care in allowing a person to enter a garden in which there were two territorially defensive dogs. It is not impossible that a worker who has to lift animals could raise a case based on the manual handling regulations, if not the common law.[11]

---

[6] *Clark v Armstrong* (1862) 24 D. 1315.
[7] The Winter Herding Act 1686 survived and was used until the new legislation came into force.
[8] 1963 S.C. 245; and see also *Hill v Lovett*, 1992 S.L.T. 994.
[9] *Dobbie v Henderson*, 1970 S.L.T. (Sh. Ct) 27.
[10] 1992 S.L.T. 994.
[11] See the facts of the unsuccessful common law case of *McCormick v City of Aberdeen District Council*, 1993 S.L.T. 1123.

Common law: negligence: animals on the roads

It has often been accepted that, as in the law of England, the **20–4**
presence of an animal on the road does not infer liability.[12] But
reasonable care must still be taken, albeit in the context of the
existence of open countryside.[13] In *Fraser v Pate*,[14] Fraser, a
motorcyclist, sued the farmer said to have allowed his sheep to stray
on to the highway. Considerable reliance was placed on an English
case, *Heath's Garage Ltd v Hodges*.[15] The court accepted the Lord
Ordinary's analysis that there was no liability because there was no
duty. It may, however, be observed that there was a curious
examination of the domestic/wild animal dichotomy, which in the
circumstances is of doubtful relevance. While the distinction is a
valid one so far as the conduct of animals by way of biting, goring
or otherwise injuring people according to their nature is concerned it
can hardly be said that a man-eating tiger equally infers liability to its
keeper should it decide instead to throw itself upon someone's motor
cycle. On the actual point, the case may well have been properly
decided on the law of negligence on the facts of the use of roads at
the time. It is an open question how far animals may be allowed to
stray without inferring negligence in today's conditions where many
people expect to be able to drive without even seeing a horse. Lord
Anderson, it should be noted, concurred on the basis that "nothing
we are deciding in this case is to be taken as encouraging carelessness on the part of farmers in the discharge of their duty of taking
all proper precautions to ensure their gates and fences are sufficient
to confine bestial to their grazings."[16]

The trend now is to permit proof before answer to evaluate factors
such as the locality and the conditions. In *Sinclair v Muir*,[17] the
Second Division allowed a proof before answer on appeal in the case
of a motorcyclist knocked over by a charging bull on the road. In
Gardiner v Miller,[18] the pursuer collided with a horse that had
escaped, the basis of the case, however, being the failure to have a
gate that could not easily be left open by strangers. A proof before
answer was allowed. In *Wark v Steel*,[19] the pursuer was a pedal
cyclist who collided with a horse, the sheriff substitute followed

[12] *Clark v Armstrong* (1862) 24 D. 1315; *Milligan v Henderson*, 1915 2 S.L.T. 156;
Fraser v Pate, 1923 S.L.T. 457 and *Anderson v Wilson's Trs*, 1965 S.L.T. (Sh. Ct)
35 in which it was held that darkness did not constitute a special circumstance
attracting liability.
[13] *Sinclair v Muir*, 1933 S.N. 42, 62; *Colquhoun v Hannah*, Unreported October 31,
1942; *Gardiner v Miller*, 1967 S.L.T. 29.
[14] 1923 S.L.T. 457.
[15] [1916] 2 K.B. 370.
[16] *ibid.* at 460.
[17] 1933 S.N. 42, 62.
[18] 1967 S.L.T. 29.
[19] 1946 S.L.T. (Sh. Ct) 17.

Fraser and dismissed. On appeal, the sheriff allowed a proof before answer and the pursuer succeeded at the proof. Note the distinction in that case between the "great unfenced areas in the highlands" and the "populous country" where there is regularly fencing to be found. The authorities were reviewed in *Swan v Andrew Minto & Sons*,[20] where the pursuer collided with one of two black cows belonging to the defenders, which had strayed on to an A-road from adjacent land. The cows were grazing on opposing grass verges and so blocked the whole road. It was alleged, *inter alia*, that the defenders ought to have erected a stockproof fence and inspected it and to have taken care that it should have remained so. The defenders averred, *inter alia*, that the cows jumped over the fence and the pursuer while denying that, said that the fence should then have been higher.[21] The sheriff founding on the cases after *Fraser*, correctly it is submitted, allowed a proof before answer.[22]

20–5 It is also worth noting a different approach to liability argued in *Bennett v J Lamont & Sons*,[23] in which livestock got onto the road through a wall that had allegedly fallen into disrepair. The pursuer averred that under common law a roads authority had a duty to take reasonable care to keep the road safe for road users as a result of their statutory duty under section 1(1) of the 1984 Act. This included a duty to take reasonable care to avoid dangers to road users from reasonably foreseeable hazards that could arise on the road from adjacent land and its use and to carry out inspections annually to this end. The roads authority, therefore, knew or ought to have known about the wall and the potential danger arising, and should have taken reasonable care to see to it that the wall was maintained in a way that obviated danger to road users and was sufficient to contain livestock. It was held that to impose a duty of care on a roads authority would be a considerable and onerous extension of the duties imposed on roads authorities given the many miles of unfenced road in Scotland adjacent to which animals might roam, and would not be fair, just or reasonable. This case of course raises bigger issues. By not suing the keeper of the animals, the pursuer perilled his case on the difficult cases discussed elsewhere in the text relating to the liability of public authorities.[24]

---

[20] 1998 Rep. L.R. 42.

[21] *Inter alia*, the defenders relied on Walker *Delict*, pp.632–634; on *Clark v Armstrong* (1862) 24 D. 1315 and of course *Fraser, op. cit.* They also relied on *Milne v Macintosh*, 1952 S.L.T. 84 which was a droving case and *Fraser v Lyle*, unreported, Paisley Sheriff Court, February 3, 1998.

[22] In the most recent case, proof before answer was allowed in a case where a motorist sued for injuries sustained when he collided with one of the defenders cows. It was necessary to know the facts: *Wormald v H J Walker & Co.* 2004, G.W.D. 55.

[23] 2000 S.L.T. 17.

[24] See Ch.12.

The Animals (Scotland) Act 1987

The Act covers many matters relating to animals and only the parts **20–6** dealing with liability for animals are dealt with in this book. It creates a new form of strict liability, specifically replacing that set out above[25] while preserving any liability under the general law relating to negligence.[26]

Upon whom does liability fall?

The Act imposes liability on a "keeper of an animal". The **20–7** meaning of this is defined by the Act.[27] A person is a keeper if he owns the animal or has possession of it, or he has actual care and control of a child under the age of 16 who owns the animal or has possession of it. If the animal has been abandoned or has escaped, liability is not avoided until another person acquires ownership or comes into possession of it.[28] The Crown does not acquire ownership of an animal if it is abandoned. A person is not liable as a keeper if he is detaining a stray animal under section 3 of the Act, nor if he is otherwise temporarily detaining it with a view to restoring it as soon as is reasonably practicable to its owner or a possessor of it. Beware the Queen's corgis for, although the Act expressly binds the Crown, proceedings cannot be brought against Her Majesty.[29]

Types of animals

Reading the Act as a whole it is possible to put animals into three **20–8** categories:

(1) Animals belonging to a species whose members generally are by virtue of their physical attributes or habits likely (unless controlled or restrained) to injure severely or kill persons or animals, or damage property to a material extent.

(2) Dogs and dangerous wild animals (as defined by the Dangerous Wild Animals Act 1976).[30]

---

[25] s.1(8)(a). The argument that essentially fault was required and that the Act had been intended to simplify the previous law rather than radically alter it was (it is submitted, rightly) rejected in *Foskett v McClymont* (1998) Rep. L.R. 13, discussed at 7.31 below.

[26] A negligence case was run in parallel to a statutory case in *Fairlie v Carruthers*, 1995 S.L.T. (Sh. Ct) 56.

[27] s.5.

[28] Contrast this with the common law position where a strict liability case was not allowed where a bullock had escaped from the custody of its owner: *Stillie v Wilson*, 1988 S.C.L.R. 108. However, the Inner House held that the facts should be established first: 1990 S.L.T. 145.

[29] s.6.

[30] s.1(3)(a). The Act was applied to a dog without difficulty in *O'Neil v Coyle*, 1995 G.W.D. 21–1185.

(3) Cattle, horses, asses, mules, hinnies, sheep, pigs, goats and deer.[31]

These are not distinct categories. The first category is the general category and the other two are specific statutory examples of animals which will fall within the Act. Thus animals in the second category are "deemed to be likely (unless controlled or restrained) to injure severely or kill persons or animals by biting or otherwise savaging, attacking or harrying." That is not to say that other animals not listed in the Dangerous Wild Animals Act might not yet fall within the first category. This view is now confirmed by the decision in *Foskett v McClymont*,[32] a case in the best tradition of the *Dandy*. The pursuer, a research student, siting a radar installation with permission, was returning from his work. He said he met an animal that would not let him past. He said the defender had told him how to deal with such an eventuality — he waved his arms at it, shouted at it and tapped it on the nose twice. The bull (as it turned out to be) charged him and tossed him over a wall on to stinging nettles. There was no argument about a common-law case. The argument that because cattle are deemed to damage land meant that a bull could not cause personal injury was rightly rejected. More difficult was the decision that an averment that a bull is a species of animal whose members are by virtue of their physical attributes or habits likely severely to injure persons, etc., was held sufficiently specific. While it was appreciated that some bulls are docile and some not, it is not clear whether this was thought to be as a result of genetics (which is the foundation of the language of "species"). The defender's were probably entitled to more specification. The Act incorporates the Dangerous Wild Animals Act 1976. That Act, in its Schedule (and see Dangerous Wild Animal Act 1976 (Modifications) Order 1984, art.1, (SI 1984/1111), makes zoological Linnaen descriptions of species authoritative and so it might reasonably be assumed that the proper course was to plead a zoological species. The defender's experts would really need to know what animal was being discussed. Similarly, animals in the third category are "deemed to be likely (unless controlled or restrained) to damage to a material extent land or the produce of land, whether harvested or not."

The phrase "attack or harry" was considered in *Fairlie v Carruthers*,[33] and was held not to include a case where a frisky dog knocked a person over while it was being exercised. It was not harrying as it was one single incident. Attack was more difficult because it seemed to require some form of intent and it would not be appropriate to look into the mind of a dog! With respect, the decision

---

[31] s.1(3)(b).
[32] (1998) Rep. L.R. 13.
[33] 1995 S.L.T. (Sh. Ct) 56.

is correct but there is no question of looking for intent — if objectively the act is an attack, that is the end of the matter. What the sheriff really did was to look objectively at the evidence and see whether he was satisfied that it was an attack or an accident.

Causation

Once a keeper of an appropriate animal has been found it need **20–9** only be shown that the injury or damage complained of is "directly referable" to (as opposed to "caused by") the physical attributes or habits of the animal.

Defences

The Act provides its own defences and exclusions:[34] **20–10**

(1) There is no liability for injury in the form of a disease transmitted by means unlikely to cause severe injury. Thus, if your panther licks my hand and I acquire some hideous disease I do not have the benefit of the strict liability.

(2) The mere presence of an animal does not incur strict liability where, for example, I ski into a reindeer in the Cairngorms, or again, where I trip over the proverbial sleeping dog lying on the pavement or drive into it.[35]

(3) There can be apportionment of liability between owner and possessor.

(4) The fault of the pursuer is a defence, in effect allowing the defence of contributory negligence.[36]

(5) There is statutory provision to allow for the voluntary assumption of risk. If you stick your head in the lion's mouth and you lose your head you have probably taken a chance that will leave the keeper free of liability. (If he said, as owners of animals tend to say, "It's all right, he'll not hurt you", that might affect the nature of the risk which was accepted and might in any event be a negligent mis-statement.)

(6) There is a defence if the person (or other animal) injured had been on the land where the beast was without authority, *unless* the animal was kept wholly or partly for the purpose of protecting persons or property, in which case there is no defence *unless* the keeping of the animal and the use made of it was reasonable and, if the animal is a guard dog within the terms of the Guard Dogs Act 1975, there has been

---

[34] Set out in s.2.

[35] Although such may be actionable in negligence: see above para.20–4 *et seq.*

[36] Such a plea was taken but not argued and would not have found favour in *Fairlie v Carruthers*, 1995 S.L.T. (Sh. Ct) 56.

compliance with section 1 of the Act. The Guard Dogs Act 1975 penalises the use of a guard dog unless its handler (being a person who is capable of controlling the dog) is present and the dog is under his control, if not actually tied up. Notice of the dog's presence must be displayed at every entrance to the property. The Dangerous Wild Animals Act 1976 forbids the keeping of any dangerous wild animal as defined in the Act without a licence. The keeper must insure against third party liabilities, which seemed to imply a right of action (now confirmed by the 1987 Act). The list of dangerous animals includes: wolf, jackal, foxes and dogs (except the domestic dog and the common red fox), cassowary, old world monkey, mangabey, baboon or mandrill, alligator, emu, cobra or mamba, lions, tigers, cheetahs, gibbons and gila monsters, orangutans and chimpanzees, ostriches and grizzly bears, vipers and rattlesnakes.[37]

When all of the above is taken into account, this new liability places liability without proof of fault on the keeper of the appropriate type of animal for injury or damage (providing it is referable to the category of beast) unless the claimant is at fault, has assumed the risk or failed to take care for his own safety. It is not a defence to show *damnum fatale*, nor the intervention of a third party.

---

[37] Note that the common names, such as those listed, are not definitive — that is only the case with the zoological terms listed in the Schedule.

CHAPTER 21

EMPLOYERS' LIABILITY

COMMON LAW

For some time, an employer has been held to have a personal duty to **21–1** take reasonable care for his employees' safety.[1] At an early stage in the industrial revolution, it was appreciated that the common law did not adequately provide for the victims of industrialisation and so there has been a long series of statutory interventions creating various forms of absolute liability.[2] Nonetheless, the common law developed to a stage where it was held that an employer personally owed a duty of reasonable care to his workmen — a duty which was not fulfilled by entrusting it to a competent foreman. The classic statement of the duty is in *English v Wilsons & Clyde Coal Co*:[3]

> "To take reasonable care, and to use reasonable skill, first, to provide and maintain proper machinery, plant, appliances, and works; secondly, to select properly skilled persons to manage and superintend the business; and thirdly, to provide a proper system of working."

Provide and maintain proper machinery, plant, appliances, and works

So, where a plaintiff was injured when a piece of a drift (a kind of **21–2** chisel) broke and entered his eye, a claim was made under the first head. As the drift had been purchased from a reputable supplier, this was held sufficient to discharge the employer's duty of reasonable care — the employer is not, at common law, an insurer of his workman's safety.[4] However, the result of that particular decision was changed by the Employers' Liability (Defective Equipment) Act 1969, which deems the negligence of the supplier to be the

---

[1] See *Hislop v Durham* (1842) 4 D. 1168.
[2] See the Employers' Liability Act 1880 and the Workmen's Compensation Act 1897.
[3] 1937 S.C. (HL) 46. For an up-to-date statement of the law including developments after publication, see Stewart, *Reparation: Liability for Delict*.
[4] *Davie v New Merton Board Mills* [1959] A.C. 604.

negligence of the employer, while allowing the employer to maintain a claim against the supplier.[5]

Select properly skilled persons

21–3 The second head comprises the duty to provide the employee with competent fellow workers, a duty breached in the case of *Hudson v Ridge Manufacturing*,[6] where an employee, well known to the employer as a practical joker, tripped up a fellow employee, who was a cripple, causing him injury. That the duty is, however, still one of reasonable care is illustrated by a contrasting Scottish case of *McLean v Remploy Ltd*,[7] in which the pursuer tripped over a length of yarn tied across her path by fellow employees. There was no liability as such conduct could not be expected.[8]

System of working

21–4 Finally, the third head demands that the working system should be reasonably safe. For example, an employer was held liable where he failed to provide a window cleaner with blocks that would prevent the window he was cleaning falling on his fingers.[9] On the other hand, in a recent Scottish case an employer was absolved when a workman used the top end of a ladder, which had wheels at the top, upside down so that the wheels were on the ground. Worse, the pursuer ordered the apprentice (who was holding the foot of the ladder) to move away. The pursuer fell.[10] Another ladder case further illustrates the wide scope of "system". In *McGregor v AAH Pharmaceuticals*,[11] the employee did not use the stepladders provided but clambered up shelves, despite a booklet instructing that this ought not to be done. The employee won. The ladders were not close enough and, although there had been reprimands for a failure to use ladders, there had been no disciplinary proceedings.

A generalised common law duty

21–5 Nonetheless, merely because a case does not fall within one of these three heads does not signify that it is of no merit. It might still

---

[5] See para.21–24.
[6] [1957] 2 Q.B. 348.
[7] 1994 S.L.T. 687.
[8] And see the similar but more gruesome English case, *Smith v Crossley Bros Ltd* (1951) 95 Sol. Jo. 655.
[9] *General Cleaning Contractors v Christmas* [1953] A.C. 180.
[10] *Russell v Motherwell Bridge Fabricators Ltd*, 1992 G.W.D. 14–827; see now reg.16 of the Workplace (Health, Safety and Welfare) Regulations 1992 (see para.7.45 below).
[11] 1995 G.W.D. 32–1656.

fall within the general obligation to take reasonable care for the workman's safety.[12]

Stress at work

Perhaps the most interesting line of cases in recent years, giving **21–6** substance to the general category, are those where the injury has not been physical. In *Walker v Northumberland C.C.*,[13] a local authority was held liable for failing to relieve the pressure of work on an employee who then had a nervous breakdown. However, he had already had one. So far as the first breakdown was concerned, it had not been reasonably foreseeable. After that it was foreseeable.[14] It has accordingly been accepted that stress is potentially actionable in Scotland and cases have been settled on that assumption. In *Rorrison v West Lothian College*,[15] it was held that a case of psychiatric injury could not succeed because the foundation in earlier complaints was not made out[16] and, in any event, the resulting psychiatric injury was difficult to pin down. In *Catleugh v Caradon Everest Ltd*,[17] a "stress" case was dismissed. The pursuer a double-glazing engineer complained of an overloaded and disorganised system of work exacerbated by an overbearing and bullying management style. He alleged that he could not refuse work. The dismissal was because of the inadequate specification of the contractual or other relationship between the parties. Otherwise, Lord Marnoch would have allowed the case to proceed in many other ways — general specification of the mental illness was relevant, forseeability could be established by two breakdowns in tears and averments that his workload should be reduced were also relevant.[18] In *Fraser v State Hospitals Board for Scotland*,[19] it was accepted that the conditions at the employees' workplace — disciplinary proceedings and the like — were in law a cause of his later breakdown. However, while there was no reason why the general duty on an employer to avoid exposing employees to unnecessary risk of injury should be restricted to physical injury, in this case, that there was nothing that the employers did which was,

---

[12] *Longworth v Coppas International (UK) Ltd*, 1985 S.L.T. 111, although see *Forsyth v Lothian Regional Council*, 1995 G.W.D. 4–204.

[13] [1995] 1 All E.R. 737.

[14] See also *Petch v Customs and Excise Commissioners* [1993] I.C.R 789.

[15] 1999 Rep. L.R. 102.

[16] A case will often be doomed to fail if there is not even an averment why the defender knew or ought to have known that the pursuer was at risk: *Smith v Advocate General for Scotland*, 2001 G.W.D. 3–139.

[17] 1999 G.W.D. 1554. Proof before answer has been allowed in a work-related stress case where there are averments of recognised mental illness and averments which could support a conclusion that the employers ought to have known that there could be a problem. (*Mather v British Telecommunications*, May 30, 2000)

[18] See also *Logan v Falkirk NHS*, 1999 G.W.D. 30–1431.

[19] 2001 S.L.T. 1051

or ought to have been perceived by them as, a potential cause of psychiatric illness. The present position is that the *Hatton*[20] guidelines are considered valuable in Scotland. They are accordingly worthy of repetition:

(1) There are no special control mechanisms applying to claims for psychiatric (or physical) illness or injury arising from the stress of doing the work the employee is required to do. The ordinary principles of employer's liability apply.

(2) The threshold question is whether this kind of harm to this particular employee was reasonably foreseeable: this has two components (a) an injury to health (as distinct from occupational stress) which (b) is attributable to stress at work (as distinct from other factors).

(3) Foreseeability depends upon what the employer knows (or ought reasonably to know) about the individual employee. Because of the nature of mental disorder, it is harder to foresee than physical injury, but may be easier to foresee in a known individual than in the population at large. An employer is usually entitled to assume that the employee can withstand the normal pressures of the job unless he knows of some particular problem or vulnerability.

(4) The test is the same whatever the employment: there are no occupations which should be regarded as intrinsically dangerous to mental health.

(5) Factors likely to be relevant in answering the threshold question include:
   (a) The nature and extent of the work done by the employee. Is the workload much more than is normal for the particular job? Is the work particularly intellectually or emotionally demanding for this employee? Are demands being made of this employee unreasonable when compared with the demands made of others in the same or comparable jobs? Or are there signs that others doing this job are suffering harmful levels of stress? Is there an abnormal level of sickness or absenteeism in the same job or the same department?
   (b) Signs from the employee of impending harm to health. Has he a particular problem or vulnerability? Has he already suffered from illness attributable to stress at work? Have there recently been frequent or prolonged

---

[20] [2002] 2 All E.R. 1.

absences which are uncharacteristic of him? Is there reason to think that these are attributable to stress at work, for example because of complaints or warnings from him or others?

(6) The employer is generally entitled to take what he is told by his employee at face value, unless he has good reason to think to the contrary. He does not generally have to make searching enquiries of the employee or seek permission to make further enquiries of his medical advisers.

(7) To trigger a duty to take steps, the indications of impending harm to health arising from stress at work must be plain enough for any reasonable employer to realise that he should do something about it.

(8) The employer is only in breach of duty if he has failed to take the steps which are reasonable in the circumstances, bearing in mind the magnitude of the risk of harm occurring, the gravity of the harm which may occur, the costs and practicability of preventing it, and the justifications for running the risk.

(9) The size and scope of the employer's operation, its resources and the demands it faces are relevant in deciding what is reasonable; these include the interests of other employees and the need to treat them fairly, for example, in any redistribution of duties.

(10) An employer can only reasonably be expected to take steps which are likely to do some good: the court is likely to need expert evidence on this.

(11) An employer who offers a confidential advice service, with referral to appropriate counselling or treatment services, is unlikely to be found in breach of duty.

(12) If the only reasonable and effective step would have been to dismiss or demote the employee, the employer will not be in breach of duty in allowing a willing employee to continue in the job.

(13) In all cases, therefore, it is necessary to identify the steps which the employer both could and should have taken before finding him in breach of his duty of care.

(14) The claimant must show that that breach of duty has caused or materially contributed to the harm suffered. It is not enough to show that occupational stress has caused the harm.

(15) Where the harm suffered has more than one cause, the employer should only pay for that proportion of the harm suffered which is attributable to his wrongdoing, unless the harm is truly indivisible. It is for the defendant to raise the question of apportionment.

(16) The assessment of damages will take account of any pre-existing disorder or vulnerability and of the chance that the claimant would have succumbed to a stress related disorder in any event.[21]

21–7 *Hatton* was influential in two recent Scottish cases. In *Stevenson v East Dunbartonshire Council*,[22] Lord Bonomy allowed proof before answer, albeit with considerable hesitation, in a stress at work case where there had been two letters from a GP one mentioning severe mental and physical stress. In *Taplin v Fife Council*,[23] Lord Philip dismissed a case alleging psychiatric injury from stress. The pursuer had been moved in 1995 as a result of a diagnosis of hypothyroidism and on account of stress due to working conditions. She broke down again in 1998 having complained about a lack of resources. His Lordship applied dicta in *Hatton*: there had to be foreseeability of actual psychiatric injury in the pursuer as an individual. The complaints in this case were about resources rather than any effect on the pursuer.[24]

Staffing levels and robbery

21–8 This is a tentative category arising out of the decision in *Collins v First Quench Retailing Ltd*.[25] The employers of a shop assistant were liable when the shopkeeper was robbed. She had expressed concerns in the past. Double-manning would have prevented a robbery like this even although there were two robbers and a look-out. From the evidence, one of the things important about double-manning was not so much to balance up the numbers but because of the criminal fraternities knowledge of the requirement for corroboration in criminal cases. Robbery was likely in the area and in particular at this off-sales shop. General warnings had been issued by the police So the case does not mean that every shop needs to have two members of staff. There may be other precautions, such as physical screens, or in other areas there may be no need to do anything at all. The case can be seen as an ordinary third-party intervention case and not requiring any special treatment. It is possible to restrict it to potential robbery in vulnerable situations, issues of staffing levels being

---

[21] *Sutherland v Hatton* [2002] P.I.Q.R. P21 at 42.

[22] 2003 S.L.T. 97. See discussion in A.J. Bowen, "*Stevenson v East Dunbartonshire Council*, 2003 S.L.T. 97" 2003 S.L.T. (News) 29.

[23] 2003 G.W.D. 1–27.

[24] See also the recent English case *Bonser v UK Coal Mining Ltd*, 2003 T.L.R. 388 which failed absent sufficient prior indicators which would have alerted the employer.

[25] 2003 S.L.T. 1220. For a case note see E. Russell, "Lone Workers — The Employer's Duty in Respect of Double Manning and Security Screens," 2003 S.L.T. (News) 241.

relatively familiar in other areas of employers' liability for example, where a helper may be required to foot a ladder or to back out a lorry. Finally, it is notable for the rejection of any economic argument relating to the cost of double-manning where double-manning was actually in use in other shops and on occasions when weighed against the danger arising to a person — especially where there had been an earlier incident.

STATUTORY LIABILITY

There is an enormous amount of material on this topic. It is **21–9** impossible, and for students, undesirable, to include it all. The batch of European-inspired regulations does however provide a partial code for employers' liability, it is reasonably internally coherent and it has now been frequently litigated. Thus that is the selection made for this section — it will illustrate the general approach of the law and set out the detail of the most frequently litigated provisions. It can no longer seek to be comprehensive even in relation to these regulations.[26] Students who do not engage in some study of detailed rules that are imposed outside of the common law will find it harder to engage in more advanced discussions about strict liability, distributive justice and the economics of compensation. Some cases will turn on existing UK statutes and regulations, but by far the bulk of cases are taken under a new batch of regulations derived from EU legislation. There is an interpretative background built up over years of considering UK statutory cases. This will yield to an EU interpretation where appropriate. A "eurorep" action is possible for defective transposition and such is certainly possible in relation to these regulations.[27] The fact that the United Kingdom chose to retain many of its linguistic formulations opens the possibility of such challenge. The main attraction for pursuers is that duties may be absolute such that if equipment must be safe by statute, it is not a defence to say that the required precautions would make the machine unusable.[28] Down the scale from absolute, some duties are expressed as if absolute, but the defender is given the provisio that he is only

---

[26] For a much fuller treatment and the up to date text of the regulations see Stewart, *Reparation: Liability for Delict.*

[27] *McTighe v East & Midlothian NHS Trust*, 1998 S.L.T. 969; 1998 S.C.L.R. 203; 1998 Rep. L.R. 21. The pursuer argued without objection (and without success) that regulation 5 of the Provision and Use of Work Equipment Regulations 1992 in allowing suitability to be judged by reference to reasonable foresight did not comply with the foundation European Directive allowing the pursuer to make a claim under the euro-rep head, the defenders being an emanation of the state. See also *Cross v Highland and Islands Enterprise*, 2001 S.L.T. 1060 and *Taylor v Glasgow City Council*, 2002 S.L.T. 689.

[28] *Summers v Frost* [1955] A.C. 740.

liable insofar as it was not reasonably practicable to provide some effective precaution. The phrase "practicable" was defined and its practical effect as effecting a reversal of the onus of proof was established in *Nimmo v Alexander Cowan & Sons Ltd*,[29] a Scottish House of Lords decision:

> "In construing a statute and determining the incidence of the burden of proof the parties' respective means of knowledge and spheres of responsibility are important factors to be taken into account together with the form and content of the relevant statutory provisions. On a true construction of section 29(1) it is for the defenders to aver and prove by way of excuse for the unsafety of the working place that they had made it safe so far as reasonably practicable or that it was not reasonably practicable to make it any safer".[30]

Finally, there was a major revision of the approach to United Kingdom statutory language in the mid-nineties. In *Mains v Uniroyal Englebert Tyres Ltd*,[31] it was held that it was proper to construe section 29(1) in a way more favourable to the pursuer than heretofore — that is by not glossing the statute by making "safe" depend upon reasonable foreseeability.[32]

The "European" Rules

21–10   The European Council Directive 89/391 of June 1989 on the Introduction of Measures to Encourage Improvements in the Safety and Health of Workers at Work,[33] often known as the "Framework Directive", provided for the introduction of measures to encourage improvements in the safety and health of workers at work.[34] It was not intended to reduce levels of protection already achieved in individual Member States. It declared a general duty on employers "to ensure the safety and health of workers in every aspect related to the work."[35] The measures necessary for the safety and health of the employees were to be implemented and reviewed by avoiding risks, evaluating the risks which cannot be avoided and combating the risks

---

[29] 1967 S.L.T. 277.
[30] See *Rae v Strathclyde Joint Police Board*, 1999 S.C.L.R. 793 for s.7 of the Offices Shops and Railway Premises Act 1963.
[31] 1995 S.L.T. 1115.
[32] Followed in *Beggs v Motherwell Bridge Fabricators*, 1998 S.L.T. 1215; 1997 S.C.L.R. 1019; 1997 Rep. L.R. 87. See the discussion of the case in a different context in *McGhee v Strathclyde Fire Brigade*, 2002 S.L.T. 680. Mains was, it is submitted correctly, influential in *Taylor v Glasgow City Council*, 2002 S.L.T. 689.
[33] OJ 1989, L183.
[34] Art.1.1.
[35] Art.5.

at source.[36] The Framework Directive is applicable subject only to any more stringent requirements imposed by a particular directive. The following domestic legislation should be interpreted "purposively" so as to give effect to the objectives of the European legislation.[37]

Management of Health and Safety at Work Regulations 1992

These regulations are the principal mode of implementation by the **21–11** UK of the aforementioned Framework Directive. When originally promulgated, by virtue of regulation 15, breach of a duty imposed by these regulations did not confer a right of action in any civil proceedings, subject to some exceptions later introduced. With effect from October 2003, that has changed. So while in the past attempts to base a case on regulation 3 have failed,[38] that might change.

Workplace (Health Safety and Welfare) Regulations 1992

A "workplace" is defined in a complicated way and some **21–12** applications of it require reference to the principal Act, but the basic definition is "any premises or part of premises which are not domestic premises and are made available to any person as a place of work, and included (a) any place within the premises to which such person has access while at work; and (b) any room, lobby, corridor, staircase, road or other place used as a means of access to or egress from the workplace or where facilities are provided for use in connection with the workplace other than a public road."[39] The workplace equipment, devices and systems must be maintained in an efficient state (from a health and safety point of view), in an efficient working order and in good repair. Cleaning must take place as appropriate.[40] The regulation can comprehend failures of maintenance or provision.[41] Regulation 6 provides for ventilation. Regulation 7 provides for the temperature being reasonable, but not by means of any injurious or offensive fumes. Sufficient thermometers must be produced.

Regulation 8 provides for suitable and sufficient light which, so far as is reasonably practicable, shall be by natural light. Emergency lighting is required if there would otherwise be exposure to danger. In *Miller v Perth and Kinross Council*,[42] the defenders were held liable for a failure to provide suitable and sufficient lighting in part

---

[36] Art.6.2
[37] *Taylor v Glasgow City Council*, 2002 S.L.T. 689 *per* Lord Carloway at 697.
[38] *Mitchell v Campbeltown Shipyard Ltd*, 1998 G.W.D. 12–616. *Cross v Highland and Islands Enterprise*, 2001 S.L.T. 1060.
[39] As defined in the Roads (Scotland) Act 1984, s.151 (reg.2(1)).
[40] reg.5.
[41] *Butler v Grampian University Hospital NHS Trust*, 2002 S.L.T. 985.
[42] 2001 G.W.D. 40–1530.

of their school, which resulted in the pursuer, a cleaner, falling. Cleanliness and freedom from waste is required by Regulation 9 and extends to the floor wall and ceiling. So far as is reasonably practicable, waste material must not be allowed to accumulate.[43] This is in addition to the provisions set out below in relation to slipping, tripping and falling. Regulation 10 on room dimensions and space requires free space to work and move about in.

Regulation 11 provides for the worker to have a suitable work station with a suitable seat, suitable referring as much to the person actually using it as the task in hand.[44] In *Simmons v British Steel plc*,[45] a worker was injured when the tubes that supplied his cutting tool his tool became snagged, causing him to fall. It was possible for the tubes to be safely contained in drums. The employers were held liable under regulations 11(2) and 12(3) as the workstation was not suitable. In *Butler v Grampian University Hospital NHS Trust*,[46] it was held that a toilet was not a workstation albeit the outpatient assistant alleged injury at that place while working at taking a patient to the toilet — work*station* suggested a set up for work. (It was however, a work*place*.)

Regulation 12 states *inter alia*:

> "(1) Every floor in a workplace and the surface of every traffic route in a workplace shall be of a construction such that the floor or surface of the traffic routes is suitable for the purpose for which it is used. (2) Without prejudice to the generality of paragraph (1), the requirements in that paragraph shall include requirements that (a) the floor, or surface of the traffic route, shall have no hole or slope, or be uneven or slippery so as, in each case, to expose any person to a risk to his health or safety; (b) every such floor shall have effective means of drainage where necessary. (3) So far as is reasonably practicable, every floor in a workplace and the surface of every traffic route in a workplace shall be kept free from obstructions and from any article or substance which may cause a person to slip, trip or fall."[47]

21–13 In *Gilmour v East Renfrewshire Council*,[48] a teacher, slipped on a chip on a ramp leading from the school canteen. There was no system of checking for chips on the ramp and she did not offer to allege an

---

[43] reg.9(3).

[44] In addition to the Code of Practice there is an HSE guidance publication called "Seating at Work' ": HAS(G) 57 (HMSO, 1991 ISBN 0118854313).

[45] 2002 S.L.T. 711.

[46] 2002 G.W.D. 610.

[47] Employers cannot ignore articles which are part of the manufacturing process as opposed to usual fixtures: *Simmons v British Steel plc*, 2001 G.W.D. 303.

[48] May 29, 2002.

inspection regime. Cases on regs 5(1), 12(2) and (3) were held relevant as was a common law case. The chip was inefficient, the ramp was physically in a state of unevenness and it was not kept free from any article which might cause a person to slip trip or fall.[49]

Regulation 13 provides against falls or falling objects, which should normally be prevented other than by providing personal protective equipment such as hard hats and the like. So far as is practicable (note, not "reasonably"), every tank, pit or structure where there is a risk of a person in the workplace falling into a dangerous substance (as defined) in the tank, pit or structure, must be securely covered or fenced.[50] Where necessary, for reasons of health and safety, windows or other translucent surfaces in a wall must be of safety material or protected against breakage of the material and be[51] marked to make it apparent. Windows, skylights and ventilators must be capable of being opened and closed[52] and cleaned safely.[53] Regulation 17 provides that workplace must be organised in such a way that pedestrians and vehicles can circulate in a safe manner and the traffic routes[54] must be suitable, but the duty is only to the standard of reasonable practicability for a workplace which is not a new workplace, modification, extension or conversion. Sensibly, motor vehicles and pedestrians are to be kept apart.

Doors and gates must be suitably constructed, including being fitted with any necessary safety devices.[55] In *Beck v United Closures & Plastics plc*,[56] Lord McEwan held that doors that had to be used to make machinery work were encompassed by the protection of regulation 18 and rejected the argument that they were excluded as not being part of the workplace.[57]

Escalators and moving walkways must function safely and have an emergency stop button which is easily identifiable and readily accessible.[58] Suitable and safe sanitary conveniences must be provided at readily accessible places and they must be ventilated and lit,

---

[49] There is an interesting series of cases considering whether this provision allows a person who is not a worker to claim to be owed the same duty. See para.18–1.

[50] reg.13(5).

[51] reg.14.

[52] reg.15. See also BS 8213 Part 1: 1991.

[53] reg.16. Account may be taken of devices fitted to the building.

[54] By reg.2 a "traffic route" is a route for pedestrian traffic, vehicles or both and includes any stairs, staircase, fixed ladder, doorway, gateway, loading bay or ramp.

[55] reg.18.

[56] 2001 S.L.T. 129.

[57] He did, however, hold that reg.5(1) of the Workplace Regulations did not apply, the doors neither constituting a "workplace" nor a "device".

[58] reg.19. See also HSE "Ergonomic Aspects of Escalators used in Retail Organisations" CRR12/1989 (HMSO, 1989, ISBN 0118859382); BS 5656:1983 "Safety rules for the construction and installation of escalators and passenger conveyors".

clean and orderly. Men and women must not share facilities.[59] Suitable and sufficient washing facilities must be available at readily accessible places. There must be showers if required by the nature of the work.[60] An adequate supply of wholesome drinking water must be provided which must be readily accessible at suitable places and provided with cups unless supplied in a convenient jet.[61] This explains the many "water-coolers" that have sprung up in offices all over the country.[62] Suitable and sufficient "accommodation" must be provided for clothing[63] and facilities for changing.[64] Suitable and sufficient rest facilities must be provided and facilities to eat meals.[65] Rest rooms and rest areas must include suitable arrangements to protect non-smokers from discomfort caused by tobacco smoke.[66] Exemptions may be made from all the regulations in respect of the home forces or visiting forces.[67]

Provision and Use of Work Equipment Regulations 1992

21–14   "Use" in relation to work equipment means any activity involving work equipment and includes starting, stopping, programming, setting, transporting, repairing, modifying, maintaining, servicing and cleaning, and related expressions must be construed accordingly. Driving a forklift truck could be use.[68]

"Work equipment" means any machinery, appliance, apparatus or tool and any assembly of components which in order to achieve a common end, are arranged and controlled so that they function as a whole.[69] It was held and had been a matter of dispute, in *Beck v United Closures & Plastics plc*,[70] that heavy doors required to be used to start machinery were in fact "work equipment".[71] A forklift

---

[59] reg.20.

[60] reg.21. Perhaps had this been in place *McGhee* might never have happened. Detailed guidance is given in the Code of Practice right down to the number of "wash stations" per person which ought to be there.

[61] reg.22.

[62] But only to the extent that it has given the vendors a reason to sell the product. It seems clear from the Code of Practice that a sink with cups which can be washed is fine.

[63] reg.23.

[64] reg.24.

[65] reg.25.

[66] reg.25(3). See also HSE "Passive smoking at work" IND(G) 63L (Rev) 1992.

[67] reg.26. See also *Mulcahy v Ministry of Defence* [1996] T.L.R. 39 for a general consideration of the army as employer.

[68] *Hunter v Murray*, 2002 G.W.D. 13–445.

[69] reg.2. For comment generally see C. Goddard, "Work Equipment" [2000] J.P.I.L. 220.

[70] 2001 S.L.T. 1299.

[71] Obviously the cases discussed below provide other examples of what is or may be work equipment.

truck can be work equipment.[72] A table which was not being used for working was not work equipment.[73]

"Suitable" means suitable in any respect which it is reasonably foreseeable will affect the health and safety of any person.[74] Every employer must ensure that work equipment is so constructed or adapted as to be suitable for its purpose.[75] The doors in *Beck v United Closures & Plastics plc*[76] were not suitable. They had a faulty locking mechanism, which combined with the force needed to close them and the positioning of the handles made them unsuitable. In another case, Lord Mcfadyen appears from the digest note to have held that if a case had otherwise been well founded, he would not have upheld a case on the Provision and Use of Work Equipment Regulations, regulation 5 where there was no history of previous incidents of injury.[77] Another regulation 5 case failed where although it was accepted that an L-Bar was work equipment, the use to which it had been put was the problem — it had been jumped upon: it was perfectly *suitable* if used as intended.[78] In *Horton v Taplin Contracts Ltd*,[79] it was held in relation to scaffolding that where the accident had been caused by the deliberate act of a fellow servant during an altercation, this was not to say the *equipment* was unsuitable.

In selecting work equipment, the employer must have regard to the working conditions and to the risks that exist including the risks posed by use of the equipment.[80] The employer must ensure that work equipment is used only for operations for which, and under conditions for which, it is suitable.[81] The risk of a forklift truck being dragged back when trying to move a heavy lorry is the kind of risk which might be encompassed.[82]

Maintenance

There is a general duty to ensure work equipment is maintained in **21–15** an efficient state, in efficient working order and in good repair.[83] In *McMullan v Glasgow Council*,[84] the pursuer was a 21-stone electrician, who fell from a swing-back stepladder. He said one of the treads broke off. A common law case failed, but a statutory case

---

[72] *Hunter v Murray*, 2002 G.W.D. 13–445.
[73] *Mackie v Dundee City Council*, 2001 G.W.D. 11–398.
[74] reg.5.
[75] reg.5(1).
[76] 2001 S.L.T. 1299. See also *Simmons v British Steel plc*, 2001 G.W.D. 8–303.
[77] *Hurley v William Muir (Bond 9) Ltd*, 2000 G.W.D. 4–158.
[78] *Paton v Tube Developments Ltd*, May 30, 2001.
[79] [2002] T.L.R. 492.
[80] reg.5(2).
[81] reg.5(3). See the facts of *Smith v Crossley Bros* (1951) 95 S.J. 655.
[82] *Hunter v Murray*, 2002 G.W.D. 13–445.
[83] reg.6.
[84] 1998 G.W.D. 17–874.

based on the absolute duty in the regulation succeeded.[85] In *McTighe v East & Midlothian NHS Trust*,[86] a nurse in a lifting case failed in a case based on regulations 5 and 6. The equipment in question was the bed in which the patient was positioned, a part of which gave way. In *McLaughlin v East and Midlothian NHS Trust*,[87] a hospital employee was injured when a curtain rail surrounding a bed fell on her and she succeeded in her case based on regulations 5 and 6.

Information, instruction and training must be given. In *Barrie v Glasgow City Council*,[88] the pursuer was injured by his slab-cutting Stihl saw. The petrol-driven saw jammed in use and the pursuer said that he could not switch it off and put it down because of the location of the switch. He alleged breaches of regulations 8 and 9. He had had training. However, the case failed because jamming was not seen as a possible source of danger as opposed to a nuisance. In any event, the pursuer failed to establish that the alleged breach caused his injuries. So far as reasonably practicable, maintenance must be possible when the machine is stopped.[89]

Effective measures have to be taken to keep dangerous machinery safe.[90] Regulation 12 provides that special hazards must be prevented especially by using appropriate measures to minimise the effect of the hazards as well as to reduce the likelihood of it occurring, those hazards being parts falling or being ejected from the work equipment; rupture or disintegration of its parts; its catching fire or overheating; or its discharging gas or liquids which are used or stored in the equipment; the explosion of the equipment or article or substance produced, used or stored in it.[91] Employers must ensure protection from things at a very high or low temperature against burns scalding or searing.[92] Where appropriate, equipment must have controls to start and vary equipment. It must only be possible to operate said control by deliberate action of the control unless part of the normal operating cycle of an automatic device.[93] A safe stop control must be provided where appropriate and one which operates

---

[85] Note that it was conceded in *Beck v United Closures & Plastics plc*, 2001 S.L.T. 1299 that the duty under reg.6 was absolute. This is consonant with *Stark v The Post Office* [2000] T.L.R. 236 in which the Court of Appeal, in allowing an appeal, held that reg.6(1) imposed an absolute liability and so the defenders would be liable even if it could be argued the Euro directives behind the UK legislation did not require absolute liability. The plaintiff was injured when part of the front brake of his delivery bike broke.

[86] 1998 S.L.T. 969; 1998 S.C.L.R. 203; 1998 Rep. L.R. 21.

[87] 2000 Rep. L.R. 87.

[88] 2000 Rep. L.R. 46.

[89] reg.22.

[90] reg.11.

[91] reg.12(3) specifies the risks.

[92] reg.13.

[93] reg.14.

in priority to other controls.[94] In some circumstances, an emergency stop device needs to be fitted.[95] Suitable sufficient lighting must be provided.[96] So far as reasonably practicable, maintenance must be possible when the machine is stopped.[97] Every employer must ensure that work equipment is marked in a clearly visible manner with any appropriate marking for reasons of health and safety.[98] Warnings unambiguous, easily perceived and easily understood must be displayed where appropriate.[99]

Personal Protective Equipment at Work Regulations 1992

Personal protective equipment (PPE) means all equipment (includ- **21–16** ing clothing affording protection against the weather) which is intended to be worn or held by a person at work and which protects him against one or more risks to his health or safety, and any accessory designed to meet that objective.[1] It has been held in the circumstances of one case that a bolt was not PPE.[2] The regulations do not apply to ordinary working clothes which do not specifically protect health and safety; offensive weapons; portable devices for detecting and signalling risks and nuisances; PPE used for travelling on the road; where used during the playing of competitive sports or where there is other statutory provision as defined.[3] Every employer must ensure that suitable PPE is provided to his employees who may be exposed to risk to their health or safety while at work, except where and to the extent that such risk has been adequately controlled by other means which are equally or more effective. PPE is not suitable unless it is appropriate for the risk involved, it takes account of ergonomic requirements and the state of health of the person who wears it, it fits, so far as reasonably practicable it is effective without itself increasing the overall risk, it complies with the law.[4] The PPE is to be compatible where more than one item is in use.[5] Before choosing the PPE the employer has to carry out an assessment which, in all but the most routine cases, ought to be recorded.[6] An employer was found liable where a workman having to mow grass with a

---

[94] reg.15.
[95] reg.16.
[96] reg.21.
[97] reg.22.
[98] reg.23.
[99] reg.24.
[1] reg.2. For a case under the common law considering the benefits and problems of PPE in the form of padded protective trousers for a chain saw operator see *Douglas v L.Adv*, 1996 G.W.D. 1981.
[2] *Kelly v First Engineering Ltd*, 1999 S.C.L.R. 1025; 1999 Rep. L.R. 106.
[3] reg.3.
[4] reg.4.
[5] reg.5.
[6] reg.6.

lawnmower on wet grass did not have suitable non-slippy shoes.[7] The PPE must be maintained in an efficient state, in efficient working order and in good repair which includes replacement and cleaning.[8] Accommodation has to be provided for the PPE when not in use.[9] The employee is to be provided with such information, instructions and training as is adequate and appropriate to enable the employee to know the risks, the manner in which it is to be used and any action the employee is to take to make it work properly.[10] The information must be "comprehensible to the persons to whom it is provided".[11] The code indicates that the help is extensive including theoretical and practical training. Reasonable steps must be taken to ensure that the kit is properly used.[12] The employee is himself under a duty to use the kit and report its loss or defective condition.[13]

Health and Safety (Display Screen Equipment) Regulations 1992

21–17 These regulations are new, in the sense of that there was barely any regulation at all in this field.[14] After the legislation, a case at common law was successful before the Court of Appeal for a form of work-related upper limb disorder (not repetitive strain injury but PDA4) in connection with work like that covered by these regulations, but it failed before the House of Lords.[15] The key definitions are as follows: "display screen equipment" means any alphanumeric or graphic display screen, regardless of the display process involved (in what follows, such are called screen); "use" means use in or in connection with work; "user" means an employee who habitually uses display screen equipment as a significant part of his normal work; "workstation" means an assembly comprising: (i) display screen equipment (whether provided with software determining the interface between the equipment and its operator or user, a keyboard or any other input device); (ii) any optional accessories to the display screen equipment; (iii) any disk drive, telephone, modem, printer,

---

[7] *Mitchell v Inverclyde District Council*, 1998 S.L.T. 1157; 1998 S.C.L.R. 191; 1997 Rep. L.R. (Quantum) 29.

[8] reg.7.

[9] reg.8.

[10] For a case which failed on the regulations see *Cameron v Kvaerner Govan*, 2000 G.W.D. 1058 but it may be noted that a common law case of vicarious liability in respect of the failure by fellow workmen to appreciate the danger in the operation succeeded.

[11] reg.9.

[12] reg.10.

[13] reg.11.

[14] These implement Directive 90/2701. See Lloyd and Simpson, "The Computer at Work", 1992 S.L.T. (News) 177.

[15] *Pickford v Imperial Chemical Industries Plc.* [1998] 1 W.L.R. 1189. See generally B. Langstaff, "Upper Limb Disorders: Work Related or Unrelated?" [1994] J.P.I.L. 14.

document holder, work chair, work desk, work surface or other item peripheral to the display screen equipment; and (iv) the immediate work environment around the display screen equipment.[16] The guidance indicates that an ordinary television screen is outside the rules, but microfiche readers are within the rules. The guidance also shows that there may be some difficulty in ascertaining who is a user. The guidance offers seven criteria that can be weighed up in making a decision. They are dependency, discretion, training, prolonged spells of over one hour, daily use, fast information transfer and criticality of errors. Drivers' cabs, screens on board a means of transport, portables (not in prolonged use), calculators and window typewriters are excluded from the regulations.[17] A suitable assessment must be carried out.[18]

Daily work on screens is to be planned to provide interruptions to reduce the workload.[19] In the guidance, it is pointed out that short, frequent breaks are better than occasional, long breaks.[20] The employer must provide eye tests,[21] Adequate health and safety training in relation to the equipment used is to be given.[22] The users must be told about all aspects of health and safety relating to their workstations and the measures taken by the employer to comply.[23]

Manual Handling Operations Regulations 1992

This regulation, at the time of writing, has been the most **21–18** commonly litigated, probably because such injuries are so frequent.[24] Fatalities are rare but as at 1992 HSE information suggested that more than a quarter of all reported accidents were due to manual handling and about a third of three-day injuries. The regulations should be interpreted purposively in accord with the European background.[25]

Manual handling operation

"Manual handling operations" means any transporting or support- **21–19** ing of a load (including the lifting, putting down, pushing, pulling,

---

[16] reg.1.
[17] reg.1(4).
[18] reg.2.
[19] reg.4.
[20] This was thought to be common sense for secretaries with tasks other than typing in the House of Lords decision in *Pickford*, n.4 above.
[21] reg.5.
[22] reg.6.
[23] reg.7.
[24] For comment generally, see J. Levy, "Manual handling" [2001] J.P.I.L. 130, J.H. Zindani, "Manual Handling Law: The End of Laissez-faire" 2000 J.P.I.L. 2, A.J. Bowen, "Manual handling: A Foreseeable Possibility or a Duty of Insurance," 2002 S.L.T. (News) 189.
[25] *Taylor v Glasgow City Council*, 2002 S.L.T. 689.

carrying or moving thereof) by hand or by bodily force. "Load" includes any person and any animal.[26] Many of the cases considered in the other paragraphs of this section directly, or indirectly apply this definition.

In *Cullen v North Lanarkshire Council*,[27] an employee had to unload debris consisting of old wooden fencing from the back of a pickup truck. He stood on the materials to be unloaded and threw them into a skip, which stood beside the truck. While he was holding a section of fencing above his head, he caught his heel on some of the remaining material and fell backwards off the platform of the truck, sustaining injuries when his left shoulder struck the ground. After proof, the defenders were absolved — their argument that this was not so much handling as the imposition of a load. However, the Inner House, it is submitted correctly, held that neither the terms in which the regulations were expressed, nor the terms of the directive which they were intended to implement, restricted the applicability of the regulations to a risk of injury arising from the *imposition* of a load, as opposed to activities *with* a load.[28]

In the earlier case of *Fraser v Greater Glasgow Health Board*,[29] a nursing auxiliary, who hurt her back lifting a patient, sued. She was assisting a staff nurse who had already trained her in lifting. The staff nurse instructed a certain mode of lifting. The defenders were held liable primarily because the lift had not been properly co-ordinated, the pursuer having one of her hands in the wrong place. While she was successful at common law, *obiter*, the Manual Handling Regulations were held not to be applicable as they were said to apply to regular operations and not to an emergency. In *Nicolls v City of Glasgow*,[30] the pursuer had to shift bales of hay with a wheelbarrow. The bales restricted the worker's view. The injury due to a jolt on the uneven surface rather than straining and was within the regulations. In *McBeath v Halliday*[31] it was accepted that fitting electrical wiring to a floodlighting column was a manual handling operation. Cases not encompassed within the regulation include a complaint of tennis

---

[26] Lord Carloway has pointed out that this formulation differs from the European directives in that it speaks only of Manual handling operations and does not include in the definition any reference to risk of injury. *Taylor v Glasgow City Council*, 2002 S.L.T. 689.

[27] 1998 S.L.T. 847.

[28] Subsequent and similar is *Purdie v City of Glasgow Council*, 2002 Rep. L.R. 26. where the pursuer was injured while shovelling magazines into a JCB. A magazine blew under the pursuers foot causing him to lose his footing. While the movement of the load was a less prominent feature, it was still the case that the facts could give rise to the inference that the risk had not been properly addressed and a PBA was allowed.

[29] (1996) Rep. L.R. 58.

[30] Unreported, Glasgow Sheriff Court, December 23, 1996.

[31] 2000 G.W.D. 2–75.

elbow from using a spanner to tighten bolts.[32] Where it is clear the operation in question is to be carried out mechanically, and not manually, the regulations are not engaged.[33]

Regulation 4

This regulation has been extensively considered. Each employer **21–20** must, so far as reasonably practicable, avoid the need for his employees to do any manual handling which involves a risk of their being injured.[34] If manual handling is necessary then the employer must assess the risk of their being injured according to the details in the schedule to the regulations.[35] Where it is not reasonably practicable to avoid the need for his employees to undertake any manual handling operations at work which involve a risk of their being injured the employer must take appropriate steps to reduce the risk of injury to the lowest level reasonably practicable[36] and must give general indications and, where possible, precise indications on the weight of each load and the heaviest side of any whose centre of gravity is not positioned centrally.[37] Employees have a duty to make use of any system laid down to comply with regulation 4(1)(b)(ii).[38] Not unreasonably, standing the language, cases have split consideration of circumstances according to whether they fall within regulation 4(1)(a) or 4(1)(b).

Risk of injury

It is not yet entirely settled as to how risk of injury is to be treated. **21–21** It is possible to look to the general kind of operation which could have been foreseen as likely to bring about the kind of injury which happened.[39] Such a view is not that different to the common law. It is possible to desiderate that the particular task be within the foreseeable risk.[40] It is possible to say that the word should be read unencumbered by foreseeability — that the actual facts complained of are examined to see if there is a manual handling operation and whether these facts involve a risk of injury — if so, there is an almost irresistible inference of liability absent the reasonably practicable

---

[32] *King v Carron Phoenix Ltd* 1999 Rep.L.R. 51 (obiter).

[33] *Delaney v McGregor Construction (Highlands) Ltd*, 2003 G.W.D. 290.

[34] reg.4(1)(a).

[35] reg.4(1)(b)(i).

[36] reg.4(1)(b)(ii).

[37] reg.4(1)(b)(iii). Assessments of risk must be reviewed: reg.4(2).

[38] reg.5.

[39] *Taylor v Glasgow City Council*, 2002 S.L.T. 689, *per* Lord Marnoch at 690–691. See generally the helpful note A.J. Bowen, "Manual Handling: A foreseeable Possibility or a duty of insurance?" 2002 S.L.T. (News) 189.

[40] *Taylor v Glasgow City Council*, 2002 S.L.T. 689, *per* Lord Reed at 692–693.

defence which precludes this regulation establishing a duty of insurance.[41] It is respectfully submitted the third is the best view. In analysing the facts of a case, it can be easy to say that there was a risk of injury — not necessarily based on foreseebility, but upon history, whether personal or communal. This is a jury question, perhaps instructed in the context. So while a danger foreseen is a risk, so is a danger well-known without having to foresee it. When we wonder whether we expose our children or our workers to a risk, we utilise the foreseeability of our reason — we also consult our written, folk and craft experience. The language of the law is here both logic and experience. A category of danger foreseen does not necessarily mean that a particular operation was risky.

The relationship of 4(1)(a) and 4(1)(b)

21–22   The first analysis is whether or not it is reasonably practicable to avoid the need for manual handling at all. The employer should ask himself whether he can simply say to his staff — "do not lift those bales". He can and should say this if he has a bale-lifting machine to hand. If it is not reasonably practicable for him to do this — perhaps there is no such thing as a bale-lifting machine — then he must follow 4(1)(b). The defender carries the onus of raising the reasonably practicable proviso.[42]

The elements of 4(1)(b)

21–23   There are elements: (i) the making of a risk assessment; (ii) the taking of appropriate preventative measures and (iii) provision of information. There is no need for the assessment to take any particular form.[43] A training course attended by a worker can constitute a suitable and sufficient assessment of the manual handling operations to be undertaken.[44] A particular assessment, in order to be suitable and sufficient, must be related to the manual handling operations which may require to be performed in each discrete task.[45] The present state of the cases is that the failure to prepare an assessment is not itself sufficient for liability.[46] Where the defender has complied with 4(1)(b)(ii) and (iii), he ought to be able to argue that any breach of 4(1)(a) is not causitive. Most certainly, a failure to carry out the desiderated assessment ought to be admitted as relevent to show the care which was or was not being lavished on the

---

[41] *Taylor v Glasgow City Council*, 2002 S.L.T. 689, *per* Lord Carloway at 697–698; specifically critiqued by Lord Reed in detail at 691–692.

[42] *Aiken v Board Of Management Aberdeen College*, 2000 G.W.D. 74.

[43] *Brown v East and Midlothian NHS Trust*, 2000 S.L.T. 342.

[44] *ibid.*

[45] *ibid.*

[46] *Logan v SRC*, unreported, January 12, 1999, *Birse v ALPS Electric (Scotland) Ltd*, 2002 G.W.D. 513.

pursuer.[47] A failure to provide written instructions in relation to he fitting of electrical wiring can be a breach of 4(1)(b)(ii).[48] An employer has been found liable in relation to the lifting of a slab with a crowbar.[49] Where the employer has provided and instructed the use of proper equipment but this is ignored by the worker will still result in the employee failing even under these new regulations.[50]

In *McIntosh v City of Edinburgh Council*,[51] decided after the leading current case *Taylor*, a worker hurt himself while trying to return a three piece ladder weighing 50kg to his van. It got stuck in grass causing him to lose his balance. It was held that the ladder was a load in terms of regulation 2(1). A man lifting a ladder of this weight involved a foreseeable possibility of injury engaging the regulations. Some helpful judicial guidance on the interpretation of *Taylor* can be found in the decision of Lord McEwan in *McIntosh*. He read *Taylor* as a majority decision, which he would have had to have followed despite his own sympathies being with the opinion of Lord Carloway. The opinion of the Court in *McDougall v Spiers*, 25 February 2003 is content that risk includes "foreseeable possibility" and it is even better if that possibility is that which allegedly occurs. The Inner House agreed, in what must have been a marginal case before them, that proof was needed.

In what could be an important decision for many workers, in one English case, the regulations supported a case where there had been no accident during an actual manual handling operation but an eventual collapse due to extended heavy lifting.[52]

Employer's Liability (Defective Equipment) Act 1969

This Act sets out to help the workman who is injured by his work **21–24** equipment. The basic law is that reasonable care is required and so a workman injured by equipment purchased from a responsible supplier would be forced to sue the supplier and not his employer.[53] The Act provides that the fault is that of the employer if an employee suffers personal injury in the course of his employment in consequence of a defect in equipment provided by his employer for the purposes of the employer's business and the defect is attributable wholly or partly to the fault of a third party (whether identifiable or

---

[47] *Birse v ALPS Electric (Scotland) Ltd*, 2002 G.W.D. 513.

[48] *McBeath v Halliday*, 2000 G.W.D. 2–75.

[49] *Skinner v Aberdeen City Council*, 2001 G.W.D. 16–657

[50] *Urquhart v Biwater Industries Ltd*, 1998 S.L.T. 576; 1998 S.C.L.R. 198: the pursuer did not use the crane provided but tried to lift concrete blocks himself.

[51] 2003 S.L.T. 827.

[52] *Knott v Newham Healthcare NHS Trust*, [2002] All E.R. (D) 216: See the note H. Immanuel, "Causation — justice for nurses?" 2002 P.I.L.J. Nov/Dec 1.

[53] *Davie v New Merton Board Mills Ltd* [1959] A.C. 604.

not).[54] Contributory negligence is a defence and the employer has a right of indemnity against the supplier. "Equipment" includes any plant and machinery, vehicle, aircraft and clothing. "Equipment" has been held to include a ship,[55] soap,[56] and a ventilation system,[57] but not actuators which were a part of the product being assembled as opposed to a tool.[58]

A weakness in the Act is that it has been interpreted as there still being a necessity to show something wrong with the article. Thus a man failed to recover damages when he was injured when a knife he was using broke. It was held that the most probable cause of the breakage was a previous fall and thus the provisions of the Employer's Liability (Defective Equipment) Act 1969 did not apply.[59]

A "defect" includes everything which renders the plant, etc. unfit for the use for which it is intended when used in reasonable way and with reasonable care.[60] Thus soap, which was in itself not said to be in any way defective, was defective within the Act where it could be used safely with gloves but was not safe without. A ventilation system was defective where clips which provided the suspension link from roof trusses for the support of ducting and trunking were insufficient for their purpose.[61] In *Edwards v Butlins*,[62] the Inner House reversed the decision to decide that where the defenders pleadings can be read as accepting that the equipment was defective, then the pursuer does not have to bring home liability to one of the two possible actual wrongdoers.

---

[54] s.1(1).

[55] *Coltman v Bibby Tankers Ltd* [1988] A.C. 276.

[56] *Ralston v Greater Glasgow Health Board*, 1987 S.L.T. 386.

[57] *Yuille v Daks Simpson Ltd*, 1984 S.L.T. 115.

[58] *Loch v British Leyland UK Ltd*, 1975 (Notes) S.L.T. 67.

[59] *Marshall v D.B. Marshall (Newbridge) Ltd*, 1991 G.W.D. 30–1807.

[60] *Yarmouth v France* (1887) 19 Q.B.D. 647, *per* Lindley L.J. at 658 quoted with approval by Lord Kincraig in *Ralston v Greater Glasgow Health Board*, 1987 S.L.T. (Notes) 386 at 387.

[61] *Yuill v Daks Simpson Ltd*, 1984 S.L.T. 116.

[62] 1998 S.L.T. 500.

CHAPTER 22

PROFESSIONAL LIABILITY

There are two main reasons why it is appropriate to treat professional **22–1** liability separately. The first is that the existence of a duty of care in certain professional areas has been the subject of decision. The second is that the standard of care differs — the reasonable man, although he might be prepared to give it a try, will not make a very successful attempt at brain surgery.[1] One thing that has to be made clear immediately is that the word "profession" is used here as a matter of convenience. As will be seen, the legal considerations do not depend upon the defender being a member of a professional body as opposed to, say, a trade association: "If I engage a man to exercise his expertise on my behalf . . . it matters not whether he is to prepare a conveyance of land or to drive a straight furrow across it."[2]

The delictual duty

Professional liability can, of course, occur contractually because **22–2** the pursuer agrees with the defender that a service be provided. In Scotland, there is no need for consideration and so, frequently, there will be a contract in place and a contractual analysis, perhaps based on implied terms will be the starting point. The existence of a contract does not, however, preclude the existence of a delictual duty. That was clear in Scotland even before *Donoghue*.[3] Generally, the standard of care required is the same in contract as in delict, but it is always possible as a matter of express contract for a party to bind himself to a higher standard of care or agree a lower standard. Sometimes there will be professional liability based on duties other than that to take care to prevent foreseeable harm. Thus, often the

---

[1] For a full up to date treatment with developments after publication, see Stewart, *Reparation: Liability for Delict.*

[2] *Arenson v Casson Beckman* [1977] A.C. 405, *per* Lord Kilbrandon at 430.

[3] *Edgar v Lamont*, 1914 S.C. 277. Resistance in England in relation to concurrent liability (*Tai Hing Cotton Mill Ltd v Liu Chong Hing Bank* [1986] A.C. 80; *National Bank of Greece v Pinios Shipping Co. (No. 1) (The Maria)* [1989] 1 All E.R. 213; *Greater Nottingham Co-operative Society Ltd v Cementation Piling and Foundations Ltd* [1988] 3 W.L.R. 396 and *Pacific Associates Inc. v Baxter* [1990] Q.B. 993 yielded to the House of Lords' decision in *Henderson v Merrett Syndicates Ltd* [1994] 3 W.L.R. 761.

delict of fraud will provide a remedy if there has been the necessary intention to deceive. As we shall see later, there may, in respect of medical treatment, be liability based on assault. However, in the main, liability is usually in issue because of unintentional harm due to a lack of the care required by law: professional people are generally trying to assist the recipient of their skills and not to cause harm. A complicating factor is that professional services are often rendered on the basis of oral or written advice rather than doing or omitting to do something.

Perhaps the easiest place to start is with physical injury caused by a lack of due care. It is clear from the cases like *Hunter v Hanley*[4] that there is a duty to take care to prevent such harm by acts or omissions. There was authority in England that there was also a duty not to cause foreseeable physical harm by the giving of negligent advice. In *Clayton v Woodman & Son (Builders) Ltd*,[5] an architect gave instructions direct to a bricklayer. The architect knew the instructions would be promptly obeyed and should have realised that they could result in serious injury. In fact, the wall on which the plaintiff was working collapsed, injuring him.

The court at first instance held that there was a breach of duty, but the decision was reversed on the facts, in that the Court of Appeal did not accept the finding that the architect had given any direct order. However, the greatest difficulty was, and often still is, negligent advice that does not cause damage to property or injury to person. That problem began to unravel with *Hedley Byrne*.[6]

The standard of care

22–3 The professional person is judged in professional matters, by the standard of his profession, not that of the reasonable man. This was established in the case of *Hunter v Hanley*,[7] a case where a doctor used an inappropriate needle in treating a patient. Lord President Clyde said:

> "In the realm of diagnosis and treatment there is ample scope for genuine difference of opinion and one man clearly is not negligent mealy because his conclusion differs from that of other professional men . . . The true test for establishing negligence in diagnosis or treatment on the part of a doctor is whether he has been proved to be guilty of such failure as no

---

[4] 1955 S.L.T. 213.

[5] [1962] 2 Q.B. 533.

[6] See para.9–7 and para.10–3 *et seq.*

[7] 1955 S.L.T. 213; and see *Bolam v Friern Hospital Management Committee* [1957] 1 W.L.R. 582. See also *Moyes v Lothian Health Board*, 1990 S.L.T. 444; Anon "Medical Negligence: Hunter v Hanley 35 Years On", 1990 S.L.T. (News) 325.

doctor of ordinary skill would be guilty of if acting with ordinary care."[8]

So the ordinary practitioner is not judged by the standard of the consultant nor let off by application of the ordinary reasonable man test. This test has been applied and considered many times, but its precise scope is debated.[9] However, the person who holds himself out as possessing a higher degree of skill may well be held liable in delict if he fails to reach that higher standard. The basic test refers to what it is other professionals do. In England, the test was put in a different way (intended to have similar effect) in *Bolam v Friern Hospital Management Committee*,[10] McNair J. stating that the professional would not be liable if he has acted in accordance with a practice accepted as proper by a responsible body of medical men skilled in that particular art. That has been interpreted as meaning that even a small group of practitioners can constitute a responsible body of opinion.[11] The English courts have also addressed another very important question — whether the courts have the final say in what is or is not negligent in professional cases. There were some indicators that the court retained an overall locus to adjudicate on the evidence or indeed to declare a professional practice negligent.[12]

However, in *Bolitho v City and Hackney Health Authority*,[13] the House of Lords retreated from interference. A senior nurse conveyed her serious concerns about a child's treatment, but no doctors came. Eventually his respiratory system collapsed and in trying to revive the child, he suffered serious brain damage. Breach of duty was established on the failure of the senior doctor, called regularly by the nurse, to have the boy treated. It was common ground that intubation so as to provide an airway in any event would have ensured that the respiratory failure that occurred did not lead to cardiac arrest. The judge had evidence from eight medical experts, all of them distinguished. Five for the plaintiff said neglect and three for the defendants said no negligence. The defendants won on the *Bolam* test even although the judge had a feeling that the defendants' evidence

---

[8] At 217.

[9] *ibid.* See also contributed, "Medical Negligence: Hunter v Hanley, 35 Years On' " 1990 S.L.T. 325. D.K. Feenan, "Medical Negligence (Hunter v Hanley 35 Years On: A Reply)" 1991 S.L.T. 321; L. Sutherland, "A Single Standard of Care" (1995) Rep. B. 6–11; K. Norrie, "Common Practice and the Standard of Care in Medical Negligence" (1985) J.R. 145.

[10] [1957] 2 All E.R. 118.

[11] *De freitas v O'Brien* [1995] T.L.R. 86.

[12] *Hucks v Cole* [1993] 4 Med. L.R. 393; *Edward Wong Finance Co. Ltd v Johnson, Stokes & Master* [1984] 1 A.C. 296; *Sidaway v Governors of the Bethlem Royal Hospital* [1985] 1 All E.R. 643.

[13] [1997] 3 W.L.R. 1151.

did not make sense. The House of Lords retained a very limited place for the courts:

> "The court is not bound to hold that a defendant doctor escapes liability for negligent treatment or diagnosis just because he leads evidence from a number of medical experts who are genuinely of opinion that the defendant's treatment or diagnosis accorded with sound medical practice . . . The use of 'responsible, reasonable and respectable' all show that the court has to be satisfied that the exponents of the body of opinion relied upon can demonstrate that such opinion has a logical basis. In particular in cases involving, as they so often do, the weighing of risks against benefits, the judge before accepting a body of opinion as being responsible, reasonable or respectable, will need to be satisfied that, in forming their views, the experts have directed their minds to the question of comparative risks and benefits and have reached a defensible conclusion on the matter."

22–4   It may be hoped the word "defensible" in *Bolitho* is taken and expanded beyond the apparent intention of its author. It ought to be within the power of the courts in cases where they understand the essence of the conflict of expert evidence to take a position that one body, however reputable, is unacceptable.[14] *Duffy v Lanarkshire Health Board*,[15] while merely refusing an appeal against an earlier absolvitor, in view of the reasons in the case not being sufficiently clearly stated, the court did look at the matter *de novo*. The court went so far as to say that the pursuer's expert was not well founded in generalising his own view to that of any competent consultant.

Finally by way of caution, an attempt to use the *Hunter* test to exculpate builders failed in *Morrisons Associated Companies Ltd v James Rome & Son Ltd*.[16] Lord Cameron said:

> "Counsel argued for the defenders that the position of a builder was the same as a doctor, and that it would, therefore be necessary to show that the defenders had acted in a way which no builder of reasonable skill exercising reasonable care would have acted in the circumstances. I do not think this is so. The practise of medicine is only permitted to those who have attained a fixed standard of professional qualifications. Further,

---

[14] Important decisions helping the Court keep some degree of control cited in support by Lord Browne-Wilkinson in *Bolitho* were: *Hucks v Cole* [1993] 4 Med. L.R. 393 and *Edward Wong Finance Co. Ltd v Johnson Stokes & Master* [1984] 1 A.C. 296.

[15] 2001 G.W.D. 10–368.

[16] 1962 S.L.T. (Notes) 75.

the practise of medicine is not an exact science and methods of practice and treatment vary with the movement of professional opinion and the expansion of the horizon of scientific knowledge. The standard of qualification of a builder is not recognised and defined in the same way. An old established craft of the builder is not subjected to the same divisions and movements in professional opinion or fluctuations in diagnosis and prescription . . . A builder or any other skilled tradesman is only required to possess a reasonable degree of competence and to display it in his work . . . What is the measure of the standard in each case must be judged against the practice ruling in the particular trade at the particular time. I think also that where different opinions as to method may reasonably be held by persons equally skilled in the particular trade or craft, selection of one which has in fact led to certain injurious consequences in preference to another which might have led to a different result is not necessarily proof of negligence . . . unless these consequences were within the realm of the reasonably foreseeable as certain or likely to ensue. On the other hand error of judgement however honestly arrived at, does not necessarily exculpate from liability."

He went on to examine the issue of practice and found that it had not been criticised by any practical builder. If it had that would make a difference for a builder but not for a doctor.[17]

Some particular problems in professional liability cases

1. Medical cases

Medical cases have raised some difficult problems that are worth **22–5** special consideration. The professional error must still cause the loss. If after medical treatment someone is worse off than when they went into hospital, they still have to show that it was the doctor's fault that caused the loss. This was re-emphasised in the case of *Kay's Tutor v Ayrshire and Arran Health Board*.[18] Although the hospital admitted administering a huge overdose of penicillin, the pursuer failed because he could not show that the child's deafness was caused by the overdose rather than the meningitis that had taken the child into hospital in the first place. If there are a number of possible causes, it must be shown that the breach of duty, on the balance of probabilities, was an operative cause of the loss.[19]

Another issue is the interrelation of liability based on negligence and liability based on assault. The House of Lords has refused to

---

[17] The defenders were held liable in contract but not in delict.
[18] 1987 S.L.T. 577.
[19] *Wilsher v Essex Area Health Authority* [1988] 2 W.L.R. 557.

accept the so-called informed consent doctrine as part of English law. This doctrine is based upon the law of assault, *i.e.* in England, trespass to the person. It will result in a doctor being held liable if the whole procedure and risks are not explained to the patient. The basis of the doctrine is that the patient cannot be touched unless he gives his full consent. In theory, the consent that the patient gives is not effective unless the consent is informed, *i.e.* based on all the relevant available information. Instead, the House of Lords held that the general rule in *Hunter* is applicable in this area of medical work and the issue is now resolved by asking whether the risk is one which the ordinary doctor exercising ordinary care would reveal to the patient. This question will generally be answered by considering the views of medical witnesses.[20] A particularly interesting case is *Gold v Haringey Health Authority*,[21] in which the failure complained of was to advise of an alternative and more efficient method of contraception. The case was decided on the basis of the *Hunter* test, but it might be thought that the other view which was argued — that the doctor was giving contraceptive advice and should have been judged by the standard of, say, a family planning adviser — is at least as attractive. However, the court was reluctant to dissect a doctor's work functionally: it refused to accept that there was a different standard of care in giving advice as opposed to carrying out medical treatment. In principle, this does not seem to be right — the protection of *Hunter* is really functional rather than titular.

Causation in medical cases

22–6   Causation is often difficult in negligence cases.[22] Thus where a women suffered a non-haemorrhagic stroke a week after being prescribed a low dose contraceptive pill, it was held on evidence mainly from medical journals that the cause was cryptogenic.[23] Equally difficult are cases where the breach of duty has cause the patient to lose the chance of a cure or to recover. It is not unlikely that the decision in *Fairchild*[24] will be prayed in aid in a medical case.

---

[20] *Sidaway v Governors of the Bethlern Royal Hospital* [1985] 1 All E.R. 643; and see *Moyes v Lothian Health Board*, 1990 S.L.T. 444 for a Scottish "Warning of risks" case; see, too, *Cameron v Greater Glasgow Health Board*, 1993 G.W.D. 6–433.

[21] [1987] 3 W.L.R. 649.

[22] See Ch.10. See also J.G. Logie, "Proof of Causation in Medical Negligence Cases", 1988 S.L.T. (News) 25; A.F. Phillips, "Further Reflections on Medical Causation", 1988 S.L.T. (News) 325; A.F. Phillips, "Medical Negligence and No-Fault Compensation", 1989 J.L.S. 239; E. Russell, "Establishing Medical Negligence — A Herculean Task", 1998 S.L.T. (News) 17. Matters are not helped by the problems faced by poor pursuers, see generally D. Sandison, "Medical Negligence Claims: The Paucity of Funding", 1995 J.L.S. 309. The new private legal insurers charge higher premiums for medical negligence cases.

[23] *Ingram v Ritchie*, 1989 G.W.D. 27–1217.

[24] Discussed in para.9–22.

While on its facts to do with mesothelioma, it arguably establishes that where it can be shown that knowledge does not exist as to a cause and there is a proof of a risk which materialised to produce the actual harm, causation may be made out.

2. *Legal advisers*

In the House of Lords case of *Robertson v Fleming*,[25] a solicitor **22-7** prepared documents for his client that were also to be useful to his client's creditors in the event of the client's insolvency. When the client became insolvent, it was found that the solicitor had failed to take necessary steps to make the security documents effective. The creditors suffered a loss. They were held unable to recover in delict but were allowed to recover on the basis of an implied contract, or a *jus quaesitum tertio*. It was thought to be clear that a solicitor could only be liable to his own client. This is a House of Lords case in a Scottish appeal and is thus, to the extent that its ratio is in point, binding. However, it is entirely at odds with the neighbour principle, established by the House of Lords in *Donoghue*. It is also contrary to the principle that the professional should answer for his lack of skill, emphatically laid down by the House of Lords in *White v Jones*.

Liability for economic loss based on *Hedley Byrne* in particular seems clearly applicable to solicitors if they have assumed responsibility or come within the special relationship. In *Weir v J.M. Hodge*,[26] Lord Weir felt himself bound by *Robertson*. *Robertson* was also followed by Lord Cameron of Lochbroom in *MacDougall v Clydesdale Bank Trustees*.[27] In *Bolton v Jameson & Mackay*,[28] Lord Wylie took the view that *Robertson* had been overtaken and allowed proof before answer on the averments that solicitors had acted improperly in paying a sum to their own client without, in the special circumstances, taking account of the pursuer's interests. It is submitted that it is correct to say that *Robertson* is still in force and binding, albeit (if that is correct) doomed to being departed from in a Scots appeal. However, other views on this particular decision are tenable and Professor Norrie's strongly expressed view that the decision is *obiter* does indeed have support by inference from *White v Jones*,[29] discussed above, where (as he points out) Lord Goff did not consider that the case required the use of the practice direction (it would have had the case been binding).[30] It must be noted, however, that the case, being Scottish, was not binding in *White* in any event.

---

[25] (1861) 4 Macq. 167.
[26] 1990 S.L.T. 266.
[27] 1993 S.C.L.R. 832.
[28] 1987 S.L.T. 291, reversed on other grounds 1989 S.L.T. 222.
[29] See 5.21 above.
[30] Norrie, "Disappointed beneficiaries, the House of Lords and Scots Law", 1995 Rep. L.R. 32 — because the case was obiter and irrelevant.

At every opportunity the rule is passed over.[31] The position has been reached where in *Holmes v Bank of Scotland*,[32] the defenders were held to have to go to PBA on a case at the instance of an intended beneficiary of their alleged failure to implement a testators instructions. The argument from *Robertson v Fleming* was rejected on the basis of the unreported decision of an extra division in *Robertson v Watt & Co.* In any event, his lordship would have himself decided that there was no reason why Scots law would not extend *Hedley Byrne* in the same way as had the English in *White*. Whatever one's view, *Robertson v Fleming* is a dead letter save for its actual holding that obligations similar to delictual obligations can be accommodated within contract itself by virtue of the doctrine *jus quaesitum tertio*.[33]

22–8   There was until recently another unusual exception to liability for professional negligence and that was in the case of the lawyer who is conducting a court action. In that the House of Lords has reviewed and restated the law the history can be cut short but remains important for the student to see the background to the leading modern case. *Rondel v Worsley*[34] was an action raised by a criminal against the dock brief (a barrister who appears without prior instruction to act for anyone who might instruct him) who appeared for him at the Old Bailey. He claimed his defence had been badly run and that if it had been done properly he would not have been convicted. The House of Lords held that barristers (in Scotland, Advocates) were immune from suit in respect of their conduct and management of a case in court and the preliminary work connected therewith such as the drawing of pleadings. It also seemed to be the case that the immunity would extend to a solicitor carrying out advocacy work. Such a statement in favour of lawyers by lawyers required some justification. The immunity was not, said the court, based on the absence of contract but upon policy and long usage and there were three good reasons for it: a barrister had to be able to carry out his duties fearlessly and independently; there would be a retrying of the original action if actions were allowed — to see if with the right conduct the case would have been won; barristers are compelled by their own professional rules to accept clients. An opportunity arose shortly afterwards to examine the extent of the immunity. In *Saif Ali v Sydney Mitchell & Co.*,[35] it was held that a barrister could be liable for advice that was not intimately connected with the

---

[31] See *Robertson v Watt & Co.*, Second Division, July 4, 1995, discussed, R. Rennie, "Solicitors' Negligence: Third Parties Join the Queue," 2001 6 S.L.P.Q. 304.

[32] 2002 G.W.D. 8–269.

[33] See Woolman (2nd ed.) p.160 *et seq. Strathford East Kilbride Ltd v HLM Design Ltd*, 1997 S.C.L.R. 877.

[34] [1969] 1 A.C. 191.

[35] [197813 All E.R. 1033.

actual conduct of a case, such as the giving of opinions. Interestingly, the two Scottish law lords dissented on this point, preferring that there be a blanket immunity for *all* work, even work where litigation was only in contemplation. In this particular case, the barrister had left the plaintiff with no one to sue and was himself sued.

The position is now that so far as England is concerned, the barrister's immunity has fallen. In *Hall & Co v Simons*,[36] the House of Lords convened as a seven judge bench and stated that the immunity created by the judges and restated in *Rondel v Worsley* should no longer exist. In civil cases, the position is probably the same in Scotland, but it is essential to note the reservations in *Hall* of Lord Hope, a former Lord President. Even then it may be impossible to exclude at least the possibility of a negligence case in criminal cases, however inconvenient. The ability to reopen criminal proceedings within the criminal system itself for negligent representation[37] means that the damage can be limited, but also that a bar on civil action based on uninhibited freedom of action is difficult to maintain. In the first consideration of the matter in Scotland since *Hall*, *Wright v Paton Farrell*,[38] absolvitor was granted in favour of solicitors who had represented the pursuer in a criminal case. Had it not been for a finding of an immunity based on *Batchelor* and declining to follow *Hall*, there would have been proof before answer. For all the case is on the criminal side, it looks like it could be analysed as the loss of the chance of an earlier acquittal and thus seems no different to the loss of a chance brought about by the failure to raise a damages writ within the time bar.

3. Negligent misstatements and contracts

If a negligent misstatement induces a contract then it may well be **22–9** a negligent misrepresentation. In the law of contract, if one party to the contract misrepresents facts to the other deliberately, negligently, or innocently, there may be a remedy by way of rescission of the contract. However, for a long time the rule in *Manners v Whitehead*[39] held sway. Even although there had been a negligent misrepresentation, if it were made by the other contracting party then damages in delict were only available if there was proof of fraud. The position was changed by the Law Reform (Miscellaneous Provisions) (Scotland) Act 1985, section 10(1), which provides that:

"A party to a contract who has been induced to enter into it by negligent misrepresentation made by or on behalf of another

---

[36] 2000 3 All E.R. 673. For a full analysis see M. Seneviratne, "The rise and fall of advocates' immunity," (2001) 21 L.S. 644.

[37] *Anderson v H.M. Advocate*, 1996 S.L.T. 155.

[38] 2002 G.W.D. 26–988.

[39] (1898) 1 F. 171.

party to the contract shall not be disentitled, by reason only that the misrepresentation is not fraudulent, from recovering damages from the other party in respect of any loss or damage he has suffered as a result of the misrepresentation; and any rule of law that such damages cannot be recovered unless fraud is proved shall cease to have effect."

In *Hamilton v Allied Domecq*,[40] Lord Carloway held that it was *not* necessary for a pursuer to aver special relationship or other facts necessary to support a *Hedley Byrne* case for negligent misrepresentation where the parties contracted and the case was brought under the relaxation in the Law Reform (Miscellaneous Provisions) (Scotland) Act 1985. All that had to be shown was that an inducing misrepresentation was made negligently. The best support for that ruling is that the parties being in a contract, all worries about proximity or the floodgates are unfounded.

4. Damages issues

22–10   Medical and legal cases have shown that professional cases are likely to raise the issue of claims for lost chances. That is a general damages issue and is accordingly dealt with below.[41]

---

[40] 2001 G.W.D. 13–517.
[41] Ch.26.

SECTION VI: GENERAL MATTERS

CHAPTER 23

THE LITIGANTS

INTRODUCTION

This Chapter describes most of the different types of litigants found **23–1** in delict actions. Most have specialities that can affect the result of the litigation. Included here are some of the exciting "life-cycle" issues, which could equally have been presented in Chapter 10 on Economic Loss. Many litigants are included here because they are entitled to immunities, not available to others.

Any litigant requires title and interest to sue. In delict, title to sue is a curious and ill-defined requirement for a successful action. Often it operates simply as a procedural device to filter *certain* claims that are legally irrelevant. This view is strengthened when it is remembered that the requirement of title and interest to sue is present in, *inter alia*, the law of contract and the law of property. Thus, in certain cases it can be said that the pursuer has no title to sue and the claim will be disposed of immediately or after a preliminary proof on the particular point — so, for example, a pursuer generally has no title to sue if someone else is harmed.[1] Title to sue depends upon the existence of a legal right. Thus, in cases where legal rights are well established and clear, the idea is perhaps helpful, such as where a person destroys the pursuer's heritable property or assaults the pursuer. Where the law is developing, there can be few fixed categories of cases where there is no title to sue, but an attack may be mounted under a plea of title to sue.[2] Once an area of law becomes contentious, it is not helpful to consider it in terms of title to sue for the law underlies the plea, not vice versa. However, outside developing areas of delict, it is a valuable and effective plea preventing time, effort and money being wasted on the proof of what must ultimately be a hopeless case. A pursuer must have title and interest to sue: "interest" means that the pursuer has suffered some loss or infringement of a civil right, protected by law. It is not necessary that there

---

[1] *McLachlan v Bell* (1895) 23 R. 126.
[2] See *Nacap v Moffat Plant Ltd*, 1987 S.L.T. 221, *North Scottish Helicopters Ltd v United Technologies Corp. Inc.*, 1988 S.L.T. 77; (No.2), 1988 S.L.T. 778, *Hand v North of Scotland Water Authority*, 2002 S.L.T. 798, TCS *Holdings Ltd v Ashtead Plant Hire*, 2003 S.L.T. 177.

be what is sometimes called a patrimonial interest — a loss to a person's estate.[3] If there is title to sue, interest is usually presumed.

The Crown, its Judges, its Government and the State

The Crown and the Parliaments

The Sovereign

23–2   The Sovereign is immune from action.[4]

The Crown

23–3   At common law, the Crown is not vicariously liable for the actings of its agents or employees, but the liability of the Crown is now governed by the Crown Proceedings Act 1947, which generally makes the Crown liable.[5] The Crown is liable both as an employer and as an occupier.[6] The Crown is bound by statute if express or by necessary implication.[7] Scotland has its own devolved Parliament.[8] Prior to the key provisions coming into force, actions against the Crown had to be raised against the Lord Advocate. He required the prior authority of whomsoever he represents.[9] This could not be challenged by a private party.[10] The Secretary of State for Scotland was called as the defender in cases where one of his departments was involved.

Normally interdicts cannot be granted against the Crown and instead declarator needs to be sought.[11] Where it is sought to prevent a breach of European Union law interdict may be appropriate.[12]

Scottish Parliament and devolution

23–4   In terms of the devolution legislation, the Lord Advocate and the Solicitor General for Scotland are now Scottish law officers to the

---

[3] For a recent review in contract: *Gunstone v Scottish Women's Athletic Association*, 1987 S.L.T. 611.

[4] But this may require review: I. Dickinson, "Crown Immunities Post-1998", 2003 S.L.T. (News) 107.

[5] Previously it was necessary to seek declarator of the wrong and seek *ex gratia* damages.

[6] s.2(1) and the Occupiers' Liability (Scotland) Act 1960, s.4.

[7] s.2(2).

[8] Scotland Act 1998.

[9] Crown Suits (Scotland) Act 1857, ss.1 and 2.

[10] 1857 Act, s.3.

[11] Crown Proceedings Act 1947, s.43(a), s 21(a); *Lord Advocate v SRC*, 1990 S.L.T. 158, *McDonald v Secretary of State for Scotland*, 1994 S.L.T. 692.

[12] *R. v Secretary of State for Transport, ex p. Factortame Ltd (No 2)* [1991] 1 A.C. 603.

Scottish Executive. The Advocate General for Scotland became the adviser to the UK Government on Scottish legal matters. Between May 20, 1999 and July 1, 1999 any action that would previously have been raised against the Lord Advocate as representing the Crown was raised against the Advocate General for Scotland.[13] Actions which would have been raised against the Lord Advocate in UK matters are raised against the Advocate General for Scotland.[14] So far as the Scottish Parliament is concerned, the court cannot make an order for suspension, interdict, reduction or specific performance if the effect of doing so would be to give any relief against the Parliament.[15] It can, however, interdict a wrong by a member of the Scottish Parliament in the conduct of his duties under its statutes.[16]

The armed forces

In respect of injuries suffered by members of the armed forces, the **23–5** law is special. By section 10(1) of the Act there was no liability in delict if the injuries were certified as pensionable. In *Adams v War Office*,[17] certification was made, but no pension was actually awarded.[18] The Crown Proceedings (Armed Forces) Act 1987 prevented this apparent injustice: "Section 10 of the Crown Proceedings Act 1947 shall cease to have effect except in relation to anything suffered by a person in consequence of an act or omission committed before the date on which this Act is passed."[19] The Secretary of State can revive the effect of section 10 if it appears necessary or expedient to do so by reason of any imminent national danger, any great emergency or for the purposes of any warlike operations in any part of the world outside the United Kingdom. Perhaps surprisingly, no such order was made when the Gulf War against Iraq broke out. Thus the Crown did not have this defence when sued by a soldier who claimed that the Crown was vicariously liable for the fault of his fellow soldier in not arranging a safe system of work as he fired a

---

[13] Between May 20, 1999 and July 1, 1999 any action against the Scottish Ministers including the Lord Advocate in that capacity should be raised against the Lord Advocate. After July 1 actions within the competence of the Scottish Parliament and Ministers are raised either against the Ministers or the Lord Advocate.

[14] Scotland Act 1998 (General Transitory, Transitional and Savings Provisions) Order 1999 (SI 1999/901); Scotland Act 1998 (Commencement) Order 1998 (SI 1998/3178); Transfer of Property (Scottish Ministers) Order 1999 (SI 1999/1104).

[15] s.40 (4) of the Scotland Act 1998.

[16] *Whaley v Lord Watson of Invergowrie*, 2000 S.L.T. 475.

[17] [1955] 3 All E.R. 245.

[18] A Scottish example, from before the 1987 Act is *Brown v Lord Advocate*, 1984 S.L.T. 146 in which the Lord Advocate represented the Ministry of Defence. A certificate was lodged and the action held to be incompetent. It would also have been held irrelevant.

[19] May 15, 1987.

howitzer at the Iraqis.[20] In *Derry v Ministry of Defence*,[21] it was held that section 10(1) of the Crown Proceedings Act applied to protect the Crown from a claim based on an allegation that the military doctor failed to diagnose the plaintiff's cancerous condition. Because the condition predated the act or omission, the State was protected. The persuasive argument that it was the omission to diagnose properly that led to a loss of a chance of better treatment seems to have failed mainly because it is difficult to fit the common law concept of a loss of a chance into the statutory language of the 1947 Act, which talks of a thing suffered. In *Mathews v MOD*,[22] section 10 was pled in an asbestosis action in respect of matters before the repeal. It was held at first instance that the Act was incompatible with Article 6 of the ECHR. However, on appeal, it was held that section 10 did not affect a fair trial — rather it dealt with substantive rights.

Local authorities

23–6   Local authorities have been sued in delict for a very long time. Cases now are raised against the appropriate statutory body. Frequent reorganisation of local government means that for all practical purposes the responsible bodies will be creatures of statute and liable to that extent. At present, actions are in the main likely to be directed towards the "new" unitary authorities, who are sued in their statutory name. Earlier actions were against the magistrates or other officers depending on the status of the organisation.[23] Local authorities are treated more kindly at present in the law of negligence, at least where they are acting as a public body.[24]

In a particularly principled decision, it has been held in England that a local authority cannot sue for defamation at all.[25] The reason is to allow criticism of the authority an important civil right. Lord Keith followed with approval some American decisions, one as old as 1923, in coming to the conclusion that English law would not permit such an action[26]: "Every citizen has a right to criticise an inefficient or corrupt government without fear of civil as well as criminal prosecution". It was appreciated that the truth might be known, but no evidence available to substantiate it and thus the immunity was necessary to allow criticism to be made. Lord Keith

---

[20] *Mulcahy v MOD* [1996] T.L.R. 39. However it was held there was no duty to provide a safe system of work at war.

[21] [1998] T.L.R. 364.

[22] [2002] 3 All E.R. 513.

[23] A perusal of the table of cases will show just how many cases involve such parties as pursuers and defenders.

[24] See Ch.10.

[25] *Derbyshire County Council v Times Newspapers Ltd* [1993] T.L.R. 87.

[26] Supreme Court of Illinois: *City of Chicago v Tribune Co.* (1923) 139 N.E. 86.

agreed with Lord Goff in *Guardian Newspapers (No.2)*[27] that so far as the law of England was concerned, it was in concert with Article 10 of the ECHR. Local authorities are the very kind of bodies that may be sued directly for just satisfaction by a victim of a breach of human rights legislation.[28]

Judges

Judges have had extensive immunities for a very long time. In **23–7** *Haggart's Trs v Lord President*,[29] the pursuers were the trustees of an advocate who had raised an action for damages against the Lord President in respect of certain remarks of censure made from the bench about the conduct of his practice. These remarks were alleged to be motivated by malice and to injure John Haggart in his practice. There were in fact two cases eventually conjoined. Absolvitor was granted in the Outer House and a reclaiming failed. A further appeal was taken to the House of Lords, who dismissed the appeal. Lord Gifford said that an action for damages is not maintainable against a judge for words delivered from the bench in the exercise of judicial duty. If it was otherwise, this would subvert due administration of justice. The judges had a public responsibility, but it did not follow how this action could be maintained.[30] On the other hand, in the House of Lords in *Allardice v Robertson*,[31] the House held, affirming the judgment of the Court of Session, that a justice of the peace is not protected against an action of damages for verbal slander made maliciously in delivering judgment against a party to a trial before him.

The immunity was upheld in a rare modern case. In *Russell v Dickson*,[32] after finding an accused person guilty at the conclusion of a summary criminal trial, a sheriff remanded the accused in custody for investigations to be made into certain aspects of the conduct of the defence by the accused persons solicitor! The accused was released by the High Court of Justiciary, which commented that the sheriff's decision to remand the accused in custody had been in excess of his common law powers, and that his actions had been an excessive and unreasonable step. The accused brought an action of damages against the sheriff for wrongful imprisonment, arguing that, in the circumstances, the sheriff's decision to remand could not be described as a judicial act, and that he was not therefore entitled to the absolute immunity from being sued for damages that applied to the judicial actings of a sheriff. It was held that even although the

[27] [1990] 1 A.C. 109.
[28] See Ch.17.
[29] (1824) 2 Shaw's App. 125.
[30] *ibid.*, 143.
[31] (1830) 2 W. & S. 102.
[32] 1998 S.L.T. 96.

sheriff's decision to remand the accused in custody was wrong and unreasonable, it was still *an act done in his judicial capacity*, and as the averments of malice which had been made were not relevant, the sheriff was protected by absolute immunity.

Emanations of the State

23–8   The law of the European Union has provided that the Government shall be responsible to its citizens for failure to carry through properly or at all certain community laws.[33]

Public authorities

23–9   The Human Rights Act gives direct rights to reparation from public authorities to a victim.[34]

CORPORATIONS

Incorporated bodies

23–10   Incorporated bodies whether incorporated by Royal Charter, under the Companies Acts or otherwise, may sue and be sued in their own name so long as the wrong is one done to the organisation. An incorporated body being a legal person cannot have hurt feelings and, therefore, cannot be awarded *solatium*. It can, however, be injured in its reputation.[35] In *Waverley Housing Management Ltd v British Broadcasting Corporation*,[36] the defenders argued that the pursuers' action should be dismissed as the company could not sue for *solatium*. It was held that while indeed a company cannot sue for *solatium*, the pursuers could maintain the action by way of general damages for future loss of business, although not for damages based on particular contracts or diminution of turnover. Although shareholders may lose money by damage to company property, it is the company who must sue.[37]

Incorporated bodies having no actual physical body. Technically they are always vicariously liable. No distinction is made between *ultra vires* and *intra vires* acts.[38] It must be determined when suing a corporation that it is indeed the corporation and not the individuals

---

[33] See Ch.16.

[34] See Ch.17.

[35] *Solicitors of Edinburgh v Robertson* (1781) Mor. 13935; *Dumfries Fleshers v Rankine*, Dec. 10, 1816, F.C.; *North of Scotland Bank v Duncan* (1857) 19 D. 881; *Glebe Sugar Refining Company v Lusk* (1866) 2 S.L.R. 9; 3 S.L.R. 33.

[36] 1993 G.W.D. 17–1117.

[37] *Scottish Australian Emigration Society v Borland* (1855) 18 D. 239; *Dunnett v Mitchell* (1887) 15 R. 131.

[38] *Houldsworth v City of Glasgow Bank* (1880) 7 R. (HL) 53.

in their own right who have done the wrong.[39] However dependent on the wrong, the actual wrongdoer is likely to be as liable as the corporation if the wrong is also a corporation wrong.[40]

Directors of a company may be held personally liable where in the conduct of the company's affairs they have broken a statutory duty owed to the pursuer. Every case depends upon the duty in question and it would not be internally inconsistent for the law of delict routinely to pierce the veil of incorporation. However, one recent instance can be found in *Quinn v McGinty*.[41] The pursuer sued a director of his employer company for his failure to comply with the statutory obligation to insure in terms of the Employer's Liability (Compulsory Insurance) Act 1969. The sheriff found against him, but the Sheriff Principal allowed the action. Whether discussed as title to sue or relevancy, a shareholder has generally no right to sue for loss of profits due to injury to that shareholder himself, even where he is the largest shareholder and earns most of its profits.[42]

Unincorporated bodies

Generally

An unincorporated body can sue in its own right, although some **23–11** patrimonial interest need be averred and proved.[43] An unincorporated body as defender will be liable to the extent of any property held in trust for all the members and to the extent of the members interest in the body, *e.g.* a club subscription.[44]

Clubs

The former rule that a club cannot be sued in its own name — **23–12** actions required to be raised against the club and the office bearers[45] — has been departed from by Rules of Court. Arguably, all that does is to allow a decree to be enforced against club assets. It has already allowed an action of interdict against nuisance to be raised against a golf club and it was thought that suitable parties could be found to answer for any breach.[46] It has also been said that it is not necessary to sue the association as constituted at the time of the wrong, but it may be designed as it exists at the time of raising the action.[47]

---

[39] *Gordon v Metaline Company* (1886) 14 R. 75.
[40] *Dunbar v Presbytery of Auchterarder* (1849) 12 D. 284.
[41] 1999 S.L.T. (Sh. Ct) 27.
[42] *Young v Ormiston*, 1936 S.L.T. 79; *Fox v P Caulfield & Co Ltd*, 1975 S.L.T. (Notes) 71.
[43] *Highland Dancing Board v Alloa Printing Co.*, 1971 S.L.T. (Sh. Ct) 50.
[44] *Gibson v Smith* (1849) 21 Sc.J. 331.
[45] *Somerville v Rowbotham* (1862) 24 D. 1187.
[46] *Borland v Lochwinnoch Golf Club*, 1986 S.L.T. (Sh. Ct) 13.
[47] *Gorrie v The Marist Brothers*, 2001 G.W.D. 39–1484.

However, prudence suggests that the actual wrongdoers personally or in association at the time ought to be sued at least until parties of substance come forward as opponents. It is more likely that a particular office bearer will be personally liable, or all members approving a certain course of conduct will be liable. However, where the personal wrong of individuals can be established they are personally liable. In *Matthew v Perthshire Cricket Club*,[48] the pursuer sued "the Perthshire Cricket Club, and the officials and Committee of the Club, for damages in respect of personal injuries sustained by him through the collapse of a grand stand on the North Inch of Perth on August 1, 1903."[49]

Members suing the Association

23–13   It may be questioned whether a member has a right to sue for injuries or wrongs by the association. Analogies with partnership suggest a case might well fail.[50] In *Graham and Simpson v Hawick Common Riding Committee*,[51] the pursuers sued for declarator under the Sex Discrimination Act 1975 and for "nominal" damages of £1. The defenders were a committee, but it was not clear of what. A plea of no title to sue was repelled and that course approved on appeal. The Sheriff Principal did not find it necessary to comment on the English cases *Prole* and *Robertson*, although he could see some force in the view that, if an association consists of its own members and has no independent existence, then on the basis that a person cannot sue himself, those decisions might well be followed in Scotland.[52] In *Milne v Duguid*,[53] Sheriff Kelbie reviewed the authorities, applied *Prole* and held that a member of an unincorporated association could not sue an association. However, he allowed proof before answer on a case against a member who was being sued on the independent ground of his activities as greenkeeper. In *Carmichael v Bearsden & District Rifle and Pistol Club*,[54] the pursuer, a former member of the defender unincorporated club, sued in respect of alleged negligence

---

[48] (1904) 12 S.L.T. 635.

[49] More marginal (being before the Division on exceptions) is *Glass v Leitch*, (1902) 5 F. 14, in which a case for damages based on the collapsing of structure was brought against the race committee who acted gratuitously and had a lease of the premises.

[50] See para.2–28 below. For England see *Robertson v Ridley* [1989] 2 All E.R. 474, doubted by Clerk and Lindsell, *The Law of Torts*, paras 10–11 and 4–93 and distinguished in *Jones v Northampton Borough Council* [1992] 156 L.G. Rev. 23. See also *Prole v Allen* [1950] 1 All E.R. 476 and *Shore v Ministry for Works* [1950] 2 All E.R. 228.

[51] 1997 S.C.L.R. 917.

[52] *ibid.*, at 932.

[53] 1999 S.C.L.R. 512.

[54] 2000 S.L.T. (Sh. Ct) 49; 2000 Rep. L.R. 55.

resulting in lead poisoning over a period of time. The sheriff and the sheriff principal held that the rule in *Mair v Wood* applied.

In *Harrison v West of Scotland Kart Club*,[55] Lady Paton addressed **23–14** the issue and reviewed the authorities. It is accordingly an authoritative statement of the present understanding of the law. The pursuer's case was that, while karting, as he slowed down to enter the pits, the kart suddenly accelerated out of control and collided with an unprotected wall. Decisions regarding track safety were made jointly by the office bearers. For various reasons, it was alleged that they knew or ought to have known that, without some crash protection in the area of the building, there was a danger that a driver might similarly lose control and collide with the wall. The first defenders sought dismissal of the case against them on the basis that a member of an unincorporated club could not sue the club. The action against the club and the committee as representing the club was dismissed. The action so far as directed towards the committe members as individuals was allowed PBA. Lady Paton established a number of propositions that are transferable to other cases (authorities omitted):

1. The fact that the five were at all relevant times members of the same club as the pursuer did not give them any immunity.
2. Nor was it the fact that the five were members or office bearers which fixed them with a duty of care.
3. It was their knowledge coupled with their de facto assumption of the responsibility for taking executive decisions relating to track safety.
4. Liability *ex delicto* does not arise from membership of the club *per se*.
5. The first defenders were correct in contending that, in the context of delict, by suing the "West of Scotland Kart Club" the pursuer was in effect suing himself. Where a member of the club seeks to recover damages in respect of negligence on the part of another member or members, he cannot seek to recover damages from all the members of the club.[56]

Only perhaps on the last point is there scope for reconsideration. At the very least there ought to be scope for an argument that the pursuer in a club of 100, all of whom *along with him* are blameworthy, can sue the other 99, who can seek relief from him qua member for his share. He then actually does not sue himself, for he does not appear as a defender but as a third party called by one — or all — of the 99.

---

[55] 2001 S.L.T. 1171.
[56] 1183–1184.

To call this "suing yourself" is stretching a practically useful rule to produce injustice. What if there are 200,000 members?[57]

The Club suing the member

23–15 On analogy with partnership cases discussed below, there may be specialities.

Partnerships

Non-partners suing the partnership

23–16 Partners are jointly and severally liable.[58] They are so liable for the matters set out in the Partnership Act 1890:

> "Where, by any wrongful act or omission of any partner acting in the ordinary course of the business of the firm, or with the authority of his co-partners, loss or injury is caused to any person not being a partner in the firm, or any penalty is incurred, the firm is liable therefor to the same extent as the partner so acting or omitting to act."

The scope of the partnership business determines the scope of the liability.[59] In *Kirkintilloch Equitable Co-operative Society Ltd v Livingstone*,[60] there was an allegation of negligence by a member of a firm of accountants who acted as auditor. The fee was paid to the firm and members of the firm assisted in the audit. However, neither the partners nor the firm were entitled to be appointed as auditors under the appropriate legislation. It was argued that, accordingly, the work was not within the ordinary course of business of the partnership. It is clear from the opinion of Lord President Clyde that section 10 of the Act provides two alternative modes of liability: "ordinary course" and "authority" cases. In *Kirkintilloch Co-op*, the acts were within the scope of the business and in any event the averments as to authority were sufficient. Section 11 makes provision for liability in the following cases, namely: (a) where one partner acting within the scope of his apparent authority receives the money or property of a third person and misapplies it; and (b) where a firm in the course of its business receives money or property of a third person, and the money is misapplied by one or more of its partners while it is in the custody of the firm. The firm is liable to make good

---

[57] The reclaiming motion in this case was heard and the decision arrived while this text was in manuscript. Note Lord Marnoch's support for the exclusionary common members rule, concurred in by the Lord President and Lady Cosgrove.

[58] 1890 Act, s.12. For practical difficulties in suing partners and a partnership see: *Smith v Goldthorpe*, 2002 G.W.D. 10–303.

[59] *Lloyd v Grace Smith* [1912] A.C. 716.

[60] 1972 S.L.T. 154.

loss. An Extra Division considered this section in *New Mining and Exploring Syndicate Ltd v Chalmers & Hunter.*[61] This was a case against a partner in a firm of solicitors in respect of the transactions of his partner who was secretary to the pursuers. The firm was not secretaries to the company and was not its law agents. The Inner House upheld the decision to assoilzie the defenders.

The new approach to vicarious liability in intentional cases applies to partnership cases. In *Dubai Aluminium Co. Ltd v Salaam and Others,*[62] the House of Lords decided in these contribution proceedings that the firm were vicariously liable for the actings of a partner who was alleged to have dishonestly assisted in a breach of trust — he was acting in the ordinary course of the business even although without the knowledge or authority of the partners. The acts complained of were so closely connected with acts that he was authorised to do that this conclusion followed.[63] Where no "corporate" or systematic failure by the firm can be shown, then it remains essential that the professional failing be identified.[64]

Partners suing the partnership

It was held by in the first division, in *Mair v Wood,*[65] that a partner **23–17** injured by the negligence of his co-partner cannot sue the firm. Lord President Clyde accepted that a partner could in principle sue and *confusio* would not operate initially, but would restrict the claim to the amount of the claim minus the "suing partner's" share. However, negligence was a different matter because *culpa tenet suos auctores.* It has to be suggested, however, that the law of vicarious liability has now moved on so much in its ordinary sphere of employment that the decision could usefully be reviewed.[66] There is some support in Erskine:

> "It also proceeds from the mutual confidence inherent in this contract, that the several partners are not always obliged to use that middle kind of diligence which prudent persons employ in their own affairs; they are secure if they manage the company's concerns as they would do their own. If, therefore, a partner should fall into an error in management, for want of a larger share of prudence or skill than he was truly master of, he is not answerable for the consequences. He did his best; and the other

---

[61] 1911 2 S.L.T. 386.

[62] [2002] 3 W.L.R. 1913.

[63] See the note C. Mitchell, "Partners in Wrongdoing" 2003 L.Q.R. 364.

[64] *Duncan v Beattie,* 2003 G.W.D. 28–798.

[65] 1948 S.L.T. 326.

[66] It is accepted in Walker, *Delict,* p.81 and in Clerk and Lindsell, *The Law of Torts,* para.4–100 but now under reference *Ross Harper & Murphy v Banks.* See n.71 below.

partners have themselves to blame that they did not make choice of a partner of greater abilities."[67]

In *Bruce v Clapham*,[68] the question was the liability of the crew of a fishing boat for the negligence of the skipper. The boat was operated as a joint adventure. It was held, *obiter*, that even if the parties were in a joint adventure, the injured workman joint adventurer would have been an employee *quoad* the Captain.[69]

The partnership suing a partner

23–18   In *Blackwood v Robertson*,[70] in an action of payment by a consulting engineer against his former partners, the defender partners counter-claimed for damages in respect of alleged negligence on the part of the pursuer as a result of which the partnership suffered loss. It was held by Sheriff Macvicar that a partner might in serious cases be made liable to his fellow partners for loss occasioned to the partnership business by his lack of care or skill, but that a minor blunder would not give rise to a right of action and so a proof before answer was needed. He also considered the counter-claim contractual, contrary to the argument before him which was delictual. In *Ross Harper & Murphy v Banks*,[71] it was held that partners were entitled to PBA in a case against a former partner who had rendered them liable to third parties in a conveyancing transaction for recovery of the sum they lost by way of their insurance excess.

Limited liability partnership

23–19   The Limited Liability Partnership Act 2000[72] was passed as a response to the precarious situation arising for partners in large businesses structured as partnerships.[73] The former "intermediate" solution of the limited partnership was very uncommon.[74] The new scheme provides for a "limited liability partnership" or "LLP",[75]

---

[67] III, iii, 21.

[68] 1982 S.L.T. 386.

[69] See generally, G. Junor, "Reparation at Sea: Being a Share Fisherman," 1999 30 Rep. B. 2.

[70] 1984 S.L.T. (Sh. Ct) 68.

[71] 2000 S.L.T. 699.

[72] With effect from April 6, 2001.

[73] *ADT Ltd v BDO Binder Hamlyn*, [1996] B.C.C. 808. Since then the problem has been emphasised by the problems arising out of the Enron collapse. See generally Cross, "Limited Liability Partnerships — Draft Bill and Consultation paper" (1999) J.R. 137.

[74] See C. Villiers, "The Limited Liability Partnership Act 2000: Extending opportunities for business." 2001 S.L.P.Q. 112. At 113. See however the note in the same article for practical ways in which this form had been utilised, at 123.

[75] Schedule 1.

which is an incorporated body corporate.[76] It cannot grant floating charges. It requires an incorporation document and of relevance to reparation, the document delivered to the registrar must identify whether some or all of the members are to be designated members.[77] Each member of the LLP is an agent for the firm.[78] Associated regulations provide that the LLP must indemnify every member in respect of payments made and personal liabilities incurred by him in the ordinary and proper conduct of the business of the LLP or in or about anything done for the preservation of the business or management of the LLP. A negligent or otherwise wrongful member is liable to the full extent of his professional liability. It is the other members who benefit from the business arrangement. That said, it is submitted that where the LLP contracts to render services, it may at least attempt to limit liability to the overall liability of the LLP. The "consumer" knows he is dealing with an LLP and it may well be that such a restriction would not be unfair or unreasonable.

Incorporated practices

It is worth noting that it is possible for solicitors at least to form **23–20** incorporated practices. They are in all respects like incorporated companies, save that the professional rules that allow incorporation must be followed.[79] Only solicitors and incorporated practices can be directors.

Trade unions

Trade unions are unincorporated bodies. Their ability to sue and be **23–21** sued is subject to constraints and immunities as befits organisations that have essentially come to have constitutional significance in the twentieth century from having been primarily illegal combinations in the nineteenth.[80] Article 23(4) of the Universal Declaration of Human Rights declares: "Everyone has the right to form and to join Trade Unions for the protection of his interests." The more practical European Convention on Human Rights provides in Article 11 the right for a person to form and join trade unions for the protection of his interests, but this is subject to restrictions necessary in a democratic society in the interests of national security or public safety, for the prevention of disorder or crime, for the protection of health or morals or for the protection of the rights and freedoms of

---

[76] s.1.
[77] s.2.
[78] s.6.
[79] Originally Solicitors (Scotland) (Incorporated Practices) Practice Rules 1997, now S(S)(IP)PR 2001. See W. Semple, "Why conduct a Legal Practice as a Limited Company" 2001 Journal of the Law Society of Scotland (March).
[80] See the review in *Wilkie v King*, 1911 S.C. 1310.

others. Thus delict, which protects and enforces the interests of persons, must treat trade unions specially.

A trade union is an organisation which consists mainly or wholly of workers whose principal purpose includes the regulation of worker/employer relations.[81] Workers and employers are specially defined.[82] A trade union is not an incorporated body by statute.[83] A union may sue or be sued in its own name and any judgment is enforceable against any property that is held in trust for its benefit. In so far as unions are entitled to protection from certain delictual actions, these have to have been authorised or endorsed under the legislation, which sets out which officials and committees are effective for this purpose.[84] In relation to certain heads of liability, there are fixed limits on the extent of liability.[85] Trade unions are liable for any negligence, nuisance or breach of duty resulting in personal injury to any person or from any breach of duty imposed in connection with the ownership, occupation, possession, control or use of property, without the protection of the statutory limitation.[86] Unions cannot sue for defamation.[87]

There is a general immunity in respect of "an act done by a person" in respect of acts done "in contemplation or furtherance of a trade dispute." There is protection against an action based on inducing a breach of contract or interfering (or inducing another to interfere) with its performance[88]; and where there is a threat that a contract (whether or not the threatener is a party to it) will be broken or its performance interfered with or that the threatener will induce another to break or interfere with a contract.[89] An agreement between two or more persons to do or procure the doing of any act in contemplation or furtherance of a trade dispute, if the act is one which, if done without any such agreement, would not be actionable, is protected.[90]

For all of these immunities to apply, the acts must be in contemplation or furtherance[91] of a trade dispute. This is defined in the Trade Union and Labour Relations (Consolidation) Act 1992. The dispute must be between workers and their employers (not with other workers), which relates wholly or mainly to and not just connected with, one or more of the following statutory factors: (a)

---

[81] Trade Union and Labour Relations (Consolidation) Act 1992, s.1.

[82] ss.30, 295, 296.

[83] s.10(1).

[84] TULRCA, s.20(2).

[85] TULRCA, s.22. The Union funds are protected from enforcement by s.23.

[86] Employment Act 1982, s.15.

[87] *EETPU v Times Newspapers Ltd* [1980] Q.B. 585.

[88] s.219(1)(a).

[89] s.219(1)(b).

[90] s.219(2).

[91] *Milligan v Ayr Harbour Trustees*, 1915 S.C. 937.

terms and conditions of employment, or the physical conditions in which any workers are required to work; (b) engagement or non-engagement, termination or suspension of employment, or the duties of employment of one or more workers; allocation of work or the duties of employment as between workers or groups of workers; (d) matters of discipline; (e) the membership or non-membership of a trade union on the part of a worker; (f) facilities for officials of trade unions; and (g) machinery for negotiation or consultation, and other procedures, relating to any of the foregoing matters, including the recognition by employers or employers' association of the right of a trade union to represent workers in any such negotiation or consultation or in the carrying out of such procedures.

In *Square Grip Reinforcement Co. v MacDonald*,[92] officials and **23–22** members of the union attended building sites where contractors known to be customers of the company were operating and induced workers there to refuse to offload lorries carrying materials supplied by the company, and to threaten that if the lorries were offloaded all the workers on the site who were members of the union would cease work. The customers were forced to refuse to take delivery of the company's materials, and so to break their contracts with the company. It was held that there was a "trade dispute". The conduct, which was an inducement to break a commercial contract, was not protected by the legislation. There are many English cases.[93] A political protest is not a trade dispute.[94]

Picketing is expressly declared to be lawful,[95] and often it would be anyway. On occasion, the protection is needed where the conduct constitutes perhaps a trespass or a nuisance.[96] The following conditions must be met — the picket must be at or near his place of work (unless a union official) and be there for the purpose only of peacefully obtaining or communicating information, or peacefully persuading any person to work or abstain from working.[97]

---

[92] (OH) 1968 S.L.T. 65. A case under the earlier Trade Disputes Act 1906 and Trade Disputes Act 1965.

[93] See Craig and Miller, *Employment Law in Scotland*, Ch.11. see the English Court of Appeal Decision in *Unison v Westminster City Council*, 2001 T.L.R. 263. This was a dispute over privatisation of council services. The case shows that it is important to show the practical importance of the issue to actual persons employed as opposed to being about high minded disputes about public policy.

[94] *Mercury Communication Ltd v Scott-Garner* [1983] I.C.R. 74 and the *Post Office Engineering Union* [1984] Ch. 37. See also *Express Newspapers Ltd v McShane* [1980] A.C. 672; *Duport Steels Ltd v Sirs* [1980] 1 W.L.R. 142; *Dimbleby & Sons Ltd v NUJ* [1984] 1 W.L.R. 427.

[95] TULCRA, s.219(3).

[96] See *Thomas v N.U.M (South Wales Area)* [1985] 2 W.L.R. 1081.

[97] See *Timex Electronic Corporation v Amalgamated Engineering Union*, The Scotsman, April 14, 1993.

"Secondary action", *i.e.* action taken against someone not a party to the dispute will not, generally, attract the immunity.[98]

The immunity has been restricted in respect of interference with contracts to contracts of employment only. Interference with other contracts is not protected in this way as, for example, a charter-party.[99] Secondary action is permitted only to attack the supply of goods between the employer in dispute and the employer of workers who are supplying goods.

The Trade Union Act 1984 made it necessary to hold a secret ballot before taking certain strike action that would require the immunity as a defence against the delict of interference in contract. The protections of section 219(1) and (2) is lost by virtue of section 226 where there is not the support of a ballot according to the rules.[1]

The Life Cycle[2]

The Nasciturus Doctrine

23–23   Birth is an obvious stage at which a bright line might be drawn. A person is certainly a person when alive out from the womb, whether naturally or untimely plucked. It is all the time prior to birth which is difficult for political, religious and moral reasons. For those reasons, it is best not to be coy in this text and say that there are at least two very strong views that have been dominant for some time: the one, that human life begins at conception; and the other, that life begins at some later stage.[3] Scotland has no statutory regime expressly covering litigation by or for things not yet born.[4] The

---

[98] See *Star Offshore Services plc v National Union of Seamen*, 1988 S.L.T. 836
[99] *Merkur Island Shipping Co. v Laughton* [1983] A.C. 570.
[1] The provisions have been amended by the Trade Union Reform and Employment Rights Act 1993 and the Employment Relations Act 1999.
[2] A mode of exposition suggested and used by Edwards and Griffiths, *Family Law* (W. Green, 1997). The cycle chosen here will be objectionable to those who do not consider marriage or parenting part of the cycle, although this text is probably on safe ground, even in a post-modern era in accepting birth and death as extreme nodes on the cycle. It is fair to say that many of the issues decided by the courts, sometimes decided on a purely juridical or jural basis, involve ethical and moral issues. At the time of writing it is thought that generally such issues are best left to the legislature or the Law Commission where broader views may be canvassed.
[3] That difference in belief or view or analysis became very focused in the U.K. by the decriminalisation of some forms of abortion by the Abortion Act 1967. The Act lays down an arbitrary line for potential abortion. Many of the points discussed today were canvassed in D. Bogie, "Personality in relation to the Law of Abortion", 1967 S.L.T. (News) 145. He points out that for the stoics and Baron Hume, the foetus was *pars ventris* or *portio viscerum* or *pars viscerum matris*.
[4] Foetus is the term most normally used in legal discussions but strictly speaking denotes the three to nine month period after conception, before which the term denoted by the scientist is embryo.

Scottish Law Commission[5] did not consider it necessary to legislate, considering that Scots law would permit recovery if the thing became a child. The English legislated.[6] The basis of the Scottish Law Commission's view that no legislation was required was the *nascituri* doctrine often discussed in such cases. The maxim or brocard is *nasciturus pro iam nato habetur quotiens de eius commodo agitur.* The doctrine is set out in Bankton as follows:

> "A child in the mother's womb is esteem'd as already born, in all things that concern its own interest, but is not reckoned among children in relation to questions to the advantage of parents from a certain number of children. By our law, rights may be granted in favour of children *nascituri* of any particular person, tho' not begotten at the time, and upon their existence they are entitled thereto, in the same manner as if they had been born at the date of the rights."[7]

The doctrine had already received judicial approval in a succession case.[8] The Scottish Law Commission's position was criticised at the time.[9]

The foetus's right to continued incubation in the womb

In *Kelly v Kelly*,[10] a husband sought to interdict his wife from **23–24** aborting their foetus.[11] It was accepted that interdict would be available to a person's representative to prevent damage being caused to that person if it would result in an award of damages. If abortion had been an actionable wrong, the father could have sued. However, because the foetus itself had no right to continued existence while in the womb, it could not be represented as a matter

---

[5] Liability for Antenatal Injuries, (Scot. Law. Com. No.30 (1973)).

[6] Congenital Disabilities (Civil Liability) Act 1976. This was after the report of the English Law Commission Report on Injuries to Unborn Children (Law Com. No.60 (1974)).

[7] I, i, 7.

[8] *Elliot v Joicey*, 1935 S.C. (HL) 57 at 70, *per* Lord Macmillan. The Canadian case of *Montreal Tramways v Leveille* [1933] 4 D.L.R. 337 is often cited. See also *Reid's Trustees v Dashwood*, 1929 S.L.T. 619; *Allan's Trs v Allan*, 1949 S.L.T. (Notes) 3; *Cox's Trs v Pegg*, 1950 S.L.T. 127. In *Dunbar of Kilconzie, Petr*, 1986 S.L.T. 463 the House of Lords refused to extend the doctrine in a rather esoteric and unprecedented heraldry case.

[9] A. Rodger, "Antenatal injury", 1974 J.R. 83.

[10] 1997 S.L.T. 896. E. Robertson, "Consider the Foetus", 1997 S.L.T. (News) 319. E.J. Russell, "Abortion Law in Scotland and the Kelly Foetus", 1997 S.L.T. (News) 187.

[11] *ibid.*, at 897: "from instructing, consenting or submitting to a termination of pregnancy' ". Interdict was also sought against those who would have actually carried out the act.

of law.[12] The question was considered to be one of law and not of policy.[13] On the legal point, all that was said was that there had been no authority adduced for protection. Nonetheless, the court then went on to consider other matters in, what it is submitted was an inadequate degree of detail.[14] To protect the foetus might cause problems with the "right" to terminate a pregnancy, according to the Act. It might be suggested *contra* that the law should balance the interests identified rather than ruling one out altogether, although in most cases the decision would favour the mother, particularly because under the United Kingdom abortion legislation, the health of the woman is one of the key grounds for termination. Another point was that if abortion could be interdicted then so could other harmful acts like smoking or certain sports. This seems an obvious point but, even if there were a right, it would hardly be enforced on the point of a mother playing a game of squash. It is, however, harder to make the point to the extent of allowing intravenous drug use, or worse the use of a drug known to produce a serious birth defect. The difficulty is in agreeing that this is a necessary legal or jural result, rather than a policy decision. Statute is often seen as superimposed on the common law, and if that were applied here it is clear that if the law takes any view it is against termination.[15] From a title to sue point of view, it should be noted that *Kelly* was at the instance of the father, in England wardship was attempted and it is no doubt possible that some other person may be thought to have some jurisdiction in these matters. This is an important point because the woman's "right to terminate", even if protection of a foetus were possible, could not be vindicated by the public at large or a section of it, such as anti-abortion activists.

A person, born alive, injured while a foetus

23–25   Moving on from the right, which the foetus does not have, to remain in the womb or be allowed to be born in due course, to cases where there is injury to the foetus, the law has settled. Many of the cases are decided against the background of the Damages (Scotland) Act 1976. Section 1(1) provides that where a person dies in consequence of personal injuries sustained by him as a result of an

---

[12] *ibid.*, at 901. The decision in *Hamilton v Fife Health Board*, 1993 S.L.T. 624 discussed below at para.2–10 was influential in the overall approach to the legal point. Reference was made to a number of English and Commonwealth authorities. See, *inter alia*, *Paton v British Pregnancy Advisory Service* [1979] 1 Q.B. 276; *B v Islington Health Authority* [1991] 1 Q.B. 638; *Borowski v Att. Gen for Canada* (1987) 39 D.L.R. (4th) 731; *F (in utero)* [1988] 2 W.L.R. 1288; *Dehler v Ottawa Civic Hospital* (1979) 101 D.L.R. (3d) 686.

[13] *Kelly* at 901C.

[14] *Kelly* at 901F.

[15] As the court accepted under reference to Gordon, Criminal Law (2nd ed. W Green), para.28–01.

act or omission of another person, then the person responsible for that death will also be liable to pay damages to any relative of the deceased as long as the person responsible would have been liable to pay. The law is considered in detail in *Cohen v Shaw*.[16] The pursuer claimed, *inter alia*, for damages on behalf of a child born alive after the death of its father. Lord Cullen allowed a jury trial. He accepted that the *nascituri* doctrine could apply unless it were excluded by statute. The 1976 Act did not exclude it.[17] The definition of relative in Schedule 1, paragraph 1(b) includes a person who "was" a child of the deceased. Lord Cullen took this to mean that the focus was on the time of the death, in which case the claimant would not have been a child.[18] It has to be asked again whether this is truly a decision of juristic necessity or a policy decision.

Parents' claim for the death of person injured while a foetus

The law was extensively canvassed in *Hamilton v Fife Health Board*.[19] A child died three days after birth. The parents alleged it was due to fault. They were parents of the deceased in terms of the Damages (Scotland) Act 1976. However, the claims being based on statute, the other requirements had to be met. The important point of interpretation was that the Act applies "where a person dies in consequence of injuries sustained by him." Lord Prosser held that this was not satisfied. His view was that the injuries were not "sustained" by the child but by the foetus.[20] It was accepted by the pursuers that prior to being born a "child" is not a person. It was accepted by the defenders that the *nascituri* principle is recognised in Scotland, subject to the limitation that the fiction operates "only for the purpose of enabling the child to take a benefit to which, if born it would be entitled" and cannot be invoked in the interests of any third party. On a close reading of the Act, Lord Prosser concluded that Parliament had not intended a foetus to be a person capable of sustaining personal injuries. In addition, he held the section to be unambiguous and that it did not accordingly require to be interpreted according to the mischief rule. In any event, he could see no mischief

23–26

---

[16] 1992 S.L.T. 1022.

[17] This decision consolidates the Law Commission view. It is also supported by earlier cases which made such awards but without discussion. *Moorcraft v W. Alexander & Sons*, 1946 S.C. 466; *Leadbetter v N.C.B.*, 1952 S.C. 19; *Riddell v James Longmuir & Sons Ltd*, 1971 S.L.T. (Notes) 33. Professor Norrie argued that it may not have been necessary to apply the fiction at all. K. McK. Norrie, "Liability for injuries caused before birth", 1992 S.L.T. (News) 65, especially at 66.

[18] Norrie's argument appears to be that the word "was" is not indicating a *punctum temporis* but rather is required grammatically to reflect the fact that the father is dead.

[19] 1992 S.L.T. 1026; 1993 S.L.T. 624 (IH).

[20] Norrie objected to this decision on the basis that a foetus, not being a legal person, cannot sustain injuries, n.43 at p.67.

being cured by the Act. This, perhaps unlike *Kelly*, is indeed a juristic approach and one entirely justified because the Damages (Scotland) Act 1976 was intended to be a statement of who could sue in respect of fatal injuries. Shortly afterwards, the first instance hearing of *Hamilton, McWilliams v Lord Advocate*[21] was decided. In this case, the defender founded on *Hamilton*, and sought dismissal. Lord Morton of Shuna considered that the section had to be interpreted in the context of the whole section. Furthermore, he considered there was precedent for considering the Report of the Scottish Law Commission.[22] In accepting and adopting a large passage from the Law Commission Report, Lord Morton considered that the 1976 Act could not have intended to change the law, which was that in principle Scots law would allow the claim, without need to refer to the *nasciturus* fiction.

The conflict was resolved when the Inner House reversed *Hamilton* on appeal. Injuries caused to a foetus are personal injuries and "properly and sensibly" described as "personal injuries" even although when inflicted the "victim" did not enjoy legal personality. "To suppose that only one who enjoys legal personality can sustain 'personal injuries' is to attach an artificial legal meaning to the adjective 'personal' in s.1(1)."[23] The court stated that the case depended not on a fiction, but on the neighbour doctrine of *Donoghue*. This does however beg the question because there is no neighbour until the foetus is born alive. While the effect of the decision may well be generally acceptable, it remains the case that the reasoning is not sufficiently convincing to prevent further argument in different cases raising the same policy issues.

Parents claim for the birth of a healthy child

23–27   This subheading might mislead. As Mason has helpfully pointed out, the cases can be subdivided and approached in different ways.[24] There are cases where a pregnancy was wanted and cases where one was not. Across that divide there are cases where there are healthy children born and where disabled children are born.

The issue in this section is that of the birth of a healthy child that the parents had relied upon the defenders to prevent thus incurring cost. It is fair to say that such cases can be treated and are properly treated under discussions of negligence. In this text they are treated here because with a House of Lords ruling on the point, the issue becomes very like title to sue. That said, this is one of these party/

---

[21] 1992 S.L.T. 1045.

[22] See generally on this topic G. Maher, "Statutory Interpretation and Scottish Law Commission Reports", 1992 S.L.T. (News) 277.

[23] 1993 S.L.T. 624 (IH), *per* Lord McCluskey at 629.

[24] J.K. Mason "Wrongful Pregnancy, Wrongful Birth and Wrongful Terminology," (2002) 6 Edin. L.R. 46.

title to sue issues that can be at home in a discussion of general negligence. Early on it seemed obvious. In *Allan v Greater Glasgow Health Board*,[25] Lord Cameron had opined that such a claim was justiciable and could result in damages. In doing so, he followed the path of English decisions.[26] This seemed a secure position.[27]

It was sought to settle the position in *McFarlane v Tayside Health Board*,[28] which must, despite many doubts and arguments, be taken as the law. The case arose from an unwanted pregnancy that resulted from an error by the consultant surgeon who had informed the pursuer that "your sperm counts are now negative and you may dispense with contraceptive precautions". At first instance, Lord Gill decided that such a claim must fail. He excluded the pain and suffering caused by the pregnancy itself as a head of claim as it is outweighed by the benefit of bringing a life into the world. Lord Gill took a firm view that the birth of a healthy child was simply not actionable. It was not a personal injury. In any event, it was such a good thing that it could not be measured in damages as a bad thing happening.[29] On reclaiming, the decision was reversed.[30]

In the House of Lords, for Lord Slynn the case was one of **23–28** economic loss notwithstanding that it arose from what he held to be an actionable pregnancy. The doctors did not assume responsibility for this economic loss. People who want to do that should recover by an appropriate contract. Lord Steyn's speech is one of the most radical in respect of delict theory in a century. He based his decision on distributive justice although he would have, if required, dismissed the claim on the basis of the fair, just and reasonable text in economic loss. Lord Hope accepted most of the key points for the pursuer. Patients are entitled to expect reasonable care and pregnancy through

---

[25] November 25, 1993.

[26] *Emeh v Kensington, Chelsea and Westminster Area Health Authority* [1985] 1 Q.B. 1012; *Thake v Maurice* [1986] 1 Q.B. 644; *Allen v Bloomsbury Health Authority* [1993] 1 All E.R. 651. *Jones v Lanarkshire Health Board*, 1990 S.L.T. 19 seems to be a similar case although as it was a procedural decision the fundamentals are not discussed in the report.

[27] See A. Stewart, "Damages for Birth of a Child" (1995) J.L.S. 298 and the sequel after the Outer House decision A. Stewart, "Live Issue — Damages for Wrongful Birth" (1996) J.L.S. 443. L. Sutherland, "Damages for the Birth of a Healthy Child", Rep. B. 14–3. For trenchant, reasoned criticism of the decision see J.K. Mason, "Unwanted pregnancy: a case of retroversion?" (2000) 4 Edin. L.R. 191, J.K. Mason "Wrongful Pregnancy, Wrongful Birth and Wrongful Terminology," (2002) 6 Edin. L.R. 46. See also J.A. Devereux, "Actions for Wrongful Birth" (1996) Tort L. Rev. 107.

[28] 2000 S.C. (HL) 1.

[29] See for support abroad, T. Weir, "The Unwanted Child" (2002) 6 Edin. L.R. 244.

[30] *McFarlane v Tayside Health Board*, 1998 S.C.L.R. 126. *Anderson v Forth Valley Health Board*, 1998 S.C.L.R. 97 decided before the reclaiming motion in *McFarlane* but reported after *McFarlane* was decided, is to the same effect as the successful Inner House decision.

natural methods can be an injury or a wrong and contraception is a legitimate aspect of freedom of choice. This meant that the claim for *solatium* for having the child and the financial loss while having the child were valid. However, the costs of raising the child could not be recovered as being an economic loss. It was not fair, just or reasonable to impose liability for these costs. Lord Clyde expressed his opinion as being based on remoteness of damage rather than duty or no duty. The case was soon applied in the Court of Appeal to disallow a claim by woman for, *inter alia*, the loss of post-natal earnings.[31] However, that was not the end of the matter. The trenchant criticism of the case and the fact that it had not been followed in the Commonwealth mean that sooner than usual it came up for reconsideration before a seven-member House of Lords. In *Rees v Darlington Memorial Hospital Trust*,[32] the case was a "factual varient" of *McFarlane*. A disabled mother was sterilised because it would be harder for her to care for a child. It failed and she had a healthy child. The case failed on a 4:3 vote. To an extent, the House did not want to be seen to be changing the law according to the personnel of the court every few years. It shows just what a difficult issue this is. It does suggest that there is no simple juridical solution and that the legislature on the advice of the Law Commissions might be the best way forward. The House behaved in a legislature like way of granting a new award — a conventional award of damages — for the wrong done, which was not to be seen as compensatory.

It is interesting to note, perhaps in support of (or sympathy for) this extremely pragmatic approach that in *Cattanach v Melchior*,[33] the High Court of Australia did not follow *McFarlane* although by a 4:3 majority. So, clearly, it is one of these issues that is not truly juridical but reflects views on peoples rights to plan their families and the view of others on the general worth of human life and no doubt other fundamental philosophical or moral views. What is additionally interesting is that the pragmatic award arrived at by the House of Lords is in a way reflected by the situation in Australia where as a result of the pro-plaintiff decision, two states, Queensland and New South Wales, have started to legislate to abolish the claim the court allowed, while allowing it for case of disabled children!

---

[31] *Greenfield v Irwin*, [2001] 1W.L.R. 1279. *McFarlane* was not followed the Court of Appeal in Queensland. See generally L. Sutherland, "Update — Medical Negligence (post-MacFarlane decisions)," 2001 39 Rep. B. 3; M. Bickford-Smith, "Damages for Failed Sterilisation," [2001] J.P.I.L. 404, J.K. Mason "Wrongful Pregnancy, Wrongful Birth and Wrongful Terminology," (2002) 6 Edin. L.R. 46.

[32] [2003] T.L.R. 568.

[33] High Court of Australia, July 16, 2003.

Parents' claim for the birth of an abnormally expensive child

If a child is born alive and, through lack of care, disabled, and thus **23–29** different from the way it would have been born but for the carelessness, it seems obvious that it will, over its life, be much more expensive to raise.

As a result of *McFarlane*, it has been held by a majority in *McLelland v Greater Glasgow Health Board*[34] in the Inner House that the *extra* costs of the disablement are recoverable where the fault was in not detecting it and allowing a termination, but following *McFarlane*, the basic costs of maintenance cannot be recovered. This case was one of a wanted child and not a completely unwanted child.[35] It is submitted that it is important to see this case with its powerful dissent and to read it against the background that Lord Marnoch, in this case on the evidence that the parents agreed they got pleasure from the child, was compelled to follow *McFarlane*.

A person's claim for having been wrongfully allowed to be born

Another question is the action of a child born in some way **23–30** different from the norm to claim in its own right for damages for a wrongdoing, such as the failure of the medical practitioner to advise or advise in sufficient time for the parents to consider deciding to seek a legal abortion. The difficulty is expressed by Norrie: "there have been times when we all were, in fact, non-existent but we have never experienced that state."[36] Causation is another important issue, but that is not a matter of title to sue. Norrie's conclusion that "a child's action based upon the denial of a 'right' to have had its life prevented has, and ought to have, no chance of success," is sound. The issue was tested in *P's C.B. v CICB.*[37] A child was born, it was alleged, as a result of an incestuous rape by her maternal grandfather on her mother. She was born with severe congenital mental and physical abnormalities. Her curator bonis applied for a payment from the CICB.[38] The Board refused the claim and the curator bonis applied for judicial review. The legal background to the claim was the statutory phrase "personal injuries". Nonetheless, the case is valuable for a wide-ranging examination of cases from Scotland,

---

[34] 2001 S.L.T. 446, the case had to be continued to hear argument on *McFarlane*.

[35] See J.K. Mason "Wrongful Pregnancy, Wrongful Birth and Wrongful Terminology," (2002) 6 Edin. L.R. 46 which probably went to press before the Inner House decision in *McLelland* and the English cases considered therein. It is not unlikely this issue will find itself back in the House of Lords.

[36] K. McK. Norrie, "Wrongful Life in Scots Law: No Right, No Remedy", 1990 J.R. 217; C.J. Grainger, "Wrongful Life: A wrong without a remedy" (1994) 1 Tort L. Rev. 164.

[37] 1997 S.L.T. 1180.

[38] The Criminal Injuries Compensation Board, now replaced by the Criminal Injuries Compensation Authority.

England, the Commonwealth and the United States.[39] Lord Osborne's decision is expressed in terms such that it is reasonable to say that the ratio might be wider than the narrow point of interpretation of the scheme. He essentially agreed that a definition of injury depends upon a "pre-injury state which is capable of assessment and comparison with the post-injury state."[40] In the case before him, it was clear that the child had not and could not have had any life other than "a defective state".[41]

Children

23–31   The foetus, which after these many hazards, is born becomes a child and thus entitled to all the protections due to a human being. People who are not adults are nowadays called children in many statutory contexts. However, that word has many different connotations and statutory inflexions. The law of delict was not altered by the Age of Legal Capacity (Scotland) Act 1991, so technically there is still a difference between pupils — boys under 14 and girls under 12; and minors — non-pupils under 18.[42] It is submitted that a pupil may be liable in civil law for his or her own delicts in Scotland, but probably subject to a minimum age of seven.[43] The basis for this distinction is the civilian distinction within "pupils", that of the *infans*.[44] Thus an *infans* will not be liable but an older pupil will be. The rationale might be if the *infans* cannot speak it cannot concoct a crime or delict. However, since the advent of negligence, it is not necessary to have an intention to harm, so it might be said that there can be liability. However, as there is often no liability for a pure omission, the *infans* must still be held to have known or that it should have known the consequences of its conduct. It should have reasonably foreseen something. It is submitted this cannot hold as a basis of distinction. Either the *infans* is liable for intention and negligence, or neither. The argument becomes complicated by the issue of contributory negligence because children are forever being injured. But this is mere verisimilitude.

---

[39] See the position in France described in T. Weir, "The Unwanted Child" (2002) 6 Edin. L.R. 244. Judicially a claim was allowed only to be reversed by legislation.

[40] *P.'s C.B.*, 1997 S.L.T. 1180 at 1199.

[41] *ibid.*

[42] s.1(3)(c).

[43] *Somerville v Hamilton* (1541) Mor. 8905. W.J. Stewart, "A Note on the Liability of Pupils in Delict", 1989 S.L.T. (News) 404.

[44] See for example the German Civil Code: 828. A person who has not completed his seventh year of age is not responsible for any damage which he does to another. A person who has completed his seventh but not his eighteenth year of age is not responsible for any damage which he does to another, if at the time of committing the damaging act he did not have the understanding necessary to realise his responsibility. The same applies to a deaf mute.

The Age of Legal Capacity (Scotland) Act 1991 did not intend to change the legal position of children so far as liability in delict is concerned. It has, however, introduced a regime governing, *inter alia*, reparation litigation. Children aged 16 or over can give consent to medical treatment.[45] Children under 16 can consent to a procedure or treatment so long as the doctor considers the child can understand the nature and consequences of the treatment. Non-therapeutic research is excluded. The Act governs the bringing or defending of or taking any step in civil proceedings.[46] If 16 or over, the minor can proceed without a curator *ad litem*. A minor needs the concurrence of their guardian. The right of a minor to set aside transactions does not apply to civil proceedings,[47] although discharges granted can be set aside until the minor reaches 21. It is possible to apply to the sheriff by way of summary application asking the court to ratify the settlement in which case it cannot be set aside. It is submitted that this position is not satisfactory. Too much can go on in the course of a litigation to prejudice the minor — an example being the deletion of some aspect of the case or the decision not to call evidence in support of it in which case it would be lost. All that can be said is that in the court process there is a lawyer who, although probably brought into the case by the parents, must look after the interests of the minor. The Children (Scotland) Act 1995 gave effect to the international desire to protect the rights of children. A person under the age of 16 has legal capacity to instruct a solicitor in connection with any civil matter where that person has a general understanding of what it means to do so and a person of 12 or older is presumed to have that general understanding.[48] Such a person has legal capacity to sue in civil proceedings.[49] There are procedural rules concerning the payment of damages to children under the Children (Scotland) Act 1995.[50]

Cohabitation

There are different views on cohabitation. Some see it as a shadow **23–32** of a real marriage; others see it as a deliberate alternative. The latter seems the correct view, especially in a system that recognises an irregular marriage. That said, the existing irregular marriage by habit and repute is difficult to establish. Were that to be relaxed, then it would be much easier to define cohabitation. As it is, many people

---

[45] s.1(1)(b).
[46] s.9.
[47] s.3(3)(d).
[48] s.2(4A) of the 1991 Act inserted by the 1995 Act.
[49] s.2(4B).
[50] s.13. See D. Kinloch and C. McEachran, "Damages for Children — some reflections" 2003 (51) Rep. B. 2 considering issues such as publicity and the appointment of judicial factors.

cohabit not because they make an intelligent choice so to do, but out of habit and circumstance. Partially in recognition of that, the legal system now makes allowance in reparation for persons who are not married.

Homosexual relationships

23–33   Recently decriminalised in stages, the law is moving, under the influence of the ECHR, to a state of recognition of such relationships, as far as title to sue is concerned. Although that has not yet happened it is wise to be aware of the trend lest within the time bar period and subject to whatever transitional provisions appear, a client may in the future have a case.[51]

Married people

23–34   The child may in due course marry another person. Marriage, to this day, constitutes a change in the status of a person. Historically, women were disadvantaged in delict cases. The nineteenth and twentieth centuries saw the legal regime changing with the political and social "emancipation" of women.[52] Some important changes have only come about towards the end of the century. A married woman in minority is not under the curatory of her husband.[53] A spouse is not liable for the act or omission of the other unless on a basis other than marriage, such as agency, employment or as a joint wrongdoer. The Law Reform (Husband and Wife) Act 1962, section 2 removed the difficulties that formerly existed from the doctrine of the common law, that husband and wife were one person, which prevented them suing each other.[54] The court may still exercise a discretion to dismiss an action if it is shown that no substantial benefit would accrue to either party if the action continued.[55] A spouse may be able to claim losses of the nature of personal services sustained by the other spouse, in a claim of their own.[56] A spouse suffering the loss has no title to sue.[57] So, if a wife is injured in a car

---

[51] See Scot. Law Com. 2002 No.120.

[52] Married Women's Property (Scotland) Act 1881; Married Women's Property (Scotland) Act 1920.

[53] Law Reform (Husband and Wife) Act 1984, s.3.

[54] See *Harper v Harper*, 1929 S.L.T. 187; *Gormanley v Evening Citizen Ltd*, 1962 S.L.T. (Sh. Ct) 61; *Bush v Belling*, 1963 S.L.T. (Notes) 69.

[55] The Scottish Law Commission recommended this last anomaly be removed: Scot. Law Com. No.135, paras 10–1 — 10–8. It has gone in England: Civil Procedure (Modification of Enactments) Order 1998 (SI 1998 /2940) para.4.

[56] Administration of Justice Act 1982, ss.7–9.

[57] s.8(2) and (4).

accident, a claim may be made in the wife's action for the cost to her husband of paying for a housekeeper.[58] A spouse has no title to sue for the enticement[59] of the other spouse.[60]

In the law of damages, there have been two decisions, one in an English[61] case and one in a Scottish case, which have practical effects in many ordinary cases. In the Scottish case, *Kozikowska v Kozikowski*,[62] the case turned on the terms of the Administration of Justice Act 1982, section 8 which provides that a person who has sustained personal injuries may recover from the wrongdoer damages representing reasonable remuneration for any necessary services rendered to the injured person by a relative as a consequence of the injury. The injured person has a duty to account to the relative for damages recovered on this ground. In *Kozikowska*, a wife sued her husband and a roads authority for damages in respect of injuries suffered when her husband's car skidded on an icy road. The wife's claim included a claim for necessary services rendered to her by her husband and by their children. Lord Coulsfield, following the English case, held that it was incompetent for the wife to recover from her husband remuneration in respect of his own services.

Parents

Parents are not as such liable for the delicts of their children.[63] **23–35** They can, however, be vicariously liable or liable themselves for putting an inadequate person in charge of dangerous things.[64] An averment that the driver of a car was the defender's 19-year-old son was irrelevant absent "employment" or that the son was an improper or inadequate driver.[65] Issues were allowed on an allegation of

---

[58] See Ch.26.

[59] See *Stedman v Stedman* (1744) Mor. 13909.

[60] Law Reform (Husband and Wife) Act 1984, s.2(2).

[61] *Hunt v Severs* [1994] 2 A.C. 350.

[62] 1996 S.L.T. 386.

[63] *Davie v Wilson* (1854) 16 D. 956; *Mckay v McLean*, 1920 1 S.L.T. 34. Compare the position under the German Civil Code: 832 "A person who is bound by law to exercise supervision over a person on account of minority, or of his mental or physical condition, is bound to make compensation for any damage which the latter unlawfully does to a third party." The duty to compensate does not arise if he fulfils his duty of supervision, or if the damage would have occurred notwithstanding the proper exercise of supervision. The same responsibility attaches to a person who takes over by contract the exercise of supervision. Thus the parents of a seven-year-old child who got hold of easily available matches were liable, although not the parents of a 15-year-old playing football. Markesinis, *The German Law of Torts*, p.662.

[64] See Ch.24.

[65] *Mckay v McLean*, 1920 1 S.L.T. 34.

putting a 14-year-old in charge of a horse of which it was said he was incapable of handling.[66] Parents can sue children just as children can sue their parents.[67] Parents and children are "relatives" for the purposes of the Administration of Justice Act 1982 and in terms of the Damages (Scotland) Act 1976

The terminally ill

23–36 The terminally ill are as entitled to the protection of the law as all others. Cases arise where out of duty or affection, it is sought to bring to an end the life of a person who is in distress. Much like the foetus cases, these cases raise moral, ethical, religious, political and economic questions. In considering euthanasia there is a symmetry with abortion, which has now legalised what was killing. So much depends on point of view: abortion seems on one view to be much more controversial because the abortee has no voice and never had one, as opposed to euthanasia where a view can have been expressed in the past; on another view, the abortion case is easier because the foetus must be disposed of according to the woman's right to choose. The delict system is involved because there is likely to be sought either a declarator that to take a certain course is not a legal wrong or an interdict to prevent certain steps. The party to the action may therefore be a relative or a doctor seeking declarator or a relative or other seeking an interdict. The wrong in question, of course, need not be a pure delict. For interdict or declarator, "wrong" is enough. However, if neither procedure were followed, then a claim for compensation for the euthanasia of relative would be a case of reparation, if it has not already attracted the criminal law.

The leading case in Scotland is a decision of a five-bench court in *Law Hospital NHS Trust v Lord Advocate*.[68] Janet Johnstone, suffered from irreversible damage to the cerebral cortex and had been in a persistent vegetative state in the hospital since 1992. She had no prospect of recovery and was unable to give a valid consent. She remained alive only because feeding and hydration were provided to her artificially and because of the nursing care she received in hospital. Medical experts considered her case hopeless and there were no useful avenues of treatment to explore. The family agreed with the experts that the treatment should stop was in form. The action was in the form of the hospital concluding for declarator that the cessation of treatment was lawful and would not constitute a delict or crime. The Lord Advocate appeared as defender in the

---

[66] *Brown v Fulton* (1881) 9 R. 36.
[67] *Wood v Wood*, 1935 S.L.T. 431.
[68] 1996 S.L.T. 848.

public interest along with the curator *ad litem* to the patient. The main problem in the actual case was jurisdiction, with which this text is not directly concerned. Certainly, the Court of Session confirmed that it had no jurisdiction to say whether or not something was a crime or not. The court had jurisdiction in matters such as this where there was no one to consent and delegated the case to the Lord Ordinary. The leading English case on withdrawal of treatment was followed.[69] For the law of delict, the main point is that made by Lord Clyde. It is no part of a doctor's duty to continue treatment which serves no purpose beyond the artificial prolongation of existence. They would be in no breach of their general duty of care to the patient in discontinuing such treatment in such circumstances and the substance of their continuing duty would be towards securing the comfort and dignity of the patient for the concluding days of the patient's life.[70] That probably represents the present general view of many people. However, where issues like nervous shock and the title to sue of same-sex couples are the subject of Law Commission consideration, it is easy to agree with Lord Milligan that legislation — at least in core cases — might be beneficial.[71]

Dead people

A deceased person's estate can be sued in delict for wrongs **23–37** done.[72] Actions by relatives for wrongs causing death are now governed by the Damages (Scotland) Act 1976.[73] The claim that the

---

[69] *Airedale NHS Trust v Bland* [1993] A.C. 789. *L, Petr,* 1996 S.C.L.R. 538 was approved.

[70] at 861. For a full up-to-date discussion of the issues raised by withdrawal of treatment and euthanasia referring to English authority since *Bland,* see J. Keown, "Beyond Bland: a critique of the BMA guidelines on withholding and withdrawing medical treatment," (2000) 20 L.S. 66, D. Price, "Fairly Bland: an alternative view of a supposed new 'death ethic' and the BMA guidelines," (2001) 4 L.S. 618. The BMA Guidelines (2nd ed.) are published by the BMA, BMJ Books.

[71] at 866.

[72] See, *e.g. Bourhill v Young,* 1942 S.C. (HL) 78. The estate is liable only to the extent of the estate. It is worth mentioning *Thomson v Duggie,* 1949 S.L.T. (Notes) 53 in case anyone else has the same idea. There was a collision between a motor ship called *Resplendent* and another motor ship, *Marinia.* The master of the *Marinia* died suddenly some time after the accident and before action was raised. The owners of *Resplendent* brought an admiralty action in personam against the widow of the master of *Marinia* in which they claimed damages for loss due to the fault of her husband. The pursuers complained that the widow, or her solicitor, had failed to disclose who were the true representatives of the deceased. Lord Birnam dismissed the case.

[73] See Ch.26. There is a Roman law maxim sometimes encountered: *actio personalis moritur cum persona.* It is not of itself of any assistance today. See generally *Bern's Ex. v Montrose Asylum* (1893) 20 R. 859.

person had before they died transmits to a certain extent to the executor, including, now, pain and suffering.[74]

Defamation raises interesting questions because traditionally people take insults upon their kin or clan seriously. In *Broom v Ritchie & Co.*[75] a widow on her own behalf and for her children sought damages for defamation for the publication in the press of a false statement that her late husband had committed suicide.[76] She claimed *solatium* only. The defenders pleaded, *inter alia*, no title to sue. The Lord Ordinary (Kincairney) sustained the plea primarily on the basis of there being no clear principle on which the case was based, and only some very old doubtful authority to support it. The pursuer reclaimed and the court adhered to the Lord Ordinary's judgment. The Lord Justice-Clerk (MacDonald) said that "an aspersion on a person after death cannot, I hold, give right to anyone else to recover damages as for a wrong done to the deceased."[77] However, it was thought that a slander against the character of a deceased person, which by necessary implication injured others, *e.g.* stamping his children as bastards, would be different and would give right in persons to sue for the effect on their status or patrimonial interests.[78] But this case was for *solatium* only.[79] In *Agnew v Laughlan*,[80] the pursuer sought reduction of a sheriff's order under which his now deceased wife had been detained in an asylum, and of certain certificates by medical practitioners. He brought the action both as an individual and as tutor of his son. The sheriff's order was said to be wrongfully obtained and the doctor's certificates were said to be false and inaccurate. The wife had just given birth and died a few days later. After a procedure roll debate held by the Lord Ordinary (MacKintosh) that the pursuer had no title to sue as the document sought to be reduced had long since been spent and inoperative. The action was dismissed. Any prejudice to the pursuer or to his son attaching to the family was too vague and remote to found a patrimonial interest. Any stigma attending to relatives of the deceased because she was put in an asylum was irrelevant. The right to sue for defamation was the deceased's alone and no claim for defamation arises after the death of the defamed.[81]

---

[74] So far as the latter is concerned as a result of reforms in 1993. See Ch.18.

[75] (1904) 6 F. 942.

[76] It being remembered that then, much more so than now, suicide carried a stigma and indeed was a crime in England.

[77] Broom, *op. cit.* at 945.

[78] Bastardy as a status no longer exists in Scotland.

[79] Note that Lord Young agreed with the result but not with the reasoning of the Lord Ordinary or the other judges of the Division. He thought the claim irrelevant on the facts.

[80] 1948 S.L.T. 512.

[81] A rule retained when the law was reformed by the Damages (Scotland) Act 1993.

Human material and body parts[82]

Dealing first with the body of the deceased, this should be viewed **23–38** as a matter of the law of property. That is why it is legitimately a title to sue matter in a delict case for say wrongful intromission or spuilzie of the corpse. The dead person's body is, of course, no longer his. Interference with it is probably wrongful unless authorised by the next of kin who themselves probably only have the body for disposal and cannot, for example, sell it.[83]

Families in particular often have views as to what should or should not happen to parts after death as to individuals in life. Any action for wrongful use of parts is restrained by the permissions in the present legislation. The law is to be found in the Human Tissue Act 1961 as amended by the Anatomy Act 1984 and the Corneal Tissue Act 1986. Broadly, these permit in life donations for certain purposes that are to be given effect to by the person "lawfully in charge of the body".

---

[82] See generally, L. Skene, "Proprietary Rights in human bodies, body parts and tissue: regulatory contexts and proposals for new laws" (2002) 22 L.S. 102. Skene reports that "body parts" was defined for the purposes of the interim report of the Inquiry into the management and care of children receiving complex heart surgery, to include tissue, organs and parts of organs and amputated limbs. Skene thinks it best to keep tissue preserved in glass slides as a separate concept. At 102 n.1. Brownsword reports that The Council of Europe, Convention for the Protection of Human Rights and Dignity of the Human Being with regard to the application of Biology and Medicine: Convention on Human Rights and Biomedicien (DIR/JU (96) 14) (Strasbourg, Directorate of Legal Affairs, November 1996) defines body parts as including "organs and tissues proper, including blood," but excluding "hair and nails, which are discarded tissues, and the sale of which is not an affront to human dignity." R. Brownsword, "Freedom of Contract, Human Rights and Human Dignity," in Friedman and Barak-Erez, *Human Rights in Private Law*, Hart 2001 p.190.

[83] *Pollack v Workman* (1900) 2 F 354. Recently in England an artist who stole old body parts from the Royal College of Surgeons to draw them was convicted of theft: *R v Kelly*, [1998] 3 All E.R. 741. See, however, the McLean report, Independent Review Group on the Retention of Organs at Post-Mortem in Scotland: "para 113 Can human tissue be sold or otherwise transferred to the ownership of another in Scots law? In principle, there is no reason why it may not — always provided that it is not an organ. No Scottish court has ruled on the question of whether human tissue can or cannot be owned, although Roman law (which has considerably influenced Scots law) suggests that it cannot be. There is no authority to the contrary in any institutional writings of Scots law. If human tissue is a res (a thing), then it can only be excluded from the normal civil law rules if it is deemed to be extra commercium. A court might declare human tissue to be extra commercium on grounds of principle, but that would have the result of effectively excluding the legal protection of the sale of any medicinal product which was manufactured from human bodily materials, unless the critical factor was not the origin of the materials, but rather the way in which they had been processed or treated." The review Group made extensive recommendations to reform the law: *www.show.nhs.uk/scotorgrev*. See also J.K. Mason and G.T. Laurie, "Consent or property: Dealing with the body and its parts in the shadow of the Bristol and Alder Hey" (2001) Mod. L.R. 710.

There are issues, again initially of the law of property in relation to DNA.[84]

Bringing this section around full circle, there has *reportedly* been a tort action for conversion by a woman of the plaintiff's sperm where he alleged she became intentionally pregnant.[85]

THE MENTALLY ILL

23–39 It all depends what is meant by "insane". A recent case on prescription had to consider the term in relation to the protection from the effects of prescription on an insane pursuer and the discussion therein gives a better view of what is thought to be alienation of reason in current Scots law.[86] Ultimately, the law is likely to look at its own view of the voluntariness of the conduct. It might be that the recent liberalisation of the criminal law on automatism would provide some guidance, especially in cases where it is the defender's voluntary conduct that brings about an insane state. The tests in the criminal cases are that the external factor must not be self-induced, that it must be one which the accused was not bound to foresee, and that it must have resulted in a total alienation of reason amounting to a total loss of control of his actions in regard to the crime with which he is charged.[87]

When reparation was about deliberate harm, then those who could not form such an intention through alienation of reason had to be exempted from liability. Thus the law in the Digest would be correct in Scots law in such cases: "accordingly the question is asked whether there is an action under the *lex Aquilia* if a lunatic causes damage. Pegasus says there is not, for he asks how there can be any accountable fault in him who is out of his mind; and he is undoubtedly right."[88] This is supported by the reasoning in *Waugh v James K. Allan Ltd*.[89] In that case, the defenders' driver who was suddenly disabled by an attack of coronary thrombosis ran down a pedestrian. Lord Reid said: "One must have great sympathy with the appellant who has suffered so severely through no fault of his own, but I find it impossible to blame the driver." It is voluntary human

---

[84] *e.g. Moore v Regents of the University of California*, 793 P 2d 479 Cal. S.C. (1990). discussed in Skene (n.82).

[85] See S. Sheldon, " 'Sperm bandits', birth control fraud and the battle of the sexes," (2001) 21 L.S. 460. The author lists reported cases from the US on other grounds such as fraud, deceit and misrepresentation in n.11. See a peripheral discussion in *Bell v McCurdie*, 1981 S.C. 64; 1981 S.L.T. 159.

[86] *Bogan's C.B. v Graham*, 1992 S.C.L.R. 920.

[87] See *Ross v H.M. Advocate*, 1991 S.L.T. 564; *Ebsworth v H.M. Advocate*, 1992 S.L.T. 1161; *Cardle v Mulrainey*, 1992 S.L.T. 1152.

[88] Dig. IX 2, 5, 2.

[89] 1964 S.C. (HL) 102.

conduct that is regulated by delict. Practically, it can be seen from *Waugh* that there can be liability if the person knew or ought to have known his condition would develop.[90]

Individuals

Bankruptcy takes the estate into the hands of the trustee subject to **23–40** the exceptions in the Act. So far as natural persons are concerned, the debtor has title and interest to sue for personal wrongs such as assault, unintentional personal injury or defamation.[91] The trustee in bankruptcy has title and interest to sue and if the bankrupt recovers compensation, the damages go to the estate.[92] It may be that a person whose estates are insolvent has no title to sue unless he can show that the trustee and the creditors have abandoned a claim.[93] In the Inner House decision, *Coutt's Trustee v Coutts*,[94] a trustee sought a declarator that the debtor's right to *solatium* in a claim vested in the trustee and that the trustee should receive that sum. The debtor was injured, then sequestrated, then he raised his action and was automatically discharged and he then settled his action. It was held in the First Division that once the action was raised it lost its personal character and vested in the trustee.[95] Again in the Inner House, in *Watson v Thompson*,[96] the trustee in bankruptcy was held entitled to be sisted as a party in a claim for *solatium* raised by the debtor after

---

[90] See *Roberts v Ramsbottom*, [1980] 1 All E.R. 7, where a man was held liable although he had been in a state of automatism, but on the basis that he should have taken steps to prevent himself causing harm to others. And generally by comparison, see the German Civil Code: BGB 827 — a person who does damage to another in a condition of unconsciousness, or in a condition of morbid disturbance of the mental activity, incompatible with a free determination of the will, is not responsible for the damage. If he had brought himself into a temporary condition of this kind by spiritous liquors or similar means, he is responsible for any damage which he unlawfully causes in this condition in the same manner as if negligence were imputable to him; the responsibility does not arise if he has been brought into this condition without fault, Markesinis, *The German Law of Torts*, p.11. Note the defender might still have to make equitable compensation to the extent his supervisor is not compelled to indemnify (para.832) providing it does not leave the defender without the means of living his normal life (para.829). Means includes however the availability of insurance. *Markesinis*, p.662.

[91] *Muir's Trs v Braidwood*, 1958 S.C. 169.

[92] *Jackson v MacKenzie* (1875) 3 R. 130.

[93] *Grindall v John Mitchell (Grangemouth) Ltd*, 1984 S.L.T. 335.

[94] 1998 S.C. 798.

[95] Under reference to *Watson, ibid.*

[96] 1990 S.L.T. 374.

his sequestration in respect of injuries sustained before his sequestration.[97] The right was no longer personal after the action had been raised. It should always be remembered that although a person whose estates have been made bankrupt may be discharged, his estate might still be subject to the administration of the trustee.

Liquidators, receivers and administrators

23–41   So far as insolvent incorporated bodies are concerned, it is essential that if a *liquidator* has been appointed, the permission of the court is sought to maintain the action. It has been held that where a joint liquidator is being sued in delict, there is no need to convene the other liquidator.[98] In terms of the applicable legislation, the actions cannot proceed against the company without the permission of the court.[99] The court that should be approached is the one dealing with the liquidation and not the one where the reparation action is taking or is to take place.[1] The court looks at the matter from the point of view of expediency and the interests of third parties, such as the pursuer, as an important factor.[2] The liquidator can waive any objection.[3] Without leave the action is incompetent.

A *receiver* has power[4] to bring and defend any action or other legal proceedings in the name of and on behalf of the company.[5] In *Myles J Callaghan Ltd v Glasgow DC*,[6] it was pointed out that the action should be raised in the name of the company with an indication that the receivers were bringing it. The company is the pursuer. A failure to do so led to an action for count reckoning and payment being dismissed.[7]

An *administrator* — in place by definition because it is considered more beneficial to trade the failing company — has general power to do all such things as may be necessary for the management of the affairs, business and property of the company.[8] No proceedings for reparation can proceed without the permission of the administrator or the court.[9]

---

[97] Affirmed 1992 S.C.L.R. 78; 1991 S.L.T. 683.
[98] *Highland Engineering Ltd v Anderson*, 1979 S.L.T. 122.
[99] Insolvency Act 1986, s.130(2).
[1] *Martin v Port of Manchester Insurance*, 1934 S.C. 143; *Coclas v Bruce Peebles & Co* (1908) 16 S.L.T. 7; *D.M. Stevenson & Co. v Radford & Bright Ltd* (1902) 10 S.L.T. 82.
[2] *Coclas, ibid.*
[3] *Hill v Black*, 1914 S.C. 913.
[4] *Radford & Bright Ltd v Stevenson* (1904) 6 F. 429.
[5] Insolvency Act 1986, Sch. 2, para.5.
[6] 1988 S.L.T. 227.
[7] *Ritchie and Redman v EFT Industrial Ltd*, 1997 S.C.L.R. 955.
[8] Insolvency Act 1986 s.8–27.
[9] s.11(3)(d).

Miscellaneous

Assignees

Once it has been accepted, as it has been in Scotland, that a right **23–42** of action vests on the wrong, the right to recover can be assigned *mortis causa* or *inter vivos* subject to the usual rules on assignation.[10] Thus, a victim can settle a claim by selling an assignation to one of several defenders who can then use the assignation to pursue the other defenders.[11] A party without title to sue may acquire such by way of assignation.[12] Care must be taken though to consider the authorities, which suggest that a person who has been paid out has nothing to assign — a view that is probably incorrect. A full examination of assignation, reviewing the older authorities, took place in *Purdon's Curator Bonis v Boyd*.[13] Two straightforward rules were also therein stated: (1) if a person other than an alleged joint-wrongdoer pays a sum to obtain an assignation of the injured person's claims for damages, he can sue for the full sum which the injured person could have recovered; the sum which he paid is irrelevant; and (2) if the injured person claims and receives compensation from an alleged wrongdoer and then sues a joint-wrong-doer, his action is competent (in the absence of a full discharge which releases the defender) — but as he cannot be allowed to receive compensation twice, the sum which he has already received must be deducted from the damages which would otherwise be payable.[14] In case of damage to the property of others[15] the issue of assignation is practically very important. An assignation should come before the action is raised to demonstrate the title to sue.[16]

In *GUS Property Management Ltd v Littlewoods Mail Order Stores Ltd*[17] a recent decision of the House of Lords, a building owned by Rest Property Co. Ltd ("Rest") was damaged by building operations being carried out on a neighbouring property. Rest was a wholly-owned subsidiary of a company, which transferred its properties to a newly-created, wholly-owned subsidiary company — the pursuers. Rest conveyed the building in question to the pursuers for a figure representing its book value. After that, Rest assigned to the pursuers all claims competent to them arising out of the building

---

[10] *Traill & Sons Ltd v Actieselskabat Dalbeattie Ltd* (1904) 6 F. 798; *Purden's C.B. v Boyd*, 1963 S.L.T. 157.
[11] *National Coal Board v Thomson*, 1959 S.C. 353, at 356; *Esso Petroleum Co Ltd v Hall Russell & Co. Ltd*, 1988 S.L.T. 874 at 885.
[12] *Nacap v Moffat Plant*, 1987 S.L.T. 221 at 224.
[13] 1963 S.L.T. 157.
[14] *ibid.,* at 160.
[15] See Ch.10.
[16] *Symington v Campbell* (1894) 21 R. 434.
[17] 1982 S.L.T. 533.

operations. The pursuers raised an action of damages against the neighbouring proprietors and those involved in the building operations. The Inner House agreed that the action should be dismissed, both because of the title to sue having been with Rest and because, the building having been transferred at book value, there was no loss. The House of Lords reversed this decision. As a general rule, the owner of a property damaged by delict did not by parting with it to another lose his title or interest to pursue a claim for damages. In this particular case, the depreciation in value and the cost of reinstatement of the building were alternative approaches to estimating the damages, the appropriate measure requiring evidence.

Judicial factors

23–43   In *Thurso Building Society's Judicial Factor v Robertson*,[18] a judicial factor appointed on the estate of an unregistered building society set up as a joint venture by five individuals in 1878 sued a solicitor in respect of alleged professional negligence. The defender pled no title to sue, arguing that there was no continuing legal persona in the joint venture, that only the descendants of the venturers had proprietary rights and therefore title to sue, and that there had been no sequestration of the estate of the joint venture, taking the management away from the descendants. Lady Paton held that the circumstances in which a judicial factor might competently be appointed were not rigidly defined or closed. What was essential was the existence of an estate in the sense of a collection of property, rights and obligations, requiring collection, preservation, administration and distribution, for which purposes the management of the estate was entrusted by the court to the factor. In this particular case, while at the time of the alleged acts of negligence, a duty of care was owed to the descendants, who had the interests in the estate, sequestration of the estate in the sense of removing the descendants' right or title was not necessary in the circumstances, especially where the descendants had never taken steps to hold or administer any of the estate. Accordingly, the pursuer did have title to sue.

Executors

23–44   See below.[19]

Members of the public

23–45   One practical benefit of the plea of title to sue and the requirement of interest is that it keeps members of the public out of the courts in matters that do not concern them. The policy of keeping the courts

---

[18] 2001 S.L.T. 797
[19] See para.26–18 *et seq.*

free to deal with live issues is still strong as can be seen from judicial review cases where the courts are open in principle to many more claimants over many issues, including the challenge of government decisions. Yet the courts will not deal in matters that are, when they come before the court, academic. *Scottish Old People's Welfare Council, petitioners*[20] is an example. The petitioners were challenging the Secretary of State's decision as erroneous in law and *ultra vires*. There was no claim for damages, but the possibility of claiming damages exists in Scottish judicial review. In this case, the petitioners were considered too remote to challenge the circular. It was, however, accepted in that case by both sides that members of the public might have title and interest to sue. The problem in this case was that the complaint, although sincere and public spirited, was against a circular about benefits and nobody had claimed under the circular at that stage.

Diplomats

The Diplomatic Privileges Act 1964 implementing the Vienna **23–46** convention on Diplomatic Relations 1961 protects a number of parties from actions. Immunity is conferred by agreement. The United Kingdom must have approved the individual. The head of mission and diplomats are generally immune,[21] but not in respect of their own houses, private succession matters or personal, professional or commercial activity. Administrative and technical staff are immune, but not for acts outside the course of their duties. Service staff are immune in respect of acts carried out in the course of their duties. Families are protected in the same way.[22] There are detailed rules as to the duration of the protection.[23] The protection can be expressly waived.[24] A protected person who raises an action is not immune from a counterclaim.[25]

State immunity

The State Immunity Act 1978 provides for immunity for the acts **23–47** of officials and governmental acts of States.[26] Foreign States have general immunity including from defamation,[27] but are not immune from actions for personal injury, death or damage. Economic loss

---

[20] 1987 S.L.T. 179–186.
[21] Art.31(1).
[22] Art.37(1)(2).
[23] Art.39.
[24] Arts 32(1) and (2).
[25] Art.32(3).
[26] It does not contravene the ECHR right to a fair hearing: *Holland v Lampen-Wolfe*, [2000] T.L.R. 575.
[27] See *Holland v Lampen-Wolfe*, [2000] T.L.R. 575.

cases do not obviously fit into this catalogue. Commercial transactions are not protected.[28] Being widely defined, "commercial transactions" covers financial and professional activities, or many things outside the exercise of sovereign authority.[29] The 1978 Act provides that the Diplomatic Privileges Act 1964 applies to Heads of State, members of their family forming their households and their private servants. The extent of the immunity of a Head of State was litigated under English law in *R. v Bow Street Metropolitan Stipendiary Magistrate, ex parte Pinochet Ugarte (No.3)*.[30] It was sought to extradite a former Head of State for various crimes allegedly committed when he was in power. At the time of the proceedings, he was in the United Kingdom for medical treatment. It was held that the former Head of State could be extradited in respect of a limited number of charges. He was entitled to immunity in respect of charges of murder and conspiracy to murder, but it was permissible to extradite in respect of torture after the date when the Head of State lost his immunity.

Foreign States are liable as occupiers in respect of heritage unless the case relates to the embassy or similar property. Section 13 (6) of the Act provides, *inter alia*, (as respects Scotland):

> "(b) the property of a State shall not be subject to any diligence for enforcing a judgment or order of a court or a decree arbitral or, in an action in rem, to arrestment or sale".[31]

There are detailed rules on separate entities not appearing to be the state itself, such as news agencies or tourist agencies or airlines and the like. One such issue has been litigated in Scotland. In *Coreck Maritime GmbH v Sevrybokholodflot*,[32] it was held that the defenders, (i) having undergone the process of privatisation to the extent that there were private stockholders holding a majority of the stock in the company; (ii) being a commercial company with its own legal personality intended to be controlled by a board of directors; and (iii) substantially free of government control and exercising no governmental functions, could not be regarded as an organ of the Russian Federation. Immunity may be waived.[33]

Visiting forces

23–48   The immunity of armed forces of Foreign States is covered by the Visiting Forces Act 1952 creating a general immunity in their favour.

---

[28] s.3.
[29] s.3(3).
[30] [1999] T.L.R. 222.
[31] For a discussion see *Forth Tugs Ltd v Wilmington Trust Co.*, 1987 S.L.T. 153, reviewing the authorities.
[32] 1994 S.L.T. 893.
[33] s.2.

The details of which countries are encompassed within the primary legislation are set out in many and various statutory instruments. The Secretary of State for Defence may make payment in satisfaction for any order made against a visiting force or as agreed between the claimant and the minister.[34] A member of the US armed forces was not permitted to sue the US Government in respect of allegedly negligent medical treatment.[35] A claim for defamation by one US citizen against another, where they worked at a US base, could not be sustained in the face of the visiting forces exception from the State Immunity Act.[36]

---

[34] s.9(1).
[35] *Littrell v Government of USA*, [1993] T.L.R. 589.
[36] *Holland v Lampen-Wolfe*, [2000] T.L.R. 575.

CHAPTER 24

VICARIOUS LIABILITY

24–1 As the name suggests, vicarious liability enables a person who has done no wrong himself to be held liable for a wrong done by another. This type of liability is now clearly established[1] and it satisfies a desire to transfer liability to pay damages to the person who has been gaining, in a general way, from the actings of the actual wrongdoer. Some maxims are often found in connection with it. The most significant is *culpa tenet suos auctores* (fault adheres to its author).[2] This is said to be a fundamental principle of the law to that vicarious liability is an exception.[3] The other maxim which is encountered is *qui facit per alium per se* (he who does something through another does it himself). This can be seen as an exception to the *culpa tenet maxim* or as an application of it! When reading older cases it should be noted that for a time, the law of Scotland followed the English doctrine of common employment. This held that an employer would not be vicariously liable for injury caused to a workman by a fellow workman on the dubious basis that the workman had, in taking the job, assumed the risk of injury by his fellow workers.[4] Eventually, the common employment doctrine was abolished (both in Scotland and in England) by the Law Reform (Personal Injuries) Act 1948. Vicarious liability is an example of joint and several liability. Accordingly, if it applies, the actual wrongdoer and the person who

---

[1] See *Baird v Hamilton* (1826) 4 S. 790. For history and historical analysis see Walker, *History VI*, 823, 826–7; *MacQueen & Seller HPLS II*, 534–5, 584–611; *Simpson HPLS II*. For a full up-to-date treatment including developments since publication see Stewart, *Reparation: Liability for Delict.*

[2] Or more colourfully, "the fox must pay his own skin": *Wood v Fullerton* (1710) Mor. 13960.

[3] As MacCormack pointed out, "the principle is cited only in cases where one of the issues is: which of two or more persons is the appropriate defender" G. MacCormack, "*Culpa Tenet Suos Auctores*: The Application of a Principle", 1973 J.R. 159.

[4] *Bartonshill Coal Co. v Reid* (1858) 3 Macq. 266. The existence of this doctrine made it more attractive to a court sympathetic to an injured pursuer to find a duty personal to the employer which had been broken, for then common employment would not apply.

is vicariously liable for his actings, are both liable.[5] The most common example of vicarious liability is for employees. This chapter also looks at the similar liability for an agent and the apparently similar liability for independent contractors. It concludes with some miscellaneous cases.

Vicarious liability for agent

The first point relates to the law of contracts. There is a distinction **24–2** between the contract of agency (and mandate (gratuitious agency)) and employment (*locatio operarum*). As a result of the different nature of these contracts, the delictual consequences differ. The obligations of the agent depend upon the instructions given to the agent. In relation to third parties, the agent's ability to affect his principal depends upon his authority, express or implied; therefore, the principal's delictual liability is formulated by reference to this relationship.

While the liability in respect of an agent and the liability in respect of an employer can be distinguished, it is quite possible for someone to be vicariously liable both as an employer of an employee and as the principal of an agent. This is particularly important, for an act may be outside the scope of an employee's employment but within the scope of his authority, express or implied, as an agent.

A principal will be liable for the acts of an agent where:

1. The acts complained of were expressly authorised
For example, where a solicitor writes defamatory letters on the instructions of a client, the client will be vicariously liable.[6]

2. The principal ratifies the act after it has been done
There seem to be few cases of this (understandably, for in the normal case it would amount to an acceptance of liability for an act one had not instructed). However, in *Buron v Denman*,[7] a British naval commander destroyed certain property and released certain slaves belonging to a Spanish subject resident abroad. The Foreign and Colonial Secretaries of State ratified the act of the commander. This was not a charitable act. By ratifying the act it became an act of State and therefore non-justiciable.

---

[5] While Trade Unions were, or remain, powerful, insurers have been wary of exercising their rights of relief against workers — many of whom might now own their own homes. R. Lewis, "Insurers Agreements not to Enforce Strict Legal Rights" (1985) 48 M.L.R. 275.

[6] *Crawford v Adams*; *Crawford v Dunlop* (1900) 2 F. 987.

[7] (1848) 2 Ex. 167; and see Lord Denning, Landmarks in the Law, pp. 223–227; see also *Att.-Gen. v Nissan* [1969] 1 All E.R. 629.

3. The act complained of is within actual or ostensible authority of the agent

This requires an understanding of the contractual position because liability is established by reference to the scope of the agent's authority.[8] However, for the purposes of the law of delict, it seems that the courts will often hold someone vicariously liable as a principal where they would perhaps not hold the "agent" able to bind the principal in contract. In the case of *Launchbury v Morgans*,[9] this area of the law was examined by the House of Lords. Mrs Morgans was the owner and registered keeper of a motor car. There were five people in the car: Mr Morgans, Mr Cawfield and three passengers (who were the plaintiffs in the case). Mr Morgans had gone out drinking and passed the keys to Mr Cawfield. They picked up the three plaintiffs. Mr Morgans fell asleep in the back seat. Mr Cawfield, driving without due care, crashed the car at 90mph. Mr and Mrs Morgans considered the car as "our car". The issue before the House of Lords was whether Mrs Morgans could be held vicariously liable for the actions of Mr Cawfield. The court rejected this argument. Lord Wilberforce said, "I regard it as clear that in order to fix vicarious liability on the owner of a car in such a case as the present, it must be shown that the driver was using it for the owner's purposes, under delegation of a task or duty." The argument that the car should be treated as a matrimonial car, making the owner liable for its use, was also rejected.

Vicarious liability for employee

24–3 The first matter to be determined is whether in fact the person who committed the delict is an employee and the proposed other defender an employer. In other words, the contract must be one of employment for service (*locatio operarum*) as opposed to, for example, a contract for services (*locatio operis, faciendi*). "Employee" for the purposes of vicarious liability is not dependent upon any period of continuous employment, which is a distinctive feature of the "employment rights" given to "employees" as variously defined by various statutes. The most difficult area is to distinguish between *locatio operarum* or employment as a servant (for example, a chauffeur) and *locatio operis faciendi* or employment as an independent contractor (for example, a taxi-driver). The element of control is an important factor and solves many of the most common cases. Since a chauffeur must take the precise route given by his employer, he is employed

---

[8] *Percy v Glasgow Corp.*, 1922 S.C. (HL) 144. See *Scobie v Steele & Wilson Ltd*, 1963 S.L.T. (Notes) 45 for a company's liability for a company director.
[9] [1973] A.C. 127.

locatio operarum; whereas the cab driver, who undertakes only to take the "fare" to a destination and himself chooses the route, is "employed" under a contract *locatio operis Jaciendi*.

However, in modern society, the control test may not be sufficient to resolve all cases, mainly because of the existence of many highly technical employments where the employer may not understand what it is the employee is doing, let alone control how he performs his task. The courts now look to various factors in resolving the question.[10] It is said that courts would consider the following: (1) the intention of the parties; (2) freedom of selection of employees; (3) duration of the contract; (4) whether payment is by salary or wages and whether made by the job or by the piece; (5) whether the tools and equipment belong to the employer or employee; (6) the nature of the arrangements for termination.[11] Thus it is now the case that resident doctors working under the NHS scheme are considered to be employees for the purposes of vicarious liability.[12] There is a trend in some recent English cases (mainly dealing with employment rights under various employment statutes) for the court to look for a mutuality of obligations: the one party to make work available and the other to do it.[13]

Once it has been established that the person who committed the delict is an employee, then the question arises whether the employer should be liable. The problem is to decide whether or not the actings complained of were within the scope of the employee's employment: it is well settled that this extends beyond his duties expressed in the contract. The overall thrust of the authorities is summarised by Lord President Clyde in the following passage from *Kirby v NCB*[14]:

"But, in the decisions, four different types of situation have been envisaged as guides to the solution of this problem. In the first place, if the master actually authorised the particular act, he is clearly liable for it. Secondly, where the workman does some work which he is appointed to do, but does it in a way which his master has not authorised and would not have authorised had he known of it, the master is nevertheless still responsible, for the servant's act is still within the scope of his employment. On the other hand, in the third place, if the servant is employed only to do a particular work or a particular class of work, and he does

---

[10] See, generally, *Short v J. & W. Henderson*, 1946 S.C. (HL) 24.

[11] See *United Wholesale Grocers Ltd v Sher*, 1993 S.L.T. 284 for a recent examination of the key factors.

[12] *McDonald v Glasgow Western Hospitals Board*, 1954 S.C. 453.

[13] *O'Kelly v Trusthouse Forte plc* [1984] Q.B. 90; *Nethermere (St Neots) Ltd v Taverna* [1984] I.C.R. 612; *McLeod v Hellyer Bros Ltd* [1987] I.R.L.R. 232. It is now spreading to ordinary tort cases: *McMeechan v Secretary of State for Employment* [1997] I.R.L.R. 353.

[14] 1958 S.C. 514 at 532–533.

something outside the scope of that work, the master is not responsible for any mischief the servant may do to a third party. Lastly, if the servant uses his master's time or his master's tools for his own purposes, the master is not responsible."

24–4 In most cases where an employee is driving to or from his work, the employer will not be liable — the act is outwith the scope of his employment. But if he is driving between places of work and in so doing decides to stay overnight at his own home, he will be within the scope of his employment.[15] It is cases two and three above which are the trickiest to distinguish and this is done on the basis of distinguishing scope of the employment from mode of execution of the work. This distinction is particularly apparent in the case of *Williams v Hemphill*.[16] A driver, instructed by his employers to drive from Benderloch to Glasgow, was persuaded by some passengers to drive round by Dollar, a considerable deviation. An accident happened as a result of the driver's fault. A passenger who had not instigated the deviation was injured. It was held that when the accident took place the driver was still acting within the scope of his employment: i.e. the driver was still implementing his master's purpose. Interestingly, opinions were reserved as to the position if the action had been raised by one of the passengers who had requested the deviation.

Cases like *Williams* must be distinguished from cases where the driver goes off "on a frolic of his own".[17] But it is important not to be misled by the rhetorical force of the handy phrase "frolic of his own" and, indeed, the Queen's Bench were not in the case of *Harrison v Michelin Tyre Co.*[18] The plaintiff had been standing on a duck board and a fellow employee tipped up the duck board. Although this was a frolic, it was not the employee's own frolic, but was part and parcel of the employment "a frolic on the job", it could be said. The point is clearly made *in Rose v Plenty*.[19] A milkman was employed by a dairy company to drive a milk float to deliver milk. At his place of work there was a notice prohibiting milkmen using boys to help them or giving boys lifts. In breach of this prohibition, this particular milkman used the services of a 13-year-old boy and allowed him to ride on the back of the float. Unfortunately, the boy was injured when the milkman drove the float without due care. In the lower court, it was held that the acts were outside the scope of the

---

[15] *Thomson v BSC*, 1977 S.L.T. 26.

[16] 1966 S.C. (HL) 31.

[17] *Joel v Morison* (1834) 6 C. & P. 501. Practical jokes by fellow workers were "frolics of the employees for which their employers were not liable": *Mclean v Remploy*, 1994 S.L.T. 687 at 688.

[18] [1985] 1 All E.R. 918.

[19] [1976] 1 All E.R. 97.

milkman's employment. On appeal, the view was taken that the instructions only affected the mode of execution of the job and did not limit or define the scope of the employment. The milkman was effectively still delivering milk, which is what he was employed to do; he was simply doing it in a forbidden way. Accordingly, his employer was vicariously liable.

Until recently, if the act has nothing to do with the work, then the employer was not vicariously liable. In *Kirby* itself, a workman on a temporary work break left his place of work and went into adjacent waste ground where he had no business to be and struck a match contrary to certain statutory provisions. It was held that at the time of the accident he was not mining but was smoking, and so the act was outwith the scope of the employment. In this case, the court contrasted these facts with those in *Century Insurance Co. v Northern Ireland Transport Board*,[20] where a match was struck while petrol was being transferred. In *Century*, this was held to be an incidence of doing a proper act negligently as opposed to doing an act unconnected with the employment. Recent cases in England, discussed below, make this fine, yet reasonable, distinction less significant.

Fraud and perhaps other intentional wrongs raise difficult issues. **24–5** In the most recent case, *Taylor v Glasgow District Council*, which eventually came before the Division,[21] Lord Sutherland (giving the opinion of the court) stated that since *Lloyd* it had not been necessary to show that the employer received any benefit from the fraud and that since *Uxbridge Permanent Building Society v Pickard*[22] it has not been necessary to show that the employers and the defrauded party have been in some contractual relationship.[23] The matter is often considered in relation to actual and ostensible authority. In the Outer House, reliance was placed on the following passage from Lord Keith of Kinkel, the Scots Lord of Appeal in an English appeal, *Armagas Ltd v Mundogas Ltd S.A.; The Ocean Frost*:

> "At the end of the day the question is whether the circumstances under which a servant has made the fraudulent representation which has caused loss to an innocent third party contracting with him are such as to make it just for the employer to bear the loss. Such circumstances exist where the employer by words or conduct has induced the injured party to believe the servant was acting in lawful course of the employer's business. They do not exist where such belief although it is present, has been brought about through misguided reliance of the servant himself, when

---

[20] [1942] A.C. 509.
[21] *Taylor v City of Glasgow*, 1997 Rep. L.R. 17; 1996 Rep. L.R. 69.
[22] [1939] 2 K.B. 248.
[23] at 4–07.

the servant is not authorised to do what he is purported to do when what he is purporting to do, is not within the class of acts that an employee in his position is usually authorised to do and when the employer has done nothing to represent that he is authorised to do it."[24]

The House of Lords in an English appeal has probably liberalised the law, widening the scope of vicarious liability, certainly in cases of intentional harm, but probably also for all cases. In *Lister & Others v Hesley Hall Ltd*,[25] it was held that those running a school boarding house were vicariously liable for the sexual offences of the warden. This was on the basis (*per* Lord Steyn) that it would be fair and just so to do. The case relies to some extent on Canadian decisions based on "close connection" with the job and some academic comments against the more traditional "unauthorised mode" approach. In that vicarious liability is about "policy" or "expediency", it is in order for attitudes to when and in what circumstances it should be applied to change over time. All previous decisions will have to be reconsidered against this case. It has already been followed repeatedly. In *Dubai Aluminium Co. Ltd v Salaam and Others*,[26] the House of Lords decided in these contribution proceedings that the firm were vicariously liable for the actings of a partner who was alleged to have dishonestly assisted in a breach of trust — he was acting in the ordinary course of the business even although without the knowledge or authority of the partners. The acts complained of were so closely connected with acts that he was authorised to do that this conclusion followed.[27] In *Mattis v Pollock*,[28] the Court of Appeal held the defendant night club owner vicariously liable where one of his bouncers ran home to get a knife to come back and stab a patron. This was on the basis of *Lister and Dubai Aluminium Co Ltd v Salaam*, and because the job involved the need for violence — albeit the incident could have stopped at stages along the train of events.[29]

---

[24] [1986] 1 A.C. 717 at 782.

[25] [2001] T.L.R. 308. See generally, P. Cane "Vicarious Liability for Sexual Abuse" (2000) 116 L.Q.R. 21 written before the House of Lords decision in *Lister*. See the earlier *Gower v Bromley LBC*, [1999] T.L.R. 726, making it clear that vicarious liability did not arise only from staff outside the council. The case was sufficiently influential to assist the allowance of an amendment in *Gorrie v The Marist Brothers*, 2001 G.W.D. 1484. It was also influential in *Royal Bank v Bannerman* 23 July 2002, a case involving allegations of fraud.

[26] [2002] 3 W.L.R. 1913.

[27] See the note C. Mitchell, "Partners in Wrongdoing" 2003 L.Q.R. 364.

[28] [2003] T.L.R. 418.

[29] See S. Habib, "Vicarious Liability: beating off the blame", 2003 P.I.L.J. August p.11.

Pro hac vice

There is one last major complication. Quite often in building, **24–6** engineering or manufacturing, a worker will be sent to a place outwith his own place of employment. He may have tools or machines from his usual employer with him. When he arrives, he may well be ordered about by a third party. If he is negligent and injures someone else, the question will arise — which of the two people who order him around is vicariously responsible? The law is quite clear on this matter, although each case must turn on its own particular facts and will always be a matter of degree. In *Mersey Docks and Harbour Board v Coggins and Griffith (Liverpool) Ltd*,[30] the harbour authority let a mobile crane to Coggins, a firm of stevedores, for loading a ship. They also provided Coggins with a crane man who was employed and paid and liable to be dismissed by the Board. However, the agreement between the Board and Coggins stated that the craneman should be the servant of the hirers. The craneman negligently injured a workman and the question was which of the two "bosses" (Coggins or the Board) was vicariously liable. The court refused to follow the contractual provision (certainly where the workman himself was not a party to it) and held that the general employer (the Board) would be liable unless it could be shown that the temporary employer had intervened to direct how a specific task was to be carried out. Accordingly, there is a heavy onus on the "original" employer who wishes to prove that a workman has been transferred *pro hac vice* to a third party. There are at least two Scots cases where *pro hac vice* has been established.[31] In *McGregor v J.S. Duthie & Sons*,[32] two passengers in a lorry were injured by the fault of the driver who was in the general employment of a partnership who had contracted to saw timber for a company. By agreement, the driver drove a lorry belonging to the company from the site to a railway station when required by the company, and the partnership was reimbursed for his wages by the company. The driver delivered timber on the company's instructions to the station. On his normal route back he stopped, as instructed by one of the partners, to pick up two passengers, who were expected in due course to become employees of the partnership, on work for the company. At the time of the accident, one of the partners was actually sitting beside the driver in the cab of the lorry. The passengers brought actions against the company and the survivor of the partnership claiming damages for the driver's negligence. The sheriff-substitute assoilzied the surviving partner and found that at the time the driver was in the *pro hac vice* employment of the company. The company

---

[30] [1947] A.C. 1; and see also *Park v Tractor Shovels Ltd*, 1980 S.L.T. 94.
[31] This may be more than in England.
[32] 1966 S.L.T. 133.

appealed. The Inner House held that in the very special circumstances, the pursuer had discharged the onus of showing that the driver was in the *pro hac vice* employment of the company. In *Sime v Sutcliffe Catering (Scotland) Ltd*,[33] Lord Caplan found *pro hac vice* employment established in a situation quite often found nowadays, where the catering in the pursuer's normal place of work was being provided by an outside contractor rather than her general employer.[34]

Liability for independent contractor

24–7   Generally, a person is not vicariously liable for the delicts committed by an independent contractor hired to do a job as opposed to an employee under a contract *locatio operarum*. As Lord Bridge said in the House of Lords: "It is trite law that the employer of an independent contractor is, in general, not liable for the negligence or other torts committed by the contractor in the course of the execution of the work."[35] In the ultimate legal analysis, the issue is a matter of fact and degree

On the basis of one difficult decision, *Marshall v Sharp*,[36] there can be vicarious liability for some not so independent contractors. The actual decision in *Marshall* was an extension of the law or it was wrong. The facts were as follows. Marshall entered a burner/dryer to see if it was sparking properly. An electrician, Dean, was operating the button which made the sparks. There was also a button that sent fuel to the sparks. He pressed this button at the same time as the spark button. Marshall was burned to death. The court accepted that there was no case of employers' personal liability made out on record, particularly no averment of a failure to implement a safe system. The court held that the electrician was not an employee of the defenders, nor of anyone else. Lord Ross called him "an independent contractor or in any event a contractor with a degree of independence", yet went on to hold the employer liable. Lord Dunpark stated: "On the evidence in this case, even if one regards Dean as a contractor rather than a servant, he was certainly not an independent contractor." Later he concluded: "While one may say that Dean was a contractor of his own labour, he cannot reasonably be classified as an independent contractor, for whose negligence the

---

[33] 1990 S.L.T. 687.

[34] See also the discussion in *Royal Bank v Bannerman*, July 23, 2002; *Easton v Consafe (Burntisland) Ltd Aberdeen* Sh. Ct, April 2, 2002 — *pro hac vice* not disputed.

[35] *D. & F. Estates v Church Commissioners* [1988] 3 W.L.R. 368. See *Baxter v Pritchard*, 1992 G.W.D. 24–1385 where the sheriff principal correctly upheld a decision not to remit averments of vicarious liability for an independent contractor to proof.

[36] 1991 S.C.L.R. 104.

defenders are not liable." The benefit of this formulation is that it supports the general rule that there is no liability. The effect of the case seems to be to apply the doctrine of *pro hac vice* employment, by which a servant is transferred from a *dejure* employer to a *defacto* employer. In this case, for the first time, the Inner House may have transferred a *sui juris* worker to a *de facto* employer. That is innovatory and unsupported by any authority. It is also remarkable in that the onus against transfer in *pro hac vice* vicarious liability cases is so high yet, in this case of a new application of the doctrine, the onus of transfer from the *sui juris* workman to the *defacto* defender was achieved.

However, it is possible that a person employing an independent contractor can incur liability as a result of his own actings. This can only be personal, and not vicarious liability: the employer is held liable for his own fault and not the fault of the independent contractor. This may occur in three categories of cases: (1) Where a person employs an incompetent or clearly unqualified contractor, *i.e.* where someone puts "*an improper person* to do some act which, if done by an improper person is likely to result in mischief."[37] (2) Where the duty that has been entrusted to the contractor is really that of the employer and is a *non-delegable duty*. Usually, these are statutory duties.[38] In one case, the House of Lords confirmed that there was no non-delegable duty upon a main contractor undertaken to subsequent occupiers, so that the main contractor was not liable for the defective workmanship of an otherwise competent subcontractor.[39] (3) Where the work to be done by the independent contractor is of a dangerous nature or *an extra-hazardous nature* where those who instruct the work have a duty to see that precautions are taken by the contractor. Examples include excavations or other work on public roads and streets or on private property.[40] Extrahazardous work does not cease to be such as a result of the work being the ordinary kind of work that the wrongdoer does — it is the nature of the work as being much more likely to cause harm that makes the principal liable.[41]

---

[37] See *Wolfson v Forrester*, 1910 S.C. 675.

[38] See *Stephen v Thurso Police Commissioners* (1876) 3 R. 535; Factories Act 1961, ss.12, 13 and 14, imposing absolute liability; Carriage of Goods by Sea Act 1971; *Riverstone Meat Co. Pty Ltd v Lancashire Shipping Co. Ltd* [1961] A.C. 807.

[39] See *D. & F. Estates Ltd v Church Commissioners*, n.28 above, *per* Lord Bridge at 387–388.

[40] *Sanderson v Paisley Burgh Commissioners* (1899) 7 S.L.T. 255. See *Alcock v Wraith* [1991] T.L.R. 600 for a modern example between private parties. For a most interesting Scottish case where the bungle was by the sub-contractors, see *MTM Construction Ltd v William Reid Engineering Ltd*, 1998 S.L.T. 211.

[41] *Honeywill and Stein Ltd v Larkin Bros Ltd* [1934] 1 K.B. 191; *Alcock v Wraith*, n.35.

Miscellaneous cases

Company directors

24–8   In *Scobie v Steele & Wilson Ltd*,[42] a pedestrian was injured when he was in collision with a motor vehicle owned by a limited company, which, at the time of the accident was being driven by one of the directors of the company. The pedestrian brought an action claiming damages against the company. The company contended that the pursuer had not made a relevant case of vicarious liability inasmuch as the doctrine of vicarious liability applied only in the case of an employee or servant of a company, and a director not being a servant of a company, could not therefore involve the company in vicarious liability:

> "If it is relevantly averred that a company director is driving a company vehicle with the knowledge and on the authority of the company upon company business, and through his negligent driving is involved in an accident, the company may be made vicariously liable for that negligence. That seems to me commonsense and sound law."[43]

That is the alleged vicarious liability of the company for the director. While a director causes the company to do things, directors are not generally liable for the acts of the company because of the concept of corporate personality — the director is the controlling mind rather than instructing.

By statute, the chief constable is liable to pay damages in respect of delicts committed by officers under his control,[44] but this may not make him generally liable (see lawburrows, above at para.2–8). *Cropper v Chief Constable, Dumfries, and Galloway Constabulary and Secretary of State*[45] sounds a warning that not all police officers are under the direction of a chief constable.

The Crown's immunity from action has been severely curtailed by statute. As a general rule, the Crown is now liable for the delicts of its servants or agents.[46]

At common law, trade unions had been held vicariously liable for the unofficial acts of their shop stewards,[47] but special rules have been introduced by statute. In addition, the Act sets out a statutory scheme of vicarious liability if, but only if, the delictual act (being an economic or industrial tort) was authorised or endorsed by the union

---

[42] 1963 S.L.T. (Notes) 45.
[43] *ibid., per* Lord Cameron at 45.
[44] Police (Scotland) Act 1967, s.39.
[45] 1998 S.L.T. 548.
[46] Crown Proceedings Act 1947; Crown Proceedings (Armed Forces) Act 1987.
[47] *Heaton's Transport (St Helens) Ltd v TGWU* [1972] I.C.R. 308.

or by a responsible person. "Responsible person" is defined by the legislation as being (1) the executive committee, (2) the president or general secretary, (3) a person empowered by the rules to authorise industrial action, (4) employed officials, and (5) any committee of the union to whom an employed official reports. For persons in categories (1) and (2) the union will be liable even if the person has acted outside the rules. However, for persons in categories (4) and (5) the union will not be vicariously liable if those persons acted outside union rules or the union repudiated their actions.[48]

It has been held that the procurator fiscal for the time being is not in the same position as a chief constable, that is liable for his deputes or assistants.[49] A named individual must be cited.

[48] Trade Union and Labour Relations (Consolidation) Act 1992, s.20.
[49] *McLaren v Procurator Fiscal for the Lothians and Borders*, 1991 G.W.D. 24–1407.

CHAPTER 25

DEFENCES, TRANSFER AND EXTINCTION

25–1 This chapter considers defences that may be put forward against an otherwise prima facie valid claim. Where a particular litigant is protected from being sued, this is treated as an immunity and considered in the context of the particular litigant. It should be appreciated that it is possible to defend an action based on delict for many reasons not set out in this Chapter. Many actions are defended on issues of fact — the defender simply denying one or more of the essential requirements of the delict. In an assault case, for example, the defender denies that he struck the blow. In an unintentional harm case, the defender may say that he did not know some fact which, if he had known it, would have imposed upon him a duty to take care. Sometimes a case can be defended upon the basis of some contractual exclusion of liability in delict. The effectiveness of such exemption clauses is now generally, and properly, considered in works on contract.[1]

Cases of transfer of liability are considered here, as are cases of the extinction of a delictual obligations. When a person dies, aspects of the claim he would have had, transfer to his executor and the surviving relatives have an independent claim of their own for the wrongful death. These related items are regulated by the Damages (Scotland) Act and so while including an instance of statutory transfer, these rules are dealt with all together in the chapter on damages.

Statutory authority

25–2 If Parliament has authorised some conduct, then it will not be actionable unless it could as easily be done without causing harm. In *Lord Advocate v North British Railways*,[2] waste that was being disposed of under statutory authority was left near an army barracks. The purpose of the statute could as easily have been served by not leaving it, so the defence was not available.

---

[1] Although see the discussion in relation to the creation of a duty above at para.10–7 *et seq.*

[2] (1894) 2 S.L.T. 71.

Justification

Justification can provide a defence in certain limited circum- **25–3**
stances (see *Crofter Co.*[3] and *Findlay*[4]). The common law also
protects conduct such as the reasonable chastisement of children.[5]

Necessity

Necessity may protect a defender against action in certain circum- **25–4**
stances, particularly where there has been an emergency. So it is
permissible to trespass in order to save life or property.[6] So too,
force-feeding of a prisoner has been held not to be actionable on this
basis.[7] If there are general principles of law crossing pedagogic and
doctrinal boundaries, then cases from the criminal law, used carefully, should assist. The High Court has recently reviewed and clearly
acknowledged the defence, which for a long time has been regarded
with suspicion. In *Moss v Howdle,*[8] it was decided that a defence of
necessity (albeit it is a form of a wider defence of coercion) is
available where the accused had no choice but to do what he did, as
where he is in immediate danger of death or serious bodily harm.

Self-defence and provocation

Defending oneself or one's property is a defence. Provocation may **25–5**
be a complete defence to an assault in civil law. Generally, it will
reduce damages rather than exculpate.[9]

Damnum fatale, Act of God and Force Majeur

Damnum fatale is one of the few defences available to a defender **25–6**
who is subject to strict liability. It refers to a happening that no
human foresight could provide against — such as an earthquake in
Edinburgh or a volcanic eruption in Thurso, but not heavy rain in
Greenock (see *Caledonian Ry*[10]).

Consent, waiver and volenti non fit injuria

Speaking generally, because delictual actions are usually between **25–7**
two parties, if one has in some way agreed or accepted that he should
be injured, corrective justice is not engaged. Applying that general
philosophical approach is more difficult. Different wrongs have

---

[3] See para.5–11 *et seq.*
[4] See para.5–13.
[5] See discussion above at para.2–4.
[6] *Cope v Sharpe* [1912] 1 K. B. 496.
[7] *Leigh v Gladstone* (1949) 26 T.L.R. 139.
[8] 1997 S.C.C.R. 215.
[9] *Ross v Bryee*, 1972 S.L.T. (Sh. Ct) 76.
[10] See para.3–11.

different aims and to that extent the efficacy of the law could be compromised by applying the same "consent" rule across all wrongs.

Where there is a deliberate conduct wrong, such as assault, then acceptance or agreement to that conduct is a defence. This explains why one boxer cannot sue another for a punch. The consent is particular (to conduct with the rules and customs, *i.e.* a punch not a stab wound) and prior. The same applies to medical treatment. Issues may then arise as to the quality of the consent. If the consent is extorted, then it does not provide a bar to recovery.[11] We have seen that Scots law has not, in the medical sphere, taken the route of seeking, for example, informed consent.[12] In Scots criminal law it is not possible to consent to inflict serious injury on another, as by a "square go".[13] Similar, policy considerations might apply to a civil case.

When we turn to harm through negligence, there is an immediate difference. The defender does not set out to harm. The pursuer cannot therefore, consent in particular and in advance. Yet justice still requires that in some cases the defender be released due to the "consent" of the pursuer. It is here that two phrases are encountered, "*volenti non fit injuria*" and "assumption of risk". Unfortunately they are used in all sorts of sense and can cause all sorts of confusion and difficulty. *Volenti* was, in origin, of the nature of a consent defence to particular conduct in advance — a freeman who was allowed to be sold as a slave was denied his right to be declared free.[14] There are many cases and articles that can be and ought to be read in attempting to understand the position of "consent" in negligence.[15] However, the following structure, based to an extent on American learning, is, it is submitted, the easiest way to understand the processes. It is further submitted that Scots cases do indeed recognise this analysis.

There are two principal ways in which "consent" operates as a defence. Because *volenti* is presently used to cover all (fairly so as a general principle of justice), it is better not to use the phrase at all. Instead, we may speak of two forms of assumption of risk. It is important to realise that there are two forms. The primary form is

---

[11] *Adamson v Martin*, 1916 S.C. 319.

[12] See paras 2–2 and 22–5.

[13] *Smart v H.M.A.*, 1975 S.L.T. 65. See also *Laskey v UK*, (1997) 24 E.H.R.R. 39.

[14] T. Ingman, "A History of the Defence of Volenti Non Fit In juria", 1981 J.R. 1. A.E. Jaffey, "Volenti Non Fit Injuria", 1985 C.L.J. 87.

[15] J.B. Stewart, "Football: Civil Aspects", 1981 S.L.T. (News) 157. W.J. Stewart, "Skiing and the Law: the First Case" (1990) 3 5 J.L.S.S. 27. A. Duff, "Civil Actions and Sporting Injuries Sustained by Professional Footballers", 1994 S.L.T. (News) 175. R. Kidner, "The Variable Standard of Care, Contributory Negligence and Volenti", 1991 L.S. 1. C.G.S. Tan, "Volenti Non Fit Injuria: An Alternative Framework", 1995 Tort L. Rev. 208.

where the pursuer has assumed a risk inherent in the activity which has materialised. This is the kind of *volenti* case that the judges call "no duty" cases. Because my opponent in a football match knows that a bona fide tackle can break my leg, if he does break my leg (which is entirely foreseeable), he is not liable because I have assumed the risk of that harm. I did not really consent to it, but was willing to run the risk. I took a chance and it came out against me. There is no need to examine issues of consent. On ordinary principles of fact finding, the pursuer can lose if he knew or if he ought to have know of the risk: the visiting martian cannot say that he was unaware of the risks inherent in a game of football. Secondary assumption is more like the classic *volenti* — where there is, or on ordinary principles of fact finding, can be held to be, a prior consent to a course of conduct.

Turning to actual cases, the law has turned against *volenti* generally, although when presented as "no duty" the anti-*volenti* cases might be avoided. So in employment cases there must be the clearest possible evidence that the pursuer accepted the risk of the actual harm: it is not sufficient to show that the pursuer continued working knowing of the risk.[16] A tenant had been held *volenti prior* to the Occupiers' Liability (Scotland) Act 1960 by remaining in a house that was in ill repair,[17] but that has not been followed in a thoughtful Sheriff Court decision.[18] It is often mentioned in sports cases, especially in regard to spectators, but it is seldom that a spectator can actually be said to have assumed a risk of injury.[19] In Scotland's first skiing decision, the sheriff correctly, it is submitted, would not have applied *volenti nonfit injuria*, but would rather have found the pursuer's damages to be reduced by contributory negligence. This would have been the case even although the sheriff considered participants generally accepted some degree of danger.[20]

Illegality, *ex turpi causa*

The maxim *ex turpi causa non oritur actio*,[21] which applies in **25–8** contract, has been applied as a defence to delict claims too. Its appearance in delict arises from the reluctance of courts to award

---

[16] See generally *ICI v Shatwell* [1965] A.C. 656.
[17] *Shields v Dalziel* (1894) 24 R. 849. *Hughes' Tutsix v G.D.C.*, 1982 S.L.T. (Sh. Ct) 70.
[18] See *Murray v Harringay Arena* [1951] 2 K.B. 529; see especially *Wooldridge v Sumner* [1962] 2 All E.R. 978.
[19] *Garven v White Corries*, Fort William Sheriff Court, June 21, 1989, unreported. See *Lamond v Glasgow Corporation*, 1968 S.L.T. 291 for a full statement in the context of sport.
[20] *Pitts v Hunt* [1991] 1 Q.B. 24. *Ashton v Turner* [1981] Q.B. 137 takes a firm line.
[21] No action arises out of an immoral transaction.

damages to one wrongdoer caused by another wrongdoer.[22] However, instances of such situations range from the safe-blower who blows up his confederate who is keeping watch, to a case where a person injures a passenger when infringing some traffic regulation.[23] The question has been regularly debated in England and has been considered recently in some detail by the Court of Appeal.[24] Australian cases have shown something of a lead in moving away from a rigorous application of the maxim.[25] The general approach for Scots law has been set out in *Weir v Wyper*,[26] which reconsidered much previous authority. A 16-year-old girl went on a trip with two men and another girl. One of the men and the other girl left the car, leaving the girl with the defender at night, in the dark, in a place she did not know. Knowing that he held only a provisional licence, she asked the defender for a lift home. The defender began showing off by driving very fast and braking violently when it was necessary to stop. The car left the road and overturned. Lord Coulsfield, it is submitted, quite properly concluded that the maxim was not to be rigorously applied nor, if the defence was restated or explained as an aspect of public policy, was it to be a complete bar to claims. The proper course was to take each case on its merits and it is probably only in cases of significant criminal activity that the defence would have a chance of success. The defence was treated as applicable to a case of an injured passenger who was knowingly in a stolen car, which on the balance of probabilities it was accepted he had helped steal.[27] It should be mentioned that such cases are sometimes argued on the basis of a public policy against recovery and yet others are argued on the basis that, in negligence cases, it is impossible to fix a standard of duty of care — for example, as between the safe-blower and his lookout, the court will not trouble to inquire as to the standards of the reasonable man out doing a burglary.[28] This latter

---

[22] See generally, A.H. Hudson, "Crime, Tort and Reparation — What Solution?" 1984 S.L.T. (News) 321.A.H. Hudson, "Crime, Tort and Reparation: A Common Solution", 1992 S.L.T. (News) 203.

[23] See, *e.g. Currie v Clamp's exec.*, 2001 G.W.D. 319.

[24] See *Jackson v Harrison* (1978) 138 C.L.R. 438; *Progress and Properties v Craft* (1976) 135 C.L.R. 651 moving away from *Smith v Jenkins* (1970)119 C.L.R. 397. The Australian position was analysed in Weir, below. See also R.W. Kostal, "Currents in the Counter-reformation: illegality and the duty of care in Canada and Australia" (1995) Tort L. Rev. 100.

[25] 1992 S.L.T. 579, considering the earlier Scottish authority *Sloan v Triplett*, 1985 S.L.T. 294; *Ashcroft's C.B. v Stewart*, 1988 S.L.T. 163; *Duncan v Ross Harper & Murphy*, 1993 S.L.T. 105; *Wilson v Price*, 1989 S.L.T. 484 and *Winnik v Dick*, 1984 S.L.T. 185.

[26] 1992 S.L.T. 579; 1992 S.C.L.R. 483, (OH). See also *Duncan v Ross Harper & Murphy*, 1993 S.L.T. 105.

[27] The Scottish Law Commission Report No.115 proposes a classification of the defence in cl. 9 of its draft Contribution in Damages (Scotland) Bill.

[28] For a case along these lines see the case of the escaping prisoner *Vellino v Chief Constable of Manchester*, [2002] 1 W.L.R. 218.

argument seems unnecessary and may well have been a way out of the otherwise draconian effect of subscribing fully to the *turpis causa* rule.

Contributory negligence

Contributory negligence is a plea to the effect that the defender **25–9** failed to take reasonable care for his own safety. Formerly this was a complete defence, so older cases should be read with caution. All that need be shown is that the pursuer's carelessness was a co-operating cause of his injuries or loss — there is no need to show a breach by the pursuer of a duty of care. The onus is on the defender to establish the defence. As a result of the Law Reform (Contributory Negligence) Act 1945, contributory negligence ceased to be a complete defence and, instead, the court was allowed to attribute fault between the parties in proportion to their share of the responsibility. Conduct that consists of a response to an emergency created by the defender does not constitute contributory negligence, in terms of the so-called "agony rule".[29] Another exemption from the defence is available under the "dilemma rule" where the pursuer picks the wrong course of two open to him in a situation created by the defender.[30]

The defence has been held available against children. In *Banner's Tutor v Kennedy's Trustees*,[31] a five-year-old girl got out of the back of a minibus and ran into a lorry. She had been expressly warned by the minibus driver not to go out until he opened the door but he did not take any actual steps to prevent her getting out. The court held that she was a girl of usual intelligence and had parental guidance about roads and had seen heavy traffic. She was held to be 20 per cent liable for the accident and her damages were reduced accordingly.

It is commonly encountered in workers' cases, slipping and tripping cases and in road traffic accident cases. While it is a contradiction in terms, it is thought that findings of 100 per cent may be made.[32] In England, a sensible approach has been taken of not finding contributory negligence unless the finding is of the order of at least 10 per cent.[33] There are many English cases applying the Act to cases of economic loss. Again, in England, it has been held to be unlikely for a pedestrian to be held to be more liable than a car driver.[34]

---

[29] *Laird Line v U.S. Shipping Board,* 1924 S.C. (HL) 37.
[30] *Clayards v Dethick* (1848) 12 Q.B. 439.
[31] 1978 S.L.T. (Notes) 83.
[32] See, *e.g. obiter* in *Robb v Salamis*, 2003 G.W.D. 33–949. *Skipton Building Society v Lea Hough & Co* [2000] P.N.L.R. 545.
[33] *Johnson v Tennant Bros Ltd,* (CA), unreported, November 19, 1954.
[34] *Eagle v Chambers* [2003] EWCA Civ 1107.

Prescription and limitation

25–10   This is a very important subject in practice. Lawyers are often consulted well after an accident has taken place. It may be professional negligence on the part of a lawyer to fail to take notice of the many and various periods of prescription and limitation. Accordingly, it has to be emphasised that what follows is merely an outline account which is necessary for an understanding of the law. The position is now almost entirely statutory.[35] The difference between limitation and prescription is a simple but important one: prescription completely extinguishes the obligation and will be judicially noticed by a court without a plea being taken; limitation simply prevents an action being raised — the obligation remains and a plea has to be taken by the defender. Most personal injury cases raise limitation issues; most property damage or economic loss cases raise prescription questions. Limitation is, therefore, a defence and prescription could be considered a mode of extinction, but they are usefully considered together.

Limitation

25–11   Personal injuries cases are subject to a three-year limitation period.[36] Time begins to run from the date on which the injuries were sustained, or where there was a continuing act or omission (like pollution) then runs from the date on which the injuries were sustained or the date on which the act or omission ceased, whichever is the later.[37] However, the action will not be limited if one of the statutory exemptions is available, such as where the injured person is under a legal disability — for example, nonage or mental disability.[38] The period is also extended where it was not reasonably practicable for the pursuer to know that the injuries in question were sufficiently serious to justify his bringing an action of damages, on the assumption that the person against whom the action was brought did not dispute liability and was able to satisfy a decree. The extension is also available where the pursuer was unaware that the injuries were attributable in whole or in part to an act or omission; and where he

---

[35] Prescription and Limitation (Scotland) Act 1973, as amended by the Law Reform (Miscellaneous Provisions) (Scotland) Act 1980, the Prescription and Limitation (Scotland) Act 1984, the Law Reform (Miscellaneous Provisions) (Scotland) Act 1985, and the Consumer Protection Act 1987. See Casebook, Ext. 93.

[36] 1973 Act, s.17.

[37] For a contentious case, see *Hunter v NSHB*, 1989 G.W.D. 15–645.

[38] For a detailed investigation of s.17(3) and the meaning of "unsoundness of mind", see *Bogan's C.B. v Graham*, 1992 G.W.D. 32–1898, 32–1907. See, in relation to those between the ages of 16 and 18, s.8 of the Age of Legal Capacity (Scotland) Act 1991 applying a transitional provision. The period runs from the commencement of the Act (September 25, 1991), not from when the pursuer was 16 years of age.

is ignorant that the defender was a person to whose act or omission the injuries were attributable in whole or in part, or was the employer or principal of such person, *i.e.* was vicariously liable. In the case of *Elliott v J. & C. Finney*[39] the court refused to extend the period to take account of the entire period when an injured person was in hospital because he had had a conversation with a policeman and could have asked him, from his hospital bed, for the information necessary to pursue the action.

Even where the pursuer is not entitled to an extension, the court has a discretion (a "section 19A discretion") to admit a claim if it seems equitable to do so. The court has to consider where the balance of the equities lies. *In Donald v Rutherford*,[40] a man was injured on November 3, 1975, and an action was begun on February 13, 1981. There was even a letter in this case written by representatives of the proposed defender saying that for certain purposes they accepted the writ as having been served on February 7, 1977. Negotiations continued. A plea having been taken and upheld, the court, on appeal, refused to allow the pursuer to get back into the action since he had a claim against the insurers of the solicitors who had not raised the action on time! The court refused to offer guidance on how the discretion would be used, saying that it would always depend upon the case in question. The court did suggest, however, that it might often be appropriate to hold a preliminary proof on the facts relating to the making of the claim. Indeed, in the case of *Elliott*, above, the court, although refusing to extend on the basis of the time in hospital, did allow an extension on the equitable ground, for although an action for negligence against the solicitors might well be successful, it was not thought to be straightforward and, as the pursuer was not entitled to legal aid, would involve outlay. That is in contrast to a similar case, *Donald v Galloway*,[41] in which the claimant had spent some time sedated in hospital, unable to find out who was responsible for his accident. While a preliminary proof was allowed on the claim for a section 17(2)(b)(iii) extension, it was denied on the section 19A equitable grounds. The running of the limitation period is stopped by the raising of a court action.

Where a person dies within three years of the date of an accident, there is a three-year limitation period from the date of the death for

---

[39] 1989 S.L.T. 208 (OH). The decision on the s.19A question was upheld in the Inner House, 1989 S.L.T. 605. See also *Ford v Union Insulation Co. Ltd*, 1989 G.W.D. 16–696; *Blake v Lothian Health Board*, 1992 G.W.D. 32–1908.

[40] 1984 S.L.T. 70. For other examples of the s.19A discretion, see *Pritchard v Tayside Health Board*, 1989 G.W.D. 15–643; *Comber v Greater Glasgow Health Board*, 1989 S.L.T. 639; *Ford v Union Insulation*, 1989 G.W.D. 16–696; *Clark v McLean*, 1993 S.L.T. 492; *Griffen v George MacLellan Holdings Ltd*, 1992 G.W.D. 30–1787; *Bogan's C.B. v Graham*, 1992 G.W.D. 32–1907; *Blake v Lothian Health Board*, 1992 G.W.D. 32–1908.

[41] 1988 G.W.D. 24–1042.

the raising of a case based on the death, unless one of the statutory exemptions outlined above applies or the section 19A discretion is exercised. Where the case is not based on the death, then the three years runs as in any other case. So where a man has his leg broken and then a year later dies of natural causes, the executor has two years to raise the case. Had he died of the broken leg then the three year period would run. Because it takes some time to appoint an executor, there is often not a full three years to process the action.

Defamation actions are subject to a three-year limitation. The section 19A discretion applies to such claims also.

Prescription

25–12   The main example of prescription in delict is in relation to other obligations to make reparation. This describes cases where there is no personal injury, for example, pure economic loss cases or cases of damage to property. In such cases there is no limitation period, but a five-year prescription that completely extinguishes the obligation. Time begins to run from the time when there is concurrence of loss and a legal wrong and there can be only one point of concurrence.[42] If, however, the harm is a continuing one like that resulting from nuisance, the time runs from when the continuing act ceased. If the pursuer was not aware of the damage and could not with all reasonable diligence have become so aware, then time does not run until he becomes aware of it. This is known as the "discoverability formula" and may assist pursuers in cases of latent damage. In the case of *Dunfermline District Council v Blyth & Blyth*,[43] Lord MacDonald considered *(obiter)* that the pursuers had to know that the damage was caused by a legal wrong of the defenders before time would begin to run. It has been held that the prescriptive period will not begin to run until there has been actual damage.[44] In the case of a solicitor's professional negligence in failing to take a proper title, it was held in the Inner House that time did not run until the defect was noticed rather than when the error was made.[45] Not only that, in cases such as this, there was no real place for reasonable diligence.[46] The prescriptive period is interrupted by the raising of an action or the relevant acknowledgment of the claim. Nonage precludes the

---

[42] Or, as is often put, the *terminus a quo* is the concurrence of *damnum and injuria*: see *Dunlop v McGowans*, 1979 S.C. 22; 1980 S.C. (HL) 73. And see also *George Porteous (Arts) Ltd v Dollar Rae*, 1979 S.L.T. (Sh. Ct) 51.

[43] 1985 S.L.T. 345.

[44] *Renfrew Golf Club v Ravenstone Securities*, 1984 S.L.T. 170.

[45] *Glasper v Rodger*, 1996 S.L.T. 44.

[46] There is some considerable argument over the precise operation of s.11. See Johnstone, *Prescription and Limitation*, 1999, *Ghani v Peter T Mccann & Co.*, 2002 G.W.D. 17–578, *Lloyd v Campbell Riddell*, March 25, 2003, Glasgow Sh. Ct.

running of the period.[47] The onus of proof of prescription is on the defender.[48]

The long negative presciption

The long negative prescription of 20 years' "mops up" obliga- **25–13**
tions, which might otherwise be kept outstanding forever; for
example, economic loss cases where the claimant did not reasonably
know he had a ground of action. It is worth noting that the mopping-
up period for the new statutory regime of product liability is only 10
years from the date when the product is put into circulation. The long
negative prescription no longer applies to claims for personal injuries
— effectively making such claims imprescriptible, although still
subject to the limitation period.

The positive prescription

This is of no relevance to the law of delict save that it actually **25–14**
confers rights — mainly to land — and thus would entitle a person
acquiring a prescriptive right to exercise any rights of a proprietor.
The "right" of a defender to commit a nuisance cannot be acquired
under the positive prescription (of 10 years), but the right of a
pursuer to complain about it can be lost after the 20 years of the long
negative prescription.

TRANSFER

Assignation[49]

It is quite clear that a claim maybe assigned at anytime to someone **25–15**
else. Any defences available against the original party will be valid
against the assignee.[50] A claim may be transferred by way of
subrogation — that is, where the insurer has indemnified his insured
for a loss for which another person is legally liable, he is entitled to
proceed against that party without the need of an assignation. By the
Third Parties (Rights Against Insurers) Act 1930, if an insured
person becomes bankrupt or unable to pay, then anyone who has
incurred a loss covered by the insurance may proceed directly against
the insurer. The Road Traffic Act 1972 makes insurance compulsory
in respect of the risk of death or personal injury to third parties

---

[47] See also n.71 above with regard to s.8 of the Age of Legal Capacity (Scotland) Act
1991.
[48] *Strathclyde R.C. v W.A. Fairhurst*, 1997 S.L.T. 658.
[49] See para.23–42.
[50] See Young, "Rights of Relief on Assignation in Settlements", 1992 S.L.T. (News)
225.

(including passengers). The insurer[51] must satisfy any judgment against any insured, notwithstanding that they may be entitled to avoid the policy.[52] There is a similar arrangement in respect of employers in terms of the Employers' Liability (Compulsory Insurance) Act 1969.

Contribution and relief

25–16   The Law Reform (Miscellaneous Provisions) (Scotland) Act 1940, section 3(1) (as amended) provides:

> "Where in any action of damages in respect of loss or damage arising from any wrongful acts or negligent acts or omissions two or more defenders are in pursuance of the verdict of a jury or the judgment of a court found jointly and severally liable in damages or expenses, they shall be liable inter se to contribute to such damages or expenses in such proportions as the jury or the court, as the case may be, may deem just."

This allows the court to apportion liability between defenders sued jointly and severally according to their responsibility for the loss. As liability is generally joint and several, the pursuer will be entitled to enforce his decree in full against any party. The party paying then has to recover the proportions for which he is not responsible from the other wrongdoers and to do that he may have to exercise his right of relief. If all the wrongdoers are not parties to the one action, the position is more complicated. While there may remain a common-law right of relief, in practice the position is now regulated by statute. Section 3(2) of the 1940 Act provides that:

> "Where any person has paid any damages or expenses in which he has been found liable in any such action as aforesaid [a section 3(1) action] he shall be entitled to recover from any other person who, if sued, might also have been held liable in respect of the loss or damage on which the action was founded, such contribution, if any, as the court may deem just."

At common law, there is a right of relief against a wrongdoer by a person who is vicariously liable for him. So, for example, where an employee injured another employee, the employer's liability insurers were held entitled to proceed against him.[53] In this particular area,

---

[51] Or the Policyholders Protection Board if the insurance company is in liquidation: Policyholders Protection Act 1975, s.6. Or after November 30, 2001, the Financial Services Compensation Scheme under the Financial Services and Markets Act 2000.

[52] But there is some safeguard where the policy is obtained, for example, by a misrepresentation.

[53] *Lister v Romford Ice & Cold Storage Co. Ltd* [1957] 1 All E.R. 125.

there are a number of extra-legal considerations, the most significant of which is that certain insurers have agreed not to exercise this legal right against employees unless there has been collusion or wilful misconduct.

The facts, read short, of *Caledonia North Sea Ltd v London Bridge* **25–17** *Engineering Ltd*,[54] were that an oil platform, the Piper Alpha, exploded with enormous loss of property and loss of life. The owner-occupiers settled damages actions with the various claimants on the owner-occupiers. The owner occupiers then sought indemnity from the 146 sub-contractors for the payments made by their insurers and underwriters. At first instance, six of seven test cases were dismissed. Because the contractors by their indemnity and the insurers by their contracts covered the same loss, they were co-debtors and the insurers would be able to sue for a proportion of their losses by way of contribution. It was also found at first instance that the insurers could have proceeded by subrogation and the owners would have had to have transferred their rights against the contractors to the insurers. On reclaiming it was held that as between the contract of insurance and the contract containing the indemnity, the latter was the primary obligation, being part of a mutual arrangement in a wider contractual relationship whereas the pursuers' insurance arrangements were intended for their own benefit and were *res inter alios acta* as respects the defenders and that the actions were properly brought by the insurers in name of the pursuers. Although decree had been pronounced in respect of the claims by the relatives and the claims had thereby been extinguished, the sums paid in terms of those decrees remained sums paid in respect of liabilities arising from the injuries or deaths, and could be recovered by the pursuers if the settlement was reasonable in the circumstances. After a hearing before the House of Lords, all but one appeal was settled (*Norton No.2 Ltd*) which was dismissed. It was also held that a settlement taking into account the possibility of an award of damages in a foreign court which is later relied upon as a claim of indemnity, is not a matter of asking a Scottish court to award foreign damages and is permitted.[55]

The use of third party procedure, available in the sheriff court as well as the Court of Session, allows a defender to call any party who might be liable to contribute or indemnify as a third party to the action. This frequently prevents the need for a separate action of contribution or relief. Actions of contribution and relief are subject to a two-year limitation period, commencing on the date when the right to contribution or relief accrued.[56] It is essential for a claim of relief

---

[54] 2000 S.L.T. 1123; 2002 S.L.T. 278.

[55] *Caledonia North Sea Ltd v London Bridge Engineering Ltd*, 2000 S.L.T. 1123; 2002 S.L.T. 278.

[56] See s.8A of the Prescription and Limitation (Scotland) Act 1973.

that there should be a Scottish decree against the claimant, but it does not have to have been obtained in a contested action.[57]

EXTINCTION

Decree and *res judicata*

25–18   A delictual claim is discharged by decree and satisfaction of the decree. The cause — providing, of course, that the decree was not taken in absence — is *res judicata* and cannot be raised again. Decree of *absolvitor* (of the defender) prevents the action being raised on a different basis, as where an action is raised for personal injuries instead of for damage to property, or for a negligent misstatement instead of fraud.[58] An acquittal in a criminal matter is not *res judicata* and a victim of crime, or their family if the victim is deceased, may raise a civil action to vindicate the wrong.[59] Common law negligence and breach of statutory duty are in most circumstances not different *media concludendi*[60] but it depends on the nature of the negligence and the terms of the statutory duty. A finding of an employment tribunal may constitute *res judicata* in a later civil action.[61] There is a divergence of authority on the common practical point that arises where accidents cause both personal injuries and property damages. In *Mcphee v Heatherwick*,[62] a motorcyclist sued the driver of a motorcar in the small debt court, on the ground of his negligent driving, for damages consisting of the excess on his insurance policy and the value of his crash helmet. The driver admitted liability and consented to decree. The motorcyclist's insurers, who were unaware of the small debt action, raised a summary action against the driver in the name of the motorcyclist, on the same ground, for the cost of replacing the motorcycle. The defender pleaded *res judicata*. This was upheld by Sheriff McPhail. The point in *McSheehy v MacMillan*[63] was different. The pursuer raised a small claim against the defender for damages consisting of the excess on his insurance policy, loss of a vehicle and non-reclaimable insurance. The defender admitted the claim and decree was granted of consent. The pursuer's

---

[57] *Comex Houlder Diving Ltd v Colne Fishing Co. Ltd*, 1987 S.L.T. 443. The Scottish Law Commission have reported on the questions of contribution and relief, annexing a draft Contribution in Damages (Scotland) Bill (Scot. Law Com. No.115). See the analysis of relief in Young "Rights of Relief", 1992 S.L.T. (News) 225 and *Comex Houlder Diving Ltd v Colne Fishing Co. Ltd* (No.2), 1992 S.L.T. 89.

[58] On this point see, generally, *Gibson & Sinipson v Pearson*, 1992 S.L.T. 894.

[59] *Mullan v Anderson*, 1996 Rep. L.R. 47; see Ch.1.

[60] *Matuszczyk v NCB*, 1955 S.C. 418.

[61] *British Airways plc v Boyce*, 2001 S.L.T. 275.

[62] 1977 S.L.T. (Sh. Ct) 46.

[63] 1993 S.L.T. (Sh. Ct) 10.

insurers subsequently raised a summary cause against the defender in the name of the pursuer in respect of the same collision for the cost of repairing the vehicle. The defender pleaded *res judicata*. The sum sued for in the action of £798 represented the sum paid by the pursuer's insurance company to the pursuer in settlement of his claim under his policy. In terms of the policy, there was a right of subrogation to the insurance company to use the pursuer's name in an action to recover their outlay. It should be noted that for the purposes of this case it was accepted that the *media concludendi* were the same — the negligent driving. That may not be the case where different claims are put forward but whatever the case this was not argued out in *McSheehy*. Instead, Sheriff Lockhart considered that the subject-matter was different and on that basis he came to a different result.

Decree of dismissal (in favour of the defender) only prevents an action being raised on the same point of law and so an action may be raised again on the same facts but on a different ground of law.

Discharge, compromise and settlement

A delictual action can be discharged on any terms and the **25–19** discharge can be in any form. Acceptance of social security benefits does not imply a discharge. Only the party in whose favour the discharge is granted can found upon it. If an action is raised against a number of persons jointly and severally, a discharge may be a discharge of one and not the others, but may be read as a discharge of the whole ground of action. The discharge of one joint wrongdoer does not prevent others subsequently claiming a right of relief against that party. A case can be compromised or settled with or without the court's permission on any terms. It is important that the settlement is clearly expressed. The onus of establishing a discharge by settlement is on the defender.[64] An advocate, but not a solicitor, can compromise a case without authority from his client. In practice, discharge may be effected by a separate minute which is a formal offer of settlement and if it includes an offer of the expenses of the action it will have the effect of imperilling the offeree for expenses if he is not subsequently awarded more than the offer by the court. It is one of the skills of the experienced agent to pitch such offers at the right level. In defamation cases, the offer must include a withdrawal of the alleged defamatory statement.[65]

In a recent reparation case, *Irving v Hiddleston*,[66] the facts and legal background are different from the *res judicata* cases discussed above, although all the same authorities were canvassed. The

---

[64] *Irving v Hiddleston*, 1998 S.C.L.R. 350, a useful review of the authorities.
[65] See para.9.12, above, with regard to minors.
[66] 1998 S.C.L.R. 350.

pursuer's first solicitors settled her claim for damages. A sum was accepted in respect of *solatium*. Payments were also made in respect of her excess and loss of use. The pursuer's condition got worse and she sued in the Outer House. It was accepted that the claim for *solatium* was ruled out. However, no claims had previously been put forward for loss of wages or employability or for services. The actual ruling in this case was that the compromise did not encompass the new claims. Thus it is essentially a contract case deciding the meaning of certain terms agreed between the parties. (Accordingly, it is submitted that the comments following *McPhee* and not following, *inter alia*, *McSheehy* are *obiter*.[67])

---

[67] In *Thomson v Coutts*, 2001 G.W.D. 25–923, the Sheriff upheld a defence of *res judicata* where a second action was raised for uninsured losses. He followed *McPhee* and did not follow *McSheehy* and regretted that the parties had not cited *Irving*.

CHAPTER 26

DAMAGES AND OTHER REMEDIES

There are rules that apply to damages no matter what area of the law **26–1** triggers the remedy. An example is the rules applying in cases of fatal accidents where the same rules apply to cases of delict or breach of contractual duties. *Aquilian* liability depends upon damage and so the existence of an actionable head bears upon liability itself.[1] No attempt is made to track current awards even indicatively.[2] Damages for defamation are sufficiently different that they are treated in context.[3] Damages issues are properly separate from liability. Where the rule of liability is for loss wrongfully caused, then it is no surprise and equally proper to ask, "what, in that context, is loss?" If an apparent head of damage is not a loss for this purpose, there is no liability at all.[4]

PRINCIPAL THEMES

Compensatory damages

Damages awarded for a wrong may seek to compensate the pursuer **26–2** for the wrong. This is said to be by way of *restitutio in integrum* — restoring the situation, so far as money can, to where it was before the wrong was committed. There are innumerable dicta on this matter.[5] One often cited is: "The dominant rule of law is the principle of *restitutio in integrum* and subsidiary rules can only be justified if they

---

[1] For an exposition of that important relationship see Stapleton "The Gist of Negligence" (1988) 104 L.Q.R. 213.

[2] See McEwan and Paton, *Greens Reparation Bulletin* and *Greens Reparation Law Reports*.

[3] See para.8–32.

[4] It has recently been well put by Lord Hoffman in the House of Lords: "Before one can consider the principle on which one should calculate the damages to which a plaintiff is entitled as compensation for a loss, it is necessary to decide for what kind of loss he is entitled to compensation." *Banque Bruxelles Lambert v Eagle Star Insurance Co.* [1997] A.C. 191.

[5] See the complete theoretical overhaul in J. Stapleton, "The Normal Expectancies Measure in Tort Damages" (1997) 113 L.Q.R. 257.

give effect to that rule".[6] Another oft-cited passage[7] is that containing Lord Dunedin's four propositions in the "Susquehanna"[8]: "(1) There is no difference in this matter between the position in Admiralty law and that of the common law, and the common law says that the damages due either for breech of contract or for tort are damages which, so far as money can compensate, will give the injured party reparation for the wrongful act and for all the natural and direct consequences of the wrongful act. (2) If there be any special damage which is attributable to the wrongful act that special damage must be averred and proved . . . (3) If the damage be general, then it must be averred that such damage has been suffered, but the quantification of such damage is a jury question. (4) For a jury question no rigid rules, or rules that apply to all cases, can be laid down, but in each set of circumstances certain relevant considerations will arise which, were the matter before a judge, it would be the duty of the judge in the case to bring before the jury."[9] The Scottish courts generally like to keep the issue open. A good example is the following hypothesis from Lord Normand in *Hutchison v Davidson*[10]:

> "The law of damages ought not, it has been said, to be reduced to a mere rule of thumb, and, whatever subordinate rules may be formulated, there must be some cases which cannot fairly be brought within them. If the garage of a country house is destroyed, and it would cost £300 to replace it, it would in my view be less than just to award £100 because a garage could be bought for that sum in a neighbouring town. The defender's counsel conceded that in such a case the reasonable cost of restoration was the proper measure of damages, and I think that this concession was in no way rash, for a garage in the neighbouring town is not comparable as regards the proprietor's convenience with a garage which is an adjunct of his country house."

Penal, punitive and exemplary damages

26–3   Scots law, differing from English law,[11] appears to have given up the idea that, whether or not there is compensation, there can be

---

[6] *Liesbosch Dredger v S.S. Edison* [1933] A.C. 449, *per* Lord Wright at 463. However, the result in that case has not always been followed and indeed has recently been comprehensively rejected in the House of Lords *Lagden v O'Connor*, 2003 T.L.R. 667.

[7] See, *e.g. Hutchison v Davidson*, 1946 S.L.T. 11.

[8] [1926] A.C. 655, at 661.

[9] At 661.

[10] 1946 S.L.T. 11 at 19.

[11] See generally Clerk and Lindsell (18th Ed., 2000) 29–121 *et. seq.* For the current English approach see *Kuddus v Chief Constable of Leicestershire* [2001] 2 W.L.R. 1789.

damages to punish or make an example of, the wrongdoer.[12] So far as English law is concerned, the position is that "exemplary damages theoretically can be given in actions of negligence but they are virtually unknown." Violent profits, which is an almost defunct remedy, can on one view be said to be partly penal, but can reflect a primitive attempt to ensure that the pursuer does not suffer in the mensuration process where consequential losses are sought.

Mitigation

Mitigation is a principle of the law of damages and thus applies to **26–4** damages for delict.[13] So if something damaged can be more cheaply repaired than replaced, that ought to be attempted. In practice, it is found very seldom in personal injuries cases, where the plea is usually that the sum sued for is excessive, and the pursuer is put to proof of his losses.[14] In personal injuries cases, it may be suggested that the pursuer could have gone back to work sooner, could have found other work, has not tried to find other work or is malingering. So while the phrase "mitigation" can be found in some delict cases, it is often used in the sense of a plea in mitigation — to lower the penalty otherwise properly imposed.

Super-mitigation and *res inter alios acta*

Here the defender says that a gain that the pursuer has acquired **26–5** should go to reduction of the damages. The pursuer argues to the contrary, saying that this benefit is nothing to do with the case between them — that it is *res inter alios acta*. This can be seen at work in the Scots case *Cantwell v Criminal Injuries Compensation Board*.[15] Loss of pension rights is a recognised head of recovery of damages for personal injury. The question before the court was the effect of section 10 of the Administration of Justice Act 1982 as amended, which provides that in assessing damages pensions are not to be taken into account. (For the purposes of *Cantwell* the police statutory pension was treated as if contractual.) The First Division applied the letter of section 10, allowed a claim for lost pension rights, but did not reduce the award by the actual ill-health pension that was received. The House of Lords upheld an appeal, holding that the proper approach is, first of all, to identify the category of loss: Loss up to retirement is loss of earnings, loss after that is pension

---

[12] *Gibson v Anderson* (1846) 9 D. 1; *Muckarsie v Dixon* (1848) 11 D. 4; *Black v NB Rly*, 1908 S.C. 44.

[13] A particular problem touching on mitigation is considered below and should be read in conjunction with this section.

[14] For a theoretical discussion which also takes this view of mitigation in tort see J. Stapleton, "The Normal Expectancies Measure in Tort Damages" (1997) 113 L.Q.R. 257.

[15] 2001 S.L.T. 966.

loss. The next task is to assess that loss before considering any deductions. In this case, there was a loss of pension and a gain of a pension from the same source and they had to be aggregated as a first step. This is an exercise prior to any possible exercise of mitigation. The purpose of section 10 was to protect, say, loss of earnings from the deduction of a pension. This decision clarified the law on the particular practical point.[16] Another leading example of these issues being worked out, this time not a personal injury case, is in the important English House of Lords Appeal, *Dimond v Lovell*.[17] The issue arose in the following way. The plaintiff's car was damaged by the defender and she obtained a substitute car pending repair from a credit hire company. As it turned out, the House of Lords accepted that because of consumer protection legislation, the credit hire agreement was legally unenforceable and so the pursuer did not need to pay for the hire and so did not require to recover it from the defendant. This was a windfall for the defendant, who would otherwise have had to pay for some loss of use of the vehicle at the very least.

Lost chances and opportunities

26–6   The defender argues that the pursuer has actually been unable to show that a wrong has actually caused a loss and should thus lose. The pursuer reformulates the case as the loss of a chance. A basic example is *Kyle v P & J Stormonth Darling W.S.*,[18] a leading modern Scots case, but one that did not engage the range of dispute and argument that surrounds cases like this one and cases more difficult. The actual blunder in *Kyle* was the failure to lodge appeal papers in a case the pursuer had lost before the sheriff and the sheriff principal. It was held by an Extra Division that even the loss of the chance to press a legal right, if it had an ascertainable value, was actionable. It was not necessary to show that the action, which it was alleged had not been raised, would have been successful. The actual appeal had been marked and legal aid granted. This case involved a consideration of two important cases on the general topic of loss of a chance, namely *Kenyon v Bell*[19] and *Yeoman's Executrix v Ferries*.[20] The former was distinguished and the latter followed.[21] So legal right cases appear to be easier. It may also be that misrepresentation cases to are easily amenable to this approach. Reece cites Lord Lowry in

---

[16] See generally, McEwan and Paton, para.8–09; S.A. Bennet, "Setting Off on the Wrong Foot" 2000 S.L.T. (News) 214.

[17] [2000] 2 W.L.R. 1121.

[18] 1994 S.L.T. 191.

[19] 1953 S.C. 125.

[20] 1967 S.L.T. 332.

[21] See also *Eldin v Campbell Middleton Burness & Dickson*, 1989 S.L.T. 122 in the Inner House.

Spring v Guardian Assurance Plc,[22] the case where the worker got a "kiss of death" reference: "Once the duty of care is held to exist and the defendants negligence is proved, the plaintiff only has to show that by reason of that negligence he has lost a reasonable chance of employment . . . he does not have to prove that but-for the negligent reference, Scottish Amicable would have employed him."[23]

Discussion presently centres on the English House of Lords appeal, *Hotson v East Berkshire Health Authority*.[24] After trial and in the Court of Appeal, the plaintiff had been entitled to 25 per cent of full damages where it was shown that a condition arose as a result of a failed diagnosis but where there was a 75 per cent chance of this arising anyway. The House of Lords held that this finding was the cause of the condition was more likely to be natural than as a result of the failure of diagnosis and so the case failed completely. There was a 1 in 4 chance that the breach did not prevent the loss. *Hotson* was not the last word on the topic. It may be assumed to have settled the law, but it was not universally welcomed: "The House of Lords decision is a decision of striking analytical poverty and legal cowardice. It is remarkable for what it did not decide."[25] It has been applied since.[26]

Even where it is right to value a chance, there are problems about how to go about it.[27]

While it is possible to identify "legal right" cases as one category, that does not mean that all other cases must fall outside it. A good example of an attempt to distinguish between cases, which has not yet found favour in the courts, is that of Reece.[28] Phenomena are

---

[22] [1994] 3 W.L.R. 354.

[23] *ibid.*, at 375–376. Quoted in Reece, *op. cit.*, at p.203.

[24] [1987] A.C. 750.

[25] C. Foster, "A Plea for a Lost Chance: Hotson Reconsidered" (1995) N.L.J. 228, citing Lord Mackay at [1987] A.C. 750 at 786, 789 and Lord Bridge at 782–783.

[26] *Tahir v Haringey Health Authority* [1998] Lloyd's Rep. Med. 104; *Hardaker v Newcastle Health Authority* [2001] Lloyd's Rep Med 512 and *Gregg v Scott* [2002] EWCA civ 1471.

[27] In one English case account was taken of the possibility of a winning a sporting championship and going on to coach by working out the future losses in slices and discounting the increased amounts by the chances that they would not be achieved: *Lanford v Hebron*, [2001] P.I.Q.R. Q160. See the note C. Hough, "Damages — what might have been," 2002 P.I.L.J. Nov/Dec p.2. Compare this to the Scottish case *Paul v Ogilvie*, 2001 S.L.T. 171 (on professional negligence) criticised in, M. Hogg, "Paul v Ogilvy: A Lost Opportunity for Lost Chance Recovery", 2003 7 Edin. L.R. 86: "Lost chances which proceed from contradictory factual hypotheses should not be awarded in conjunction" at 92.

[28] H. Reece, "Losses of Chances in the Law" (1996) M.L.R. 188. Other academic studies of value to practitioners are J.G. Fleming, "Probabalistic Causation in Tort Law" (1989) 68 Can. Bar Rev. 661; J.G. Fleming, "Probabilistic Causation in Tort Law: A Postscript" (1991) 70 Can. Bar Rev. 136; M. Lunney, "What Price Chance?" (1995) L.S. 2; H.H.A. Stewart, "Medical Lost Chances: challenging the new orthodoxy," 2000 2(5) S.L.P.Q. 147.

"deterministic when their past uniquely determines their future".
Phenomena are "indeterministic when they have a random component".[29] The consequence of adopting this analysis is that many
medical cases, which, unlike *Hotson*, are indeterministic, can and
ought to be resolved by a loss of a chance approach. *Kyle* has perhaps
unnecessarily committed Scots law to the "but-for" test in "non-
legal-right" cases worthy of a loss of a chance approach in its desire
to respect earlier authority.

Once and for all

26–7   The general rule is that all loss must be recovered in one action. A
further extension of this is that all heads of loss are assumed to have
been sought in any action raised (although that is wider and more
debatable). There are exceptions and indulgences.

Re-opening the proof

26–8   In personal injury cases, and perhaps in any other case where the
damages incorporate an attempt to measure future loss, it is possible
to alter what is claimed for even if it has the effect of opening up a
proof or requiring further proof. This was decided by a court of seven
judges in *Rieley v Kingslaw Riding School*,[30] in which, pending
appeal on liability, the pursuer's leg required to be amputated. The
Lord Ordinary had indicated that a higher award would have been
appropriate had the leg needed to be amputated. The Inner House in
these circumstances agreed to hear the additional proof. Such cases
are exceptional.

Renewed claims

26–9   A possible exception to the once and for all rule is that a further
claim (*e.g.* after conclusion of a first action or after a time limit) may
be regarded as being so different that it constitutes a new claim. Such
cases are likely to be found under either (i) prescription and
limitation — it being too late to include a new head — or (ii) *res
judicata*.[31]

Interim damages

26–10   By virtue of special rules, a pursuer may get an advance payment.[32] This is not so much an exception in spirit but in the letter, in

---

[29] Reece, *op.cit.* at 194.
[30] 1975 S.L.T. 61.
[31] These issues are discussed above at 25–18.
[32] There is a full treatment in *McEwan & Paton*, Ch.1. For a general discussion, albeit
    regarding English law, see S. Ashcroft, "Law Commission Paper No. 224:
    Structured Settlements and Interim and Provisional Damages — A Practitioner's
    Review" [1995] J.P.I.L. 3.

that the pursuer obtains damages "twice or more and for all".[33] There is a balancing exercise at the end, and the pursuer might have to repay in certain circumstances.[34] The application of the rule has been settled to a considerable degree by *Cowie v Atlantic Drilling*,[35] in which the Division upheld a finding of interim damages (in terms of rule 89A of the 1965 Rules of the Court of Session) in favour of a workman injured on a North Sea oil rig. There were a number of alleged breaches of duty and a plea and averments of contributory negligence. There were two issues: (1) Would the pursuer succeed on liability to any extent? The court considered this matter well settled by an existing line of authority[36]: the test is whether the pursuer will succeed, or will certainly succeed, or will almost certainly succeed. In this case, the accident was admitted; an absolute duty was applicable and the court was satisfied that the test was met. (2) Would the pursuer succeed without any substantial finding of contributory negligence? Here the court settled a divergence of view on the proper interpretation. The court preferred the view that said it meant "considerable" or "big", which was defined as more than a quarter or a third.[37] The First Division found it impossible to come to an estimate; however, that operated in the pursuer's favour as the court was, therefore, unable to say that there would be a considerable finding.[38]

Provisional damages

The public policy arguments that cases should finish or that people **26–11** should not be troubled too often by the same action has less force when the defender is a public authority or an insured body. On that assumption, UK legislation provides for provisional damages.[39] This is still, as will be seen from the text following, not a true exception to the common law,[40] but, practically, it is a huge divergence. Section

---

[33] The practice is governed by rule 43.9 of the 1994 Rules of Court and the Sheriff Court Rules, rule 36.8–10. The payment may itself be by instalments: Damages Act 1996, s.2.

[34] See observations in *Walker v Infabco Diving Services Ltd*, 1983 S.L.T. 633.

[35] 1995 S.L.T. 1151.

[36] *Douglas's C.B. v Douglas*, 1974 S.L.T. (Notes) 7; *Walker v Infabco Diving Services Ltd*, 1983 S.L.T. 633; *Nelson v Duraplex Industries Ltd*, 1975 S.L.T. (Notes) 31 and *Reid v Planet Welding Equipment Ltd*, 1980 S.L.T. (Notes) 7.

[37] *McNeill v Roche Products Ltd*, 1988 S.L.T. 704.

[38] In *Hogg v Carrigan*, 2001 Rep. L.R. 60 an interim award was made in face of a possible no-seatbelt contribution of 25%.

[39] There is a full treatment in McEwan & Paton, Ch.2. See generally J. Blaikie, "Provisional damages: A Progress report", 1991 36 J.L.S. 109; J. Blaikie, "Provisional damages: Please may I have some more?", 1995 S.L.P.Q. 65 and albeit regarding English law, S. Ashcroft, "Law Commission Paper No.224: Structured Settlements and Interim and Provisional Damages — A Practitioner's Review" [1995] J.P.I.L. 3, R. Milligan, "Provisional Damages," 2002 Rep B. 2.

[40] See Lord Weir in *Potter v McCulloch*, 1987 S.L.T. 308 at 310.

12 of the Administration of Justice Act 1982, which applies in Scotland, provides that if there is proved or admitted to be a risk that at some definite or indefinite time in the future the injured person will, as a result of the act or omission which gave rise to the cause of the action, develop some serious disease or suffer some serious deterioration in his physical or mental condition the court may, on the application of the injured person order that damages may be paid and the right granted to come back at some specified later time for more. It is a condition of such an indulgence that the person responsible for paying the damages is a public authority or public corporation; or insured or otherwise indemnified in respect of the claim.

In *White v Inveresk Paper Co. Ltd (No.2)*,[41] as anticipated in *Potter* the word "serious" in section 12 had to be considered. Lord Murray, accepting there was a 5–10 per cent risk of osteoarthritis, found this to be material and not *de minimis*, and did not consider this to be serious deterioration. "Serious" qualifies "deterioration" rather than "effects". The persuasive factor seems to have been the argument that was put by counsel that a clear line needed to be drawn in such cases. Lord Murray pointed out that "the deterioration in question does not provide a clear cut and severable threshold of the kind which is really needed to enable the reservation to be properly applied in future. The line between permanent minor residual restrictions of the knee and the onset, probably gradually, of osteoarthritic symptoms would be difficult or impossible to draw."[42] In *Meek v Burton's Gold Medal Biscuits Ltd*,[43] Lord Prosser rejected the idea that the Act could not be used where the subsequent claim would depend upon a subsequent triggering event. However, in this case an award was not made. Although there was a risk of serious deterioration, even then there might not be serious consequences.

Quantification of damages (property and economic loss)

26–12   There are certain general approaches. The approach to moveable property can be seen in the following opinion of Lord Jamieson in *Pomphrey v James A. Cuthbertson Ltd*[44]:

> "The owner of an article which has been damaged through the fault of another is entitled to reparation for the wrongful act and for all the natural and direct consequences of the wrongful act. He is entitled to *restitutio in integrum*. To give effect to that general principle of law certain rules have been evolved in practice. If the article can be economically repaired the measure

---

[41] 1988 S.L.T. 2.
[42] At 5; see also *McMenemy v Argyll Stores Ltd*, 1992 S.L.T. 971.
[43] 1989 S.L.T. 338.
[44] 1951 S.L.T. 191.

of damages is the cost of the repairs, together with any consequential damage naturally and directly flowing from the wrongful act. If on the other hand the article is totally destroyed or cannot be economically repaired, and is an article which has a marketable value, the measure of damages is in the general case its value immediately before it was damaged. The owner of a damaged article must therefore decide whether the article is capable of being economically repaired or is to be treated as a constructive total loss. If he makes a wrong decision, he may lay himself open to the charge by the wrongdoer that he has failed in his duty to minimise the damage. The test is: What would a prudent owner, who had himself to bear the loss, do in the circumstances?"[45]

In a professional negligence case where, for example, there has been a negligent valuation, the basic rule is the difference between the careless valuation and the valuation that ought to have been made at the time. Repairs are a cross-check.[46]

South Australia Asset Management principle ("SAAMCO", "Banque Bruxelles")

Some economic loss cases give rise to real difficulties where there **26–13** has been a change in market conditions. There is authoritative guidance on these problems as a result of many cases at the end of the last century. The leading case is now *South Australia Asset Management Corporation v York Montague Ltd.*[47] Damages issues are properly separate from liability. Where the rule of liability is for loss wrongfully caused, then it is no surprise and equally proper to ask, what in that context is loss. If an apparent head of damage is not a loss for this purpose there is no liability at all. The present position is most easily seen in the decision in the *Nykredit* associated appeal. The lenders, on March 12, 1990, advanced £2.45 million on the security of a property valued by the defendants at £3.5 million. The correct value had been said by the judge to be between £2 and £2.375 million. The price obtained at auction in February 1993 when the market had taken a fall was £345,000. The judge quantified the

---

[45] At 196–197. For an example which makes a practical point, see *McQueen v Hepburn*, 1979 S.L.T. (Sh. Ct) 38 which considers some of the older dicta.

[46] *Stewart v H.A. Brechin & Co.*, 1959 S.C. 306, assumed to be the correct measure in the delict case *Martin v Bell Ingram*.

[47] [1996] 3 All E.R. 365 and other related cases The case is sometimes known as the Banque Bruxelles Lambert appeal because that decision in the Court of Appeal was the leading decision. It settled before getting to the Lords. See P.J. Wade, "High Valuations versus Bad Lending", 1995 Rep. B. 4–2 and *Leeds Permanent Building Society v Fraser & Steele*, 1995 S.L.T. (Sh. Ct) 72, both ante-dating South Australia Asset Management.

damages at £3,058,555. On appeal, the House of Lords said the figure should be the difference between £3.5 million and the true value at the date of the valuation. So the negligent surveyors escaped the consequences of the fall of the market. The reasoning of the House of Lords was based on limiting the scope of the duty itself — the surveyors were not advising on a course of conduct, but relaying information upon which the pursuers would act. The test in tort was: how much worse off were the pursuers because the information was wrong? Lord Hoffmann explained the reasoning by way of the doctor and mountaineer analogy. The mountaineer, who is worried about his knee, goes to the doctor who says it is OK. He goes mountaineering and is injured, but not through anything wrong with his knee. The doctor cannot be liable to the mountaineer. It has been followed (but not applied) in Scotland in *Newcastle Building Society v Paterson, Robertson & Graham*.[48]

Quantification of damages (personal injuries)

26–14   There are a number of special rules about the computation of damages, particularly in the area of personal injuries or in respect of the death of a relative. A distinction is made between loss to a person's estate or wealth, known as patrimonial loss and, on the other hand, pain and suffering, which is compensated by an award of *solatium*.

Patrimonial loss: items recoverable

26–15   (i) Wages lost to the date of the proof, together with an award for projected future loss due to the continuing effects of the injury are recoverable. In computing the amount to be paid in respect of wage loss, the following calculation is made:

> — calculate a figure for annual wage loss (called the multi-plicand);
> — multiply by a figure (called the multiplier) which reflects the years over which there will be a wage loss.

The multiplier is necessarily less than the actual number of years over which wages are prima facie lost (*e.g.* until retirement at 65) because of two main factors: (a) the fact that damages are paid in a lump sum and can, therefore, gain interest; and (b) the possibility that the injured person would die at some time during the period over which damages are being awarded. Thus there is usually a bigger multiplier for a young person than an old person, especially (in the latter case) if the pursuer is soon to retire. Until recently lawyers

---

[48] 2002 S.L.T. 747

were content to look at previous cases and the facts of a case to come to a suitable multiplier. After some consideration, reflected clearly in *O'Brien's C.B. v British Steel*,[49] the position has been reached as a result of the House of Lords' decision in *Wells v Wells*,[50] where "official" Ogden tables are used to start finding the multiplier. Further, in using the tables, it has now been accepted that in working out the rate of return, which a prudent pursuer would seek, the pursuer does not need to be a risk taker. That suggests that the return will be quite low, which in turn provides a bigger damages award. The particular rate of return to be selected is that set by statutory instrument.[51] The Ogden tables provide only for the contingency of mortality and judicial experience is still needed to enhance or discount multipliers from the tables.

Section 9 of the Damages (Scotland) Act 1976[52] provides that the court should take into consideration lost wages that a pursuer would have earned if his life expectancy had not been reduced by the accident. In personal injuries cases, the multiplier is to be applied from the date of the proof, whereas in fatal accident cases, the multiplier applies from the date of death. Alternatively, rather than apply a multiplier to a multiplicand, and especially if it seems that the pursuer will be able to find work or continue working, the court may award a lump sum to reflect general disadvantage in the job market.

(ii) Medical expenses generally are recoverable and will cover the cost of necessary transport between hospital and home. The cost of wheelchairs, crutches and prosthetics is recoverable.

(iii) Interest on such damages is due (subject to the court's discretion) usually from the date of the accident, by virtue of the Interest on Damages (Scotland) Act 1971. The damages are divided between prior and future loss. Thus, interest is given on the actual loss sustained to the date of the proof. Interest at half the "court rate" is usually awarded, to reflect the fact that the loss occurred, on a week-by-week basis.

Deductions from patrimonial loss

These are as follows: **26–16**

(i) Any benefits received, other than from the injured person's own estate which the person would, in the court's opinion, have received or have been acquired.

(ii) Income tax from the loss of earnings sum.

---

[49] 1991 S.L.T. 477. See generally See S.A. Bennett, "The Future's Bright; the Future's Ogden," 2001 S.L.T. (News) 54, I. Artis, "The Present is Brighter for Ogden," 2001 S.L.T. (News) 153.

[50] [1998] 3 W.L.R. 329.

[51] Presently the Damages (Personal Injuries) (Scotland) Order 2002.

[52] See Casebook, App. Ext. 11.

(iii) In terms of the Social Security (Recovery of Benefits) Act 1997, benefits are effectively taken back from damages awards.[53] The defender compensator is made liable to the Secretary of State.[54] The pursuer will appreciate that the defender has this liability and must know the extent of the clawback to enable decisions as to settlement or continued conduct of the litigation to be made. The compensator is allowed to deduct the payments he is obliged to make from the pursuer.[55] The Act provides how this is to be done, the principle being "like for like".[56] Deductions from each category of damages awarded may only extend to those paid over the relevant period, normally five years from the accident.[57] A full and final settlement brings the relevant period to a premature end.[58] Compensation has to be broken into three heads from which associated benefits are recoverable: (1) earnings lost during the relevant period[59]; (2) cost of care incurred during the relevant period[60]; (3) loss of mobility during the relevant period.[61] Courts must now specify in their orders the amount of any compensation payment that is attributable to each of these three heads over the relevant period.[62] Settlements and tenders will have to be arranged to take account of recoupment. The 1992 Scheme allowed for a small settlements figure of £2,500. The 1997 Act permits this, but it has not been reintroduced at the time of writing.

The effect of the scheme is that if the defender or insurer is liable for a penny, they are liable for all the benefits. Under the previous scheme, this State clawback could come out of the injured person's solatium or pain and suffering money — but no longer.

(iv) The full amount of any earnings from employment, or unemployment benefit, and any payment made by the wrongdoer (unless through a trust).

---

[53] And the associated Social Security (Recovery of Benefits) Regulations 1997 (SI 1997/2205). See generally F. Maguire, "Compensation Recovery", 42 J.L.S.S. 352.

[54] s.6.

[55] s.8.

[56] Sch.2.

[57] In the case of disease, it is five years from the first listed benefit claim.

[58] s.3(4).

[59] Benefits recoverable are: disability working allowance; disablement pension payable under s.103 of the Social Security Contributions and Benefits Act 1992; incapacity benefit; income support; invalidity pension and allowance; jobseekers allowance; severe disablement allowance; sickness benefit; statutory sick pay; unemployability supplement; unemployment benefit.

[60] Recoverable benefits are: attendance allowance; care component of disability living allowance; disablement pension increase payable under s.104 or s.105 of the Social Security Contributions and Benefits Act 1992.

[61] Recovered from mobility allowance; mobility component of disability living allowance.

[62] s.15.

(v) Again against income, there is to be deducted any saving made by the injured person by being maintained at the public expense, *e.g.* in a hospital.

No account is to be taken of any contractual pension, or pension or retirement benefit from public funds, nor of any payment made by an employer subject to any obligation to repay in the event of the recovery of damages, nor of the proceeds of an insurance policy.[63]

There is a modern approach to compensation damages in general (this applies to *solatium* below) which argues for a structured settlement: "A structured settlement is an extra-judicial settlement under which the defender's insurers undertake to pay periodic payments to the insured party in lieu of the whole or part of the traditional lump sum. The defender's insurers (the general insurers) then reinsure their obligation using a life office."[64] There are tax advantages to such schemes and it may be argued by the defender that the benefit should be split.[65] The system, seldom seen in practice, has now been approved and enhanced by the legislature.[66]

Solatium

The injued person can recover for among other things pain and **26–17** suffering, loss of faculties; and shortened expectation of life. Section 5 of the Damages (Scotland) Act 1993 added a new section 9A to the Damages (Scotland) Act 1976. The amended Act allows loss of expectation of life to be taken into account in awarding solatium, whereas before the provision in section 9 only allowed this in relation to patrimonial loss. If the injured person's expectation of life has been reduced by the injuries and the injured person is, was, or at any time would be, likely to become aware of that reduction, the court must have regard to the consequence of that awareness he has suffered or is likely to suffer.[67] There are complicated rules on interest on damages that are beyond the scope of this book.[68] Generally, past *solatium*, *i.e.* pain and suffering suffered before the proof — will attract interest at a figure representing approximately the average "court rates" for the period from the date the injuries

---

[63] Administration of Justice Act 1982, s.10. The common-law position is the same: *Parry v Cleaver* [1970] A.C. 1; *Forgie v Henderson* (1818) 1 Murray 410; *Davidson v UCS Ltd*, 1990 S.L.T. 329.

[64] Eden, "Structured Settlements" (1992) 37 J.L.S.S. 207.

[65] The English Law Commission has issued a consultation paper on this and related topics.

[66] Damages (Scotland) Act 1996, ss.4, 5 and 6; Casebook, App.18.

[67] s.5; new s.9A(1). This overturns the rule in *Dalgleish v Glasgow Corp.*, 1976 S.C. 32 in which an award was made to a comatose child.

[68] The reader is referred to the Interest on Damages (Scotland) Act 1971 and McEwan & Paton (3rd ed.).

were healed, or approximately one-half the average rate where pain continues and part of the *solatium* is apportioned to the past.[69]

The courts will generally take a broad brush approach to questions of quantification. Courts are assisted by awards in clearly similar cases, but obviously every case has its own peculiarities.[70] It should be remembered that inflation affects the value of money and that care should be taken in comparing awards in older cases. Awards in England still tend to be higher than those in Scotland and those in the United States are many times higher.[71] Until recently, jury trials were rare, yet judicial awards were based on what reasonable men would award. At the time of writing, jury cases are more common and, while subject to control of excess, the trend is for jury awards to be published and for them to help to inform judicial awards.[72] This has led to an increase in awards.[73]

Transmission on death and the relatives' claim on death

26–18   The law is regulated by the Damages (Scotland) Act 1976 as amended by the Damages (Scotland) Act 1993.[74] This law applies where a person dies in consequence of personal injuries sustained by him as a result of an act or omission of another person, being an act or omission giving rise to liability to pay damages to the injured person or his executor.[75]

In brief, it allows the deceased's pain and suffering to be inherited by his executor and it allows various relatives to have a claim in their own right for the wrongful death. There are detailed procedural rules to pull all of these individuals together. While, by the Damages (Scotland) Act 1976 (as originally enacted), no right to *solatium* for personal injuries transmitted to the representatives, the right to damages of a claimant in consequence of personal injuries will (subject to exceptions) now transfer to the executor in the same way

---

[69] The court rates are laid down in various Acts of Sederunt.

[70] See *Barker v Murdoch*, 1979 S.L.T. 145; *Bowers v Strathclyde R.C.*, 1981 S.L.T. 122.

[71] This leads to what is sometimes called forum shopping — considering in detail whether jurisdiction can be established in a more generous state. Regular reference to the Judicial Studies Board Guidelines may be bringing Scottish and English awards closer in practice.

[72] *Girvan v Inverness Farmers Dairy (No.2)*, 1998 S.L.T. 21.

[73] A.M. Hajducki, "Changing Values: Bereavement Awards in the post-Shaher World," 2003 S.L.T. (News) 189.

[74] For a detailed record of the genesis of this Act, including extracts from newspapers and Hansard and the Law Commission papers, see Ch.1 of Casebook.

[75] There is certainly now an element of transmission in the claim and it is accordingly dealt with here. The calculation of damages, meanwhile, is different-another reason for separating it from the treatment of quantification in Ch.12. However, there are related issues and the two sections might usefully be read together.

as patrimonial loss cases.[76] The *solatium* is calculated up to the date of death.[77] The unamended 1976 Act gave certain relatives of a deceased person the right to recover "loss of support" and a right to certain relatives to recover "loss of society". The 1993 Act introduced a new "relative's non-patrimonial award", discussed below, to replace loss of society and in a way that will make the award more substantial. The relatives' claims depend upon the category or categories into which they fall. Everyone who is in the immediate family is a relative, but not all relatives are in the immediate family: "immediate family" is a subset of "relatives". Loss of support is dealt with under "immediate family", below, but is also relevant to the treatment of "relative".

"Immediate family"

This is defined as parents and children of the deceased. It includes **26–19** the deceased's spouse and a cohabitee, *i.e.* any person, not being the spouse of the deceased, who was, immediately before the deceased's death, living with the deceased as husband or wife, and recently has been held to cover a woman who married a man after the delict had been committed.[78] It includes in-laws.[79] The Scottish Law Commission has responded to the vast majority of views on consultation that brothers and sisters should have title to sue. Following their general approach that would not be extended to brother and sisters in law. It is proposed to extend title to sue to *de facto* brothers and sisters — those brought up in the same household as the deceased as reflection of modern family life. They recommend extension to grandparents and grandchild, but not remoter ascendants. The Commission proposes to treat "same-sex cohabitants" as broadly equivalent to "opposite-sex cohabitants". On balance, the Commission did not recommend extension to persons engaged the one to the other.

(i) Loss of support

These persons are entitled to claim loss of support, which is based **26–20** on the actual amount of support that was usually received.[80] It is

---

[76] 1993 Act, s.3, inserting new s.2 of the 1976 Act. 1993 Act, s.3; new s.2(1) of the 1976 Act.

[77] In relation to verbal injury cases, a claim in respect of injury transmits to the executor, but, with the exception of patrimonial loss cases, only if the claimant brought an action while alive. The term "personal injuries" in the 1976 Act and the Administration of Justice Act 1982 was amended to include injury from defamation, verbal injury or any other verbal injury or injury to reputation.

[78] See Administration of Justice Act 1982; *Phillips v Grampian Health Board*, 1988 S.L.T. 628.

[79] *McAllister v ICI Plc*,1997 S.L.T. 351; *Monteith v Cape Insulations*, 1997 G.W.D. 28–1431.

[80] See *Hatherley v Smith*, 1989 S.L.T. 316 (necessary averments).

appropriate to take account of likely increases in support that would have followed,[81] but not speculative matters.[82] In assessing loss of support, the court will not take into account remarriage prospects.[83] Nor will the court deduct social security benefits paid or money that will accrue from the deceased's estate, such as insurance policies. Reasonable funeral expenses are recoverable.[84]

(ii) Non-patrimonial award. Contemplation, grief and non-patrimonial benefit award

26–21   Alternatively or in addition to a loss of support claim there is the "contemplation, grief and non-patrimonial benefit award" or an amended section 1(4) award.[85] In legislation passed or made before the Damages (Scotland) Act 1993, the phrase "loss of society award" is to be construed as an amended section 1(4) award.[86] To call this a loss of society award would be to risk confusion with cases under the unamended Act and to call it the non-patrimonial award might risk leaving out of account the other elements. Such an award is competent only to relatives who are members of the deceased's immediate family.[87] The three elements to such an award, being such damages as the court thinks just, are: (1) distress and anxiety endured by the relative in contemplation of the suffering of the deceased before his death; (2) grief and sorrow of the relative caused by the deceased's death; (3) the loss of such non-patrimonial benefit as the relative might have been expected to derive from the deceased's society and guidance if the deceased had not died. The court may take a broad brush to this award and need not ascribe particular sums to any head. The last part is essentially the same as the loss of society award previously provided for and decisions on that will be useful in relation to subsection (3) cases.[88] Note that the transfer provisions noted above mean that if a wife dies shortly after her husband who died as a result of the defender's negligence, her section 1(4) claim, having vested, will transmit to her executor. However, of the various heads it is more likely that the grief and sorrow element will transfer than the non-patrimonial element because of the restriction on the transfer to the position before the death of the relative. The new phrasing of the award was not intended by the Commission to change

---

[81] *Smith v Comrie's Exrs*, 1944 S.C. 499.

[82] *Daniell v Aviemore Station Hotel Co.*, 1951 S.L.T. (Notes) 76.

[83] Law Reform (Miscellaneous Provisions) Act 1971, s.4.

[84] s.1(3); *Porter v Dickie*, 1983 S.L.T. 234; *Prentice v Chalmers*, 1985 S.L.T. 168.

[85] There is no short form for this in use. "Grief" would be too narrow and cause problems for mistaken cross-referencing to nervous shock.

[86] 1993 Act, s.7(1).

[87] See above. A child in utero is a child for these purposes — *Cohen v Shaw*, 1992 S.L.T. 1022.

[88] See *Dingwall v Walter Alexander & Sons*, 1981 S.L.T. 313; *Donald v SPTE*, 1986 S.L.T. 625.

but to clarify the law so previous decisions are still relevant — nonetheless, the general view of pursuers' agents, now supported to an extent by the courts, is that the Commission intended to allow the courts to award the higher sums that the 1976 Act might have envisaged.[89] An award is also competent for any personal services rendered to the deceased and it is a legitimate head of claim to include a sum in respect of the services that the deceased would have rendered to the relative in terms of the Administration of Justice Act 1982.

Relatives

Relatives, according to Schedule 1 to the 1976 Act (as amended), **26–22** are immediate family as defined above, with the addition of the following: ascendants and descendants; any person who was, or was the issue of, a brother, sister, uncle or aunt of the deceased, and any person who, having been a spouse of the deceased, had ceased to be so by virtue of a divorce. It does not matter that the relationship is through the mother's line rather than the father's, nor that a child or parent is a stepchild or step-parent, nor that a child is illegitimate. These persons can recover loss of support suffered or likely to be suffered. They may recover reasonable funeral expenses. The relatives, who are not also members of the immediate family, have no right to a loss of society award. By section 9 of the 1982 Act, the same extended body of relatives are entitled to claim for personal services, which (i) were or might have been expected to be rendered by the deceased, (ii) were of a kind which when rendered by a person other than a relative would ordinarily be obtainable on payment, and (iii) the deceased might have been expected to render gratuitously. This allows, *inter alia*, a working widow or widower to claim for the services of, for example, a cook or a housekeeper.

REMEDIES OTHER THAN DAMAGES

Interdict

Interdict, even in the sheriff court, is governed by a specialised **26–23** body of rules relevant to such actions. The reasons may be that ultimately the defender can be imprisoned for breach of interdict, and that urgent action is often required. There is also a set of other rules that apply to the granting of interim interdict. The need for interim interdict is obvious — it might be useless to await the outcome of a contested case if the damage is already done. Many of the cases have to be dealt with immediately, when the balance of convenience is an

---

[89] A.M. Hajducki, "Death Payments — A New Approach", 1999 S.L.T. (News) 77. See *McManus v Babcock Energy*, 1999 G.W.D. 21–1013.

important consideration and often operates in favour of the status quo. The essential requirements for an interim interdict are title and interest to sue, a *prima facie* case[90] and the balance of convenience being in the applicant's favour.[91]

Normally, interdict cannot be granted against the Crown and the Scottish executive. In cases involving wrongs to the person there is little difficulty. Interdict will be granted against, for example, apprehended assault.[92] In the same way, molestation[93] will be interdicted. For some time, in the case of parties who are married, a matrimonial interdict — one that restrains or prohibits any conduct of one spouse towards the other or a child of the family or prohibits a spouse from entering or remaining in a matrimonial home or in a specified area in the vicinity of a matrimonial home — had the special privilege of being able to be fortified by a power of arrest.[94] More recently, this has been extended to parties who are not married.[95] Conduct that amounts to harassment[96] is restrained by a special statutory remedy.[97]

Economic delicts[98] may be restrained. Many cases involving economic delicts involve trade unions and account must be taken of their immunities in delict.[99] Unless the immunity applies, strikers, sitters-in and illegal picketers will be restrained.[1] An important rule is that interdict cannot be granted in absence if the defender claims or is likely to claim that he acted in contemplation or furtherance of a trade dispute.[2]

Passing-off is a delict that is regularly restrained by interdict: by its nature, if it continues, irreparable damage may be done.[3] The balance of convenience in interim interdict applications will normally favour an established trader.

---

[90] *Osborne v British Broadcasting Corporation*, 2000 S.L.T. 150, *Discovery Communications Inc v Discovery FM Ltd*, 2000 S.L.T. 212.

[91] *Deane v Lothian Regional Council*, 1986 S.L.T. 22.

[92] para.4–3 *et seq.*

[93] In the contemporary sense of harassment rather than the traditional sense of troubling of possession in lands: see Stair I, 9, 26 which also imported a right to obtain an order ordering the wrongdoer to desist.

[94] Matrimonial Homes (Family Protection) (Scotland) Act 1981, s.14(1); s.15(1)

[95] See para.2–15.

[96] See para.2–15 above for a discussion of the right.

[97] See para.2–15.

[98] See Ch.5.

[99] See Ch.23. See also K. Ewing, "Interdicts in Labour Law", 1980 S.L.T. (News) 121.

[1] See dicta in *Galt v Philp* 1984 S.L.T. 28; *Phestos Shipping Co. v Kurmiawan*, 1983 S.L.T. 388; *Timex Electronic Corporation v AEEU*, 1994 S.L.T. 438.

[2] *Scotsman Publications Ltd v SOGAT*, 1986 S.L.T. 646.

[3] See Ch.5.

An anticipated breach of confidence may be restrained.[4] In relation to heritage, interdict operates as a possessory remedy as well as preventing wrongs. It is best to see these cases as adjuncts of the rights conferred by the law of property rather than as wrongs to property.[5]

Cases of nuisance have proved to be difficult to analyse. While from the standpoint of interdict, nuisance incurs a strict liability, so far as damages are concerned "nuisance" *culpa* must be averred and proved, albeit this may be by inference.[6]

A fear of repeated trespass can be restrained.[7] So far as moveables are concerned, it is clear from *Leitch & Co. v Leyden*[8] that where appropriate, wrongs to moveables will be interdicted.[9] Interdict against a repeat of a defamatory statement is an obvious and uncontroversial protection from harm on the basis of an existing finding of wrongdoing.[10] Even before the coming home of human rights, cases of interdict prior to publication have been treated as much more of a problem. An application is competent.[11] At the interim stage, the balance of convenience remains the test, taking into account the reparabilility of the harm in damages and the public interest.[12] It may be that asking simply whether or not the statement is prima facie defamatory[13] may not give enough protection to the freedom of speech.[14] The same issues arise in relation to breach of confidence.

Professor Munro, re-examined the issue against the background of Human Rights Law in Scotland and readers are respectfully referred

---

[4] Indeed that is the best way of implementing the obligation. The topic is dealt with in Chs 8 and 17. See *A Family v BBC*, The Scotsman, November 6, 1992; *Osborne v British Broadcasting Corporation*, 2000 S.L.T. 150.

[5] See, *e.g. Calquhoun v Paton* (1859) 21 D. 996; *Maxwell v GSW Railway Co.* (1866) 4 M. 447. And for a third party enforcing a real burden see *Lees v North East Fife District Council*, 1987 S.L.T. 769. See also *Wills Trs v Cairngorm Canoeing and Sailing School Ltd*, 1976 S.L.T. 162; *Cowie v SRC*, 1985 S.L.T. 333; *Nicol v Blott*, 1986 S.L.T. 677; *Burton's Trs v Scottish Sports Council*, 1983 S.L.T. 418.

[6] See Ch.3. For a recent example of interdict and nuisance damages see *G B & A M Anderson v White*, 2000 S.L.T. 37.

[7] *Hay's Trustees v Young* (1877) 4 R. 398; *Stuart v Stephen* (1877) 4 R. 873; *Colquhoun and Cameron v Mackenzie* (1894) 22 R. 23; *Wallace-James v Mont gomerie & Co.* (1899) 2 F. 107.

[8] 1931 S.C. (HL) 1.

[9] See also Ch.3.

[10] Walker, *Delict*, 453.

[11] *Waddell v BBC*, 1973 S.L.T. 246.

[12] In *Waddell* the balance of convenience favoured the publishers.

[13] As in, *e.g. McMurdo v Fergusson*, 1993 S.L.T. 193.

[14] Traditionally the English approach was to be in favour of publication, *e.g. Ferris-Bank (Anguilla) Ltd v Layar and others* [1991] T.L.R. 68 unless there was a clear exception such as a conspiracy to injure, *e.g. Gulf Oil Ltd v Page* [1987] Ch. 327. (A case described by Tony Weir as egregious and disgraceful: Weir, *Economic Torts*, (Oxford, 1997) pp 19–20.)

to that study,[15] which considers, *inter alia*, ECHR jurisprudence[16] suggesting that in future issues of pressing social need and the necessity of intereference will be live issues — there is no bright line rule against prior judicial restraint.[17] Permanent orders are less controversial.

Declarator

26–24   A litigant may ask the court to declare that a certain course of conduct is a civil wrong. In such a case, the right to the remedy may depend upon the law of delict. A simple declarator might well be sufficient when dealing with a responsible body, which would follow the decision of the court. Indeed, before the enactment of the Crown Proceedings Act 1947, this process was necessary in ordinary reparation cases. A declarator may be sought to declare conduct not delictual if that will have a practical effect in the actual case, although because the Inner House cannot bind the High Court of Justiciary, a declarator of non-criminality is incompetent.[18] The ECHR considers declarations of infringement can be sufficient to constitute just satisfaction and there is no reason at all why Scots courts could not deal with a human rights reparation case in the same way.

Judicial review

26–25   This is a procedure to obtain remedies in matters that concern the Court of Session's supervisory jurisdiction. It is not restricted to matters of public law, but applies also to cases where a jurisdiction is given to a body to take decisions.[19] It might well be the only remedy where there is an alleged liability by omission by a local authority that is causing a continuing loss. While this may well be actionable in damages, a better remedy might be to obtain an order against the authority to prevent further loss.[20] Indeed, it is possible to obtain any remedy in an application for judicial review, including damages and including restitution, unlike the equivalent English Jurisdiction.[21] If a case raises a several case for reparation that might

---

[15] C.R. Munro, "Prior Restraint of the Media and Human Rights Law", 2002 J.R. 1.

[16] Such as, *e.g. Handyside v UK* (1976) A 24, 1 E.H.R.R. 737, *Observer Ltd and Guardian Newspapers Ltd v UK* (1991) A 216, 14 E.H.R.R. 153.

[17] Professor Munro also provides an incisive analysis of the effect of section 12 of the HRA in this context. In particular he emphasises the need for an applicant for an order to comply with section 12(2) to take all practicable steps to notify the applicant for an order for prior restraint. See also *Dickson Minto WS v Bonnier Media Ltd*, 2002 G.W.D. 551.

[18] *Law Hospital NHS Trust v Lord Advocate*, 1996 S.L.T. 848.

[19] See, generally, *West v Secretary of State for Scotland*, 1992 S.L.T. 636.

[20] See *Rowling v Takaro Properties Ltd* [1988] 2 W.L.R. 418 for an illustration.

[21] See *Woolwich v Inland Revenue* [1992] 3 W.L.R. 366.

best be pursued as an ordinary action rather than being tacked on to a judicial review.[22] Damages for abuse of office[23] may be in a different category and might perhaps best be considered in the context of the judicial review action.

Actions of harassment

The Protection from Harassment Act 1997[24] is implemented, *inter* **26–26** *alia*, by a separate action of harassment.

State systems

At various times, the reparation system has not been adequate to **26–27** meet the ends of social policy, either domestic, supra-national or international. Thus many wrongs may be compensated, for example through Workers Compensation systems, the Criminal Injuries Compensation Scheme or the Motor Insurers Schemes.[25]

Court of Session simplified procedure

The Court of Session has introduced special procedures for **26–28** allowing reparation cases to be case managed and fast-tracked. Pleadings are reduced in significance and complexity. The law of delict is not affected by any of these rules, but it is likely that more cases will go to proof and more decisions will be reached after proof, which should make the law less abstract but more difficult to state concisely!

---

[22] *Shetland Line (1984) Ltd v Secretary of State for Scotland*, 1996 S.L.T. 653.
[23] See Ch.7.
[24] See para.2–15.
[25] All of which are detailed in Stewart, *Reparation, Liability for Delict*.

BIBLIOGRAPHY

Adams, J., "Is There a Tort of Unfair Competition?" 1985 J.B.L. 26 5–10
Adams, J. and R. Brownsword, "The *Aliakmon* and the Hague Rules", 1990
    J.B.L. 23 10–8
Anon "Medical Negligence: Hunter v Hanley 35 Years On", 1990 S.L.T.
    (News) 325 22–3
Anton, A.E., *Private International Law* (2nd ed., 1990) 1–5
Anton, A.E. and P.R. Beaumont, *Civil Jurisdiction in Scotland* (2nd ed.,
    1995) 1–5
Arnell, S., "Causation reassessed", 2002 S.L.T. 265 9–22
Artis, I., "The Present is Brighter for Ogden", 2001 S.L.T. (News) 153 26–15
Ashcroft, S., "Law Commission Paper No. 224: Structured Settlements and
    Interim and Provisional Damages—A Practitioner's Review" [1995]
    J.P.I.L. 3 .... 26–10, 26–11
Atiyah, *Accidents, Compensation and the Law* (3rd ed., 1980), p.44 9–10
    pp.116–121 9–20
Atiyah, *Rise and Fall* (Oxford, 1979), Ch.20 1–2

BMA Guidelines (2nd ed.) 23–36
Bailey, S.H. and M.J. Bowman, "Public Authority Negligence Revisited",
    2000 C.L.J. 59(1), 85 12–3
Bailey, S.H. and M.J. Bowman, "The Policy/Operational Dichotomy—a
    Cuckoo in the Nest", 1986 C.L.J. 430 12–3
Balen, P., "An introduction to product liability claims" [2002] J.P.I.L. 3 19–3
Bankton, I, iv, 32 4–3
Bates, F., "What must be foreseen?" 1970 S.L.T. (News) 97 9–5
Bender, L., "A Lawyer's Primer on Feminist Theory and Tort" (1988) 38 J.
    Legal Educ. 3 9–9
Bennet, S.A., "Setting Off on the Wrong Foot" 2000 S.L.T. (News) 214 26–5
Bennett, S.A., "The Future's Bright; the Future's Ogden", 2001 S.L.T. (News)
    54 26–15
Bickford-Smith, M., "Damages for Failed Sterilisation" [2001] J.P.I.L. 404 23–28
Bigwood, R., "Economic Duress by (Threatened) Breach of Contract" (2001)
    117 L.Q.R. 376 5–16
Birks, "The Concept of a Civil Wrong" in *Philosophical Foundations of Tort
    Law* (Owen ed., Oxford, 1995), p.39 1–1
    pp.42–45 1–17
Birks, *Introduction to the Law of Restitution* (Oxford, 1989) 1–2
Black, "Delict and the Conflict of Laws", 1968 J.R. 40 1–5
Black, *Historical Survey*, p.326 9–1
Black, R., "An Historical Survey of Delictual Liability in Scotland for
    Personal Injuries and Death", 1975 C.I.L.J.S.A. 46, 189, 316
Blackie, HPLS II, 633 8–1
    702 8–36
    705 8–34
Blackie, J., "Enrichment and Wrongs in Scots Law" [1992] Acta Juridica
    23 1–2
Blackie, J., "The Provoking Dogs Problem 2", 1993 J.L.S. 148 20–1
Blackie, J., "Enrichment Wrongs and Invasion of Rights in Scots Law'" in *The
    Limit of the Law of Obligations* (Visser ed., 1997) 1–2

Blaikie, J., "Negligent Solicitors and Disappointed Beneficiaries", 1989 S.L.T. (News) 317 10–11
Blaikie, J., "Nervous Shock: Traumatised Fellow Workers and Bystanders", 1994 S.L.T. (News) 297 11–2
Blaikie, J., "Product Liability" (1987) 32 J.L.S.S. 325 .... 19–3, 19–8
Blaikie, J., "Provisional damages: A Progress report", 1991 36 J.L.S. 109 26–11
Blaikie, J., "Provisional damages: Please may I have some more?", 1995 S.L.P.Q. 65 26–11
Blom-Cooper, L., "The Right to be Let Alone" [1989] J.L.S. 402 1–19
Boberg, P.Q.R., *The Law of Delict* (Jutta, 1989)
pp.26–27 1–4
pp.31–32 1–18
Boch, C. and R. Lane, "A New Remedy in Scots Law: Damages from the Crown for Breach of Community Law", 1992 S.L.T. 145 16–2
Bogie, D., "Personality in relation to the Law of Abortion", 1967 S.L.T. (News) 145 23–23
Bonnington, A.J., "Privacy: Letting the Right Alone", 1992 S.L.T. (News) 289 .... 1–19, 8–37
Bowen, A.J., "Manual handling: A Foreseeable Possibility or a Duty of Insurance", 2002 S.L.T. (News) 189 .... 21–18, 21–21
Bowen, A.J., "*Stevenson v East Dunbartonshire Council*, 2003 S.L.T. 97", 2003 S.L.T. (News) 29 21–7
Brodie, D., "Negligence in the Convention," in *A Practical Guide to Human Rights Law in Scotland* (Reed ed., W. Green, 2001) 17–1
Brodie, D., "Nervous Shock and Professional Rescuers" (1997) Rep. B. 13–2 11–2
Brodie, D., "Public Authorities and the Duty of Care", 1996 J.R. 127 12–1
Brownsword, R., "Freedom of Contract, Human Rights and Human Dignity," in Friedman and Barak-Erez, *Human Rights in Private Law* (Hart, 2001) p.190 23–38
Burchfield, "Controversial Vocabulary in the Oxford English Dictionary" in *Unlocking the English Language* (Faber, 1989), p.96 5–6

Cameron, Gordon D.L., "Strict Liability and the Rule in *Caledonian Railway Co v Greenock Corporation*", 2000 (5) S.L.P.Q. 356 3–11
Cameron, J.T., "Intimidation and the Right to Strike", 1964 S.L.T. (News) 81 5–15
Cane, P., *Atiyah's Accidents Compensation and the Law* (6th ed., Butterworths, 1999) 1–10
Cane, P., "Contract Tort and the Lloyd's Debacle" in *Consensus in Idem* (Oxford, 1996) 1–2, 10–1
Cane, P., "Does No-Fault Have a Future", 1994 J.P.I.L. 302 1–10
Cane, P., "Vicarious Liability for Sexual Abuse" (2000) 116 L.Q.R. 21 24–5
Carey Miller, D.L., "A Statutory Substitute for Scienter" (1973) J.R. 61 20–1
Carey Miller, D.L., "The Scottish Institutional Writers on Animal Liability" (1974) J.R. 1 20–1
Carey Miller, D.L. and H. Lardy, "Calcutt II: Comments from a Scots Perspective", 1993 S.L.T. (News) 199 .... 1–19, 8–37
Carter, "Choice of Law in Tort and Delict" (1991) 107 L.Q.R. 405 1–5
Carty, H., *An analysis of the Economic Torts* (OUP, 2001) 5–9
Carty, H., "Intentional Violation of Economic Interests: the Limits of Common Law Liability" (1988) 104 L.Q.R. 242 .... 5–9, 5–10
Cave, P., "Contract, Tort and the Lloyd's Debacle" in *Consensus ad Idem* (Rose ed., Sweet & Maxwell, 1996), p.5 10–10
Cheer, U., "New Zealand Court of appeal rejects the 'Murphy' approach to tort liability for defective buildings" (1995) Tort L. Rev. 90 12–4

Clark, *Product Liability* (Sweet & Maxwell, 1989) 19–3
  Ch.8 19–8
Clark, A., "Conceptual Basis of the Product Liability" (1985) 48 M.L.R.
  325 19–3
Clark, A., "Liability for Defective Products" (1981) 26 J.L.S. 398 19–3
Clark, A., "Product Liability: The New Rules", 1987 S.L.T. (News) 257 19–3
Clark, A., "US Product Liability" (1982) 27 J.L.S. 514 19–3
Clerk, J.F. and Lindsell, W.H.B., *The Law of Torts*, (18th ed., 2000)
  para.4–100 23–17
  para.10–11 23–13
  29–121 *et. seq* 26–3
  Chs 15, 24, 26 and 27 5–1
  27–37 5–4
  24–85 5–16
Clive, "Goods by Any Other Name", 1963 S.L.T. (News) 106 5–6
Colbey, R., "Personal Injury Claims Arising out of Food Poisoning" [1994]
  J.P.I.L. 294 19–4
Conaghan, J. and W. Mansell, *The Wrongs of Tort* (Pluto Press, London,
  1993) 1–9
Concise Oxford Dictionary of Current English (9th ed.) 5–6
Conway, *Personal Injury Practice in the Sheriff Court* (2nd ed., W. Green,
  2003) 1–6
  p.303 18–10
  Ch.18 18–10
Craig and Miller, *Employment Law in Scotland*, Ch.11 23–22
Crawford, E., *International Private Law* (W. Green, 1998) 1–5
Cross, "Limited Liability Partnerships—Draft Bill and Consultation paper"
  (1999) J.R. 137 23–19
Cusine and Paisley, *Servitudes and Rights of Way* 18–3

"Damn *Injuria* Again", 1984 S.L.T. (News) 85 1–7
Davidson, P.F., "Nuisance and Negligence", 1986 J.R. 107 3–8
Davies, "The End of the Affair: Duty of Care and Liability Insurance" (1989)
  9 L.S. 67 1–11
Davies, M., "The Road from Morocco: Polemis, Donoghue, No Fault" (1982)
  45 M.L.R. 534 9–25
Denning, Lord, *Landmarks in the Law*, pp.223–227 24–1
Devereux, J.A., "Actions for Wrongful Birth" (1996) Tort L. Rev. 107 23–27
Dickinson, I., "Crown Immunities Post–1998", 2003 S.L.T. (News) 107 23–2
Dig. IX 2, 5, 2 23–39
Downie, G.H., "New Right to Damages in Community Law" (1992) 37
  J.L.S.S. 424 16–2
Doyle, J.J., "The Liability of Public Authorities (1994) 1 Tort L. Rev. 189 12–1
Duff, A., "Civil Actions and Sporting Injuries Sustained by Professional
  Footballers", 1994 S.L.T. (News) 175 25–7

Eden, "Structured Settlements" (1992) 37 J.L.S.S. 207 26–16
Edwards and Griffiths, *Family Law* (W. Green, 1997) 23–23
Eekelaar, J., "Corporal Punishment, Parents' Religion and Children's Rights",
  2003 L.Q.R. 370 .... 2–4, 17–11
English Law Commission Report on Injuries to Unborn Children (Law Com.
  No.60 (1974)) 23–23
Erskine J., *An Institute of the Law of Scotland*, (J.B. Nicholson) (2 vols,
  1871)
  III, i, 16 5–2
  III, 1, 13 1–8

Ervine, W.C.H., "Product Liability and Part 1 of the Consumer Protection Act 1987" (1988) SCOLAG 21 .... 19–3, 19–8

Evans-Jones, *The Civilian Tradition in Scots Law* (Stair Society, 1995) 1–7

Ewing, K., "Interdicts in Labour Law", 1980 S.L.T. (News) 121 26–23

Fairgrieve, "The Human Rights Act 1998, Damages and Tort law" [2001] P.L. 695 17–1

Feenan, D.K., "Medical Negligence (Hunter v Hanley 35 Years On: A Reply)", 1991 S.L.T. 321 22–3

Feldthusen, "Failure to Confer Discretionary Public benefits: The Case for Complete Negligence Immunity", 1997 Tort L. Rev. 17 12–3

Ferguson, P.R., "Compensation for Alleged Vaccine Injury" (1994) 39 J.L.S. 80 19–3

Ferguson, P.R., "Pharmaceutical Products Liability", 1992 J.R. 226 19–3

Fleming, J.G., "Probabalistic Causation in Tort Law" (1989) 68 Can. Bar Rev. 661 26–6

Fleming, J.G., "Probabilistic Causation in Tort Law: A Postscript" (1991) 70 Can. Bar Rev. 136 26–6

Fleming, J.G., "The Fall of the Crippled Giant" (1995) 3 Tort L. Rev. 56 3–10

Fleming, J.G., "Tort in a Contractual Matrix" (1995) 3 Tort L. Rev. 12 9–7

Foster, C.,"A Plea for a Lost Chance: Hotson Reconsidered" (1995) N.L.J. 228 26–6

Fraser, W.L.R., *Constitutional Law* (Hodge, 1938)
p.179 1–4
p.194 1–4
p.200 1–4

Freeman, R., "Product Liability, defective goods" [2001] J.P.I.L. 26 19–3

Gloag and Henderson, *The Law of Scotland* (11th ed., W. Green, 2001) Chs 25, 26 and 27 .... 4–6, 5–9

Goddard, C., "Work Equipment" [2000] J.P.I.L. 220 21–14

Goldberg, "The Development Risk Defence and Medicinal Products" (1991) 36 J.L.S.S. 376 19–8

Gordley, J., "Contract and Delict: Towards a Unified Law of Obligations", (1997) 1 Edin.L.R. 345 1–2

Gordley, J., "Tort Law in the Aristotelian Tradition" in Owen "Why Philosophy Matters to Tort Law" 1–15
p.131 1–15

Gordon, *Criminal Law* (2nd ed., W Green), para.28–01 23–24

Gordon, W.M., "Householders' Liabilities" (1982) 27 J.L.S.S. 253 4–3

Gore, A., "Asbestos claims" [2002] J.P.I.L. 105 9–22

Gow, J.J., "Is culpa ammoral?" (1953) 65 J. R. 17 1–17

Grainger, C.J., "Wrongful Life: A wrong without a remedy" (1994) 1 Tort L. Rev. 164 23–30

Grundy, P.M.D. and A.P. Gumbs, "Bolam, Sidaway and the Unrecognised Doctrine of Informed Consent: A Fresh Approach'" [1997] J.P.I.L. 211 2–2

Guthrie-Smith, *The Law of Damages*, p.241 8–36

Habib, S., "Vicarious Liability: beating off the blame", 2003 P.I.L.J. August p.11 24–6

Hajducki, A.M., "Changing Values: Bereavement Awards in the post-Shaher World", 2003 S.L.T. (News) 189 26–17

Hajducki, A.M., "Death Payments—A New Approach", 1999 S.L.T. (News) 77 26–21

Handford, P., "The Dog Act in the New South Wales Court of Appeal" 1995 Tort Law Rev. (Note), p.5 20–1

Harris, D.R., et al, *Compensation and Support for illness and Injury* (Oxford, 1984) 1–10

Hepple, B., "Negligence: the Search for Coherence" [1998] C.L.P. 69 9–1

Heuston, R., "Judicial Prosopography" (1986) 102 L.Q.R. 90 5–10

Hogg, "Relational Loss, the Exclusory Rule and the High Court of Australia" (1995) 3 Tort L. Rev. 26 10–1

Hogg, "The Very Private Life of the Right to Privacy" (EUP, 1994), Hume Paper Vol. 2, No. 3 8–37

Hogg, M., *Obligations* (Avizandum, 2003) 1–2, 10–1

Hogg, M., "Paul v Ogilvy: A Lost Opportunity for Lost Chance Recovery", 2003 7 Edin. L.R. 86 26–6

Hogg, M.A., "Privacy: A Valuable and Protected Interest in Scots Law", 1992 S.L.T. 349 .... 1–19, 8–37

Holyoak, J. and F. Mazzocchetti, "The Legal Protection of Economic Interests", (1993) 1 Tort L.R. 185 5–10

Hough, C., "Damages—what might have been", 2002 P.I.L.J. Nov/Dec p.2 26–6

HSE guidance publication: "Seating at Work": HAS(G) 57 (HMSO, 1991 ISBN 0118854313) 21–12

HSE "Ergonomic Aspects of Escalators used in Retail Organisations" CRR12/1989 (HMSO, 1989, ISBN 0118859382) 21–13

HSE "Passive smoking at work" IND(G) 63L (Rev) 1992 21–13

Hudson, A.H., "Crime, Tort and Reparation: A Common Solution", 1992 S.L.T. (News) 203 25–8

Hudson, A.H., "Crime, Tort and Reparation—What Solution?", 1984 S.L.T. (News) 321 25–8

Hume, Lectures, III, 186 4–3

208 3–12

Immanuel, H., "Causation—justice for nurses?", 2002 P.I.L.J. Nov/Dec 1 21–23

Ingman, T., "A History of the Defence of Volenti Non Fit Injuria", 1981 J.R. 1 25–7

Inst I, i, 3 1–15

Jackson, B.S., "Liability for Animals in Scottish Legal Literature", 1 J.R.139 20–1

Jaffey, A.E., "Volenti Non Fit Injuria", 1985 C.L.J. 87 25–7

Jamieson, *Summary Applications* GPL (W. Green, 2000) 2–8

Johnston, D., "Owners and Neighbours: from Rome to Scotland" in *The Civil Law Tradition in Scotland* (Evans-Jones ed., 1995), Stair Society Supplementary Volume 2 5–10

p.176 3–12

Jones, "Breach of Confidence after Spycatcher" [1989] C.L.P. 49 5–3

Junor, G., "Beyond the Common Law—The (potential) reach of product liability", 2001 Rep. B. 41–5 19–3

Junor, G., "Reparation at Sea: Being a Share Fisherman", 1999 30 Rep. B. 2 23–17

Junor, G., "Road Authorities on Ice: A postscript or new chapter?", 2003 50 Rep. B. 4 .... 12–7, 18–11

Kamba, W.J., "Concept of Duty of Care and Aquilian Liability in Roman Dutch Law", 1975 J. R. 252 1–17

Kames, I, i, 1 4–3

Keown, J., "Beyond Bland: a critique of the BMA guidelines on withholding and withdrawing medical treatment", (2000) 20 L.S. 66 23–36

Kidner, R., "Remoteness of Damage: the Duty Interest Theory and the Re-interpretation of The Wagon Mound", 1989 L.S. 1 9–25

Kidner, R., "Resiling from the *Anns* principle: the variable nature of proximity in negligence" (1987) 7 L.S. 319 9–8
Kidner, R., "The Variable Standard of Care, Contributory Negligence and Volenti", 1991 L.S. 1 25–7
Kilbrandon, Lord, "The Law of Privacy in Scotland" (1971) 2 Cambrian L. R. 35 8–37
Kinloch, "Slippery Substances", 1995 Rep. B. 4–7 18–4
Kinloch, D., "*Salter v UB Frozen and Chilled Foods Ltd.*" 2003 S.L.T. (News) 261 11–2
Kinloch, D. and C. McEachran, "Damages for Children—some reflections", 2003 (51) Rep. B. 2 23–31
Kolbert (1989) 1–7
Kostal, R.W., "Currents in the Counter-reformation: illegality and the duty of care in Canada and Australia" (1995) Tort L. Rev. 100 25–8

Langstaff, B., "Upper Limb Disorders: Work Related or Unrelated?" [1994] J.P.I.L. 14 21–17
Laurie, G.T., "Privacy, Paucity and the Press", 1993 S.L.T. (News) 285 .... 1–19, 8–37
Law Commission Consultation Paper on Liability for Psychiatric Illness, 1995 CP No.137 11–5
Levy, J., "Manual handling" [2001] J.P.I.L. 130 21–18
Lewis, R., "Insurers Agreements not to Enforce Strict Legal Rights" (1985) 48 M.L.R. 275 24–1
Liability for Antenatal Injuries (Scot. Law. Com. No.30 (1973)) 23–23
Liability for Psychiatric Illness (Law Com. No.249, 1998) 11–5
Lloyd and Simpson, "The Computer at Work", 1992 S.L.T. (News) 177 21–17
Logie, "Affirmative Action in the Law of Tort: the Case of the Duty to warn" (1989) 48 C.L.J. 115 9–3
Logie, "Special Relationships, Reasonable Foreseeability and Distinct Probabilities: the Duty to Prevent Damage to the Property of Others", 1988 J.R. 77 13–1
Logie, "The Final Demise of Junior Books", 1989 J.R. 5 10–4
Logie, J.G., "Proof of Causation in Medical Negligence Cases", 1988 S.L.T. (News) 25 22–6
"Lord Macmillan's Speech" (1992) 108 L.Q.R. 236 19–2
Lunney, M., "What Price Chance?" (1995) L.S. 2 26–6

McBryde, W.W., "Bourhill v Young: the Case of the Pregnant Fishwife" in *Comparative and Historical Essays in Scots Law* (Carey Miller and Meyers, eds, Butterworth, 1992), p.66 .... 9–4, 11–1
McBryde, W.W., "The Advantages of Fault", 1975 J.R. 32 1–17
MacCormack, G., "Aquilian Culpa" in *Daube Noster* (Watson ed., 1974) 1–7, 1–17
MacCormack, G., "Culpa in the Scots Law of Reparation", 1974 J. R. 13 1–17
MacCormack, G., "Culpa Tenet Suos Auctores: The Application of a Principle", 1973 J.R. 159 24–1
McEwan and Paton on *Damages for Personal Injuries in Scotland* 26–1, 26–17
  Ch.1 26–10
  Ch.2 26–11
  para.8–09 26–5
McKendrick, E., "Economic Duress—A Reply", 1985 S.L.T. (News) 277 5–16
McKenzie, A.P., "Privacy: A New Right in UK law?", 2002 S.L.T. (News) 98 8–37
Mckenzie, D., et al., "Civil Liability for Injury and Damage Arising from Access to the Scottish Countryside'" (1997) 2 S.L.P.Q. 214 18–3
McKenzie, D.W. and Evans-Jones, R., "The Development of Remedies for Personal Injuries and Death" in *The Civilian Tradition in Scots Law* (Evans-Jones ed., Stair Society, supplementary volume 2 (1995)) 1–8

Mackenzie Stuart, "Liability of Common Carriers" (1926) 3 8 J.R. 205 4–6
MacKintosh, J., "The Edict nautae caupones stabularii" (1891) 3 J.R. 306 4–5
McLaren, J., "Nuisance Law and the Industrial Revolution—Some Lessons
    from Social History" [1983] 3 O.J.L.S. 155 1–8
McLean report, *Independent Review Group on the Retention of Organs at
    Post-Mortem in Scotland* 23–38
McManus, F., "Bye-bye Rylands-Again!", 1995 J.R. 194 3–10
McManus, F., "Culpa and the Law of Nuisance", 1995 J.R. (note) 462 .... 1–17, 3–8
McManus, F., "Culpa and the Law of Nuisance", 1997 J.R. 259 1–17
McManus Russell et al, *Delict: A comprehensive Guide to the Law* (Wiley),
    xvii 1–19
MacNair's *Law of the Air* (4th ed.) p.107 3–3
MacQueen, H.L., "The Wee McGlen case: Representations of Scottishness
    —Passing off and Unfair Trading" (1983) 5 E.I.P.R. 18 5–7
MacQueen, H.L., "Wee McGlen and the Action of Passing Off", 1982 S.L.T.
    (News) 225 5–7
MacQueen, H. and D. Brodie, "Private Rights, Private Law and the Private
    Domain", in *Human Rights and Scots Law: Comparative Perspectives on
    the Incorporation of the ECHR* (Boyle, Himsworth et al eds, Hart,
    2002) 17–1
MacQueen and Thomson, *Contract Law in Scotland* (LexisNexis, 2000) 1–2
MacQueen, H. and W.D.H. Sellar, "Negligence", *HPLS* 517 9–1
    534–535 24–1
    584–611 24–1
Maher, G., "Statutory Interpretation and Scottish Law Commission Reports",
    1992 S.L.T. (News) 277 23–26
Malcolm, (The Hon David K.), A.C., "The High Court and Informed Consent:
    The Bolam Principle Abandoned" (1994) 1 Tort L. Rev. 81 2–2
Markesinis, *The German Law of Torts*,
    p.10 1–18
    p.11 23–39
    p.35 1–18
    pp.37–43 1–18
    pp.51–58 1–18
    p.56 1–18
    p.58 1–17
    p.60 1–17
    pp.95–109 1–18
    pp.148–239 1–18
    p.662 .... 23–35, 23–39
Markesinis, B.S., "Negligence, nuisance and affirmative duties of action"
    (1989) 105 L.Q.R. 104 .... 3–8, 9–3
Markesinis, B.S., "The not so Dissimilar Tort and Delict" (1977) L.Q.R. 78 1–14
Mason, J.K., "Unwanted pregnancy: a case of retroversion?" (2000) 4 Edin.
    L.R. 191 23–27
Mason, J.K., "Wrongful Pregnancy, Wrongful Birth and Wrongful Terminol-
    ogy" (2002) 6 Edin. L.R. 46 .... 23–27, 23–28, 23–29
Mason, J.K and G.T. Laurie, "Consent or property: Dealing with the body and
    its parts in the shadow of the Bristol and Alder Hey" (2001) Mod. L.R.
    710 23–38
Middleton, K.G., "Reform of UK Competition Law", 1998 S.L.T. (News)
    47 5–12
Milligan, R., "*Fairchild v Glenhaven Funeral Services*", 2002 46 Rep. B. 1 9–22
Milligan, R., "Provisional Damages", 2002 Rep B. 2 26–11
Mitchell, C., "Partners in Wrongdoing", 2003 L.Q.R. 364 .... 23–16, 24–5
Mullany, "Common-sense Causation—an Australian View", 1992 O.J.L.S.
    431 9–21

Munro, C.R., "Prior Restraint of the Media and Human Rights Law", 2002 J.R. 1 26–23

Newdick, C., "The Development Risk Defence", 1988 C.L.J. 455 19–3
Newdick, C., "The Future of Negligence in Product Liability" (1987) 103 L.Q.R. 288 .... 19–3, 19–8
Norrie, "Disappointed beneficiaries, the House of Lords and Scots Law", 1995 Rep. L.R. 32 22–7
Norrie, *HPLS*
495 5–2
497–500 2–8
Norrie, K., "Common Practice and the Standard of Care in Medical Negligence" (1985) J.R. 145 22–3
Norrie, K., "Defamation, Negligence and Employers' References" (1994) 39 J.L.S.S. 418 8–28
Norrie, K., "Hurts to Character, Honour and Reputation: a Reappraisal", 1985 J.R. 163 8–1
Norrie, K., "Informed consent and duty of care", 1985 S.L.T. (News) 289 2–2
Norrie, K., "Liability for injuries caused before birth", 1992 S.L.T. (News) 65 23–25
Norrie, K., "Liability of Solicitors to Third Parties", 1988 S.L.T. (News) 309 10–11
Norrie, K., "Wrongful Life in Scots Law: No Right, No Remedy", 1990 J.R. 217 23–30

O'Brien, L.S., "The Validity of the Diagnosis of Post-Traumatic Stress Disorder" [1994] J.P.I.L. 257 11–1
O'Carroll, M., "Nervous Shock: Proposals for Reform" (1995) 40 J.L.S. 231 11–5
Owen, "Why Philosophy Matters to Tort Law" 1–15

Patrick, H., "New Act Heralds Major Reform of Scottish Mental Health Law", 2003 S.L.T. (News) 255 2–11
Pearson Commission: Cmnd 7054 (1978) 19–3
Phillips, A.F., "Further Reflections on Medical Causation", 1988 S.L.T. (News) 325 22–6
Phillips, A.F., "Medical Negligence and No-Fault Compensation", 1989 J.L.S. 239 22–6
Phillips, J. and A. Coleman, "Passing Off and the Common Field of Activity" (1985) 101 L.Q.R. 242 5–6
Phillipson's, G., "Transforming Breach of Confidence? Towards a Common Law Right of Privacy under the Human Rights Act" (2003) 66 M.L.R. 726 8–37
Powles, D., "Product Liability—A Novel Dimension in Scots Law", in A.J. Gamble (ed.), *Obligations in Context* (W. Green, 1990) at p.33 19–3
Price, D., "Fairly Bland: an alternative view of a supposed new 'death ethic' and the BMA guidelines" (2001) 4 L.S. 618 23–36
"Professional negligence: the dilatory solicitor and the disappointed legatee", 1996 S.L.P.Q. 245 10–11

Reece, H., "Losses of Chances in the Law" (1996) M.L.R. 188 26–6
Reid, C.T., "Damages for Deliberate Abuse of Power", 1988 S.L.T. (News) 121 7–1
Rennie, R., "Solicitors' Negligence: Third Parties Join the Queue", 2001 6 S.L.P.Q. 304 22–7
Reparation Law Reports (W. Green) 1–1, 26–1
Reparation Bulletin (W. Green) 1–1, 26–1
Reparation: Liability for Delict (W. Green) 1–1

Report on Liability for Psychiatric Illness, Law Com No.249 11–5
Robertson, E., "Consider the Foetus", 1997 S.L.T. (News) 319 23–23
Rodger, "Bouygues and Scottish Choice of Law Rules in Delict", 1995
    S.L.P.Q. 58 1–5
Rodger, "Lord MacMillan's Speech in *Donoghue v Stevenson*" (1992) 108
    L.Q.R. 236 .... 1–14, 9–1
Rodger, "Mrs Donoghue and Alfenus Varrus", 1988 C.L.P. 1 and (1992) 108
    L.Q.R. 236 9–1
Rodger, "Spuilzie in the Modern World", 1970 S.L.T. (News) 33 3–13
Rodger, A., "Antenatal injury", 1974 J.R. 83 23–23
Russell, E., "Abortion Law in Scotland and the Kelly Foetus", 1997 S.L.T.
    (News) 187 23–24
Russell, E., "Establishing Medical Negligence—A Herculean Task", 1998
    S.L.T. (News) 17 22–6
Russell, E., "Lone Workers—The Employer's Duty in Respect of Double
    Manning and Security Screens", 2003 S.L.T. (News) 241 21–8
Russell, P., "The Commercial Exploitation of Fictitious Names" (1980) 130
    N.L.J. 256 5–7

Sales, P., and D. Stilitz, "Intentional Infliction of harm by Unlawful Means"
    (1999) 115 L.Q.R. 411 .... 5–2, 5–10
Sandison, D., "Medical Negligence Claims: The Paucity of Funding", 1995
    J.L.S. 309 22–6
Scottish Law Commission No.135, paras 10–1 — 10–8 23–34
Scottish and English Law Commissions: Cmnd 6831 (1977) 19–3
Scottish Law Commission Discussion Paper on Damages for Psychiatric
    Injury, 2002 S.L.C. DP No.120 .... 11–5, 11–6
Scottish Law Commission Report 2002 No. 187 11–6
Semple, W., "Why Conduct a Legal Practice as a Limited Company", 2001
    Journal of the Law Society of Scotland (March) 23–20
Seneviratne, M., "The rise and fall of advocates' immunity" (2001) 21 L.S.
    644 22–8
Sheldon, S., " 'Sperm bandits', birth control fraud and the battle of the sexes"
    (2001) 21 L.S. 460 23–38
Simpson HPLS II 24–1
Skene, L., "Proprietary Rights in human bodies, body parts and tissue:
    regulatory contexts and proposals for new laws" (2002) 22 L.S. 102 23–38
Smith, "When the Truth Hurts", 1998 S.L.T. (News) 1 8–36
Smith, T.B., "Designation of Delictual Actions: Damn Injuria Damn", 1972
    S.L.T. (News) 125; "Damn Injuria Again", 1984 S.L.T. (News) 85 1–7
Sopinka, J., "The Liability of Public Authorities: Drawing the Line" (1993) 1
    Tort L. Rev. 123 12–1
Spink, P., "The Consumer Protection Act the State of the Art Defence" (1997)
    42 J.L.S.S. 416 19–8
Stair Memorial Encyclopaedia, Vol. 10 .... 16–1, 16–2
    para.81 16–2
    paras 239–244 16–2
Stair Memorial Encyclopaedia, Vol. 14 3–4
    para.2087 .... 1–17, 3–8
Stair Memorial Encyclopedia, Vol. 15, para.558 8–36
    Stair I, i, 7 23–23
    Stair, I, ix, 4 8–1
    Stair, I, ix, 5 1–19
    Stair, I, ix, 8 5–15
    Stair, I, ix, 16 3–13
    Stair, 1, ix, 25 3–1
    Stair III, iii, 21 23–17

Stair Society, Vol. 20, "Delict", p.268 8–1
Stanton et al., *Statutory Torts* (Sweet & Maxwell, 2003) 15–2
Stapleton "The Gist of Negligence" (1988) 104 L.Q.R. 213 26–1
Stapleton, J., "Duty of Care: Peripheral Parties and Alternative Opportunities
    for Deterrence" [1995] 111 L.Q.R. 301 1–9
    305 1–9
    306 1–9
    317 1–9
Stapleton, J., "Products Liability Reform—Real or Illusory", 1986 6 O.J.L.S.
    392 .... 19–3, 19–8
Stapleton, J., "Software, Information and the Concept of Product" (1989) 9 Tel
    Aviv Stud. in Law 47 19–4
Stapleton, J., "The Normal Expectancies Measure in Tort Damages" (1997)
    113 L.Q.R. 257 .... 26–2, 26–4
Steele, J., "Private law and the environment: nuisance in context", 1995 L.S.
    236 3–4
Stein, P., "*The actio de effusis vel dejectis* and the Concept of Quasi-Delict in
    Scots Law" (1955) 4 I.C.L.Q. 356 4–3
Stein, P.G., *Romisches Recht und Europa: Die Geschichte einer Rechtskultur*
    (1996), 38 1–1
Stewart, *A Casebook on Delict*, App. Ext. 5 8–17
    Appendix, Ext. 11 .... 1–7, 26–15
    Ext. 11. 2.1.3 1–7
    Ext. 11 1–19
    Ext. 12 1–8
    Ext. 14 1–7
    App. 18 26–16
    Ext. 42 10–4
    Ext. 86 8–29
    Ext. 93 25–9
Stewart, "Damages for Birth of a Child" (1995) J.L.S. 298 23–27
Stewart, *Reparation: Liability for Delict* 3–2, 3–13, 4–1, 7–1, 11–1, 11–6, 12–1,
                  13–1, 14–1, 15–1, 17–1, 18–1, 19–1, 20–1, 21–1,
                        21–9, 22–1, 24–1
    Ch.2 1–5
    Ch.8 5–1
    Ch.29 1–13
    Ch.33 1–6
Stewart, A., "Live Issue—Damages for Wrongful Birth" (1996) J.L.S. 443 23–27
Stewart, A., "Smith's question-mark", 1990 J.R. 71 1–1
Stewart, H.A., "Medical Lost Chances: challenging the new orthodoxy", 2000
    2(5) S.L.P.Q. 147 26–6
Stewart, J.B., "Football: Civil Aspects", 1981 S.L.T. (News) 157 25–7
Stewart, Q., "The Law of Passing-Off—A Scottish Perspective" (1983) 5
    E.I.P.R. 64 5–7
Stewart, W.J., "A Note on the Liability of Pupils in Delict", 1989 S.L.T.
    (News) 404 23–31
Stewart, W.J., "Lawburrows: Elegant Remedy or Absurd Form", 1988 S.L.T.
    181 2–8
Stewart, W.J., "Skiing and the Law: the First Case" (1990) 3 5 J.L.S.S. 27 25–7
Stoppa, "The Concept of Defectiveness in the Consumer Protection Act 1987:
    a critical analysis", 1992 L.S. 210 19–5
Sutherland, L, "A Relationship of Mutual Trust", Rep. L.B. 5–4 2–2
Sutherland, L., "A Single Standard of Care" (1995) Rep. B. 6–11 22–3
Sutherland, L., "Damages for the Birth of a Healthy Child", Rep. B. 14–3 23–27
Sutherland, L., "Update—Medical Negligence (post-MacFarlane decisions)",
    2001 39 Rep. B. 3 23–28

Tan, C.G.S., "Volenti Non Fit Injuria: An Alternative Framework", 1995 Tort
L. Rev. 208 25–7
Teff, H., "Liability for Negligently Inflicted Nervous Shock" (1983) 99 L.Q.R.
100 .... 11–1, 11–3
Thomson, A., "Economic Duress", 1985 S.L.T. (News) 85 5–16
Thomson, J.M., "Abandoning the Law of Delict", 2000 S.L.T. (News) 43 1–15
Thomson, J.M., "An Island Legacy—the Delict of Conspiracy" in *Compar-
ative and Historical Essays in Scots Law* (Carey Miller & Mayers, eds,
Butterworths, 1992), p.137 5–11
Todd, S., "Negligence Liability of Public Authorities: Divergence in the
Common Law" (1986) 102 L.Q.R. 370 12–4
Turnbull, G.J., "Post-Traumatic Stress Disorder—a Psychiatrist's Guide"
[1997] J.P.I.L. 234 11–1
Turnbull, *The Spycatcher Trial* (Heinemann, London, 1988) 5–3
Turner, D., "Pre-action protocol: tripping up over disclosure", 2003 P.I.L.J.
August p.2 18–10
"The Dilatory Solicitor and the Disappointed Legatee", 1993 S.L.T. (News)
329 10–11
"The Right to be Let Alone" (1989) 34 J.L.S.S. 402 8–37

Upton, "Crown Liability in Damages under Community Law [Parts 1 & 2]",
1996 S.L.T. (News) 175 and 211 16–3

Van Gerven, *Cases, Materials and Text on National, Supranational and
International Tort Law* (Hart, 2000) 10–8
Visser & Whitty, *HPLS*
p.424 1–1
pp.432–434 1–3
p.438 1–8
pp.464–470 1–1
Villiers, C., "The Limited Liability Partnership Act 2000: Extending opportu-
nities for business", 2001 S.L.P.Q. 112 23–19

Wade, P.J., "High Valuations versus Bad Lending", 1995 Rep. B. 4–2 26–13
Waelde, C., "Wet? Wet?—a little mystery unresolved", 1996 S.L.T. (News)
1 5–7
Walker, *Delict*, p.81 23–17
pp.285–286 4–1
pp.296–297 .... 8–33, 15–1
p.453 26–23
pp.632–634 20–4
p.698 2–14
p.713 2–9
Walker, *A History of Private Law in Scotland*, II, pp.615–616 2–8
p.542 .... 1–7, 1–8
p.736 8–36
p.737 1–17
Walker, *A History of Private Law in Scotland*, IV, p.695 1–18
Walker, *A History of Private Law in Scotland*, V, p.240 8–13
Walker, *A History of Private Law in Scotland*, VI, p.823 24–1
pp.826–827 24–1
Walker, "Reflections on a Leading Case" (1992) 37 J. L. S.S. 394 9–5
Walker, D.M., *The Scottish Legal System*, (7th revised ed., 1997) at 395 *et
seq.* 15–2
Walker, D.M., "The Development of Reparation" (1952) 64 J. R. 101 1–7
Walker, D.M., "Strict Liability in Scotland" (1954) 66 J. R. 231 1–10

Wallinga, Tammo, "Effusa vel deiecta in Rome and Glasgow," 2002 Edin.
L.R. Vol. 6, 123 4–4
Wei, G., "Surreptitious Takings of Confidential Information", 1992 L.S.
302 5–4
Weir, T., *Economic Torts* (1997), Ch.3 1–19
    pp.19–20 26–23
    p.28 5–10
    p.29 5–14
Weir, T., "The Unwanted Child" (2002) 6 Edin. L.R. 244 .... 23–27, 23–30
Wheat, K., "Nervous Shock: Proposals for Reform" [1994] J.P.I.L. 207 11–5
Whitty, N., "Nuisance", para.2107 3–8
Whitty, N., "The Source of the Plus Quam Tolerabile Concept in Nuisance",
2003 7 Edin L.R. 218 3–5
Wilkinson, A.B., and Forte, A.D.M., "Pure Economic Loss—a Scottish
Perspective", 1985 J. R. 1 10–1
Williams, J.M., "Product Liability—Hepatitis C litigation" [2001] J.P.I.L.
238 .... 19–5, 19–8
Williams and Mead, "Abolition of the Double Actionability Rule: Questions
still to be answered" [1996] J.P.I.L. 112 1–5
Wilson, W.A., "The Product Liability Directive", 1980 S.L.T. 1 19–8
Woolman (2nd ed.) p.160 *et seq.* 22–7
Wright, "Standards of Care in Negligence Law" in *Philosophical Foundations
of Tort Law* (Owen, ed., 1996) 9–9
Wright, R., "Right Justice and Tort Law" in *Philosophical Foundations of Tort
Law* (Owen ed., 1995) 1–9

Young, "Rights of Relief on Assignation in Settlements", 1992 S.L.T. (News)
225 .... 10–8, 25–15, 25–18

Zimmerman, *The Law of Obligations: Roman Foundations of the Civilian
Tradition* (Oxford, 1996) 1–7
    p.201 1–17
    p.202 1–17
    pp.998–1004 1–17
    p.1018 1–17
    p.1021 1–2
    p.1031 1–17
    p.1032 1–15
    p.1033 .... 1–15, 1–17
    p.1034 1–17
    p.1037 1–18
Zimmerman and Simpson, *HPLS II*, 612–632 3–4
    615 3–7
    631–632 3–8
Zindani, J.H., "Manual Handling Law: The End of Laissez-faire", 2000
J.P.I.L. 2 21–18

INDEX

Abortion, 23–24
Abuse, 2–15
Abuse of process, 6–1
 civil litigation, 6–2
 crime, 6–3
Act of God, 15–6
Act of the Queen's enemies, 4–5, 4–6,
 4–7, 4–8
Actio de effuses vel dejectis, 4–2, 4–3
Actio de positis vel suspensis, 4–2,
 4–3, 4–4
Actio injuriarum, 1–7, 2–1, 8–1
Actio legis Aquiliae, 1–7, 1–17, 3–15,
 8–1, 8–32
Adultery, 2–14
Advocate General for Scotland, 23–4
Aemulationem vicini, 5–10
 use of land in, 3–12
Affront, 8–1
Animals, liability for, 20–1—20–10
 animals on roads, 20–4, 20–5
 Animals (Scotland) Act 1987, 20–6
  attack or harry, 20–8
  causation, 20–9
  defences, 20–10
  keeper of an animal, 20–7
  strict liability, 20–6, 20–7
  types of animals, 20–8
 attack or harry, 20–8
 causation, 20–9
 common law
  negligence, 20–3, 20–4
 dogs
  guard dogs, 20–2
  injury to cattle, 20–2
 history, 20–1
 keeper of an animal, 20–7
 negligence, 20–3
  animals on roads, 20–4, 20–5
 strict liability before 1987 Act, 20–2
  defences, 20–2
 types of animals, 20–8
Aristotle, 1–15
Armed forces
 injuries suffered by members, 23–5
  pensionable injuries, 23–5
 visiting, 23–48
Arrest, 2–10
 police powers, 2–12

Assault, 1–7, 2–1
 causation, 2–3
 consent, 2–2
 defences
  justification, 2–4
  self-defence, 2–7
 definition, 2–1
 motive, 2–2
 notional, 2–1
 police, 2–5
 professional liability
  medical cases, 22–5
 provocation, 2–6
 reasonable chastisement, 2–4
 remoteness of damage, 2–3
Assignation, 25–15
Assignees, 23–42
 settling a claim by assignation,
  23–42
Assythment, 1–7

Bankruptcy *see* **Insolvents**
Body parts, 23–38
 donation of, 23–38
Breach of confidence, 5–3, 5–4
 breach of commercial confidence,
  5–4
 public interest right to disclose, 5–4
Breach of duty of care, 9–20, 9–22
 reasonable care
  above average person, 9–17
  availability of precautions, 9–14
  below average person, 9–16
  cost/benefit analysis, 9–10—9–14
  degree of probability, 9–11
  expense involved in taking
   precautions, 9–14
  higher standard for above average
   person, 9–17
  immoral standards, 9–18
  impractical standards, 9–18
  knowledge of precautions, 9–14
  lower standard for below average
   person, 9–16
  magnitude of harm, 9–12
  multi-layered standards, 9–19
  professional people, 9–17, 9–19
  reasonable man, 9–9, 9–15
  risk and economics, 9–10—9–14
  skilled person, 9–17

Breach of duty of care—*cont.*
　reasonable care—*cont.*
　　value of activity, 9–13
　statutory duty, 15–7
　usual practice, 9–15

Calcutt report, 8–37
　Calcutt report, 8–37
　and *convicium*, 8–37
　Government review, 8–37
Carriage, 1–2
Carriers
　of goods, 4–5, 4–6
　　act of the Queen's enemies, 4–6
　　damnum fatale, 4–5, 4–6
　wrongful refusal to contract, 5–9
Causation, 1–16, 2–3, 9–20
Causing loss by unlawful means,
　5–10
　aemulationem vicini, 5–10
Caution, 2–8, 3–1
Character reference, 8–24
Chief constable
　vicarious liability for officers, 24–8
Child protection, 12–3
Children
　abnormally expensive, 23–29
　civil proceedings, 23–31
　delicts
　　infans, 23–31
　　parents not liable, 23–35
　　pupils, 23–32
　healthy
　　unwanted pregnancy, 23–27
　legal capacity, 23–31
　medical treatment
　　consent, 23–31
　minors, 23–31
　over 16
　　consent to medical treatment,
　　　23–31
　pupils, 23–31
　　delictual liability, 23–31
　　infans, 23–31
Church courts, 8–1
Civil litigation
　abuse of process, 6–2
Clubs
　suing, 23–12
　　club suing member, 23–15
　　members suing association, 23–13,
　　　23–14
　　office bearers, 23–12

Cohabitation, 23–32
　irregular marriage by habit and
　　repute, 23–32
Compensation
　state system, 26–27
Compensation, 1–10
Compromise, 25–19
Concurrent liability, 1–2
Consent, 25–7
　informed, 2–2
　medical treatment
　　children, 23–31
Conspiracy, 5–10
　aemulationem vicini, 5–10
　breach of EEC Treaty competition
　　provisions, 5–12
　conspiracy to injure by lawful means,
　　5–11
　conspiracy to injure by unlawful
　　means, 5–11, 5–12
　English law, 5–12
Constitution, 1–4
Contempt of court, 2–9
Contract
　inducing breach of *see* **Inducing
　　breach of contract**
　third parties, 1–2
Contravention of lawburrows, 2–8,
　3–1
Contributory negligence, 1–9, 15–10,
　25–9
Contumelia, 8–1
Convicium, 8–2, 8–9, 8–35, 8–36
　business cases, 8–2
　non-business cases, 8–2
　and privacy, 8–37
　public hatred, 8–2
　veritas convicium non excusat, 8–36
Corporal punishment *see* **Reasonable
　chastisement**
Corporations, 23–10—23–22
Corrective justice, 1–15
Correspondence, right to respect for,
　17–10
Court of Session
　simplified procedure for reparation,
　　26–28
Crime
　abuse of process, 6–3
**Criminal Injuries Compensation
　Scheme**, 1–13
Crown
　declarator, 23–3
　and European Union law
　　interdict, 23–3
　liability of, 23–3
　　vicarious, 24–8

Culpa tenet suos auctores, 23–17
Culpa, 1–7, 1–8, 1–15, 1–17, 3–1, 3–8,
    3–11, 3–14, 4–4, 9–1

Damages, 26–1—26–22
  compensatory, 26–2
  exemplary, 26–3
  interim, 26–10
  loss of a chance, 26–6
  loss of opportunity, 26–6
  mitigation, 26–4
  nuisance, 3–8
  once for all, 26–7
    interim damages, 26–10
    provisional, 26–11
    renewal claims, 26–9
    re-opening the proof, 26–8
  patrimonial loss, 26–15
    deductions from, 26–16
  penal, 1–3, 26–3
  provisional, 26–11
  punitive, 26–3
  quantification, 26–12, 26–14
    patrimonial loss, 26–15, 26–16
    South Australia Asset Management
      principle, 26–13
  relatives' claim on death, 26–18,
    26–22
    immediate family, 26–19
    loss of support, 26–20
    non-patrimonial award, 26–21
  res inter alios acta, 26–5
  solatium, 23–27, 26–17
  super-mitigation, 26–5
  transmission on death, 26–18
Damnum fatale, 4–5, 35–6
Death penalty, 17–19
Deceased person
  body, 23–38
    wrongful use of parts, 23–38
  delict
    defamation of deceased person,
      23–37
    suing estate, 23–37
Declarator, 26–24
Defamation, 8–1, 8–2, 8–3
  accidental, 8–7
  character reference, 8–24
  communication, 8–4
  damages, 8–32
    basis, 8–32
    mitigating factors, 8–32
  of deceased person, 23–37
  defences, 8–11—8–31
    absolute privilege, 8–18—8–21
    apology, 8–13
    disclaimer, 8–12

Defamation—*cont.*
  defences—*cont.*
    fair retort, 8–16
    in rixa, 8–14
    qualified privilege, 8–22—8–31
    veritas, 8–17
    vulgar abuse, 8–15
  falsity, 8–6
  and free speech, 8–3, 8–28, 8–33
  imputations about solvency, 8–9
  innuendo, 8–10
  intention, 8–7
  interdict, 8–33
  of local authority, 23–6
  of and concerning the pursuer, 8–5
  offer of amends, 8–30
  offer of apology, 8–32
  privilege, 8–3, 8–18
    parliament, 8–18
    Scottish parliament, 8–20
  qualified privilege, 8–3, 8–22
    fair comment, 8–29
    between persons having common
      interest, 8–25
    complaint to appropriate authority,
      8–23
    discharge of a duty, 8–23
    protection of interests of another,
      8–24
    protection of one's own interests,
      8–26
    published reports, 8–28, 8–32
    responsible journalism privilege,
      8–22, 8–27
    Reynolds privilege, 8–22, 8–27
  rehabilitation of offenders, 8–17
  statement must be defamatory, 8–8
  statements about fitness for
    occupation or profession, 8–9
  statements imputing immorality or
    criminality, 8–9
  unintentional, 8–31
Defences, 25–1—25–14
  act of God, 25–6
  consent, 2–2, 23–31, 25–7
  contributory negligence, 1–9, 15–10,
    25–9
  damnum fatale, 4–5, 4–7, 25–6
  ex turpi causa, 25–8
  illegality, 25–8
  force majeur, 25–6
  justification, 2–4, 25–3
  limitation, 25–10, 25–11
  necessity, 25–4
  prescription, 25–10, 25–12, 25–23,
    25–14
  provocation, 2–6, 25–5

Defences—*cont.*
self-defence, 2–7, 25–5
statutory authority, 25–2
volenti non fit injuria, 1–9, 15–10, 18–7, 25–7
waiver, 25–7
Definition of delict, 1–1
connotations, 1–1
mens rea, 1–1
Detention, 2–10
lawful, 17–5
and right to liberty and security, 17–5
statutory, 2–11
Deterrence, 1–9
over-deterrence, 1–9
Diplomats, 23–46
Discharge, 25–19
Discrimination prohibition, 17–15
Distributive justice, 1–15
Diversion of natural course of a stream, 3–11
Doctors *see* **Professional liability**
Dolus, 1–17
Duty of care
breach of duty *see* **Breach of duty of care**
developments, 9–7
indirect damage and injury *see* **Indirect damage and injury**
neighbour principle, 9–3, 9–7
owed to particular pursuer, 9–4
reasonable foreseeability, 9–3, 9–7
acts or omissions, 9–3
damnum injuria datam, 9–5
economic loss, 9–7, 9–8
reasonable man, 9–3
what is to be foreseen, 9–5, 9–6
third party interventions *see* **Third party interventions**
Economic loss, 10–1—10–12
assumption of liability, 10–3
bright line non-recovery rule, 10–8, 10–9
contractual losses, 10–8
derived from non-pursuer, 10–8, 10–9
disclaimers of liability, 10–7
employment reference, 10–5
Hedley Byrne liability, 10–3, 10–4, 22–7
Henderson v Merrit liability, 10–10
negligent mis-statement, 10–3, 10–4
professional negligence, 22–7
proximity, 10–6, 10–9
special relationship cases, 10–3
statutory intervention, 10–12

Economic loss—*cont.*
unwanted pregnancy, 23–28
White v Jones liability, 10–11

Economic wrongs, 5–1—5–16
Education, right to, 17–17
Ejection
from property, 3–1
remedies, 3–1
Elections, right to free, 17–18
Emmanations of the State, 12–8, 23–8
and European Community laws, 23–8
Employee health and safety *see* **Employers' liability**
Employees
harbouring *see* **Harbouring employees**
Employers *see* **Employers' Liability**
vicariously liable for employees, 1–11
Employers' liability, 21–1—21–24
common law, 21–1—21–8
appliances, 21–2
Hatton guidelines, 21–6
personal duty to take reasonable care for employees' safety, 21–1
plant, 21–2
safe system of work, 21–4
selection of skilled persons, 21–3
staffing levels and robbery, 21–8
stress at work, 21–6
works, 21–2
statutory liability, 21–9—21–24
computer display screens, 21–17
defective equipment, 21–24
display screen equipment, 21–17
Employer's Liability (Defective Equipment) Act 1969, 21–24
European inspired regulations, 21–9
European Rules, 21–10
Health and Safety (Display Screen Equipment) Regulations 1992, 21–17
machinery, 21–2, 21–14, 21–15
training, 21–15
maintenance of work equipment, 21–15
Management of Health and Safety at Work Regulations 1992, 21–11
Manual Handling Operations Regulations 1992, 21–18—21–23

Employers' liability—*cont.*
statutory liability—*cont.*
Personal Protective Equipment at
Work Regulations 1992,
21–16
protective equipment, 21–16
Provision and Use of Work
Equipment Regulations 1992,
21–14
risk assessment, 21–22, 21–23
risk of injury, 21–21
Workplace (Health Safety and
Welfare) Regulations 1992,
21–12, 21–13
work equipment, 21–14, 21–15
workplace defined, 21–12
Employment reference, 10–5
Enforcement mechanism, 1–12
England
economic and monetary union with,
1–8
differences in law, 1–14
English Law Commission, 11–5, 11–6
Enticement, 2–9
spouse, 2–9
**European Committee for the
Prevention of Torture and
Inhumane or Degrading
Treatment or Punishment**, 17–3
European Human Rights law, 1–12
see also **Human rights**
**European Union law, failed or
inadequate transposition**,
16–1—16–5
compensation claims
conditions for, 16–2
competition policy, 16–1
direct effect
directives, 16–2
regulations, 16–2
Treaty Articles, 16–2
directives
direct effect, 16–2
EEC
competition provisions
breach of, 5–12
legislation contrary to UK law, 16–3
loss sustained by third party, 16–4
non-contractual liability of the
Community
reparation conditions, 16–4
regulations
direct effect, 16–2
and statutory liability, 16–1

Euthanasia *see* **Terminally ill**
Evidence, 1–6
Ex turpi causa, 25–8
Extinction
decree, 25–18

Fair trial *see* **Right to a fair trial**
Fame, reputation and honour, 8–1
**Family life and enjoyment of
property**, 3–9, 12–5
Foetus
aborting, 23–24
injury to, 23–25
child born alive, 23–25
death after born alive, 23–26
death while foetus, 23–26
parents' claim, 23–26
personal injuries, 23–26
right to incubation in womb, 23–24
unable to be represented, 23–24
Force majeur, 25–6
Fornication, 2–14
Forum non conveniens, 1–5
Fraud, 5–2
damages, 5–2
definition, 5–2
Free speech, 1–4
and defamation, 8–3, 8–28, 8–33
Freedom of assembly and association,
17–13
armed forces, 17–13
Freedom of expression, 17–12
**Freedom of thought, conscience and
religion**, 2–4, 17–11
French Civil Code, 1–8
Function of delict, 1–9—1–13

German Code, 1–18
Globalisation, 1–8
Grotius, 1–15

Hague-Visby rules, 14–1
Hansard
and defamation, 8–18
Harassment, 2–15
actions, of, 23–26
Harbouring employees, 5–8
Hatton **guidelines**, 21–6
Healthy child
unwanted pregnancy, 23–27
Hedley Byrne **liability**, 10–3, 12–8,
22–7
and Scottish law, 10–4
Henderson v Merrit **liability**, 10–10
Heritable property
ejection, 3–1
remedies, 3–1

Heritable property—*cont.*
  intrusion, 3–1
    remedies, 3–1
History of delict, 1–7, 1–8
Home, right to respect for, 17–10
Homosexual relationships, 23–33
Hotel proprietors, 4–5
  see also **Innkeepers**
  act of the Queen's enemies, 4–7
  damnum fatale, 4–5, 4–7
Human life
  foetus *see* **Foetus**
  when begins, 23–23
Human rights, 17–1—17–25
  against other citizens, 17–1
  against the state, 17–1
  death penalty abolished, 17–19
  defamation, 8–1
  discrimination prohibition, 17–15
  European law, 1–12
  family life and enjoyment of
    property, 3–9, 12–5, 17–10
  freedom of assembly and association,
    17–13
  freedom of expression, 17–12
  freedom of religious expression, 2–4,
    17–12
  freedom of thought, conscience and
    religion, 17–11
  infringement, 1–4
  inhuman or degrading treatment or
    punishment, 17–3, 17–11
  just satisfaction, 17–1
  no punishment without law, 17–9
  and nuisance, 3–9
  protection of property, 17–16
  and public authorities, 12–8, 17–1
  reparation for breach, 17–1,
    17–20—17–25
    causation, 17–24
    character and conduct of pursuer,
      17–23
    claimants, 17–22
    costs and expenses, 17–21
    just satisfaction, 17–20, 17–21
    non-pecuniary loss, 17–21
    pecuniary loss, 17–21

Illegality, 25–8
Imprisonment
  wrongful, 2–13
Incorporated bodies, 23–10
  directors, 23–10
  reputation
    injury to, 23–10
  suing, 23–10
  vicarious liability, 23–10

Incorporated practices, 23–20
Independent tribunal, 17–6
Indirect damage and injury,
    14–1—14–2
Inducing breach of contract, 5–13
  direct intervention, 5–14
  direct persuasion, 5–14
  indirect intervention, 5–14
Informed consent doctrine, 2–2
**Inhuman or degrading treatment or
    punishment**, 17–3
  European Committee for the
    Prevention of Torture and
    Inhumane or Degrading
    Treatment or Punishment, 17–3
  life sentence for murder, 17–3
  slopping out, 17–3
Innkeeper
  wrongful refusal to contract, 5–9
Insolvents
  administrators, 23–41
  individuals, 23–40
    injuries sustained before
      sequestration, 23–40
    suing for personal wrongs, 23–40
    trustee in bankruptcy, 23–40
  liquidators, 23–41
  receivers, 23–41
Insult, 8–1
Insurance, 1–11
Interdict, 26–23
Interests
  protection of, 1–18, 1–19
Interference in contract, 5–10
  aemulationem vicini, 5–10
International law
  choice of law, 1–5
  private, 1–5
Intimidation, 5–10
  aemulationem vicini, 5–10
Intimidation, 5–15, 5–16
  three-party, 5–16
  two-party, 5–16
Intrusion
  on to property, 3–1
  remedies, 3–1

Judex qui litem suam feceritI, 4–1
Judges
  immunities, 23–7
Judicial proceedings
  and defamation, 8–21
Judicial review, 26–25
  and misfeasance in office, 7–1
  members of the public, 23–49

Jus quaesitum tertio, 1–2
Justice, 1–15
  corrective, 1–15
  distributive, 1–15
Justification, 25–3
Justinian
  three precepts of law, 1–15

Kant, 1–15

Land
  escape of dangerous things from, 3–10
  non-natural use of, 3–10
  ownership
    a caelo usque ad centrum, 3–2
  use in *aemulationem vicini*, 3–12
Law
  choice of, 1–5
Lawburrows
  contravention of, 2–8, 3–1
Lex Aquiliae see *Actio legis Aquiliae*
Liability
  fair, just and reasonable, 1–15
Liberty and security see **Right to liberty and security**
Limitation, 25–10, 25–11
Lis alibi pendens, 1–5
Litigants, 23–1—23–48
  title and interest required to sue, 23–1
Local authorities
  defamation of, 23–6
  delict, 23–6
  unitary authorities, 23–6
Lord Advocate, 23–3, 23–4
Lord President, 23–7

Magistrates
  wrongful imprisonment by, 2–13
Malicious falsehood, 8–35
  heads, 8–35
  slander of business, 8–35
  slander of goods, 8–35
  slander of property, 8–35
  slander of title, 8–35
Marriage
  and delict, 23–34
    women disadvantaged, 23–34
  irregular, by habit and repute, 23–32
  married woman in minority, 23–34
  spouses
    enticement of spouse, 23–34
    suing one another, 23–34

Medical liability see **Professional liability**
Medical treatment
  assault, 2–2
  informed consent doctrine, 2–2
Members of the public
  remoteness, 23–49
Mens rea, 1–1, 2–1
Mental illness
  damaged caused by insane person, 23–39
  Hatton guidelines, 21–6
  meaning of insane, 23–39
  nervous shock see **Nervous shock**
  stress at work, 21–6
Misfeasance in office, 7–1, 7–2, 12–8
Mis-statements
  defamatory see **Defamation**
  negligent see **Economic loss; Professional liability**
Moveables
  spuilzie see **Spuilzie**
  wrongful interference with see **Wrongful interference with moveables**

Nascituras **Doctrine**, 23–23, 23–26
Natural Lawyers, 1–15
Nautae caupones stabularii, 4–5
Necessity, 25–4
Negligence, 1–4
Negligence, 9–1
  causation, 9–20, 9–21
    "but for" test, 9–20
    causa causans, 9–20
    causa sine qua non, 9–20
    material contribution, 9–22
    novus actus interveniens, 9–23
  duty of care see **Duty of care**
  economic loss see **Economic loss**
  history, 9–1
  nervous shock see **Nervous shock**
  public authorities see **Public authorities**
  remoteness of damage, 9–25
Nervous shock, 11–1—11–6
  aftermath doctrine, 11–3
  control mechanisms, 11–1
  damage to property, 11–4
  English Law Commission
    consultation paper, 11–5, 11–6
  foreseeability, 11–1, 11–3
  primary victims, 11–2
    reasonable fortitude, 11–2
  proximity, 11–1
  reasonable fortitude, 11–2
  rescuers, 11–2

Nervous shock—*cont.*
Royal College of Psychiatrists
Mental Health Group, 11–5
Scottish Law Commission discussion
paper, 11–6
secondary victims, 11–2, 11–3
category of plaintiff, 11–3
sufficient participation, 11–2
Non-physical personal injury *see*
Nervous shock
Nuisance
basis of liability, 3–8
coming to the nuisance, 3–5
conduct *plus quam toerablie*, 3–4
culpa, 3–8
damages, 3–8
definition, 3–4
escape of dangerous things from
land, 3–10
and human rights, 3–9
locality, 3–7
neighbourhood, 3–7
non–natural use of land, 3–10
statutory authority, 3–6

Occupiers liability, 18–1
acceptance of risk, 18–7
actings of others, 18–5
definition of occupier, 18–2
possession and control test, 18–2
duty and standard of care, 18–4
excluding duty
agreement, 18–7
notices, 18–7
and higher duties of care, 18–8
landlord and tenant, 18–9
mode of entry, 18–6
premises covered, 18–3
pursuer, 18–6
roads and pavements, 18–3, 18–10
statutory, 18–1
trespassers, 18–6
volenti non fit injuria, 18–7

Parents
not liable for delicts of children,
23–35
Parliament
and defamation, 8–18
Partnerships
limited liability partnership, 23–19
non-partners suing partnership, 23–16
partners suing partnership, 23–17
confusio, 23–17
partnership suing a partner, 23–18
scope of business
and scope of liability, 23–16

Partnerships—*cont.*
vicarious liability, 23–16
Passing off, 5–5, 5–6, 5–7
damages, 5–5
five elements in support of action,
5–6
market in which parties operate, 5–6
image of the product, 5–7
restitutionary remedy, 5–5
Pavements
liability for, 18–3, 18–10, 18–11
Gibson averments anent
inspection, 18–10
Personal injuries
foetus, 23–25, 23–26
Picketing, 23–22
Plagium, 2–9
Police
arrest, 2–12
assault, 2–5
misfeasance in office, 7–2
Praetor, 4–5, 8–36
Pregnancy
right to terminate, 23–24
unwanted, 23–27, 23–28
economic loss, 23–27
solatium, 23–27
Prescription, 25–10
long negative, 25–13
positive, 25–14
Privacy, 8–37
Private and family life, respect for,
3–9, 12–5, 17–10
Private international law, 1–5
Procedure, 1–6
Procurator fiscal
not vicariously liable for deputes or
assistants, 24–8
Product liability, 19–1–9
common law, 19–2
Consumer Protection Act 1987, Part
1, 19–3
and EEC diretive, 19–3
damages, 19–7
defect
definition, 19–5
hidden and unknown to consumer,
19–2
defences, 19–8
compliance with legal
requirements, 19–8
defect did not exist at relevant
time, 19–8
defender did not supply, 19–8
state of scientific and technical
knowledge, 19–8

Product liability—*cont.*
  defences—*cont.*
    supply not in the course of
      business, 19–8
    negligence liability, 19–8
    producer's liability, 19–6
    product
      definition, 19–4
    services, 19–2
    strict liability, 19–3, 19–8
    supplier's liability, 19–6
    time bar, 19–9
Professional liability, 22–1–10
  contract, 22–2
    standard of care, 22–2
  damages, 22–10
  delictual duty, 22–2
    and contract, 22–2
    standard of care, 22–2
  failure to deliver professional skill,
    1–2
  legal advisers, 22–7
    court actions, 22–8
    economic loss, 22–7
  medical cases, 22–5
    assault, 22–5
    causation, 22–6
    negligence, 22–5
  negligent mis-statements and
    contracts, 22–9
  physical injury, 22–2
  standard of care, 22–1, 22–2, 22–3,
    22–4
Property, protection of, 17–16
Protection of rights and interests,
  1–18, 1–19
Proximity, 10–6, 10–9, 11–1
Public authorities, 12–1–12–8
  arguments from English cases, 12–7
  child protection, 12–3
  discretionary areas, 12–2
  economic loss, 12–3
  emanations of the state, 12–8
  Hedley Byrne liability, 12–8
  and human rights legislation, 12–8,
    17–1
  local authorities *see* **Local
    authorities**
  and misfeasance in office, 12–8
  operational areas, 12–2
  and private, law, 1–4
  protection of, 12–4, 12–8
  roads and pavements, 18–3, 18–10,
    18–11
  Scotland, 12–6
  victim's right to reparation, 23–9
  wrongful administration, 1–4

Public hatred, 8–2
Public interest right to disclose, 5–4
Public office
  misuse of, 1–4
Public officers
  misfeasance in office, 7–1, 7–2
Pufendorf, 1–15
Punishment
  no punishment without law, 17–9

Quasi-delicts, 1–1, 4–1
  act of the Queen's enemies, 4–6,
    4–7, 4–8
  actio de effuses vel dejectis, 4–2, 4–3
  actio de positis vel suspensis, 4–2,
    4–3, 4–4
  culpa, 4–4
  damnum fatale, 4–5
  nautae caupones stabularii, 4–5, 4–6,
    4–7
  occupier of premises, 4–2, 4–3
  placed and suspended, 4–4
  poured and thrown, 4–3

Rape, 2–14
Reasonable chastisement, 2–4, 17–11
  teachers, 2–4
Rehabilitation of offenders
  and defamation, 8–17
Religious cult
  enticement, 2–9
Religious expression
  freedom of, 2–4
Reparation, 1–1
  branch of private law, 1–4
  and state, 1–4
Res ipsa loquitur, 4–4
Responsible journalism privilege,
  8–22, 8–27
Restitutio in integrum, 26–2
Reynolds **privilege**, 8–22, 8–27
Right to a fair trial, 17–6
  civil cases, 17–7
    personal injury, 17–7
  criminal cases, 17–8
    defence, 17–8
    examination of witnesses, 17–8
    interpreter, 17–8
    language, 17–8
    minimum rights, 17–8
    time to prepare defence, 17–8
  independent tribunal, 17–6
  public, 17–6
Right to liberty and security, 17–5
  compensation for detention in
    contravention, 17–5
  lawful detention, 17–5

Right to life, 17–2
Right to marry and found a family,
  17–14
Rights
  protection of, 1–18, 1–19
Risk allocation, 1–11
Roads
  animals on, 20–4, 20–5
  liability for, 18–3, 18–10, 18–11
  Gibson averments anent
    inspection, 18–10
Roman law, 1–7
Roman quasi-delicts *see* **Quasi-delicts**
Royal College of Psychiatrists Mental
  Health Group, 11–5

Scotsman
  Spycatcher case, 5–4
Scottish Law Commission, 5–3, 11–6,
  23–23
Scottish parliament, 23–4
  courts' powers, 23–4
  and defamation, 8–20
  law making powers, 1–8
  member of
    interdict, 23–4
Seduction, 2–14
Self–defence, 2–7
Settlement, 25–19
Shoplifting
  detention of suspect by store
    detectives, 2–10
Sic utere tuo ut alienum non laedas,
  3–7
Sin
  and commission of delict, 1–2
Slander, 8–1, 8–2, 8–5
  see also **Malicious falsehood**
Slavery and forced labour
  prohibition, 17–4
Social workers
  misfeasance in office, 7–2
Software, 3–14
South Australia Asset Management
  principle, 26–13
Sovereign's immunity, 23–2
Spondet peritiam artis, 1–2
Spouse
  enticement, 2–9
Spuilzie, 3–13
  property destroyed, 3–15
  property detained, 3–15
  property of another taken, 3–15
  property of another used without
    permission, 3–15
  restoration of goods, 3–13
  violent profits, 3–13

Stable keepers, 4–5
  act of the Queen's enemies, 4–8
  damnum fatale, 4–5
State
  and arguments about reparation, 1–4
  immunity, 23–47
Statutory authority
  defence, 25–2
Statutory detention, 2–11
Statutory duty, 15–1—15–10
  breach, 15–7
    defences, 15–10
  causation, 15–8
  and civil liability, 15–1, 15–2, 15–5
  common law delict, 15–1
    as mechanism for enforcement
      only, 15–1
  contributory negligence, 15–10
  enforced by civil action, 15–5
  intended to protect pursuer, 15–4
  intention of statute, 15–6
  must be in force and applicable to
    defender, 15–3
  remoteness of damage, 15–9
  and right to damages, 15–1
  and *volenti non fit injuria*, 15–10
Sterilisation
  failed, 23–27, 23–28
Store detectives
  detention of shoplifting suspect, 2–10
Stream
  diversion of natural course, 3–11
Stress
  at work, 21–6
  nervous shock *see Nervous shock*
Strict liability, 1–15
  compensation, 1–10
Sunday Times
  Spycatcher case, 5–3

Teachers
  reasonable chastisement, 2–4
Terminally ill
  ending life, 23–36
Theft, 1–7
Third party interventions, 13–1–3
  allurement and danger argument,
    13–2
  reasonable foreseeability, 13–1
Threats of harm, 2–1
Torture prohibition, 17–3
  European Committee for the
    Prevention of Torture and
    Inhumane or Degrading
    Treatment or Punishment, 17–3

Trade unions
immunity in respect of act done by a
person, 23–21
interference with contracts of
employment, 23–22
secret ballots, 23–22
picketing, 23–22
right to join, 17–13, 23–21
strike action, 23–22
suing, 23–21
trade dispute, 23–22
and political protest, 23–22
vicarious liability, 24–8
Transfer
assignation, 23–42, 25–15
contribution, 25–16
relief, 25–16, 25–17
Treaty Articles
direct effect, 16–2
and United Kingdom courts, 16–2
Trespass, 3–2
airspace, 3–2, 3–3
defences, 3–3
UK experience, 17–25
respect for private and family life,
17–10
right to education, 17–17
right to a fair trial, 17–6—17–8
right to free elections, 17–18
right to liberty and security, 17–5
right to life, 17–2
right to marry and found a family,
17–14
slavery and forced labour prohibition,
17–4
torture prohibition, 17–3
trade unions, 17–11

Unincorporated bodies, 23–11
United States of America, 2–2
Unjust enrichment, 1–2

Verbal injury, 1–4, 8–1, 8–2, 8–34
Veritas convicium non excusat, 8–36
Vicarious liability, 24–1—24–8
agent, 24–2
actual or ostensible authority, 24–2
authorised acts, 24–2

Vicarious liability—*cont.*
agent—*cont.*
liability in respect of, 24–2
principal ratifies, 24–2
chief constable, 24–8
company directors, 24–8
Crown, 24–8
employer
for employees, 1–11, 24–3, 24–4,
24–5
independent contractors, 24–7
pro hac vice, 24–6
incorporated bodies, 23–10
independent contractor, 24–7
partnerships, 23–16
procurator fiscal, 24–8
trade unions, 24–8
Violent profits
spuilzie, 3–13
wrongful interference with
moveables, 3–13
Volenti non fit injuria, 1–9, 15–10,
18–7, 25–7

Waiver, 25–7
Welfare, 1–13
White v Jones **liability**, 10–11
Wilberforce dictum, 12–1
Women
and delict cases, 23–34
married woman in minority, 23–34
Wrongful administration, 1–4
Wrongful birth, 23–30
Wrongful imprisonment, 2–13
magistrates, 2–13
**Wrongful interference with
moveables**, 3–13
civil liability, 3–16
property destroyed, 3–15
property detained, 3–15
property of another taken, 3–15
property of another used without
permission, 3–15
restoration of goods, 3–13
violent profits, 3–13
Wrongful interference with trade,
5–10
aemulationem vicini, 5–10
Wrongful refusal to contract, 5–9